BUSINESS STRUCTURES

Third Edition

■ ■ ■

By
David G. Epstein
George E. Allen Chair Professor of Law
University of Richmond

Richard D. Freer
Robert Howell Hall Professor of Law
Emory University School of Law

Michael J. Roberts
Senior Lecturer and
Executive Director of the Arthur Rock Center
for Entrepreneurship
Harvard Business School

George B. Shepherd
Professor of Law
Emory University School of Law

AMERICAN CASEBOOK SERIES®

WEST®
A Thomson Reuters business

Mat #40785241

© West, a Thomson business, 2002, 2007
© 2010 Thomson Reuters
    610 Opperman Drive
    St. Paul, MN 55123
    1–800–313–9378
Printed in the United States of America

ISBN: 978–0–314–20059–4

DEDICATION

We wrote *Business Structures* primarily for students who did not take any "business courses" in college. Two of us did not take any "business courses" in college. And then we took this course in law school, and it was our worst law school experience (until, years later, we attended our first law school faculty meeting). We wrote this book to spare you that fate.

We also dedicate *Business Structures* to the wonderful people at West who market and sell law school books. *Cf.* page 1.

PREFACE

We understand that many of you are taking this course because your law school requires it or because the last bar exam had both a corporation question and a partnership question or because the class meets at 11 on Tuesdays, Wednesdays and Thursdays. Regardless of the reason, we are glad that you are taking the course.

All law students and lawyers need to understand business structures. For law students, business structures are building blocks in other courses. For lawyers, business structures are building blocks in the lives of their clients, in the lives of their communities.

And, like law students, lawyers, clients and communities, business structures have "lives." This book covers the life cycle of a business, Bubba's Burritos, from birth to death. We will see how Bubba's Burritos' "life" and legal issues change as the business changes from a sole proprietorship to a partnership, to a corporation, to a limited partnership, to a limited liability company. We will also consider how the life and legal issues of Bubba's Burritos differ from those of a larger, more mature business such as McDonalds.

We will look not only at businesses but also at their owners. Generally, people buy a business or an interest in a business to make money. We will consider how the structure of a business affects the ability of its owners to make money from business operations or from the sale of ownership interests.

While the stuff you will be learning is important, it can't be that difficult. After all, Kyle and Stan were able to learn about corporations and corporate takeovers from the underwear gnomes in *South Park*, episode 217. [*See* http://en.wikipedia.org/wiki/Underpants_Gnomes.]

DAVID G. EPSTEIN
RICHARD D. FREER
MICHAEL J. ROBERTS
GEORGE B. SHEPHERD

v

ACKNOWLEDGMENTS AND CONVENTIONS

First and foremost we want to acknowledge our thanks to the students and professors who have used the book and made suggestions about improving the book (Freer, Roberts, and Shepherd are especially grateful for the repeated comment—"You can't let Epstein say something like that in a casebook."). A special word of thanks to Scott Ward, an extraordinary teacher and friend.

It is customary to thank, in passing, our research assistants for their contributions. In this case, a passing sentence is not nearly enough. We're grateful to Sean Diamond, Emory Law class of 2011, and Maggie White, Emory Law class of 2010, for their diligent and insightful research assistance. And, we very much appreciate the extraordinary efforts of our co-workers who converted our scribbled text into this camera-ready book, especially Jacqueline Archer of the Harvard Business School Case Services Center.

We are grateful for permission to use the following copyrighted materials:

Chancellor William T. Allen, "Ambiguity in Corporation Law," 22 Del. J. Corp. L. 894 (1997).

Janet C. Arrowood, "The Buy–Sell Agreement: Alternative Forms," 22 Colo. Law 381 (1993). Reprinted by permission of the Colorado Bar Association.

Adolph A. Berle, Jr., "The Theory of Enterprise Entity," 47 Colum. L. Rev. 343 (1947). Reprinted by permission.

Margaret M. Blair, "A Contractarian Defense of Corporate Philanthropy," 28 Stetson L. Rev. 27 (1998).

Jeffrey Brent Brams, "Franchisor Liability: Drafting Around the Problems with Franchisor Control," 24 Okla. City U.L.Rev. 65 (1999).

James A. Cohen, "Lawyer Role, Agency Law and the Characterization Officer of the Court," 48 Buff. L. Rev. 349 (2000).

James D. Cox, "Private Litigation and the Deterrence of Corporate Misconduct," 60 Law & Contemp. Probs. 1 (1997).

Stuart R. Cohn, "The Impact of Securities Laws on Developing Companies: Would the Wright Brothers Have Gotten Off the Ground?" 3 J. Small & Emerging Bus. L. 315 (1999).

Deborah A. DeMott, "A Revised Prospectus for a Third Restatement of Agency," 31 U.C. Davis L. Rev. 1035 (1998). This work, copyright 1998 by Deborah DeMott, was originally published in 31 U.C.Davis L. Rev. 1035

(1998), copyright 1998 by the Regents of the University of California. Reprinted with permission.

Deborah A. DeMott, "The Lawyer As Agent," 67 Fordham. L. Rev. 301 (1998).

George W. Dent, Jr., "Venture Capital and the Future of Corporate Finance," 70 Wash.U.L.Q. 1029 (1992).

Frank H. Easterbrook & Daniel R. Fischel, "Corporate Control Transactions," 91 Yale L.J. 698 (1982). Reprinted by permission of The Yale Law Journal and Company and William S. Hein Company.

Amy Fantini, "Youthful Indiscretions," reprinted with permission from the May 2001 edition of *The American Lawyer*.

Lawrence J. Fox, "Lawyers' Ethics According to Nader: Let the Corporate Clients Beware," 12 Georgetown Journal of Legal Ethics, 367–376 (1999), Reprinted with the permission of the publisher, Georgetown Journal of Legal Ethics.

Philippe Francq and Jean Van Hamme, "Largo Winch—Hostile Takeover Bid," copyright Dupuis (1991).

Richard D. Freer, "Business Organizations," *Oxford Companion to American Law* (2002).

Roland J. Gilson, "Value Created by Business Lawyers: Legal Skills and Asset Pricing," 94 Yale L. J. 239 (1985). Reprinted by permission of The Yale Law Journal Corporation and William S. Hein Company.

Susan Pace Hamill, "The Origins Behind the Limited Liability Company," 59 Ohio State L. J. 1459 (1998).

Robert Hillman, "Business Partners as Fiduciaries: Reflections on the Limits of Doctrine," 22 Cardozo L. Rev. 51 (2000).

Henry Martin, "money" cartoon, The New Yorker Collection, copyright cartoonbank.com.

Douglas K. Moll, "Shareholder Oppression v. Employment at Will in the Close Corporation: The Investment Model Solution," 1999 U.Ill. L. Rev. 517. Copyright to the University of Illinois Law Review is held by the Board of Trustees of the University of Illinois.

Edward R. Rock & Michael L. Wachter, "Waiting for the Omelet to Set: Match Specific Assets and Minority Oppression in Close Corporations," volume 24, issue 4 (1999) *Journal of Corporation Law*, Reprinted with permission of the *Journal of Corporation Law*.

Gary Roma, Charity Frappe, copyright Iron Frog Productions (1991).

Carolyn Rosenberg & Duane Sigleko, "Yes, D & O Coverage Needs to Be Negotiated," *Business Law Today*, Volume 9, No. 1, September/October 1999, Reprinted by Permission.

Kevin Shelley & Susan Morton, " 'Control' in Franchising and the Common Law," *Franchise Law Journal*, Volume 19, No. 3, Winter 2000, Reprinted by Permission.

James Surovwiecki, "Gadfly, Inc.," *The New Yorker*, September 10, 2001.

Robert B. Thompson, "Piercing the Corporate Veil Within Corporate Groups: Corporate Shareholders as Mere Investors," 13 Conn.J. Int'l L 379 (1999).

Business Structures also includes non-copyrighted materials from public websites such as the Delaware Division of Corporations' *www.state.de.us./corp/index.htm* and the SEC's *www.sec.gov/edgar.shtml*.

So *Business Structures* can "hold" this rich array of non-case materials and "hold" all the traditional cases that law professors like to teach and, most important, "hold" your interest, we have heavily edited the cases and omitted citations in the cases, other than citations to other cases in the book. We indicate an omission of text by * * *. We have also edited out almost all of the footnotes in cases, and have not indicated the omission of footnotes. However, footnotes in cases are indicated by the original numerical references, rather than by an asterisk. If you see a footnote in a principal case, it is important. To make these footnotes easier to identify, they appear in bold print.

Summary of Contents

TABLE OF CONTENTS

TABLE OF CASES

The principal cases are in bold type. Cases cited or discussed in the text are in roman type. References are to pages. Cases cited in principal cases and within other quoted materials are not included.

BUSINESS STRUCTURES

Third Edition

CHAPTER ONE

WHAT DO BUSINESSES DO AND WHAT DO LAWYERS FOR BUSINESSES DO?

■ ■ ■

A. WHY DOES SOMEONE OWN A BUSINESS OR AN INTEREST IN A BUSINESS?

1. THE EPSTEIN–FREER VIEW AND THE ROBERTS–SHEPHERD VIEW

Co-author Epstein believes that most people own a business (or an interest in a business) to make money. He asked all of his relatives who own businesses why they do so, and got the same answer from all: "to make money."

"Remember a few years ago when everything was sex, sex, sex?"

To eliminate the possibility that this empirical research was flawed, co-author Freer went to the exclusive Piedmont Driving Club in Atlanta to inquire of members why they own businesses or interests in businesses. He was able to speak with only two people before being asked to leave. But those two gave him the same answer: "to make money."

Co-authors Roberts and Shepherd, who suffer from more sophisticated economic training than Epstein and Freer, believe that the Epstein/Freer view is basically correct, but incomplete. They say that a business is some form of activity that is organized to "create value" for its owners. This means that the business must create a profit in some sense, but not necessarily in the conventional sense.

First, a business can "make money" without creating value. For instance, suppose an erstwhile entrepreneur used her hard-earned savings to purchase a business for $100,000, which generated a profit of $5,000 per year. While this may seem like it is "making money," no real value has been created. She could have put the $100,000 in a savings account at a bank and earned that same 5% interest, without the risks, and work, of starting a business.

Second, a business can create value without "making money." Fast-growing, technology-based businesses often require a long cycle—many years—of continued investment and reinvestment on the part of the owners before the business starts throwing off cash—"making money." Still, if these investments create new products that customers want to buy, and develop a competitive advantage for the company in its marketplace, then ownership in the company will be attractive to potential purchasers, and the company will be able to sell its stock at an increasingly high price. Even if the business is spending profusely and earning nothing, potential purchasers' willingness to pay a higher price demonstrates the creation of value. Whether it is a person selling tomatoes from a table in the front yard or a joint venture between Google and Verizon, the usual defining characteristic of a business is that economic activity is organized for the purpose of earning a profit.

But co-author Shepherd is a more sensitive guy, and thinks that the goals of businesses can be broader than just earning profit. Businesses can be established not only to make money, but also—or even primarily—to help people. Some people who are not the least bit greedy start, invest in, and run corporations and other businesses.

For example, several public-interest lawyers may form a professional corporation the purpose of which is to help low-income victims of domestic abuse. Although the lawyers hope to make a modest living from their corporation, the business form is used to limit liability, not maximize profits. Likewise, George Steinbrenner may run the New York Yankees to win the most games, even if the team loses money.

The law makes careful distinctions between business structures. These distinctions are based upon who the owners are (a sole proprietor, partners, shareholders, etc.), what rights and obligations the owners have, and whether the business itself is a legal "entity" separate from the owners. We will study these distinctions later. What is important now is to understand that businesses—regardless of their legal structure—are the forum for economic activity, the objective of which is often, but not always, to earn an economic return, profit, or other increased value to the proprietor.

2. VIEWS OF OTHER "GONTSER MACHERS"*

The late Milton Friedman, who won the Nobel Prize in Economics in 1976, is widely regarded as the leader of the so-called "Chicago School" of economics. He described his views on the role of business in a *New York Times Magazine* article:

> In a free-enterprise, private-property system, a corporate executive is an employee of the owners of the business. He has direct responsibility to his employers. That responsibility is to conduct the business in accordance with their desires, which generally will be [to] make as much money as possible while conforming to the basic rules of the society, both those embodied in law and those embodied in ethical custom. * * *

> * * * [T]he key point is that, in his capacity as a corporate executive, the manager is the agent of the individuals who own the corporation * * * and his primary responsibility is to them.* * *

> Of course, the corporate executive is also a person in his own right. As a person, he may have many other responsibilities that he recognizes or assumes voluntarily—to his family, his conscience, his feelings of charity, his church, his clubs, his city, his country. * * * If we wish, we may refer to some of these responsibilities as "social responsibilities." But in these respects he is acting as a principal, not an agent; he is spending his own money or time or energy, not the money of his employers or the time or energy he has contracted to devote to their purposes. If these are "social responsibilities," they are the social responsibilities of individuals, not of business.* * *

> * * * [T]he doctrine of "social responsibility" [is] * * * a "fundamentally subversive doctrine" in a free society, and [I] have said that in such a society there is one and only one social responsibility of business—to use its resources and engage in activities designed to increase its profits so long as it stays within the rules of the game, which is to say, engages in open and free competition without deception or fraud.

Milton Friedman, *The Social Responsibility of Business Is to Increase Its Profits*, N‍EW Y‍ORK T‍IMES M‍AGAZINE, September 13, 1970.

---

* You should know that "gontser macher" is a Yiddish expression for "big shot."

QUESTIONS

1.   Reconsider Professor Friedman's phrase "acting as a principal, not as an agent." What is the difference between a "principal" and an "agent"? *See* Restatement (Second) of Agency § 1 (or Restatement (Third) of Agency § 1.01). What is the difference between "acting as a principal" and "acting as an agent?" What problems can arise when an agent has different objectives from her principal?

2.   Would Professor Friedman agree with this "mission statement" set out on the Ben & Jerry's Homemade, Inc. website in 1998?

> Ben & Jerry's gives away 7.5 percent of its pre-tax earnings in three ways: The Ben and Jerry's Foundation; employee Community action Teams at five Vermont sites; and through corporate grants made by the Director of Social Mission Development. We support projects which are models for social change—projects which exhibit creative problem solving and hopefulness. The Foundation is managed by a nine-member employee board and considers proposals relating to children and families, disadvantaged groups, and the environment.

Do the company's practices harm shareholders? If they do, would that deter you from purchasing stock in the company?

3.   Would Rob Feckner, president of the board of the California Public Employees Retirement System ("CALPERS"), which has over $160 billion dollars to invest to provide for medical care and retirement benefits for California state employees, agree? Should he be permitted to refuse to invest the money in tobacco companies or in non-union companies, even if this might lower returns?

Another gontser macher, Warren Buffett, the noted investor,* viewed business philanthropy in zoological terms:

> What many big shots love is what I call elephant bumping. I mean they like to go to the places where other elephants are, because it reaffirms the fact that when they look around the room and they see all these other elephants that they must be an elephant too. * * * So my friend [a fundraiser] always takes an elephant with him when he goes to call on another elephant. [A]s long as the visiting elephant is appropriately large, my friend gets his money. * * * And in the process of raising this eight million dollars from 60 corporations from people who nod and say that's a marvelous idea, it's prosocial, etc., not one CEO has reached in his pocket and pulled out ten bucks of his own to give to this marvelous charity.

---

* Roberts and Shepherd objected to our explaining who Warren Buffett is until Epstein and Freer assured them that many students would think Warren Buffett was that "Margaritaville guy" their parents listen to. *Cf. Time Magazine*, July 10, 2000. (Former Secretary of the Treasury Robert Rubin was described as believing that "any normal person would say that Jimmy Buffett is Warren Buffett's son.")

KNIGHTS, RAIDERS AND TARGETS: THE IMPACT OF HOSTILE TAKEOVERS 14 (John C. Coffee et al. eds. 1988).

3. VIEWS OF COURTS AND LEGISLATURES

In reading the following case, please consider these questions:

1.   Who owned the A.P. Smith Mfg. Co.?

2.   Who is suing whom for what?

3.   Why did stockholders of A.P. Smith Mfg. Co. complain about the contribution to Princeton? How did A.P. Smith Mfg. Co. get the $1,500 it contributed to Princeton? Why would stockholders care what A.P. Smith Mfg. Co. did with corporate funds? Did the stockholders know that A.P. Smith Mfg. Co. would make a contribution to Princeton before becoming stockholders? Was that relevant to the court? Should it have been?

4.   Did Hubert F. O'Brien attend Princeton? Was that relevant? Should it have been?

A.P. SMITH MFG. CO. v. BARLOW

Supreme Court of New Jersey, 1953
98 A.2d 581

JACOBS, J.

The Chancery Division, in a well-reasoned opinion by Judge Stein, determined that a donation by the plaintiff The A. P. Smith Manufacturing Company to Princeton University was intra vires.* * *

The company was incorporated in 1896 and is engaged in the manufacture and sale of valves, fire hydrants and special equipment, mainly for water and gas industries. Its plant is located in East Orange and Bloomfield and it has approximately 300 employees. Over the years the company has contributed regularly to the local community chest and on occasions to Upsala College in East Orange and Newark University, now part of Rutgers, the State University. On July 24, 1951 the board of directors adopted a resolution which set forth that it was in the corporation's best interests to join with others in the 1951 Annual Giving to Princeton University, and appropriated the sum of $1,500 to be transferred by the corporation's treasurer to the university as a contribution towards its maintenance. When this action was questioned by stockholders, the corporation instituted a declaratory judgment action in the Chancery Division and trial was had in due course.

Mr. Hubert F. O'Brien, the president of the company, testified that he considered the contribution to be a sound investment, that the public expects corporations to aid philanthropic and benevolent institutions, that they obtain good will in the community by so doing, and that their charitable donations create a favorable environment for their business operations. In addition, he expressed the thought that in contributing to liberal arts institutions, corporations were furthering their self-interest in assuring the free flow of properly trained personnel for administrative and other corporate employment. Mr. Frank W. Abrams, chairman of the board of the Standard Oil Company of New Jersey, testified that corporations are expected to acknowledge their public responsibilities in support of the essential elements of our free enterprise system. He indicated that it was not "good business" to disappoint "this reasonable and justified public expectation," nor was it good business for corporations "to take substantial benefits from their membership in the economic community while avoiding the normally accepted obligations of citizenship in the social community." * * *

The objecting stockholders have not disputed any of the foregoing testimony nor the showing of great need by Princeton and other private institutions of higher learning and the important public service being rendered by them for democratic government and industry alike. Similarly, they have acknowledged that for over two decades there has been state legislation on our books which expresses a strong public policy in favor of corporate contributions such as that being questioned by them. Nevertheless, they have taken the position that (1) the plaintiff's certificate of incorporation does not expressly authorize the contribution and under common-law principles the company does not possess any implied or incidental power to make it, and (2) the New Jersey statutes which expressly authorize the contribution may not constitutionally be applied to the plaintiff, a corporation created long before their enactment.

In his discussion of the early history of business corporations Professor Williston refers to a 1702 publication where the author stated flatly that the general intent and end of all civil incorporations is for better government. And he points out that the early corporate charters, particularly their recitals, furnish additional support for the notion that the corporate object was the public one of managing and ordering the trade as well as the private one of profit for the members. However, with later economic and social developments and the free availability of the corporate device for all trades, the end of private profit became generally accepted as the controlling one in all businesses other than those classed broadly as public utilities. As a concomitant the common-law rule developed that those who managed the corporation could not disburse any corporate funds for philanthropic or other worthy public cause unless the expenditure would benefit the corporation. During the 19th Century when corporations were relatively few and small and did not dominate the country's wealth, the common-law rule did not significantly interfere with the public interest. But the 20th Century has presented a different climate. Control of economic wealth has passed largely from individual entrepreneurs to dominating corporations, and calls upon the corporations for reasonable philanthropic donations have come to be made with increased public support. In many instances such contributions have been sustained by the courts within the common-law doctrine upon liberal findings that the donations tended reasonably to promote the corporate objectives. * * *

When the wealth of the nation was primarily in the hands of individuals they discharged their responsibilities as citizens by donating freely for charitable purposes. With the transfer of most of the wealth to corporate hands and the imposition of heavy burdens of individual taxation, they have been unable to keep pace with increased philanthropic needs. They have therefore, with justification, turned to corporations to assume the modern obligations of good citizenship in the same manner as humans do. Congress and state legislatures have enacted laws which encourage corporate contributions, and much has recently been written to indicate the crying need and adequate legal basis therefore. * * *

It seems to us that just as the conditions prevailing when corporations were originally created required that they serve public as well as private interests, modern conditions require that corporations acknowledge and discharge social as well as private responsibilities as members of the communities within which they operate. Within this broad concept there is no difficulty in sustaining, as incidental to their proper objects and in aid of the public welfare, the power of corporations to contribute corporate funds within reasonable limits in support of academic institutions. * * *

In 1930 a statute was enacted in our State which expressly provided that any corporation could cooperate with other corporations and natural persons in the creation and maintenance of community funds and charitable, philanthropic or benevolent instrumentalities conducive to public welfare, and could for such purposes expend such corporate sums as the directors "deem expedient and as in their judgment will contribute to the protection of the corporate interests." * * *

The appellants contend that the foregoing New Jersey statutes may not be applied to corporations created before their passage. Fifty years before the incorporation of The A. P. Smith Manufacturing Company our Legislature provided that every corporate charter thereafter granted "shall be subject to alteration, suspension and repeal, in the discretion of the legislature." * * *

State legislation adopted in the public interest and applied to preexisting corporations under the reserved power has repeatedly been sustained by the United States Supreme Court above the contention that it impairs the rights of stockholders and violates constitutional guarantees under the Federal Constitution. * * *

It seems clear to us that the public policy supporting the statutory enactments under consideration is far greater and the alteration of preexisting rights of stockholders much lesser than in the cited cases sustaining various exercises of the reserve power. In encouraging and expressly authorizing reasonable charitable contributions by corporations, our State has not only joined with other states in advancing the national interest but has also specially furthered the interests of its own people who must bear the burdens of taxation resulting from increased state and federal aid upon default in voluntary giving. It is significant that in its enactments the State has not in any way sought to impose any compulsory obligations or alter the corporate objectives. And since in our view the corporate power to make reasonable charitable contributions exists under modern conditions, even apart from express statutory provision, its enactments simply constitute helpful and confirmatory declarations of such power, accompanied by limiting safeguards.

In the light of all of the foregoing we have no hesitancy in sustaining the validity of the donation by the plaintiff. There is no suggestion that it was made indiscriminately or to a pet charity of the corporate directors in furtherance of personal rather than corporate ends. On the contrary, it was made to a preeminent institution of higher learning, was modest in amount and well within the limitations imposed by the statutory enactments, and was voluntarily made in the reasonable belief that it would aid the public welfare and advance the interests of the plaintiff as a private corporation and as part of the community in which it operates. We find that it was a lawful exercise of the corporation's implied and incidental powers under common-law principles and that it came within the express authority of the pertinent state legislation. * * *

The judgment entered in the Chancery Division is in all respects affirmed.

QUESTIONS AND NOTES

1. Questions about the law.

1.1   What does *intra vires* mean? The Revised Model Business Corporation Act (MBCA) uses the term *ultra vires* in § 3.04. How is *intra vires* different from *ultra vires*? What is a "stockholder"? The MBCA uses the term "shareholder." *See* MBCA § 1.40(21). The terms are interchangeable.

1.2   Who made the decision to contribute to Princeton? What is a "board of directors"? *See* MBCA § 8.01; Delaware § 141(a).

1.3   In approving the contribution, was the board of directors acting as an agent or a principal? If it was acting as an agent, who was the principal?

1.4   What is a "certificate of incorporation?" The MBCA uses the phrases "certificate of existence," § 1.28, and "articles of incorporation," § 2.02. Which, if either, phrase is like a "certificate of incorporation"? Why did the objecting stockholders argue that "[A.P. Smith Mfg. Company's] certificate of incorporation does not authorize the contribution"? What if the certificate of incorporation expressly authorized charitable contributions to universities in New Jersey? What if it expressly prohibited such charitable contributions?

1.5   In *A.P. Smith*, the court indicated that the applicable New Jersey statute allowed corporations to make charitable contributions that the directors "deem expedient and [which] in their judgment will contribute to the protection of the corporate interests." Today, a typical statute simply provides that a corporation can "make donations for the public welfare or for charitable, scientific, or educational purposes." MBCA § 3.02(13). Does such a statutory provision permit corporate giving beyond that permitted by the reasoning of the court in *A.P. Smith*? Why would states permit corporate managers to give away shareholders' money?

1.6   Roberts owns 100 shares of Unilever stock. Unilever is acquiring Ben & Jerry's. Although Roberts loves Ben & Jerry's ice cream, he disagrees with its corporate philanthropy and wants nothing to do with Ben & Jerry's. What can Roberts do?

1.7   When *A.P. Smith* was decided, stock ownership was largely for the relatively well-to-do. So a decision by corporate managers to give away some portion of corporate assets for charitable purposes seemed somehow noble—rich people were giving away money that would otherwise go to rich people to support charitable causes (including rich people's schools like Princeton). Since then, far more Americans have become invested in stocks. Indeed, through pension plans and mutual funds, a considerable proportion of working-class Americans are invested in stocks. So today, corporate philanthropy may consist of a (highly paid) corporate executive giving away money that otherwise might go into a blue-collar worker's pension. What is so noble about that?

1.8   Can corporations make *political* contributions? The New York Business Corporation Law (BCL) provides that they can, "irrespective of corporate benefit," § 202(a)(12), but New York Election Law imposes a ceiling of $5,000 per year to any political candidate or organization. New York Elec. Law § 14–116. Why should there be an express statutory ceiling on political contributions but not on charitable contributions? Why would the political contribution provision allow such grants "irrespective of corporate benefit"?

2.   Notes.

2.1   Over seven decades ago, Owen D. Young, then the chief executive officer of General Electric, took the position that his obligations were not limited to shareholders:

> [I]t makes a great deal of difference in my attitude toward my job as an executive officer of the General Electric Company whether I am a trustee of the institution or an attorney for the investor. If I am a trustee, who are the beneficiaries of the trust? To whom do I owe my obligations?
>
> My conception is this: That there are three groups of people who have an interest in that institution. One is the group of fifty-odd thousand people who have put their capital in the company, namely, its stockholders. Another is a group of well toward one hundred thousand people who are putting their labor and their lives into the business of the company. The third group is of customers and the general public.

E. Merrick Dodd, Jr., *For Whom Are Corporate Managers Trustee?* 45 HARV. L. REV. 1149, 1154 (1932).

Would Professor Friedman agree with Mr. Young?

2.2   The MBCA and other corporate codes now expressly authorize corporations to make charitable contributions. *E.g.*, MBCA § 3.02(13); Delaware § 122(9); New York BCL § 202(a) (12). Since 1935, the federal tax laws have made charitable contributions by corporations tax deductible. As Professor Blair explains, the law is clear but the basis for the law is not:

Although a lively debate raged in the law from the mid–19th century to the mid–20th century about whether, and under what circumstances, corporations could give away funds to humanitarian, charitable, or philanthropic causes, this question appeared to be settled by the 1950s. Since then, both statutory and case law have made it clear that corporate officers and directors have very wide discretion to direct reasonable amounts of corporate resources toward artistic, educational, and humanitarian causes, even those that have only a remote connection (or no obvious connection at all) to the business goals and profitability of the firm.

This stance of the law has been defended primarily by reference to an entity theory of the firm. Under this theory, the corporation is itself a separate legal "person," with individual rights under the law, and it is therefore appropriate to expect, and even demand, that corporations be "good citizens," and that they behave in "socially responsible" ways, including contributing to "socially responsible" causes. Corporate officers and directors, who act for this entity, must therefore be protected when they expend corporate resources on philanthropy.

But while the law appears to be settled, there is still an influential strand of legal thinking, particularly among scholars steeped in the jurisprudence of law and economics, that argues that corporate giving, if it is permitted at all, should be strictly limited to those situations where the benefit to the firm in the form of higher expected profits is clear and compelling. The argument against corporate philanthropy of a more general nature, as well as against other forms of gratuitous acts by corporations in the name of corporate "social responsibility," was made forcefully by Milton Friedman in 1962 in a famous and often-quoted essay. Friedman's view was that a corporation is a special purpose institution for managing and governing private property—in particular, the private property of the shareholders. For corporate managers and directors to do anything with that property other than what the shareholders want them to do (which, presumably, is to increase profits) would be tantamount to expropriating resources that do not belong to them, and would violate the terms of their employment agreement. Arguments to the same effect by subsequent contractarian legal scholars have generally been couched in terms of "principal-agent" theory (in which the central contractual relationship in a corporation is understood as an agency relationship between the shareholders, who are the real "owners" of the corporation's property and act as "principals," and the directors and managers who serve as their "agents").

Margaret M. Blair, *A Contractarian Defense of Corporate Philanthropy*, 28 STETSON L. REV. 27–29 (1998).

2.3   The business in the *A.P. Smith* case was a corporation. While we will spend more time on corporations than on any other business structure, we will study other forms of business structures, such as sole proprietorships in Chapter 2 and partnerships in Chapter 3. When we get into Chapter 2, consider how the New Jersey Supreme Court would have ruled if A.P. Smith Mfg. Co. had been a sole proprietorship and the objecting parties were employees. And in Chapter 3, consider how the New Jersey Supreme Court would have ruled if A.P. Smith Mfg. Co. had been a partnership and the parties objecting to the Princeton contribution were partners.

———————

Why is *A.P. Smith* in the book? Why is it the first case in the book? Why do we not simply say: "Corporations have the legal authority to make charitable contributions" and leave it at that? What does this case have to do with the introductory "empirical research" on why people own businesses?

One answer to these questions (as well as further issues raised by the respective answers) follows: We have included the *A.P. Smith* case and the questions based on the *A.P. Smith* case to show students the following general building-block concepts:

- The law views a business, at least a business in the corporate structure, as a separate entity, a separate legal person;
- A body of law—both statutory law and case law—has developed to control the actions of that separate entity or person;
- Real persons act for that corporation—they are "agents";
- A business with more than one owner, at least a business with more than one owner that is a corporation, can distribute and use its funds in ways that are opposed by at least some of its owners.

Accordingly, owners of businesses who want to make money and persons acting as lawyers for owners of businesses who want to make money (and persons studying the law of business structures) should consider questions such as: (i) who makes decisions for the business? (ii) on whose behalf are they acting as agents? (iii) can an owner profitably dispose of her ownership interest in a business if she does not agree with the decisions others are making? and (iv) how does the legal structure of the business affect the answers to the above questions?

B. HOW DOES THE OWNER OF A BUSINESS MAKE MONEY FROM THE BUSINESS?

There are two general ways an owner of the business can make money from the business. First, she can receive distributions of all or part of the money the business has earned. Second, she can sell all or part of her ownership interest in the business for more than she paid for it.* But how does the owner of a business (and her lawyer) know how much money the business has made and how much money the business is worth?

———————

* Of course, an owner of a business can also make money from the business by working for the business and receiving a salary for her work. And one does not have to be an owner of a business to work for the business and receive a salary for her work. We deal here with making money specifically in return for one's role *as an owner*.

C. HOW DOES THE OWNER OF A BUSINESS (AND HER LAWYER) KNOW HOW MUCH MONEY THE BUSINESS HAS MADE AND HOW MUCH MONEY THE BUSINESS IS WORTH?

In the *A.P. Smith* case, we dealt with the question of who had a legal right to the money a corporation earned—Princeton or the corporation's owners. The legal question was complicated by the business structure of A.P. Smith Mfg. Co., a corporation with a board of directors and shareholders who were not on the board of directors. Legally, then, there were three groups of persons or entities: (1) the business; (2) its managers; and (3) its owners.

While the legal question in *A.P. Smith* is arguably complicated, the facts were simple—the fight was over $1,500 that had been paid by the corporation to Princeton. In many fights over a business's money, there are very difficult fact questions about where the money is or where the money went. To win these fights for your clients, you will need to understand the business's accounting records and financial statements.

Generally, business entities are required to keep "appropriate accounting records" and to make those records available to the owners of the business. *See, e.g.*, MBCA §§ 16.01(b) and 16.02(b)(2); Delaware § 220(b). *See also* Revised Uniform Partnership Act (RUPA) §§ 403(a) and 403(b). Businesses typically maintain several financial statements, which are provided to investors, the company's managers, and—in the case of large public companies (ones for which the stock is publicly traded)—to the public and to public enforcement authorities. Much as medical instruments measure a patient's vital signs, the financial reports measure the company's financial health. Without accurate reports, the company can sicken or die without managers or the public knowing until too late.

The main financial statements are (1) the income statement, which computes profit during a given period (e.g., month or year) based on data about revenues and costs; (2) the cash flow statement, which measures the cash made available to a business from its operations during a given period; and (3) the balance sheet, which shows the company's assets, liabilities and the owners' "equity" in the business. There are several things you should know about these three statements.*

---

* An American Lawyer article on the summer work experiences of a Stanford law student [Janar Wasito] supports this view: "Law students throughout the country are clamoring for more training in business as they realize that serving start-ups goes beyond grinding out legal documents ... 'From what I have seen, the best attorneys are business planners who help chart out the pitfalls and opportunities of a company.' He [Wasito] also plans to take a *second* accounting class this year, noting that if he can't read a balance sheet, 'I'm just a well-spoken guy

Financial statements are prepared according to GAAP—Generally Accepted Accounting Principles.[†] We will not get into intricate accounting rules, but two important generally accepted accounting principles are: (1) *matching*: costs or expenses should be "booked" in the same period as the revenues those expenditures helped generate, and (2) *conservatism*: the data should be conservative—that is, they should present the firm's financial data in an accurate way, but err on the side of understating its revenues and the value of its assets, and on overestimating its costs and liabilities.

Perhaps the most famous example of what can happen when the principle of conservatism is violated is the case of Enron. This large energy firm engaged in a tactic called "off-balance-sheet" financing. The theory of off-balance-sheet financing is that certain activities of the firm may be carried out in other legal entities (e.g., subsidiaries, joint ventures) and that the firm need not show the obligations of those entities on its balance sheet as long as there is no chance that it, the parent company, could be forced to make good on those obligations (this is known as "nonrecourse" debt). When Enron disclosed the existence of the partnerships it had created as sources of off-balance-sheet financing, it did not disclose the partnership's debt, claiming that the debt in these entities was nonrecourse to Enron.

It turned out, however, that the debt *was* recourse to Enron under certain conditions after all. That is, the parent could be forced to make good on these obligations. This revelation brought the house of cards tumbling down. Under the principle of conservatism, Enron (and its accountants) should have made worst-case assumptions about what might happen, and should have disclosed these obligations to Enron's shareholders. By the time everyone learned of this, it was too late. Enron's stock, which had reached a high of $84 per share, plummeted to less than $1, taking with it the jobs and pensions of many Enron employees.

1. THE INCOME STATEMENT

We begin our analysis with an income statement. In its simplest form, an income statement computes the profit of a business for the period in question—usually one year. The computation involved in an income statement is pretty easy: Profit before taxes equals Revenue minus Costs. Let's take the example of an individual—Melvin Propp—who purchases mouse pads for $1 each and sells them for $2. If he buys and sells a thousand mouse pads in 2010, Propp's income statement looks like this:

who has some contacts. Those are fleeting qualities.'" Susan Orenstein, *Golden Boy*, THE AMERICAN LAWYER 80, 82, 84 (October 1999) (emphasis in original).

† The Securities and Exchange Commission has proposed what it calls a "roadmap" toward adoption of International Financial Reporting Standards by American companies by 2014. The idea is to promote a global standard for accounting. *See* www.sec.gov/rules/proposed/ 2008/33–8982.pdf.

Propp's Mousepads (PM) Income Statement 2010

Revenue (from sales)	$2,000	($2 × 1,000)
− Cost of Goods Sold [COGS]	1,000	($1 × 1,000)
= Profit Before Taxes [PBT]	$1,000	

Let's suppose Propp is pleased with his profit and hires two people to work for him in 2011. If he hires two employees at $100 each, and each of them also sells 1,000 mousepads (at $2 per mousepad), Propp's income statement looks like this:

PM Income Statement 2011

Revenue (sales)	$6,000	(3 × 1,000 × $2)
− COGS	3,000	($1 × 3,000)
− Salaries	200	(2 × $100)
= PBT	$2,800	

Now suppose in 2012 Propp bought a $5,000 mousepad manufacturing machine, and the machine was expected to last for five years. If we followed the process we've been using, we would add an item to the income statement for machinery expense and note a $5,000 expense for this item.

But this would be misleading. Profits would be understated in the first year. We would be charging the business's profits for the entire cost of the machine in one year, even though Propp will use the machine over five years. In subsequent years, profits would be overstated because we would be charging the business nothing for the machine, even though we were getting the benefit from its use.

The solution to this problem is to use something called *depreciation*. For example, we could charge the income statement for one-fifth of the machine ($1,000) each year. This one-fifth figure comes from the fact that the machine has a useful life of five years. Thus, at the end of that time we will have charged the business fully for the machine. This $1,000 figure reflects that the machine is getting less valuable each year, since we are "using" part of it up. The portion that we use up is called depreciation.*

Now let us assume that in 2012 Propp did the following:

- bought the mousepad machine;
- depreciated it at $1,000 a year;
- manufactured and sold 5,000 mousepads for $2 each;
- paid $500 for the materials for the 5,000 mousepads;
- paid someone a salary of $500 to run the machine;
- paid someone a salary of $500 to sell mousepads for him; and

---

* The approach we used above is called straight-line depreciation. We simply take the value of the equipment, divide it by the number of years of useful life, and then deduct this much each year from the income statement as depreciation. It is called straight-line depreciation because the value of the equipment decreases by the same amount each year in a straight line. Other forms of depreciation, called accelerated methods, deduct proportionally more of the cost of the equipment in the earlier years and less later on.

   • paid $100 for phone calls and other general and administrative (G & A) expenses.

Then Propp's income statement would look like this:

PM Income Statement 2012

Revenue (sales)	$10,000
– COGS	500
– Salaries	1,000
– G & A	100
– Depreciation	1,000*
= PBT	$ 7,400

Up to now, we have been ignoring taxes. You simply cannot do that (even if you work for the federal government). For this exercise, we will assume that Propp's tax rate is 50%. We have to add two more lines to the bottom of Propp's 2012 income statement:

PM Income Statement 2012

Revenue (sales)	$10,000
– COGS	500
– Salaries	1,000
– G & A	100
– Depreciation	1,000
= PBT	$ 7,400
– Taxes	3,700
= Net Income	$ 3,700

An income statement provides a useful perspective on a business. By looking at an income statement, we can learn a great deal about the operations of a business in a particular year. And looking at income statements for several years allows us to see how a business's performance changes.

One thing we cannot see from an income statement is how much cash a business may be generating or using up in a given year. This is because some entries in the income statement, such as depreciation, do not represent any actual movement of cash. To measure the cash, we need to look at a cash flow statement.

2. THE CASH FLOW STATEMENT: A FIRST LOOK

The cash flow statement is a measure of how much more or less cash a business has at the end of the year than it had at the beginning of that

---

* Consider the effect of depreciation and depreciation methods on PBT and on taxes. If Propp could choose an accelerated method of depreciation so that he could allocate more of the $5,000 cost of the machine to 2012, his 2012 PBT would be lower, his taxes would be lower, and he could keep more of his 2012 earnings. Of course, in future years, his depreciation would be lower, his PBT would be higher, and his taxes would be higher. But, of course, Propp would rather have the money now. The sooner he gets the money, the sooner he can invest it and begin earning a return on it. This is why business groups lobby hard for accelerated depreciation.

year. Cash flow would be easy to measure if all of a business's cash went into the bank; cash flow would simply be the change in the amount in the bank account.

But that is not what happens in the real world, or even in the hypothetical world of Propp's Mousepads. Recall that we saw from Propp's income statement that Propp could buy a machine for $5,000 and charge the business only $1,000 on the income statement. (The remaining $4,000 still comes out of the cash at the bank, but it does not show up as an expense on the income statement.) Conversely, in the years after Propp buys the machine, he will be charging the income statement $1,000 but he will not have to pay this in cash, because he's already paid for the machine. The $1,000 is just a charge for the portion of the machine that was "used up" in that year.

We can readily see how depreciation changes the relationship between the business's income statement and its real cash flow. In our simple model, until we added depreciation, the income statement was also a cash flow statement; whatever the profit after tax was, this amount was also the cash profit the business had made. Now, when we add depreciation, we see this relationship has changed.

In the first year of the machine's use, cash flow is less than profit because we have a cash outflow of $5,000 to buy the machine, but this appears nowhere on the income statement. The only figure we see is a $1,000 charge for depreciation. In future years, cash flow will be more than profit, because we will be charging the income statement $1,000 in depreciation, but there is no real cash outflow for this.

Thus, we can see there are two components to the differences we are talking about. One is the depreciation figure, and we've seen where that comes from. The other figure is called investment. It represents the money spent to purchase equipment. The company's cash declines because it exchanges cash for the equipment. When the business buys something that will be used for more than one year, this is an investment and only the depreciation appears on the income statement. In contrast, if the company buys something that it will use up within the year, it is called an expense, and the total amount appears on the income statement. Salaries, G & A, and COGS are expenses.

Accounting for depreciation, and investment, the general formula that converts an income statement to a cash flow statement is: Cash Flow equals Profit after Tax plus Depreciation minus Investment. We can convert Propp's income statements for the first and second years of the machine's life to cash flow statements:

PM Cash Flow Statement

Year	2012	2013*
Revenue (sales)	$10,000	$10,000
COGS	500	500
Salaries	1,000	1,000
G & A	100	100
Depreciation	1,000	1,000
PBT	7,400	7,400
Taxes	3,700	3,700
Profit After Taxes	$ 3,700	$ 3,700
+ Depreciation	1,000	1,000
− Investment	5,000	0
= Cash Flow	$ - 300	$ 4,700

This example shows why both the income and cash flow statements provide valuable information about a business. The income statement indicates the business was just as profitable in 2013 as it was in 2012. From a cash flow perspective, however, the two years are dramatically different. Due to the investment in equipment, there is a severe cash drain on the business in 2012. In 2013, the business is getting the benefit of that piece of equipment, but the business does not have to lay out any additional cash to do so. Although profits are the same in both years, the business might well be able to survive an unexpected crisis better in 2013 than 2012.

To understand the difference between an income statement and a cash flow statement more fully, we need to understand what information is provided by a balance sheet.

3.   THE BALANCE SHEET

The last financial statement we will consider is the balance sheet. The income and cash flow statements capture activity *during a period,* showing how much profit or cash flowed into (or out of) the business during the period. In contrast, the balance sheet is a snapshot of a particular moment.

A balance sheet has three main sections.

(a) *Assets*: These are the things that the company owns that have value. Assets are the business's "stuff." The typical assets on a balance sheet are cash, land, buildings, accounts receivable (money owed to the company by its customers) and machinery and equipment (such as the mousepad machine). When equipment such as the mousepad machine is depreciated, the dollar amount of that depreciation charge is deducted as an expense on the income statement; the same amount is deducted from the value of the asset on the balance sheet. Assets like cash are not depreciated because they don't get used up. Similarly, accounts receivable are not depreciated but may be "written off." For example, if one of Propp's credit customers files for bankruptcy, its accounts payable would likely go unpaid. Propp would then "write off" the account receivable due from the customers. This would ensure that the overall accounts receiv-

---

* This assumes that business operations in 2013 mirror business operations in 2012.

able figure is an accurate reflection of the business's expectations for getting paid.

(b) *Liabilities*: Liabilities are the opposite of assets: they are what the company owes. Typical liability items are accounts payable (what the company owes its suppliers), wages that it owes to its employees, and any debts the company incurs (for example, when it borrows money).

(c) *Owners' Equity*: Owners' equity is what is left over after you subtract the liabilities from the assets. Simply put, owners' equity equals assets minus liabilities.

This is why a balance sheet is called a balance sheet—it balances. When you put the assets on the left-hand side of the balance sheet, and the liabilities and owners' equity on the right hand side, then the balance sheet *will* balance. By definition, it must.*

And it makes sense. If the assets are all of the company's things that have value, and the liabilities are all the "claims" on that value, then the difference between the two is the value of the business to the owners—the owners' equity. Even if a company has $1 billion in assets, the value of the owners' equity is zero if the company also has $1 billion in debt. When liabilities exceed assets, the owners' equity is negative—the condition otherwise known as insolvency.

Let's look at what a balance sheet for Propp's Mousepad might look like. First, assume that on January 15, 2011, Propp invested $666 of his own money in the business. In that case, the balance sheet would look like this:

PM Balance Sheet
January 15, 2011

Assets		Liabilities & Equity	
Cash	$666	Liabilities	$0
		Equity	$666
Total	$666	Total	$666

Or Propp could have lent the money to the business, in which case the balance sheet would look like:

PM Balance Sheet
January 15, 2011

Assets		Liabilities & Equity	
Cash	$666	Note due Propp	$666
		Equity	$0
Total	$666	Total	$666

* Note that the principle of conservatism means that assets appear on the balance sheet at the lower of cost or market. So, a piece of land purchased in 1950 would appear on the balance sheet with a value equal to its original purchase price. Thus, the balance sheet may not accurately reflect the current market value of the company's assets and might not tell a prospective buyer how much to pay for the business.

After the first year of operation, we said that Propp had a profit of $1,000. Assuming for a minute that this was equal to cash flow, that cash would have built up in the Propp's Mousepads' bank account over the course of the year, and thus, at year end, the balance sheet would have looked like:

PM Balance Sheet
December 31, 2011

Assets		Liabilities & Equity	
Cash	$1,666	Liabilities	$666
		Equity	$1,000
Total	$1,666	Total	$1,666

Note that profits accrue to equity. Let's suppose that, just before year-end, Propp has decided Propps Mousepads should pay back his loan. He could write himself a check for $666, and then both cash and liabilities would decrease by $666, and the balance sheet would still balance. If Propp instead decided to have Propps Mousepads distribute $100 of the profits to himself—as owner of the business—these would be a deduction from owners' equity.*

After several years of business operation and expansion, a more complete balance sheet for Propp's business might look like this:

PM Balance Sheet
December 31, 2015

Assets		
Cash	5,000	
Accounts Receivable	22,000	
Inventory	33,000	
Security Deposits	6,000	
Current Assets		**66,000**
Equipment—Gross	147,000	
Depreciation	24,000	
Equipment—Net		**123,000**
Total Assets		*189,000*
Liabilities & Equity		
Accounts Payable	19,000	
Taxes Payable	5,000	
Total short-term liabilities		**24,000**
Bank Note		**85,000**
Liabilities		*109,000*
Net Total Equity		**80,000**
Total Liabilities + Equity		*189,000*

---

* This assumes that Propp lent the business the initial $666.

Let's see what we can learn from this balance sheet. For example: PM is relatively low on cash, having only $5,000 to satisfy $19,000 in "bills" (Accounts Payable) which it must pay to its suppliers; and PM is a relatively heavy user of debt* (the bank note is for more than 100% of the company's equity; that is, the note is for $85,000, while the equity is $80,000—so the note is for 106% of the equity); and PM has spent $147,000 on equipment, and charged $24,000 in depreciation against it.

4. THE CASH FLOW STATEMENT: A SECOND LOOK

In our first view of cash flow statements, we compared the impact of purchasing and depreciating equipment on both the income statement and cash flow statement. Now we need to see the possible impact of changes on balance sheet items on a cash flow statement.

Consider for example the impact of changes in accounts receivable on the cash flow statement. Assume that in 2015 Propp's credit sales are approximately $22,000 every month and that typically his customers pay within 30 days. If in December of 2015, Propp's collections from prior credit sales total only $18,000 instead of the anticipated $22,000, Propp's cash entry on his balance sheet for December 31, 2015, will be $4,000 lower and the accounts receivable entry on his December 31, 2015 balance sheet will be $4,000 higher. More important, Propp's cash flow statement for 2015 will show that the business produced $4,000 less cash. In sum, an increase in a balance sheet asset account other than cash results in a decrease in cash flow. The business owns the other asset (here the accounts receivable) instead of cash.

In contrast, an increase in a balance sheet liability account can result in an increase in the cash account on the balance sheet and an increase in cash flow. Suppose Propp borrows $20,000 in December of 2015. That increases liability shown on the December 31, 2015 balance sheet by $20,000 but also increases the balance sheet cash account by $20,000. And that increase in liability increases cash flow by $20,000. Obviously (we hope), if Propp spent the $20,000 he borrowed in December of 2015 to buy inventory in December of 2015, that $20,000 inventory expenditure would increase the inventory account on the balance sheet by $20,000 and reduce the cash account and eliminate the $20,000 from the cash flow statement.

Likewise, suppose that the business sold shares of its stock for $100,000. This would appear on the balance sheet as increase in cash of $100,000, and an increase in shareholder equity of the same amount.

---

* Debt in the business world is just like debt in personal life. When you borrow money, you are in debt. PM used a lot of borrowed money.

Note that not only do the balance sheet totals balance, but every transaction has a balancing effect: an increase in bank borrowings (a liability) also creates an increase in cash (an asset) when the borrowed money is deposited in the company's bank account. This is why accounting—or bookkeeping—is often called a "double entry" system: every transaction has two effects, which always serve to balance.

Accordingly, the definition of a cash flow statement should be expanded to include the effect of changes in balance sheet accounts:

Cash flow equals profits from income statement plus depreciation minus net change in balance sheet asset accounts other than cash plus net change in liabilities and funds from new issues of stock.

And, accordingly, in reviewing a cash flow statement for a particular year, it is helpful to look at the balance sheets for several years and compare the changes in asset accounts and liabilities.

5. FINANCIAL STATEMENTS AND THE VALUE OF A BUSINESS

Is it helpful to review the financial statements in determining what a business is worth? Please consider the following problems.

PROBLEMS: USE OF FINANCIAL STATEMENTS

1. Review the PM balance sheet for December 31, 2015. In January of 2016, would you recommend that a client buy Propp's business for $189,000? For $80,000? Does the balance sheet help a prospective buyer determine how much she should pay for the business? Does the balance sheet help a prospective investor determine how much he should pay for a share of the business? Does the balance sheet help a prospective lender determine how much it can safely lend to the business? How?

2. Review the PM cash flow statements for 2012 and 2013. In January of 2014, would you recommend to Propp that he sell the business for $3,700? For $4,700? For $20,350? Does the cash flow statement help a prospective buyer determine how much she should pay for the business? Does the cash flow statement help an investor determine how much she should pay for a share of the business? Does the cash flow statement help a prospective lender determine how much it can safely loan the business?

D. THE SARBANES-OXLEY ACT AND CORPORATE GOVERNANCE

The Sarbanes–Oxley Act of 2002 ("Sarbanes–Oxley," "Sarbox," or "SOX") was passed by the 107th Congress in reaction to the widely perceived breakdown of financial accounting and corporate accountability in the wake of the financial scandals in the 2000 time frame. (Note that the phrases "corporate governance" and "corporate accountability" apply to all forms of business organizations, not just corporations.) Enron was certainly the most widely known financial scandal, but far from the only one.

Before describing the intent and effect of Sarbanes–Oxley, it is worth understanding for a minute, both the general nature—and the general motivation—for these accounting frauds.

As backdrop, it is important to understand that these frauds all transpired in public companies; that is, companies whose shares were publicly traded and held broadly by the investing public. It is certainly possible to have accounting fraud in privately held companies and in non-corporate entities, but Congress and the regulatory agencies are much more concerned with frauds perpetrated on the general public.

These frauds have as their main feature the use of false financial statements—the balance sheet, income and cash flow statements that we have been discussing in this chapter. In well-functioning corporate governance systems, the public shareholders rely upon the board of directors, who in turn delegate a fair amount of responsibility for the oversight of the company's accounting to its audit committee (a subcommittee of the board). The audit committee oversees the work of the company's financial accounting staff (typically under the direction of a chief financial officer), chooses an auditor, oversees their work auditing the firm's accounting statements, engages with the auditors in any discussion of accounting issues that arise, and ultimately, recommends to the board that they accept the firm's audited financials for inclusion in the firm's SEC filings (e.g., the quarterly 10–Q reports, or the annual 10–K filings).

When auditors audit a firm's financials, they look to see that the firm's stated accounting policies have been consistently applied, they assess the reasonableness of these policies, and they "test" the data that the firm's financial statements are based upon. That is, for example, they look and see if the sales transactions reported did in fact occur. They check and see that the company really does have a bank account with $12 million dollars in it, if that's what the company's financial statements say.

Of course, it is impossible to test every single piece of data, and the audit firm relies upon the principle of "sampling" certain random transactions, as well as looking at any transactions that look suspicious or are the types of transactions the auditors know are prone to mistakes or even fraud.

Auditors have always been careful to say that their audit cannot be guaranteed to find fraud. That is, a group of smart people, who set out to defraud a company, can usually fool the auditors for at least some period. The auditors simply don't have the time to look at every piece of data. Similarly, an audit committee cannot spend the time to look at and analyze every transaction. The whole system relies upon a fair amount of trust in management by both the auditors and the audit committee.

1. THE MOTIVATION FOR FRAUD

As we have discussed, the financial markets look carefully at the company's financial statements to assess its business prospects, and use such information as an important input to coming to a point of view on the value of a company's stock. If the numbers are good, then fundamental performance is good, then the price of the stock should go up. That is a bit of an oversimplification, but not by much. So, managers at firms have an incentive to put out good numbers to satisfy their investors, just as all of us would prefer to make the people we work for happy as opposed to upset at us. However, managers often have another set of incentives. In some cases, they earn cash bonuses for delivering good financial results. In many cases, senior managers own stock in the company, or have stock options, that are worth more when the price of the company's stock rises.

2. TYPES OF FRAUD

There are various types of fraud. In the Enron case, the company engaged in various forms of "off-balance-sheet" transactions where it tried to move liabilities off its balance sheet through a complicated series of steps. There may have been some thread of legitimacy at each step but, in sum, the overall result clearly misrepresented the company's financial state. In the footnotes to the financials—where such complex machinations should be disclosed so that at least investors understand what is going on—the descriptions were less than transparent. It seems as though the fraud was pervasive at various layers of management, and was condoned by the auditors. These transactions also involved serious conflicts of interest, in that some officers of the company were owners of the entities that the company was conspiring with, and these executives made substantial sums from these transactions.

There are a host of other types of fraud, but most come down to either representing the company's financial condition as better than it is, or misappropriating the wealth of the company for private gain. It is worth pointing out that, when executives or board members sell stock during a time period when they have misrepresented the company's financial status, this is a form of securities law violation as well, as the executives could be deemed to be trading based upon inside information i.e., information that was not generally known in the market.

3. THE INTENT OF SARBANES–OXLEY

Sarbanes–Oxley attempts to clarify certain responsibilities of auditors, company management, and boards and audit committees, as well as impose new process and responsibilities on these parties.

For example, the Act specifies that companies must disclose whether their audit committees have an "audit committee financial expert"— someone whose experience makes her qualified to deal with the range of accounting issues and practices at the company. It also requires that other members of the audit committee have a degree of financial literacy that was previously not required.

One of the most important parts of the act is "Section 404" which specifies that the company must evaluate its own internal controls, and that it must do so with a set of procedures that both evaluate the design of those controls as well as test their operating effectiveness. The same section requires that auditors then audit management's assessment and opine on the state of internal controls at the company.

Another section of the Act requires that the CEO and the Chief Financial Officer "attest to the accuracy of the firm's financial statements." That is, to sign a statement—under threat of criminal liability—verifying that the statements are accurate.

All of these rules are designed to prevent much of the finger pointing, blame shifting and lack of accountability that frustrated investigators and analysts as they tried to get to the bottom of fraud situations: that is, CEOs saying, "I didn't understand the company's financial statements and trusted the CFO."

Other aspects of the Act address the perceived conflicts that developed within an auditing firm. That is, many accounting firms do other kinds of financial consulting work. In many of the fraud situations, these accounting firms were making lots of money from these non-audit services. There was a belief that this compromised their independence i.e., made it much less likely for them to blow the whistle on poor accounting out of a fear of losing all of this other profitable work at the client. The Act specifies both the degree to which firms could do other work for audit clients and the procedures which would need to be followed when such work was done. The Act also specifies that the partner running the audit must rotate off of the account at least every five years, in an attempt to prevent a too-cozy relationship from developing between the auditor and the client.

E.   WHAT DOES A LAWYER FOR A BUSINESS DO?

If we are right in saying that a person usually owns a business to make money, then that business owner hires an attorney (1) to help the business make money or (2) to help her get money from the business or (3) to help the business and her protect that money from the claims of others. Ralph Nader put it less charitably. According to Nader (who is a lawyer), "lawyers for businesses are largely responsible for the perversion of justice in America":

> Power attorneys crush the powerless populace and smaller businesses to assure that their clients prevail. The tools they use and the places they control twist the nation's political economy to serve corporate purposes. These attorneys do not have to go on television to advertise—their image precedes them on the corporate grapevine.

In a society officially dedicated to the rule of law, economic power needs its counselors to legitimize, mystify, facilitate, extend, immunize, shield, and entrench. For these services, attorneys are the central organizers and catalysts for the entry of other professions, such as accountants and even scientists, advancing corporate agendas. The complex systems and structures that corporate attorneys have constructed over the past 130 years are intellectual as well as practical achievements. Hardly a fraction of the brainpower of the profession was ever arrayed on the side of shareholders or small businesses, much less workers, the environment, consumers, citizens, voters, or the poor.

Corporate attorneys developed dazzling techniques of raising and investing capital, avoiding accountability and disclosure, concentrating power within and outside of companies, limiting liability from the early stages of corporate chartering to the recent maneuvers of voluntary Chapter 11 bankruptcy. Rarely do historians attribute to the work of these attorneys the difficulties faced by labor, consumers, suppliers, franchisees, shareholders, and local communities dealing with corporate management. Simply stated, these attorneys are masterminds of choreographing contests that are, in fact, no contest at all. To many corporate lawyers such deeds are their finest hour.

Ralph Nader and Wesley J. Smith, No Contest—Corporate Lawyers and the Perversion of Justice in America xxiv–xv (1996).

Questions and Notes

1. Principles of professional ethics provide that a lawyer has an obligation to represent his or her client zealously. *See* ABA Model Rules of Professional Conduct 1.3 and ABA Model Code of Professional Responsibility DR 7–101(A)(1). Are Mr. Nader and Mr. Smith arguing that an attorney for a corporation or other business should not zealously represent her client? *Cf.* George A. Riemer, *Zealous Lawyers: Saints or Sinners*, 59 Ore. St. Bar Bull. 31, 32 (1998) ("While every human activity is subject to extremes, we should not water down the core duty of lawyers: to be zealous advocates on behalf of clients.").

2. Who is the client the business attorney is to represent zealously? Assume, for example, that your firm represents A. P. Smith Mfg Co. Who is your client: Mr. O'Brien? the board of directors? the stockholders? the employees? the community? Can your client be a combination of these?

3. A partner in a large Philadelphia law firm, i.e., a "power lawyer," suggests two problems with Ralph Nader's views:

> First, it undermines what one would think Nader would believe to be fundamental tenets of our society—that everyone, including the largest conglomerate in America, is entitled to effective legal representation no matter how unpopular, so long as they are pursuing nonfraudulent, noncriminal goals. Moreover, they are entitled to that representation

from a lawyer whose loyalty is not compromised by representation of other clients that are adverse to the first group.

Second, Nader offers us no guidance as to (a) how lawyers are supposed to decide when these other societal considerations act as limitations on their representations of clients and (b) who decides what those limitations are. If we were to leave it to Nader, we know that lawyers would not be allowed, for example, to participate in what he calls "the tort deform process." But is it Nader that each lawyer is to consult with every morning to find out where the limitations are?

Lawrence J. Fox, *Lawyers' Ethics According to Nader: Let the Corporate Clients Beware,* 12 GEO. J. LEGAL ETHICS 367, 372–73 (1999).

4. Ralph Nader's NO CONTEST is not really a book about "business lawyers"—at least not as practicing lawyers use that term. Practicing lawyers think of business lawyers as "deal lawyers." It is more a book about the trial lawyers who represent businesses in their litigation. If a business lawyer is doing her job right, litigation should be a small part of her work.

5. As the following excerpt from Ronald Gilson, *Value Creation By Business Lawyers: Legal Skills and Asset Pricing,* 94 YALE L.J. 239, 241–43 (1984), suggests, business lawyers are criticized not only by activists like Ralph Nader, but even by their clients:

What do business lawyers really do?

Clients have their own, often quite uncharitable, view of what business lawyers do. In an extreme version, business lawyers are perceived as evil sorcerers who use their special skills and professional magic to relieve clients of their possessions.

Clients frequently advance other more charitable but still negative views of the business lawyer that also should be familiar to most practitioners. Business lawyers are seen at best as a transaction cost, part of a system of wealth redistribution from clients to lawyers; legal fees represent a tax on business transactions to provide an income maintenance program for lawyers. At worst, lawyers are seen as deal killers whose continual raising of obstacles, without commensurate effort at finding solutions, ultimately causes transactions to collapse under their own weight.

Lawyers, to be sure, do not share these harsh evaluations of their role. When my question—what does a business lawyer really do—is put to business lawyers, the familiar response is that they "protect" their clients, that they get their clients the "best" deal. But both sides do seem to agree on the appropriate standard by which the performance of business lawyers should be judged: If what a business lawyer does has value, a transaction must be worth more, net of legal fees, as a result of the lawyer's participation.

6. Despite the criticism, most business lawyers are justifiably proud of what they do. They spend most of their time helping distinctly middle-class clients start, manage, grow, and ultimately sell small and medium-size businesses. The businesses, in turn, provide the products and services that people

need and enjoy. Lawyers can take pride that they help produce, perhaps a bit indirectly, AIDS drugs, organic healthy foods, and the movie *Wassup Rockers*.

F. WHAT ARE THE LEGAL STRUCTURES FOR BUSINESSES?

For the most part, the rest of this book is about the various forms of legal structures for businesses. By way of preview, the following is an overview of what co-author Roberts teaches people going to business school (which we call "client school" because many of your clients will have gone there) about the legal structures for businesses.

The decision regarding a business structure is driven chiefly by the objectives of the business's founder and the firm's investors, in terms of tax status, exposure to legal liabilities, and flexibility in the operation and financing of the business. The choices are made difficult by the inherent tradeoffs imposed by the law. To get the most favorable tax treatment, one may sometimes have to give up some protection from liability exposure, flexibility or both.

1. WHAT CHOICES ARE AVAILABLE?

The basic legal forms of business organization include:

The sole proprietorship

The partnership

- general partnership
- limited partnership

The corporation

The limited liability company (LLC)

For the owner, the two most important differences in these various business structures are (1) tax treatment of the business's profits and (2) liability exposure of the owners for the business's debts and other potential liabilities. These differences can be seen most readily by comparing sole proprietorships and corporations. Other business structures such as partnerships, limited partnerships, and limited liability companies are, in a sense, combinations of features from the corporation and partnership structures.

a. The Sole Proprietorship

The sole proprietorship is the oldest and simplest form of organization: a person undertakes a business without any of the formalities associated with other forms of organization; the individual and the business are one and the same for tax and legal liability purposes.

The proprietorship does not pay taxes as a separate entity. The individual reports all income and deductible expenses for the business on her personal income tax return. These earnings of the business are taxed to the individual regardless of whether they are *actually* distributed in cash. There is no vehicle for "sheltering" income from tax.

For liability purposes, the individual and the business are also one and the same. Thus, legal claimants can pursue all assets of the owner, not simply the assets used in the business.

b. The Corporation

The corporation is the most common legal structure for large businesses.* One major advantage of the corporation, compared to the sole proprietorship, is that a corporation's owners (stockholders or shareholders) are generally protected from personal liability.

In exchange for this protection, the corporation is considered a tax-paying entity. A corporation must pay taxes on its income, just like a real person.

And, because the business does not get any deduction for dividends paid, the earnings of a corporation are, in essence, taxed twice. First, the corporation pays a tax on its income. Second, the owners of the corporation pay a tax on the part of the corporation's earnings that is distributed to them as dividends.

The current maximum income taxation rate on corporate income is 35%; the maximum rate on individual income is likely to be approximately 40% when federal and state taxes are considered. Thus, $1.00 of pre-tax corporate income becomes $0.39 when it is distributed as dividends and taxed at the personal level $[1.00 \times (1-.35) \times (1-.40)]$.

This double taxation of corporations—taxation first of the corporations on its earnings and then second of its shareholders on their dividends—creates powerful incentives for enterprises that anticipate distributing earnings to use a form of business structure which is not taxed on its earnings, such as a partnership or limited liability company.

Other forms of organization can best be understood in relation to the sole proprietorship and the corporation. Do not think of these business forms as hermetically sealed; in fact, there is a great deal of overlap among them, and a lawyer may be able to suggest more than one potential business structure to achieve the client's goals. It is helpful to note that the law continues to evolve, and one reason for the multiple business forms is that states have reached various stages of development. Eventually, some people believe, there will be only two basic business forms, the corporation for large businesses and the limited liability company for small ones. The law is not there yet, though, so the lawyer must be facile with the characteristics of various business structures.

c. The (General) Partnership

Partnerships are businesses that consist of two or more owners. A partnership is treated like a sole proprietorship for tax and liability

---

* We refer here to "C" corporations. We briefly discuss "S" corporations a bit further down.

purposes. Earnings are distributed according to the partnership agreement, and taxes are paid only at the personal level on the partner's share
of that income (this is called "pass-through" taxation). For liability
purposes, each of the partners is jointly and severally liable. Thus, an
injured party may pursue one or more of the partners for any amount.
The claim need not be proportional to invested capital or to the distribution of earnings.

d. The Limited Partnership

Limited partnerships are a hybrid form of organization. It is like a
partnership or sole proprietorship for tax purposes. And, it is somewhat
like a corporation for liability purposes. A limited partnership is a partnership that has *both* limited and general partners. The general partner
assumes the management responsibility *and* unlimited liability for the
business. The limited partner has little voice in management and is not
individually liable for the company's debts. The limited partner thus looks
a lot like a shareholder in a corporation.

e. The Limited Liability Company (LLC)

The limited liability company is a business structure developed to
provide both the protection from liability of a corporation and the protection from double taxation of a partnership. The owners of a limited
liability company are not individually liable for the company's debts. The
limited liability company is not a tax paying entity. Income taxes are only
paid once—by the owners of the limited liability company when a part of
the company's earnings is distributed to them.

The existence of an LLC depends on compliance with the state limited
liability company law. These laws differ from state to state.*

f. The S Corporation and Not–For–Profit Corporations

Although we won't discuss them further in this book, you should
know a little about two additional business forms. Like the LLC, the S
Corporation is afforded the tax status of a partnership, but the protection
from legal liability of a corporation. This advantageous tax treatment
comes at a cost. To qualify for S Corporation tax status, the business must
meet a number of rather restrictive conditions in the Internal Revenue
Code, including being a domestic corporation, owned wholly by human
(not entity) citizens of the United States, with 100 or fewer stockholders.

The IRS and individual states have established that certain corporations that, in narrowly specified ways, operate for the public benefit need
not pay corporate income tax. In addition, individuals can deduct gifts to
these "non-profit" corporations from their tax returns. Internal Revenue

---

* Similar to an LLC, a Limited Liability Partnership (LLP) is a general partnership that files
the documents required by state law to provide partners with limited liability—that is, the
partners, who ordinarily would be liable for partnership debts, are not personally liable; they can
lose nothing more than their investments in the firm. The law varies from state-to-state on
whether this freedom from liability is total or partial, depending on the type of claim asserted.

Code 501(c)(3). Churches and universities are examples. Most normal businesses do not qualify.

2. HOW DO YOU CHOOSE?

The right choice depends upon a balance of factors to be assessed in light of the client's needs:

> Persons setting up any business must address certain core questions, including (1) who will own the business, (2) who will manage it, (3) who will reap any profit, (4) who will bear the risk of any loss, and (5) who will pay income tax on any business profit. * * * The development of [various] forms of business organization in the United States is largely the story of attempting to maximize benefit while reducing risk. One example might be assessing the possibility of whether an owner could limit his liability for business debts while sharing in profits and decision-making.

Richard D. Freer, *Business Organizations*, OXFORD COMPANION TO AMERICAN LAW 77 (2002), edited by Kermit Hall, copyright by Oxford University Press, Inc. Used by permission of Oxford University Press, Inc.

CHAPTER TWO

WHAT IS A SOLE PROPRIETORSHIP AND HOW DOES IT WORK?

■ ■ ■

A. WHAT IS A SOLE PROPRIETORSHIP? WHAT IS SOLE PROPRIETORSHIP LAW? WHAT ARE THE PROBLEMS IN STARTING A BUSINESS AS A SOLE PROPRIETORSHIP?

The most common form of business is the sole proprietorship. A sole proprietorship is a business structure without a legal structure. In a sole proprietorship, the business and its owner are the same actual person and the same legal person. Assume, for example, that Melvin Propp, a 25–year–old recent college graduate, has decided that he has figured out the next food fad: southern-style burritos.* He wants to lease a building near a college campus and open what he hopes will be the first of thousands of Bubba's Burritos stores. What does Propp need to do?

Propp does not need a lawyer to create the sole proprietorship. He does not need to do anything to create the sole proprietorship. Propp is the sole proprietorship, and the sole proprietorship is Propp. There is no need to draft any legal document, and no need to file anything. The sole proprietorship is the "default" structure for a business with one owner. Unless the owner files papers to create some other structure, such as a corporation, his business is automatically a sole proprietorship.

---

* According to Amy Culbertson, a restaurant reviewer for the Cincinnati Post, burritos "are a major food fad. * * * The most visible aspect of the trend is the use of international ingredients and flavors—fusion cuisine with a vengeance." Amy Culbertson, *Invasion of the Burrito*, Scripps–Howard News Service, Birmingham Post–Herald, February 23, 2000. And the beat goes on. According to an article on a website, dated February 6, 2006, "Hot trend or convenient meal? Are burrito joints the coffeehouses of the 21st century? It might be too early to tell, but if you follow the crumbs from a burrito restaurante, they just might lead to a ... college campus." www. krtcampus.com/stories,campusnews.htm. *But cf.* Rod Patterson, Living, Portland Oregonian, 2000, March 16, 2000. ("In a civilized society, a burrito is not an entree; it is a symbol of man's inhumanity to man.")

The use of a trade name such as "Bubba's Burritos" can present various legal issues. For example, there are statutory procedures for reserving and obtaining a trade name and there are statutory and case law requirements that the trade name not be deceptively similar to existing trade names. The use of a trade name does not, however, create or require a new legal entity. Propp is Bubba's Burritos and Bubba's Burritos is Propp.

Similarly, as a sole proprietor, Propp will not need a lawyer's help in dealing with the questions that confronted the corporation in the *A.P. Smith* case: (1) who decides what the business does; and, (2) who gets the money the business makes. In a sole proprietorship, there is no legal separation of the business, the people who manage the business, and the people who own the business. Propp simply is Bubba's Burritos. Propp makes the business decisions and Propp gets the profits from the business.

Propp is also responsible for the debts and obligations of the business. For liability purposes, Propp is Bubba's Burritos. Propp reports the business's income on his personal tax return and pays the taxes on that income (at his personal rate). People who extend credit to the business or otherwise have legal claims (including tort claims) against the business can sue Propp personally and collect those claims from Propp. To summarize:

> The sole proprietorship is as old as business itself. With it, * * * one person owns the enterprise, is responsible for management decisions, receives all profit and bears all loss. The business is indistinguishable from its proprietor. Business income is part of the proprietor's taxable income for federal and state personal income tax purposes. The law imposes no formalities for forming a sole proprietorship. The proprietor simply owns and operates a business, which is a sole proprietorship even if the proprietor is unaware of that fact.

Richard D. Freer, *Business Organizations,* OXFORD COMPANION TO AMERICAN LAW 77 (2002).

B. WHAT ARE THE PROBLEMS IN OPERATING A BUSINESS AS A SOLE PROPRIETORSHIP?

1. EMPLOYEES AND INTRODUCTION TO PRINCIPLES OF AGENCY

Sometimes, the sole proprietor will be the only person actively involved in the business. It is very common, however, for the sole proprietor to hire employees to discharge various business functions. In fact, a sole proprietorship can have thousands of employees—it remains a sole proprietorship so long as one person *owns* the business.

Clearly, Propp will need employees for Bubba's Burritos. The relation-

ship between Propp and his employees is largely a matter of contract law.*
An important legal question arises, however, when claims are asserted
against Propp by third parties. Specifically, is Propp liable to third parties,
in contract or in tort, for the acts or omissions of his employees? The
answer is found in the application of the law of agency.

Courts developed the principles of agency as part of common law. In
some states, the principles were eventually codified. Your professor will
ask you to study these principles as they have been recorded in a
Restatement. Courts tend to find the law of agency in the Restatements.†

Agency law involves *delegation*. Someone (the principal) has a task to
perform or an agreement to make. Instead of doing it herself, she engages
someone else (the agent) to do it on her behalf. Businesses regularly act
through agency relationships, but agency relationships are not limited to
business.

Indeed, all of us are regularly involved in agency relationships (perhaps without even knowing it). Suppose your roommate knows you are
going to the store and says "would you pick up some popcorn for me—you
know, that kind with all the cheese on it?" You say "sure." You are now
an agent for your roommate. Your roommate is your principal.

But why? Read Restatement (Second) of Agency (R–2) § 1, and note
these three points:

First, agency is a "fiduciary relation"—we will discuss that concept in
great detail later. For now, realize it means that the agent owes duties—
fiduciary duties—to the principal in discharging the act.

Second, there must be some "manifestation of consent by one person
[the principal] to another [the agent] that the other [the agent] shall act
on his [the principal's] behalf and subject to his [the principal's] control."

Third, there also must be "consent by the other [the agent] so to act."

Exactly the same three points are made in Restatement (Third) of
Agency (R–3) § 1.01.

---

* Other bodies of law affect the relationship between employer and employee, of course. These
include laws on taxation, wages and hours, employment discrimination and others that are
beyond the scope of our book.

† The ALI has addressed agency law in three Restatements. The original Restatement of
Agency was promulgated in 1934 and is of no concern to us. But we must deal with the other two
efforts. The ALI published the Restatement (Second) of Agency (which we will call "R–2") in
1958. Through the decades, courts have cited R–2 approvingly in thousands of cases. In 2006, the
ALI approved the Restatement (Third) of Agency (which we will call "R–3"). It is beginning to
gain a following, but certainly has not supplanted R–2 (and might never).

Your professor probably required you to buy a statutory supplement. That book will contain
either R–2 or R–3 (in fact, it may have both). In general, R–3 is written somewhat more clearly
then R–2, and in a couple of areas R–3 has adopted different terminology. In addition, R–3
addresses the application of agency law in organizational contexts, such as corporations, that R–2
did not. Nonetheless, courts readily have applied R–2 in such contexts. In all but one substantive
area (inherent agency power, discussed below), however, the answers to our questions will be the
same under R–2 and R–3. So, for us, there no appreciable substantive difference between the two.

Throughout these materials, we will cite the relevant provisions of both R–2 and R–3. This will
allow your professor to adopt either one for your class. When we quote the language of a
Restatement, it will generally be to R–2 (with a citation to the complementary section in R–3).

Your roommate, the principal, made the manifestation as required in the second step. Notice that the "control" required does not mean that the roommate told you how to do what he wanted done. He did not spell out every detail of how you were to acquire the popcorn. But he did tell you what the job was, and it was clear that he was "in charge" for that act.

And you consented, as required in the third step. Thus you formed an agency relationship regardless of whether you called it that and regardless of whether you knew that. Agency is a result of *conduct*, and not of the words used. The conduct manifests that one will do something for another, who is in charge.

Here we focus on one important aspect of agency law: how agents interact with third parties. Specifically, do the agent's acts bind the principal to the third party? And do the agent's acts bind the third party with the principal? Common sense and experience will tell us a great deal here. So does R–2 § 7, which defines "authority" as the "power of the agent to affect the legal relations of the principal by acts done in accordance with the principal's manifestations of consent to him."

Let's talk first about contractual liability. Suppose you call a travel agent and ask him to make a reservation for you on Delta's 8:00 PM flight from Atlanta to Paris on July 13. He does so. When you show up two hours before the flight, Delta cannot say "We don't need to let you on that flight because we never made a deal with you." Indeed, the airline *did* make a deal with you—*through* your agent. That deal binds the third party (the airline). Think of the chaos that would ensue if we could not enter *binding* deals through agents.

But what about the other way around? Does a deal by your agent with a third party bind you? The answer will be yes *if* your agent had "power" (or, as most courts will say, "authority") to bind the principal. Take the airline example. You call a travel agent and ask him to make a reservation for you on Delta's 8:00 PM flight from Atlanta to Paris on July 13. He does so. Can you refuse to pay for the Delta ticket on the theory that you have never dealt directly with Delta? Of course not. You are bound because your agent had authority to bind you in the purchase of that ticket. More specifically, your travel agent had *actual authority*.

Actual Authority (R–3 §§ 2.01, 3.01; R–2 § 26 (R–2 simply calls this "authority")). This is created by manifestations from the principal (P) to the agent (A) that the agent reasonably believes create authority. The principal—P—simply tells A that A is empowered to act on P's behalf in accomplishing some task.

> Epstein tells his chauffeur, Freer, that Freer has authority to have the car serviced at Roberts Service Station. Freer takes the car to Roberts for servicing. Epstein is obliged to pay for the service. Freer had actual authority to bind Epstein to the deal. Epstein gave that authority to Freer.

Sometimes the manifestation by P to A is not direct.

> Roberts goes to see his stockbroker, Shepherd, to place an order for 500 shares of Coca–Cola stock. When he sees that Shepherd is not at his desk, Roberts jots a note saying "Please purchase 500 sh. Coca–Cola for my account," which he signs. Roberts places it on what he thinks is Shepherd's desk. In fact, though, it is the desk of another broker, Epstein, who fills the order for Roberts. Epstein has actual authority to make the purchase for Roberts. The communication from Roberts can reasonably be interpreted to make Epstein believe that he was authorized. Roberts is bound to pay for the stock.

To be precise (always a good thing), what we have seen is "actual *express* authority," because P expressly gave A the power to undertake the act on her behalf.

> There is also "actual *implied* authority," which recognizes that an agent has the authority to do what is reasonably necessary to get the assigned job done, even if P did not spell it out in detail. In other words, there is interstitial authority for the agent to do what needs to be done to accomplish the task assigned.

> Freer asks his assistant to make travel arrangements for him to attend a law professor conference. Although he does not say anything specifically about airline reservations, his assistant has the implied actual authority to make such a reservation for him.

R–2 § 35 reflects this idea by providing that an agent's authority "includes authority to do acts which are incidental to it, usually accompany it, or are reasonably necessary to accomplish it." The same notion is found in R–3 § 2.02(1), which provides that the agent may take action "necessary or incidental to achieving the principal's objectives."

> An agent can also bind a principal on the basis of "apparent authority."

Apparent Authority (R–2 § 27; R–3 §§ 2.03, 3.03). The term "apparent authority" is somewhat misleading because, in apparent authority fact situations, P does not really authorize A to act on her behalf. Indeed P may have privately forbidden A to act. Instead, apparent authority is created by manifestations by P to a third party (TP). The manifestation (1) must be attributable to P, (2) must get to TP, and (3) must lead TP reasonably to conclude that A is an agent for P. Note that the provision does not require detrimental reliance by TP on P's manifestation.

> Epstein tells Roberts, who runs Roberts Service Station, that Freer is Epstein's agent for having the car serviced. Freer has apparent authority. This is true even if Epstein had privately told Freer that Freer had no authority to get the car fixed.

We will call this "apparent authority" (as R–2 and R–3 do) but you should know that some courts refer to this power as "implied authority."

Inherent Agency Power (R–2 § 8A). This power of A to bind P to deals with TP arises from the agency relationship itself. There is a sense that the power to do so just goes with the territory of the agency created. The best example arises in the corporate field. As we will see when we study corporations later in the book, corporate officers are agents of the corporation. One such officer is the corporate president. Generally, the office of corporate president carries with it the power to bind the corporation to contracts entered in the ordinary course of business.

> Shepherd is president of XYZ Corporation. In that capacity, he signs a contract that obligates XYZ Corporation to buy ordinary supplies from TP. Shepherd did not have actual authority to do this. Neither (to most courts) did he have apparent authority, because the corporation made no manifestation to TP that Shepherd could bind it. Rather, the corporation is bound on the contract because Shepherd, as president, had inherent agency power to bind it.

It is here that we encounter the only substantive distinction we will address between R–2 and R–3. While R–2 recognizes the concept of inherent agency power in § 8A, R–3 purports to abolish it. This abolition was a subject of substantial debate. *Compare, e.g.,* Thomas A. Simpson, *A Comment on an Inherently Flawed Concept: Why the Restatement (Third) of Agency Should Not Include the Doctrine of Inherent Agency Power*, 57 ALA. L. REV. 1163 (2006) *with* Gregory Crespi, *The Proposed Abolition of Inherent Agency Authority by the Restatement (Third) of Agency: An Incomplete Solution*, 45 SANTA CLARA L. REV. 337 (2005).

In the big picture, however, it is not clear that the abolition will change the way cases are decided. Instead, R–3 simply expands the notion of what constitutes a "manifestation" by P to TP, and hence broadens the scope of apparent authority. So in the hypothetical above about Shepherd, a court applying R–3 would hold the corporation liable on the contract with TP by concluding that the corporation had essentially manifested to TP—by giving Shepherd the title of president—that Shepherd had authority to bind it to deals in the ordinary course of business. That is, Shepherd had "apparent authority by position."

With this background, how do you answer the following problems?

PROBLEMS: LIABILITY OF THE SOLE PROPRIETOR FOR CONTRACTS OF HER EMPLOYEE

1. Propp hires Agee as cook, and tells her that part of her job will be to order the food for the restaurant. Agee does so by ordering grits and the other essential ingredients for Southern-style burritos for Bubba's Burritos from TeePee Distributing Co. (TP). TP delivers the food to Bubba's Burritos.

a. Is Propp legally obligated to pay for the food? *See* R–2 §§ 1, 7, 26, 140. *See* R–3 §§ 1.01, 1.02, 3.01, 3.02.

b. Is Agee legally obligated to pay for the food? *See* R–2 §§ 4, 320, 321, 322, 326. *See* R–3 §§ 1.04(2), 6.01, 6.02, 6.03, 6.04.

2. After several months, it becomes clear that Agee has been ordering too much food. Propp instructs Agee to reduce food purchases from TP from $2,200 a month to no more than a $1,000 a month. Notwithstanding this clear instruction, for the next month Agee orders $2,200 of new food from TP.

a. Is Propp legally obligated to pay $2,200 to TP? *See* R–2 §§ 8, 27, 140. *See* R–3 §§ 2.03, 3.03.

b. Is Agee legally obligated to pay $2,200 to TP? *See* R–2 § 320. *See* R–3 § 6.01.

c. Is Agee liable to Propp for violating her fiduciary duty to Propp? *See* R–2 § 377. *See* R–3 §§ 8.07, 8.09.

3. Agee (the cook) calls the local newspaper and tells the advertising director that she is running Bubba's Burritos for Propp (which is simply not true). She then places a series of full-page ads for Bubba's Burritos with the newspaper.

a. Is Propp liable to the newspaper for the Bubba's Burritos advertisements? *See* R–2 § 140.

b. Is Agee liable? *See* R–2 §§ 8A, 320, 321, 322. *See* R–3 §§ 6.01, 6.02, 6.03.

c. In this hypothetical, is there a principal at all?

What about tort liability? Suppose, for example, that Agent (A) is negligent and injures third party (TP) or damages her property. Is Principal (P) liable for that? You may remember the doctrine of *respondeat superior* from Torts. Through that doctrine, P can be liable even though P is not personally negligent. For example, P might hire A to make deliveries for her, and might train A appropriately for the job. If A is negligent and injures TP, however, the doctrine of *respondeat superior* will impose liability on P—even though P did nothing wrong. P's liability is "vicarious" or "secondary," and does not depend on P's being negligent.*

But *respondeat superior* does not apply in all cases of agency. Instead, it applies only to a subset of principal-and-agent relationships traditionally referred to as "master-and-servant." This is antiquated terminology, used in R–2 and still employed by many courts. R–2 defines this relationship at §§ 2 and 220. The more modern terminology, reflected in R–3, is "employer-and-employee." The principles are the same, no matter which terminology is used. Problems will work out the same way under both.

The important ingredient is that the master (or employer) has the right to control the details of how the servant (or employee) does the job. This requirement goes beyond the basic control inherent in all agency relationships, which we discussed above in connection with R–2 § 1 and

----

* We are concerned only with vicarious liability of P—that is, P's liability for something A did or failed to do, even though P did nothing wrong. P may commit a separate tort by hiring someone negligently who is inappropriate for the job or by failing to supervise an agent. We are not addressing such separate bases of liability here.

R–3 § 1.01. Here the master (employer) has control over the day-to-day performance of the servant's (employee's) task. Even here, though, it is not necessary that the master detail *every* move the servant must make. Just so there is enough from which we can say (or, more properly, a court can say) there is "control" over the details of the job. For example, in a normal employment relationship, Bubba's Burritos could tell its cook when to show up, how to cook the burritos, etc.*

A servant (employee) is to be distinguished from an *independent contractor*, who is hired to do a job, but is not told specifically how to do it. *See* R–2 § 2(3). The torts of an independent contractor generally are *not* attributable to the person who hires him. So vicarious tort liability comes from the fact that the person engaging someone controls the details of how the job is to be done. The dividing line between a servant and an independent contractor is often hazy, and is always fact-specific. *See* R–2 §§ 220, 228, 229. *See* R–3 § 7.07.

> Roberts hires Shepherd to build a sunroom. Roberts knows nothing about construction. He doesn't care how Shepherd does the job—just so it gets done to Roberts's satisfaction. Shepherd is an independent contractor, and is not a servant. Roberts would not be liable for Shepherd's torts. For example, Roberts would not be liable when Shepherd accidentally hands someone an operating power saw blade-first.

An independent contractor might be an agent or a non-agent for contract purposes.

> Suppose that when Roberts hires Shepherd, he gives him actual authority to purchase necessary supplies at Home Depot and charge them to Roberts' account. Shepherd is an "agent independent contractor." Although Roberts would be liable in contract to Home Depot for the supplies that Shepherd purchases on Roberts' behalf (he has actual authority), Roberts would not be liable for any torts that Shepherd commits.

> Suppose instead that when Roberts hires Shepherd, he gives him neither actual nor apparent authority to purchase supplies and charge them to his account. Shepherd is a "non-agent independent contractor." Roberts would be liable for Shepherd's actions neither in contract nor tort.

Finally, note that the master (employer) is liable for the torts of a servant (employee) *only* if the tort was committed within the scope of employment. *See* R–2 § 219. *See* R–3 § 7.07(1). An employer would not be liable when an employee injures his friends when he drops a blender in the hot tub after work.

---

* Part of the problem with the older terminology is the inference that a "servant" performs menial tasks. This is not necessarily so. A highly-skilled and highly-paid professional can be a "servant." Again, the modern terminology, "employee," is more accurate.

Although it might seem that an intentional tort would never be within the scope of one's employment, circumstances might indicate otherwise.

Freer hires Epstein as bouncer for a party. Epstein punches a guest in the nose. Although Freer did not instruct Epstein to do this, such a tort may go with the territory. Freer is probably vicariously liable. *See* R–2 § 228(1)(d). *See* R–3 § 7.07.

Sometimes a servant/employee leaves the appointed job to engage in personal business. Case law would say that such a servant/employee was on a "frolic." Torts committed during such periods should not be a basis for vicarious liability. Obviously, though, the dividing line here is hazy, and courts may strain to say that a servant was merely on a "detour" (as opposed to a "frolic"), during which torts committed by the servant would create vicarious liability.

Freer moonlights as a delivery driver for Bubba's Burritos. On his way to make a delivery, he makes a side trip to the stadium to buy tickets to an upcoming game. He commits a tort in the stadium parking lot. This side trip might well be a "frolic," meaning that the master would not be liable. The side trip was not motivated in any way to serve the master. *See* R–2 § 228(1)(c). *See* R–3 § 7.07.

On his way to make a delivery, Freer goes slightly out of his way to get lunch at McDonald's. He commits a tort in the McDonald's parking lot. This side trip might well be merely a "detour," meaning that the master would be vicariously liable. Although Freer deviated from the most direct route, he is entitled to lunch, and was on his way to do the master's job.

With this background, how do you answer the following problems?

PROBLEMS: *LIABILITY OF THE SOLE PROPRIETOR FOR TORTS OF HER EMPLOYEE*

1. Propp hires Servantes to work as a waiter at Bubba's Burritos. Is Servantes a "servant"? Are all "agents" also "servants"? Are all "servants" also "agents"? Are all employees "servants"? Is Propp a "master"?

2. Is the CEO of General Motors a servant? Is the pilot of a Boeing 747 airplane a servant of the airline? Are you liable if your accountant accidentally burns someone with cigar ash while doing your taxes?

3. Servantes negligently spills scalding coffee on a customer.

a. Is Propp liable in tort to the customer?

b. What if Propp specifically told Servantes, both orally and in writing, that his job description did not include spilling scalding liquids of any kind on customers?

c. Is Servantes also liable in tort to the customer?

4. While driving to work, Servantes negligently injures a pedestrian.

a. Is Propp liable in tort to the pedestrian?

   b.   Is Servantes liable in tort to the pedestrian?

   5.   Propp hires Agee to work as a cook. When Agee overhears a customer criticizing her cooking, she hits the customer over the head with a skillet.

   a.   Is Agee liable in tort to the customer?

   b.   Is Propp liable in tort to the customer?

   c.   Is Servantes (the waiter) liable in tort to the customer?

   6.   Can Propp eliminate the need to hire an attorney to answer the preceding questions simply by purchasing insurance?

2.   OTHER AGENCY RELATIONSHIPS IN BUSINESS

The application of agency law is not limited to the employment relationship. The owner of a business will encounter agency law issues in many other situations.

a.   Attorney–Client

The previous problems suggest that Propp might be hiring an attorney to defend him in various tort and contract actions arising from the business operations of Bubba's Burritos. Is Propp's attorney an agent? If so, for whom? In reading the following case, consider three questions about its facts:

   1.   What facts support a conclusion that Hayes's attorney was her agent?

   2.   What facts support a conclusion that Hayes's attorney had actual authority to settle her lawsuit?

   3.   What facts support a conclusion that Hayes's attorney had apparent authority to settle her lawsuit?

HAYES v. NATIONAL SERVICE INDUSTRIES, INC.

United States Court of Appeals, Eleventh Circuit, 1999
196 F.3d 1252

HOEVELER, SENIOR DISTRICT JUDGE, sitting by designation.

Robin Hayes appeals from the decision below enforcing the settlement agreement negotiated by her attorney as to Hayes' action brought pursuant to Title VII, 42 U.S.C. § 2000e. We must decide whether the nature of the underlying action, i.e., the employment discrimination claim, requires a departure from our general reliance on state law principles in determining whether to enforce a settlement agreement. We conclude that under the specific facts of this case it is proper to apply Georgia law to the construction and enforceability of this settlement agreement. Finding no abuse of discretion in the lower court's conclusion that Hayes' attorney had apparent authority to enter into the settlement on Hayes' behalf and that Hayes therefore was bound by the agreement, we affirm.

GA law

Hayes sued National Linen Service and its parent company, National Service Industries, Inc. (collectively, "National"), alleging wrongful discharge from her employment as a sales representative. The attorneys for the two parties settled the case. Hayes rejected the settlement, and National filed a motion to enforce the settlement agreement. The Magistrate Judge to whom the motion was referred issued a report finding that Rogers [Hayes's attorney] had apparent authority, and in fact believed he had actual authority, to settle the case. The report found that "the terms of the settlement are clear; plaintiff only contends that she did not consent," but noted that such issue was "irrelevant so long as her attorney has the apparent authority to settle her case [under Georgia law]." Hayes filed her objections to the report, claiming that she did not give Rogers the authority to settle the case on her behalf.

The district court overruled Hayes' objections, and adopted the report and recommendation [of the Magistrate Judge], specifically agreeing that Rogers had "apparent, if not actual, authority" to settle Hayes' claims. Defendants' motion to enforce was granted and Hayes' complaint was dismissed.

We must determine whether the trial judge abused his discretion in deciding to enforce the settlement agreement. * * *

An attorney of record is the client's agent in pursuing a cause of action and under Georgia law "[a]n act of an agent within the scope of his apparent authority binds the principal." The attorney's authority is determined by the representation agreement between the client and the attorney and any instructions given by the client, and that authority may be considered plenary unless it is limited by the client and that limitation is communicated to opposing parties.

"The client is therefore 'bound by his attorney's agreement to settle a lawsuit, even though the attorney may not have had express authority to settle, if the opposing party was unaware of any limitation on the attorney's apparent authority.'" *Ford v. Citizens and Southern Nat. Bank, Cartersville*, 928 F.2d 1118, 1120 (11th Cir. 1991). While Hayes asserts that her attorney lacked authority to settle this matter, it is undisputed that Hayes' attorney, Andrew Rogers, spoke with counsel for National, Sharon Morgan, and expressly told Morgan that he had authority from Hayes to settle the case for $15,000.00. According to Georgia law, an attorney has the apparent authority to enter into a binding agreement on behalf of a client and such agreement is enforceable against the client. Thus, the agreement is enforceable against Hayes according to Georgia law.

Careful attention to the arguments raised by Hayes reveals that her challenge is simply as to the authority of her attorney to enter into the agreement. Her attack on the formation of the contract is answered conclusively by our discussion above. Hayes' attorney told counsel for National that he had authority to settle this matter. An agreement was reached, and it is enforceable against Hayes. We affirm.

QUESTIONS AND NOTES

1. Questions about the law.

1.1 Did the court conclude that Hayes's attorney had "actual authority" or "apparent authority"? Did the court conclude that the attorney had both types of authority?

1.2 What is the difference, if any, between actual authority and apparent authority?

1.3 What is the legal significance of the fact that Hayes's attorney told counsel for National that he had authority to settle this matter?

1.4 Can an agent create his own authority to bind his principal? Is that what happened in this case?

1.5 Would the Eleventh Circuit have decided the question differently if Hayes's attorney had simply accepted the settlement offer without expressly saying that he had authority to settle?

1.6 Is the court's decision consistent with R–2 § 27? Is it consistent with R–3 §§ 2.03 and 3.03?

1.7 Does Hayes have a basis on which to sue her former attorney?

2. Notes.

2.1 Deborah A. DeMott, *The Lawyer As Agent*, 67 FORDHAM L. REV. 301, 301 (1998):

> The law of agency provides the foundational structure for many of the legal consequences that follow from the relationship between a lawyer and a client, as well as the relationship between an individual lawyer and a law firm. Definitional precision in the law aside, the lawyer-client relationship is a commonsensical illustration of agency. A lawyer acts on behalf of the client, representing the client, with consequences that bind the client. Lawyers act as clients' agents in transactional settings as well as in litigation. In any agency relationship, for example, the agent's loyalty to the interests of the principal is a dominant concern, as is the loyalty of a lawyer to the client.
>
> Despite its foundational significance, the law of agency does not by itself capture all of the legal consequences of relationships between lawyers and clients and between lawyers and others to whom the lawyer owes duties. In this context, agency is roughly comparable to the structural steel members that support a building and define its size and basic shape but do not govern how the building functions and looks. Lawyers are agents, but lawyers perform functions that distinguish them from most other agents. That a lawyer is an agent is sometimes irrelevant to the legal consequences of what the lawyer has done or has failed to do, making an unswerving focus on agency misleading. It is not surprising, then, that courts on occasion differentiate among agency's consequences, rather than according agency a monolithic or inexorable set of consequences.

2.2   James A. Cohen, *Lawyer Role, Agency Law and the Characterization "Officer of the Court,"* 48 BUFF. L. REV. 349, 404–05 (2000):

> The law of agency has governed American lawyers since before the Revolution, but recent scholarship about legal ethics and professional role almost entirely ignores it. Most commentators would concede that attorneys are agents, but would quickly add that the lawyer is also an "officer of the court" who has obligations to seek justice. However, analysis of the phrase "officer of the court" reveals that it has surprisingly little content; it is mostly rhetoric, caused by self-love and self-promotion.
>
> The agent must be obedient to the instructions of the principal. The client sets the goals and the lawyer simply tries to accomplish them.
>
> Following client instructions is central to both lawyer and agent role, but obedience does not mean that the lawyer must follow any and all lawful instruction. Because of the expertise, training, skill, and judgment, the lawyer has considerable license in selecting the means to accomplish the client's goals, subject to only two general conditions: (1) Lawyers may decline to abide by client instructions that may interfere with, or do not promote, accomplishment of the clients goals and (2) decline to engage in wrongdoing.

b.   Franchises and Other Business Relationships

The relationship of agency law to the franchisor-franchisee relationship is even less clear:

> An agency relationship involves consent and control. The parties must have consented that one is to act as a fiduciary on the behalf, and subject to the direction and control, of the other. Whatever the verbalization by the parties about the nature of their relationship, the external facts govern. Agency will then arise if the franchisor-principal has the requisite degree of control over the franchisee-agent, notwithstanding the customary boilerplate provision in the franchising agreement that the parties do not intend an agency relationship.
>
> When a court concludes that in the franchise relationship in issue, the franchisor has retained such control over the operations of the franchisee and its employees as to make the franchisee (and its employees) an agent (or subagents) of the franchisor, long-established principles of relational law come into play. By virtue of its status as a principal, the franchisor becomes liable to third parties for certain acts of its franchisee in its role as an agent. Finally, the control of the franchisor may be so reduced and the relationship sufficiently distant that the franchisee is not viewed as an agent at all. In such event, by definition, vicarious liability can only arise under those agency principles extending agency liability to non-agents under such doctrines as apparent agency or agency by estoppel.

Phillip L. Blumberg & Kurt Strasser, THE LAW OF CORPORATE GROUPS—ENTERPRISE LIABILITY 340–41 (1998).

What are Professors Blumberg and Strasser saying? If Bubba's Burritos prospers and Propp sells franchises, will he be liable to a customer of the Charlottesville franchisee who finds a snuff can lid in his burrito? Is the following case involving a foreign object in a Big Mac helpful in answering this question?

In reading the case, please consider these questions about the facts:

1.   How did the heart-shaped sapphire stone get into the Big Mac? Was that relevant to the court? Should it have been?

2.   Are the employees of 3K "servants" of 3K? Was that relevant to the court? Should it have been?

3.   Are the employees of 3K "servants" of McDonald's Corporation?

4.   How important is it to the court that McDonald's promulgated a manual laying out various requirements for 3K?

MILLER v. McDONALD'S CORPORATION

Oregon Court of Appeals, 1997
945 P.2d 1107

WARREN, P.J.

Plaintiff seeks damages from defendant McDonald's Corporation for injuries that she suffered when she bit into a heart-shaped sapphire stone while eating a Big Mac sandwich that she had purchased at a McDonald's restaurant in Tigard. The trial court granted summary judgment to defendant on the ground that it did not own or operate the restaurant; rather, the owner and operator was a non-party, 3K Restaurants (3K), that held a franchise from defendant. Plaintiff appeals, and we reverse.

Most of the relevant facts are not in dispute. To the degree that there are disputes, we read the record most favorably to plaintiff, the non-moving party, and review the evidence to determine whether an objectively reasonable juror could return a verdict in her favor on the subject of the motion. 3K owned and operated the restaurant under a License Agreement (the Agreement) with defendant that required it to operate in a manner consistent with the "McDonald's System." The Agreement described that system as including proprietary rights in trade names, service marks and trade marks, as well as "designs and color schemes for restaurant buildings, signs, equipment layouts, formulas and specifications for certain food products, methods of inventory and operation control, bookkeeping and accounting, and manuals covering business practices and policies."

The manuals [promulgated by McDonald's for franchisees] contain "detailed information relating to operation of the Restaurant," including food formulas and specifications, methods of inventory control, bookkeeping procedures, business practices, and other management, advertising, and personnel policies. 3K, as the licensee, agreed to adopt and exclusively use the formulas, methods, and policies contained in the manuals, including any subsequent modifications, and to use only advertising and pro-motional materials that defendant either provided or approved in advance in writing.

The Agreement described the way in which 3K was to operate the restaurant in considerable detail. It expressly required 3K to operate in compliance with defendant's prescribed standards, policies, practices, and procedures, including serving only food and beverage products that defendant designated. 3K had to follow defendant's specifications and blue-prints for the equipment and layout of the restaurant, including adopting subsequent reasonable changes that defendant made, and to maintain the restaurant building in compliance with defendant's standards. 3K could not make any changes in the basic design of the building without defendant's approval.

The Agreement required 3K to keep the restaurant open during the hours that defendant prescribed, including maintaining adequate supplies and employing adequate personnel to operate at maximum capacity and efficiency during those hours. 3K also had to keep the restaurant similar in appearance to all other McDonald's restaurants. 3K's employees had to wear McDonald's uniforms, to have a neat and clean appearance, and to provide competent and courteous service. 3K could use only containers and other packaging that bore McDonald's trademarks. The ingredients for the foods and beverages had to meet defendant's standards, and 3K had to use "only those methods of food handling and preparation that [defendant] may designate from time to time." In order to obtain the franchise, 3K had to represent that the franchisee had worked at a McDonald's restaurant; the Agreement did not distinguish in this respect between a company-run or a franchised restaurant. The manuals gave further details that expanded on many of these requirements.

In order to ensure conformity with the standards described in the Agreement, defendant periodically sent field consultants to the restaurant to inspect its operations. 3K trained its employees in accordance with defendant's materials and recommendations and sent some of them to training programs that defendant administered. Failure to comply with the agreed standards could result in loss of the franchise.

Despite these detailed instructions, the Agreement provided that 3K was not an agent of defendant for any purpose. Rather, it was an independent contractor and was responsible for all obligations and liabilities, including claims based on injury, illness, or death, directly or indirectly resulting from the operation of the restaurant.

Plaintiff went to the restaurant under the assumption that defendant owned, controlled, and managed it. So far as she could tell, the restaurant's appearance was similar to that of other McDonald's restaurants that she had patronized. Nothing disclosed to her that any entity other than defendant was involved in its operation. The only signs that were visible and obvious to the public had the name "McDonald's,"* **[2]** the employees wore uniforms with McDonald's insignia, and the menu was the same that plaintiff had seen in other McDonald's restaurants. The general appearance of the restaurant and the food products that it sold were similar to the restaurants and products that plaintiff had seen in national print and television advertising that defendant had run. To the best of plaintiff's knowledge, only McDonald's sells Big Mac hamburgers.

In short, plaintiff testified, she went to the Tigard McDonald's because she relied on defendant's reputation and because she wanted to obtain the same quality of service, standard of care in food preparation, and general attention to detail that she had previously enjoyed at other McDonald's restaurants.

Under these facts, 3K would be directly liable for any injuries that plaintiff suffered as a result of the restaurant's negligence. The issue on summary judgment is whether there is evidence that would permit a jury to find defendant vicariously liable for those injuries because of its relationship with 3K. Plaintiff asserts two theories of vicarious liability, actual agency and apparent agency. We hold that there is sufficient evidence to raise a jury issue under both theories. We first discuss actual agency.

The kind of actual agency relationship that would make defendant vicariously liable for 3K's negligence requires that defendant have the right to control the method by which 3K performed its obligations under the Agreement. The common context for that test is a normal master-servant (or employer-employee) relationship. The relationship between two business entities is not precisely an employment relationship, but the Oregon Supreme Court, in common with most if not all other courts that have considered the issue, has applied the right to control test for vicarious liability in that context as well. We therefore apply that test to this case. * * *

A number of other courts have applied the right to control test to a franchise relationship. The Delaware Supreme Court, in *Billops v. Magness Const. Co.*, 391 A.2d 196 (Del. 1978), stated the test as it applies to that context:

> If, in practical effect, the franchise agreement goes beyond the stage of setting standards, and allocates to the franchisor the right to exercise control over the daily operations of the franchise, an agency relationship exists.

* * *

As the various cases show, it may be difficult to determine when a franchisor has retained a right not only to set standards but also to control the daily operations of the franchisee. Two examples show the

---

* **[2]** This is plaintiff's testimony in her affidavit. Representatives of 3K testified in their depositions that there was a sign near the front counter that identified Bob and Karen Bates and 3K Restaurants as the owners. There is no evidence of the size or prominence of the sign, nor is there evidence of any other non-McDonald's identification in the restaurant.

different conclusions that the courts have reached and provide some guidance for this case. In *Wood v. Shell Oil Co.*, 495 So.2d 1034 (Ala.1986), the franchise agreement required a Shell gasoline dealer to maintain the station premises, including the appearance, design, color, style, and layout, in accordance with Shell's specifications or recommendations, to promote the sale of the products that the dealer purchased, to require all employees to wear Shell uniforms, and to let Shell inspect its books. The dealer had to maintain a competent staff of employees and to perform all mechanical work in a workmanlike manner, using only first class parts. Shell might offer supplemental training for the employees. The Alabama court held that the agreement did not establish actual agency because it did not control how the dealer complied with the requirements.

In contrast, in *Billops* the franchise agreement for a Hilton Inn hotel incorporated a detailed and, in part, mandatory operating manual that covered identification, advertising, front office procedures, cleaning and inspection service for rooms and public areas, minimum room standards, food purchasing and preparation standards, staff procedures and standards for booking group meetings, function, and room reservations, accounting, insurance, engineering, maintenance and numerous other details. The franchisee had to keep detailed records so that the franchisor could ensure compliance with those guidelines, while the franchisor retained the right to enter the premises to ensure compliance. The franchisor could terminate on 20 days notice for an uncorrected violation. The court held that those facts created a jury issue of whether an actual agency relationship existed.

The essential distinction between *Wood* and *Billops* is the extent to which the franchisor retained control over the details of the franchisee's performance. In *Wood*, the franchisor required only that mechanical work be done in a workmanlike manner. In *Billops*, however, the franchisor issued a manual that described the methods by which the franchisee was to carry out its responsibilities in considerable detail. The agreement in *Wood*, thus, could only be read as providing standards that the franchisee had to meet, while the agreement in *Billops* could be read as retaining the right to exercise control over the franchisee's daily operations.

The facts of this case are close to those in *Billops*. For that reason, we believe that a jury could find that defendant retained sufficient control over 3K's daily operations that an actual agency relationship existed. The Agreement did not simply set standards that 3K had to meet. Rather, it required 3K to use the precise methods that defendant established, both in the Agreement and in the detailed manuals that the Agreement incorporated. Those methods included the ways in which 3K was to handle and prepare food. Defendant enforced the use of those methods by regularly sending inspectors and by its retained power to cancel the Agreement. That evidence would support a finding that defendant had the right to control the way in which 3K performed at least food handling and preparation. In her complaint, plaintiff alleges that 3K's deficiencies in those functions resulted in the sapphire being in the Big Mac and thereby caused her injuries. Thus, * * * there is evidence that defendant had the right to control 3K in the precise part of its business that allegedly resulted in plaintiff's injuries. That is sufficient to raise an issue of actual agency.

Plaintiff next asserts that defendant is vicariously liable for 3K's alleged negligence because 3K was defendant's apparent agent.* [4] The relevant standard is in Restatement (Second) of Agency, section 267. [That section provides: "One who represents that another is his servant or other agent and thereby causes a third person justifiably to rely upon the care or skill of such apparent agent is subject to liability to the third person for harm caused by the lack of care or skill of the one appearing to be a servant or other agent as if he were such."]

We have not applied section 267 to a franchisor/franchisee situation, but courts in a number of other jurisdictions have done so in ways that we find instructive. In most cases the courts have found that there was a jury issue of apparent agency. The crucial issues are whether the putative principal held the third party out as an agent and whether the plaintiff relied on that holding out.

We look first at what may constitute a franchisor's holding a franchisee out as its agent. In the leading case of *Gizzi v. Texaco, Inc.*, 437 F.2d 308 (5th Cir. 1971), the plaintiff purchased a used Volkswagen van from a Texaco service station. He was injured when the brakes failed shortly thereafter. The franchisee had worked on the brakes before selling the car. The station prominently displayed Texaco insignia, including the slogan "Trust your car to the man who wears the star." Texaco engaged in considerable national advertising to convey the impression that its dealers were skilled in automotive servicing. About 30 percent of Texaco dealers sold used cars. There was a Texaco regional office across the street from the station, and those working in that office knew that the franchisee was selling cars from the station. Based on this evidence, the court concluded, under New Jersey law, that the question of apparent agency was for the jury. * * *

In *Billops*, the franchise agreement required the franchisee to display the Hilton logo and sign to the exclusion of all others, forbade the mention of any name other than Hilton as the management of the Hotel, and required the franchisee to identify itself with the Hilton "system," including the color scheme and design of the hotel. There was no reasonable way, based on the method of operation or physical environment of the hotel, by which an ordinary customer would know that he or she was dealing with anything other than the Hilton Corporation. The Delaware

---

* [4] Apparent agency is a distinct concept from apparent authority. Apparent agency creates an agency relationship that does not otherwise exist, while apparent authority expands the authority of an actual agent. *See Crinkley v. Holiday Inns, Inc.*, 844 F.2d 156, 166 (4th Cir. 1988). In this case, the precise issue is whether 3K was defendant's apparent agent, not whether 3K had apparent authority. However, because courts in Oregon and elsewhere often use the terms interchangeably, we will treat the parties' arguments as based on apparent agency, whichever term they actually use.

Supreme Court held that that evidence was sufficient to support a finding of apparent agency.

In *Crinkley v. Holiday Inns, Inc.*, 844 F.2d 156 (4th Cir.1988), the defendant required the use of the Holiday Inn trade name and trademarks, was the original builder of the hotel, and engaged in national advertising that promoted its system of hotels without distinguishing between those that it owned and those that it franchised. The only indication that the defendant did not own this particular Holiday Inn was a sign in the restaurant that stated that the franchisee operated it. Based on this evidence, the court concluded, under North Carolina law, that apparent agency was a question for the jury.

In each of these cases, the franchise agreement required the franchisee to act in ways that identified it with the franchisor. The franchisor imposed those requirements as part of maintaining an image of uniformity of operations and appearance for the franchisor's entire system. Its purpose was to attract the patronage of the public to that entire system. The centrally imposed uniformity is the fundamental basis for the courts' conclusion that there was an issue of fact whether the franchisors held the franchisees out as the franchisors' agents.

In this case, for similar reasons, there is an issue of fact about whether defendant held 3K out as its agent. Everything about the appearance and operation of the Tigard McDonald's identified it with defendant and with the common image for all McDonald's restaurants that defendant has worked to create through national advertising, common signs and uniforms, common menus, common appearance, and common standards. The possible existence of a sign identifying 3K as the operator does not alter the conclusion that there is an issue of apparent agency for the jury. There are issues of fact of whether that sign was sufficiently visible to the public, in light of plaintiff's apparent failure to see it, and of whether one sign by itself is sufficient to remove the impression that defendant created through all of the other indicia of its control that it, and 3K under the requirements that defendant imposed, presented to the public.* **[7]**

Defendant does not seriously dispute that a jury could find that it held 3K out as its agent. Rather, it argues that there is insufficient evidence that plaintiff justifiably relied on that holding out. It argues that it is not sufficient for her to prove that she went to the Tigard McDonald's because it was a McDonald's restaurant. Rather, she also had to prove that she went to it because she believed that McDonald's Corporation operated both it and the other McDonald's restaurants that she had previously patronized. It states: "All [that] the Plaintiff's affidavit proves is that she went to the Tigard McDonald's based in reliance on her past experiences at other McDonald's. But her affidavit does nothing to link

---

* **[7]** In addition, operation of the restaurant by a franchisee is not inconsistent as a matter of law with a finding of agency. An agency relationship necessarily requires that the principal and the agent be separate entities.

her experiences with ownership of those restaurants by McDonald's Corporation.''

Defendant's argument both demands a higher level of sophistication about the nature of franchising than the general public can be expected to have and ignores the effect of its own efforts to lead the public to believe that McDonald's restaurants are part of a uniform national system of restaurants with common products and common standards of quality. A jury could find from plaintiff's affidavit that she believed that all McDonald's restaurants were the same because she believed that one entity owned and operated all of them or, at the least, exercised sufficient control that the standards that she experienced at one would be the same as she experienced at others.

Plaintiff testified in her affidavit that her reliance on defendant for the quality of service and food at the Tigard McDonald's came in part from her experience at other McDonald's restaurants. Defendant's argument that she must show that it, rather than a franchisee, operated those restaurants is, at best, disingenuous. A jury could find that it was defendant's very insistence on uniformity of appearance and standards, designed to cause the public to think of every McDonald's, franchised or unfranchised, as part of the same system, that makes it difficult or impossible for plaintiff to tell whether her previous experiences were at restaurants that defendant owned or franchised.

Other courts have not required the specificity of reliance on which defendant insists. In *Crinkley*, the plaintiffs stayed at a Holiday Inn because they thought that it would be a good place to stay. They were unable to get a room at the first Holiday Inn that they tried and used a Holiday Inn directory to find the one where they did stay. One plaintiff testified that he did not know the difference between a franchised inn and a company-owned inn and would be greatly surprised to find that Holiday Inns (the franchisor) was not involved in the operation of the inn where he stayed. The court held that that evidence was sufficient to raise a jury issue of reliance. * * *

In *Billops* there was evidence that the plaintiffs relied on the Hilton name and on the quality that the name represented. That was sufficient to avoid summary judgment. In *Gizzi* the plaintiff's testimony that Texaco's advertising had instilled in him a sense of confidence in the corporation and its products created an issue of fact on reliance. * * *

In this case plaintiff testified that she relied on the general reputation of McDonald's in patronizing the Tigard restaurant and in her expectation of the quality of the food and service that she would receive. Especially in light of defendant's efforts to create a public perception of a common McDonald's system at all McDonald's restaurants, whoever operated them, a jury could find that plaintiff's reliance was objectively reasonable. The trial court erred in granting summary judgment on the apparent agency theory.

Reversed and remanded.

QUESTIONS AND NOTES

1. Questions about the law.

1.1 Would 3K be liable for the negligence of its employee? If so, why did Miller sue McDonald's?

1.2 The Court noted that the agreement between 3K and McDonald's provided that 3K was not an agent of McDonald's. Was that important to the court? Should it have been?

1.3 McDonald's benefits from its franchises being part of a large, consistent international organization. Would it be fair to permit McDonald's to escape liability costs when the organization causes injury?

1.4 Do you agree with the following advice from the general counsel for Speedy Sign–A–Rama, USA, Inc.:

> The franchisor should draft a direct disclaimer of agency into its franchise agreement. This disclaimer is usually written as an Independent Contractor's clause. Unfortunately, rather than operating as a "get out of jail free" card, the Independent Contractor's clause is quickly swept aside by the court in preference of a control-based analysis. However, the courts inevitably comment on the existence of such a clause, proving that they do examine the franchise agreement for it and give it some consideration. A sample agency disclaimer follows:

> INDEPENDENT CONTRACTOR AND INDEMNITY (1) This agreement does not create the relationship of principal and agent between the Franchisee and EGN.* Franchisee is an independent contractor and, except as expressly permitted under this Agreement for certain rights of EGN, neither the Franchisee nor EGN will under any circumstances, act or hold itself out as agent or representative of the other, nor incur any liability or create any obligation whatsoever in the name of the other. The Franchisee shall further indemnify EGN against all claims, demands, damages, cost or expenses which may be incurred or received by EGN resulting from any finding by any Court or regulatory agency that Franchisee is an agent of EGN. (2) The Franchisee agrees to take such affirmative action as may be requested by EGN to indicate that the Franchisee is an independent contractor, including placing and maintaining a plaque in a conspicuous place within the Premises and a notice on all stationery, business cards, sales literature, contracts and similar documents, which states that the EGN Restaurant is independently owned and operated by the Franchisee. The content of such plaque and notice is subject to the prior written approval of EGN.

Jeffrey Brent Brams, *Franchisor Liability: Drafting Around the Problems With Franchisor Control*, 24 OKLA. CITY U. L. REV. 65, 70–71 (1999).

1.5 How is "apparent agency" (discussed by the court in footnote 4 in *Miller*) different from "apparent authority"? Is apparent agency a basis for imposing contract liability, or tort liability, or both?

---

* The sample agency disclaimer is taken from a law review article that focuses on a peanut butter-based restaurant chain, "Everything's Gone Nuts (EGN)."

1.6   Is the story of the snuff can lid in the Charlottesville Bubba's Burritos customer's burrito distinguishable from the *Miller* case?

1.7   Are all franchisors liable as principals? Do all franchise arrangements create agency relationships?

2.   Notes.

2.1   One of Miller's arguments was that McDonald's, a corporation, was liable for the acts of 3K, another corporation, because McDonald's control over 3K's performance made 3K McDonald's agent. While the relationship between the two corporations in this case was franchisor-franchisee, the concept that a corporation can be liable under agency law principles for the acts of another corporation if it controls that corporation's performance of the acts is not limited to franchises. *Cf.* R–2 § 14M. *See generally* Maung Ng We & Massive Atlantic Limited v. Merrill, Lynch & Co., Inc., 2000 WL 1159835 (S.D.N.Y. 2000). We will talk more about this when we know enough about corporations that we can compare "piercing the corporate veil" and agency law.

2.2   Deborah DeMott, *A Revised Prospectus for a Third Restatement of Agency,* 31 U.C. DAVIS L. REV. 1035, 1044 (1998):

> Since 1958, much case law has considered circumstances, apart from formal and explicit appointment, that justify treating one person as another's agent. The most troubling cases apply concepts termed "apparent agency" and "estoppel" to hold liable a party who benefits from a relationship in which the parties did not intend the legal consequences of agency. Frequently, the party who ultimately benefits economically through another's activity fails to notify the public that the relationship is other than agency. It is likely that parties to such relationships value their ability to structure the way they do business in order to minimize legal risks.
>
> Some cases strain to apply this estoppel doctrine to protect third parties who are injured in their dealings with, for example, a nonemployee physician in a hospital emergency room or an independent franchisee in a seemingly unified national chain of business establishments. Jurisdictions differ on the plaintiff's burden of establishing detrimental reliance on an appearance of agency and in the probative significance assigned to a party's failure to correct misimpressions that others may draw about the nature of a relationship.

2.3   Kevin Shelley & Susan Morton, *"Control" in Franchising and the Common Law,* 19 FRANCHISE L. J. 119 (2000), make these observations:

> In Chicago, it is illegal to fish in your pajamas. In Atlanta, the law says that you may not tie a giraffe to a telephone pole. Maine has a statute that makes it illegal to bite a landlord. And in Connecticut (pay attention, you fast-food franchisors), it is illegal to open a restaurant that does not feature both nose-blowing and non-nose-blowing sections.
>
> They are all antiquated, silly, and absurd rules of law. However, they are no more antiquated, silly, and absurd than the rules of law that predate franchising's advent by decades and in some cases centuries but that are blindly applied by the judiciary without an understanding of the

fundamental business structures and precepts of franchising. Perhaps nowhere is this unfortunate practice more evident than in the judiciary's continued application of traditional principal-agent and employer-employee "control" doctrines to the franchisor-franchisee relationship without regard to the controls inherent in that relationship—controls that, in fact, form part of the definition of the term "franchise" in every federal and state franchise law, rule, and regulation.

2.4 Can you see now why a franchisee's stationary and advertising often state, "This company is independently owned and operated."

C. HOW DOES A SOLE PROPRIETORSHIP GROW?

Presumably, Propp needs money to start Bubba's Burritos and make it grow. Let's begin discussing how Propp might obtain the necessary funds.

1. FUNDING BY THE OWNER

A business is often at greatest risk when it is just starting. Accordingly, the first investment in the business almost always will be from the business's owner. One reason is that the entrepreneur's investing in her own business can demonstrate her commitment to the business. Investors and lenders perceive (rightly) that the entrepreneur will be more committed to the venture if she has invested her personal assets in it.

There is another, more practical, reason this start-up phase will usually be financed with the entrepreneur's own funds. To raise money, you typically need more than an idea. The entrepreneur will have to invest some money in the idea, perhaps to build a prototype or to do a market study, to convince potential providers of capital that the idea has potential.

This is not to say that these funds must be the owner's own money in the purest sense. The entrepreneur can obtain these funds by mortgaging personal assets like a house or car, borrowing from friends or relatives, or even by using a personal bank loan or credit card advances. The important fact is that when the money goes into the business, it goes in as an investment (or "equity"), not as a loan (or "debt") to be repaid to the entrepreneur. Balance sheet, remember?

2. OVERVIEW OF DEBT AND EQUITY

In essence, all financing for a business is either (1) debt or (2) equity or (3) some combination of debt and equity. Debt funding is a loan that the business is legally obligated to repay—generally with interest. Equity funding is an investment that the business receives for selling part ownership in the business. Unlike with a loan, the business is not legally obligated to repay this investment.*

Debt and equity financing differ in such important respects as:

- The degree of risk each represents to the provider of funds. When a business borrows money, the creditor is entitled to receive both repayment of the amount borrowed—the principal—and interest on that principal, according to a set schedule. In contrast, if someone provides equity funds, the business is not legally obligated to pay her anything, although the business may choose to distribute some cash as dividends. The main benefit these equity holders receive is an ownership interest in the firm. Compared to being a creditor, being an owner has higher risk, both up and down. The risk is higher, but so is the potential return. A creditor can expect at most repayment of the debt with interest. In contrast, the owner can get fabulously rich if the business does fabulously well. However, the owners can also more readily lose everything. The creditors of a failing business must be paid in full before anything is distributed to the business's owners. If nothing is left after paying creditors, the owners get nothing.

- Another difference is the degree of risk debt and equity represent to the business. Debt is riskier to the business. Suppose that the business borrows money, and then times get tough. If the business fails to repay either the debt or the required interest, the lender can sue and even force the business into bankruptcy. This is not true with equity. The equity owner has no right to repayment. So an equity investment will permit a business to weather hard times easier than a borrowing of equal size. Indeed, if the business keeps on borrowing—getting more "leveraged"—then its interest obligation may grow so large that even a modest downturn in sales will endanger the company's survival. In contrast, selling additional equity will not make the company riskier.

- A final difference between debt and equity is the cost of each to the business. Debt has a fixed cost: the interest rate the business pays to borrow the money is the cost of those funds. On the other hand, at the time the equity is sold, the cost to the business of the equity is uncertain. If we own the company, and if we sell equity to investors, then those investors share in the success of the company. If the company does extremely well and the equity becomes worth a great deal of money, then the cost to the initial owners is large. The new investors get some of the large value of the company, instead of the original entrepreneur's getting all of it. In contrast, if the company does poorly or fails, the ownership that the first owners have sacrificed is worth little. Another cost of equity is the control we give up. If investors own equity, they have a right to have a

---

* The exact nature of the ownership of the company which this investment represents is determined by the legal form of business organization. For instance, in a general partnership, an owner is a partner. In a limited partnership, owners can be general or limited partners. And in a corporation, an owner is a shareholder.

voice in how we run the business. In contrast, creditors are not entitled to any control over the company, unless they bargain for it specifically.

Equity is ownership. If Bubba's Burritos obtains outside equity funding, then Propp will no longer be the sole owner of Bubba's Burritos, and Bubba's Burritos will no longer be a sole proprietorship. Because this chapter is on sole proprietorship, we will focus here on growing the business by debt funding. Although the *Fenimore* case (a few pages ahead) discusses the implications of a court's characterizing an investment as equity rather than debt, detailed consideration of making a business grow through equity funding awaits later chapters.

3.   BORROWING MONEY

A bank or other lender will typically make loan decisions by evaluating risks and return. To state the obvious, the lender will demand either a higher interest rate or some other form of higher return if it perceives a higher risk.

Propp's objective, of course, is to obtain funds for Bubba's Burritos at the lowest possible cost. The art of successful borrowing lies in obtaining funds in a manner that providers of funds view as relatively less risky. They will then charge less for their money.

Propp can do several things to structure the loan so it will be perceived as low risk:

* pledge personal or corporate assets against the loan, as a form of collateral to secure the loan.

* promise to pay the money back in a short time, when the creditor can more easily judge the health of the business, rather than over the long term, when predictions about the business's financial strength are less certain.

* give the creditor some measure of control over the business, either through loan covenants or participation in business decisions. An example would be a seat on the board of directors of a corporation.

In addition, the owner of a sole proprietorship such as Propp often encounters requests by creditors for a share of the business's profits. A lender may seek a share of the profits as a form of repayment, or as a part of its payment in addition to or instead of interest. What are the possible legal consequences of any such profit sharing?

4.   SHARING PROFITS WITH A LENDER

The following case shows the adverse legal consequences to a Mrs. Serge (whose name was Watt at the time she entered the relevant deal) of agreeing to share profits in a business with her brother. The ultimate question is whether the agreement they entered was a loan, or whether it instead was an equity investment by which Mrs. Serge became co-owner in what therefore had been transformed into a partnership. The case introduces some of the next chapter's partnership material, including the conditions under which a partnership results if another owner is added to a sole proprietorship. In reading the case, consider the following questions:

1.   Who owes money to whom? Were the creditors referred as to "Villabona" owed money by the car business? Was that important to the court?

2.   Who is contending that the agreement between Mrs. Serge and her brother, Donald Fenimore, was a partnership agreement? (As we will see in Chapter 3, regardless of what business associates call their relationship, a partnership is "an association of two or more persons to carry on as co-owners a business for profit.") Revised Uniform Partnership Act (which we call "RUPA") § 202. Who is suggesting instead that the agreement between Mrs. Serge and her brother is a loan? Why?

3.   Did the agreement between Mrs. Serge and her brother use the word "partnership"?

4.   Was Mrs. Serge involved in the operation of the car business?

5.   Is anyone contending that Fenimore did not receive at least $15,000 from Mrs. Serge which has not been repaid?

6.   The agreement is reproduced below. Did a lawyer prepare the agreement between Mrs. Serge and her brother? If so, was she a good lawyer?

* * * * *

This Agreement between Donald R. Fenimore, Sr. and Audrey F. Watt made this Sixth day of November Nineteen Hundred Eighty-nine sets forth our understanding of our business arrangements.

Audrey F. Watt has advanced Twenty-five Hundred Dollars ($2,500.00) and Ten Thousand Dollars ($10,000.00) to Donald R. Fenimore in order for him to conduct the business of buying and selling of motor vehicles.

Donald R. Fenimore hereby agrees to divide the profits from each vehicle bought and sold with Audrey F. Watt immediately upon the sale of each or as soon as feasible thereafter. Donald R. Fenimore will pay the expenses incident to his conducting the business and Audrey F. Watt will pay the costs incident to her borrowing the said sums of money.

Donald R. Fenimore agrees to execute this document and a Last Will and Testament which will make Audrey F. Watt his sole heir and sole beneficiary of all his assets upon his demise and this shall be in force until his death unless Audrey F. Watt executes a release contrary to this.

Should Donald R. Fenimore die or become incapacitated prior to the settling of the estate of his mother, Annie F. Fenimore, he hereby gives and bequeaths all his rights and interests therein to his sister, Audrey F. Watt, and gives her sole control over his share of his mother's estate.

Donald R. Fenimore appoints his sister, Audrey F. Watt, as his executrix without giving Bond for his Last Will and Testament. However, should he die prior to executing a Will, this will serve as his Last Will and Testament.

Donald R. Fenimore appoints Audrey F. Watt to be the sole individual to make all the arrangements for his funeral and burial. His wish is to be buried in the cemetery plot where his father, Harvey C. Fenimore, and his mother, Annie F. Fenimore, are buried in Silverbrook Cemetery, of which he is an equal owner together with his nine brothers and sisters. His five children or any other person(s) are not to interfere with any arrangements that she makes. His five children will be adequately taken care of by their mother in life and in death. They have no recourse as to their father's estate. This provision is solely the Will of Donald R. Fenimore and Audrey F. Watt has no influence as to his decision and desire.

Should Donald R. Fenimore still have a live-in relationship with Joyce D. Middleton at the time of his death, she shall be given adequate time to move the mobile home and the household furnishings in which they reside and it will be hers solely. However, the time to remove said mobile home will not exceed 60 days unless agreed to in writing by Audrey F. Watt. The personal effects of Donald R. Fenimore in the mobile home shall be turned over immediately to Audrey F. Watt at the time of his death.

This Agreement shall be subject to any additional amount(s) of money that Audrey F. Watt may advance to Donald R. Fenimore. All monies advanced will be due upon the dissolution of this Agreement or upon Donald R. Fenimore's death or incapacitation wherein Audrey F. Watt is appointed Power of Attorney for the protection of Donald R. Fenimore and for her rights and investments under his domain.

If Audrey F. Watt should predecease Donald R. Fenimore, this Agreement will bind Donald R. Fenimore to her heirs, successors and assigns. However, if she should predecease him, Donald R, Fenimore shall be given reasonable and adequate time of at least 90 days to make arrangements to reimburse her estate for any and all debts that may be then due.

This Agreement shall become null and void should a subsequent Agreement be entered into between Donald R. Fenimore and Audrey F. Watt to nullify this Agreement.

Willard H. Middleton Jr.	**Donald R. Fenimore 11/6/89**
Witness	Donald R. Fenimore
Billy Middleton	**Audrey F. Watt 11/6/89**
Witness	Audrey F. Watt

IN RE ESTATE OF FENIMORE

Delaware Court of Chancery, 1999
1999 WL 959204

CHANDLER, CHANCELLOR (adopting the report of the master):

[Donald Fenimore is insolvent. Creditors collectively referred to as Villabona have a judgment against Fenimore for $32,000. These creditors are seeking to recover a part of that judgment from approximately $20,000 of property Fenimore recently inherited. Mrs. Serge is also seeking to recover that $20,000 from Fenimore, contending that she is also a creditor of Donald Fenimore and that Fenimore's debt to her should be paid first.]

* * * Mrs. Serge's story is a very sad one. She testified that after the death of her first husband, whose last name was Watt, she owned her own home in Hockessin and the home was debt free. As time passed, Donald Fenimore asked her for money to get him out of a variety of scrapes, leading her to mortgage her home. The house is now mortgaged to the hilt and much of her income goes to servicing the mortgage debt. For the most part, she paid Donald in cash because that is the way he wanted it. On one occasion, it was not possible to get cash quickly, and so she gave him a check for $10,000.00, which he negotiated. The date on the front of the check is October 26, 1989. The date stamp on the back indicates that it was paid by the bank that same day. About ten days after Mrs. Serge gave the $10,000.00 to her brother, she and he made an agreement that appears to address this money and another $2,500.00 that she gave him about the same time. Mrs. Serge testified that she has given her brother much more than that over the years, and specifically gave him another $2,500.00 in 1988 or 1989.

Mrs. Serge has been in court a number of times in connection with her litigation with her siblings over their mother's estate. One thing that has been evident throughout all these proceedings is that she is very familiar with the need for paper trails and so it comes as no surprise that, loving her brother but knowing better than to trust him too much, she had him sign an agreement, dated November 6, 1989, memorializing their understanding. The mortgage came about a year later. Mrs. Serge testified that she believes her brother owes her vastly more than the $15,000.00 she testified about with some detail. She also testified that when the mortgage was given as security for the previous loans on October 31, 1990, she did not know about the Villabona judgment.

A judgment binds lands from the time it is entered by the Prothonotary,* and a properly recorded mortgage has priority over a judgment subsequently obtained. Because the mortgage was recorded before the judgment was entered on the records of the Prothonotary for the county

---

* Editors' note: This statement simply refers to the traditional rule that a judgment against someone operates as a lien against that person's real property from the moment the judgment is recorded with the proper officer, here the Prothonotary.

in which the real estate is located, Villabona must somehow invalidate the effect of the mortgage in order to prevail. * * *

Villabona addresses the financial relationship between Mrs. Serge and her brother. It argues that if the 1989 agreement is indicative of anything, it is a partnership between Mrs. Serge and Donald Fenimore. Villabona notes that the agreement gives their "understanding of [their] business arrangements." It specifically does not characterize the $12,500.00 as a loan, but states that Mrs. Serge "advanced" this money to her brother "for him to conduct the business of buying and selling of motor vehicles." Note that the word used before "business" is a definite article, it is not a possessive. In other words, she is not described as lending him money to operate his business, she is "advancing" money for him to conduct a specific business, the owner(s) of which is not identified. This distinction takes on significance when one reads the next paragraph, in which they agree that Mrs. Serge will pay the costs of her borrowing money for this venture, and Donald Fenimore will pay the ordinary operating expenses of the business, and they will "divide the profits from each vehicle bought and sold . . . ." The balance of the agreement is concerned with securing Mrs. Serge's interests in the event of her brother's death and stating terms of dissolution of the partnership.

The partnership argument is based on 6 Del. Code Ann. § 1507 [which is modeled on § 7 of the Uniform Partnership Act]: "In determining whether a partnership exists, the following rules shall apply: . . . (4) The receipt by a person of a share of the profits of a business is prima facie evidence that he is a partner in the business, but no such inference shall be drawn if such profits were received in payment: (a) As a debt by installments or otherwise; (b) As wages of an employee or rent to a landlord; (c) As an annuity to a widow or representative of a deceased partner; (d) As interest on a loan, though the amount of payment vary with the profits of the business; (e) As the consideration for the sale of a goodwill of a business or other property by installments or otherwise." The November, 1989 document clearly provides for a division of profits and a division of responsibility for debts. The right to receive a share of the profits is nowhere indicated as falling into any of the five exceptions to evidence of a partnership just quoted. Therefore, the language of the 1989 agreement, as evaluated in light of the statute, would seem to be enough to conclude that the relationship between Mrs. Serge and her brother so far as the agreement is concerned is that of partners.

Our courts have taken the view that it is not essential to the existence of a partnership that all partners have the right to make decisions and a duty to share liabilities on dissolution, but at least one of these factors must be present, and there must also be an intent to share profits. The standard of proof necessary to prove the existence of a partnership is stricter when the action is between two partners than if it is between the alleged partners and a third party claiming that a partnership exists as to his opponents. Nonetheless, one must show the existence of the partnership by a preponderance of the evidence, and to do so one may demonstrate an intention to share profits and losses, and may use acts, the dealings and conduct of the parties, and admissions of the parties to do so.

When one examines the November, 1989 agreement in terms of the principles just stated, it is easy to conclude that at the very least the arrangement looks like a partnership. There is a written declaration of the intent of the parties, and it specifically calls for the sharing of profits and the allocation of expenses, that is, liabilities. There is even a plan of dissolution should things not work out. Based on this, and noting that the standard of proof is less strict when between two non-partners (in this case, Villabona and Mrs. Serge) than it would be between the partners themselves, I conclude that a partnership existed in fact between Audrey Serge and Donald Fenimore as of November 6, 1989. One may conclude that the partnership continues to exist because the record is silent as to the occurrence of any of the events that the agreement states will trigger dissolution of the partnership: a decision to dissolve, or the death of either Mrs. Serge or her brother. More importantly, there is no evidence that any of these factors had come about in 1990 when Villabona received its judgment, or in 1991 when the judgment was recorded in New Castle County.

The real thrust of this discussion is the consequence of a finding that a partnership existed. The money referred to in the 1989 agreement amounts to an investment in the partnership. It is part of a "business arrangement," but nowhere in that document or elsewhere is it characterized as a loan. If Mrs. Serge is to claim priority status as a creditor because of the agreement, she must show that she was not a partner and thereby convert the investment to a loan to her brother. Once a determination has been made that she is a partner, the provisions of 6 Del. Code § 1540 [modeled on § 40 of the Uniform Partnership Act] come into play.

The key part of § 1540 is subsection (9) [modeled on § 40(i) of the Uniform Partnership Act]: "Where a partner has become bankrupt or his estate is insolvent the claims against his separate property shall rank in the following order: a. Those owing to separate creditors; b. Those owing to partnership creditors; c. Those owing to partners by way of contribution." What this means for the present case is, that once Mrs. Serge is determined to have been her brother's partner, her right to collect under the agreement from him as to his inheritance, which is not partnership property, is subordinate to the claims of his "separate creditors", that is, Villabona. If they are creditors of the partnership, even then her interests would be subordinate to theirs. * * *

QUESTIONS AND NOTE

1. Why is Villabona arguing that the 1989 agreement is "indicative of" a partnership between Mrs. Serge and her brother? Why does the court (or, more accurately, the master) wait until the end of the opinion (master's report) to tell us "the consequence of finding that a partnership exists"?

2. What is the basis for the court's conclusion that a partnership exists?

2.1   Would the court have reached a different result if the agreement had used the word "lends" instead of the word "advances"?

2.2   We noted in the opinion that the Delaware statute was modeled on the Uniform Partnership Act (which we will call the "UPA"). Suppose instead that the applicable statute was § 202(c) of the *Revised* Uniform Partnership Act (we met RUPA in the notes before the case). Would the result be the same?

2.3   How could a lawyer for Mrs. Serge have drafted the agreement to avoid a finding of partnership?

3.   Suppose Capel lent Propp $250,000 on June 4, 2010 and the loan agreement provided that the loan was to be repaid not later than April 15, 2012 and that until the loan was repaid

- Capel was to receive 40% of the profits of the firm, not exceeding $50,000 and not less than $10,000;

- Propp was to consult Capel as to important matters in the conduct of Bubba's Burritos;

- Capel could veto any business that she thinks highly speculative or injurious;

Under the *Fenimore* decision, would Capel be Propp's partner? How about under RUPA § 202?

4.   The facts in Question 3 were adapted from *Martin v. Peyton*, 158 N.E. 77 (N.Y. 1927), which is the classic case concerning whether a lender has become a partner by having power essentially to call the shots in the business. In that case, Peyton made a loan of $2,500,000 to Martin under terms similar to those outlined in Question 3. Martin became insolvent. Martin's creditors argued that (i) Peyton's sharing in profits coupled with Peyton's power to veto certain business decisions made Peyton a partner with Martin and (ii) Peyton, as a partner, was liable for the partnership's debts. In finding that Peyton was not a partner, the court distinguished between active control and reactive control. Specifically, the court emphasized that Peyton "may not initiate any transactions as a partner may do." *See generally* Howard P. Walthall, Sr., *What Do You Mean "We," Kemo Sabe? Partnership Law and Responsibilities of Office Sharing Lawyers*, 28 CUMB.L. REV. 601, 620–28 (1998). Is *Fenimore* consistent with *Martin v. Peyton*?

5.   Reconsider the *Miller* case, in which the court found that McDonald's might be liable under a theory of apparent agency. Can you now think of another theory for holding McDonald's liable?

6.   Because *Fenimore* quotes from §§ 1507 and 1540 of the Delaware partnership statute, which is based on the UPA, and because we have also asked you to read RUPA provisions, we might as well move on to the study of the partnership.

CHAPTER THREE

WHAT IS A PARTNERSHIP AND HOW DOES IT WORK?

■ ■ ■

Propp does not know what a partnership is but he knows that he needs some help running Bubba's Burritos. He also knows that he needs to keep Agee as a cook and a manager of Bubba's Burritos, and Agee has said that she will leave unless she shares in the profits and has a "say" in business decisions. And Propp knows that he needs money to expand Bubba's Burritos, money that is available from Capel, who also wants to share in the profits and to participate in business decisions.

Propp also knows that if he brings Capel or anyone else into the business there will be questions about (1) how the profits and losses from the business should be divided, and (2) who makes the various business decisions that affect profitability. This chapter (and the rest of the book) will focus on these questions of who gets the money and who makes the decisions. This chapter will consider what else Propp's attorney (and Agee and Capel's attorneys) should know about starting, operating, growing, profiting from and selling a business as a partnership.

A. WHAT IS A PARTNERSHIP?

Of course, a partnership is a form of business. The two primary differences between a sole proprietorship and a partnership are (i) the number of owners and (ii) the number of legal entities.

Obviously, as we saw in Chapter 2, a *sole* proprietorship is a business with only one owner. A partnership, in contrast, is a business with more than one owner. All of the statutory and common law definitions of a partnership refer to owners, plural. (Recall the Delaware statute discussed in the *Fenimore* case at the end of Chapter 2.) The operative language of all statutory definitions is the same: a partnership is "an association of two or more persons to carry on as co-owners a business for profit." *See* Uniform Partnership Act (UPA) § 6(1) and Revised Uniform Partnership Act (RUPA) §§ 101(6), 202(a).

We will see below that UPA and RUPA are the two leading models of partnership statutes; some states adopt one and some states adopt the other, and some states adopt modifications. Throughout the chapter, we will compare and contrast UPA and RUPA provisions.

Not only is the sole proprietorship business structure limited to businesses with one owner, but that business and its one owner are treated as a single legal entity. That means that the assets of the business are also the assets of its owner; the obligations of the business are also the obligations of its owner. Partnerships are different—sort of. While the obligations of a business operated as a partnership are also the obligations of its owners, we will see that a partnership is, in some other respects, treated legally as an entity separate from its owners.

RUPA § 201 provides that a partnership is "an entity distinct from its partners." In contrast, UPA generally embraces an "aggregate theory", i.e., it considers a partnership not as a separate legal person but rather as merely the aggregate of its partners. The debate as to whether a partnership is treated as an aggregate or entity is of very limited practical significance. There are provisions in RUPA that are more consistent with the aggregate theory than the entity theory, and there are provisions in UPA that are more consistent with the entity theory than the aggregate theory.

For some purposes, the partnership is routinely seen as an entity and for some it is not. In the area of taxation, which (happily) is beyond our scope, the partnership is seen as an aggregate of partners. Thus, the partnership itself does not pay tax on its profits. Instead, only the partners pay tax on the business's profits. This is called "flow-through" taxation, and is a distinct advantage over the corporation, which is universally regarded as an entity separate from those who run and own it. Thus, the corporation itself pays taxes on its profits *and* its shareholders pay taxes on distributions they receive, so-called "double taxation." But enough about tax.

As a bottom line, your answers to specific questions posed by your professors or by clients or judges will not be based upon whether you embrace an aggregate or entity status, but on the language of the relevant statutory provisions. *See* Robert W. Hillman, Allan W. Vestal & Donald J. Weidner, GENERAL AND LIMITED LIABILITY PARTNERSHIP UNDER THE REVISED UNIFORM PARTNERSHIP ACT 52 (1996) ("Neither practitioners, arbitrators, or courts should place too much reliance on either the aggregate theory or the entity theory.") Or as Paul McCartney and Stevie Wonder might have put it:

> *Aggregate and entity, live together in perfect harmony;*
> *Side by side in RUPA and UPA;*
> *Oh Lord, why don't we?*

QUESTIONS

1. Can a business be both a sole proprietorship and a partnership? Can I start a partnership by myself?

2. Can a business be both a corporation and a partnership? *See* RUPA § 202(b). *See also* the Official Comments to RUPA § 202.

3. Can a corporation serve as a partner in a partnership? *See* UPA §§ 2 and 6(1); RUPA §§ 101(10) and 202(a).

B.   WHAT IS PARTNERSHIP LAW?

Partnership law deals with the rights and obligations of partnerships and the rights and obligations of the partners. For centuries, this law was common law. Early in the twentieth century, however, state legislatures started to codify partnership law.

In 1914, the Commission on Uniform State Laws promulgated UPA. Eventually, every state except Louisiana adopted UPA. In 1994, the National Conference of Commissioners on Uniform State Laws approved RUPA, which has been adopted by about half the states, including major commercial states.

Although every state (including Louisiana) now has some form of general partnership statute, case law remains an important part of partnership law. Case law is important not only in interpreting the provisions in partnership statutes, but also in filing gaps in such statutes. State partnership laws usually contain a provision similar to UPA § 5 and RUPA § 104, which state that "the principles of law and equity" govern to the extent not provided for by statute.

At first blush, this combination of state partnership statutes and case law would seem to be the place to look for answers to all questions about the rights and obligations of partnerships and partners. Blush again. So long as the question involves only the rights and obligations of the partnership and its partners, the primary source of partnership "law" will not be a statute or case law at all. It will be the *partnership agreement*. As the Official Comments to RUPA § 103 state in part: "The general rule * * * is that relations among the partners and between the partners and the partnership are governed by the partnership agreement. To the extent that the partners fail to agree upon a contrary rule, RUPA provides the default rule." Similarly, UPA § 18 provides that the rules for determining the rights and duties of partners are "subject to any agreement between them."

In other words, as to these issues, UPA and RUPA are fall-back provisions—they apply *only* if the partners have not agreed to the contrary. The statutes provide default rules, not immutable prescriptions, and thus provide great flexibility.

> The resultant flexibility is important, and reflects the clear policy choice that the businesspeople should be left to structure their relationship as best suits them. For example, suppose three people form a partnership. Alpha contributes 70 percent of the capital to start the business, while Beta and Omega each contribute 15 percent. Because of her larger investment and risk, Alpha may naturally expect that

she should have the authority to make major business decisions. Similarly, Alpha may naturally expect to receive 70 percent of any profits. Unless such understandings are reflected in a partnership agreement, however, Alpha is subject to the default rules of UPA and RUPA, which provide that management decisions are to be made by majority vote of the partners and that profits will be shared equally.

Richard D. Freer, *Business Organizations*, OXFORD COMPANION TO AMERICAN LAW 78 (2001).

C.   WHAT ARE THE LEGAL PROBLEMS IN STARTING A BUSINESS AS A PARTNERSHIP?

Starting a business as a partnership, like starting a business as a sole proprietorship, requires no formal legal steps. Both sole proprietorships and partnerships can be viewed as "residual" or "default" business structures. If one person owns a business and she does not take any action to qualify it as a corporation or some other particular form of business structure, it will be a sole proprietorship. If two or more people own a business and they do not take any action to qualify it as a corporation or some other particular form of business structure, it will be a partnership.

Creating a partnership does not require that papers be filed in the public records. Partnership law does not even require that there be a written partnership agreement. If two or more persons are operating a business as co-owners, that business will be a partnership—even if there is no formal partnership agreement, and even if the partners do not realize that they have formed a partnership. In fact, we saw exactly that in the *Fenimore* case at the end of Chapter 2.

Although partnership agreements are not legally required, in the real world these documents are *extremely* important. First, a partnership agreement is a contract and is enforceable to the same extent as contracts generally. Second, always remember that partnership agreements can change much of the statutory law that otherwise would govern. But not all businesses that are partnerships bother, or can afford, to create a partnership agreement. There are many partnerships that do not have a partnership agreement. For these, UPA and RUPA provide reasonable rules that most people would put in a partnership agreement, if they had thought about it. Although these standard rules might be fine for a two-person lawn-mowing business, they would be a disaster for a 500–lawyer law firm. Study UPA § 18 and RUPA § 103 and consider the following problems.

PROBLEMS: PARTNERSHIP AGREEMENT

1. To operate Bubba's Burritos as a partnership, do Propp, Agee and Capel need a written partnership agreement?

2. Do Propp, Agee, and Capel need a lawyer? Do they need more than one lawyer?

3.   Consider the following provisions from a form partnership agreement provided in continuing legal education materials. Are the provisions effective under RUPA § 103(a)? Do you think the doctors had a lawyer prepare these provisions? More than one lawyer? Good lawyers?

a.   The net profits of the partnership shall be divided among, and any net losses of the partnership shall be borne by, the partners in the following percentages during the periods indicated:

Partner	August 1, 2007 through July 31, 2008	Effective August 1, 2008 and thereafter
Dr. Alpha	27.67%	25%
Dr. Bravo	27.67%	25%
Dr. Charlie	27.67%	25%
Dr. Motherlover	17.00%	25%

The foregoing agreements as to distribution of net profits are subject, however, to the special provisions hereinafter set out.

b.   Withdrawals of net profits by the partners shall be in such amounts and at such times as the partners shall determine by mutual agreement.

c.   The partnership shall maintain a bank account or bank accounts in such bank or banks as may be agreed upon by the partners. Checks on such account or accounts shall be drawn only for partnership purposes, including distributions of profits agreed upon by the partners, and may be signed by any partner, except that any check for an amount in excess of $6,000 must be signed by two partners.

d.   No partner may, without the written consent of the other partners, assign, encumber or in any manner dispose of all or any part of the interest of such partner in the partnership.

e.   No partner may, on behalf of the partnership, without the express consent of the other partners, borrow or lend money, or make, deliver or accept any commercial paper, or execute any mortgage, deed or bill of sale to secure debt, bond, lease, contract to sell any property of the partnership, or contract to purchase any property for the partnership other than ordinary medical and office supplies. William R. Patterson, *Drafting the Partnership Agreement*, CA86 ALI–ABA COURSE OF STUDY, May 2, 1996, Partnerships, LLCs and LLPs.

3.1   Note that paragraph b provides for withdrawals by "mutual agreement." What does that mean? Does it require unanimity?

3.2   If you were a partner in this business, would you want to require unanimity for withdrawals? Wouldn't such a requirement give each partner the power to veto withdrawals by any others? Is that a good idea?

3.3   Note that paragraph c of the agreement provides for a decision "as agreed upon by the partners." How is that different from "mutual agreement," which is used in paragraph b? Why would the partnership agreement use different language concerning consent in paragraphs b and c? Does the use of different terms for agreement reflect good lawyering?

3.4   If the partners wanted to provide that a decision requires unanimity, why not use the word "unanimity"? Any time you fail to provide precision for your clients, you may be inviting litigation. Again, what does "mutual consent" mean? Doesn't the fact that "mutual consent" may be subject to two interpretations invite litigation? If so, doesn't that mean the business planning lawyer failed?

3.5   Suppose the partnership agreement also provided: "Neither the partners nor the partnership will be liable for injuries to the public." Would the provision be enforceable? Note that RUPA § 103(b) lists certain topics in which the partners lack power to contract. Particularly, for the question asked here, note § 103(b)(10).

D.   WHAT ARE THE PROBLEMS IN OPERATING A BUSINESS AS A PARTNERSHIP?

1.   WHO OWNS WHAT?

Under both UPA and RUPA, partnerships can and do own property. In other words, both Acts envision the partnership as an entity for this purpose. *See* UPA §§ 8 and 25 and RUPA §§ 201, 203, and 204. The individual partners do *not* own partnership property. *See* UPA §§ 24 and 26 and RUPA §§ 501 and 502. Apply these sections to the following problems. (Hint: it is usually a good idea to read the Official Comments to the various sections too.)

PROBLEMS: PARTNERSHIP PROPERTY

1.   Propp, Agee, and Capel decide to operate Bubba's Burritos as a partnership. How can the partnership acquire property?

2.   Did the cooking equipment that belonged to Propp and that was used in the restaurant before formation of the partnership automatically become partnership property?

3.   Are the cash and credit card receipts from the operation of Bubba's Burritos partnership property?

4.   After formation of the partnership, suppose Bubba's Burritos acquires new tables and chairs. Are these partnership property?

5.   After formation of the partnership, suppose Bubba's Burritos uses funds provided by Capel to buy Blackacre. Is Blackacre partnership property? What if the seller deeds Blackacre to Capel?

6.   Is the following partnership agreement provision helpful in answering the preceding questions?

(a) *Partnership property.* Subject to the provisions of Article VII (b) and (c), all property originally paid or brought into, or transferred to, the partnership as contributions to capital by the partners, or subsequently acquired by purchase or otherwise, on account of the partnership, is partnership property.

(b) *Title to Property to Remain in Partner*. It is agreed that the following described property: [description], is being made available to the partnership by ___ solely for the use of the partnership and is to remain the property of ___ and is to be returned to him on [date], or when the partnership is dissolved, if prior to that date.

(c) *Property to be in Partnership Name*. The title to all partnership property shall be held in the name of the partnership.

(d) *Rights in Specific Partnership Property*. It is agreed that [name of partner] has the right at any time during the existence of this partnership to [assign or describe other right] the following specific partnership property: [describe property]. NY LF § 18.10.

2. WHO DECIDES WHAT THE PARTNERSHIP WILL DO?

Questions regarding who makes decisions for a partnership arise in two ways: (1) disputes between the partnership and some outside third party, and (2) disputes among the partners. Assume, for example, that Bubba's Burritos is structured as a partnership with Agee, Propp, and Capel as the partners, and Capel enters an agreement with Roberts for Bubba's Burritos to lease a building that Roberts owns. This can result in:

(1) A dispute between Bubba's Burritos and Roberts over whether Capel had the power to make this decision for Bubba's Burritos— i.e., a dispute over whether Bubba's Burritos is legally obligated to Roberts; and,

(2) A dispute among Agee, Capel and Propp over whether Capel had the right to make this decision for Bubba's Burritos—i.e., a dispute over whether Capel is legally obligated to Agee and Propp.

In situations such as (1)—in which the issue is whether a partner had the power to obligate the partnership to some third party—courts look to the provisions of the relevant partnership statute and then to agency principles such as actual and apparent authority. In situations such as (2)—in which the issue is whether a partner had the right to act on behalf of the partnership—courts look to the provisions of the partnership agreement first, and then to provisions of the relevant partnership statute and then to common law agency principles. Consider the following problems.

PROBLEMS: PARTNERSHIP DECISION-MAKING

1. Bubba's Burritos is a partnership. Agee, Propp and Capel are the partners. Agee and Capel want the partnership to lease a building from Roberts. Propp disagrees. Propp comes to you with the question of whether

the partnership can lease the building even though he is opposed. How do you answer his question? Please assume that there is no partnership agreement provision concerning this issue. *See* UPA § 18(e) and RUPA §§ 103 and 401(f).

2. What if the partners wanted to do something "extraordinary" (BTW, what does that mean?)? What vote would be required? *See* UPA § 18(h) and RUPA § 401(j).

3. Bubba's Burritos is a partnership. Agee, Propp and Capel are the partners. The partnership agreement provides that "Capel shall serve as managing partner, and, as such, shall have the authority to lease property on behalf of the partnership without consulting any other partner." Capel, without consulting Agee or Propp, rents a building for the partnership from Roberts for ten years at $10,000 a year. Is the partnership legally obligated to pay Roberts? *See* UPA § 18(e) & (h) and RUPA §§ 103 and 401(f) & (j).

4. Same facts as Question 3 except that the partnership agreement does not make Capel a managing partner. Instead, the partnership agreement provides "No partner may, without the express consent of the other partners, lease property on behalf of the partnership." Notwithstanding this provision, Capel, without consulting Agee or Propp, rents a building for the partnership from Roberts for ten years at $10,000 a year. Is the partnership legally obligated to pay Roberts on this lease? *See* UPA §§ 5, and 9 and RUPA §§ 103(b)(10), 104, and 301.

5. Same facts as Question 4. What would Bubba's Burritos have to do to ensure that Roberts knows that Capel lacks authority to bind the partnership? Is doing so easier under UPA or RUPA?

6. Same facts as Question 4. Can Agee and Propp take any legal action against Capel? *See* RUPA § 405(b).

—————

These problems illustrate possible questions relating to *who* makes decisions for a partnership. A lawyer for such a business (or for one of the partners) will also encounter questions about *how* such decisions are to be made. In particular, a lawyer will have to consider whether these decisions are affected by any duties a partner may owe to the partnership or to her fellow partners.

For example, suppose Capel, as managing partner with express authority to rent buildings for the partnership, rents a building for the partnership from his brother-in-law Epstein at a rate significantly above the market rate. Or suppose Capel, as managing partner, learns of an opportunity to rent a building significantly below market rate, but rents the building for himself rather than for the partnership. Common sense (and, as it turns out, common law) tell us there are problems with these examples.

The next case involves somewhat analogous facts. It is the most–cited case on (i) what things a partner has the right to do and (ii) what are the right things for a partner to do.

MEINHARD v. SALMON

Court of Appeals of New York, 1928
164 N.E. 545

CARDOZO, C.J.

[Walter Salmon was a real estate developer. He had the opportunity to rent a seven-story building on the corner of Fifth Avenue and Forty-second Street in New York and the lease was for a term of 20 years. The building needed improvements, however, which Salmon could not afford. So Salmon leased the building from the building's owner, Elbridge Gerry. Salmon also entered a separate agreement with Morton Meinhard, a wool merchant. Under this agreement, Meinhard provided the money for renovations to the building in exchange for a share of the profits from the building over the course of the 20–year lease. Their agreement also provided that Salmon and Meinhard were to share any losses equally but that Salmon had the sole power to manage the building.

After more than nineteen years, shortly before the 20–year lease was to expire, Gerry, the building's owner, approached Salmon with a proposal. Gerry, who also owned five adjacent buildings, wanted someone to lease all of these properties, to destroy the existing buildings, and to put up a new, single, larger building. This was valuable real estate. It was three blocks from the site of the Chrysler building, which was being planned at approximately the same time.

Salmon accepted Gerry's proposal and entered into a lease and development agreement with Gerry. Meinhard was not a party to this new agreement. Indeed, Meinhard did not even know of this agreement. When Meinhard learned of the deal, he initiated this litigation, suing for an interest in the new, expanded development.]

[Meinhard and Salmon] were coadventurers, subject to fiduciary duties akin to those of partners. As to this we are all agreed. The heavier weight of duty rested, however, upon Salmon. He was a coadventurer with Meinhard, but he was manager as well. * * *

When the lease was near its end, Elbridge T. Gerry had become the owner of the reversion. He owned much other property in the neighborhood, one lot adjoining the Bristol building on Fifth Avenue and four lots on Forty–Second Street. He had a plan to lease the entire tract for a long term to someone who would destroy the buildings then existing and put up another in their place. In the latter part of 1921, he submitted such a project to several capitalists and dealers. He was unable to carry it through with any of them. Then, in January 1922, with less than four months of the lease to run, he approached the defendant Salmon. The result was a new lease to the Midpoint Realty Company, which is owned and controlled by Salmon, a lease covering the whole tract, and involving a huge outlay. * * * The existing buildings may remain unchanged for seven years. They are then to be torn down, and a new building to cost

$3,000,000 is to be placed upon the site. The rental, which under the Bristol lease was only $55,000, is to be from $350,000 to $475,000 for the properties so combined. Salmon personally guaranteed the performance by the lessee of the covenants of the new lease until such time as the new building had been completed and fully paid for.

The lease between Gerry and the Midpoint Realty Company was signed and delivered on January 25, 1922. Salmon had not told Meinhard anything about it. Whatever his motive may have been, he had kept the negotiations to himself. Meinhard was not informed even of the bare existence of a project. The first that he knew of it was in February, when the lease was an accomplished fact. He then made demand on the defendants that the lease be held in trust as an asset of the venture, making offer upon the trial to share the personal obligations incidental to the guaranty. The demand was followed by refusal, and later by this suit.
* * *

Joint adventurers, like copartners, owe to one another, while the enterprise continues, the duty of the finest loyalty. Many forms of conduct permissible in a workaday world for those acting at arm's length are forbidden to those bound by fiduciary ties. A trustee is held to something stricter than the morals of the market place. Not honesty alone, but the punctilio of an honor the most sensitive, is then the standard of behavior. As to this there has developed a tradition that is unbending and inveterate. Uncompromising rigidity has been the attitude of courts of equity when petitioned to undermine the rule of undivided loyalty by the "disintegrating erosion" of particular exceptions. Only thus has the level of conduct for fiduciaries been kept at a level higher than that trodden by the crowd. It will not consciously be lowered by any judgment of this court.

The owner of the reversion, Mr. Gerry, had vainly striven to find a tenant who would favor his ambitious scheme of demolition and construction. Baffled in the search, he turned to the defendant Salmon in possession of the Bristol, the keystone of the project. He figured to himself beyond a doubt that the man in possession would prove a likely customer. To the eye of an observer, Salmon held the lease as owner in his own right, for himself and no one else. In fact he held it as a fiduciary, for himself and another, sharers in a common venture. If this fact had been proclaimed, if the lease by its terms had run in favor of a partnership, Mr. Gerry, we may fairly assume, would have laid before the partners, and not merely before one of them, his plan of reconstruction. The pre-emptive privilege, or, better, the pre-emptive opportunity, that was thus an incident of the enterprise, Salmon appropriated to himself in secrecy and silence. He might have warned Meinhard that the plan had been submitted, and that either would be free to compete for the award. If he had done this, we do not need to say whether he would have been under a duty, if successful in the competition, to hold the lease so acquired for the benefit of a venture then about to end, and thus prolong by indirection its responsibilities and duties. The trouble about his conduct is that he excluded his coadventurer from any chance to compete, from any chance to enjoy the opportunity for benefit that had come to him alone by virtue of his agency. This chance, if nothing more, he was under a duty to concede. The price of its denial is an extension of the trust at the option and for the benefit of the one whom he excluded.

No answer is it to say that the chance would have been of little value even if seasonably offered. Such a calculus of probabilities is beyond the science of the chancery. Salmon, the real estate operator, might have been preferred to Meinhard, the woolen merchant. On the other hand, Meinhard might have offered better terms, or reinforced his offer by alliance with the wealth of others. * * *

The very fact that Salmon was in control with exclusive powers of direction charged him the more obviously with the duty of disclosure, since only through disclosure could opportunity be equalized. If he might cut off renewal by a purchase for his own benefit when four months were to pass before the lease would have an end, he might do so with equal right while there remained as many years. He might steal a march on his comrade under cover of the darkness, and then hold the captured ground. Loyalty and comradeship are not so easily abjured.

Little profit will come from a dissection of the precedents. None precisely similar is cited in the briefs of counsel. What is similar in many, or so it seems to us, is the animating principle. Authority is, of course, abundant that one partner may not appropriate to his own use a renewal of a lease, though its term is to begin at the expiration of the partnership. The lease at hand with its many changes is not strictly a renewal. Even so, the standard of loyalty for those in trust relations is without the fixed divisions of a graduated scale. * * *

Salmon had put himself in a position in which thought of self was to be renounced, however hard the abnegation. He was much more than a coadventurer. He was a managing coadventurer. For him and for those like him the rule of undivided loyalty is relentless and supreme. A different question would be here if there were lacking any nexus of relation between the business conducted by the manager and the opportunity brought to him as an incident of management. For this problem, as for most, there are distinctions of degree. If Salmon had received from Gerry a proposition to lease a building at a location far removed, he might have held for himself the privilege thus acquired, or so we shall assume. Here the subject-matter of the new lease was an extension and enlargement of the subject-matter of the old one. A managing coadventurer appropriating the benefit of such a lease without warning to his partner might fairly expect to be reproached with conduct that was underhand, or lacking, to say the least, in reasonable candor, if the partner were to surprise him in the act of signing the new instrument. Conduct subject to that reproach does not receive from equity a healing benediction.

A question remains as to the form and extent of the equitable interest to be allotted to the plaintiff. * * *

ANDREWS, J. (dissenting).

* * * I am of the opinion that the issue here is simple. Was the transaction, in view of all the circumstances surrounding it, unfair and inequitable? I reach this conclusion for two reasons. There was no general partnership, merely a joint venture for a limited object, to end at a fixed time. The new lease, covering additional property, containing many new and unusual terms and conditions, with a possible duration of 80 years, was more nearly the purchase of the reversion than the ordinary renewal with which the authorities are concerned. * * *

Under these circumstances the referee has found and the Appellate Division agrees with him, that Mr. Meinhard is entitled to an interest in the second lease, he having promptly elected to assume his share of the liabilities imposed thereby. This conclusion is based upon the proposition that under the original contract between the two men "the enterprise was a joint venture, the relation between the parties was fiduciary and governed by principles applicable to partnerships," therefore, as the new lease is a graft upon the old, Mr. Salmon might not acquire its benefits for himself alone.

Were this a general partnership between Mr. Salmon and Mr. Meinhard, I should have little doubt as to the correctness of this result, assuming the new lease to be an offshoot of the old. Such a situation involves questions of trust and confidence to a high degree; it involves questions of good will; many other considerations. * * *

We have here a different situation governed by less drastic principles. I assume that where parties engage in a joint enterprise each owes to the other the duty of the utmost good faith in all that relates to their common venture. Within its scope they stand in a fiduciary relationship. * * *

It seems to me that the venture so inaugurated had in view a limited object and was to end at a limited time. There was no intent to expand it into a far greater undertaking lasting for many years. The design was to exploit a particular lease. Doubtless in it Mr. Meinhard had an equitable interest, but in it alone. * * *

What Mr. Salmon obtained was not a graft springing from the Bristol lease, but something distinct and different—as distinct as if for a building across Fifth Avenue. I think also that in the absence of some fraudulent or unfair act the secret purchase of the reversion even by one partner is rightful. Substantially this is such a purchase. Because of the mere label of a transaction we do not place it on one side of the line or the other. Here is involved the possession of a large and most valuable unit of property for 80 years, the destruction of all existing structures and the erection of a new and expensive building covering the whole. No fraud, no deceit, no calculated secrecy is found. Simply that the arrangement was made without the knowledge of Mr. Meinhard. I think this not enough.

The judgment of the courts below should be reversed and a new trial ordered, with costs in all courts to abide the event.

QUESTIONS AND NOTES

1. Questions about the law.

1.1   What did Salmon do wrong? What should he have done differently? What is this case really about: "the duty of finest loyalty" or money?

1.2   Assume that Salmon, through research, learned of Gerry's landhold-ings and that he then approached Gerry about a new expanded lease and development agreement. Would Judge (later Justice) Cardozo have reached the same result?

1.3   Assume that Gerry had approached and contracted with Meinhard rather than Salmon. If Salmon then sued Meinhard when he learned of the new expanded lease, would Judge Cardozo have reached the same result?

1.4   Were Salmon and Meinhard partners? Was that important to Judge Cardozo and the majority? Why? Was it important to Judge Andrews in dissent? Why?

1.5   Would Salmon and Meinhard have been partners under UPA or RUPA? *See* UPA § 7 and RUPA § 202.

1.6   What is a punctilio?

2. Notes.

2.1   One scholar describes the *Meinhard* case as "a culmination of Cardozo's efforts to implant a sense of honorable conduct into law." Andrew L. Kaufman, CARDOZO 241 (1998). In an earlier book about Justice Cardozo, Judge Posner refers to *Meinhard* as the most famous of Cardozo's "moralistic opinions" and praises Cardozo's language as "memorable words and they set a tone. They make the difference between an arm's length relationship and a fiduciary relationship vivid and unforgettable." Richard A. Posner, CARDOZO: A STUDY IN REPUTATION 574, 576 (1990).

2.2   *Meinhard* involved a joint venture. Indeed, the dissent is based on the fact that "there was no general partnership, merely a joint venture." Nonetheless, as the language in *Meinhard* indicates, the principles applied in the case are not limited to joint ventures. The fiduciary principles espoused in the case transcend the business structure involved. We will reconsider not only the language of *Meinhard* but the *Meinhard* fact pattern of taking an "opportunity" that was "an incident of the enterprise" in later chapters on corporations, limited partnerships and limited liability companies. When you reconsider *Meinhard*, consider also Professor Hillman's comments:

> *Meinhard* has aged well. No case of its period is of comparable contemporary influence in the business law area. *Meinhard* is cited today for the power and vitality of the idea it expresses rather than as a window to an era the values of which have long since been abandoned. The "punctilio of an honor" precept is as enduring as any expression of partnership or corporate law and continues to guide courts in determin-ing the duties business partners owe one another.

> To be sure, care must be taken to distinguish how standards are stated from how they are applied * * *. As a matter of common sense, we

may know that the *Meinhard* statement is too extreme and inflexible to represent a workable standard for those fiduciary relationships that are business partnerships. At the same time, to dismiss the case as nothing more than a vehicle of exaggerated rhetoric is to ignore the proven staying power of the landmark opinion.

Robert Hillman, *Business Partners as Fiduciaries: Reflections on the Limits of Doctrine,* 22 CARDOZO L. REV. 51, 53 (2000).

Fiduciary duties were developed by judges, as part of the common law. RUPA attempts to codify these fiduciary duties and then to allow the partners in their partnership agreement to modify the duties that a partner owes to her fellow partners and the partnership. *See* §§ 103 and 404. These provisions have no counterparts in the UPA. Study the provisions carefully. It may seem astounding, but, together, §§ 103 and 404 permit waiver of some fiduciary duties.

QUESTIONS

1. What duties do partners owe under § 404? To whom do they owe these duties?

2. Which of the duties can be eliminated completely? Which can be modified but not eliminated? How can they be modified?

3. What language in § 404 would have been most helpful to Meinhard?

4. What language in § 404 would have been most helpful to Salmon?

5. Suppose the agreement between Meinhard and Salmon had contained this language:

> *Other Business Activities of Partners.* Any partner may have other business interests or may engage in other business ventures of any nature or description whatsoever, whether presently existing or hereafter created, including, without limitation, the ownership, leasing, management, operation, franchising, syndication and/or development of real estate and may compete, directly or indirectly, with the business of the Partnership. No partner shall incur any liability to the Partnership as the result of such Partner's pursuit of such other business interests and ventures and competitive activity, and neither the Partnership nor any of the partners of Record Holders shall have any right to participate in such other business interests or ventures or to receive or share in any income derived therefrom.

See Richard A. Booth, *Fiduciary Duty, Contract and Waiver in Partnerships and Limited Liability Companies,* 1 J. SMALL & EMERGING BUS. L. 55 (1998).

In answering, consider § 103.

6. Professor Hynes argues that "The restrictions on waivability in [RUPA] sections 103(b)(2)–(4) should be deleted because they interfere with the right of partners to define their relationship as they wish. Persons

entering into a partnership ordinarily bargain from an approximately equal position, an equality created by the fact that each party typically has something of near-equal value to offer the other. This should give presumptive validity to the bargain of the parties." J. Dennis Hynes, *Fiduciary Duties and RUPA: An Inquiry Into Freedom of Contract*, 58 LAW & CONTEMP. PROB. 29, 39 (1995). Do you agree? By the way, why does Professor Hynes *not* include § 103(b)(5) in his proposed deletions?

Professor Hynes's views reflect the "contractarian school" of economic thought. This school holds that business people ought to be free to agree to the terms of their relationship, with minimal statutory imposition. The provision in RUPA for modification or waiver of fiduciary duties reflects the degree to which this school has affected modern thought on business formation.

7.   What are the policy arguments *for* the contractarian notion permitting parties to agree to modifications or even elimination of fiduciary duties? What are the policy arguments *against* permitting parties to agree to modification or even elimination of fiduciary duties? *See generally* Scott FitzGibbon, *Fiduciary Relationships Are Not Contracts*, 82 MARQ. L. REV. 303 (1999). We will revisit these questions when we consider contractual modifications of fiduciary duties in businesses structured as corporations, limited partnerships, and limited liability companies. And we will also consider the policy arguments for different answers to these questions depending on the form of business structure.

8.   Do UPA §§ 103(b)(10) and 404 ensure protection for third parties who deal with the partnership or with partners?

3.   WHO IS LIABLE FOR WHAT TO WHOM?

a.   Liability of the Partnership

Recall that under RUPA § 201, a partnership is a legal person—an entity. As such, a partnership can be held liable and can sue or be sued. The same is also true under UPA, even though UPA does not expressly adopt the entity theory. *See* UPA §§ 13 and 14 and RUPA §§ 305 and 307.

A third party can sue the *partnership* for the contracts entered by its agents and for the torts committed by its agents. If, for example, a waiter at Bubba's Burritos negligently drops a platter of sizzling grits fajitas on a customer, Vic Timm, Mr. Timm can sue Bubba's Burritos.

Also, under RUPA, a *partner* can sue the partnership to enforce her rights under the Act or under the partnership agreement. *See* RUPA § 405(b). If, for example, Bubba's Burritos refuses to provide Capel with access to its books and records, she can sue Bubba's Burritos. There is no similar provision in UPA; that Act limits partners' ability to sue to seeking the dissolution of the partnership.

b.   Liability of the Partners

Under RUPA, partners are jointly and severally liable for all obligations of the partnership. *See* RUPA §§ 305, 306 and 307. In contrast, under UPA § 15, partners are jointly (but not severally) liable in contract but jointly and severally liable in tort. The difference is significant. With joint liability, the plaintiff must sue *all* of the partners together in a single suit. With joint and several liability, however, the plaintiff is free to sue one or more of the partners. For example, the plaintiff could recover the partnership's entire liability to him from just one partner. Apply RUPA §§ 305, 306, and 307 to the following problems. (Stay focused; these get tough).

PROBLEMS: PARTNERSHIP AND PARTNER LIABILITY

1.   A, C, and E are partners in the ACE partnership. In the course of her work for the partnership, A, through her negligence, injures P.

1.1   Can P sue and recover from the partnership, ACE?

1.2   Instead, can P sue and recover from A (who is, after all, the tortfeasor)?

1.3   Instead, can P sue and recover from E?

2.   Suppose P sues ACE and obtains a judgment against the partnership. How can she enforce (collect on) that judgment? (In other words, whose assets are available from which to collect the judgment?)

3.   Suppose P sues both ACE and A in a single suit and obtains a judgment against both. From whose assets can she collect on the judgment?

4.   Suppose P sues both ACE and E in a single suit and obtains a judgment against both. From whose assets can she collect on the judgment?

5.   If P successfully sues A and collects from A, does A have any right of contribution or indemnity? If so, from whom? Study RUPA § 401(c).

6.   Professor Hamilton has predicted that in states adopting RUPA, "sophisticated creditors will change their forms so as to routinely require that all partners guarantee all loans and other significant contractual obligations." Why?

c.   Note About Limited Liability Partnerships (LLPs)

One of the drawbacks of the partnership, as we have seen, is that the partners are generally liable for the partnership debts. The RUPA provisions we studied in the preceding problems bring significant protection from the traditional rule of liability by protecting the assets of vicariously liable partners from collection by a judgment creditor; as we saw, generally a successful plaintiff cannot collect her judgment from partners' individual assets until exhausting partnership assets.

The law has developed more profound protection from liability for those engaged in business. Indeed, one important theme throughout the rest of this book will be how various business structures might protect the owners of the business from liability for its debts.

Starting in the 1980s, most states have permitted partners to enjoy limited liability; that is, they have provided that partners are not liable for partnership debts. These statutes vary considerably from state to state, but one common element in such a "limited liability partnership" (LLP) is the public filing of a document that serves as notice that partners will not be personally liable for what the partnership does. The LLP has proven especially popular for professionals; many law firms are LLPs. Indeed, in some states, the LLP can be used only by partnerships practicing a profession, and not for general business. In some states, partners in an LLP are protected only from liability for negligence claims, and thus remain vicariously liable in contract and for intentional torts of other partners.

Section 306(c) of RUPA is particularly broad. It provides that "[a]n obligation of a partnership while the partnership is a limited liability partnership, whether arising in contract, tort, or otherwise, is solely the obligation of the partnership. A partner is not personally liable, directly or indirectly, by way of contribution or otherwise, for such an obligation solely by reason of being or so acting as a partner."

E.   HOW DOES A PARTNERSHIP BUSINESS GROW?

Making a business grow usually requires money. This money usually comes from one of four sources: (1) the existing owners; (2) outside lenders; (3) new investors (i.e. additional owners); and (4) earnings from business operations.

1.   EXISTING OWNERS

All or some of the existing owners of a partnership might decide to make further investments in the partnership. RUPA refers to a partner's investment in the partnership as a contribution of capital. However, there is no statutory requirement that partners make initial or additional capital contributions. Partners themselves agree on capital contributions—by whom, how much and when.

These arrangements can often be found in the partnership agreement. It is common for the partnership agreement to contain provisions requiring initial and additional capital contributions from partners. Properly drafted, such provisions will state (1) the vote or events that trigger the obligation to contribute, (2) the amount of each partner's contribution obligation, (3) the time in which to make the additional contribution, and (4) the consequences of a failure to contribute.

PROBLEM: CAPITAL CONTRIBUTION REQUIREMENT IN PARTNERSHIP AGREEMENT

Your client Agee is forming a partnership with Capel and Propp. The proposed partnership agreement provides in part:

Subsequent Capital Contributions. Subsequent capital contributions, as called for by the Managing Partner, shall be made by each partner in proportion to his or her respective distributive share. In the event any partner fails to make such subsequent capital contribution, the partners who have contributed their shares may consider the sums so advanced as loans to the partnership.

How would you modify this provision before advising a client to sign it?

The provision concerning subsequent capital contributions provides that advances by some (but not all) partners will be treated as loans. This fact raises three questions. First, can a partner make a loan to the partnership? Second, does a partner care whether the money she provides to the partnership is treated as a capital contribution or a loan? Third, does anyone else care?

RUPA § 404(f) makes answering the first question easy: "A partner may lend money and transact other business with the partnership...." We hope Chapters 1, 2, and 3 (and your common sense) make the two other questions in the preceding paragraph equally easy. (Remember the *Fenimore* case at the end of Chapter 2.)

2.   OUTSIDE LENDERS

Recall the discussion of borrowing in Chapter 2, where we addressed the concepts of risk and return and what a business can do to lower a lender's risk so the lender will agree to accept a lower return such as a lower interest rate. Recall also Professor Hamilton's prediction that lenders to partnerships in RUPA states are likely to request guarantees from individual partners. How would you resolve the following partnership loan problem?

PROBLEM: PARTNER'S GUARANTEE OF LOANS TO THE PARTNERSHIP

You represent the Bubba's Burritos partnership. AmSouth Bank is willing to lend the partnership the money it needs to grow, but only if Capel personally guarantees the loan. Capel asks for your advice as to whether she should sign such a guarantee.

3.   ADDITIONAL OWNERS (i.e., INVESTORS)

a. Financial Issues

Raising money by selling a part ownership interest in the business to an investor raises obvious financial questions such as: What does the investor get for her money? What percentage of the business belongs to her, and what will be paid to her when the business is sold? What percentage of the earnings of the business go to her when the business's earnings are distributed to its owners?

Investors, like lenders, are going to be balancing risk and return. If the risk to the investor is high, then the short-term or the long-term return to the investor has to be high to induce the investment. Otherwise, she will invest elsewhere.

One common way of measuring return on investment is by comparing the amount of cash flow—i.e., cash from business operations that could (at least in theory) be paid to the business's owners—with the amount of the owner's investment in a business. Assume for example that Propp invested $1,000 to start the Propp Mousepad (PM) business and that PM generated an annual cash flow of $220. Finance mavens would say the PM "return on equity" was 22% ($220 divided by $1,000).

An owner's risk and his return on equity are affected not only by the business's cash flow but also by the business's financial structure. The higher the amount of debt a business has, the higher the risk to the owner, and the higher the rate of return that the investor will look for.

Assume that Roberts starts his own mouse pad business, RP. Like Propp, Roberts needs $1,000 to get his mouse pad business started. But instead of investing the whole $1,000 himself, he invests $500 of his own money in RP, and borrows the other $500 from Cambridge Bank, which he is obligated to repay at $50 a year. If RP's sales and all other expenses are the same as PM's, RP's annual cash flow is lower than MP's because of the debt repayment—only $170 ($220–$50). *But RP's return on equity is higher than PM's return on equity, because of the debt.* It is 34 percent ($170 divided by $500).

The preceding paragraph illustrates the reason that the use of debt to finance a business is sometimes called "leverage." Debt, in essence, levers up the return on equity. Why wouldn't business owners always use leverage? Didn't it almost double the investor's return in the previous example? Yes, but it also substantially increases the investment's risk. Suppose that the two companies each experience a lean year, with cash flow falling from $220 to $20. Because it has no debt to service, PM will survive safely. In contrast, RP will be in deep trouble. Because the $20 of cash flow will be inadequate to pay its $50 debt repayment obligation, RP will become insolvent unless it has other cash available, perhaps saved from earlier years. Although leverage helps when times are good, it can kill when times are bad.

b. Legal Issues

Raising money for new partnership growth by bringing in new investors as new partners raises two legal questions that are not especially tricky. First, do all existing partners have to approve any new partner? RUPA § 401(i) requires the consent of all existing partners—unless the partnership agreement provides otherwise. (Remember UPA § 18 and RUPA § 103.) Second, is the new partner personally liable for all of the partnership's existing debts? Under RUPA § 306(b), a new partner is not personally liable for partnership obligations "incurred before the person's admission as a partner." The following problems illustrate these two legal issues.

PROBLEMS: NEW PARTNERS

1.   The Bubba's Burritos partnership agreement is silent as to admitting new partners. Shepherd has offered to invest $100,000 in Bubba's Burritos. Agee and Propp favor taking Shepherd's money and making him a partner. Capel is opposed. Agee and Propp come to you with the question of whether they can amend the partnership agreement to provide that admission of new partners requires the approval of a simple majority of the partners. How do you answer their question? *See* RUPA §§ 401(j); 103.

2.   Shepherd has some questions about becoming a partner in Bubba's Burritos. He wants to know whether he will be personally liable on:

- Bubba's Burritos' existing ten-year lease of its Tuscaloosa location;

- Bubba's Burritos' anticipated construction mortgage on its new Boston location.

How do you answer his questions?

4.   EARNINGS FROM BUSINESS OPERATIONS

Existing partners fund the growth of their business not only by deciding to put new money into the partnership, but also by deciding not to take money out of the partnership. In deciding whether to retain earnings, the partnership should evaluate whether the partnership can earn a higher return than the partners could earn individually if the money were distributed to them. Earnings should be distributed unless the partnership has some lucrative use for the funds. Who should make that decision about whether to distribute earnings? Consider the following introductory problem and then the materials in the next part of this chapter on how the owners of a partnership make money.

PROBLEM: USE OF PARTNERSHIP EARNINGS

You represent Bubba's Burritos, a partnership, which had net income of $250,000 last year. Propp and Capel want to use that money to expand the business. Agee needs her share of the money to pay school loans. What do you advise? By the way, can you advise everybody?

F.   HOW DO THE OWNERS OF A PARTNERSHIP MAKE MONEY?

Recall that all of Epstein's relatives said that they owned businesses to make money. Generally an owner of a business makes money by (1) being paid a salary by that business or (2) receiving all or part of the profits from that business or (3) selling her interest in the business.

1. SALARY

RUPA provisions with respect to partnership salaries are easy to understand and easy to apply. And once you understand these RUPA provisions, you will understand why they are rarely applicable. Nonetheless, apply the cited RUPA provisions in the following problems.

PROBLEMS: PARTNERSHIP SALARY

1. Propp, Agee and Capel are the partners in the Bubba's Burritos partnership. Agee and Propp work at the partnership, but Capel does not. Can Agee and Propp receive a salary from the partnership? *See* RUPA §§ 401(h), 401(j), 103(a).

2. Assume the partnership agreement provides that Agee shall receive an annual salary of $30,000 and that Propp is to receive an annual salary of $25,000. Can Capel prevent Agee and Propp from increasing their salaries?

3. Can Capel compel the partnership to employ him and pay him a salary?

4. Can the partnership pay Capel a salary even though he does not do any work for the partnership? Do the other partners care? (Is RUPA § 404(d) relevant?) Why would they agree to this? Do the partnership's creditors care? Does the Internal Revenue Service care?

2. PROFITS

The law with respect to partnership profits, like the law with respect to partnership salaries, is found primarily in the partnership agreement and other contracts and laws—not in the partnership statute or partnership case law. The only provision in RUPA that expressly deals with partners' rights to partnership profits is § 401(b): "Each partner is entitled to an equal share of the partnership profits and is chargeable with a share of the partnership losses in proportion to the partner's share of the profits." *See also* UPA § 18(a). Does this help you answer the following problems about profits and losses?

PROBLEMS: PARTNERSHIP PROFITS

1. Who gets what if there is no partnership agreement provision on allocation of profits? Bubba's Burritos is a partnership. Agee, Capel and Propp are the partners. Capel invests $1,000,000 in the partnership. Propp invests $20,000. Agee does not make a contribution of capital; she works for the partnership and draws a salary. The partnership makes a profit of $99,000 in 2010. How will that profit be shared among Agee, Capel and Propp?

2. Who gets what if there is a partnership provision? Would your answer to (1) be different if the partnership agreement provided that 2/3 of the profits shall be allocated to Capel, 1/6 of the profits shall be allocated to Agee and 1/6 of the profits shall be allocated to Propp?

3.   Who decides when the partners receive a distribution in a good year? Again assume that the partnership earned $99,000 in 2010 and that the partnership agreement provides that 2/3 of the profits are to be allocated to Capel. Agee and Propp take the position that the partnership should not make any distribution to partners but rather should use the $99,000 for advertising. Capel comes to you with the question of whether she can compel the partnership to distribute her share of the profits to her. How do you answer her question? *Cf.* RUPA §§ 401(f) & (j).

4.   Who decides whether the partners receive a distribution in a bad year? Now assume that 2010 was a bad year for Bubba's Burritos. It had to use earnings retained from prior years' operations to pay its bills. That same year was also a bad one for Agee and Propp personally. They come to you with the question of whether the partnership can make a distribution to partners notwithstanding the bad year. How do you answer their question? *Cf.* RUPA § 807.

5.   Often the answers to questions such as those above can be found in the partnership's loan agreements. It is common for a lender to require a business borrower to agree that it will not make any distributions to its owners until the loan is repaid.

3.   SALE OF OWNERSHIP INTEREST TO A THIRD PARTY

Assume again that Bubba's Burritos is a partnership and that the partners are Agee, Capel, and Propp. Propp wants to make money by selling his part of the partnership to a non-partner—he wants to sell his ownership interest and use that money on some new business.

Recall the business and legal problems that a partnership encountered when it tried to sell new partnership interests to new investors:

- finding a buyer;
- gaining any necessary approval from existing partners; and,
- dealing with the question of preexisting obligations.

Propp, a partner, will encounter all of these problems when he tries to sell his existing partnership interest to some new investor. And Propp will encounter an additional, unavoidable, statutory problem, RUPA § 502: "The only transferable interest of a partner in the partnership is the partner's share of profits and losses of the partnership and the partner's right to receive distributions." *See also* UPA § 26.

PROBLEMS: SALE OF PARTNERSHIP INTEREST

1.   If Roberts buys Propp's partnership interest, will Roberts have a right to participate in partnership decisions? What is the policy reason for this?

2.   If Roberts buys Propp's partnership interest, will Propp retain the right to participate in the management of the partnership? *See* RUPA

§ 503(d). What incentive does Propp have to participate actively in partnership management at this point?

3. If Roberts buys Propp's partnership interest, does Propp remain liable for partnership obligations?

4. Instead of buying Propp's partnership interest, suppose Roberts buys a partnership interest from the partnership itself. Will Roberts have a right to participate in partnership decisions?

5. Review: RUPA § 502 refers to both the "partner's share of profits" and the "partner's right to receive distributions." What is the difference?

4. SALE OF OWNERSHIP INTEREST BACK TO THE PARTNERSHIP

a. Buy–Sell Agreements

The partner might also make money by selling her share of the partnership back to the partnership itself. Because of the business and legal problems in an existing partner's selling her partnership interest to an outsider, it is common for the partnership agreement or some separate agreement among partners to provide for sale of partnership interests back to the partnership or to other partners. Such agreements are commonly referred to as "buy-sell agreements."

Any buy-sell agreement should answer the following questions:

(1) Are the other partners or the partnership obligated to buy or do they instead have the option to buy?

(2) What events trigger this obligation or option?

(3) How is the selling partner's interest to be valued?

(4) What is the method of funding the payment?

Special attention should also be given to the tax effects of the payout (but not in these materials).

Even if there is no buy-sell agreement, a partner has the power to compel the partnership to pay for her partnership interest by withdrawing from the partnership. How much and when a withdrawing partner is paid by the partnership is covered by (i) partnership agreements, (ii) partnership statutes, and (iii) the next part of this chapter.

b. Withdrawal of a Partner

The first thing that happens when a partner withdraws from a partnership is that you have to master a new vocabulary. If UPA controls, you need to study UPA §§ 29, 30, and 31 and to know these terms:

(1) dissolution;

(2) winding up;

(3) termination.

Interestingly, "dissolution" does not mean that the partnership ceases to exist. It is not the end of the partnership. It is simply the beginning of the end. After "dissolution," as defined in UPA § 29, there will be a winding up (or "liquidation") of the business, after which the partnership will actually terminate.

If RUPA controls the withdrawal of the partner, you need to know:

(1) dissociation as discussed in RUPA § 601 and the materials below;

(2) dissolution as covered in RUPA § 801 and the materials below;

(3) winding up;

(4) termination.

Whichever statute and set of terms you are using, you will be using them to answer the questions of (i) what happens to the withdrawing partner if there is no dissolution of the partnership and (ii) what happens to the partnership and to its partners if there is dissolution.

Under RUPA § 602, any partner has the power to dissociate (withdraw) at any time. While there can be no question about whether a partner has the power to withdraw, there can be important questions about whether the withdrawal was "wrongful" under common law rules or under the partnership statute.

If the withdrawal or dissociation violates the partnership agreement, or occurs before the expiration of the partnership term, or satisfies any other circumstance set out in § 602(b), it is "wrongful." And if the dissociation is wrongful, the partner may be paid less than otherwise for her partnership interest and, more importantly, may be paid later. *See* RUPA §§ 602(c), 701(c) and 701(h). How much a withdrawing partner is paid depends not only on whether the dissociation was wrongful but also on (i) whether there is any provision in the partnership establishing the payment to a withdrawing partner and (ii) what happens to the partnership after the withdrawal. An important point: unless the partnership agreement says otherwise, a partner in a "partnership at will" (a partnership with neither a specified end date nor a specific undertaking to complete) can quit at any time without its being wrongful.

In the following problems, assume that the partnership is not dissolved after the partner's withdrawal. Instead, it makes a payment to the withdrawing partner and continues business operations. After these problems, we will consider what happens to the partnership and all the partners when the partnership is dissolved.

PROBLEMS: PARTNER WITHDRAWAL

1.   Bubba's Burritos is a partnership. Agee, Capel, and Propp are the partners. The partnership agreement has no provision with respect to withdrawal or dissociation of a partner. The partnership agreement does provide that the partnership is to have a ten-year term. Can Propp withdraw from the partnership in the partnership's third year? Will such withdrawal be "wrong-

ful"? When will Propp be paid for his partnership interest? *See* RUPA §§ 602(b), 603, 701(e) and 701(h).

2.   What are the consequences of a wrongful dissociation? *See* RUPA §§ 602(c) and 701(h).

3.   How much will Propp be paid for his partnership interest? *See* RUPA §§ 701(b) and (c).

4.   Would your answers be different if the partnership agreement specified that it would continue until it completed the construction of a large-scale electric generator powered by fermented ketchup?

5.   What if the partnership agreement, like that of many law firms, indicated instead that it had no end date or specific task to complete?

In reading the next case on partnership dissolution, please consider the following questions:

1.   Why is Mrs. Creel arguing that the only way to determine the value of her deceased husband's interest in the partnership is to liquidate all of the assets? Why did Altizer and Lilly reject her demand that they liquidate the partnership's assets?

2.   Will the amount received at such a liquidation sale be greater than the amount based on the accountant's valuation?

3.   How did the accountant determine the value of the partnership?

CREEL v. LILLY

Court of Appeals of Maryland, 1999
729 A.2d 385

CHASANOW, JUDGE.

The primary issue presented in this appeal is whether Maryland's Uniform Partnership Act (UPA) permits the estate of a deceased partner to demand liquidation of partnership assets in order to arrive at the true value of the business. Specifically, Petitioner (Anne Creel) maintains that the surviving partners have a duty to liquidate all partnership assets because (1) there is no provision in the partnership agreement providing for the continuation of the partnership upon a partner's death and (2) the estate has not consented to the continuation of the business. Respondents (Arnold Lilly and Roy Altizer) contend that because the surviving partners wound up the partnership in good faith, in that they conducted a full inventory, provided an accurate accounting to the estate for the value of the business as of the date of dissolution, and paid the estate its proportionate share of the surplus proceeds, they are under no duty to liquidate the partnership's assets upon demand of the deceased partner's estate.
* * *

I. Background

On approximately June 1, 1993, Joseph Creel began a retail business selling NASCAR racing memorabilia. His business was originally located in a section of his wife Anne's florist shop, but after about a year and a half he decided to raise capital from partners so that he could expand and move into his own space. On September 20, 1994, Mr. Creel entered into a partnership agreement—apparently prepared without the assistance of counsel—with Arnold Lilly and Roy Altizer to form a general partnership called "Joe's Racing." * * *

II. Discussion and Analysis

We begin our analysis by reviewing the law of partnership as it pertains to the issues in this case. Maryland enacted UPA in 1916. * * *

Under UPA, partners may avoid the automatic dissolution of the business upon the death of a partner by providing for its continuation in their partnership agreement. Sophisticated partnerships virtually always use carefully drafted partnership agreements to protect the various partners' interests by providing for the continuation of the business, the distribution of partnership assets, etc., in the face of various contingencies such as death. * * *

Over time, the UPA rule requiring automatic dissolution of the partnership upon the death of a partner, in the absence of consent by the estate to continue the business or an agreement providing for continuation, with the possible result of a forced sale of all partnership assets was viewed as outmoded by many jurisdictions including Maryland. The development and adoption of RUPA by the National Conference of Commissioners on Uniform State Laws (NCCUSL) mitigated this harsh UPA provision of automatic dissolution and compelled liquidation.

RUPA's underlying philosophy differs radically from UPA's, thus laying the foundation for many of its innovative measures. RUPA adopts the "entity" theory of partnership as opposed to the "aggregate" theory that the UPA espouses. Under the aggregate theory, a partnership is characterized by the collection of its individual members, with the result being that if one of the partners dies or withdraws, the partnership ceases to exist. On the other hand, RUPA's entity theory allows for the partnership to continue even with the departure of a member because it views the partnership as "an entity distinct from its partners." Section 9A–201.

This adoption of the entity theory, which permits continuity of the partnership upon changes in partner identity, allows for several significant changes in RUPA. Of particular importance to the instant case is that under RUPA "a partnership no longer automatically dissolves due to a change in its membership, but rather the existing partnership may be continued if the remaining partners elect to buy out the dissociating partner." In contrast to UPA, RUPA's "buy-out" option does not have to be expressly included in a written partnership agreement in order for it to be exercised; however, the surviving partners must still actively choose to exercise the option, as "continuation is not automatic as with a corporation." This major RUPA innovation therefore delineates two possible paths for a partnership to follow when a partner dies or withdraws: "[o]ne leads to the winding up and termination of the partnership and the other to continuation of the partnership and purchase of the departing partner's share." Critically, under RUPA the estate of the deceased partner no longer has to consent in order for the business to be continued nor does the estate have the right to compel liquidation.

Like UPA, RUPA is a "gap filler" in that it only governs partnership affairs to the extent not otherwise agreed to by the partners in the partnership agreement. See § 9A–103(a), which states: "[R]elations among the partners and between the partners and the partnership are governed by the partnership agreement. To the extent the partnership agreement does not otherwise provide, this title governs relations among the partners and between the partners and the partnership." There are certain RUPA provisions, however, that partners cannot waive, such as unreasonably restricting the right of access to partnership books and records, eliminating the duty of loyalty, unreasonably reducing the duty of care, and eliminating the obligation of good faith and fair dealing. See § 9A–103(b).

Along with 18 other states, Maryland has adopted RUPA, effective July 1, 1998, with a phase-in period during which the two Acts will coexist. As of January 1, 2003, RUPA will govern all Maryland partnerships. In adopting RUPA, the Maryland legislature was clearly seeking to eliminate some of UPA's harsh provisions, such as the automatic dissolution of a viable partnership upon the death of a partner and the subsequent right of the estate of the deceased partner to compel liquidation. In essence, the NCCUSL drafted RUPA to reflect the emerging trends in partnership law. RUPA is intended as a flexible, modern alternative to the more rigid UPA and its provisions are consistent with the reasonable expectations of commercial parties in today's business world. * * *

[W]e want to clarify that while UPA is the governing act, our holding is also consistent with RUPA and its underlying policies. The legislature's recent adoption of RUPA indicates that it views with disfavor the compelled liquidation of businesses and that it has elected to follow the trend in partnership law to allow the continuation of business without disruption, in either the original or successor form, if the surviving partners choose to do so through buying out the deceased partner's share.

In this appeal, however, we would arrive at the same holding regardless of whether UPA or RUPA governs. Although our holding departs from the general UPA rule that the representative of the deceased partner's estate has a right to demand liquidation of the partnership, our position of "no forced sale" hardly represents a radical departure from traditional partnership law. * * * Because a partnership is governed by any agreement between or among the partners, we must begin our analysis of the compelled liquidation issue by examining the Joe's Racing partnership agreement. We reiterate that both UPA and RUPA only apply when there is either no partnership agreement governing the partnership's affairs, the agreement is silent on a particular point, or the agreement contains provisions contrary to law. * * * Thus, when conflicts between partners arise, courts must first look to the partnership agreement to resolve the issue.

The agreement, whatever its form, is the heart of the partnership. One of the salient characteristics of partnership law is the extent to which partners may write their own ticket. Relations among them are governed by common law and statute, but almost invariably can be overridden by the parties themselves. * * *

The pertinent paragraph and subsections of the Joe's Racing partnership agreement are as follows:

> 7. TERMINATION
>
> (a) That, at the termination of this partnership a full and accurate inventory shall be prepared, and the assets, liabilities, and income, both in gross and net, shall be ascertained: the remaining debts or profits will be distributed according to the percentages shown above in the 6(e).
>
> (d) Upon the death or illness of a partner, his share will go to his estate.
>
> If his estate wishes to sell his interest, they must offer it to the remaining partners first.

Even though the partnership agreement uses the word "termination," paragraph 7(a) is really discussing the dissolution of the partnership and the attendant winding-up process that ultimately led to termination. Paragraph 7(a) requires that the assets, liabilities, and income be "ascertained," but it in no way mandates that this must be accomplished by a forced sale of the partnership assets. Indeed, a liquidation or sale of assets is not mentioned anywhere in 7(a).

In this case, the winding-up method outlined in 7(a) was followed exactly by the surviving partners: a full and accurate inventory was prepared on August 31, 1995; this information was given to an accountant, who ascertained the assets, liabilities, and income of the partnership; and finally, the remaining debt or profit was distributed according to the percentages listed in 6(e). * * *

Mrs. Creel argues that the partnership agreement does not address the winding-up process and that we should look to UPA's default rules to fill in this gap. Her contention is incorrect. We only turn to UPA and its liquidation rule if there is no other option, and such is clearly not the case here. While this partnership agreement was drafted without the assistance of counsel and is not a sophisticated document that provides for every contingency, if it states the intention of the parties it is controlling. * * *

Thus, when we look to the intention of the parties as reflected in 7(a) of the partnership agreement, the trial judge could conclude that the partners did not anticipate that a "fire sale" of the partnership assets would be necessary to ascertain the true value of Joe's Racing. Paragraph 7(a) details the preferred winding-up procedure to be followed, to include an inventory, valuation, and distribution of debt or profit to the partners.

Moreover, paragraph 7(d), which discusses what happens to a partner's share of the business upon his death, also makes no mention of a sale or liquidation as being essential in order to determine the deceased partner's proportionate interest of the partnership. On the contrary, 7(d) appears to be a crude attempt to draft a "continuation clause" in the form of a buy-out option by providing that the deceased partner's share of the partnership goes to his estate, and if the estate wishes to sell this interest it must first be offered to the remaining partners. In contrast to consenting to the continuation of the business, Mrs. Creel made it plain that she wanted the business "dissolved and the affairs of the company wound up;" however, this does not mean a liquidation was required. Particularly in light of Maryland's recent adoption of RUPA, paragraph 7(d) of the partnership agreement can be interpreted to mean that because Mrs. Creel did not wish to remain in business with Lilly and Altizer, they had the option to buy out her deceased husband's interest.

In short, when subsections (a) and (d) of paragraph 7 are read in conjunction, it is apparent that the partners did not intend for there to be a liquidation of all partnership assets upon the death of a partner. * * *

Assuming arguendo that the Joe's Racing partnership agreement cannot be interpreted as outlining an alternative to liquidation in winding up the partnership in the event of a dissolution caused by a partner's death, we still find that a sale of all partnership assets is not required under either UPA or RUPA in order to ascertain the true value of the business. Support for this is found in Maryland's recent adoption of RUPA, which encourages businesses to continue in either their original or successor form, and also the holdings of out-of-state cases where other options besides a "fire sale" have been chosen when a partnership is dissolved under UPA. * * *

We now explore the "true value of the partnership" issue and whether liquidation is the only way to obtain it. * * *

Mrs. Creel contends that the accountant's valuation improperly considered only the book value of the business and not its market value. "Book value" refers to the assets of the business, less its liabilities plus partner contributions or "equity." "Market value" includes the value of such intangibles as goodwill, the value of the business as an ongoing concern, and established vendor and supplier lines, among other factors. Again, we concur with the trial court's findings as to the valuation of Joe's Racing.

In making no finding of goodwill value, for example, the trial court likely considered the fact that Joe's Racing had only been operating a little over a year before the partnership was formed, and after Lilly and Altizer became partners with Mr. Creel the business was only in existence for nine months before Mr. Creel died. On these facts, it is reasonable for the trial court to conclude—without any evidence presented to the contrary—that a small business selling NASCAR memorabilia, which had been operating for barely two years, did not possess any goodwill value.

Our goal in this case, and in cases of a similar nature, is to prevent the disruption and loss that are attendant on a forced sale, while at the same time preserving the right of the deceased partner's estate to be paid his or her fair share of the partnership. With our holding, we believe this delicate balance has been achieved. For the reasons stated, we hold that paragraph 7, subsections (a) and (d), of the partnership agreement should be interpreted as outlining an alternative method of winding-up Joe's Racing and arriving at its true value other than a "fire sale" of all its assets. Even if there were no partnership agreement governing this case, however, we hold that Maryland's UPA—particularly in light of the legislature's recent adoption of RUPA—does not grant the estate of a deceased partner the right to demand liquidation of a partnership where the partnership agreement does not expressly provide for continuation of the partnership and where the estate does not consent to continuation. To hold otherwise vests excessive power and control in the estate of the deceased partner, to the extreme disadvantage of the surviving partners. We further hold that where the surviving partners have in good faith wound up the business and the deceased partner's estate is provided with an accurate accounting allowing for payment of a proportionate share of the business, then a forced sale of all partnership assets is unwarranted.
* * *

QUESTIONS AND NOTES

1.   In Part II of the opinion, the court says that the RUPA dissociation provisions permit a partnership to continue in existence after the death of a partner "if the remaining partners elect to buy out the dissociating partner." It goes on to say that such continuation is not automatic, but that the surviving partners must choose to exercise the option to continue the business.

The court was discussing an earlier version of RUPA. The more recent version, which is contained in your statutory supplement, provides that after dissociation "the partnership shall cause the dissociated partner's interest in the partnership to be purchased * * *." RUPA § 701(a).

2.   The court notes that the partnership agreement was prepared "without the assistance of counsel." Could a competent lawyer have drafted the partnership agreement to avoid this litigation? What would she have provided?

3.   Recall that Mrs. Creel contends that the "accountant's valuation improperly considered only the book value of the business." How is book

value determined? Will book value be higher or lower than the amount received by liquidating the assets?

4. Would the result in *Creel* have been different if there were no partnership agreement, so that the case was instead decided under RUPA's default rules? *See* RUPA §§ 601(7), 602(b), and 701(b).

5. One more time: RUPA is a gap filler. Don't leave dissociation gaps in the partnership agreements you draft. Review how this partnership agreement for doctors fills the gap with respect to payment to a withdrawing partner:

> 20. Except as otherwise provided herein, the partnership shall continue until dissolved by mutual consent; provided, however, that any partner shall have the right to withdraw from the partnership after sixty days' notice in writing to the other partners (except during a period when a totally disabled partner is entitled to a share of partnership net profits under paragraph 17(a) or to payments in liquidation of the partnership interest under paragraph 17 (b) or the estate of a deceased partner is entitled to a percentage of partnership net profits or to other payments under paragraph 18(b) or a withdrawn, expelled or retired partner is entitled to payments under paragraph 22(b)); and provided, further, that a partner may be expelled from the partnership by the other partners for any of the following reasons:

> (a) Revocation or suspension of the license of such partner to practice medicine or other major disciplinary action against such partner as a physician by any duly constituted authority.

> (b) Professional misconduct which violates the ethical standards of the medical profession, if such misconduct continues after its desistance is required by the other partners.

> (c) Insolvency or bankruptcy of the partner or assignment of the assets of such partner for the benefit of creditors.

> (d) Any other reason which the other partners unanimously determine is an adequate reason for the expulsion of such partner.

> 21. Upon the withdrawal or expulsion of a partner, such partner shall be entitled to the following payments by the partnership in liquidation of the interest of such partner in the partnership:

> (a) The amount of the interest of such partner in the capital of the partnership, which shall equal the capital account of such partner as shown on the partnership books as of the date of withdrawal or expulsion, including any undrawn share of profits but not including accounts receivable, and adjusted to reflect the appraised value of the partnership x-ray equipment as provided in paragraph 18 (a)(3).

> (b) A portion of the following amounts, which portion in each case shall be the percentage interest of such withdrawn or expelled partner in the accounts receivable of the partnership immediately prior to withdrawal or expulsion:

> (1) the amount of collections of accounts receivable on the partnership books as of the date of withdrawal or expulsion which are made by

the partnership, under established practices as to billings and use of collection agencies, within three months after such date, less 20 percent of all such collections for costs of collection; and

(2) an amount equal to 70 percent of the uncollected balances at the end of the aforesaid three-month period of accounts receivable which were on the partnership books as of the date of such withdrawn or expelled partner's withdrawal or expulsion. The portion of the amounts of collections specified in clause (1) above to which a withdrawn or expelled partner is entitled shall be paid to such partner, without interest, in three monthly installments, each of which shall be computed on the basis of collections during one of the three months specified in clause (1) and shall be made as soon as reasonably possible after the end of such month. The portion of the amount specified in clause (2) above to which a withdrawn or expelled partner is entitled shall be paid to such partner, without interest, within six months after withdrawal or expulsion.

William R. Patterson, *Drafting the Partnership Agreement,* CA86 ALI–ABA 837 (May 2, 1996).

6.   We have left a gap in our coverage: the liability of a dissociating partner and her ability to bind the partnership after leaving. Study RUPA §§ 702 and 703. Assume that Capel, a partner in the Bubba's Burritos partnership, dissociates from the partnership on April 5. (All dates given are in the same year). Is Capel liable:

a.   To Roberts on the ten-year real property lease that Bubba's Burritos and Roberts executed on January 15?

b.   To Shepherd on his slip and fall claim against Bubba's Burritos based on an alleged July 13 accident there?

c.   To TeePee Distributors, Inc., a long-time supplier of Bubba's Burritos, for food ordered and delivered on April 11?

d.   Can Capel bind the partnership to an agreement with Tee Pee Distributors, Inc. on April 7? In other words, does Capel retain what is sometimes called ''lingering authority'' to bind the partnership even after dissociating?

7.   Would any of your answers in Question 6 change if the Bubba's Burritos partnership agreement provided that a partner's liability ends on dissociation? *See* RUPA § 103(b)(10).

G.   PARTNERSHIP ENDGAME

1.   DISSOLUTION, WINDING UP, AND TERMINATION AS ENDGAME FOR THE PARTNERSHIP

As the *Creel* case showed, under RUPA the partnership faces two choices when a partner dies or otherwise withdraws from the partnership. Either (1) the remaining partners can purchase the departing partner's interest and continue the partnership business, or (2) the partnership can dissolve, liquidate, and terminate. The latter is the path less traveled.

Nonetheless, a lawyer (and so a law student) needs to be able to answer three questions about dissolution, winding up and termination:

1. What causes dissolution?

2. What happens during winding up?

3. Who gets what when on termination?

Under RUPA, the first question is answered by §§ 601, 801, 802(b) and the partnership agreement. Work through the following problems using these RUPA sections. Then consider whether the partnership agreement should have provided a different answer.

PROBLEMS: PARTNERSHIP DISSOLUTION

1. Propp, Agee, and Capel are partners in Bubba's Burritos. The partnership agreement contains no provision relating to dissolution or to the duration of the partnership. Capel withdraws. Can Propp and Agee continue to operate the partnership?

2. Same facts as Question 1. What if Capel wants the partnership to dissolve but Propp and Agee want to continue to operate the partnership?

3. Same facts as Question 1 except that Capel dies, and her widower, Mr. Capel, wants the partnership to dissolve. Again, Agee and Propp do not want the partnership to dissolve. What result? (By the way, does this fact pattern sound familiar?)

4. Drs. A, B, C, and D are in a partnership. The partnership agreement has a ten-year term. In year three of the partnership, Dr. A. withdraws. Can Doctors B, C, and D continue the partnership?

5. Does your answer to Question 4 change if Dr. B wants to dissolve the partnership?

———————

Dissolution is not the end of the partnership. At most, as we said earlier, it is the beginning of the end. As Comment 2 to RUPA § 801 explains:

Under RUPA, "dissolution" is merely the commencement of the winding up process. The partnership continues for the limited purpose of winding up the business. In effect, that means the scope of the partnership business contracts to completing work in process and taking such other actions necessary to wind up the business. Winding up the partnership business entails selling its assets, paying its debts, and distributing the net balance, if any, to the partners in cash according to their interests. The partnership entity continues, and the partners are associated in the winding up of the business until winding up is completed. When the winding up is completed, the partnership entity terminates.

Consider the following problems about the "paying its debts" part of winding up a partnership:

PROBLEMS: WINDING UP

1. On dissolution, Bubba's Burritos owes $100,000 to its creditors, including $20,000 lent to the partnership by one of its partners, Capel. Should the debt owed to Capel be treated differently from the debt owed to the other creditors? *See* RUPA § 807(a) and Comment 2 of Official Comments to § 807.

2. Suppose that the partnership has no assets. Can the inside and outside creditors collect the unpaid balance of their claims from the partners individually? Recall RUPA §§ 306, 807(b).

If the partnership agreement does not address the issue effectively, the parties can encounter significant problems in trying to distribute assets to the partners "according to their interests." RUPA provides default rules in this area in §§ 401 and 807. These provisions establish four basic concepts:

Unless partners agree to the contrary:

1. They share responsibility not only for the losses from operation of the partnership business, but also for any partners' losses from investments in the partnership. *See* RUPA § 401(b);

2. The amount of each partner's loss from her investment in the partnership is determined from her partnership account, a bookkeeping device which keeps track of how much a partner puts into the partnership, how much she has taken out of the partnership, and her share of the partnership's profits and losses. *See* RUPA §§ 401(a), 807(a)–(b);

3. When the partnership is dissolved, the partnership is legally obligated to pay each partner an amount measured by the balance in her partnership account. *See* RUPA § 807(b). Summarizing and distilling the calculations in § 401, the amount in each partner's account will be:

● The value of each partner's investment in the partnership of money or property, but no credit for the value of a partner's labor (we'll discuss in a bit whether this is fair);

● Minus any distributions to the partner—remember, profits can be either retained or disbursed;*

● Plus an equal share of whatever of value remains in the partnership, after paying both creditors and the above amounts. If there are insufficient partnership funds to cover the amounts above, the loss will be divided equally among the partners' accounts.

4. It is possible that, at the time of dissolution, a partner will have a negative balance in his account. For example, this could occur if a partner,

---

* Sometimes these first two items are called the partner's "capital account."

relative to the other partners, has contributed little property or money, but has received relatively large distributions, and the partnership has suffered large losses. Such a partner will have to contribute additional funds to the partnership in the amount of the negative balance. RUPA § 807(b). Only this will ensure that the other partners—such as those who received no distribution—are dealt with fairly.

Apply these concepts in the following problems.

PROBLEMS: PARTNERSHIP ACCOUNTS

1. At the start of the Bubba's Burritos partnership, Capel invests $250,000 in the partnership. Propp deeds land to the partnership worth $150,000. Agee contributes $2,000 of cookware and agrees to work for the partnership as manager. They agree to share profits from the partnership equally. Do they also need to agree as to partnership accounts? If so, can you represent all three of them?

2. Suppose that, at the dissolution of the Bubba's Burritos partnership described in the first problem, the partnership has cash and property worth $200,000 after paying all of its creditors. Capel earlier received distributions of $150,000, Propp received $142,000, and Agee received nothing. How should the $200,000 be distributed?

3. Same facts as Question 2 except that after paying its creditors the partnership has only $20,000. (This may have happened, for instance, because the value of the assets that the partners contributed has declined). How is the $20,000 distributed? This one is tougher because there is not enough money to compensate everyone for her contributions. To jump-start these calculations, here are some helpful questions. How much money is owed to compensate each partner for what she has contributed, but that has not yet been distributed to her? How much money does the partnership have to cover that amount? (The hypo says $20,000.) How much is that short? That amount is a loss, to be shared equally. Now do the numbers.

———

Were your answers for Question 2: Capel gets $130,000, Propp gets $38,000, and Agee gets $32,000? Were your answers for Question 3: Propp pays $22,000, Agee pays $28,000, and Capel receives $70,000? Do you think it's fair that Agee received the least of all the partners, even though he worked full time for the partnership? If so, you will probably disagree with the next case. At any rate, read the next case and, as you do, consider the following:

1. Were the creditors of the partnership paid? Do the creditors of the partnership "have a dog in this fight?"

2. Was the defendant paid for the work that he did for the partnership?

KOVACIK v. REED

Supreme Court of California, 1957
315 P.2d 314

SCHAUER, J.

In this suit for dissolution of a joint venture and for an accounting, defendant appeals from a judgment that plaintiff recover from defendant one half the losses of the venture. We have concluded that inasmuch as the parties agreed that plaintiff was to supply the money and defendant the labor to carry on the venture, defendant is correct in his contention that the trial court erred in holding him liable for one half the monetary losses, and that the judgment should therefore be reversed. * * *

Plaintiff, a licensed building contractor in San Francisco, operated his contracting business as a sole proprietorship under the fictitious name of "Asbestos Siding Company." Defendant had for a number of years worked for various building contractors in that city as a job superintendent and estimator.

Early in November, 1952, Kovacik [plaintiff] told Reed [defendant] that Kovacik had an opportunity to do kitchen remodeling work for Sears Roebuck Company in San Francisco and asked Reed to become his job superintendent and estimator in this venture. Kovacik said that he had about $10,000.00 to invest in the venture and that, if Reed would superintend and estimate the jobs, Kovacik would share the profits with Reed on a 50–50 basis. Kovacik did not ask Reed to agree to share any loss that might result and Reed did not offer to share any such loss. The subject of a possible loss was not discussed in the inception of this venture. Reed accepted Kovacik's proposal and commenced work for the venture shortly after November 1, 1952. * * * Reed's only contribution was his own labor. Kovacik provided all of the venture's financing through the credit of Asbestos Siding Company, although at times Reed purchased materials for the jobs in his own name or on his account for which he was reimbursed. * * *

The venture bid on and was awarded a number of remodeling jobs in San Francisco. Reed worked on all of the jobs as job superintendent. During August, 1953, Kovacik, who at that time had all of the financial records of the venture in his possession, informed Reed that the venture had been unprofitable and demanded contribution from Reed as to amounts which Kovacik claimed to have advanced in excess of the income received from the venture. Reed at no time promised, represented or agreed that he was liable for any of the venture's losses, and he consistently and without exception refused to contribute to or pay any of the loss resulting from the venture. The venture was terminated on August 31, 1953.

Kovacik thereafter instituted this proceeding, seeking an accounting of the affairs of the venture and to recover from Reed one half of the losses. Despite the evidence above set forth from the statement of the oral proceedings, showing that at no time had defendant agreed to be liable for any of the losses, the trial court "found"—more accurately, we think, concluded as a matter of law—that "plaintiff and defendant were to share equally all their joint venture profits and losses between them," and that defendant "agreed to share equally in the profits and losses of said joint venture." Following an accounting taken by a referee appointed by the court, judgment was rendered awarding plaintiff recovery against defendant of some $4,340, as one half the monetary losses* [1] found by the referee to have been sustained by the joint venture.

It is the general rule that in the absence of an agreement to the contrary the law presumes that partners and joint adventurers intended to participate equally in the profits and losses of the common enterprise, irrespective of any inequality in the amounts each contributed to the capital employed in the venture, with the losses being shared by them in the same proportions as they share the profits.

However, it appears that in the cases in which the above stated general rule has been applied, each of the parties had contributed capital consisting of either money or land or other tangible property, or else was to receive compensation for services rendered to the common undertaking which was to be paid before computation of the profits or losses. Where, however, as in the present case, one partner or joint adventurer contributes the money capital as against the other's skill and labor, all the cases cited, and which our research has discovered, hold that neither party is liable to the other for contribution for any loss sustained. Thus, upon loss of the money the party who contributed it is not entitled to recover any part of it from the party who contributed only services. The rationale of this rule is that where one party contributes money and the other contributes services, then in the event of a loss each would lose his own capital—the one his money and the other his labor. Another view would be that in such a situation the parties have, by their agreement to share equally in profits, agreed that the values of their contributions—the money on the one hand and the labor on the other—were likewise equal; it would follow that upon the loss, as here, of both money and labor, the parties have shared equally in the losses. Actually, of course, plaintiff here lost only some $8,680—or somewhat less than the $10,000 which he originally proposed and agreed to invest. * * *

It follows that the conclusion of law upon which the judgment in favor of plaintiff for recovery from defendant of one half the monetary losses depends is untenable, and that the judgment should be reversed. * * *

---

* [1] The record is silent as to the factors taken into account by the referee in determining the 'loss' suffered by the venture. However, there is no contention that defendant's services were ascribed any value whatsoever. It may also be noted that the trial court 'found' that 'neither plaintiff nor defendant was to receive compensation for their services rendered to said joint venture, but plaintiff and defendant were to share equally all their joint venture profits and losses between them.' Neither party suggests that plaintiff actually rendered services to the venture in the same sense that defendant did. And, as is clear from the settled statement, plaintiff's proposition to defendant was that plaintiff would provide the money as against defendant's contribution of services as estimator and superintendent.

The judgment is reversed.

QUESTIONS AND NOTES

1. Questions about the law.

1.1   Would the result in this case have been different if the court had applied RUPA? Compare RUPA §§ 401(a) and 401(b) with RUPA §§ 807(b) and 807(d). Be sure to look at the Official Comments, especially to RUPA § 401.

1.2   Does the court regard the business in this case as a partnership? Why?

1.3   Would a court that applied RUPA regard the business in this case as a partnership? Why? How about a court that applied UPA? Why?

2. Note.

It is important to understand the difference between the questions of (i) who is liable to third parties for unpaid obligations of the partnership and (ii) who must bear the partnership's losses. The questions arise at different times and have different answers.

The question of liability to third parties for unpaid obligations of the partnership can arise at any time during the existence of a partnership. Assume, for example, that Freer and Roberts form a partnership (FR) to do kitchen remodeling. FR buys sinks and disposals on credit from Epstein Sales, Inc. (ES). If FR does not pay, can ES collect from Freer or Roberts personally? That question is answered by RUPA § 306: "all partners are liable jointly and severally for all obligations of the partnership." That question is different from the question in *Kovacik*.

In *Kovacik,* the partnership had already paid its obligations to creditors; it had paid these third-parties with partnership funds that had been invested in the partnership by Kovacik. The partnership had ended. It had no more debts. The question in *Kovacik* was not whether creditors of the partnership would recover on their claims, but whether Kovacik would recover anything on his investment in the partnership (which lost the money he invested). Unless it is answered in the partnership agreement, that question will be answered by RUPA § 807.

2. EXPULSION AS AN ENDGAME FOR A PARTNER

Expulsion is mentioned but not expressly dealt with by RUPA. *See* RUPA §§ 601(3)–(5) (expulsion as an event of dissociation). Section 601(3) recognizes the possibility that partnership agreements might provide for the expulsion of partners. For example, the excerpt from the doctors' partnership agreement set forth in Note 5 at the end of Section F of this chapter, above, set out grounds for expulsion of a doctor/partner.

The following case involves a lawyers' partnership agreement that provided the procedures but not the substantive grounds for expulsion. In the case, a partner was expelled from her law firm because she (in good faith, but in error) accused another partner of unethical conduct. She sued the partnership, alleging a breach of fiduciary duty and a breach of the duty of good faith and fair dealing.

BOHATCH v. BUTLER & BINION

Supreme Court of Texas, 1998
977 S.W.2d 543

ENOCH, JUSTICE.

Partnerships exist by the agreement of the partners; partners have no duty to remain partners. The issue in this case is whether we should create an exception to this rule by holding that a partnership has a duty not to expel a partner for reporting suspected overbilling by another partner. The trial court rendered judgment for Colette Bohatch on her breach of fiduciary duty claim against Butler & Binion and several of its partners (collectively, "the firm"). The court of appeals held that there was no evidence that the firm breached a fiduciary duty and reversed the trial court's tort judgment; however, the court of appeals found evidence of a breach of the partnership agreement and rendered judgment for Bohatch on this ground. We affirm the court of appeals' judgment.

Bohatch became an associate in the Washington, D.C., office of Butler & Binion in 1986 after working for several years as Deputy Assistant General Counsel at the Federal Energy Regulatory Commission. John McDonald, the managing partner of the office, and Richard Powers, a partner, were the only other attorneys in the Washington office. The office did work for Pennzoil almost exclusively.

Bohatch was made partner in February 1990. She then began receiving internal firm reports showing the number of hours each attorney worked, billed, and collected. From her review of these reports, Bohatch became concerned that McDonald was overbilling Pennzoil. * * *

On July 15, 1990, Bohatch met with Louis Paine, the firm's managing partner, to report her concern that McDonald was overbilling Pennzoil. Paine said he would investigate. * * *

In August, Paine met with Bohatch and told her that the firm's investigation revealed no basis for her contentions. He added that she should begin looking for other employment, but that the firm would continue to provide her a monthly draw, insurance coverage, office space, and a secretary. After this meeting, Bohatch received no further work assignments from the firm.

In January 1991, the firm denied Bohatch a year-end partnership distribution for 1990 and reduced her tentative distribution share for 1991 to zero. In June, the firm paid Bohatch her monthly draw and told her that this draw would be her last. Finally, in August, the firm gave Bohatch until November to vacate her office.

By September, Bohatch had found new employment. She filed this suit on October 18, 1991, and the firm voted formally to expel her from the partnership three days later, October 21, 1991. * * *

The jury found that the firm breached the partnership agreement and its fiduciary duty. It awarded Bohatch $57,000 for past lost wages, $250,000 for past mental anguish, $4,000,000 total in punitive damages (this amount was apportioned against several defendants), and attorneys' fees. The trial court rendered judgment for Bohatch in the amounts found by the jury, except it disallowed attorneys' fees because the judgment was based in tort. After suggesting remittitur, which Bohatch accepted, the trial court reduced the punitive damages to around $237,000.

All parties appealed. The court of appeals held that the firm's only duty to Bohatch was not to expel her in bad faith. The court of appeals stated that " '[b]ad faith' in this context means only that partners cannot expel another partner for self-gain." Finding no evidence that the firm expelled Bohatch for self-gain, the court concluded that Bohatch could not recover for breach of fiduciary duty. However, the court concluded that the firm breached the partnership agreement when it reduced Bohatch's tentative partnership distribution for 1991 to zero without notice, and when it terminated her draw three months before she left. The court concluded that Bohatch was entitled to recover $35,000 in lost earnings for 1991 but none for 1990, and no mental anguish damages. Accordingly, the court rendered judgment for Bohatch for $35,000 plus $225,000 in attorneys' fees.

We have long recognized as a matter of common law that "[t]he relationship between * * * partners * * * is fiduciary in character, and imposes upon all the participants the obligation of loyalty to the joint concern and of the utmost good faith, fairness, and honesty in their dealings with each other with respect to matters pertaining to the enterprise." Yet, partners have no obligation to remain partners; "at the heart of the partnership concept is the principle that partners may choose with whom they wish to be associated." The issue presented, one of first impression, is whether the fiduciary relationship between and among partners creates an exception to the at-will nature of partnerships; that is, in this case, whether it gives rise to a duty not to expel a partner who reports suspected overbilling by another partner.

At the outset, we note that no party questions that the obligations of lawyers licensed to practice in the District of Columbia—including McDonald and Bohatch—were prescribed by the District of Columbia Code of Professional Responsibility in effect in 1990, and that in all other respects Texas law applies. Further, neither statutory nor contract law principles answer the question of whether the firm owed Bohatch a duty not to expel her. The Texas Uniform Partnership Act, Tex.Rev.Civ. Stat. Ann. art. 6701b, addresses expulsion of a partner only in the context of dissolution of the partnership. In this case, as provided by the partnership agreement, Bohatch's expulsion did not dissolve the partnership. Finally, the partnership agreement contemplates expulsion of a partner and prescribes procedures to be followed, but it does not specify or limit the grounds for expulsion. Thus, while Bohatch's claim that she was expelled in an improper way is governed by the partnership agreement, her claim that she was expelled for an improper reason is not. Therefore, we look to the common law to find the principles governing Bohatch's claim that the firm breached a duty when it expelled her. * * *

The fiduciary duty that partners owe one another does not encompass a duty to remain partners or else answer in tort damages. Nonetheless, Bohatch and several distinguished legal scholars urge this Court to recognize that public policy requires a limited duty to remain partners—i.e., a partnership must retain a whistleblower partner. They argue that such an extension of a partner's fiduciary duty is necessary because permitting a law firm to retaliate against a partner who in good faith reports suspected overbilling would discourage compliance with rules of professional conduct and thereby hurt clients.

While this argument is not without some force, we must reject it. A partnership exists solely because the partners choose to place personal confidence and trust in one another. Just as a partner can be expelled, without a breach of any common law duty, over disagreements about firm policy or to resolve some other "fundamental schism," a partner can be expelled for accusing another partner of overbilling without subjecting the partnership to tort damages. Such charges, whether true or not, may have a profound effect on the personal confidence and trust essential to the partner relationship. Once such charges are made, partners may find it impossible to continue to work together to their mutual benefit and the benefit of their clients.

We are sensitive to the concern expressed by the dissenting Justices [in this case] that "retaliation against a partner who tries in good faith to correct or report perceived misconduct virtually assures that others will not take these appropriate steps in the future." However, the dissenting Justices do not explain how the trust relationship necessary both for the firm's existence and for representing clients can survive such serious accusations by one partner against another. The threat of tort liability for expulsion would tend to force partners to remain in untenable circumstance—suspicious of and angry with each other—to their own detriment and that of their clients whose matters are neglected by lawyers distracted with intra-firm frictions.

Although concurring in the Court's judgment, Justice Hecht criticizes the Court for failing to "address amici's concerns that failing to impose liability will discourage attorneys from reporting unethical conduct." To address the scholars' concerns, he proposes that a whistleblower be protected from expulsion, but only if the report, irrespective of being made in good faith, is proved to be correct. We fail to see how such an approach encourages compliance with ethical rules more than the approach we adopt today. Furthermore, the amici's position is that a reporting attorney must be in good faith, not that the attorney must be right. In short, Justice Hecht's approach ignores the question Bohatch presents, the amici write about, and the firm challenges—whether a partnership violates a fiduciary duty when it expels a partner who in good faith reports suspected ethical violations. The concerns of the amici are best addressed by a rule that clearly demarcates an attorney's ethical duties and the parameters of tort liability, rather than redefining "whistleblower."

We emphasize that our refusal to create an exception to the at-will nature of partnerships in no way obviates the ethical duties of lawyers. Such duties sometimes necessitate difficult decisions, as when a lawyer suspects overbilling by a colleague. The fact that the ethical duty to report may create an irreparable schism between partners neither excuses failure to report nor transforms expulsion as a means of resolving that schism into a tort.

We hold that the firm did not owe Bohatch a duty not to expel her for reporting suspected overbilling by another partner. * * *

[The court did affirm the lower courts' rulings, however, that the firm had breached its contract with Ms. Bohatch, which permitted her to recover contract damages and attorneys' fees. The court's rejection of the fiduciary duty claim deprived Ms. Bohatch of her claims for mental anguish and punitive damages.]

QUESTIONS AND NOTES

1. Questions about the law.

1.1   In this case, Bohatch's suggestion of unethical billing conduct by another lawyer, though made in good faith, was incorrect. Would the Texas Supreme Court have reached a different result if she had been correct and was nonetheless expelled?

1.2   The Texas Supreme Court quotes the Texas Court of Civil Appeals for the proposition "partners can not expel another partner for self-gain." Can a law firm expel a partner because her practice is no longer profitable? Because they find the partner annoying?

1.3   When Bohatch was expelled, did she have a right to be paid her share of the value of the Butler & Binion partnership? *See* RUPA §§ 601(3), 701(b); *see generally* Larry E. Ribstein, *Law Partner Expulsion*, 55 BUS.LAW. 845 (2000).

2. Notes.

2.1   Dean Vestal is critical of the Texas Supreme Court's decision in *Bohatch*.

> * * * The court's analysis began with a recognition of the common law rule "that [t]he relationship between * * * partners * * * is fiduciary in character, and imposes upon all the participants the obligation of loyalty to the joint concern and of the utmost good faith, fairness, and honesty in their dealings with each other with respect to matters pertaining to the enterprise." But the court then cited as a countervailing

proposition the assertion that "partners have no obligation to remain partners; at the heart of the partnership concept is the principle that partners may choose with whom they wish to be associated." The court framed the issue presented as "whether the fiduciary relationship between and among partners creates an exception to the at-will nature of partnerships; that is, in this case, whether it gives rise to a duty not to expel a partner who reports suspected overbilling by another partner."

The Texas Supreme Court marshaled cases for the propositions that "a partnership may expel a partner for purely business reasons," "that a law firm can expel a partner to protect relationships both within the firm and with clients," and "that a partnership can expel a partner without breaching any duty in order to resolve a fundamental schism." The court declined "to recognize that public policy requires a limited duty to remain partners i.e., a partnership must retain a whistleblower partner," and held that "the firm did not owe Bohatch a duty not to expel her for reporting suspected overbilling by another partner." Using this analysis, the court concluded that "[t]he fiduciary duty that partners owe one another does not encompass a duty to remain partners or else answer in tort damages." This statement is at once both correct as far as it reaches and essentially irrelevant to the case at hand.

But what of the duty of good faith and fair dealing from which the analysis started? Properly viewed, the issue in Bohatch was not whether the partnership was an at-will partnership for purposes of dissolution; rather, the issue was whether the partners fulfilled the obligation of good faith and fair dealing that they owed Bohatch as a result of her status as a partner. Having started with a recognition of the common law rule "that '[t]he relationship between * * * partners * * * is fiduciary in character, and imposes upon all the participants the obligation of loyalty to the joint concern and of the utmost good faith, fairness, and honesty in their dealings with each other with respect to matters pertaining to the enterprise,'" the Bohatch court lost its bearings and wandered off course.

Allan W. Vestal, *Law Firm Expulsions*, 55 WASH. & LEE L. REV. 1083, 1107–09 (1998).

2.2   Professor Ribstein is critical of Dean Vestal's criticism:

There have been several recent cases involving expulsions of law partners.

It may seem appropriate in such cases to apply strong fiduciary and good faith duties to protect the helpless fired partner from the firm's career-threatening and possibly opportunistic action. Thus, one recent commentator would strongly qualify a law firm's ability to expel partners, applying a good faith requirement that implicates a cause requirement (unless explicitly disclaimed in writing) and implementation of a common purpose.

In general, there is little to be gained and much to be lost by close judicial scrutiny of law firm expulsions. The firm itself has strong incentives to avoid abusing the expulsion power, and it is very hard for courts to determine when these abuses occur. At the same time, placing

judicial constraints on the expulsion power weakens the effectiveness of
this remedy. Expulsion is an important complement to other disciplinary
mechanisms within the firm because it does not require the firm to prove
wrongdoing or precisely calibrate the penalty and the harm done. Requiring a showing of cause or that the penalty fits the harm would significantly weaken the deterrent effect of expulsion and thereby make it harder
for firms to protect their reputations. The losers would include not only
law firms, but also their clients, who rely on the firm's ability to maintain
its reputation.

Larry E. Ribstein, *Law Partner Expulsion,* 55 BUS. LAW. 845, 852 (2000).

3. FREEZE–OUT AS AN ENDGAME FOR A PARTNER

Go back to the beginnings of Bubba's Burritos. Capel is considering
investing $120,000 in the business in exchange for a partnership interest.
Capel believes that the business will lose money for several years before
becoming very profitable. She is concerned that the other partners, Propp
and Agee, may use her money, wait until the business becomes profitable,
and then try to dump her as a partner. The term "freeze out" is often
used to describe such a situation. In a freeze out, the holders of the
majority interest force a minority owner to sell or otherwise give up her
interest. *See generally* Franklin A. Gevurtz, *Squeeze–Outs and Freeze–
Outs in Limited Liability Companies,* 73 WASH.U.L.Q. 497 (1995) (which
discusses the next case, *Page v. Page,* as an example of a "freeze-out").

In *Page v. Page,* the parties wanted the court to determine whether
their agreement formed a partnership at will, which could be dissolved at
any time for any (or no) reason, without breach. But Justice Traynor
wanted to discuss a different point—whether a partner can withdraw from
a partnership so he can take the partnership's business for himself.

In reading the case, consider the following questions:

1.   Why does the plaintiff want the partnership to end? Why does the
defendant want the partnership to continue?

2.   Did either the plaintiff or the defendant do anything wrong?

PAGE v. PAGE

Supreme Court of California, 1961
359 P.2d 41

TRAYNOR, JUSTICE.

Plaintiff and defendant are partners in a linen supply business in
Santa Maria, California. Plaintiff appeals from a judgment declaring the
partnership to be for a term rather than at-will.

The partners entered into an oral partnership agreement in 1949.
Within the first two years each partner contributed approximately $43,000
for the purchase of land, machinery, and linen needed to begin the

business. From 1949 to 1957 the enterprise was unprofitable, losing approximately $62,000. The partnership's major creditor is a corporation, wholly owned by plaintiff, that supplies the linen and machinery necessary for the day-to-day operation of the business. This corporation holds a $47,000 demand note of the partnership. The partnership operations began to improve in 1958. The partnership earned $3,824.41 in that year and $2,282.30 in the first three months of 1959. Despite this improvement plaintiff wishes to terminate the partnership. * * *

Defendant testified that the terms of the partnership were to be similar to former partnerships of plaintiff and defendant, and that the understanding of these partnerships was that "we went into partnership to start the business and let the business operation pay for itself, put in so much money, and let the business pay itself out." * * *

In the instant case defendant failed to prove any facts from which an agreement to continue the partnership for a term may be implied. The understanding to which defendant testified was no more than a common hope that the partnership earnings would pay for all the necessary expenses. Such a hope does not establish even by implication a "definite term or particular undertaking" as required by section 15031, subdivision (1)(b) of the Corporations Code. All partnerships are ordinarily entered into with the hope that they will be profitable, but that alone does not make them all partnerships for a term and obligate the partners to continue in the partnerships until all of the losses over a period of many years have been recovered.

Defendant contends that plaintiff is acting in bad faith and is attempting to use his superior financial position to appropriate the now profitable business of the partnership. Defendant has invested $43,000 in the firm, and owing to the long period of losses his interest in the partnership assets is very small. The fact that plaintiff's wholly-owned corporation holds a $47,000 demand note of the partnership may make it difficult to sell the business as a going concern. Defendant fears that upon dissolution he will receive very little and that plaintiff, who is the managing partner and knows how to conduct the operations of the partnership, will receive a business that has become very profitable because of the establishment of Vandenberg Air Force Base in its vicinity. Defendant charges that plaintiff has been content to share the losses but now that the business has become profitable he wishes to keep all the gains.

There is no showing in the record of bad faith or that the improved profit situation is more than temporary. In any event these contentions are irrelevant to the issue whether the partnership is for a term or at-will. Since, however, this action is for a declaratory judgment and will be the basis for future action by the parties, it is appropriate to point out that defendant is amply protected by the fiduciary duties of co-partners.

Even though the Uniform Partnership Act provides that a partnership at will may be dissolved by the express will of any partner, this power, like any other power held by a fiduciary, must be exercised in good faith.

We have often stated that "partners are trustees for each other, and in all proceedings connected with the conduct of the partnership every partner is bound to act in the highest good faith to his copartner, and may not obtain any advantage over him in the partnership affairs by the slightest misrepresentation, concealment, threat, or adverse pressure of any kind."

A partner at will is not bound to remain in a partnership, regardless of whether the business is profitable or unprofitable. A partner may not, however, by use of adverse pressure "freeze out" a co-partner and appropriate the business to his own use. A partner may not dissolve a partnership to gain the benefits of the business for himself, unless he fully compensates his co-partner for his share of the prospective business opportunity. In this regard his fiduciary duties are at least as great as those of a shareholder of a corporation.

In the case of *In re Security Finance Co.*, 317 P.2d 1, 5 [1957] we stated that although shareholders representing 50 per cent of the voting power have a right under Corporations Code to dissolve a corporation, they may not exercise such right in order "to defraud the other shareholders, to 'freeze out' minority shareholders, or to sell the assets of the dissolved corporation at an inadequate price."

Likewise in the instant case, plaintiff has the power to dissolve the partnership by express notice to defendant. If, however, it is proved that plaintiff acted in bad faith and violated his fiduciary duties by attempting to appropriate to his own use the new prosperity of the partnership without adequate compensation to his co-partner, the dissolution would be wrongful and the plaintiff would be liable. * * *

The judgment is reversed.

QUESTIONS

1. Why did the plaintiff seek a declaratory judgment that the partnership is a partnership at-will?

2. What will the defendant receive if the partnership is dissolved? What will the defendant owe?

3. If you were representing the defendant, what amount would you recommend your client accept to settle this case?

4. Why the different result in *Bohatch*?

5. Aren't you glad you read *Meinhard v. Salmon*?

———————————

By way of review, reconsider the various ways a person's ownership interest in a partnership may end:

- freeze out;
- expulsion;
- withdrawal from the partnership followed by either the partnership's purchase of her partnership interest or dissolution of the partnership;
- sale to the partnership or an existing partner pursuant to an agreement; or,
- sale to a third party of her "transferable interest in the partnership," i.e., "share of profits and losses" and "right to receive distributions."

Another possible endgame for a partner is the sale of the entire partnership. The legal issues in such a sale are primarily contracts issues or tax issues.

Thusfar we have seen only one way for a partnership to end: dissolution, followed by winding up, followed by termination. Partnerships can also end when they are converted from a partnership to some other business structure, or when the partnership is merged into or otherwise combined with another business. These possibilities can be addressed by default provisions of RUPA, by partnership agreement, or by the next chapters of this book. Before we move to these next chapters, consider two review questions about partnerships:

1.   Assume that your client owns an interest in a business because she wants to make money. What law-related issues should most concern her about her interest? In other words, what are the down-sides of being a partner?

2.   And what, if anything, can you do in negotiating and writing the partnership agreement to address those concerns?

CHAPTER FOUR

WHAT IS A CORPORATION AND HOW DOES A BUSINESS BECOME A CORPORATION?

■ ■ ■

Remember our friends Propp, Agee and Capel? Assume again that Propp wants to start a southern-style burrito restaurant near a college campus. Agee will work as cook and day-to-day manager of the restaurant and Capel will provide needed funds. Now assume that they want to use the corporation structure for the business.

Their questions are familiar: What is a corporation? How do we set up the business as a corporation? Who owns what? Who decides what? Who is liable for what to whom? How can the business grow? How do we make money from the business? And how can the business end? Not surprisingly, some of the answers to these corporation questions are similar to the answers to the partnership questions and some are different. To answer the first of their questions, please read MBCA §§ 2.02 and 2.03, Delaware §§ 102 and 106,* and the following.

Most people tend to think of corporations as huge businesses. Indeed, most of the billion-dollar multinational businesses are corporations. But there is nothing in the corporate form that requires the business to be big. Most corporations are not big; many are owned and run by one person. Perhaps surprisingly, though, most statutes concerning the formation and running of corporations do not distinguish between large and small businesses. Courts sometimes do make the distinction, however, as we will see at various points in our chapters dealing with the corporation.

As a matter of terminology, small corporations are often called "close" or "closely-held." They have relatively few shareholders (there is no magic number, usually) and there is no public market for buying or selling interests in them. On the other hand, large corporations are often called "public," for the simple reason that they have many shareholders and the interests in them are publicly traded (for instance, on stock exchanges). There are many corporations somewhere in the middle, but

---

* Throughout the book, we refer to sections of the Delaware General Corporation Law simply as "Delaware."

lawyers tend to group corporations into these two categories—close and public. Keep them in the back of your mind as we delve into the world of the corporate form of doing business.

A. WHAT IS A CORPORATION AND WHAT IS CORPORATION LAW?

Some familiarity with the history of corporations and corporate law in the United States is helpful—you know, understanding where we have been should help us understand where we are. One of our favorite authors explains:

> * * * For as long as America has existed, the primary authority over the creation of business organizations has resided with the individual states. At America's beginnings, only two business forms existed [in addition to the sole proprietorship]: the general partnership, which requires no formal sovereign recognition, and the corporation, which has always required formal recognition by a sovereign person or government.

> * * * During America's colonial period and for a few years thereafter, the vast majority of the people in America's agriculturally based society labored on family farms producing the goods necessary for their own survival and occasional surplus to be bartered. The manufacture of goods produced by artisans in small shops and the business of merchants engaged in importing and exporting grew steadily around the cities clustered at the seaboard, with the sole proprietorship and the partnership serving as the legal forms for conducting these businesses. The crude and undeveloped state of transportation made any large-scale movement of goods from the cities prohibitively expensive and kept business at small levels. Business had not yet evolved to a point where the legal benefits of forming a corporation proved useful. The colonial assemblies and the early state legislatures granted corporate charters primarily for public purposes, including the establishment of towns, churches, cemeteries, colleges, and charities.

> Especially after 1790, state-issued corporate charters for banks proliferated in order to supply credit to the nation's rapidly growing business economy. State-chartered banks, which numbered over two hundred by 1815, played a prominent role in the nation's economy through the circulation of bank notes that served as a medium of exchange within the nation's currency. During the decades leading up to and just after the War of 1812, the number of state-issued corporate charters increased rapidly because canals and turnpikes increased rapidly, representing the first step in America's transportation revolution. Unlike the majority of purely private business enterprises, which still operated in the partnership form, banks and transportation projects needed the legal advantages offered by the

corporate form, specifically the ability to pool large amounts of capital and to exist beyond the natural life of the owners.

* * * During the 1820s, undoubtedly fueled by protective tariffs adopted a few years earlier, state-issued corporate charters for manufacturing companies grew rapidly. Although America's real Industrial Revolution remained several decades away, for most of the 1820s business and commerce steadily grew and the business corporation experienced little overt controversy. However, within the shadows of businesses' progress, the seeds of discontent were present. America's transformation from an agricultural and mercantile economy to a market economy displaced and negatively affected many individuals. The rhetoric surrounding Andrew Jackson's election in 1828 as the sixth President of the United States denounced federal powers and harshly criticized banks, business corporations, and other instruments of power oppressing the large majority of farmers and workers.

Jacksonians did not oppose corporations *per se*. Rather, they objected to the special privileges obtained in the special legislative charters. Prominent Jacksonians, wanting to cure the evils of special privileges conferred by the special corporate charters, advocated the creation of general incorporation laws that would allow equal access to the corporate form to all those meeting the statutory requirements. After President Jackson left office in 1836, state law general incorporation statutes appeared in two states. During the 1840s the idea caught on as six additional states passed general incorporation statutes. By the eve of the Civil War, sixteen additional states enacted statutes, bringing the total to well over fifty percent of the existing states.

Susan Pace Hamill, *The Origins Behind the Limited Liability Company*, 59 OHIO ST. L.J. 1459, 1484 (1999).

The nineteenth-century general incorporation statutes of which Professor Hamill speaks were designed for large businesses.

Businesses have changed. Most corporations in the twenty-first century are not large. Take a look at the yellow pages in your local phone book. You'll see entries such as Bama Floor and Tile Co. and Tide Contractors, Inc. Or take a look at government statistics.* In 2006, 5.8 million corporations filed federal tax returns. More than 80% had less than $500,000 of assets. A corporation is not only the business structure used by most large businesses with thousands of owners, but it is also the business structure used by most small businesses, some with just one owner. Indeed, in terms of economic impact, the corporation is by far the most important business structure, accounting for approximately 90% of business receipts.†

While most twenty-first century corporations have relatively few assets and relatively few owners, twenty-first century general incorpo-

---

* Internal Revenue Service Statistics of Income—2006 Corporate Income Tax Returns (2009).

† U.S. Census Bureau, Statistical Abstract of the United States, Table 725 (2005).

ration law in many ways still reflects the original large-corporation model. And, in most states, there is a single, general corporation law that applies to all corporations. We are going to learn about both small and large corporations. Part of this course will be aimed at understanding how the courts have adapted general corporate statutes based on a large business model to small businesses.

1. A CORPORATION IS . . .

A corporation is whatever the relevant state law says it is.[‡] As Professor Hamill has pointed out, corporations always have been and still are creations of state legislatures. Today every state has a general corporation statute. And every state's corporation statute provides that (i) a corporation is a separate legal entity and (ii) its owners, usually called shareholders (or stockholders), are generally not personally liable for the debts of the corporation. This means that while there is no statutory limit on how much money an owner of a corporation can make from her investment in a corporation, the most that she risks is the amount that she paid for the shares of stock. That is the limit of her liability. This is the concept of "limited liability."

Almost a hundred years ago, Nicholas Murray Butler, who was the President of Columbia University, said: "I weigh my words when I say that the . . . limited liability corporation is the greatest single discovery of modern times."[*] (Of course, he said this before the invention of the ShamWow.) More recently, William T. Allen (then a judge in Delaware) offered only slightly moderated praise of corporations and corporate law:

> Stated broadly, but I think accurately, the elemental purpose of corporation law is the facilitation of cooperative activity that produces wealth. A net increase in total wealth, other things remaining unchanged, is an absolute good. With increased wealth, all other things remaining the same, there is a greater ability to relieve human suffering and enhance life. That is an unqualified good. While we no longer take much notice of the fact, the corporate form is a powerful engine for wealth production.
>
> Corporation law facilitates wealth creation principally by creating a legal structure that makes it substantially cheaper for investors to commit their capital to risky ventures. It does this through the innovation of tradable share interests, centralized management, limited liability, and the entity concept itself. The interaction of these legal characteristics facilitates diversification of investments and centralization of management. This allows capital to subject itself to greater

---

[‡] As the Supreme Court stated in *The Trustees of Dartmouth College v. Woodward*, 17 U.S. 518, 636 (1819): "A corporation is an artificial being, invisible, intangible and existing only in contemplation of law. Being a mere creature of law, it possesses only those properties which the charter of its existence confers upon it."

[*] Quoted in James Willard Hurst, THE LEGITIMACY OF THE BUSINESS CORPORATION IN THE LAWS OF THE UNITED STATES 1780–1970 at p. 9 (1970).

risk. It is the ability to increase the degree of risk that can be rationally accepted that provides the greatest source of the efficiency of the corporate form. Much of this utility depends upon investors allowing themselves to be safely passive.

William T. Allen, *Ambiguity in Corporation Law*, 22 DEL. J. CORP. L. 894, 895–96 (1997).

Professor Gabaldon offers a different view of corporations (and other limited liability business structures):

A significant part of the story of American enterprise has been written by state legislators hoping to stimulate entrepreneurship and investment. As a result, there are several forms of business organizations that at least ostensibly will permit an economic actor to limit the amount that she puts at risk. The most popular of these forms is the corporation.

If it was ever true that limited liability was necessary to encourage economic development, it is arguably even more necessary today. The litigious society does exist. Moreover, the statistics indicating the chance of success for any new business are frightening: the majority of start-up enterprises fail, leaving debts in excess of assets. Even traditional bastions of investment security seem to be collapsing in record numbers. Since these facts logically compel a perception that the "upside" potential of entrepreneurship and investment is limited, it may make sense to assure that "downside" possibilities are limited as well.

Limited liability, of course, cannot be regarded as an unmitigated good. Even brief retrospection reveals quite an interesting picture of the historically perceived risks of limited liability. This historical perception may be described in terms of a morality play featuring two important characters. One of these characters is a hapless public, completely unaware that the smiling individual handing out cups of lemonade is not personally and completely on the line for the contents of those cups. The other is Dr. Frankenstein.

According to this Frankensteinian view, irresponsible corporate impresarios regularly dispatch inhuman corporate entities to roam the countryside in search of profits. Lacking both conscience and capital, these entities will inflict injuries for which they cannot, and their heedless inventors need not, pay. In an uncharitable, but not necessarily unrealistic, permutation, the corporate scientist quite deliberately may design the creature to generate short-run gains for the creator, while surreptitiously imposing tremendous costs on third parties.

Theresa A. Gabaldon, *The Lemonade Stand: Feminist and Other Reflections on the Limited Liability of Corporate Shareholders*, 45 VAND. L. REV. 1387, 1390–92 (1992).

Economics has become important for understanding corporations, both in the press and in judicial opinions. Let's look at three main ideas.

First, economists view the corporation as a way to reduce "transaction costs" compared to frequent transactions in markets. Each day, Bubba's Burritos's owners could hire a new cook at whatever is the daily wage, and negotiate what his tasks will be. But it's much simpler (transaction costs are lower) for the restaurant to form as a corporation, hire a permanent employee, and be able to tell him what needs to be done.*

Second, economists often view the corporation not so much as an entity, but as a set of contractual relationships among the suppliers of all of the corporation's inputs. This "nexus of contracts" links the workers who supply the labor, the shareholders and lenders who supply the money, and the managers who supply the management.

Third, economists are concerned about "agency costs." Any employee or other agent of the corporation, whether a cook or a CEO, may have an incentive to benefit himself rather than the corporation—for example, by being lazy or by causing the company to purchase an unnecessary burrito-shaped corporate jet. Much of corporate law and lawyering attempts to control agency costs.

Suppose that Bubba's Burritos hires a CEO to run the company. Can you think of ways that Bubba's might structure her employment contract to ensure that she doesn't waste the corporation's money on herself or spend all her time on the golf course?

2. CORPORATE LAW† IS ...

There are four primary sources of "corporate law": (1) state statutes, (2) articles of incorporation,‡ bylaws and other agreements, (3) case law, and (4) federal statutes.

As noted, each state has its own general corporation statute. While no two state statutes are identical, more than half of the states have modeled their statutes in some measure on the Model Business Corporation Act (MBCA).*

---

* This approach began with a famous article by Ronald Coase, *The Nature of the Firm*, 4 ECONOMICA 386 (1937).

† In a sense, "corporate law" could be defined as all laws that apply to corporations. Almost all laws apply to corporations—antitrust laws, bankruptcy laws, environmental laws, etc. In this book, we limit coverage of "corporate law" to laws that address the creation and operation of the corporate business structure.

‡ In some states, notably Delaware and New York, the articles are called the certificate of incorporation. In other states, such as Maryland, the same document is often referred to as the charter.

* The Model Business Corporations Act is the work product of an American Bar Association Committee. Over the years, there have been several versions. The first MBCA was prepared in 1969; the current version was completed in 1984 (and has been regularly revised since then). The most recent version is sometimes referred to as the Revised Model Business Corporation Act, or RMBCA. We use "MBCA" to refer to that.

In addition to the MBCA, Delaware corporation law is centrally important. Far more businesses have incorporated in this small state than in any other.

Some of the provisions in any state's statutes are mandatory. Others are default rules that apply only if the articles of incorporation or bylaws of the corporation do not contain a different provision. (We saw default provisions with UPA and RUPA.)

Thus a corporation's articles or bylaws, like a partnership's partnership agreement, can be an important source of corporate law. On some matters, the articles and bylaws will be the most important source of law.

Case law serves two separate corporate law functions. First, cases interpret and apply the provisions in corporate statutes and in a corporation's articles and bylaws. Second, cases fill gaps in the law—they resolve problems not covered or not fully covered by statutes, articles or bylaws. Perhaps the most important judicial gap-filling involves the fiduciary duties of directors, officers, and shareholders. Just as cases such as *Meinhard v. Salmon* are instrumental in establishing the fiduciary duties of partners, they are also instrumental in establishing the fiduciary duties of directors, officers, and shareholders.

There is no general federal corporation statute. There are, however, important federal statutes that govern certain corporate activities. Later chapters will discuss briefly some of the federal statutes that apply to sales of stock and other corporate securities, and to tender offers and other forms of corporate acquisitions.

B. WHAT ARE THE LEGAL PROBLEMS IN STARTING A BUSINESS AS A CORPORATION?

1. PREPARING THE NECESSARY PAPERS

The "necessary papers" are the articles of incorporation. A corporation does not exist until the articles of incorporation are properly executed and filed with the appropriate state agent or agency (usually the Secretary of State). MBCA § 2.03 sets out where the articles are to be filed, and MBCA § 2.02(a) sets out what the articles of incorporation must contain. Compare this latter provision to the older provision in Delaware § 102.

We have set out below a sample articles of incorporation available on the Delaware Division of Corporations Web site, http://corp.delaware.gov (click on "corporate forms" in the Information section). Clearly, this form satisfies the Delaware requirements. Assess, however, whether these articles would satisfy the requirements of MBCA § 2.02(a). We will later discuss whether these articles meet the needs of Bubba's Burritos, Inc.

STATE of DELAWARE
CERTIFICATE of INCORPORATION
A STOCK CORPORATION

First: *The name of this Corporation is* _____
_____.

Second: *Its registered office in the State of Delaware is to be located at* _____ *Street, in the City of* _____ *County of* _____ *Zip Code*_____. *The registered agent in charge thereof is* _____.

Third: *The purpose of the corporation is to engage in any lawful act or activity for which corporations may be organized under the General Corporation Law of Delaware.*

Fourth: *The amount of the total stock this corporation is authorized to issue is* _____ *shares (number of authorized shares) with a par value of* _____ *per share.*

Fifth: *The name and mailing address of the incorporator are as follows:*

  Name _____

  Mailing Address _____

  Zip Code _____.

I, The Undersigned, *for the purpose of forming a corporation under the laws of the State of Delaware, do make, file and record this Certificate, and do certify that the facts herein stated are true, and I have accordingly hereunto set my hand this*

  _____ *day of* _____, *A.D. 20* _____.

       BY: _____
       (Incorporator)

       NAME: _____
       (Type or Print)

The MBCA provides that a corporation comes into existence as soon as the articles are properly filed. It also permits the corporation to adopt bylaws. MBCA § 2.06(a); *see also* Delaware § 109. Traditionally, nothing has required corporations to have bylaws; adoption of bylaws is not a condition precedent to forming a corporation. Nonetheless, in the real world, almost every corporation does have bylaws.

Just as MBCA §§ 2.02(a) and (b) govern the contents of a corporation's articles, MBCA § 2.06(b) provides for the contents of a corporation's bylaws: "The bylaws may contain any provision for managing the business and regulating the affairs of the corporation that is not inconsistent with laws or the articles of incorporation." *See also* Delaware § 109.

Notice that neither the MBCA nor Delaware requires that bylaws be filed with any state agent or agency. Indeed, no state requires filing of bylaws. In other words, bylaws (unlike articles) are a completely internal document. Sample bylaws are available on the Internet. One example is found at: http://www.publiceducation.org/doc/startanlef/MS-bylaws.doc.

PROBLEMS: ARTICLES AND BYLAWS

1.   How do you decide what goes in the articles of incorporation and what goes in the bylaws? What are the differences between articles of incorporation and bylaws? *Compare* MBCA § 7.07(a) ("The *bylaws* may fix ... the record date) *with* MBCA § 7.21(a) ("unless the articles of incorporation provide otherwise, each outstanding share ... is entitled to one vote").

2.   One common statement is that "articles are a contract between the corporation and its shareholders and a corporation and the state, but bylaws are simply a contract between the corporation and its shareholders." If the articles and the bylaws were to conflict on some provision, which one should prevail?

3.   How much should a lawyer charge for preparing articles of incorporation and bylaws and filing the articles? *Incorporate USA* charges only $99.95. *See* http://www.inc123.com/.

4.   If the proprietors (or their lawyers) do it correctly under the relevant state law, they will have formed a "de jure corporation"—that is, a legal corporation.

2.   CONTRACTING BEFORE INCORPORATING

In the vocabulary of corporations, the word "promoter" has a different and less pejorative meaning than it seems to in the real world. In corporate law, a promoter is not some guy with big hair who sets up boxing matches. Instead, a promoter is someone acting on behalf of a corporation that is not yet formed.

Assume, for example, that Propp, Agee and Capel are still negotiating the provisions that will be in the articles of incorporation when Propp and Agee find the perfect site for a restaurant. Propp and Agee want to lease the building from L & L Real Estate ("L & L") before someone else gets it. This means they will sign the lease before they have a chance to file the articles of incorporation to form the corporation. Doing this will raise the following problems about who is liable on a contract entered by the promoters on behalf of a corporation not yet formed.

PROBLEMS: LIABILITY OF PROMOTERS AND OF THE CORPORATION ON PRE-INCORPORATION CONTRACTS

1.   What is the liability of the promoter if the corporation is never formed? Specifically:

a.   Propp negotiates and executes a lease with L & L. Propp simply signs the lease "Propp for Bubba's Burritos, Inc." No articles of incorporation are ever filed for Bubba's Burritos, Inc. Can L & L enforce the lease against Propp? *See* MBCA § 2.04.

b.   Same facts as a., except that Propp signs the lease "Bubba's Burritos, Inc., a corporation to be formed"?

c.   Is there any legal basis for L & L to enforce the lease against Agee or Capel in either of the two preceding questions?

2.   What is the liability of the corporation if it is formed? Assume that articles of incorporation are filed forming Bubba's Burritos, Inc. after Propp had signed the lease with L & L. Is the corporation liable on the lease?

The answer is no—at least not yet. The corporation did not exist when the lease was entered, and does not become liable on the lease automatically simply by coming into existence. When we think about it, this is clear from agency law, which we studied in Chapter 2. Propp was trying to act as an agent for the corporation (which would be the principal). But there was no principal when Propp entered the contract, for the simple reason that the corporation had not been formed then. Propp acted for a non-existent principal, and thus is liable as a party to the contract.

Does the corporation become liable as soon as it is created? No. The corporation will be liable on the lease only if it takes some action to *adopt* it. It might do so in one of two ways. First, the corporation itself might *expressly* adopt the contract. As we will see later in this book, a corporation generally acts through its board of directors. So if the board of directors of Bubba's Burritos, Inc. passes a resolution formally adopting the lease, the corporation will be liable on the lease from that moment. Second, the corporation might *impliedly* adopt the lease. Suppose, for instance, the board of directors does not take such a formal action, but a corporate official causes the corporation to use the premises that are subject to the lease. By using the premises, the corporation has adopted the lease, and is liable from that point.

3.   By adopting the lease in Question 2, the corporation has *ratified* what its "agent" did. Ratification, in the words of the Restatement (Second) of Agency (R–2), § 82, is the "affirmance by a person of a prior act which did not bind him but which was done or professedly done on his account." In the words of the Restatement (Third) of Agency (R–3), § 4.01, it is the "affirmance of a prior act done by another, whereby the act is given effect as if done by an agent acting with actual authority." These mean the same thing— ratification is the *ex post facto* adoption of something an "agent" purportedly did for a "principal."

4.   What is the liability of the promoter after incorporation? Assume that articles of incorporation are filed forming Bubba's Burritos, Inc. after Propp had signed the lease with L & L. Now—regardless of whether the corporation adopts the lease—can L & L enforce the lease against Propp?

The answer is yes. And, again, the answer comes from agency law. As a matter of agency law, why is Propp personally liable on the lease? *See* R–2 § 326. *See* R–3 § 6.04. Note that this is true *even if Bubba's Burritos adopted the* lease.

The only way for Propp to get off the hook for personal liability at this point is for the parties—meaning Bubba's Burritos, L & L, and Propp—to enter a "novation." As you may recall from Contracts, a novation here would be an agreement that Bubba's Burritos would replace Propp under the lease with L & L.

3. DE FACTO CORPORATION AND CORPORATION BY ESTOPPEL

In the preceding section, we dealt with a promoter who acted on behalf of a corporation that she knew did not exist (yet). Here, we deal with persons acting on behalf of (or with) a business that they think is a corporation—but, as it turns out, the corporation was not actually formed!

As we saw earlier in this chapter, it is pretty easy to form a corporation. The magic moment at which the entity comes into being is usually the point at which the state agency accepts the articles for filing. At that point, the entity is formed and in theory the entity is liable for its own debts. But what if the corporation was not formed?

PROBLEM: LIABILITY WHEN THERE IS DEFECTIVE INCORPORATION

1. Propp, Agee and Capel want to incorporate their business as Bubba's Burritos, Inc. They go to Freer, an attorney, who prepares all the necessary documents. Propp, Agee and Capel execute the documents and give Freer the check for the filing fee. Freer tells them that he will deliver the documents and filing fee to the appropriate state agency on March 1 and that they can start doing business as a corporation on that day. Instead, however, Freer moves to Italy and never delivers the documents to the state agency.

On March 2, Propp, Agee, and Capel meet as the directors of Bubba's Burritos, Inc. and elect Propp as president. On March 3, Propp, thinking he is president of Bubba's Burritos, Inc., acting on behalf of the corporation, signs a lease between Bubba's and L & L Realty. Propp and the people at L & L all think that Bubba's Burritos, Inc. is a corporation. When they discover that no corporation was formed, the people at L & L seek to enforce the lease against Propp personally.

a. Is Propp liable on the lease?

b. Are Agee and Capel liable on the lease? (After all, if they did not form a corporation, what kind of business did the three have?)

Obviously, the proprietors did not form a de jure corporation (because the state agency never filed the articles). The starting point, then, is that they are personally liable for the acts purportedly taken by the corporation. Over time, however, courts developed the doctrine of "de facto corporation." They concluded that if the proprietors were acting in good faith and came very close to forming a de jure corporation (usually said to have reached "colorable" compliance with the formation requirements), there was a de facto corporation. As a result, the proprietors would not be personally liable.

As it developed, de facto corporation was a broad doctrine—it applied in contract and tort. Indeed, it applied in all cases except an action brought by the state against the proprietors. De facto corporation is an equitable doctrine, so one seeking to use it must act in good faith. That means she must be unaware of the failure to form a de jure corporation.

Because today it is so easy to form a de jure corporation, many states have abolished the de facto corporation doctrine. In such states, if you fail to form a de jure corporation, the proprietors are liable for whatever they purported to do on the "corporation's" behalf.

c.   How does MBCA § 2.04 deal with the de facto corporation doctrine?

2.   A related but narrower doctrine is "corporation by estoppel." It is narrower because it generally applies only in contract cases, not tort. The name says it all—it is basically just estoppel.

Continuing the fact pattern from Problem 1, suppose on March 3, after Bubba's Burritos, Inc. was thought to have been formed, Epstein enters a contract with the corporation, by which Epstein will sell supplies to the business. Epstein treats the business as though it is a corporation, and deals with Propp as though he were president of a corporation. When he discovers that there is no corporation, can Epstein sue the proprietors individually to recover on the contract?

The starting point, again, is that there is no de jure corporation, so the proprietors will be liable personally. Here, Propp, Agee, and Capel may be able to argue de facto corporation. But they might also argue corporation by estoppel. The argument is that Epstein dealt with the business as a corporation and treated it as such, and thus should be estopped from denying that it is. The reason the doctrine is limited to contract cases is clear—Epstein, before entering the deal, could have insisted on seeing the books of the corporation to determine whether it had assets from which to pay.

4.   ISSUING STOCK*

Shares of stock are the units of ownership in a corporation. If Agee, Capel, and Propp are going to be the owners of Bubba's Burritos, Inc., they will need to own shares of Bubba's Burritos, Inc. stock. Where does this stock come from? MBCA § 6.03(a) provides "A corporation may issue the number of shares of each class or series authorized by the articles of incorporation. Shares that are issued are outstanding shares until they are reacquired, converted or canceled." There is a lot of information in those two sentences:

- a corporation sells its own stock;
- a corporation's sale of its own stock is called an "issuance";
- the articles of incorporation determine the number of shares a corporation may issue;
- this number is the number of "authorized shares";
- a corporation is not required to issue all of its authorized shares;

---

* The MBCA uses the terms "share" and "shareholder" rather than the terms "stock" and "stockholder." The terms are interchangeable.

- shares that the corporation actually does issue are called "issued shares";

- "outstanding shares" consist of issued shares that the corporation has not reacquired (the corporation can buy stock back from shareholders, and those shares that have been issued and not reacquired are "outstanding"); and,

- a corporation can have more than one type ("class or series") of stock.

To review, you need to make the following terms a part of your working vocabulary:

- issuance;

- authorized shares;

- issued shares;

- outstanding shares; and

- classes of stock.

While there is a good bit of important legal information about "issuing stock" in the two sentences of MBCA § 6.03, there is also a lot of important legal and business information about issuing stock that is not there. There are three other terms that are not important to MBCA § 6.03 (or any other MBCA provision) but are important to a law practice and (more immediately) to a law school course that includes corporations: (1) preferred stock, (2) common stock, and (3) par value.

Preferred stock is a creature of the articles of incorporation. Recall from the MBCA that the articles of incorporation can authorize more than one type or class of stock. *See* MBCA § 6.01 et seq. If the articles provide that a class of stock is to be treated more favorably than the other class of stock, then it is preferred stock. The other class of stock that does not enjoy special treatment is the common stock.

Generally, the more favorable treatment relates to one or more of the following financial attributes of ownership: (1) dividend rights, (2) liquidation rights, or (3) redemption rights. Assume for example that the articles of Bubba's Burritos, Inc. authorize 1,000 shares of Class 1 stock and 200 shares of Class 2 stock and provides that each share of Class 2 stock shall receive a dividend that is three times greater than any dividend paid to Class 1 stock. Class 2 stock would then be described as preferred stock. More precisely, it would have a dividend preference.

A more typical type of dividend preference would be a dollar amount—like $1 per preferred share. The corporation would be obligated to pay this amount per share—in full—before it could pay one cent to the common shareholders.

In this example, Class 1 would be the common stock, i.e., the class of stock that is not preferred. In the event that Bubba's Burritos, Inc. only has one class of stock, then all of its stock would be common stock.

Why would a corporation have two classes of stock? Why would some owners settle for common stock if other owners have preferred stock?

In the following example, Silicon Gaming, Inc. was unable to pay its debts and so gave its creditors 39,750 shares of $.001 par Class D preferred stock in satisfaction of $39,750,000 of debt. The following excerpt from the directors' resolution sets out some of the points of preference:

CERTIFICATION OF DETERMINATION, PREFERENCES AND RELATIVE, PARTICIPATING, OPTIONAL AND OTHER SPECIAL RIGHTS OF PREFERRED STOCK AND QUALIFICATIONS, LIMITATIONS AND RESTRICTIONS OF SERIES D CONVERTIBLE REDEEMABLE PREFERRED STOCK OF SILICON GAMING, INC.

Pursuant to Section 401 of the General Corporation Law of the State of California

Silicon Gaming, Inc. (the "Company"), a Company organized and existing under the laws of the State of California, by execution of this certificate (this "Certificate of Determination") does hereby certify and affirm, that pursuant to the authority contained in Article III of its Amended and Restated Articles of Incorporation (the "Articles of Incorporation") and in accordance with the provisions of Section 401 of the General Corporation Law of the State of California, the Board of Directors of the Company on [date], duly adopted the following resolution which resolution remains in full force and effect on the date hereof:

(a) Dividends.

(1) The holders of outstanding Series D Preferred Stock shall be entitled to receive in any fiscal year, when, as and if declared by the Board of Directors, out of any assets at the time legally available therefor, non-cumulative dividends in cash at a rate per share as declared by the Board of Directors. No cash dividends shall be paid on any share of Common Stock unless a cash dividend is paid with respect to all outstanding shares of Series D Preferred Stock in an amount for each such share of Series D Preferred Stock equal to or greater than the aggregate amount of such cash dividends for all shares of Common Stock into which each such share of Series D Preferred Stock could then be converted. The right to dividends on Series D Preferred Stock shall not be cumulative and no right shall accrue to holders of Series D Preferred Stock by reason of the fact that distributions on said shares are not declared in any prior year, nor shall any undeclared or unpaid distribution bear or accrue interest.

(b) Preference on Liquidation.

(1) In the event of any voluntary or involuntary liquidation, dissolution, or winding up, of the Company (a "Liquidation Event"), each holder

of shares of the Series D Preferred Stock shall be entitled to payment out of the assets of the Company available for distribution of an amount equal to the greater of (A) $1,000 per share of Series D Preferred Stock held by such holder before any distribution is made to the holders of Common Stock of the Company, and any other class of capital stock of the Company ranking junior to the Series D Preferred Stock and (B) the amount per share that the holders of the Series D Preferred Stock would receive if the Series D Preferred Stock held by such holder were converted as of the liquidation date and the holder were to receive assets and funds of the Company available for distribution to the holders of Common Stock.

(c) Redemption.

In the event of a Change of Control the holders of at least a majority of the shares of Series D Preferred Stock then outstanding taken together as a series may require the Company to redeem the outstanding shares of Series D Preferred Stock by delivering a Redemption Notice (as defined in Section 2(c)(4)) within the ninety (90) day period following the Change of Control. The shares of Series D Preferred Stock will be redeemed at an amount (the "Series D Redemption Amount") equal to the greater of (A) the Series D Liquidation Preference and (B) the Fair Market Value of the Common Stock into which the Series D Preferred Stock held by such holders could be converted as of the date of such Change of Control, and no payment shall be made to the holders of the Common Stock or any Capital Stock ranking junior to the Series D Preferred Stock unless such amount is paid in full.

———

Recall that Silicon Gaming, Inc. Class D stock has a "par value" of $.001. What is "par"? In a diminishing number of states, the corporation statutes require that the articles of incorporation state whether the stock, common or preferred, is to have a "par value," and, if so, what the par value amount is. In some states, including Delaware, the corporation may have par stock, but is not required to do so. *See* Delaware § 102(a)(4) and MBCA § 2.02(b)(2)(iv).

"Par value" is the *minimum* price for which a corporation can issue its shares. If, for example, the articles of incorporation of Bubba's Burritos, Inc. provide for a single class of stock with a par value of $1,000 a share, then the corporation must receive at least $1,000 for each share it issues. If the corporation issues seven shares to Propp, then the corporation must receive consideration from Propp with a value of at least $7,000.

Par value is just a minimum issuance price, not a fixed price. *See* Delaware § 153(a). Bubba's Burritos could issue $1,000–par–value stock for more than $1,000 a share; it will certainly try to sell the stock for as high a price as it can. It just could not issue $1,000–par–value stock for less than $1,000 per share. And par value affects only the *issuance* price. It would have no effect on the price for which Propp could later *resell* his

$1,000–par Bubba's Burritos stock—for example, on a stock exchange such as the New York Stock Exchange or NASDAQ. Such later sale, because it is not made by the corporation, is simply not an "issuance," and issuance rules, such as par value, therefore do not apply.

State corporation statutes that provide for par value stock also generally provide for keeping two separate funds or accounts—"stated capital" and "capital surplus." "Stated capital" includes the aggregate par value of all issued shares of par value stock. If, for example, Bubba's Burritos had issued 50 shares of $1,000–par–value stock, then its stated capital would be $50,000. This is the figure that would appear on the balance sheet as one of the items in the account for "shareholders' equity" or "owners' equity." The stated capital account cannot be distributed to shareholders. It is, in theory, a cushion to protect creditors, to ensure that the company retains at least some money to pay its bills.

Suppose Bubba's Burritos had received funds for its issuance *in excess of par*. Such excess goes into an account called "capital surplus" or "additional paid-in capital" and may be distributed back to shareholders in dividends. If, for example, Bubba's Burritos had received $99,000 from its issuance of 50 shares of $1,000–par–value stock, then its stated capital would still be $50,000 and its capital surplus / additional paid-in capital would be $49,000.

Two developments have significantly limited the practical impact of "par value," "stated capital," and "capital surplus." First, the MBCA and the corporation statutes of the majority of states have eliminated the requirements that articles of incorporation provide a "par value" for stock and that corporations maintain a "stated capital" account. Second, even in the states that require "par value" and "stated capital" (or just "capital") (*see* Delaware § 154 and New York § 510),* corporations have reduced the importance of the concepts by setting par value at a penny or even a fraction of a cent.

PROBLEMS: ISSUANCE

1.   Read Delaware §§ 152 and 153 and MBCA § 6.21(b) and (c).

a.   Can a corporation issue stock in exchange for land?

b.   How about for a promise of future services to the corporation?

c.   How about for a promissory note?

d.   How about for goodwill?

e.   How about for a release of a claim against the corporation?

2.   The articles of incorporation for C Inc., a Delaware corporation, provide that Class A stock shall have a $2 par value. Can C Inc. issue 2000 shares of Class A stock to S for $1 a share? *See* Delaware § 154.

---

* Throughout the book, we refer to sections of the New York Business Corporation Law simply as "New York."

3. Same facts as Question 2. Can C Inc. issue 3,000 shares of Class A stock to S for $5 a share? BTW, why would a corporation issue par value stock for more than par?

4. Under the facts of Question 3, what portion of the issuance price would be allocated to stated capital?

5. Can S sell her $5 par C Inc. Class A stock to T for $3 a share? Why would a shareholder sell her stock for less than its par value? Recall that when S sells the C Inc. stock, it is not an issuance. An issuance occurs only when the corporation sells its own stock. And because par is an issuance concept, it does not apply when S, rather than the corporation, sells the stock. Note that almost everyone who owns stock bought that stock on an exchange—that is, they bought it from other shareholders, and not as part of an issuance.

6. Can C Inc. issue 100,000 shares of its $2 par value Class A stock to B in exchange for Blackacre?

7. Capel invests $100,000 in Bubba's Burritos, Inc. and receives stock. Does she care what the par value of the stock is? Does she care whether the stock has a par value? Does par have any necessary relationship to the actual value of the stock?

8. Suppose that Capel owns half of the stock in Bubba's Burritos. Does she care whether Bubba's sells stock to others, or for what price?

5. CHOOSING THE STATE OF INCORPORATION AND QUALIFYING AS A "FOREIGN CORPORATION"

Bubba's Burritos, Inc. can choose to incorporate in any state, even a state in which it has no business activity. The laws of that state will then become the default rules that govern the "internal affairs" of Bubba's Burritos, Inc. *See* Restatement (Second) of Conflicts of Laws §§ 296–310 (1971). "Internal affairs" include procedures for corporate actions and the rights and duties of directors, shareholders and officers with respect to each other. For example, if Bubba's Burritos, Inc. incorporates in Hawaii, Hawaiian law will govern issues such as shareholders' right to vote and the procedures by which the board of directors acts. This is true even though none of Bubba's Burritos' shareholders, directors, officers, customers, or greasy burritos has ever been to Hawaii.

The company's internal affairs would not include the rights of third parties with respect to Bubba's Burritos. If a Bubba's customer is injured by a falling burrito, the law that governs her personal injury suit against Bubba's would be chosen by the general rules for conflicts of laws. For example, even if Bubba's were incorporated in Hawaii, Alabama law would probably govern the suit, if the burrito struck the plaintiff in Alabama.

Very, very few non-Hawaiian businesses are incorporated in Hawaii, however. In part this is because Hawaii is hard to spell and in part this is because the choice is usually between the business's home state and Delaware.

Most "Fortune 500" corporations are incorporated in Delaware. For example, General Motors is incorporated in Delaware. To paraphrase a former Secretary of Defense (and President of General Motors), what is good for General Motors is good for the rest of the country. Since General Motors incorporated in Delaware, why shouldn't Bubba's Burritos incorporate in Delaware?

Unless Delaware is where Bubba's will be doing business, though, we need to be aware that incorporating there will impose additional costs. First, consider attorneys' fees. Recall that incorporation requires the preparation and filing of articles of incorporation. And corporations also have bylaws. Will a Delaware lawyer charge more than a lawyer in the state where you intend to sell burritos? Can a lawyer from that state handle a Delaware incorporation? If so, will she charge more for Delaware incorporation than for a local incorporation?

Second, consider the fees that have to be paid to Delaware. It was recently estimated that corporations pay more than $400,000,000 a year to the State of Delaware in filing fees and franchise taxes. So we need to ask whether the Delaware fee and tax structure is more burdensome than that in the state where we will be selling burritos.

Third, if Bubba's Burritos incorporates in Delaware but operates in another state, it will have to make filings in and make payments to *both* states. It will be incorporated in Delaware but will have to qualify to do business as a "foreign corporation" in the other states. *See* MBCA §§ 1.40(10); 15.01. In corporate law, "foreign" does not refer to another country—it applies to another state. So, in Colorado, a Colorado corporation is "domestic" and a corporation formed *anywhere other than Colorado* (even Wyoming) is "foreign."

Every state requires foreign corporations transacting business there to "qualify." Qualification usually includes (1) obtaining authorization from the appropriate state agency, (2) appointing a registered agent in the state, (3) filing annual statements in the state, and (4) paying fees and franchise taxes to the state. So it can be quite expensive to incorporate in one state and qualify to do business in another.

What, then, are the benefits of Delaware incorporation? Here's what Delaware says in the frequently asked questions (FAQ) section on the Delaware Division of Corporations website:

> Why do so many companies incorporate in Delaware?
>
> Businesses choose Delaware not for one single reason, but because we provide a complete package of incorporation services. The Delaware General Corporation Law is the most advanced and flexible business formation statute in the nation. The Delaware Court of Chancery is a unique 215 year old business court that has written most of the modern U.S. corporation case law. Delaware's State

Government is business-friendly and accessible. Our Division of Corporations is a model of state-of-the-art efficiency and our staff provides prompt, friendly and professional service to clients, attorneys, registered agents and others. These factors have all contributed to making Delaware a premier legal home to companies around the world.

Do I have to live in Delaware to have a Delaware corporation?

No. Delaware law requires every corporation to have and maintain a Registered Agent in the State who may be either an individual resident, a domestic corporation, or a foreign corporation authorized to transact business in Delaware whose business office is identical with the corporation's registered office.

Must I use an Attorney to incorporate?

No, but you should contact an attorney concerning legal matters. The Delaware Division of Corporations acts solely in an administrative capacity and does not provide legal advice.

If I am incorporated in another state or jurisdiction, do I need to qualify to do business in the State of Delaware?

Yes, Delaware law requires every corporation that is doing business in this state but is formed in another state or jurisdiction to submit a completed "Foreign Qualification" form with the Division of Corporations along with a Certificate of Existence issued by that state or jurisdiction.

How quickly can I incorporate or receive back my request?

The Division of Corporations offers a variety of services including "1–Hour," "2–Hour," "Same Day," and "Next Day" Expedited Services which are designed to meet your business needs.

———————

Moreover, the Hotel du Pont in Wilmington, Delaware, is a much more elegant place to stay than the Motel 6 in Montgomery, Alabama.

Others, however, argue that Delaware law is inferior to the law of many other states. Among the reasons that corporations continue nonetheless to choose Delaware is self-reinforcing habit. Because most corporations choose Delaware, the only state's corporate law that most law schools (and casebooks) teach in detail is Delaware's. For the lawyers who advise corporations on where to incorporate, Delaware law is the only law with which they feel comfortable. *See* William Carney & George Shepherd, *The Mystery of Delaware Law's Continuing Success*, 2009 U. Ill. L. Rev. 1.

QUESTIONS

1. The tort law of some states is viewed as more favorable to plaintiffs than the tort law of other states. For example, business leaders have described Alabama as "torts hell."* Can Bubba's Burritos, Inc. avoid the application of Alabama torts law by incorporating in Delaware?

2. Assume that Bubba's Burritos, Inc., is represented by one of Epstein's country cousins, Billy Bob Epstein, a lawyer with a sole practice in Arab, Alabama. How can Billy Bob form a Delaware corporation? Does he have to travel to Delaware? Does he have to share the work (and the fees) with some Delaware attorney? *See, e.g.*, www.ctcorporation.com.

3. Why does the Delaware Division of Corporations tout the expertise of the Delaware courts? If Bubba's Burritos, Inc. is incorporated in Delaware but operates only in Alabama, will an Alabama shareholder have to go to Delaware to sue Bubba's Burritos, Inc.? Is the expertise of the Delaware courts only relevant if the lawsuit is tried in Delaware? *See generally* Jill E. Fisch, *The Peculiar Role of the Delaware Courts in the Competition for Corporate Charters*, 68 U. CINN. L. REV. 1061, 1064 (2000). ("This article offers an alternative explanation for Delaware's success in attracting corporate charters—the unique lawmaking function of the Delaware courts. The article focuses on the peculiar role of the Delaware judiciary in corporate lawmaking, a role that has received little attention from corporate law scholars. The article demonstrates that Delaware uses an unusual process to make corporate law. Delaware relies heavily on judge-made law, but the structure and operation of the Delaware courts causes Delaware's judicial lawmaking to differ from that in other states. Indeed, the process by which Delaware courts make corporate law resembles legislation in some ways.")

4. We noted that a foreign corporation must qualify to transact business in another state. And we noted that qualifying can be expensive. But the foreign corporation must qualify *only* if it is "transacting business" in the state. What level of activity is required to constitute "transacting business" under these statutes?

Delaware § 373 is typical of other statutes in which state legislatures make clear what activity does *not* constitute transacting business by a foreign corporation. These statutes are based upon the principle that the Commerce Clause of the Constitution prohibits states from excluding a corporation that is engaged in *interstate* commerce. Thus, the foreign corporation provisions apply to foreign corporations engaged in *intrastate* activities within another state.

5. California has a statute that purports to apply California law to the affairs of non-California corporations. Cal. Corp. Code § 2115 provides that the articles of a foreign corporation are deemed amended to comply with

---

* *Cf.* David Greising, *Huge Verdicts? Maybe There is a Place for Them*, CHICAGO TRIBUNE, May 12, 1999, 1999 WL 2872434.

California law and are subject to California law if, *inter alia*, more than half the stock is held by California residents. The Delaware Supreme Court refused to apply the California provision in *VantagePoint Venture Partners 1996 v. Examen, Inc.*, 871 A.2d 1108 (2005). California law would have allowed shareholders of a particular class of stock to block a merger. Delaware law would not. The Delaware court held that Delaware law governed under the internal affairs doctrine. It held that the internal affairs doctrine was not merely a choice-of-law principle, but was constitutionally based. Due process required that directors and officers of the corporation know in advance what law would govern and the Commerce Clause prohibited California from regulating the internal affairs of a Delaware corporation. *Id.* at 1113–17.

CHAPTER FIVE

HOW DOES A CORPORATION OPERATE?

■ ■ ■

A. WHO IS LIABLE TO THE CORPORATION'S CREDITORS?

Recall that a corporation is an "entity" and a "person." As such, it can sue and be sued for the actions of its agents. The corporation can be held liable to third parties for contracts, torts, violations of statutes, etc. If Bubba's Burritos, Inc. fails to pay rent to its landlord, L & L Real Estate, the landlord can sue Bubba's Burritos, Inc. and collect on any judgment by garnishing Bubba's Burritos, Inc.'s bank account or levying on other corporate assets. Similarly, if Vic Timm comes down with food poisoning because of spoiled food he ate at Bubba's Burritos, Inc., he can sue and collect from the corporation itself.

Recall also that a shareholder's protection from personal responsibility for the corporation's liability is basic to the corporate structure and to corporate law. Please read MBCA § 6.22(b) and Delaware § 162. Neither L & L Real Estate nor Vic Timm can sue and collect from Capel or any of the other Bubba's Burritos, Inc. shareholders. This is the general rule in every state.

But there are contractual and judicial exceptions to the rule that shareholders are not personally liable for the acts or debts of the corporation. The contractual exception is easy and obvious. Third parties often refuse to extend credit to a corporation with limited assets unless that corporation's shareholders agree to be personally responsible, i.e., personally guarantee payment. For example, L & L Real Estate may refuse to rent the building to Bubba's Burritos, Inc. unless Capel or the other shareholders personally guarantee the rent payments.

As the following cases indicate, however, the judicially created exceptions to the rule that shareholders are not personally liable for the acts or debts of the corporation are neither easy nor obvious. In the first case, an unpaid supplier of services to a corporation is permitted to collect its claim from the corporation's principal *shareholder*, W. Ray Flemming, because of the judicially created concept of "piercing the corporate veil." As you read the case, consider the following questions:

131

1.   Did the W. Ray Flemming Fruit Company satisfy the requirements of South Carolina law for the creation of a corporation?

2.   Did either the corporation or W. Ray Flemming individually violate any provision of the South Carolina corporate code or any other law?

3.   Is W. Ray Flemming now personally liable for all of the debts of the corporation?

4.   Are the other stockholders of W. Ray Fleming Fruit Company also personally liable to the plaintiff Dewitt Truck Brokers, Inc.?

DEWITT TRUCK BROKERS, INC. v. W. RAY FLEMMING FRUIT COMPANY

United States Court of Appeals, Fourth Circuit, 1976
540 F.2d 681

[W. Ray Flemming Fruit Company ("corporation") sold fruit for growers on commission. When the fruit was sold, the corporation would pay the growers the sales price less (i) the corporation's commissions and (ii) the corporation's transportation costs. The corporation contracted with Dewitt Truck Brokers, Inc., ("plaintiff") to transport the fruit. The corporation owes plaintiff approximately $15,000. W. Ray Flemming, the corporation's principal shareholder, orally assured plaintiff that he would personally pay for the fruit transportation if the corporation did not. This oral promise to answer for the debts of another was not legally enforceable because of the statute of frauds. Accordingly, in this litigation, plaintiff asks the court to "pierce the corporate veil."]

DONALD RUSSELL, CIRCUIT JUDGE. In this action on debt, the plaintiff seeks, by piercing the corporate veil under the law of South Carolina, to impose individual liability on the president of the indebted corporation. The District Court, making findings of fact which may be overturned only if clearly erroneous, pierced the corporate veil and imposed individual liability. The individual defendant appeals. We affirm.

At the outset, it is recognized that a corporation is an entity, separate and distinct from its officers and stockholders, and that its debts are not the individual indebtedness of its stockholders. This is expressed in the presumption that the corporation and its stockholders are separate and distinct. And this oft-stated principle is equally applicable, whether the corporation has many or only one stockholder. But this concept of separate entity is merely a legal theory, "introduced for purposes of convenience and to subserve the ends of justice," and the courts "decline to recognize (it) whenever recognition of the corporate form would extend the principle of incorporation 'beyond its legitimate purposes and (would) produce injustices or inequitable consequences.'" Krivo Industrial Supp. Co. v. National Distill. & Chem. Corp. (5th Cir. 1973), 483 F.2d 1098, 1106. Accordingly, "in an appropriate case and in furtherance of the ends of justice," the corporate veil will be pierced and the corporation and its stockholders "will be treated as identical."

This power to pierce the corporate veil, though, is to be exercised "reluctantly" and "cautiously" and the burden of establishing a basis for the disregard of the corporate fiction rests on the party asserting such claim.

The circumstances which have been considered significant by the courts in actions to disregard the corporate fiction have been "rarely articulated with any clarity." Perhaps this is true because the circumstances "necessarily vary according to the circumstances of each case," and every case where the issue is raised is to be regarded as "sui generis (to) * * * be decided in accordance with its own underlying facts." Since the issue is thus one of fact, its resolution "is particularly within the province of the trial court" and such resolution will be regarded as "presumptively correct and (will) be left undisturbed on appeal unless it is clearly erroneous."

Contrary to the basic contention of the defendant, however, proof of plain fraud is not a necessary element in a finding to disregard the corporate entity. This was made clear in Anderson v. Abbott (1944), 321 U.S. 349, 362, where the Court, after stating that "fraud" has often been found to be a ground for disregarding the principle of limited liability based on the corporate fiction, declared:

* * * The cases of fraud make up part of that exception [which allow the corporate veil to be pierced]. But they do not exhaust it. An obvious inadequacy of capital, measured by the nature and magnitude of the corporate undertaking, has frequently been an important factor in cases denying stockholders their defense of limited liability. * * *

On the other hand, equally * * * as well settled as the principle that plain fraud is not a necessary prerequisite for piercing the corporate veil is the rule that the mere fact that all or almost all of the corporate stock is owned by one individual or a few individuals, will not afford sufficient grounds for disregarding corporateness. But when substantial ownership of all the stock of a corporation in a single individual is combined with other factors clearly supporting disregard of the corporate fiction on grounds of fundamental equity and fairness, courts have experienced "little difficulty" and have shown no hesitancy in applying what is described as the "alter ego" or "instrumentality" theory in order to cast aside the corporate shield and to fasten liability on the individual stockholder.

But, in applying the "instrumentality" or "alter ego" doctrine, the courts are concerned with reality and not form, with how the corporation operated and the individual defendant's relationship to that operation. One court has suggested that courts should abjure "the mere incantation of the term 'instrumentality' " in this context and, since the issue is one of fact, should take pains to spell out the specific factual basis for [their] conclusions. And the authorities have indicated certain facts which are to be given substantial weight in this connection. One fact which all the authorities consider significant in the inquiry, and particularly so in the case of the one-man or closely-held corporation, is whether the corporation was grossly undercapitalized for the purposes of the corporate undertaking. And, "[t]he obligation to provide adequate capital begins with incorporation and is a continuing obligation thereafter * * * during the corporation's operations." Other factors that are emphasized in the application of the doctrine are failure to observe corporate formalities, non-payment of dividends, the insolvency of the debtor corporation at the time, siphoning of funds of the corporation by the dominant stockholder, non-functioning of other officers or directors, absence of corporate records, and the fact that the corporation is merely a facade for the operations of the dominant stockholder or stockholders. The conclusion to disregard the corporate entity may not, however, rest on a single factor, whether undercapitalization, disregard of corporation's formalities, or what-not, but must involve a number of such factors; in addition, it must present an element of injustice or fundamental unfairness. But undercapitalization, coupled with disregard of corporate formalities, lack of participation on the part of the other stockholders, and the failure to pay dividends while paying substantial sums, whether by way of salary or otherwise, to the dominant stockholder, all fitting into a picture of basic unfairness, has been regarded fairly uniformly to constitute a basis for an imposition of individual liability under the doctrine. * * *

If these factors, which were deemed significant in other cases concerned with this same issue, are given consideration here, the finding of the District Court that the corporate entity should be disregarded was not clearly erroneous. Certainly the corporation was, in practice at least, a close, one-man corporation from the very beginning. Its incorporators were the defendant Flemming, his wife and his attorney. It began in 1962 with a capitalization of 5,000 shares, issued for a consideration of one dollar each. At the times involved here Flemming owned approximately 90% of the corporation's outstanding stock, according to his own testimony, though this was not verified by any stock records. Flemming was obscure on who the other stockholders were and how much stock these other stockholders owned, giving at different times conflicting statements as to who owned stock and how much. His testimony on who were the officers and directors was hardly more direct. * * *

The District Court found, also, that the corporation never had a stockholders' meeting. * * * It is thus clear that corporate formalities, even rudimentary formalities, were not observed by the defendant.

Beyond the absence of any observance of corporate formalities is the purely personal manner in which the corporation was operated. No stockholder or officer of the corporation other than Flemming ever received any salary, dividend, or fee from the corporation, or, for that matter, apparently exercised any voice in its operation or decisions. In all the years of the corporation's existence, Flemming was the sole beneficiary of its operations and its continued existence was for his exclusive benefit. During these years he was receiving from $15,000 to $25,000 each year from a corporation, which, during most of the time, was showing no profit and apparently had no working capital. Moreover, the payments to Flemming were authorized under no resolution of the board of directors of the corporation, as recorded in any minutes of a board meeting. Actually, it would seem that Flemming's withdrawals varied with what could be taken out of the corporation at the moment: If this amount were $15,000, that was Flemming's withdrawal; if it were $25,000, that was his withdrawal.

To summarize: The District Court found, and there was evidence to sustain the findings, that there was here a complete disregard of "corporate formalities" in the operation of the corporation, which functioned, not for the benefit of all stockholders, but only for the financial advantage of Flemming, who was the sole stockholder to receive one penny of profit from the corporation in the decade or more that it operated, and who made during that period all the corporate decisions and dominated the corporation's operations.

That the corporation was undercapitalized, if indeed it were not without any real capital, seems obvious. In fact, the defendant Flemming makes no effort to refute the evidence of want of any capital reserves on the part of the corporation. It appears patent that the corporation was actually operating at all times involved here on someone else's capital. This conclusion follows from a consideration of the manner in which Flemming operated in the name of the corporation during the year when plaintiff's indebtedness was incurred. * * *

Were the opinion of the District Court herein to be reversed, Flemming would be permitted to retain substantial sums from the operations of the corporation without having any real capital in the undertaking, risking nothing of his own and using as operating capital what he had collected as due the plaintiff. Certainly, equity and fundamental justice support individual liability of Flemming for plaintiff's charges, payment for which he asserted in his accounting with the growers that he had paid and for which he took credit on such accounting. This case patently presents a blending of the very factors which courts have regarded as justifying a disregard of the corporate entity in furtherance of basic and fundamental fairness.

Finally, it should not be overlooked that at some point during the period when this indebtedness was being incurred, whether at the beginning or at a short time later is not clear in the record, the plaintiff became concerned about former delays in receipt of payment for its charges and, to allay that concern, Flemming stated to the plaintiff, according to the latter's testimony as credited by the District Court, that "he (i. e., Flemming) would take care of (the charges) personally, if the corporation failed to do so * * *." On this assurance, the plaintiff contended that it continued to haul for the defendant. The existence of this promise by Flemming is not disputed. When one, who is the sole beneficiary of a corporation's operations and who dominates it, as did Flemming in this case, induces a creditor to extend credit to the corporation on such an assurance as given here, that fact has been considered by many authorities sufficient basis for piercing the corporate veil. The only argument against this view is bottomed on the statute of frauds. * * *

QUESTIONS AND NOTES

1. Questions about the law.

1.1   Can a South Carolina corporation have only one shareholder? If so, is that shareholder personally liable for the corporation's debts since he is the "sole beneficiary of its obligations?"

1.2   What is "undercapitalization?" Was the corporation in this case undercapitalized?"

1.3   At what point is undercapitalization determined? If a corporation is adequately capitalized when it is formed but later loses money, is it then undercapitalized? Assume, for example, that Propp, Agee and Capel organize Bubba's Burritos, Inc. and that the amount they pay for their stock is sufficient to ensure that the corporation is adequately capitalized initially. Bubba's Burritos, Inc., however, suffers operating losses that exhaust virtually all of this initial capital. Does this mean that Propp, Agee and Capel are now at a risk of personal liability for Bubba's Burritos, Inc.'s debts through piercing the corporate veil unless they provide additional capital to the corporation?

1.4   The Fourth Circuit also mentions "disregard of corporate formalities"? What corporate formalities did the corporation disregard? How was the plaintiff adversely affected by any such disregard of corporate formalities? Other shareholders?

1.5   Are there any other factors mentioned by the Fourth Circuit that seem to have nothing at all to do with whether a shareholder should be held liable for corporate obligations? Specifically, the court noted that the corporation had not paid dividends. Wouldn't a creditor like Dewitt be *delighted* that the corporation did not pay dividends? After all, if the corporation had paid dividends to its shareholders, there would have been even less money from which creditors could recover. So it seems nonpayment of dividends is actually a *good* thing from the creditors' viewpoint. Might there be valid tax reasons for a corporation not to pay dividends?

1.6.   If you were the lawyer for Flemming or his corporation, could you have offered advice that might have helped him avoid personal liability?

1.7.   If the trial court had ruled for Flemming—had refused to pierce the corporate veil—would the Fourth Circuit have reversed?

2. More Questions.

2.1   The court in *Dewitt* (and just about every other court that has discussed piercing the corporate veil) mentions that one basis for piercing is to avoid fraud. Suppose Capel leaves her job at Bubba's Burritos. She and Bubba's enter an agreement by which Capel agrees that she will not go into competition with Bubba's in the Tuscaloosa area for at least two years. (Such agreements are called "covenants not to compete" and are usually upheld if reasonable as to temporal and geographic limitations.) The next week she forms Capel's Quesadillas, Inc., which goes into direct competition with Bubba's on the Strip in Tuscaloosa. Should she be able to say that she is not violating the covenant not to compete because it is Capel's Quesadillas, Inc. (and not she) who is competing with Bubba's? Of course not. Most people would agree that her use of the corporate form to avoid her personal covenant was fraudulent. The court would pierce the corporate veil and put Capel's Quesadillas, Inc. out of business.

2.2   In *Dewitt,* the plaintiff was invoking the piercing the corporate veil doctrine to hold an individual shareholder liable for his or her corporation's contracts or torts. What if the shareholder is itself a corporation?

A corporation can be a shareholder of another corporation. Indeed, a corporation is often the only shareholder of another corporation. A corporation whose stock is owned by another corporation is commonly referred to as a "subsidiary." More precisely, a subsidiary is a corporation, a majority or all of the outstanding stock of which is owned by another corporation, called the parent corporation.

Remember that every corporation is an entity—a legal person, with its own assets separate from those who own and run it. Accordingly, a parent corporation is not liable for the contracts, torts, and other obligations of its subsidiary corporation unless there is a contractual or judicial exception to the rule that a shareholder is not liable for the acts or debts of the corporation.

The next case involves the issue of piercing the corporate veil to hold a parent corporation liable for torts of its subsidiary.

Bristol–Myers Squibb Co. (Bristol), was the sole shareholder of Medical Engineering Corp. (MEC). MEC was a breast implant maker; Bristol was not. Both MEC and Bristol were defendants in the multidistrict litigation over silicone breast implants. One of the plaintiffs' legal theories was piercing the corporate veil. In reading the court's decision on Bristol's motion for summary judgment, please consider the following:

1.   What did Bristol do wrong?

2.   Were the plaintiffs harmed by any of Bristol's actions or inactions? Is that relevant to piercing the corporate veil?

3.   Was MEC undercapitalized?

IN RE SILICONE GEL BREAST IMPLANTS
LIABILITY LITIGATION

United States District Court, Northern District of Alabama, 1995
887 F.Supp. 1447

POINTER, CHIEF JUDGE. Under submission after appropriate discovery, extensive briefing, and oral argument is the motion for summary judgment filed by defendant Bristol–Myers Squibb Co. Bristol is the sole shareholder of Medical Engineering Corporation, a major supplier of breast implants, but has never itself manufactured or distributed breast implants. Bristol asserts that the evidence is insufficient for the plaintiffs' claims to proceed against it, whether through piercing the corporate veil or under a theory of direct liability. The parties agree that, with discovery substantially complete, this motion is ripe for decision. For the reasons stated below, the court concludes that Bristol is not entitled to summary judgment.* * *

Documents reflect that MEC has had, at least in form, a board of three directors, generally consisting of the Bristol Vice President then serving as President of Bristol's Health Care Group, another Bristol executive, and MEC's president. Bristol's Health Care Group President, who reported to Bristol's president or chairman, could not be outvoted by the other two MEC board members. Several of the former MEC presidents did not recall that MEC had a board, let alone that they were members; and one of these stated that he did not attend, call, or receive notice of board meetings in his five years of service because he had a designated Bristol officer to contact. The few resolutions that were adopted by MEC's board were apparently prepared by Bristol officials.

MEC prepared "significant event" reports for Bristol's Corporate Policy Committee. These reports included information on breast implant production, such as publicity, testing, expenses, lawsuit settlements, and backorders caused by sterilization difficulties. Neither Bristol managers nor MEC Presidents recall any orders or recommendations being issued by Bristol as a result of these reviews. Bristol also required MEC to prepare and submit a five-year plan for its review.

MEC submitted budgets for approval by Bristol's senior management. For this submission, MEC filled out a series of standard Bristol forms that included information on projected sales, profits and losses, cash flow, balance sheets, and capital requirements. Bristol had the authority to modify this budget, though it rarely, if ever, actually did so.

Cash received by MEC was transferred to an account maintained by Bristol. This money was credited to MEC, but the interest earned was credited to Bristol. Bristol was MEC's banker, providing such loans as it determined MEC needed. Bristol required MEC to obtain its approval for capital appropriations, though most, if not all, of these requests were approved.

Bristol set the employment policies and wage scales that applied to MEC's employees. Before hiring a top executive or negotiating the salary, MEC was required to seek Bristol's approval. Before hiring a vice president of MEC, MEC's president and his superior at Bristol interviewed the candidate. Key executive employees were rated on the Bristol schedule. Bristol set a target for salary increases below the key executive level and approved those for employees above that level. Key executives of MEC received stock options for Bristol stock. MEC employees could participate in Bristol's pension and savings plans.

Bristol provided various services to MEC. Zimmer International, another Bristol subsidiary, distributed MEC breast implants but did not receive any benefit for doing so. Bristol's corporate development group assisted MEC in seeking out new product lines. Bristol's scientific experts researched the hazards of breast implants and polyurethane foam. Bristol provided funds for MEC to conduct sales contests. Bristol funded tests on breast implants. Another Bristol subsidiary, ConvaTec, assisted MEC in developing its premarket approval application (PMAA) regarding breast implants for the FDA. In addition to this assistance, Bristol hired an outside laboratory to verify ConvaTec's analysis. Bristol also conducted post-market surveillance at the request of the FDA. * * *

Bristol's name and logo were contained in the package inserts and promotional products regarding breast implants, apparently as a marketing tool to increase confidence in the product. Bristol's name was used in all sales and promotional communications with physicians.

MEC posted a profit every year between 1983 and 1990. Total sales increased from approximately $14 million in 1983 to $65 million in 1990. Bristol never received dividends from MEC. Bristol prepared consolidated federal income tax returns but MEC prepared its own Wisconsin tax forms. Bristol also purchased insurance for MEC under its policy. This insurance has a face value of over $2 billion.

Bristol's executive vice president suspended MEC's sales of polyurethane coated breast implants on April 17, 1991, and determined not to submit a PMAA for the implants to the FDA. MEC ceased its breast implant business in 1991 and later that year MEC ceased all operations by selling its urology division. This sale could not have occurred without Bristol's approval, and proceeds from the sale were turned over to Bristol, which then executed a low-interest demand note for $57,518,888 payable to MEC. MEC's only assets at this time are this demand note and its indemnity insurance.

The various theories of recovery made by plaintiffs against Bristol can be generally divided between those involving "corporate control" and those asserting direct liability. The corporate control claims deal with piercing the corporate veil to abrogate limited liability and hold Bristol responsible for actions of MEC. The direct liability theories include strict products liability, negligence, negligent failure to warn, negligence per se for not complying with FDA regulations, misrepresentation, fraud, and participation.

The potential for abuse of the corporate form is greatest when, as here, the corporation is owned by a single shareholder. The evaluation of corporate control claims cannot, however, disregard the fact that, no different from other stockholders, a parent corporation is expected—indeed, required—to exert some control over its subsidiary. Limited liability is the rule, not the exception. However, when a corporation is so controlled as to be the alter ego or mere instrumentality of its stockholder, the corporate form may be disregarded in the interests of justice. So far as this court has been able to determine, some variation of this theory of liability is recognized in all jurisdictions.

An initial question is whether veil-piercing may ever be resolved by summary judgment. Ordinarily the fact-intensive nature of the issue will require that it be resolved only through a trial. Summary judgment, however, can be proper if, as occurred earlier in this litigation with respect to claims against Dow Chemical and Corning, the evidence presented could lead to but one result. Because the court concludes that a jury (or in some jurisdictions, the judge acting in equity) could—and, under the laws of many states, probably should—find that MEC was but the alter ego of Bristol, summary judgment must be denied.

The totality of circumstances must be evaluated in determining whether a subsidiary may be found to be the alter ego or mere instrumentality of the parent corporation. Although the standards are not identical in each state, all jurisdictions require a showing of substantial domination. Among the factors to be considered are whether:

- the parent and the subsidiary have common directors or officers
- the parent and the subsidiary have common business departments
- the parent and the subsidiary file consolidated financial statements and tax returns
- the parent finances the subsidiary
- the parent caused the incorporation of the subsidiary
- the subsidiary operates with grossly inadequate capital
- the parent pays the salaries and other expenses of the subsidiary
- the subsidiary receives no business except that given to it by the parent
- the parent uses the subsidiary's property as its own
- the daily operations of the two corporations are not kept separate
- the subsidiary does not observe the basic corporate formalities, such as keeping separate books and records and holding shareholder and board meetings.

The fact-finder at a trial could find that the evidence supports the conclusion that many of these factors have been proven: two of MEC's three directors were Bristol directors; MEC was part of Bristol's Health Care group and used Bristol's legal, auditing, and communications departments; MEC and Bristol filed consolidated federal tax returns and Bristol prepared consolidated financial reports; Bristol operated as MEC's finance company, providing loans for the purchase of Aesthetech and Natural Y, receiving interest on MEC's funds, and requiring MEC to make requests for capital appropriations; Bristol effectively used MEC's resources as its own by obtaining interest on MEC's money and requiring MEC to make requests for capital appropriations to obtain its own funds; some members of MEC's board were not aware that MEC had a board of directors, let alone that they were members; and the senior Bristol member of MEC's board could not be outvoted by the other two directors. These facts, even apart from evidence that might establish some of the other factors listed above, would provide significant support for a finding at trial that MEC is Bristol's alter ego.

Bristol contends that a finding of fraud or like misconduct is necessary to pierce the corporate veil. Despite Bristol's contentions to the contrary, Delaware courts—to which Bristol would have this court look—do not necessarily require a showing of fraud if a subsidiary is found to be the mere instrumentality or alter ego of its sole stockholder. In addition, many jurisdictions that require a showing of fraud, injustice, or inequity in a contract case do not in a tort situation. A rational distinction can be drawn between tort and contract cases. In actions based on contract, "the creditor has willingly transacted business with the subsidiary" although it could have insisted on assurances that would make the parent also responsible. In a tort situation, however, the injured party had no such choice; the limitations on corporate liability were, from its standpoint, fortuitous and non-consensual.

There is, however, evidence precluding summary judgment even in jurisdictions that require a finding of fraud, inequity, or injustice. This conclusion is not based merely on the evidence that, even accepting Bristol's contentions regarding the amount of insurance available to MEC, MEC may have insufficient funds to satisfy the potential risks of responding to, and defending against, the numerous existing and potential claims of the plaintiffs. Equally significant is the fact that Bristol permitted its name to appear on breast implant advertisements, packages, and product inserts to improve sales by giving the product additional credibility. Combined with the evidence of potentially insufficient assets, this fact would support a finding that it would be inequitable and unjust to allow Bristol now to avoid liability to those induced to believe Bristol was vouching for this product.

Because the evidence available at a trial could support—if not, under some state laws, perhaps mandate—a finding that the corporate veil should be pierced, Bristol is not entitled through summary judgment to dismissal of the claims against it.

QUESTIONS AND NOTES

1.   Questions on piercing the corporate veil.

1.1   Again, what did Bristol do wrong? How did it harm the plaintiffs? Are these questions relevant to the issue of piercing the corporate veil?

1.2   Do you agree with Judge Pointer that it should be easier to pierce the corporate veil in cases involving tort claims than in cases involving contract claims? Do you agree with Judge Pointer that the plaintiffs in this case, women who bought implants from MEC, were asserting tort claims?

2.   Notes on piercing the corporate veil.

2.1   In the same multidistrict silicone gel breast implant litigation, Judge Pointer earlier granted a motion by Dow Chemical Co. and Corning, Inc., sole shareholders of Dow Corning Corp., to dismiss a corporate veil piercing count against them, stating:

> There is no evidence of intermingling or commingling of funds or of any improper loans between the parents and the subsidiary * * *. There is no evidence that [the parent companies] drained Dow Corning of its assets, even after they had knowledge of the potential liability for silicone gel breast implants * * *. Although Dow and Corning have had significant contacts with their subsidiary, these contacts do not * * * rise to the level of manipulation and control that would support a piercing of the corporate veil * * *. The various business dealings between the three companies appear to have been carried out with due regard for the separate existence and interests of each, with all necessary corporate formalities being observed.

In re Silicone Gel Breast Implants Products Liability Litigation, 837 F.Supp. 1128, 1138 (N.D. Ala. 1993).

2.2   "This [the piercing the corporate veil cases] is jurisprudence by metaphor or epithet * * *. [W]e are faced with hundreds of decisions that are irreconcilable and not entirely comprehensible. Few areas of the law have been so sharply criticized by commentators." Philip L. Blumberg, THE LAW OF CORPORATE GROUPS: PROCEDURAL LAW 8 (1983).

2.3   Actually, there are thousands, not hundreds, of reported decisions on piercing the corporate veil and Professor Thompson of the Vanderbilt University Law School attempted to reconcile the decisions:

> My original empirical project, published in 1991, covered all Westlaw cases through 1985 that involved attempts to pierce the corporate veil. This study examined 1600 cases and reported both factual data (such as the year, court, law applied, number of shareholders, and substance of the claim) and the reasons courts offered to justify their decision to either pierce or not pierce the corporate veil. Some of the key findings were as follows:
>
>   1.   Courts pierced the corporate veil in approximately 40% of all reported cases;

2.   Piercing the veil is a doctrine directed exclusively at close corporations and corporate groups; piercing did not occur as to shareholders in public corporations or more precisely in corporations with more than nine shareholders;

3.   Courts pierce the veil more often to get to an individual who is a shareholder than to reach another corporation who is a shareholder, a result contrary to expectations of several commentators who have argued that limited liability within limited liability, as occurs when a corporation is a shareholder, is not necessary;

4.   Courts are less likely to pierce the veil in cases involving tort claims as opposed to those involving contractual or statutory claims; this finding is surprising given even stronger statements of commentators that a tort setting makes for a much stronger case for piercing the veil since the plaintiff had no opportunity to bargain for the lack of liability;

5.   Undercapitalization and corporate informalities often lead to piercing, but appear in a relatively small percentage of all cases in which courts pierce and an even smaller number of the tort cases.

During the last year, I have extended my initial data base from its original ending point in 1985 to include cases through 1996. This expansion generated an additional 2200 cases to go with the initial 1600. A preliminary examination of the recent data indicates that these results fit within the pattern of the original study. The new data suggest that the judiciary is still reluctant to pierce the veil in tort cases and within corporate groups.

Robert B. Thompson, *Piercing the Corporate Veil Within Corporate Groups: Corporate Shareholders as Mere Investors*, 13 CONN. J. INT'L L. 379, 383–85 (1999).

3.   Questions about holding a parent corporation liable for the subsidiary corporation's actions under agency concepts.

3.1   In the portion of the opinion dealing with piercing the corporate veil, Judge Pointer states "Equally significant is the fact that Bristol permitted its name to appear on the breast implant advertisements, packages, and product inserts to improve sales by giving the product additional credibility." Why is that relevant to piercing the corporate veil? Isn't that more relevant to holding Bristol liable under some theory of apparent agency as in the *McDonald's* case in Chapter 2?

3.2   Is the following statement of the law on holding a parent corporation liable for the subsidiary corporation's actions under agency concepts helpful?

It is beyond dispute that a corporation may not be held liable for the actions of another company merely because it has an ownership interest in it. A corporate parent may, however, be held to account for the wrongs of its subsidiary if the corporate form is disregarded under a veil piercing analysis or, as plaintiffs postulate here, under traditional principles of agency. Judge Learned Hand's lucid explanation of the rationale for branding a corporate subsidiary as the agent of the parent shows that the relationship is not likely to be found:

Control through the ownership of shares does not fuse the corporations, even when the directors are common to each. One corporation may, however, become an actor in a given transaction, or in part of a business, or in a whole business, and, when it has, will be legally responsible. To become so it must take immediate direction of the transaction through its officers, by whom alone it can act at all. At times this is put as though the subsidiary then became an agent of the parent. That may no doubt be true, but only in quite other situations; that is, when both intend that relation to arise, for agency is consensual. [*Kingston Dry Dock v. Lake Champlain Transp. Co.*, 31 F.2d 265, 267 (2d. Cir. 1929).]

This seldom is true and liability normally must depend upon the parent's direct intervention in the transaction, ignoring the subsidiary's paraphernalia of incorporation, directors and officers. The test is therefore rather in the form than in the substance of the control; in whether it is exercised immediately, or by means of a board of directors and officers, left to their own initiative and responsibility in respect of each transaction as it arises. Some such line must obviously be drawn, if shareholding alone does not fuse the corporations in every case.

See generally Deborah A. DeMott, *The Mechanisms of Control,* 13 Conn. J. of Int'l L. 233 (1999).

3.3 If, as Judge Hand suggested in *Kingston Dock* above, "liability normally must depend upon the parent's direct intervention in the transaction," is such liability the derivative liability of a parent/principal for its subsidiary/agent's acts? Or is it, instead, direct liability of the parent for its own acts?

4. Note on direct liability of a parent corporation because of its control of a subsidiary's operations.

In considering the liability of a parent corporation under CERCLA for the cleanup costs of a facility owned by its subsidiary, the United States Supreme Court addressed the possibility of a parent/shareholder's direct liability:

The Court of Appeals was accordingly correct in holding that when (but only when) the corporate veil may be pierced, may a parent corporation be charged with derivative CERCLA liability for its subsidiary's actions.

CERCLA liability may turn on operation as well as ownership, and nothing in the statute's terms bars a parent corporation from direct liability for its own actions in operating a facility owned by its subsidiary. As Justice (then-Professor) Douglas noted almost 70 years ago, derivative liability cases are to be distinguished from those in which "the alleged wrong can seemingly be traced to the parent through the conduit of its own personnel and management" and "the parent is directly a participant in the wrong complained of." In such instances, the parent is directly liable for its own actions. It is this direct liability that is properly seen as being at issue here. *United States v. Bestfoods*,* 524 U.S. 51, 63–65 (1998).

5. Note on enterprise liability.

For more than seven decades, some professors and lawyers have argued for "enterprise liability." This is a theory under which corporations that (although technically separate) are commonly-owned and engage in one enterprise should be treated as a single legal entity for purposes of liability. As you read the following classic explanation of enterprise liability, consider how it differs from (1) piercing the veil liability or (2) agency liability or (3) direct liability.

Classically, a corporation was conceived as an artificial person, coming into existence through creation by a sovereign power.

Its primary business advantage, of course, was insulation of individual stockholders composing the corporation from liability for the debts of the corporate enterprise.

As the scale of business enterprises enlarged, the process of subdivision began; hence subsidiary corporations wholly-owned or partly-owned; or holding companies combined into a series of corporations constituting a combined economic enterprise; and so forth. More often than not, a single large-scale business is conducted, not by a single corporation, but by a constellation of corporations controlled by a central holding company, the various sectors being separately incorporated, either because they were once independent and have been acquired, or because the central concern, entering new fields, created new corporations to develop them, or for tax reasons. In some instances, departments of the business are separately incorporated and operated as separate legal units. Since under modern corporation statutes any three persons can in effect request and get a corporate charter, writing their own grant of powers (with very few limitations) and thus constituting themselves an artificial person, the process has been easy to carry on, and has been a decided business convenience.

This is far from the original conception of a corporation. The legal doctrine of corporate personality was built around the idea of a sovereign grant of certain attributes of personality to a definable group, engaged in an enterprise. The so-called "artificial personality" was designed to be the enterpriser of a project. Multiplicity of artificial personalities within an enterprise unit would probably have been impossible under most early corporation laws.

The divergence between corporate theory and the underlying economic facts has occasioned a variety of problems (dealt with *ad hoc* by the courts) in which the theory of "artificial personality" simply did not work, and was consequently extended, disregarded, sometimes buttressed by further fiction, at others manipulated to get a convenient result.

---

* What a small world! Unilever, the British/Dutch conglomerate that acquired Ben & Jerry's, has also acquired Bestfoods, the parent polluter in this case. The two are probably a good match in that, according to one article, "A single serving of Ben & Jerry's ice cream was measured to contain about 2,000 times the level of dioxin that the EPA considers to be safe. Steven Milloy, *A Commentary*, January 24, 2002, WASHINGTON TIMES (D.C.), A16, 2002, WL 2903363.

All this suggests that a review of the classic conception is in order. It has seemed to the writer that one of the pressing needs in the field of corporation law is its systematization. A series of rules has been adopted in varying groups of cases as wrongs appeared and remedies were worked out. These emerged as isolated doctrines applicable to specific situations. This essay is designed to suggest the possibility that a number of rules which are regarded as separate in fact are applications of a single dominant principle.

It is the thesis of this essay:

That the entity commonly known as "corporate entity" takes its being from the reality of the underlying enterprise, formed or in formation;

That the state's approval of the corporate form sets up a prima facie case that the assets, liabilities and operations of the corporation are those of the enterprise;

But that where the corporate entity is defective, or otherwise challenged, its existence, extent and consequences may be determined by the actual existence and extent and operations of the underlying enterprise, which by these very qualities acquires an entity of its own, recognized by law.

For brevity, this hypothesis is hereafter referred to as the theory of "enterprise liability."

Adolph A. Berle, *The Theory of Enterprise Liability*, 47 Colum. L. Rev. 343, 343–44 (1943).

———————

Walkovszky v. Carlton, 223 N.E.2d 6 (N.Y. 1966), is a famous case even though its holding is not completely clear. We note the facts simply because they may exemplify the theory of enterprise liability. In *Walkovszky*, the plaintiff was injured when hit by a taxicab. The cab was operated by a corporation owned by Carlton. That corporation's assets consisted of two cabs (not fully paid for), the "medallion" allowing it to operate in New York, and the minimum amount of insurance required by law for each cab. It turns out that Carlton also owned nine other corporations, each of which was set up the same way. All ten taxicab companies were operated out of a single garage, with a single dispatching system. In other words, the ten were operated as a single business. The plaintiff alleged that Carlton continually drained all profits out of the companies, leaving them with little in the way of assets.

If the plaintiff's theory of piercing the corporate veil had been successful, he would have pierced through the one corporation that operated the cab that hit him, and recovered from Carlton. On the other hand, if the plaintiff's theory of enterprise liability had been successful, the court would have treated all ten companies as one. The plaintiff thus would have been able to recover from the combined assets of all ten companies. So, enterprise liability pierces the walls of one corporation *not* to go after the assets of a shareholder, but to go after the assets of related companies.

B. WHO GETS TO MAKE DECISIONS FOR THE CORPORATION?

There was no serious legal question about who gets to make the decisions in a sole proprietorship and in a partnership. After all, in a sole proprietorship, there is only the sole proprietor (and perhaps some employees). And in a partnership, there are only the partners (and perhaps some employees). In the corporation, however, we may have various players: promoter(s), incorporator(s), shareholder(s), director(s) and officer(s). Who decides what?

As we will see, the answer to this question of "who decides what" varies with the corporation. This was observed by A. A. Berle and Gardiner Means in their famous book THE MODERN CORPORATION AND PRIVATE PROPERTY. What they saw in 1932 was that:

- ownership of large corporations was widely dispersed;

- no single shareholder owned sufficient stock in companies such as U.S. Steel or the Pennsylvania Railroad to control the corporation's agenda;

- the larger the corporation, the smaller the proportion of stock held by management.

Berle and Means described this division of ownership and decision-making:

> * * * [T]he position of ownership has changed from that of active to passive agent. In place of the actual physical properties over which the owner could exercise direction and for which he was responsible, the owner now holds a piece of paper representing a set of rights and expectations with respect to an enterprise. But over the enterprise and over the physical property—the instruments of production—in which he has an interest, the owner has little control. * * *. The owner is practically powerless through his own efforts to affect the underlying property * * * in the corporate system, the 'owner' of industrial wealth is left with a mere symbol of ownership while the power, the responsibility and the substance which have been an integral part of ownership in the past are being transferred to a separate group [management] in whose hands lie control.

Adolph Berle & Gardiner Means, THE MODERN CORPORATION AND PRIVATE PROPERTY 64–65 (1932).

What can we see today in McDonald's, Bubba's Burritos, and other corporations?

1. BOARD OF DIRECTORS AND OFFICERS

Even though McDonald's Corporation is an entity, a person for all legal purposes, there is no Mr. or Ms. McDonald—as one person—to make decisions for the business. That is not even the role of Ronald McDonald. And that is not the role of the person who owns one or one hundred or even one thousand of the more than one billion shares of McDonald's stock now outstanding. Generally, if a corporation has more than four or five shareholders, most shareholders play virtually no role in making decisions regarding the operation of the business. (For most shareholders of corporations with more than four or five shareholders, their only important decision is when to sell their shares—a decision we will consider later.)

Under the corporation statutes of all states, it is the board of directors that is entitled to make the corporation's most important decisions. MBCA § 8.01 is typical of provisions embodying this principle. Read the section and the Official Comment to it.*

As explained by one text, the "traditional pattern of corporate governance" works as follows:

> The traditional corporate pattern is triangular, with the shareholders at the base. The shareholders, who are generally viewed as the ultimate or residual owners of the business, select the personnel at the next level—namely, the board of directors. According to accepted wisdom, the board of directors appoints the chief executive officer and other corporate officers, determines corporate policies, oversees the officers' work, and in general manages the corporation or supervises the management of its affairs. In legal theory the directors are supreme during their term of office (usually one year).

James D. Cox, Thomas Lee Hazen, & F. Hodge O'Neal, CORPORATIONS 146 (1997).

For those of you who were political science majors:

> This corporate model of organization reflects the American embrace of the republican form of government. In it, the owners elect those who make the management decisions, the directors, and may remove them with or without cause. The directors hire and monitor the officers, who implement the directors' management decisions. In turn, the officers, who hire and monitor lower-level employees, are agents of the corporation. Their actions, if made within the scope of their authority, will bind the entity, just as an employee's act might bind a sole proprietor or a partner's act might bind other partners.

Richard D. Freer, *Business Organizations,* OXFORD COMPANION TO AMERICAN LAW 79 (2002).

---

* Again, it's a good idea to read the Official Comments to all sections assigned. They often provide helpful explanations and examples.

Are these statements consistent with MBCA §§ 8.01 and 7.32? Are they consistent with the *A.P. Smith Mfg. Co. v. Barlow* case in Chapter 1?

In actual practice, is the board of directors the decision-maker for a large, publicly-held corporation like McDonald's? For a small, closely held corporation like Bubba's Burritos, Inc.?

QUESTIONS

1. Who serves as the directors of a large, publicly-held corporation? For McDonald's, the answer (in 2009) is:

McDonald's Corp. Directors (2009)

Ralph Alvarez. Mr. Alvarez is President and Chief Operating Officer of the Company, a position to which he was elected in August 2006, and also has served as a Director since January 2008. He served as President of McDonald's North America from January 2005 to August 2006 and as President, McDonald's USA from July 2004 to January 2005. From January 2003 to July 2004, Mr. Alvarez served as Chief Operations Officer for McDonald's USA. Mr. Alvarez, 53, was first employed by the Company in 1994 and is a member of the class of 2010. Mr. Alvarez is currently a director of Key Corp, but is not standing for re-election, and will continue to serve as a director until the KeyCorp Annual Meeting of Shareholders in May 2009. Mr. Alvarez also serves on the board of Eli Lilly and Company.

Susan E. Arnold. Ms. Arnold is serving in a special assignment reporting to the Chief Executive Officer with The Procter & Gamble Company, a manufacturer and marketer of consumer goods, through September 1, 2009. Ms. Arnold was the President–Global Business Units of The Procter & Gamble Company from 2007 until March 2009 when she retired from that post. Prior to that time she served as Vice Chair of P & G Beauty and Health since 2006 and Vice Chair of P & G Beauty since 2004. She is also a director of The Walt Disney Company. Ms. Arnold, 55, joined McDonald's Board in 2008 and is a member of the class of 2011.

Robert A. Eckert. Mr. Eckert is Chairman of the Board and Chief Executive Officer of Mattel, Inc., a designer, manufacturer and marketer of family products, a post he has held since May 2000. Mr. Eckert, 54, joined McDonald's Board in 2003 and is a nominee for the class of 2012.

Enrique Hernandez, Jr. Mr. Hernandez has been Chairman and Chief Executive Officer of Inter–Con Security Systems, Inc., a provider of high-end security and facility support services to government, utilities and industrial customers, since 1986. He joined McDonald's Board in 1996 and is a nominee for the class of 2012. Mr. Hernandez, 53, also serves as the Chairman of the Board of Nordstrom, Inc., and as a director of Chevron Corporation and Wells Fargo & Company.

Jeanne P. Jackson. Ms. Jackson became President of Direct to Consumer for NIKE, Inc., a designer, marketer and distributor of athletic footwear, equipment and accessories, in March 2009. Ms. Jackson was

Chief Executive Officer of Walmart.com from March 2000 to January 2002. Ms. Jackson, 57, joined McDonald's Board in 1999 and is a nominee for the class of 2012. She also serves on the board of Harrah's Entertainment, Inc.

Richard H. Lenny. Mr. Lenny was Chairman, President and Chief Executive Officer of The Hershey Company, a manufacturer, distributor and marketer of chocolate and non-chocolate candy, snacks and candy-related grocery products, from January 2002 until his retirement in December 2007. He serves as a director of ConAgra Foods, Inc. Mr. Lenny, 57, joined McDonald's Board in 2005 and is a member of the class of 2011.

Walter E. Massey. Dr. Massey retired as President of Morehouse College in June 2007, a post to which he was named in 1995. He serves as a director of Bank of America Corporation. Dr. Massey, 71, joined McDonald's Board in 1998 and is a member of the class of 2010.

Andrew J. McKenna. Mr. McKenna has been the non-executive Chairman of the Board since 2004 and is also the Chairman of Schwarz Supply Source, a printer, converter, producer and distributor of packaging and promotional materials. Mr. McKenna, 79, joined McDonald's Board in 1991 and is a nominee for the class of 2012. He is also a director of Aon Corporation and Skyline Corporation.

Cary D. McMillan. Mr. McMillan has been Chief Executive Officer of True Partners Consulting, LLC, a professional services firm providing tax and other financial services, since December 2005. From October 2001 to May 2004, he was the Chief Executive Officer of Sara Lee Branded Apparel, and Executive Vice President, from January 2000 to May 2004, of Sara Lee Corporation, a branded consumer packaged-goods company. Mr. McMillan, 51, joined McDonald's Board in 2003 and is a member of the class of 2011. He also serves as a director of American Eagle Outfitters, Inc. and Hewitt Associates, Inc.

Sheila A. Penrose. Ms. Penrose is the non-executive Chairman of the Board of Jones Lang LaSalle Incorporated, a real estate services and money management firm, since her election to that post in January 2005. She has served on Jones Lang LaSalle's Board since 2002. From October 2000 to December 2007, Ms. Penrose was the President of the Penrose Group, a provider of strategic advisory services on financial and organizational strategies. Ms. Penrose, 63, joined McDonald's Board in 2006 and is a member of the class of 2011.

John W. Rogers, Jr. Mr. Rogers is the Chairman and Chief Executive Officer of Ariel Investments, LLC, a privately held institutional money management firm that he founded in 1983. Mr. Rogers, 51, joined McDonald's Board in 2003 and is a member of the class of 2010. Mr. Rogers also serves as a director of Aon Corporation and Exelon Corporation, and as a trustee of Ariel Investment Trust.

James A. Skinner. Mr. Skinner is Vice Chairman and Chief Executive Officer, a post to which he was elected in November 2004, and also has served as a Director since that date. He served as Vice Chairman from

January 2003 to November 2004. Mr. Skinner, 64, has been with the Company for 37 years and is a member of the class of 2011. He also serves as a director of Illinois Tool Works Inc. and Walgreen Co.

Roger W. Stone. Mr. Stone has been Chairman and Chief Executive Officer of KapStone Paper and Packaging Corporation, formerly Stone Arcade Acquisition Corporation, since April 2005. Mr. Stone was manager of Stone–Kaplan Investments, LLC from July 2004 to January 2007. He was Chairman and Chief Executive Officer of Box USA Group, Inc., a corrugated box manufacturer, from 2000 to 2004. Mr. Stone has also been the non-executive Chairman and director of Stone Tan China Acquisition Corp. since January 2007. Mr. Stone, 74, joined McDonald's Board in 1989 and is a member of the class of 2010.

Miles D. White. Mr. White has been Chairman of the Board and Chief Executive Officer of Abbott Laboratories, a pharmaceuticals and biotechnology company, since 1999. Mr. White joined Abbott in 1984. He is currently a director of Motorola, Inc., but is not standing for re-election, and will continue to serve as a director until the Motorola Annual Meeting of Stockholders in May 2009. Mr. White, 54, joined the McDonald's Board in April 2009 as a member of the class of 2010.

You can see from the list that a director can also be an officer. McDonald's "inside" directors are those who are also officers. The "outside" directors are those who are not.

2. How much do directors get paid? At McDonald's, directors received compensation of roughly $220,000 per year, made up of approximately 55% cash and 45% stock. An average McDonald's director owns approximately 30,000 shares (out of the 1.1 billion shares outstanding).

3. Is the McDonald's board of directors an agent for McDonald's? For the shareholders? Are Susan Arnold and the other directors agents? According to Restatement (Second) of Agency § 14C, "Neither the board of directors nor an individual director of a business is, as such, an agent of the corporation or its members [shareholders]." Why? Why does it matter?

4. Section 3.02 of the American Law Institute's Principles of Corporate Governance lists mandatory and permissive functions of the board of directors of a publicly-held corporation:

§ 3.02. Functions and Powers of the Board of Directors

Except as otherwise provided by statute:

(a) The board of directors of a publicly-held corporation should perform the following functions:

  (1) Select, regularly evaluate, fix the compensation of, and, where appropriate, replace the principal senior executives;

  (2) Oversee the conduct of the corporation's business to evaluate whether the business is being properly managed;

  (3) Review and, where appropriate, approve the corporation's financial objectives and major corporate plans and actions;

(4) Review and, where appropriate, approve major changes in, and determinations of other major questions of choice respecting the appropriate auditing and accounting principles and practices to be used in the preparation of the corporation's financial statements;

(5) Perform such other functions as are prescribed by law, or assigned to the board under a standard of the corporation.

(b) A board of directors also has power to:

(1) Initiate and adopt corporate plans, commitments, and actions;

(2) Initiate and adopt changes in accounting principles and practices;

(3) Provide advice and counsel to the principal senior executives;

(4) Instruct any committee, principal senior executive, or other officer and review the actions of any committee, principal senior executive, or other officer;

(5) Make recommendations to shareholders;

(6) Manage the business of the corporation;

(7) Act as to all other corporate matters not requiring shareholder approval.

Why is § 3.02 limited to publicly-held corporations?

5. Who serves as a director of a small, closely held corporation? Do you think that Miles D. White or Richard H. Lenny serves as a director of a small, closely held corporation? Or Enrique Hernandez? What do the directors of a small, closely held corporation do? Does a small, closely held corporation even need a board of directors? *Cf.* MBCA § 7.32; Delaware §§ 350, 351.

6. What decisions do you think the McDonald's board of directors actually makes? Consider whether the McDonald's board of directors would have a role in the following corporate decisions:

● Personnel: (a) Whether to hire Bill Clinton as president and chief executive officer of McDonald's? (b) Whom to hire as interns in the executive office?

● Operations: (a) Whether to close all McDonald's outlets to observe the Sabbath? (b) Whether to close the McDonald's store in the Student Union at the University of Alabama?

● Acquisitions: (a) Whether to diversify by acquiring a chain of aerobic dance studios? (b) Whether to acquire Bubba's Burritos?

————

If the board of directors does not make these decisions, who does?

The MBCA and other corporation laws contemplate that a corporation will have not only a board of directors but also officers. MBCA §§ 8.40 and 8.41 permit every corporation to designate in its bylaws what officers it will have and what their duties will be. Compare Delaware § 142.

The duties of an officer of a corporation are affected not only by state corporation law and that corporation's bylaws but also by agency law. While a member of the board of directors of a corporation is not an agent of the corporation, an officer is. *See generally* Franklin Gevurtz, CORPORA-TION LAW 181–86 ("Resolution of such disputes [over the authority of an officer of a corporation] entails the application of basic rules of agency law to the corporate setting. For the most part, agents have the power to bind their principal based upon either actual or apparent authority.") As you will recall, we discussed some agency principles in Chapter 2, Section (B)(1).

PROBLEMS: CORPORATE DECISION-MAKING

1. You receive a letter from V, a Vice President–Legal of McDonald's Corporation, offering you a position as staff attorney. Does that letter obligate McDonald's to hire you? What if the letter is signed by S, who identifies himself as "Senior Attorney"?

2. Your client, First Bank, is making a substantial loan to Bubba's Burritos, Inc. The loan officer calls and asks who should sign the loan for Bubba's Burritos, Inc.:

    A. Capel, who owns 51% of the outstanding stock?

    B. Propp, who is a director?

    C. Agee, who is the corporation's president?

3. The board of directors selects officers.* *See* MBCA § 8.40(b), Delaware § 142(b). Can the directors agree to select each other as officers? What if a director does not do what she agreed to do? Assume, for example, that Agee, Capel, and Propp, the three directors of Bubba's Burritos, Inc., agree that each will vote for Agee for President and for Capel for treasurer. At the next board of directors meeting, Propp and Capel vote for Propp for president. Can Agee enforce the voting agreement?

The following case will help us answer the questions in the preceding note. In reading it, consider the following:

1. Who were the contracting parties?

2. What were the terms of their deal?

McQUADE v. STONEHAM

New York Court of Appeals, 1934
189 N.E. 234

POUND, CHIEF JUDGE. The action is brought to compel specific perform-ance of an agreement between the parties, entered into to secure the

---

* In a few states the shareholders can be empowered to select and remove the officers. Such authority must be put in the articles, however. *See, e.g.,* New York §§ 715(b) & (c).

control of National Exhibition Company, also called the Baseball Club (New York Nationals or "Giants"). This was one of Stoneham's enterprises which used the New York polo grounds for its home games. McGraw was manager of the Giants. McQuade was at the time the contract was entered into a city magistrate. * * *

Defendant Stoneham became the owner of 1,306 shares, or a majority of the stock of National Exhibition Company. Plaintiff and defendant McGraw each purchased 70 shares of his stock. Plaintiff paid Stoneham $50,338.10 for the stock he purchased. As a part of the transaction, the agreement in question was entered into. It was dated May 21, 1919. Some of its pertinent provisions are:

VIII.   The parties hereto will use their best endeavors for the purpose of continuing as directors of said Company and as officers thereof the following:

Directors:

Charles A. Stoneham,

John J. McGraw,

Francis X. McQuade

— with the right to the party of the first part [Stoneham] to name all additional directors as he sees fit:

Officers:

Charles A. Stoneham, President,

John J. McGraw, Vice–President,

Francis X. McQuade, Treasurer.

IX.   No salaries are to be paid to any of the above officers or directors, except as follows:

President....................... $45,000
Vice–President..................... 7,500
Treasurer 7,500

X.   There shall be no change in said salaries, no change in the amount of capital, or the number of shares, no change or amendment of the by-laws of the corporation or any matters regarding the policy of the business of the corporation or any matters which may in anywise affect, endanger or interfere with the rights of minority stockholders, excepting upon the mutual and unanimous consent of all of the parties hereto. * * *

XIV.   This agreement shall continue and remain in force so long as the parties or any of them or the representative of any, own the stock referred to in this agreement, to wit, the party of the first part, 1,166 shares, the party of the second part 70 shares and the party of the third part 70 shares, except as may otherwise appear by this agreement. * * *

In pursuance of this contract Stoneham became president and McGraw vice president of the corporation. McQuade became treasurer. In

June 1925, his salary was increased to $10,000 a year. He continued to act until May 2, 1928, when Leo J. Bondy was elected to succeed him. The board of directors consisted of seven men. The four outside of the parties hereto were selected by Stoneham and he had complete control over them. At the meeting of May 2, 1928, Stoneham and McGraw refrained from voting, McQuade voted for himself, and the other four voted for Bondy. Defendants did not keep their agreement with McQuade to use their best efforts to continue him as treasurer. On the contrary, he was dropped with their entire acquiescence. At the next stockholders' meeting he was dropped as a director although they might have elected him.

The courts below have refused to order the reinstatement of McQuade, but have given him damages for wrongful discharge, with a right to sue for future damages.

The cause for dropping McQuade was due to the falling out of friends. McQuade and Stoneham had disagreed. The trial court has found in substance that their numerous quarrels and disputes did not affect the orderly and efficient administration of the business of the corporation; that plaintiff was removed because he had antagonized the dominant Stoneham by persisting in challenging his power over the corporate treasury and for no misconduct on his part. The court also finds that plaintiff was removed by Stoneham for protecting the corporation and its minority stockholders. We will assume that Stoneham put him out when he might have retained him, merely in order to get rid of him.

Defendants say that the contract in suit was void because the directors held their office charged with the duty to act for the corporation according to their best judgment and that any contract which compels a director to vote to keep any particular person in office and at a stated salary is illegal. Directors are the exclusive executive representatives of the corporation, charged with administration of its internal affairs and the management and use of its assets. They manage the business of the corporation. * * *

Although it has been held that an agreement among stockholders whereby it is attempted to divest the directors of their power to discharge an unfaithful employee of the corporation is illegal as against public policy, it must be equally true that the stockholders may not, by agreement among themselves, control the directors in the exercise of the judgment vested in them by virtue of their office to elect officers and fix salaries. Their motives may not be questioned so long as their acts are legal. The bad faith or the improper motives of the parties does not change the rule. Directors may not by agreements entered into as stockholders abrogate their independent judgment.

Stockholders may, of course, combine to elect directors. That rule is well settled. As Holmes, C. J., pointedly said (Brightman v. Bates, 55 N. E. 809, 811 [1900]): "If stockholders want to make their power felt, they must unite. There is no reason why a majority should not agree to keep together." The power to unite is, however, limited to the election of directors and is not extended to contracts whereby limitations are placed on the power of directors to manage the business of the corporation by the selection of agents at defined salaries.

The minority shareholders whose interests McQuade says he has been punished for protecting, are not, aside from himself, complaining about his discharge. He is not acting for the corporation or for them in this action. It is impossible to see how the corporation has been injured by the substitution of Bondy as treasurer in place of McQuade. * * *

It is urged that we should pay heed to the morals and manners of the market place to sustain this agreement and that we should hold that its violation gives rise to a cause of action for damages rather than base our decision on any outworn notions of public policy. Public policy is a dangerous guide in determining the validity of a contract and courts should not interfere lightly with the freedom of competent parties to make their own contracts. We do not close our eyes to the fact that such agreements, tacitly or openly arrived at, are not uncommon, especially in close corporations where the stockholders are doing business for convenience under a corporate organization. We know that majority stockholders, united in voting trusts, effectively manage the business of a corporation by choosing trustworthy directors to reflect their policies in the corporate management. Nor are we unmindful that McQuade has, so the court has found, been shabbily treated as a purchaser of stock from Stoneham. We have said: "A trustee is held to something stricter than the morals of the market place" (Meinhard v. Salmon, 249 N. Y. 458, 464 [1928]), but Stoneham and McGraw were not trustees for McQuade as an individual. Their duty was to the corporation and its stockholders, to be exercised according to their unrestricted lawful judgment. They were under no legal obligation to deal righteously with McQuade if it was against public policy to do so.

The courts do not enforce mere moral obligations, nor legal ones either, unless someone seeks to establish rights which may be waived by custom and for convenience. We are constrained by authority to hold that a contract is illegal and void so far as it precludes the board of directors, at the risk of incurring legal liability, from changing officers, salaries, or policies or retaining individuals in office, except by consent of the contracting parties. On the whole, such a holding is probably preferable to one which would open the courts to pass on the motives of directors in the lawful exercise of their trust.

A further reason for reversal exists. At the time the contract was made the plaintiff was a city magistrate. * * *

The Inferior Criminal Courts Act (Laws of 1910, c. 659, as amended) provides that no "city magistrate shall engage in any other business." * * *

The judgment of the Appellate Division and that of the Trial Term should be reversed and the complaint dismissed, with costs in all courts.

QUESTIONS

1. Would the court have decided this case differently if the contract had been between McQuade and the National Exhibition Company, and that contract had provided that McQuade would serve as treasurer of the company for five years?

2. Would the court have decided this case differently if McQuade, Stoneham, and McGraw were the only stockholders of the corporation and the agreement provided that McQuade would be retained as treasurer so long as he "was faithful, efficient and competent"?

3. Would the court have decided this case differently if MBCA § 7.32 applied? *See* MBCA §§ 7.32(a)(1), (3), 7.32(b)(1). What about Delaware § 350?

2. SHAREHOLDERS' DECISIONS INSTEAD OF DIRECTORS' DECISIONS

The New York Court of Appeals had misgivings about some of the language it used in *McQuade*. Just two years later, in Clark v. Dodge, 199 N.E. 641 (N.Y. 1936), that court upheld an agreement and stated: "The broad statements in the *McQuade* opinion, applicable to the facts there, should be confined to the facts there."

In New York today, "the broad statements in the *McQuade* opinion" would not even be applicable to "the facts there." New York has adopted a statute that permits shareholders of corporations with relatively few shareholders (usually called "close" or "closely held" corporations) to enter into agreements controlling board decisions.*

Indeed, now many states have such statutes (as mentioned in Question 3 directly above, these states include both Delaware and all the states that have adopted the MBCA). The next case considers the effect of the Maine statute on an agreement between two shareholders. Their agreement was that the corporation could not pay either of them a salary. In reading the case, please consider the following questions:

---

* New York Business Corporation Law § 620:

"(a) An agreement between two or more shareholders, if in writing and signed by the parties thereto, may provide that in exercising any voting rights, the shares held by them shall be voted as therein provided, or as they may agree, or as determined in accordance with a procedure agreed upon by them.

(b) A provision in the certificate of incorporation otherwise prohibited by law because it improperly restricts the board in its management of the business of the corporation, or improperly transfers to one or more shareholders or to one or more persons or corporations to be selected by him or them, all or any part of such management otherwise within the authority of the board under this chapter, shall nevertheless be valid:

(1) If all the incorporators or holders of record of all outstanding shares, whether or not having voting power, have authorized such provision in the certificate of incorporation or an amendment thereof; and

(2) If, subsequent to the adoption of such provision, shares are transferred or issued only to persons who had knowledge or notice thereof or consented in writing to such provision.

(c) A provision authorized by paragraph (b) shall be valid only so long as no shares of the corporation are listed on a national securities exchange or regularly quoted in an over-the-counter market by one or more members of a national or affiliated securities association."

1.   Was there an oral agreement that the corporation would not pay a salary to either Villar or Kernan?

2.   Was that agreement breached? By whom—Kernan? The corporation? Both? Which one is Villar suing?

3.   Were Villar and Kernan directors of the corporation when they made that agreement? Is that relevant?

4.   Were Villar and Kernan directors of the corporation when the corporation agreed to pay Kernan consulting fees? (We will see the possible relevance of this question later in the course.)

VILLAR v. KERNAN

Supreme Court of Maine, 1997
695 A.2d 1221

DANA, JUSTICE. The United States District Court for the District of Maine has certified the following questions of state law to this Court:

> (1) Does Maine law preclude an action for breach of an oral contract between two shareholders of a closely held corporation prohibiting their receipt of salaries from the corporation?

> (2) If the answer to the first question is "no," what factors are to be considered in determining whether specific performance is available to take an oral contract outside the statute of frauds provision for contracts not to be performed within one year?

The United States District Court has prepared a statement of findings of facts. These facts disclose that in 1988 Frederick Villar and Peter Kernan agreed to go into the brick oven pizza business. Villar was responsible for operating the new business and Kernan assumed responsibility for the business's finances. When Villar and Kernan incorporated their business as Ricetta's, Inc., Villar received 49 percent of the shares and Kernan received 51 percent. * * * [T]he parties agreed that "there would never be salaries. In other words, as owners [they] would never get salaries, just distribution." At some point Ronald Stephan, the manager of the restaurant, became a two percent shareholder of Ricetta's, Inc., obtaining one percent from both Kernan and Villar.

The parties' pizza restaurant succeeded as a business but their relationship deteriorated. Villar and Stephan attempted to buy Kernan out, but the buyout was unsuccessful and ultimately Stephan became allied with Kernan.

In March 1994 Kernan entered into a "so-called consulting agreement" with Ricetta's. The agreement provided for automatic payments to him of $2,000 per week. The agreement was ratified at a shareholders' and board of directors' meeting at which Villar was not present. Kernan's obligations pursuant to the agreement were not specified, but the corporation's rights were restricted. For example, Kernan's compensation could be increased but not decreased by a majority vote of the board of directors, and his services could be terminated only for criminal violation involving dishonesty, fraud, breach of trust, or for willful engagement in misconduct in the performance of his duties. Pursuant to the agreement Kernan received $90,000 in consulting fees in 1994 and $24,000 in early 1995.

In May 1995 Villar filed a complaint in the United States District Court asserting six counts against four defendants. On Kernan's motion for a judgment on the pleadings or for a summary judgment, the court dismissed all of Villar's claims except the breach of contract claim against Kernan. A nonjury trial on Villar's breach of contract claim was held in August 1996. The court concluded that there was an oral agreement between Villar and Kernan that prohibited Kernan from receiving a salary from Ricetta's. The court determined that unless 13–A M.R.S.A. § 618 (1981)* **[1]** precluded the enforcement of an oral shareholder agreement,

---

* **[1]** 13–A M.R.S.A. § 618 provides:

Agreements among shareholders respecting management of corporation and relations of shareholders

1. No written agreement, whether contained in the articles of incorporation or bylaws or in a written side agreement, and which relates to any phase of the affairs of the corporation, including, but not limited to, the following:

A. Management of the business of the corporation; or

B. Declaration and payment of dividends or division of profits; or

C. Who shall be officers or directors, or both, of the corporation; or

D. Voting requirements, including requirements for unanimous voting of shareholders or directors; or

E. Employment of shareholders by the corporation; or

F. Arbitration of issues as to which the stockholders are deadlocked in voting power or as to which the directors are deadlocked and the shareholders are unable to break the deadlock; or

G. Which purports to treat the affairs of the corporation as if it were a partnership and the shareholders as if they were partners,

shall be deemed invalid because the agreement contains any such provision, or because it limits or restricts the powers or discretion of the directors of the corporation, or because it transfers to one or more shareholders or to one or more persons or corporations to be selected by him or them all or part of the management of the corporation, if the following conditions are satisfied:

A. Either the agreement is set forth, or its existence is clearly referred to, in the articles of incorporation, and if in an amendment of the articles, such amendment was adopted by the unanimous vote of all outstanding shares, whether or not entitled to vote by the provisions of the articles; or the agreement has been expressly assented to in writing by all shareholders of the corporation, whether or not entitled to vote; and

B. Subsequent to the making of the agreement or its adoption in the articles or bylaws, shares are transferred or issued only to persons who have notice or actual knowledge thereof, or assent in writing thereto.

2. Notwithstanding a failure to satisfy the conditions set out in subsection 1, paragraphs A and B, such an agreement shall be valid and enforceable between the parties thereto, and their assignees and successors who have notice thereof, unless it is affirmatively shown that its enforcement would be prejudicial to the rights of third parties who intervene in objection to its enforcement.

3. To the extent that it contains provisions which would not be valid but for subsection 1, an agreement authorized by subsection 1 shall be valid only so long as no shares of the corporation are traded on any national securities exchange or regularly quoted in any over-the-counter market by one or more members of a national or affiliated securities association.

4. The text of any agreement authorized by subsection 1 shall be set forth in full, or a conspicuous reference shall be made to the agreement, upon the face or back of each certificate for shares issued by the corporation.

the agreement could be enforceable in equity despite the statute of frauds. Finding no controlling precedent in Maine regarding section 618 or the factors the court should consider when determining whether enforcement of an oral agreement within the statute of frauds is appropriate, the court certified the two questions. We answer the first question in the affirmative and, therefore, do not address the second question. * * *

Section 618 operates to validate agreements that would be unenforceable under traditional notions of acceptable corporate practice.* **[2]** In short, the statute provides that written agreements between shareholders are enforceable even if they (1) relate to a phase of affairs of the corporation, such as the management of the corporation, payment of dividends, or employment of shareholders, (2) restrict director discretion, or (3) transfer management duties to shareholders, as long as such agreements satisfy certain conditions. 13–A M.R.S.A. § 618(1). Specifically, the agreement must be included in the articles of incorporation or expressly assented to by all shareholders, and after the agreement is made anyone who acquires shares must have notice or actual knowledge of the agreement. § 618(1)(A),(B). Even if those specific requirements are not met, however, the agreement may still be enforceable between the parties to the agreement if the rights of any third parties who intervene and object to the enforcement of the agreement are not prejudiced. § 618(2).

Kernan contends that the language in the first sentence of section 618(1) implies that shareholder agreements validated by section 618 must be in writing. We agree. Because the language of subsection (1) refers to written agreements between shareholders, stating that "[n]o written agreement will be invalid ...", it is logical to conclude that the Legislature intended to validate only written agreements that meet the requirements of the statute. To conclude otherwise would nullify the word "written" in the opening sentence of that subsection.

Villar argues that the parties' agreement is simply an agreement between shareholders that does not affect the corporation and that it need not rely on section 618's validation provision for its validity. We disagree. Their agreement affects the corporation's affairs because it effectively

---

5. A transferee of shares in a corporation whose shareholders have entered into an agreement authorized by subsection 1 shall be deemed to have notice thereof if the text of the agreement was set forth, or if the agreement was conspicuously noted, on the face or back of the certificate for such shares when he took them.

6. The effect of an agreement authorized by subsection 1 shall be to relieve the director or directors of, and to impose upon the shareholders consenting to the agreement, the liability for managerial acts or omissions that is imposed by law upon directors to the extent that and so long as the discretion or powers of the directors in their management of corporate affairs is controlled by any such provision.

* **[2]** * * * Section 618 was enacted at a time when shareholder agreements were viewed by courts as unenforceable infringements on traditional corporate structure and control. Other states were also enacting laws that ensured such agreements would be enforced by the courts. See also Model Business Corporation Act § 7.32, 2 Model Business Corporation Act Annotated 7–245 (1996) ("In the past, various types of shareholder agreements were invalidated by courts for a variety of reasons.... Rather than relying on further uncertain and sporadic development of the law in the courts, [the validation provision of] section 7.32 ... adds an important element of predictability....").

prohibits the corporation from hiring Kernan as a consultant. We are not persuaded by Villar's characterization of the agreement, asserted at oral argument, as one that would allow the corporation to hire Kernan but then require him to pay Villar half of the salary that he received from the corporation. Such an interpretation would effectively rewrite the parties' agreement.

Kernan contends that the agreement at issue falls within the reach of section 618's validation provision because it relates to the affairs of the corporation by affecting the employment of shareholders. We agree. The potential scope of the validation provision of section 618 is broad. It states that an agreement is not invalid because it "relates to any phase of affairs of the corporation, including, but not limited to ... [e]mployment of shareholders by the corporation...." § 618(1)(E). The agreement between Villar and Kernan relates to the corporation's affairs because it prohibits Kernan from receiving a salary and effectively precludes his employment by the corporation. In addition, the agreement may affect the declaration and payment of dividends because money that is not distributed to Kernan in a salary may be distributed as dividends among the three shareholders. § 618(1)(B). Because the agreement must rely on section 618 for its validity and falls within the validating provision of section 618(1), it must meet the section's specifications and therefore must be in writing to be enforceable.* **[3]**

Subsection (2) of section 618 does not allow enforcement of the agreement at issue here because that subsection does not excuse the requirement in subsection (1) that the agreement be in writing to be validated. Subsection (2) provides that "[n]otwithstanding a failure to satisfy the conditions set out in subsection 1, paragraphs A and B, such an agreement shall be valid and enforceable between the parties thereto * * * unless it is affirmatively shown that its enforcement would be prejudicial to the rights of third parties * * *." Although subsection (2) reflects an intent to allow enforcement of shareholder agreements despite their failure to comply with the formalities of subsection (1), the language of the subsection does not excuse the writing requirement specified in the first sentence of that subsection. Thus, only written agreements that fail to meet the requirements of subsection (1) may be enforceable among the parties to the agreement by virtue of subsection (2).

Because we conclude that to be enforceable section 618 requires a shareholder agreement prohibiting the shareholders' receipt of salaries from the corporation to be in writing, we answer the first certified question in the affirmative and do not answer the second question.

---

* **[3]** We do not interpret section 618 to provide only a safe harbor for certain agreements that would be invalid pursuant to other provisions of the Maine Business Corporation Act or the common law. Rather, we conclude that an agreement that affects the corporation in a way addressed by section 618(1) must meet the specifications of 618 to be valid, and we need not first determine whether the agreement would be invalid pursuant to the Act or the common law.* * *

1.   What was the agreement "that would be unenforceable under traditional notions of acceptable corporate practice?"

2.   Would the court have decided this case differently if the agreement between Villar and Kernan had been in writing?

3.   Would the court have decided this case differently if the MBCA § 7.32 had applied? What about Delaware §§ 350 and 351?

4.   Eighteen states (including California, Delaware (§ 342), and Texas) have special statutes for close corporations. In these states, only shareholders of corporations that have qualified as a "close corporation" can, by agreement, control or otherwise limit the discretion of the board of directors. See generally Franklin Gevurtz, CORPORATION LAW 505–11.

Most people use the terms "close" or "closely held" corporation to refer to a corporation with relatively few shareholders, the stock of which is not publicly traded, regardless of whether the corporation was incorporated in one of the eighteen states with a special close corporation statute.

5.   What can Villar do now? He is a shareholder in a corporation that has only a few shareholders, and he has no control over that corporation's decisions. What could Villar have done if the business had been structured as a partnership?

In a sense, Villar is like the plaintiff in cases that we have considered earlier such as *A.P. Smith* and *McQuade*. We will continue to explore the rights and remedies of a minority shareholder in a closely held corporation. The first question for the next part of this chapter is the easier and narrower question of why Villar was not a director at the time of the Ricetta's consulting agreement with Kernan.*

3.   SHAREHOLDERS' DECISIONS ABOUT DIRECTORS AND CUMULATIVE VOTING

As we have seen in *McQuade* and *Villar*, one person can wear several hats simultaneously. One person can be (1) a director, (2) an officer, and (3) a shareholder. Such a person plays a different role and is subject to different rules depending upon whether she is acting as a (1) a director, (2) an officer or (3) a shareholder.

One role of a shareholder is making decisions about directors. Shareholders elect directors. *See* Delaware § 211(b); MBCA § 8.03(c). And shareholders remove directors. *See* Delaware § 141(k); MBCA § 8.08.

Of course, in a large, publicly-held corporation, the role of most shareholders in electing and removing directors is of little practical consequence. They own too few shares to have any impact. The shareholders in a position to call the shots will usually be other corporations that own many shares, such as a parent corporation or mutual funds or pension funds.

---

* Ricetta's, Inc. had three directors: Kernan, Stephan and James E. Kelley. Villar v. Ricetta's, Inc., 1996 WL 118519 (D. Me. 1996).

In a small, closely held corporation, several of the shareholders can have the power to elect or remove directors. That is especially true if the state corporate code or the corporation's articles of incorporation provide for "cumulative voting" or if the shareholders have entered into a voting agreement.

Corporate lawyers (and corporate law students) need to understand the difference between cumulative voting and "straight voting." At a meeting to elect directors under straight voting, there is a separate election for each seat on the board. Each shareholder gets to cast her number of shares in any way she desires for each of these separate elections.

Assume Bubba's Burritos, Inc. has five directors and three shareholders—Capel (who owns 50 shares), Propp (who owns 30 shares), and Agee (who owns the other 10 shares). In electing the director for Seat 1 on the board, Capel has 50 votes, Propp has 30 votes and Agee has 10 votes. Obviously, then, Capel can elect her candidate for that seat—her 50 votes for that candidate will be more than Propp and Agee can muster for another candidate. In electing the director for Seat 2 on the board, the same thing will happen—Capel has 50 votes, Propp has 30, and Agee has 10. And so on for the remaining seats. A shareholder owning a majority of the stock will be able to elect every director.

With cumulative voting, however, directors are not elected seat-by-seat. There is one at-large election in which the shareholders cast votes and, on our example here, the top five vote-getters would be elected to the board (because Bubba's has five directors in this hypo). In voting, however, here the shareholders get to "cumulate." This means that each gets to multiply the number of shares she owns times the number of directors to be elected.

Under this scheme, Capel has 250 votes (50 shares multiplied by five directors to be elected at the meeting). Propp has 150 votes (30 shares multiplied by five directors to be elected at the meeting). Agee has 50 votes (10 shares multiplied by five directors to be elected at the meeting). Each shareholder can allocate her votes as she sees fit, and the top five recipients of votes are elected. If Propp and Agee vote intelligently,* cumulative voting will enable them to elect two of the five directors.

Cumulative voting does not apply to all shareholder votes. It applies only to shareholders' election of or removal of directors. Moreover, not all corporations use cumulative voting even for such matters. In some states, cumulative voting is required for all corporations, sometimes by statute and sometimes, as in Arizona, by state constitution. However, in most states, by statute the corporation can choose whether to have cumulative voting.

These states split into two camps, however, over what the "default" provision should be. In other words, if the articles say nothing about

---

* Using cumulative voting "intelligently" can be complicated. *See generally* Lewis R. Mills, *Mathematics of Cumulative Voting*, 1968 DUKE L.J. 28.

cumulative voting, does it exist? In some states, cumulative voting exists unless the articles take it away. In others, cumulative voting does not exist unless the articles affirmatively grant it.

Compare MBCA § 7.28(b) with Delaware § 214.

Many corporations choose not to employ cumulative voting. Why would a corporation make this choice?

PROBLEMS: CUMULATIVE VOTING

1. Agee, Capel, and Propp come to you to incorporate Bubba's Burritos, Inc. You explain cumulative voting to them. They ask you whether you recommend cumulative voting. How do you answer their question?

2. Villar, a 48% shareholder of Ricetta's, Inc., was not a director at the time of Ricetta's consulting agreement with Kernan. Do you think Ricetta's, Inc. had cumulative voting?

3. If cumulative voting is in effect, this formula calculates the number of shares needed for a shareholder to elect various numbers of directors:

$$[(N \times S) / (D+1)] + 1$$

N = number of directors the shareholder wants to elect

S = total number of shares voting

D = total number of directors to be chosen at the election

3.1 Assume there are nine directors to be elected to the board of Bubba's Burritos, Inc., and that the corporation has 1000 outstanding shares (all of which will be voted at the meeting). Cumulative voting is in effect. You are a shareholder and want to elect Epstein to the board. How many shares do you need to ensure that Epstein will be elected to the board? How many shares do you need to elect two directors, rather than just one?

3.2 Suppose now the board consists of only three directors. How many shares would be needed to elect Epstein?

3.3 What do the answers to these two hypotheticals tell you about the effect of a "staggered" board, in which only a fraction (usually one-third) of the entire board is elected each year? If you were interested in continuity on the board, why would you prefer a staggered board?

4. Questions about removal of directors.

4.1 On what basis or bases can shareholders vote to remove a director from office before her term expires? Compare Delaware § 141(k) with MBCA § 8.08. Can you see how the provisions protect cumulative voting? They provide identical bases for removal except if there is a staggered board. What is the difference if there is a staggered board?

4.2 Some states have oddly restrictive provisions about removal of directors. In New York, for instance, a director can be removed only for cause. She can be removed without cause only if the articles (which New York calls the "certificate") provide. *See* New York § 706.

4.3   Assume that Bubba's Burritos has three directors and 3000 shares entitled to vote, and it uses cumulative voting. Two thousand shares are represented at a meeting called for the purpose of removing a director. How many of the 2000 shares represented at the meeting would have to vote for removal to effect removal under Delaware law? Under the MBCA?

4. SHAREHOLDERS' VOTING ON DIRECTORS' DECISIONS ON "FUNDAMENTAL CORPORATE CHANGES"

Shareholders' voting is not limited to the election and removal of directors. The MBCA and other corporation statutes identify certain "fundamental corporate changes"* that require shareholder approval. These are truly profound changes in the life of the corporation, and generally include such things as: (1) amendment of the articles of incorporation; (2) dissolution; (3) merger with another corporation; and (4) sale of all or substantially all of the assets of the corporation. Because these sorts of things are not routine business decisions, the corporation codes do not leave them entirely to the board of directors. The shareholders are given a voice.

Note, however, that the shareholders' voting on these fundamental corporate changes differs from shareholders' voting on directors in three important respects. First, a shareholder vote on election or removal of directors is a shareholder decision, a shareholder *action*. In contrast, a shareholder vote on a merger or other fundamental corporate change is approval or disapproval of a board of directors' decision, a shareholder *reaction* to board of directors' action.

Second, there may be a supermajority approval requirement in either the state's corporation code or the corporation's articles for fundamental corporate changes. Third, there is no cumulative voting on fundamental corporate changes. Cumulative voting is limited to the election and removal of directors.

We will study fundamental corporate changes in more detail later (particularly in Chapter 8). For now let's focus on the mechanics of shareholder voting. Before doing so, though, reflect on the fact that shareholders have a very limited voice in corporate affairs—they elect and remove directors and they have to approve fundamental corporate changes. On other management decisions, however, the power lies in the board. That is one of the earmarks of a corporation—the separation of ownership from management. Often shareholders consider this a great benefit. In a corporation, the shareholder can be a "passive" investor, free from management responsibilities.

---

* Although the term "fundamental corporate changes" is used in cases and in commentary, it is used infrequently in corporation codes.

5. WHERE SHAREHOLDERS VOTE, AND WHO VOTES

Whether the shareholder vote is on directors or a fundamental corporate change, lawyers (and law students) need to be able to answer the questions relating to where shareholders vote, who votes, and how they can vote. This understanding requires mastery of the following terms: (1) annual meeting, (2) special meeting, (3) record owner, (4) record date, (5) street name, and (6) proxy.

An "annual meeting" is a meeting that is held annually. (Some corporate law concepts are easier than others.) *See, e.g.,* Delaware § 211(b); MBCA § 7.01. Any other meeting of shareholders is a "special meeting." *See, e.g.,* Delaware § 211(d); MBCA § 7.02.

The person who has the legal right to vote at an annual or special meeting of shareholders is the "record owner." The meaning of the phrase "record owner" is almost as obvious as the meaning of the phrases "annual meeting" and "special meeting." A corporation keeps records showing who owns its stock, i.e., the "record owners." The corporation is required to send notice of annual meetings and special meetings to its record shareholders. *See* Delaware § 213(a) and MBCA §§ 7.05 and 7.20(a).

This presents obvious practical questions for a corporation whose stock is regularly resold by its shareholders. Who gets the notice of the meeting? Who gets to vote at the meeting? "The record owner at the record date" is the answer to these questions: the corporation can fix a "record date" before the meeting, and only the record owners *as of that date* are entitled to notice of and a vote at the meeting. *See* Delaware § 213(a) and MBCA § 7.07(a), (b).

Often the person listed as owner on the corporation's records (the record owner) is not the real owner (the "beneficial owner"). An investor buying shares of a publicly traded corporation usually buys her shares through a broker, not from the issuing corporation.* She does not receive a stock certificate; she is not shown as the owner in the corporation's records. Instead, a depository company, maintained by a group of brokerage firms, holds the certificate and is shown as the owner in the corporation's records. The investor is shown as the owner in the *brokerage firm's* records. This is commonly referred to as "street name ownership."

A combination of stock exchange rules and Securities and Exchange Commission rules ensures that when stock is held in street name, the beneficial owner is informed about shareholder votes, and the shares are voted as instructed by the beneficial shareholder. You will consider these rules in great detail if you take an advanced course in securities regulation. For present purposes, consider the following problems:

---

* Accordingly, such a purchase is not an "issuance," and the various issuance rules (including par value) that we saw in section (B)(4) of Chapter 4 do not apply.

PROBLEMS: VOTING

1. Delaware § 213(a) and MBCA § 7.07(b) introduce the concept of the "record date," which is an administrative convenience for determining who gets to vote at an upcoming meeting. Read those statutes and address these hypotheticals:

1.1 Bubba's Burritos will hold its annual shareholder meeting on June 30. What is the latest date the corporation can use as its record date under the two statutes? What is the earliest date?

1.2 The corporation sets a record date of June 8. Capel, who owns 40% of the outstanding stock of Bubba's Burritos, Inc., sells her stock to Shepherd on June 10. Who votes the stock at the annual meeting?

1.3. Same facts as Question 1.2 except Capel transfers her stock to Shepherd on June 7. Who votes the stock at the annual meeting?

2. The board of directors of Bubba's Burritos, Inc. decides that the Bubba's Burritos' restaurants will sell Gefilte Fish Parmesan* instead of burritos. Do the shareholders have to approve this change in the corporation's basic business?

3. Your client, First Bank, is making a significant loan to Bubba's Burritos, Inc. The loan officer asks you whether the Bank will or should have a right to vote on Bubba's Burritos business decisions. Is the following excerpt from an article by Judge (then professor) Easterbrook and Professor Fischel helpful?

> Voting rights are universally held by shareholders to the exclusion of bondholders, managers, and other employees. The reason, we believe, is that shareholders are the residual claimants to the firm's income. Bondholders have fixed claims, and employees generally negotiate compensation schedules in advance of performance. The gains and losses from abnormally good or bad performance are the lot of the shareholders, whose claims stand last in line. As the residual claimants, the shareholders are the group with the appropriate incentives to make discretionary decisions.

Frank Easterbrook & Daniel Fischel, VOTING IN CORPORATE LAW 395, 402 (1983).

6. WHO VOTES (AND WHAT ARE PROXIES)?

A shareholder does not have to be present at the annual or special meeting to vote her shares. State corporation statutes provide for shareholder voting by "proxy." Voting by proxy simply means that the person who is entitled to vote authorizes another person to vote for her. It is a form of agency: the owner is the principal and authorizes the proxy-holder to be her agent for voting.

Assume Roberts owns 100 shares of Bubba's Burritos stock. He gives Shepherd a proxy to vote his shares at the upcoming annual meeting. If the proxy is silent as to duration, how long is the proxy effective under Delaware law? Under the MBCA? *See* Delaware § 212(b); MBCA § 7.22.

---

* Cf. Daniel Klein & Freie Vuijst, THE HALF JEWISH BOOK (2000).

A form of proxy is set out below:

PROXY

The undersigned, as record owner of the shares of _____ Corporation described below, hereby appoints_____, as the proxy of the undersigned, to attend and vote at the (annual/special) meeting of the shareholders of _____ Corporation, to be held at _____, on _____, at _____, and to represent, vote, execute, consent, waive and otherwise act for the undersigned in the same manner and with the same effect as if the undersigned were personally present at said meeting. This proxy may be revoked at any time.

The shares represented by this proxy shall be voted in the following manner:

ACTIONS PROPOSED TO BE TAKEN

	FOR	AGAINST	WITHHOLD
Proposal No. *(Describe Proposal)*	[ ]	[ ]	[ ]
Proposal No. 2 *(Describe Proposal)*	[ ]	[ ]	[ ]

FOR ELECTION AS DIRECTOR(S)

	FOR	AGAINST	WITHHOLD
_____ *(Name)*	[ ]	[ ]	[ ]
_____ *(Name)*	[ ]	[ ]	[ ]
_____ *(Name)*	[ ]	[ ]	[ ]

IF NO INDICATION IS MADE ON HOW YOU DESIRE YOUR SHARES TO BE VOTED, THE PROXY HOLDER WILL HAVE COMPLETE DISCRETION IN VOTING THE SHARES ON ANY MATTER VOTED ON AT THE MEETING.

Number and Class of Shares Owned: _____

DATED: _____   _____

                                  Signature(s)

_____

Name(s) (typed or printed)

_____

Address(es)

Note that the proxy provides that it can be revoked. What if it were silent on revocability? Remember that we said a proxy is a form of agency: the owner of the shares consents to the proxy holder's voting the shares for her. *See* Restatement (Second) of Agency (R–2) § 1. Because agency law allows a principal to terminate an agent's authority at any time, *see* R–2 § 118, a proxy that does not address revocability will be revocable.

In fact, under case law, a proxy can often be revoked even if it states that it is *irrevocable*. Drawing again on agency principles, courts hold that a proxy is irrevocable only if it both (1) states that it is irrevocable and (2) is "coupled with some interest in the stock." *See* R–2 §§ 138, 139; MBCA § 7.22.

Assume, for example, that Capel borrows $100,000 from First Bank and pledges his Bubba's Burritos, Inc. stock as collateral for the loan. First Bank wants to be able to vote the shares and so requires that Capel execute an "irrevocable proxy." Because First Bank has an interest in the stock (the stock pledge), the proxy would be irrevocable under common law. *See also* MBCA § 7.22(d)(1)–(4) for other generally recognized examples of a proxy coupled with an interest. (Later (in subsection B(9) of this chapter) we will see MBCA § 7.22(d)(5), which deals with shareholder voting agreements. Right now, we will see the federal rules dealing with the use of proxies in publicly-held corporations.)

7.   FEDERAL PROXY RULES

If Bubba's Burritos, Inc. or some other corporation with relatively few shareholders holds a shareholders' meeting,* it is likely that most of the shareholders will attend the meeting. When, however, McDonald's or some other public corporation holds a shareholders' meeting, few of the shareholders attend the meeting. Instead, most of the shareholders of a public corporation who vote use proxies.

Because the use of proxies is so important to shareholder participation in public corporations, the Securities and Exchange Commission (SEC) has promulgated a series of rules to regulate the proxy process. More specifically, the SEC has regulated the proxy solicitation process. In this course, we will address two of these provisions: Rule 14a–9, which prohibits false or misleading statements in soliciting proxies, and Rule 14a–8, which deals with shareholder proposals.

a.   False or Misleading Statements of Fact

17 C.F.R. § 14a–9. False or misleading statements.

(a) No solicitation subject to this regulation shall be made by means of any proxy statement, form of proxy, notice of meeting or other communication, written or oral, containing any statement which, at the time and in the light of the circumstances under which it is made, is false or misleading with respect to any material fact, or which omits to state any material fact necessary in order to make the statements therein not false or misleading or necessary to correct any statement in any earlier communication with respect to the solicitation of a proxy for the same meeting or subject matter which has become false or misleading.

---

* Most state corporate statutes provide that shareholders can act without a meeting with the written consent of all shareholders. MBCA § 7.04 is representative of such provisions.

VIRGINIA BANKSHARES, INC. v. SANDBERG

United States Supreme Court, 1991
501 U.S. 1083

[Virginia Bankshares, Inc. (Petitioner) owned 85% of the stock of First American Bank of Virginia (Bank). Petitioner used what we describe later in this book as a "freeze-out merger" to acquire the other 15% of the Bank's outstanding stock for $42 a share.

Virginia law governed the merger, and Virginia law required that the merger be approved by the board of directors of both Petitioner and Bank. Although Virginia law did not require that the Bank's shareholders approve the merger since Petitioner already owned 85% of the Bank's stock, the Bank's directors nonetheless solicited the other shareholders for their proxies in favor of the merger. In the proxy solicitation, the directors stated that they had approved the merger because it gave the minority shareholders "high value" for their stock. The directors also described the $42 as a "fair price."

Plaintiff, one of the minority shareholders, refused to give her proxy. Instead, she sued for damages for violation of Rule 14a–9. And won. Well, won two of three—the United States District Court and the United States Court of Appeals for the Fourth Circuit.]

SOUTER, J. Section 14(a) of the Securities Exchange Act of 1934 authorizes the Securities and Exchange Commission (SEC) to adopt rules for the solicitation of proxies, and prohibits their violation. In *J.I. Case Co. v. Borak*, 377 U.S. 426 (1964), we first recognized an implied private right of action for the breach of § 14(a) as implemented by SEC Rule 14a–9, which prohibits the solicitation of proxies by means of materially false or misleading statements.

The questions before us are whether a statement couched in conclusory or qualitative terms purporting to explain directors' reasons for recommending certain corporate action can be materially misleading within the meaning of Rule 14a–9, and whether causation of damages compensable under § 14(a) can be shown by a member of a class of minority shareholders whose votes are not required by law or corporate bylaw to authorize the corporate action subject to the proxy solicitation. We hold that knowingly false statements of reasons may be actionable even though conclusory in form, but that respondents have failed to demonstrate the equitable basis required to extend the § 14(a) private action to such shareholders when any indication of congressional intent to do so is lacking. * * *

We consider first the actionability per se of statements of reasons, opinion, or belief. * * * That such statements may be materially significant raises no serious question. The meaning of the materiality requirement for liability under § 14(a) was discussed at some length in *TSC Industries, Inc. v. Northway, Inc.*, 426 U.S. 438 (1976), where we held a fact to be material "if there is a substantial likelihood that a reasonable shareholder would consider it important in deciding how to vote." We think there is no room to deny that a statement of belief by corporate directors about a recommended course of action, or an explanation of their reasons for recommending it, can take on just that importance. Shareholders know that directors usually have knowledge and expertness far exceeding the normal investor's resources, and the directors' perceived superiority is magnified even further by the common knowledge that state law customarily obliges them to exercise their judgment in the shareholders' interest. Naturally, then, the shareowner faced with a proxy request will think it important to know the directors' beliefs about the course they recommend and their specific reasons for urging the stockholders to embrace it.

But, assuming materiality, the question remains whether statements of reasons, opinions, or beliefs are statements "with respect to ... material fact[s]" so as to fall within the strictures of the Rule. * * *

It is no answer to argue, as petitioners do, that the quoted statement on which liability was predicated did not express a reason in dollars and cents, but focused instead on the "indefinite and unverifiable" term, "high" value, much like the similar claim that the merger's terms were "fair" to shareholders. The objection ignores the fact that such conclusory terms in a commercial context are reasonably understood to rest on a factual basis that justifies them as accurate, the absence of which renders them misleading. Provable facts either furnish good reasons to make a conclusory commercial judgment, or they count against it, and expressions of such judgments can be uttered with knowledge of truth or falsity just like more definite statements, and defended or attacked through the orthodox evidentiary process that either substantiates their underlying justifications or tends to disprove their existence. * * *

Respondents adduced evidence for just such facts in proving that the statement was misleading about its subject matter and a false expression of the directors' reasons. Whereas the proxy statement described the $42 price as offering a premium above both book value and market price, the evidence indicated that a calculation of the book figure based on the appreciated value of the Bank's real estate holdings eliminated any such premium. * * * There was, indeed, evidence of a "going concern" value for the Bank in excess of $60 per share of common stock, another fact never disclosed. However conclusory the directors' statement may have been, then, it was open to attack by garden-variety evidence, subject neither to a plaintiff's control nor ready manufacture, and there was no undue risk of open-ended liability or uncontrollable litigation in allowing respondents the opportunity for recovery on the allegation that it was misleading to call $42 "high." * * *

Under § 14(a), then, a plaintiff is permitted to prove a specific statement of reason knowingly false or misleadingly incomplete, even when stated in conclusory terms. In reaching this conclusion we have considered statements of reasons of the sort exemplified here, which misstate the speaker's reasons and also mislead about the stated subject matter (e.g., the value of the shares). A statement of belief may be open to objection only in the former respect, however, solely as a misstatement of the psychological fact of the speaker's belief in what he says. In this case, for example, the Court of Appeals alluded to just such limited falsity in observing that "the jury was certainly justified in believing that the directors did not believe a merger at $42 per share was in the minority stockholders' interest but, rather, that they voted as they did for other reasons, e.g., retaining their seats on the board."

The question arises, then, whether disbelief, or undisclosed belief or motivation, standing alone, should be a sufficient basis to sustain an action under § 14(a), absent proof by the sort of objective evidence described above that the statement also expressly or impliedly asserted something false or misleading about its subject matter. We think that proof of mere disbelief or belief undisclosed should not suffice for liability under § 14(a), and if nothing more had been required or proven in this case, we would reverse for that reason.

On the one hand, it would be rare to find a case with evidence solely of disbelief or undisclosed motivation without further proof that the statement was defective as to its subject matter. While we certainly would not hold a director's naked admission of disbelief incompetent evidence of a proxy statement's false or misleading character, such an unusual admission will not very often stand alone, and we do not substantially narrow the cause of action by requiring a plaintiff to demonstrate something false or misleading in what the statement expressly or impliedly declared about its subject.

On the other hand, to recognize liability on mere disbelief or undisclosed motive without any demonstration that the proxy statement was false or misleading about its subject would authorize § 14(a) litigation confined solely to what one skeptical court spoke of as the "impurities" of a director's "unclean heart." This, we think, would cross the line that [this Court] sought to draw. * * *

[P]etitioners argue that even if conclusory statements of reason or belief can be actionable under § 14(a), we should confine liability to instances where the proxy material fails to disclose the offending statement's factual basis. There would be no justification for holding the shareholders entitled to judicial relief, that is, when they were given evidence that a stated reason for a proxy recommendation was misleading and an opportunity to draw that conclusion themselves.

The answer to this argument rests on the difference between a merely misleading statement and one that is materially so. While a misleading statement will not always lose its deceptive edge simply by joinder with others that are true, the true statements may discredit the other one so obviously that the risk of real deception drops to nil. Since liability under § 14(a) must rest not only on deceptiveness but materiality as well (i.e., it has to be significant enough to be important to a reasonable investor deciding how to vote) petitioners are on perfectly firm ground insofar as they argue that publishing accurate facts in a proxy statement can render a misleading proposition too unimportant to ground liability.

But not every mixture with the true will neutralize the deceptive. * * * The point of a proxy statement, after all, should be to inform, not to challenge the reader's critical wits. Only when the inconsistency would exhaust the misleading conclusion's capacity to influence the reasonable shareholder would a § 14(a) action fail on the element of materiality.

Suffice it to say that the evidence invoked by petitioners in the instant case fell short of compelling the jury to find the facial materiality of the misleading statement neutralized. * * *

The second issue before us, left open in *Mills v. Electric Auto–Lite Co.*, 396 U.S. 375 (1970), is whether causation of damages compensable through the implied private right of action under § 14(a) can be demonstrated by a member of a class of minority shareholders whose votes are not required by law or corporate bylaw to authorize the transaction giving rise to the claim. *J.I. Case Co. v. Borak* did not itself address the requisites of causation, as such, or define the class of plaintiffs eligible to sue under § 14(a). * * *

Although a majority stockholder in Mills controlled just over half the corporation's shares, a two-thirds vote was needed to approve the merger proposal. After proxies had been obtained, and the merger had carried, minority shareholders brought a Borak action. The question arose whether the plaintiffs' burden to demonstrate causation of their damages traceable to the § 14(a) violation required proof that the defect in the proxy solicitation had had "a decisive effect on the voting." The Mills Court avoided the evidentiary morass that would have followed from requiring individualized proof that enough minority shareholders had relied upon the misstatements to swing the vote. Instead, it held that causation of damages by a material proxy misstatement could be established by showing that minority proxies necessary and sufficient to authorize the corporate acts had been given in accordance with the tenor of the solicitation, and the Court described such a causal relationship by calling the proxy solicitation an "essential link in the accomplishment of the transaction." In the case before it, the Court found the solicitation essential, as contrasted with one addressed to a class of minority shareholders without votes required by law or by law to authorize the action proposed, and left it for another day to decide whether such a minority shareholder could demonstrate causation.

In this case, respondents address Mills' open question by proffering two theories that the proxy solicitation addressed to them was an "essential link" under the Mills causation test. They argue, first, that a link existed and was essential simply because VBI [Petitioner] would have been unwilling to proceed with the merger without the approval manifested by the minority shareholders' proxies, which would not have been obtained without the solicitation's express misstatements and misleading omissions. On this reasoning, the causal connection would depend on a desire to avoid bad shareholder or public relations, and the essential character of the causal link would stem not from the enforceable terms of the parties' corporate relationship, but from one party's apprehension of the ill will of the other.

In the alternative, respondents argue that the proxy statement was an essential link between the directors' proposal and the merger because it was the means to satisfy a state statutory requirement of minority shareholder approval, as a condition for saving the merger from voidability resulting from a conflict of interest on the part of one of the Bank's directors, Jack Beddow, who voted in favor of the merger while also serving as a director of FABI. Under the terms of Va.Code Ann. § 13.1–691(A) (1989), minority approval after disclosure of the material facts about the transaction and the director's interest was one of three avenues to insulate the merger from later attack for conflict, the two others being ratification by the Bank's directors after like disclosure and proof that the merger was fair to the corporation. On this theory, causation would depend on the use of the proxy statement for the purpose of obtaining votes sufficient to bar a minority shareholder from commencing proceedings to declare the merger void.

Although respondents have proffered each of these theories as establishing a chain of causal connection in which the proxy statement is claimed to have been an "essential link," neither theory presents the proxy solicitation as essential in the sense of Mills' causal sequence, in which the solicitation links a directors' proposal with the votes legally required to authorize the action proposed. * * *

* * * [T]hreats of speculative claims and procedural intractability are inherent in respondents' theory of causation linked through the directors' desire for a cosmetic vote. Causation would turn on inferences about what the corporate directors would have thought and done without the minority shareholder approval unneeded to authorize action. A subsequently dissatisfied minority shareholder would have virtual license to allege that managerial timidity would have doomed corporate action but for the ostensible approval induced by a misleading statement, and opposing claims of hypothetical diffidence and hypothetical boldness on the part of directors would probably provide enough depositions in the usual case to preclude any judicial resolution short of the credibility judgments that can only come after trial. Reliable evidence would seldom exist. Directors would understand the prudence of making a few statements about plans to proceed even without minority endorsement, and discovery would be a quest for recollections of oral conversations at odds with the official pronouncements, in hopes of finding support for ex post facto guesses about how much heat the directors would have stood in the absence of minority approval. The issues would be hazy, their litigation protracted, and their resolution unreliable. Given a choice, we would reject any theory of causation that raised such prospects, and we reject this one.

The theory of causal necessity derived from the requirements of Virginia law dealing with postmerger ratification seeks to identify the essential character of the proxy solicitation from its function in obtaining the minority approval that would preclude a minority suit attacking the merger. Since the link is said to be a step in the process of barring a class of shareholders from resort to a state remedy otherwise available, this theory of causation rests upon the proposition of policy that § 14(a) should provide a federal remedy whenever a false or misleading proxy statement results in the loss under state law of a shareholder plaintiff's state remedy for the enforcement of a state right. * * *

This case does not, however, require us to decide whether § 14(a) provides a cause of action for lost state remedies, since there is no indication in the law or facts before us that the proxy solicitation resulted in any such loss. The contrary appears to be the case. Assuming the soundness of respondents' characterization of the proxy statement as materially misleading, the very terms of the Virginia statute indicate that a favorable minority vote induced by the solicitation would not suffice to render the merger invulnerable to later attack on the ground of the conflict. The statute bars a shareholder from seeking to avoid a transaction tainted by a director's conflict if, inter alia, the minority shareholders ratified the transaction following disclosure of the material facts of the transaction and the conflict. Assuming that the material facts about the merger and Beddow's interests were not accurately disclosed, the minority votes were inadequate to ratify the merger under state law, and there was no loss of state remedy to connect the proxy solicitation with harm to minority shareholders irredressable under state law. Nor is there a claim here that the statement misled respondents into entertaining a false belief that they had no chance to upset the merger, until the time for bringing suit had run out.

The judgment of the Court of Appeals is reversed.

It is so ordered.

* * *

SCALIA, J., concurring in part and concurring in the judgment. As I understand the Court's opinion, the statement "In the opinion of the Directors, this is a high value for the shares" would produce liability if in fact it was not a high value and the directors knew that. It would not produce liability if in fact it was not a high value but the directors honestly believed otherwise. The statement "The Directors voted to accept the proposal because they believe it offers a high value" would not produce liability if in fact the directors' genuine motive was quite different—except that it would produce liability if the proposal in fact did not offer a high value and the Directors knew that.

I agree with all of this. However, not every sentence that has the word "opinion" in it, or that refers to motivation for directors' actions, leads us into this psychic thicket. Sometimes such a sentence actually represents facts as facts rather than opinions—and in that event no more need be done than apply the normal rules for § 14(a) liability. I think that is the situation here. In my view, the statement at issue in this case is most fairly read as affirming separately both the fact of the Directors' opinion and the accuracy of the facts upon which the opinion was assertedly based. It reads as follows:

"The Plan of Merger has been approved by the Board of Directors because it provides an opportunity for the Bank's public shareholders to achieve a high value for their shares." App. to Pet. for Cert. 53a.

Had it read "because in their estimation it provides an opportunity, etc.", it would have set forth nothing but an opinion. As written, however, it asserts both that the board of directors acted for a particular reason and that that reason is correct. This interpretation is made clear by what immediately follows: "The price to be paid is about 30% higher than the [last traded price immediately before announcement of the proposal] . . . . [T]he $42 per share that will be paid to public holders of the common stock represents a premium of approximately 26% over the book value . . . . [T]he bank earned $24,767,000 in the year ended December 31, 1986 . . . ." Id., at 53a–54a. These are all facts that support and that are obviously introduced for the purpose of supporting—the factual truth of the "because" clause, i.e., that the proposal gives shareholders a "high value."

If the present case were to proceed, therefore, I think the normal § 14(a) principles governing misrepresentation of fact would apply.

QUESTIONS AND NOTES

1. What must a shareholder, induced by a board's opinion in a proxy solicitation, show to prove that the opinion was materially misleading? What if every member on the board admits that they did not believe the statements they included in the proxy solicitation?

2. Would the proxy solicitation have been materially misleading if the directors had omitted any mention of their "beliefs about the course they recommend[ed]"? Would a reasonable shareholder consider the directors' own opinions important in how the shareholders decide to vote?

3. We omitted a footnote from the Court's opinion that expressly left open the issue of whether scienter is a requirement for liability under Rule 14(a). Although the issue remains open, many lower courts have held that negligence is sufficient. In a recent opinion, Judge Posner emphasized that "[t]here is no required state of mind for a violation of section 14(a); a proxy solicitation that contains a misleading misrepresentation or omission violates the section even if the issuer believed in perfect good faith that there was nothing misleading in the proxy materials. * * * Section 14(a) requires proof only that the proxy solicitation was misleading, implying at worst negligence by the issuer. * * * And negligence is not a state of mind; it is a failure, whether conscious or even unavoidable (by the particular defendant, who may be below average in his ability to exercise due care), to come up to the specified standard of care." Beck v. Dobrowski, 559 F.3d 680, 682 (7th Cir. 2009).

4.   Note that there are two forms of causation that shareholders must establish: loss causation and transaction causation (or but-for causation). First, loss causation requires the shareholders to show that the transaction caused some harm to them. In *Virginia Bankshares*, the shareholders were able to show loss causation because the proxy statement induced shareholders to sell their shares at $42 per share instead of the going concern value of $60 per share. However, the shareholders were unable to prove transaction causation, which requires that the transaction depended on the proxy votes.

5.   The Court left another issue open. What if the proxy solicitation had caused the shareholders to vote for the merger and thereby they lost an otherwise available state remedy? Arguably this would satisfy the transactional causation requirement.

Proxy solicitation is not limited to management. Shareholders can solicit proxies. For example, in the summer of 2001, Sam Wyly, a Computer Associates shareholder (and hedge fund manager), solicited proxies from Computer Associates shareholders, to replace the Computer Associates board of directors. The following piece from THE NEW YORKER describes the proxy contest:

>   Now that the battle for control of the giant software company Computer Associates is over—it ended when C.A.'s current board of directors was reelected by shareholders at the company's annual meeting, last Wednesday—what I'll miss most is the big, bold headlines: the plaintive "Mr. Wyly, Please Leave Our Company Alone," the sinister "Sam Wyly Is Still Pulling the Strings," and the ever-reliable "Why is This Man Smiling?"

>   Such teasers dominated the full-page ads that Computer Associates, its employees, and its erstwhile foe, a Texas dealmaker named Sam Wyly, ran regularly during that past month and a half in the *Times* and the *Wall Street Journal*. Thousands of C.A. workers put out a manifesto, declaring of Wyly, "There is nothing he can do to gain control of us." Wyly's side, meanwhile, described Charles Wang, C.A.'s chairman and co-founder, as a parasitic money-grubber who had the board of directors in his back pocket. And the company, which spent about fifteen million dollars defending itself, depicted Wyly as a nefarious villain who was determined to "derail C.A.'s future."

>   As it happens, the fight's climax didn't live up to its advance billing. The annual meeting, held in a bleak ballroom in a hotel just off the Long Island Expressway, was more pep rally than smackdown. And Wyly himself, who many had hoped would give a Gordon Gekko-style speech denouncing C.A.'s leaders, said nothing. In a way, his work was done. His months-long campaign to toss out Wang and replace C.A.'s board of directors had already shed plenty of harsh light on the company and its executives. The shareholders knew the score.

Press accounts of Wyly usually refer to him as an "entrepreneur" or a "financier," but really he's another classic American type: the crank. Short and slight, with long grey hair and a Texas twang, Wyly is a man of many enthusiasms. In the course of a checkered but lucrative career as a buyer and seller of companies, he has run two software firms, one telecom company (which lost a hundred million dollars trying to compete with A. T. & T.), the Bonanza steakhouse chain, a chain of boutiques named after his then wife, an arts-and-crafts retailer (the industry "gorilla" according to Wyly), and, most recently, a renewable-energy firm. Last year, he won some notoriety for orchestrating a $2.5–million stealth attack on John McCain for being soft on the environment. The green knight he was fighting for? George W. Bush.

When it came to C.A., though, Wyly, who sold his company, Sterling Software, to C.A. last year, chose his target well. Over the previous five years, C.A. stock had risen just eight per cent, while the S. & P. 500 had soared eighty-five per cent. At the same time, the company's board had awarded a staggering billion-dollar bonus to its three top dogs, including Wang and Sanjay Kumar, the president and C.E.O. (A shareholder lawsuit forced them to give back a couple of hundred million.) In April of this year, Business Week said that Wang had delivered shareholders less value in return for his pay than any other executive in America (and in this category the competition is pretty stiff). Wang and his cronies seemed to view the company as a private fiefdom—and Wyly's proxy challenge as a personal affront. When Wang was asked if he'd learned anything from the proxy fight, he said, "We need to communicate better. We are not the greatest politicians and campaigners." It was as though the company's dismal performance were just a matter of bad spin.

The appearance of a rabble-rouser like Wyly, with his spirited talk of shareholders rights and the virtues of managerial accountability, was inevitable. Since the nineteen-eighties, corporate raiders and shareholder activists have forced American companies to be more attentive to people who actually own them. Most C.E.O.s know that if their stock price lags they'll get the bum's rush; "shareholder value" is now corporate America's version of "Jesus saves."

Wyly's campaign to end Wang's cushy sinecure may have failed, but at least it put C.A. on notice. In fact, Wyly seems to have found his calling, as the country's wealthiest corporate gadfly. Corporate gadflies are those people who show up at annual meetings across the country to ask annoying questions about what the managers are up to. The most famous gadfly, Lewis D. Gilbert, started his career in 1933 at a Consolidated Gas meeting and hectored corporate executives for the next sixty years. Another legend, Evelyn Y. Davis, appeared at a G.M. annual meeting dressed in a bathing suit and once said to John Reed, the Citibank C.E.O., "Let me tell you something, my dear. I've got you by the balls." But these people owned tiny stakes, and tended not to have enough money to mount serious proxy challenges. Wyly could change that. As C.A. discovered, he's rich enough, and persistent enough, to be more than just a petty annoyance. Last week, after his defeat, Wyly looked rather pleased with himself as he spoke at length about his commitment to shareholder rights. He'd seen the light, and now he was going to spread the word.

The timing is good. In the bull market, almost every executive was a genius; only the surliest of shareholders begrudged the boss his bloated pay. But in a bear market the good will evaporates. Shareholders grow restless and reach for the pitchforks. These days, C.E.O.s have more explaining to do. The question of who really owns a company—the shareholders or the brass—gets played out in big, bold type. Charles Wang may have kept his job this time. But who's smiling now?

James Surowiecki, *The Financial Page: Gadfly, Inc.*, THE NEW YORKER, September 10, 2001.

Mr. Wyly spent more than $10,000,000 of his own money on this proxy contest. One of the reasons that the proxy solicitation was so expensive for both Computer Associates and Mr. Wyly is that both had to comply with the SEC's proxy rules. While shareholders can solicit proxies, any shareholder of a public company that engages in a full-fledged proxy solicitation to elect directors and effect other changes must comply with the SEC proxy rules.

b. Shareholder Proposals

It is important to distinguish between a full-fledged proxy solicitation such as Mr. Wyly's and a shareholder proposal pursuant to Rule 14a–8 such as the shareholder proposal in the McDonald's 2001 proxy statement set out below:

> Management has been advised that a shareholder intends to present the following proposal at the Annual Meeting. The name, address and share ownership of the proponent will be furnished to any person upon oral or written request to the Company's Investor Relations Department at 1–630–623–7428, or McDonalds' Plaza, Oak Brook, Illinois 60523. The Board recommends a vote AGAINST this proposal.

> Shareholder proposal

> WHEREAS: our company's business practices in China respect human and labor rights of workers. The eleven principles below were designed to commit a company to a widely accepted and thorough set of human and labor rights standards for China. They were defined by the International Labor Organization and the United Nations Covenants on Economic, Social and Cultural Rights, and Civil, and Political Rights. They have been signed by the Chinese government and China's national laws.

(1) No goods or products produced within our company's facilities or those of suppliers shall be manufactured by bonded labor, forced labor, within prison camps or as part of reform-through-labor or reeducation-through-labor programs.

(2) Our facilities and suppliers shall adhere to wages that meet workers' basic needs, fair and decent working hours, and at a minimum, to the wage and hour guidelines provided by China's national labor laws.

(3) Our facilities and suppliers shall prohibit the use of corporal punishment, and physical, sexual or verbal abuse or harassment of workers.

(4) Our facilities and suppliers shall use production methods that do not negatively affect the worker's occupational safety and health.

(5) Our facilities and suppliers shall not call on police or military to enter their premises to prevent workers from exercising their rights.

(6) We shall undertake to promote the following freedoms among our employees and the employees of our suppliers: freedom of association and assembly, including the rights to form unions and bargain collectively; freedom of expression, and freedom from arbitrary arrest or detention.

(7) Company employees and those of our suppliers shall not face discrimination in hiring, remuneration or promotion based on age, gender, marital status, pregnancy, ethnicity or region of origin.

(8) Company employees and those of our suppliers shall not face discrimination in hiring, remuneration or promotion based on labor, political or religious activity, or on involvement in demonstrations, past records of arrests or internal exile for peaceful protest, or membership in organizations committed to non-violent social or political change.

(9) Our facilities and suppliers shall use environmentally responsible methods of production that have minimum adverse impact on land, air and water quality.

(10) Our facilities and suppliers shall prohibit child labor, at a minimum comply with guidelines on minimum age for employment within China's national labor laws.

(11) We will issue annual statements to the Human Rights for Workers in China Working Group detailing our efforts to uphold these principles and to promote these basic freedoms.

RESOLVED: Stockholders request the Board of Directors to make all possible lawful efforts to implement and/or increase activity on each of the principles named above in the People's Republic of China.

Supporting statement

As U.S. companies import more goods, consumer and shareholder concern is growing about working conditions in China that fall below basic standards of fair and humane treatment. We hope that our company can prove to be a leader in its industry and embrace these principles.

The Board's recommendation

McDonald's has a well-respected and well-recognized record and reputation for business honesty and integrity, and everyone at McDonald's shares a commitment to high standards of behavior and performance on issues of social responsibility. These values and principles serve as the cornerstone of McDonald's success. McDonald's is deeply concerned about the protection of human rights in China, and we believe our existing policies and practices in this regard in many ways surpass those raised in the proposal.*.*.*

Rule 14a–8 requires a public corporation such as McDonald's to include a shareholder's proposal and supporting statement of up to 500 words in its proxy statement. Since Ralph Nader's "Campaign GM" in the 1970's, many of these Rule 14a–8 shareholder proposals, like the human rights for China's workers proposal in the McDonald's proxy statement, involve social and political concerns.

The first and most frequent use of shareholder proposals was to effect changes in corporate governance. The most frequent and famous user of Rule 14a–8 shareholder proposals was Lewis Gilbert, whom we already met in the New Yorker article. The most frequently cited case applying Rule 14a–8, SEC v. Transamerica Corp., 163 F.2d 511 (3d Cir. 1947), required Transamerica to include in its proxy statement Lewis Gilbert's shareholder proposal that shareholders rather than directors select the company's auditors.

In resolving questions relating to Rule 14a–8, lawyers look more to SEC bulletins and no-action letters. A no-action letter is a recommendation by SEC staff that the full commission not challenge specified conduct. To avoid trouble with the SEC, a person or corporation that is considering the conduct will seek the no-action letter in advance. A no-action letter does not provide complete protection. In some circumstances, an aggrieved person could bypass the SEC and challenge the conduct directly in court. Consider, for example, the following correspondence relating to a SEC no-action letter sought by Xerox. Xerox asked that the SEC not challenge exclusion from its proxy statement of a shareholder proposal relating to replacement of all inside directors.

First, the shareholder demanded inclusion of the proposal in the company's proxy statement:

December 5, 2000

XEROX CORPORATION
ATTN: SECRETARY
P.O. BOX 1600
STAMFORD CT, 06904

Dear Madam Secretary,

In accordance with proxy rules, I want to introduce a proposal for shareholder consideration at the next annual meeting of Xerox Corporation. I am a Xerox retiree, employee number 5263, and I own 209 Xerox Convertible Preferred Shares through the ESOP program. The proposal I want to submit is as follows:

As the owners of Xerox Corporation, we, the shareholders, entrust the Board of Directors and Officers to protect and enhance our investment in Xerox. The value of our investment has declined by 90% from its previous high, reflecting a serious breach of trust The Board of Directors, dominated and influenced by employee directors, must accept responsibility for this unacceptable performance.

We recognize that the current Board of Directors cannot restore our investment; therefore, we propose the following:

- Effective immediately, all Employee Directors vacate their positions on the Board Of Directors.

- The remaining Outside Directors, within two months, will fill the vacated Director positions with outside directors using guidelines that ensure needed competencies, e.g. finance, legal, management, etc.

- When this is done, the remaining Directors will resign their positions, and the new Directors will fill those vacant positions with outside Directors.

- To ensure the potential for success this reorganization fosters, each new Director must meet the following minimum qualifications:

- None are current Officers of Xerox Corporation.

- Each new Director must directly own at least 1,000 common shares of Xerox Stock

- Each new Director must state an unequivocal willingness to take an active role in the management of Xerox Corporation.

Madam Secretary, if there are any additional requirements I must meet to offer this proposal, please advise at your earliest opportunity.

Sincerely,
James D. Lehner

The company sought a no-action letter as follows:

Xerox Corporation, SEC
Publicly Available March 9, 2001

January 12, 2001

OFFICE OF CHIEF COUNSEL
DIVISION OF CORPORATION FINANCE
SECURITIES AND EXCHANGE COMMISSION
450 FIFTH STREET, N.W.
WASHINGTON, D.C. 20549
Re: Shareholder Proposal of James D. Lehner

Dear Sir or Madam:

Xerox Corporation (the "Company") has received a letter dated December 5, 2000 from James D. Lehner, a former employee of the Company, presenting a shareholder proposal for inclusion in the Company's 2001 proxy materials, copy enclosed (the "Lehner Proposal"). Pursuant to Rule 14a–8(i)(j) the Company hereby advises the Commission that it intends to exclude the proposal from its 2001 proxy materials for the reasons described below. By copy of this letter, we are advising Mr. Lehner of the Company's intention. In accordance with Rule 14a–8(j) (2) there are submitted herewith five additional copies of this letter and the enclosure.

Rule 14a–8(i)(8) Election of Directors

The Lehner Proposal may be excluded on the basis of Rule 14a–8(i)(8) because it is a proposal that relates to election of directors. The Lehner Proposal would in effect require that all of the directors standing for election at the 2001 annual meeting of the Company resign ("vacate their positions") and be replaced by individuals meeting certain criteria. First, all of the "Employee Directors" would have to resign and the remaining "Outside Directors" would be required to fill the vacated positions with individuals using "guidelines that ensure needed competencies, e.g. finance, legal, management, etc." Second, the remaining directors (presumably the "Outside Directors" who just replaced the "Employee Directors") would be required to resign as well. Then the newly elected directors would be required to fill those vacant positions with outside directors. The Lehner Proposal goes on to require that each new director must meet certain minimum qualifications. Thus, the proponent seeks to replace all of the nominees for director at the 2001 annual meeting.

Accordingly, the Lehner Proposal quite clearly involves the election of directors. The Staff's no-action letters in this area reflect the Commission's view expressed in its 1976 release which states that the principal purpose of the election to office exclusion "is to make clear, with respect to corporate elections, that Rule 14a–8 is not the proper means for conducting campaigns or effecting reforms in elections of that nature, since other proxy rules, including Rule 14a–11 [election contests], are applicable" (Release No. 34–12598—July 7, 1976). Thus, the Staff has consistently held that proposals which in effect oppose the election of specific nominees for election to the company's board of directors may be excluded. *See* Archer–Daniels–Midland (August 6, 1999) (proposal which would permit only a very narrow category of individuals to stand for election); Dow Jones & Co., Inc. (January 31, 1996) (proposal mandated that a board seat be filled by a particular individual); Storage Technology Corp. (March 11, 1998) (proposal to require the company's proxy statement to include a list of nominees selected by shareholders).

Consistent with this, the Staff has permitted exclusion of proposals questioning the suitability to hold office as relating to election of directors. The Lehner Proposal accuses incumbent board members of a "serious breech of trust," [sic] that they are "dominated and influenced by employee directors" and must "accept responsibility for [the] unacceptable performance" of the Company. It goes on to state "we recognize that the current Board of Directors cannot restore our investment" therefore the board members should resign in the two waves as described above. The Lehner Proposal clearly constitutes a contest for election by impugning the incumbent board members who, with two exceptions due to a retirements, are likely to be nominees at the 2001 annual meeting. In a recent no-action letter the Staff permitted exclusion of a proposal questioning the business judgment of board members (Honeywell International Inc. (March 2, 2000)). *See also* Black & Decker Corp (January 21, 1997) (proposal maligned CEO who was a nominee for election).

In short, the Lehner Proposal is a flagrant attempt to use the shareholder proposal process of Rule 14a–8 to replace directors and is a disguised attempt at an election contest without meeting the requirements of Rule 14a–12. It is, therefore, properly excludable under Rule 14a–8(i)(8).

Rule 14a–8(i)(3) False and Misleading Contrary to Commissions Rule 14a–9

Rule 14a–8(i)(3) provides that a proposal or the supporting statement that is contrary to any of the Commission's proxy rules and regulations, including Rule 14a–9, which prohibits false and misleading statements in proxy soliciting materials, may be excluded. One of the examples of misleading statements cited by the Commission under Rule 14a–9 contained in item (b) of the Notes states:

> "(b) Material which directly or indirectly impugns character, integrity or personal reputation, or directly or indirectly makes charges concerning improper, illegal or immoral conduct or associations, without factual foundation."

As noted above, the statement in support of the Lehner Proposal accuses the incumbent board members of a "serious breech of trust," [sic] that they are "dominated and influenced by employee directors" and must "accept responsibility for [the] unacceptable performance" of the Company. This allegation is seemingly supported solely by reference to the decline in Mr. Lehner's investment in Xerox. This is purely circumstantial and is hardly the kind of factual support envisioned by the Rule. Accordingly, the Lehner Proposal may be omitted because it contains false and misleading statements contrary to the Commission's Rule 14a–9.

* * *

For the foregoing reasons, the Company believes that it may properly exclude the Lehner Proposal from its proxy materials for the 2001 Annual Meeting.

Very truly yours,
Martin S. Wagner
Associate General Counsel
XEROX CORPORATION

The SEC then gave Xerox what it wanted:

1934 Act /s—/Rule 14A–8
March 9, 2001
Publicly Available March 9, 2001
Re: Xerox Corporation

Incoming letter dated January 12, 2001

The proposal relates to certain board members immediately vacating their positions, as well as replacing Xerox board members as specified in the proposal.

There appears to be some basis for your view that Xerox may exclude the proposal under rule 14a–8(i)(8) as relating to an election for membership on its board of directors. Accordingly, we will not recommend enforcement action to the Commission if Xerox omits the proposal from its proxy materials in reliance on rule 14a–8(i)(8). In reaching this position, we have not found it necessary to address the alternative basis for omission upon which Xerox relies.

Sincerely, Lillian K. Cummins
Attorney–Advisor

QUESTIONS AND NOTES

1. The SEC has adopted a "plain-English" question and answer format for 14a–8. It lists 13 reasons management may refuse a proffered shareholder proposal. *See* Question 9, Rule 14a–8(i).

2. How might you change Mr. Lehner's proposal to avoid exclusion? *See AFSCME v. American Int'l Group, Inc.*, 462 F.3d 121, 123 (2d Cir. 2006) ("[A] shareholder proposal that seeks to amend the corporate bylaws to establish a procedure by which shareholder-nominated candidates may be included on the corporate ballot does not relate to an election within the meaning of the Rule and therefore cannot be excluded from corporate proxy materials under that regulation"). In response to AFSCME, the SEC amended Rule 14a–8(i)(8) in 2008 to exclude proposals that allowed shareholders to include nominees in the proxy statement.

3. What could Mr. Lehner have done after Xerox sought a no-action letter, but prior to the SEC's response? *See* Question 11, Rule 14a–8(k). Notwithstanding the exclusion of Mr. Lehner's proposal from the proxy statement, could he make the proposal from the floor at the upcoming meeting?

8. SHAREHOLDERS' INSPECTION RIGHTS

Access to the corporation's books and records can be important to a shareholder who wants to act in an informed and responsible way in exercising her right to vote. (Such access could also be important to a shareholder who wants to act irresponsibly.) Every state provides for such access by statute.* These provisions vary from state to state. The next case applies the Delaware statute. In reading the case, please consider the following:

1. Who is seeking to inspect a corporation's records? Specifically, which corporation wants access?

2. What was the purpose for the inspection stated in the demand letter? Does the defendant agree with the plaintiff shareholder's statement of its purpose? Does that matter?

3. What books and records did the plaintiff want to inspect?

4. Note the broader provision for *director* access to corporate books and records. Why does this broader access make sense for directors?

KORTUM v. WEBASTO SUNROOFS, INC.

Delaware Court of Chancery, 2000
769 A.2d 113

JACOBS, VICE CHANCELLOR. This action is brought by a director and a 50% stockholder of a joint venture Delaware corporation to inspect the corporation's books and records under 8 Del. C. § 220. Two issues are presented. The first is whether the inspection rights of the director—which otherwise are conceded to be absolute—may be limited by ordering the director not to disclose those records (or information derived therefrom) to the 50% stockholder that designated the director as a board member. The second issue is whether the plaintiff stockholder's stated purpose for inspection is bona fide, and if so, whether the scope of inspection relief should be limited because of the possibility of conflicting interests between that 50% stockholder and the corporation. I conclude, in this post-trial Opinion, that (1) the plaintiff-director's inspection rights should be unrestricted, and (2) that the plaintiff-stockholder, whose purpose for seeking inspection is bona fide, should have the same inspection rights as its director-designee, but subject to certain limiting conditions applicable to both plaintiffs.

I. FACTS

A. The Parties and their Relationships

The Delaware corporation that is the subject of this dispute is Webasto Sunroofs, Inc. ("WSI"), a company that is engaged in the business of manufacturing, marketing, selling, and distributing sunroofs

---

* In addition, in many states, there is a common law right for the shareholder to inspect, which usually exists alongside the statutory right.

to the automotive industry in North America. WSI is a joint venture formed under a shareholders agreement dated May 1, 1984 (the "Shareholders Agreement") between plaintiff Webasto AG Fahrzeugtechnik ("WAG") and a subsidiary of Magna International, Inc.("Magna").* **[2]** WSI employs approximately 900 people and in 1998 it had net sales of approximately $201 million.

WAG and Magna each owns 50% of the equity of WSI, and each stockholder designates three of WSI's six directors. One of WAG's director-designees is plaintiff Franz–Joseph Kortum ("Kortum"), who is WAG's Chief Executive Officer. WAG and Kortum are the plaintiffs in this action. The defendant is WSI, but only nominally. The true respondent is Magna, the other 50% stockholder that controls WSI on a day-to-day basis and that is presently embroiled in this dispute with WAG.

The Shareholders Agreement governs the relationship between the two stockholders. Under that Agreement, WAG is to provide technical support to WSI in accordance with certain license agreements, and Magna is to provide management services under a management agreement dated as of August 1, 1984 ("Management Agreement"). Under the Management Agreement, Magna has been exercising day-to-day control over WSI's operations, and is presently exercising control over WSI's position in this litigation. But, and as WSI (Magna) concedes in its brief, for the last fifteen years WAG, through its director-designees, has "participate[d] in decision making regarding the operation, strategy and financial condition of WSI." The record shows that significant financial and other information has been routinely furnished to WAG and Magna. WAG contends, however, that much of that information is not provided to it on a regular basis or in the same detail as is provided to Magna. What is clear is that Magna, by virtue of its day-to-day control of WSI, controls access to those books and records and is now using that control to deny similar access to the other 50% stockholder and co-venturer, WAG. That denial of access is what has prompted the institution of this § 220 proceeding.

B.   Events Leading to the Demand for Inspection

Although WAG's motives for seeking inspection of WSI's books and records are disputed, the underlying background facts are not. Until 1998 the two co-venturers' relationship was more or less harmonious. In 1998 two events occurred, and from that point on the relationship between WAG and Magna deteriorated. The first event was Mr. Kortum's ascendancy as CEO of WAG and his insistence upon more adequate reporting of information to WAG. The second was WSI's 1998–year end reported profits of only $2.1 million—a 90% downward variance from the $21 million in profits that WSI had previously budgeted. Concerned about that development, Horst Winter, Executive President of WAG and a director of WSI, wrote WSI a letter requesting detailed explanations for that down-

---

* **[2]** The Magna subsidiary is Cosma International of America, Inc. ("Cosma"). Except where otherwise stated, Magna and Cosma are referred to in this Opinion as "Magna," and any references to Magna include Cosma.

ward variance. That letter was hand delivered at a meeting between Magna and WAG representatives held in Munich, Germany, in February, 1999. At that meeting, Kortum stated that he and WAG were dissatisfied with the quality of WSI's financial reporting and its explanation for the variances, and took the position that more detailed explanations were required. At that meeting Magna representatives responded that the books of WSI were fully open to WAG at any time, and they agreed to let WAG conduct an audit of WSI. Shortly thereafter, while WAG was arranging with Magna to conduct the audit, WAG was told that Magna would not allow the audit to take place.

Magna (through WSI) does not deny that these events occurred, but contends that WAG's claimed need for more information was and is pretextual. WAG's real purpose, Magna claims, is to compete directly against WSI in the North American sunroof market, free of any constraints imposed by the joint venture or the Shareholders Agreement. Magna points to several facts that, it claims, compel this conclusion. First, WAG acquired and operates Hollandia Sunroofs, Inc. ("Hollandia"), which markets and distributes sunroofs in the aftermarket industry in the United States. Second, WAG formed a new corporation (Webasto Roof and Body Systems of Lapeer, Michigan) to offer services, products, and engineering technology to its customers in North America. Third, WAG is currently distributing and selling sunroof products (including lamella sunroofs) in North America. Fourth, WAG has excluded WSI from preparing quotations to develop new business from General Motors and Daimler Chrysler. Fifth, and most important, on May 19, 1999, WAG filed an action in this Court under 8 Del. C. § 273 to discontinue WSI (the "Section 273 action"), in which WAG has proposed a plan of discontinuance and a distribution of WSI's assets. The Section 273 action is being actively prosecuted.

On May 31, 1999, two weeks after WAG filed the Section 273 action, Mr. Kortum sent a letter to WSI, pursuant to § 220, in both his capacities as a director of WSI and as Chairman of WAG, demanding to inspect WSI's books and records. Kortum's stated purpose as a director for seeking inspection was to monitor Magna's performance under the Management Agreement, especially in light of the recent profit variances. WAG's stated purpose as a stockholder was to value its shareholder interest in WSI. It is undisputed that the scope of the requested document inspection is quite broad.* **[8]**

---

* **[8]** The demand embraces all WSI books and records, including, but not limited to, the following nine categories: (1) all sales records underlying WSI's audited financial statements; (2) all documents reflecting the nature and value of WSI's assets, including, but not limited to, accounts receivable, inventories of finished goods, raw materials and work in progress, records of WSI property, plant and equipment holdings, records of cash on hand, cash equivalents and other investments, and records of any other WSI assets; (3) records of all WSI obligations and liabilities; (4) all supply contracts, tooling contracts or any other WSI contracts with third-party vendors and/or related entities; (6) all sales projections and/or business plans prepared or reviewed by WSI management; (7) any other financial records of WSI; (8) all information concerning employees of WSI, including, but not limited to, employment contracts, any employee benefit plans or other

WAG contends that it submitted the May 31 demand letter in response to Magna having reneged on its undertaking to permit WAG to conduct an audit. Magna (WSI) responds that the demand letter, and this action, are simply a part of WAG's "exit strategy" from the joint venture, and a stratagem to enable WAG to obtain sensitive information that WAG will use competitively to WSI's disadvantage. In any event, in response to the demand letter WSI agreed to permit the inspection by Kortum in his capacity as a director, subject to his written confirmation that he and any advisors would inspect and use the books and records only in that capacity; i.e., he would not disclose them to WAG or to any other third parties. WSI declined, however, to permit any books and records inspection by WAG, citing as reasons WAG's competitive status, the nature of the information WAG was demanding, and the pendency of the Section 273 action.

This proceeding followed.

II.   THE CONTENTIONS AND THE APPLICABLE LAW

This action involves two separate inspection claims: Kortum's claim for inspection in his capacity as a WSI director, and WAG's claim for inspection as one of WSI's two 50% stockholders. Those claims implicate separate rights that arise out of two distinct provisions of § 220 of the Delaware General Corporation Law, provisions that impose different burdens of proof.

A.   Director's Inspection Rights

Regarding the inspection rights of a director, § 220(d) provides that "[a]ny director ... shall have the right to examine the corporation's stock ledger, a list of its stockholders and its other books and records for a purpose reasonably related to the director's position as a director." Once the director makes a § 220 demand that is refused, a prima facie showing of entitlement to the documents has been made and the burden shifts to the corporation to show why inspection should be denied or conditioned. As Vice Chancellor Lamb has stated, there is a "presumption that a sitting director is entitled to unfettered access to the books and records of the corporation for which he sits and certainly is entitled to receive what the other directors are given."

In apparent recognition of the broad scope of a director's statutory inspection right, WSI (Magna) conceded in its response to the demand that Kortum, in his directorial capacity, was entitled to inspect all the documents described in his demand letter. WSI contends, however, that it is entitled to impose conditions that (it asserts) will assure that the inspection will be only in Kortum's directorial capacity. Specifically, in its response to the demand letter, Magna imposed the following restrictions on Mr. Kortum's inspection:

---

individual benefit plans, stock option plans, etc.; and (9) any tax balance sheets, tax returns and tax assessments for the last three years and latest WSI tax auditors reports.

- a requirement that other persons who will assist in the inspection be identified at least three business days in advance;

- a limitation on other participants to "only those persons who represent you personally in such capacity, and who do not have any other interest or representation which may conflict with the interests of WSI . . .;

- a requirement that Kortum sign a confirmation that he would be inspecting and using WSI documents only in his capacity as a WSI director, and that any other person who assists in the inspection sign a similar confirmation; and

- an agreement that, by inspecting the documents, Mr. Kortum would not disclose the information to any third parties, including any competitor or potential competitor, and WAG itself.

Magna also reserved the right to decide what documents Kortum could copy.

Accordingly, the only issue presented with respect to Kortum's claimed directorial inspection right is whether any or all of the conditions that Magna seeks to impose are reasonable. I conclude, for the reasons discussed in Part III, infra, that with one exception, they are not.

B.   Shareholder's Inspection Rights

The inspection rights of a shareholder are governed by 8 Del. C. § 220(c), which pertinently provides:

> Where the stockholder seeks to inspect the corporation's books and records, other than its stock ledger or list of stockholders, such stockholder shall first establish (1) that such stockholder has complied with this section regarding the form and manner of making demand for inspection of such documents; and (2) that the inspection such stockholder seeks is for a proper purpose.

Thus, unlike the case of a director seeking inspection, a stockholder who seeks inspection under § 220 must prove by a preponderance of the evidence: (a) its compliance with the form and manner of making a demand specified in the statute, and (b) the propriety of its purpose for seeking inspection, i.e., that the purpose is reasonably related to its interest as a stockholder. Once the shareholder demonstrates its entitlement to inspection, it must also show that the scope of the requested inspection is proper, i.e., that the books and records sought are "essential and sufficient" to the shareholder's stated purpose.

In this case WSI contends that WAG has failed to meet its burden in all three respects. That is, WSI argues that (i) WAG did not submit a demand in conformity with the "form and manner" required by the statute, because the demand was not "under oath;" (ii) WAG's stated purpose is not factually bona fide, because given the volume and kinds of documents it has already received and because it has no present ability or intent to buy Magna's shares or sell its shares, WAG has no need to inspect WSI's books and records to value its investment. Indeed, Magna argues, WAG's stated purpose is pretextual, since its true objective is to garner as much sensitive, proprietary information as it can to enable it to compete with WSI once the joint venture is dissolved. Finally, WSI (Magna) argues that (iii) inspection would harm WSI and therefore should be denied, but even if WAG can establish its entitlement to inspection, WAG has failed to show that any of the broad categories of documents it seeks to inspect is "essential and sufficient" to its stated purpose of valuing its investment.

These contentions present three issues relating to WAG's inspection rights as a shareholder:

(1) Did WAG submit a demand "under oath" as required by the statute?

(2) Has WAG shown that its stated valuation purpose is, in fact, its true purpose? and

(3) Has WAG shown that the scope of the inspection it seeks is proper?

For the reasons next discussed, I conclude that WAG's demand was "under oath" within the meaning of the statute, and that its stated valuation purpose is, in fact, its true purpose. I also conclude that Kortum is entitled to inspect all of the document categories described in the demand, and may disclose those documents to WAG, subject to certain conditions. Accordingly, it becomes unnecessary to, and I therefore do not, reach the issue of whether the documents described in the demand are "essential and sufficient" to WAG's purpose.

III. ANALYSIS

A. Kortum's Director Inspection Claim

As previously noted, because WSI (Magna) has conceded that Kortum, as a director, is entitled to inspect all the books and records listed in the demand letter subject to certain limitations, the only issue present is whether WSI's proposed limitations are warranted. I conclude that they are not.

Restrictions on Kortum's choice of agents to assist him in the inspection might be justified if the proposed agents have interests in conflict with WSI. Magna (WSI) has the burden of demonstrating such a conflict, and has not met that burden. The agents Kortum anticipates using include lawyers, accountants, members of WAG's finance staff, and Horst Winter, who is a director of WSI. None of these agents was shown to be engaging (or preparing to engage) in activities hostile to WSI. Moreover, Magna's claim that WAG is engaged in a campaign to compete with, and thereby harm, WSI, is undercut by the fact that WAG's 50% stock interest in WSI represents 20% of WAG's revenues and 25% of its profits.

Nor is it reasonable to condition Kortum's inspection upon an undertaking not to disclose to WAG any information gleaned from the document inspection. Kortum is a fiduciary of WSI, but he is a fiduciary of WAG as well. Absent a conflict between those two roles, Kortum's fiduciary duty would require him to disclose that information to WAG, which is one of WSI's 50% owners. * * *

Magna has not established a conflict between Kortum's two fiduciary roles. Although it claims that WAG intends to compete with WSI in North America to the greatest extent possible, the only evidence of any actual competition with WSI is that Hollandia currently competes in the after-market segment—a fact acknowledged by Mr. Kortum, who testified that no information received as a result of this proceeding will be shared with Hollandia. With that exception, Magna's other evidence of "competitive threat" is speculative and unpersuasive.

That evidence concerns activities that were not the subject of any protest by or dispute with Magna, until WAG filed the Section 273 dissolution action. Such activities may threaten competition with Magna, but not necessarily with WSI. At most Magna has shown that WAG has the infrastructure and potential to compete with WSI in the OEM [original equipment manufacturer] market at some point in the future. And while that might ultimately occur if WAG prevails in the Section 273 action, that possibility does not prove that WAG is threatening to do so now, or that Magna may justifiably use its day-to-day control over WSI to prevent Kortum from disclosing the results of his inspection to WAG.*
[17] For the same reason, WSI's (Magna's) attempt to limit Kortum's statutory right to make copies of inspected documents is also unwarranted.

Accordingly, Mr. Kortum's inspection rights shall be unrestricted, except for the self-imposed restriction that no information derived from the inspection will be shared with Hollandia.

B.   WAG's Shareholder Inspection Claim

As earlier noted, WSI (Magna) opposes WAG's inspection claim on the grounds that (i) the demand was not under oath as the statute requires; (ii) WAG has not shown that its stated purpose is, in fact, its true purpose; (iii) WAG has not demonstrated that the broad categories of documents WAG seeks to inspect are "essential and sufficient" to its purpose; and (iv) if inspection is allowed, its scope should be limited to protect WSI against competitive harm threatened by WAG.

Because the Court has already determined that Kortum is entitled to inspect the universe of books and records described in the demand and should not be restricted from disclosing those documents (or resulting information) to WAG, that determination obviates the need to determine

---

* [17] Magna's insistence that Kortum not disclose any information obtained as a result of the inspection to other third parties including other potential competitors, is not unreasonable on its face. I perceive no reason why Kortum would object to such a condition, so long as the nondisclosure obligation does not include WAG or its representatives. Because Magna has not shown any risk that Kortum intends to disclose the information to anyone other than WAG, however, it must be presumed that Kortum, as a fiduciary of WSI, will not disclose WSI's proprietary or confidential information to such third parties. Therefore, Kortum is encouraged, but will not be required, to bind himself to that nondisclosure restriction.

whether the documents to be inspected are "essential and sufficient" to achieve WAG's purpose. Consequently, the issues are whether (1) WAG is entitled to inspection relief (specifically, whether the form of its demand is proper and its stated purpose is bona fide), and (2) whether WAG's inspection rights (which would otherwise be coextensive with Kortum's) should be restricted, and if so, to what extent.

1. The Form-of-Demand Issue [The court concluded that the demand was made in the proper statutory form.]

2. The Bona Fides of WAG's Stated Inspection Purpose

WSI (Magna) next challenges the bona fides of WAG's stated purpose. In its demand letter, WAG stated that its purpose for seeking inspection was "to determine the value of its shareholding interest in WSI." It is well established that the purpose of valuing one's shares in the corporation is proper under § 220. In these circumstances the genuineness of that purpose appears self-evident. WAG is a 50% stockholder in a joint venture corporation owned by only one other 50% stockholder. The relationship between those two stockholders is antagonistic, and one of them (WAG) has filed a petition under Section 273 to dissolve the corporation. As part of the Section 273 action, WAG has proposed a plan to liquidate WSI's assets in a private auction limited to the two 50% owners. In its response to WAG's petition, Magna (through its subsidiary, Cosma) asks the Court to dismiss the petition or, alternatively, to conduct a public auction to sell all of WSI's outstanding shares.

Thus, if the Section 273 action proceeds to a conclusion, it is possible that: (1) WSI's assets will be sold to one or perhaps to both stockholders, or (2) all of WSI's outstanding shares will be sold at a public auction. If, however, the Section 273 proceeding is dismissed, WAG would have a strong interest in either selling its WSI shares to Magna or buying Magna's WSI shares. Under any scenario WAG would have a need to value its investment to enable it to make an informed judgment about how much to bid for WSI's assets, or for Magna's WSI shares, or about the price at which WAG should sell its WSI shares. I find that WAG's interest in valuing its WSI shares based on accurate information is both genuine and substantial: WAG's investment in WSI represents 20% of its revenues and 25% of its profits. Whether dissolved or not, WSI will not continue as a joint venture between Magna and WAG.

WSI (Magna) contends, however, that WAG's stated purpose in seeking inspection is not its true purpose because there is no imminent opportunity for WAG to exit its investment. But the facts that no specific offer to purchase or sell is pending at this moment and that WAG has not yet decided whether * * * to purchase or sell, do not—alone and without more—defeat the factual bona fides of its valuation purpose. As this Court stated in *Helmsman Management Services, Inc. v. A & S Consultants, Inc.* [525 A.2d 160, 167 (Del. Ch. 1987)]:

When a minority stockholder in a closely held corporation whose stock is not publicly traded needs to value his or her own shares in order to decide whether to sell them [and if so, for how much], normally the only way to accomplish that is by examining the appropriate corporate books and records.

That reasoning has additional force where, as here, the shareholder seeking inspection is a 50% owner of the non-publicly-held corporation.* [27] That fact is of importance because it matters greatly if the stockholder seeking inspection owns 100 shares in General Motors or owns 50% of the shares of a private corporation held by two stockholders. In the latter case, there often is no identifiable corporate interest separate and apart from the interests of the two stockholders or if there is, the interest of the corporation in protecting itself from unwarranted intrusion is considerably diminished. For that reason, in cases such as this, there should be a rebuttable presumption that the 50% shareholder's purpose for seeking inspection is valid. In this case, however, the evidence demonstrates the propriety of WAG's purpose with or without a presumption.

WSI argues that WAG's status as an actual or potential competitor also belies its professed valuation purpose. In this case that argument is factually and legally incorrect. A stockholder's status as a competitor may limit the scope of, or require imposing conditions upon, inspection relief, but that status does not defeat the shareholder's legal entitlement to relief.

Finally, WSI argues that the pendency of the Section 273 proceeding defeats WAG's inspection right. That also is incorrect. So long as the statutory requirements for inspection relief are satisfied, the mere pendency of another proceeding does not disqualify a party involved in the other lawsuit from inspecting the corporation's books and records. Nor does the possibility that the Section 273 action may result in a public auction disqualify that party. WSI (Magna) argues that if inspection is allowed, WAG will have access to WSI's competitive secrets, which would eliminate any incentives for other bidders, including WAG, to pay for them at a public auction. This argument is flawed in two respects. First, many, if not all, of the joint venture's "competitive secrets" are licensed patents and technological trade secrets and know-how developed by WAG. Second, WSI fails to explain why other bidders would be dissuaded if WAG has prior access to those secrets, but would not be if Magna, also a potential bidder, has the same access.* [30]

---

* [27] WSI also argues that WAG has already performed a preliminary valuation of its investment, which shows that WAG's stated valuation purpose is pretextual. The argument is unpersuasive, because the preliminary valuation, based on less than complete information, buttresses the credibility of WAG's claimed need to do a more reliable valuation. *See* Thomas & Betts Corp., 685 A.2d at 713; (shareholder's ability to perform a preliminary valuation based on incomplete information does not warrant denial of inspection of books and records to value shares).

* [30] I place little credence in WSI's protestation that Magna has no greater access to WSI's books and records than does WAG. Magna controls the day-to-day operations of WSI, and therefore controls access to WSI's records. Even assuming that Magna has voluntarily chosen not

I conclude, for these reasons, that WAG has demonstrated its entitlement to inspection under § 220, and that in these specific circumstances the scope of that inspection will be coextensive with the scope of the inspection granted to plaintiff Kortum. I turn to the remaining issue, which is whether any conditions upon WAG's exercise of those rights should be imposed.

3. Conditions of WAG's Inspection

There shall be one limitation, which shall apply equally to WAG and Kortum. For the same reasons that Kortum may not disclose information obtained from the inspection to Hollandia; any other officers, directors, employees or agents of WAG who receive access to such information shall be similarly prohibited. Moreover, and subject to the above condition, any information obtained from the inspection shall be disclosed only to WAG personnel (other than employees or agents of Hollandia), and persons assisting the plaintiffs in the books and records inspection.

QUESTIONS AND NOTES

1. Was Webasto Sunroofs, Inc. a corporation? A joint venture?

2. Who has the burden of proof on the issue of "proper purpose" under Delaware § 220?

3. How does Delaware § 220 differ from MBCA § 16.02?

4. The management of a corporation generally does not challenge an inspection request from a shareholder who is merely seeking information related to the value of her investment. Most litigation on the issue involves shareholders whom management believes are asserting inspection rights to gain information to use against management, perhaps to change management. We will look at such takeover attempts later. *See* Fred S. McChesney, *"Proper Purpose," Fiduciary Duties, and Shareholder–Raider Access to Corporate Information,* 68 U. CINN. L. REV. 1199 (2000) (The article begins with a quote from that great American, Little Richard: "Keep a-knocking but you can't come in. Come back tomorrow night and try it again.").

5. The MBCA, like Delaware, provides readier access to books and records for directors than for shareholders. *See* MBCA § 16.05.

9. SHAREHOLDERS' VOTING AGREEMENTS

Recall that *McQuade v. Stoneham* held that a voting agreement among *directors* was contrary to public policy and void. The next case (which, like *McQuade*, appears in most casebooks) illustrates that courts will uphold voting agreements among *shareholders*. In reading the case, consider the following questions:

1. Why did Mrs. Ringling and Mrs. Haley enter into the shareholder voting agreement?

---

to exercise that control to grant itself complete access, Magna has the ability to do that whenever it chooses. WAG, which owns the same percentage of equity as Magna, does not.

2.   Was anyone adversely affected by their agreement?

3.   Who breached the agreement? Why?

4.   Who won the lawsuit? What did she win? When did the shareholders' meeting occur? When did compliance with the voting agreement occur?

RINGLING BROS.–BARNUM & BAILEY COMBINED SHOWS, INC. v. RINGLING

Supreme Court of Delaware, 1947
53 A.2d 441

PEARSON, JUDGE. The Court of Chancery was called upon to review an attempted election of directors at the 1946 annual stockholders meeting of the corporate defendant. The pivotal questions concern an agreement between two of the three present stockholders, and particularly the effect of this agreement with relation to the exercise of voting rights by these two stockholders. At the time of the meeting, the corporation had outstanding 1000 shares of capital stock held as follows: 315 by petitioner Edith Conway Ringling; 315 by defendant Aubrey B. Ringling Haley (individually or as executrix and legatee of a deceased husband); and 370 by defendant John Ringling North. The purpose of the meeting was to elect the entire board of seven directors. The shares could be voted cumulatively. Mrs. Ringling asserts that by virtue of the operation of an agreement between her and Mrs. Haley, the latter was bound to vote her shares for a certain slate of directors. Mrs. Haley contends that she was not so bound for reason that the agreement was invalid, or at least revocable. * * *

The agreement recites that:

2.   In exercising any voting rights to which either party may be entitled by virtue of ownership of stock, each party will consult and confer with the other and the parties will act jointly in exercising such voting rights in accordance with such agreement as they may reach with respect to any matter calling for the exercise of such voting rights.

3.   In the event the parties fail to agree with respect to any matter covered by paragraph 2 above, the question in disagreement shall be submitted for arbitration to Karl D. Loos, of Washington, D. C. as arbitrator and his decision thereon shall be binding upon the parties hereto. Such arbitration shall be exercised to the end of assuring for the respective corporation's good management and such participation therein by the members of the Ringling family as the experience, capacity and ability of each may warrant.

4.   Each of the parties hereto will enter into and execute such voting trust agreement or agreements and such other instruments as, from time to time they may deem advisable and as they may be advised by counsel are appropriate to effectuate the purposes and objects of this agreement.

5. This agreement shall be in effect from the date hereof and shall continue in effect for a period of ten years unless sooner terminated by mutual agreement in writing by the parties hereto.

6. The agreement of April 1934 is hereby terminated.

7. This agreement shall be binding upon and inure to the benefit of the heirs, executors, administrators and assigns of the parties hereto respectively.

The Mr. Loos mentioned in the agreement is an attorney and has represented both parties. At the annual meetings in 1943 and the two following years, the parties voted their shares in accordance with mutual understandings arrived at as a result of discussions. In each of these years, they elected five of the seven directors. Mrs. Ringling and Mrs. Haley each had sufficient votes, independently of the other, to elect two of the seven directors. By both voting for an additional candidate, they could be sure of his election regardless of how Mr. North, the remaining stockholder, might vote.* [1]

Some weeks before the 1946 meeting, they discussed with Mr. Loos the matter of voting for directors. They were in accord that Mrs. Ringling should cast sufficient votes to elect herself and her son; and that Mrs. Haley should elect herself and her husband; but they did not agree upon a fifth director. * * * Mrs. Ringling made a demand upon Mr. Loos to act under the third paragraph of the agreement 'to arbitrate the disagreement' between her and Mrs. Haley in connection with the manner in which the stock of the two ladies should be voted. * * * Mr. Loos directed Mrs. Ringling to cast her votes:

882 for Mrs. Ringling,

882 for her son, Robert, and

441 for a Mr. Dunn, who had been a member of the board for several years. She complied.

Mr. Loos directed that Mrs. Haley's votes be cast:

882 for Mrs. Haley,

882 for Mr. Haley, and

441 for Mr. Dunn.

Instead of complying, Mr. Haley attempted to vote his wife's shares:

1103 for Mrs. Haley, and

1102 for Mr. Haley.

---

* [1] Each lady was entitled to cast 2,205 votes (since each had the cumulative voting rights of 315 shares, and there were 7 vacancies in the directorate). The sum of the votes of both is 4,410, which is sufficient to allow 882 votes for each of 5 persons. Mr. North, holding 370 shares, was entitled to cast 2,590 votes, which obviously cannot be divided so as to give to more than two candidates as many as 882 votes each. It will be observed that in order for Mrs. Ringling and Mrs. Haley to be sure to elect five directors (regardless of how Mr. North might vote) they must act together in the sense that their combined votes must be divided among five different candidates and at least one of the five must be voted for by both Mrs. Ringling and Mrs. Haley.

Mr. North voted his shares:

864 for a Mr. Woods,

863 for a Mr. Griffin, and

863 for Mr. North.

The chairman ruled that the five candidates proposed by Mr. Loos, together with Messrs. Woods and North, were elected. The Haley–North group disputed this ruling insofar as it declared the election of Mr. Dunn; and insisted that Mr. Griffin, instead, had been elected. A director's meeting followed in which Mrs. Ringling participated after stating that she would do so 'without prejudice to her position that the directors' meeting was not properly held.' Mr. Dunn and Mr. Griffin, although each was challenged by an opposing faction, attempted to join in voting as directors for different slates of officers. Soon after the meeting, Mrs. Ringling instituted this proceeding.

The Vice Chancellor determined that the agreement to vote in accordance with the direction of Mr. Loos was valid as a 'stock pooling agreement' with lawful objects and purposes, and that it was not in violation of any public policy of this state. He held that where the arbitrator acts under the agreement and one party refuses to comply with his direction, 'the Agreement constitutes the willing party * * * an implied agent possessing the irrevocable proxy of the recalcitrant party for the purpose of casting the particular vote'. It was ordered that a new election be held before a master, with the direction that the master should recognize and give effect to the agreement if its terms were properly invoked. * * *

We come now to defendants' contention that the voting provisions are illegal and revocable. They say that the courts of this state have definitely established the doctrine 'that there can be no agreement, or any device whatsoever, by which the voting power of stock of a Delaware corporation may be irrevocably separated from the ownership of the stock, except by an agreement which complies with Section 18' of the Corporation Law, Rev.Code 1935, and except by a proxy coupled with an interest. * * * The statute reads, in part, as follows:

> Sec. 18. Fiduciary Stockholders; Voting Power of; Voting Trusts:—Persons holding stock in a fiduciary capacity shall be entitled to vote the shares so held, and persons whose stock is pledged shall be entitled to vote, unless in the transfer by the pledgor on the books of the corporation he shall have expressly empowered the pledgee to vote thereon, in which case only the pledgee, or his proxy may represent said stock and vote thereon.
>
> One or more stockholders may by agreement in writing deposit capital stock of an original issue with or transfer capital stock to any person or persons, or corporation or corporations authorized to act as trustee, for the purpose of vesting in said person or persons, corporation or corporations, who may be designated

Voting Trustee or Voting Trustees, the right to vote thereon for any period of time determined by such agreement, not exceeding ten years, upon the terms and conditions stated in such agreement. Such agreement may contain any other lawful provisions not inconsistent with said purpose. Said Voting Trustees may vote upon the stock so issued or transferred during the period in such agreement specified; stock standing in the names of such Voting Trustees may be voted either in person or by proxy, and in voting said stock, such Voting Trustees shall incur no responsibility as stockholder, trustee or otherwise, except for their own individual malfeasance.

In our view, neither the cases nor the statute sustain the rule for which the defendants contend. Their sweeping formulation would impugn well-recognized means by which a shareholder may effectively confer his voting rights upon others while retaining various other rights. For example, defendants' rule would apparently not permit holders of voting stock to confer upon stockholders of another class, by the device of an amendment of the certificate of incorporation, the exclusive right to vote during periods when dividends are not paid on stock of the latter class. The broad prohibitory meaning which defendants find in Section 18 seems inconsistent with their concession that proxies coupled with an interest may be irrevocable, for the statute contains nothing about such proxies. The statute authorizes, among other things, the deposit or transfer of stock in trust for a specified purpose, namely, "vesting" in the transferee "the right to vote thereon" for a limited period; and prescribes numerous requirements in this connection. Accordingly, it seems reasonable to infer that to establish the relationship and accomplish the purpose which the statute authorizes, its requirements must be complied with. But the statute does not purport to deal with agreements whereby shareholders attempt to bind each other as to how they shall vote their shares. Various forms of such pooling agreements, as they are sometimes called, have been held valid and have been distinguished from voting trusts. Generally speaking, a shareholder may exercise wide liberality of judgment in the matter of voting, and it is not objectionable that his motives may be for personal profit, or determined by whims or caprice, so long as he violates no duty owed his fellow shareholders. The ownership of voting stock imposes no legal duty to vote at all. A group of shareholders may, without impropriety, vote their respective shares so as to obtain advantages of concerted action. They may lawfully contract with each other to vote in the future in such way as they, or a majority of their group, from time to time determine. Reasonable provisions for cases of failure of the group to reach a determination because of an even division in their ranks seem unobjectionable. The provision here for submission to the arbitrator is plainly designed as a deadlock-breaking measure, and the arbitrator's decision cannot be enforced unless at least one of the parties (entitled to cast one-half of their combined votes) is willing that it be enforced. We find the provision reasonable. It does not appear that the agreement enables the parties to take any unlawful advantage of the outside share-holder, or of any other person. It offends no rule of law or public policy of this state of which we are aware. * * *

The Court of Chancery may, in a review of an election, reject votes of a registered shareholder. The votes representing Mrs. Haley's shares should not be counted. Since no infirmity in Mr. North's voting has been demonstrated, his right to recognition of what he did at the meeting should be considered in granting any relief to Mrs. Ringling; for her rights arose under a contract to which Mr. North was not a party. With this in mind, we have concluded that the election should not be declared invalid, but that effect should be given to a rejection of the votes representing Mrs. Haley's shares. No other relief seems appropriate in this proceeding. With respect to the election of directors, the return of the inspectors should be corrected to show a rejection of Mrs. Haley's votes, and to declare the election of the six persons for whom Mr. North and Mrs. Ringling voted.

This leaves one vacancy in the directorate. The question of what to do about such a vacancy was not considered by the court below and has not been argued here. For this reason, and because an election of directors at the 1947 annual meeting (which presumably will be held in the near future) may make a determination of the question unimportant, we shall not decide it on this appeal. If a decision of the point appears important to the parties, any of them may apply to raise it in the Court of Chancery, after the mandate of this court is received there.

An order should be entered directing a modification of the order of the Court of Chancery in accordance with this opinion.

QUESTIONS

1. Is this case involving a voting agreement by shareholders of a circus distinguishable from *McQuade v. Stoneham*, a case involving a voting agreement by the directors of a baseball team? Should shareholders, but not directors, be able to enter enforceable voting agreements?

2. Was the shareholder voting agreement in *Ringling* enforceable?

3. Many corporation codes authorize shareholder voting agreements. Delaware has since codified the principle in Delaware § 218(c); *see also* MBCA § 7.31. Would the *Ringling* case have been decided differently under the present Delaware statute? How about under MBCA § 7.31? Note that MBCA § 7.31(b) expressly provides for specific enforcement of a voting agreement. How is that better than the result in *Ringling*?

4. The *Ringling* decision mentions the term "voting trust"? Was the agreement in the *Ringling* case a "voting trust"? Would the result in *Ringling* have been different if the parties had established a voting trust with Loos as the trustee? In answering, see Delaware § 218(a) and MBCA § 7.30. Can you articulate the differences between a voting trust and a voting agreement?

C. WHAT ARE THE RESPONSIBILITIES OF A CORPORATION'S DECISIONMAKERS* AND TO WHOM ARE THEY RESPONSIBLE?

1. WHAT ARE THE DECISIONMAKERS' BUSINESS RESPONSIBILITIES?

The pressures on publicly-held companies—and the executives who run them—are really quite different from those experienced by the management of privately-held businesses, such as close corporations.

As we have discussed before, it is management's job to create value for the owners. The owners of a corporation are of course its shareholders. In privately-held companies, owners and managers are often the same people; shares are usually held by the firm's senior management. In the relatively rare situations in which privately-held companies have outside professional managers running the business, shareholders usually constitute a majority of the board. In all these situations, the owners of the company know intimately what is going on in the business, and they are usually responsible for making and executing the important decisions that influence the enterprise's success or failure. Thus, managers of privately held companies are little worried about the short-term implications of their actions, or about the way in which outsiders perceive those decisions. Indeed, it is doubtful that many outsiders know—or care—about what the company or its management is up to.

Publicly-held companies, however, are different for a variety of reasons. First, their financial results are public—people do know. Second, lots of people own the stock and are therefore "owners," affected by the company's performance and the price of the stock. Third, federal securities laws and the rules of the various stock exchanges require public

---

* Most of the corporate law on duty of care and duty of loyalty involves directors as defendants. The actions of a corporation's key officers are subject to at least equal judicial scrutiny. As the Official Comment to MBCA § 8.42 states:

"[A]n officer when performing in such officer's official capacity shall meet the standards of conduct generally similar to those expected of directors under MBCA 8.30. Consistent with the principles of agency which generally govern the conduct of corporate employees, an officer is expected to observe the duties of obedience and loyalty and to act with the care that a person in a like position would reasonably exercise under like circumstances."

And shareholders who, pursuant to MBCA § 7.32 agreements, exercise the power and discretion of directors assume the same duty of care and duty of loyalty as directors. *See* MBCA § 7.32(e).

202 How Does a Corporation Operate? Ch. 5

companies to announce and explain any material actions or issues as they occur. Finally, because tremendous amounts of money can be made (or lost) by trading stocks, there is an entire industry devoted to analyzing and opining on the attractiveness of the stock of every publicly traded company—it is worth a lot of money to be right just a little bit more than average. Most stockholders and analysts do not really know—the way management or a board member knows—what is going on inside a company. Thus, they rely on what is measurable and observable—such as patterns in the company's short-term earnings—to make their judgments and pronouncements about the relative merit of the stock.

Let's look at McDonald's. On Wednesday, February 17, 2010, the stock closed at $64.26 per share, down $0.25 from its close the previous day. At $64.26 per share—and with roughly 1.1 billion shares outstanding—the company had a market value, or market "cap" (for capitalization), of nearly $70 billion.

Those 1.1 billion shares were owned by many owners. The largest owners of the stock were mutual fund companies—Fidelity (3.5%), Capital Research (1.9%), and Barclay's Bank (4.5%). In total, 10 "owners" each controlled more than one percent, for a total of 330 million shares; 30% of the total stock, or $21 billion worth, was controlled by these 10 "owners."

The word owners appears in quotes because, of course, Fidelity didn't really own the stock. It controlled it, and made the decision to buy and sell. But the millions of people who own Fidelity's mutual funds were really the shares' ultimate owners. Still, Fidelity—which attracts investors based upon the performance of its mutual funds relative to others—has a strong incentive to make good decisions about if, and when, to buy and sell the stock. Just by realizing that the fund manager controls $2.6 billion worth of McDonald's stock, you can begin to see the huge incentive a company like Fidelity has to buy and sell the stock at the right time. Each difference of $1 per share is worth $37 million. Pretty soon, those millions add up to real money.

Because McDonalds has so much outstanding stock, 20 "equity research analysts" followed the company in early 2010. These are people who work for the large investment banks that trade stocks for clients. They make their research available—for free to big owners like Fidelity—in the hope that these firms will recognize the value of this research by using their bank to buy and sell the stock, thus earning trading commissions for the bank. In addition, Fidelity and the other mutual fund firms have their own analysts who follow the industry, visit the company, talk to management, and generally try to figure out what is happening before anyone else. These private analysts don't publish their work, because their firms are the only ones who benefit from it.

Do all of the billions of dollars that are spent on investment research and analysis do any good? Do people who use research and analysis to pick stocks earn higher returns? Surprisingly, many financial economists, citing the "Efficient Capital Market Hypothesis," think that the answer is generally no. Often, a diversified group of stocks picked at random produces just as high returns as the stocks picked by the experts. That is, picking stocks by throwing darts at the stock page of the newspaper often produces as much success as the experts' choices. The substantial fees that experts charge can tip the balance further against the experts. Indeed, this is a major reason that index funds, which have low costs because they employ no expert stock-choosers, have been so successful over the past decade.

2. WHAT ARE THE LEGAL RESPONSIBILITIES?

a. Duty of Care

(i) Breach of Duty of Care by Board Action

Roberts becomes a director of Bubba's Burritos, Inc. He convinces Shepherd and the other directors that Bubba's Burritos should sell frappes[†] as well as burritos. It turns out to be a really bad idea. The corporation loses big bucks because of it. Can Roberts, Shepherd, and the other directors be held liable for their bad decision? If so, to whom? The next case considered a similar question. In addressing the case, please consider the following:

---

† Interested readers may find the following illuminating on the subject of "frappes."

1. Who is Shlensky and why does he care whether the Cubs play baseball at night?

2. Was the Cubs' decision not to play baseball at night a bad decision?

3. The last time the Cubs won the World Series, was electric lighting of the playing field an option? Had Edison been born?

Heading up to Belfast, Maine, Driving mighty slow. Was I on the correct road? I really didn't know. / I drove a bit farther If only to see, If a 3 East road sign Would appear unto me. / What did appear Was that I was lost, I must have turned onto a road I should've crossed. / I spied up ahead a sign for MILLIE'S CONFECTIONS, So I decided to pull over, And ask for advice on how to get to Belfast. / I went inside this ice cream stand, And took a look around. Not one single customer Could anywhere be found. / Millie herself Was the only soul in sight, Standing behind the counter, With a smile, oh, so bright. / "Hello, sir!" she said With a warm tone,"What can I get you -- A frappe, cup, or cone?" / "I'm sorry to say, I'm really quite lost, Can you possibly tell me How to get to Belfast?" / It didn't seem to register, What it is that I needed. "What flavor would you like?" She asked me—she pleaded. / I don't want any ice cream!" I said with such tact, The smile fled from her face Like Kurds from Iraq. / The look in her eyes Was too much to take. She was so crushed, I could see her heartbreak. / She started to cry, And said, "Business is slow." I was really hoping for this sale, Cuz I'm so low on dough." / I felt bad for poor Millie, So I thought I'd be nice, Even though this was the nineties, And it went against Zeitgeist. / So I ordered a frappe, If only to please her—To make her happy. And appease her. / That I really wanted this frappe, I tried hard to pretend to her, As she placed the milk and ice cream Into the blenderer. / She gave me directions, As she gave me the cup, "You understand how to get there? She asked. I said, Yup." / I gave her the cash, Along with a tip: "Don't worry,

Millie, Business is sure to pick up." / "Thank you," she whispered, With a tear in her eye, "I'll surely remember this Until the day that I die." / I went out to my car, Got in and drove away, Knowing that I had done My good deed for the day. / It's not very often, I could do a good deed such as that—One that happened to contain Sixteen percent milk fat. / I held the cup in my hand As if it were the Holy Grail, When it came to getting into heaven, I knew I couldn't fail. / For so long I'd been myopic In not seeing the joy of being philanthropic. / I was heading o'er to Belfast, Maine, Driving mighty fast, Determined to make up for, The time that now had passed. / I took a turn, As I took a sip, But I was going too fast, And the cup—it did slip— / Right out of my hand, And onto my lap, And all over the seat Went the rest of my frappe. / The shock was so great, That I did miss the curve, I was outta control—My car—it did swerve. / I crashed into a tree, And was crushed to death I called Millie's name, With my last dying breath. / I was so silly To take pity on Millie. For it seems my compassion, Led to my compression. / If only I'd had qualms About the giving of alms ... / And if only I'd known, 'Bout that cup o' Styrofoam ... / 'Twas indeed a rarity To buy a frappe in charity, I say with all sincerity, I see now with such clarity: that / I was such a sap To buy a charity frappe. It spilled onto my lap. It was a charity frappe That led to this mishap Because of its loose cap. I could give myself a slap Because the charity frappe, It erased me off the map. It was a charity frappe. / As to advice, let me offer you this bit: Be very wary Of charity that is dairy—It's best to keep a lid on it.

SHLENSKY v. WRIGLEY

Illinois Court of Appeals, 1968
237 N.E.2d 776

SULLIVAN, JUSTICE. This is an appeal from a dismissal of plaintiff's amended complaint on motion of the defendants. The action was a stockholders' derivative suit against the directors for negligence and mismanagement. The corporation was also made a defendant. Plaintiff sought damages and an order that defendants cause the installation of lights in Wrigley Field and the scheduling of night baseball games.

Plaintiff is a minority stockholder of defendant corporation, Chicago National League Ball Club, (Inc.), a Delaware corporation with its principal place of business in Chicago, Illinois. Defendant corporation owns and operates the major league professional baseball team known as the Chicago Cubs. The corporation also engages in the operation of Wrigley Field, the Cubs' home park, the concessionaire sales during Cubs' home games, television and radio broadcasts of Cubs' home games, the leasing of the field for football games and other events and receives its share, as visiting team, of admission moneys from games played in other National League stadia. The individual defendants are directors of the Cubs and have served for varying periods of years. Defendant Philip K. Wrigley is also president of the corporation and owner of approximately 80% of the stock therein.

Plaintiff alleges that since night baseball was first played in 1935 nineteen of the twenty major league teams have scheduled night games. In 1966, out of a total of 1620 games in the major leagues, 932 were played at night. Plaintiff alleges that every member of the major leagues, other than the Cubs, scheduled substantially all of its home games in 1966 at night, exclusive of opening days, Saturdays, Sundays, holidays and days prohibited by league rules. Allegedly this has been done for the specific purpose of maximizing attendance and thereby maximizing revenue and income.

The Cubs, in the years 1961–65, sustained operating losses from its direct baseball operations. Plaintiff attributes those losses to inadequate attendance at Cubs' home games. He concludes that if the directors continue to refuse to install lights at Wrigley Field and schedule night baseball games, the Cubs will continue to sustain comparable losses and its financial condition will continue to deteriorate. * * *

Plaintiff alleges that, except for the year 1963, attendance at Cubs' home games has been substantially below that at their road games, many of which were played at night.

Plaintiff compares attendance at Cubs' games with that of the Chicago White Sox, an American League club, whose weekday games were generally played at night. The weekend attendance figures for the two teams was similar; however, the White Sox week-night games drew many more patrons than did the Cubs' weekday games.

Plaintiff alleges that the funds for the installation of lights can be readily obtained through financing and the cost of installation would be far more than offset and recaptured by increased revenues and incomes resulting from the increased attendance.

Plaintiff further alleges that defendant Wrigley has refused to install lights, not because of interest in the welfare of the corporation but because of his personal opinions "that baseball is a 'daytime sport' and that the installation of lights and night baseball games will have a deteriorating effect upon the surrounding neighborhood." It is alleged that he has admitted that he is not interested in whether the Cubs would benefit financially from such action because of his concern for the neighborhood, and that he would be willing for the team to play night games if a new stadium were built in Chicago.

Plaintiff alleges that the other defendant directors, with full knowledge of the foregoing matters, have acquiesced in the policy laid down by Wrigley and have permitted him to dominate the board of directors in matters involving the installation of lights and scheduling of night games, even though they knew he was not motivated by a good faith concern as to the best interests of defendant corporation, but solely by his personal views set forth above. It is charged that the directors are acting for a reason or reasons contrary and wholly unrelated to the business interests of the corporation; that such arbitrary and capricious acts constitute mismanagement and waste of corporate assets, and that the directors have been negligent in failing to exercise reasonable care and prudence in the management of the corporate affairs.

The question on appeal is whether plaintiff's amended complaint states a cause of action. It is plaintiff's position that fraud, illegality and conflict of interest are not the only bases for a stockholder's derivative action against the directors. Contrariwise, defendants argue that the courts will not step in and interfere with honest business judgment of the directors unless there is a showing of fraud, illegality or conflict of interest.

The cases in this area are numerous and each differs from the others on a factual basis. However, the courts have pronounced certain ground rules which appear in all cases and which are then applied to the given factual situation. * * *

In *Davis v. Louisville Gas & Electric Co.*, 16 Del.Ch. 157 [1928], a minority shareholder sought to have the directors enjoined from amending the certificate of incorporation. The court said:

> We have then a conflict in view between the responsible managers of a corporation and an overwhelming majority of its stockholders on the one hand and a dissenting minority on the other— a conflict touching matters of business policy, such as has occasioned innumerable applications to courts to intervene and determine which of the two conflicting views should prevail. The response which courts make to such applications is that it is not

their function to resolve for corporations questions of policy and business management. The directors are chosen to pass upon such questions and their judgment unless shown to be tainted with fraud is accepted as final. The judgment of the directors of corporations enjoys the benefit of a presumption that it was formed in good faith and was designed to promote the best interests of the corporation they serve. * * *

Plaintiff in the instant case argues that the directors are acting for reasons unrelated to the financial interest and welfare of the Cubs. However, we are not satisfied that the motives assigned to Philip K. Wrigley, and through him to the other directors, are contrary to the best interests of the corporation and the stockholders. For example, it appears to us that the effect on the surrounding neighborhood might well be considered by a director who was considering the patrons who would or would not attend the games if the park were in a poor neighborhood. Furthermore, the long run interest of the corporation in its property value at Wrigley Field might demand all efforts to keep the neighborhood from deteriorating. By these thoughts we do not mean to say that we have decided that the decision of the directors was a correct one. That is beyond our jurisdiction and ability. We are merely saying that the decision is one properly before directors and the motives alleged in the amended complaint showed no fraud, illegality or conflict of interest in their making of that decision.

While all the courts do not insist that one or more of the three elements must be present for a stockholder's derivative action to lie, nevertheless we feel that unless the conduct of the defendants at least borders on one of the elements, the courts should not interfere. The trial court in the instant case acted properly in dismissing plaintiff's amended complaint. * * *

Finally, we do not agree with plaintiff's contention that failure to follow the example of the other major league clubs in scheduling night games constituted negligence. Plaintiff made no allegation that these teams' night schedules were profitable or that the purpose for which night baseball had been undertaken was fulfilled. Furthermore, it cannot be said that directors, even those of corporations that are losing money, must follow the lead of the other corporations in the field. Directors are elected for their business capabilities and judgment and the courts cannot require them to forego their judgment because of the decisions of directors of other companies. Courts may not decide these questions in the absence of a clear showing of dereliction of duty on the part of the specific directors and mere failure to "follow the crowd" is not such a dereliction.

For the foregoing reasons the order of dismissal entered by the trial court is affirmed.

Affirmed.

QUESTIONS

1. Did the trial court conclude that the Cubs playing only day games was a dumb decision? Did the trial court care whether it was a dumb decision? Did the appellate court?

2. What can Shlensky do now?

3. Why did an Illinois court quote from and rely on a decision of the Delaware Chancery Court? Though the Cubs are based in Chicago, note that the corporation was formed in Delaware. Recall from the end of Chapter 4 that the law of the state of incorporation governs the internal affairs of the corporation. So Delaware law governs the internal affairs of a corporation that runs a baseball team in Chicago!

———————

One of the most quoted modern cases on a director's duty of care is *Joy v. North*, a Second Circuit decision applying Connecticut law. The lawsuit against the officers and directors of a Connecticut bank alleged that they had breached the duty of care in making a series of loans to a real estate developer referred to in the portion of the opinion set out below as "Katz."

The following part of the majority opinion includes a discussion of both (i) the directors' duty of care and (ii) shareholder derivative suits. We will consider shareholder derivative suits in more detail later in the materials. Accordingly, much of the detail of Judge Winter's consideration of shareholder's derivative suits has been edited. Nonetheless, a general understanding of shareholder derivative suits is necessary to see how the directors' duty of care and other duties are judicially enforced.

JOY v. NORTH

United States Court of Appeals, Second Circuit, 1982
692 F.2d 880

[A shareholder brought a shareholder derivative suit against the corporation's directors and officers. The corporation's board of directors then appointed a "special litigation committee," which issued a report recommending that the suit be dismissed as to "outside" directors. The corporation filed a motion for summary judgment, based on the special litigation committee's report. The trial court granted the motion, holding that "the business judgment rule limits judicial scrutiny of its recommendations to the good faith, independence and thoroughness of the Committee." 692 F.2d 882. A divided Second Circuit here reverses and remands.]

WINTER, J. * * * Our opinion first addresses the nature and function of the business judgment rule, which played a large role in persuading the District Court to dismiss this action. It turns then to the legal oddity known as the derivative action, thought by many to be an endangered species as a consequence of the evolution of special litigation committees. * * *

A. The Liability of Corporate Directors and Officers and the Business Judgment Rule

While it is often stated that corporate directors and officers will be liable for negligence in carrying out their corporate duties, all seem agreed that such a statement is misleading. Whereas an automobile driver who makes a mistake in judgment as to speed or distance injuring a pedestrian will likely be called upon to respond in damages, a corporate officer who makes a mistake in judgment as to economic conditions, consumer tastes or production line efficiency will rarely, if ever, be found liable for damages suffered by the corporation. Whatever the terminology, the fact is that liability is rarely imposed upon corporate directors or officers simply for bad judgment and this reluctance to impose liability for unsuccessful business decisions has been doctrinally labeled the business judgment rule. Although the rule has suffered under academic criticism, it is not without rational basis.

First, shareholders to a very real degree voluntarily undertake the risk of bad business judgment. Investors need not buy stock, for investment markets offer an array of opportunities less vulnerable to mistakes in judgment by corporate officers. Nor need investors buy stock in particular corporations. In the exercise of what is genuinely a free choice, the quality of a firm's management is often decisive and information is available from professional advisors. Since shareholders can and do select among investments partly on the basis of management, the business judgment rule merely recognizes a certain voluntariness in undertaking the risk of bad business decisions.

Second, courts recognize that after-the-fact litigation is a most imperfect device to evaluate corporate business decisions. The circumstances surrounding a corporate decision are not easily reconstructed in a courtroom years later, since business imperatives often call for quick decisions, inevitably based on less than perfect information. The entrepreneur's function is to encounter risks and to confront uncertainty, and a reasoned decision at the time made may seem a wild hunch viewed years later against a background of perfect knowledge.

Third, because potential profit often corresponds to the potential risk, it is very much in the interest of shareholders that the law not create incentives for overly cautious corporate decisions. Some opportunities offer great profits at the risk of very substantial losses, while the alternatives offer less risk of loss but also less potential profit. Shareholders can reduce the volatility of risk by diversifying their holdings. In the case of the diversified shareholder, the seemingly more risky alternatives may well be the best choice since great losses in some stocks will over time be offset by even greater gains in others. Given mutual funds and similar forms of diversified investment, courts need not bend over backwards to give special protection to shareholders who refuse to reduce the volatility of risk by not diversifying. A rule which penalizes the choice of seemingly riskier alternatives thus may not be in the interest of shareholders generally.

Whatever its merit, however, the business judgment rule extends only as far as the reasons which justify its existence. Thus, it does not apply in cases, e.g., in which the corporate decision lacks a business purpose, is tainted by a conflict of interest, is so egregious as to amount to a no-win decision, *Litwin v. Allen*, 25 N.Y.S.2d 667 (N.Y.Co.Sup.Ct.1940), or results from an obvious and prolonged failure to exercise oversight or supervision. Other examples may occur.

B. Shareholder Derivative Actions

Whereas ordinary lenders may and will sue directly to enforce their rights and debentureholders look to indenture trustees to enforce obligations to them, direct actions by individual shareholders for injuries to the value of their investment would be an inefficient and wasteful method of enforcing management obligations. The stake of each shareholder in the likely return is usually too small to justify bringing a lawsuit and a multiplicity of such actions would result in corporate and judicial waste. Moreover, the costs of organizing a large number of geographically diverse shareholders to bring an action are usually prohibitively high. If an alternative remedy were not available, therefore, the fiduciary obligations of corporate management, however limited, might well be unenforceable. * * *

The derivative action is the common law's inventive solution to the problem of actions to protect shareholder interests. In its classic form, a derivative suit involves two actions brought by an individual shareholder: (i) an action against the corporation for failing to bring a specified suit and (ii) an action on behalf of the corporation for harm to it identical to the one which the corporation failed to bring. The technical structure of the derivative suit is thus quite unusual. Moreover, the shareholder plaintiffs are quite often little more than a formality for purposes of the caption rather than parties with a real interest in the outcome. Since any judgment runs to the corporation, shareholder plaintiffs at best realize an appreciation in the value of their shares. The real incentive to bring derivative actions is usually not the hope of return to the corporation but the hope of handsome fees to be recovered by plaintiffs' counsel. * * *

C. Termination of Derivative Suits by Special Litigation Committees

In the normal course of events a decision whether to bring a lawsuit is a corporate economic decision subject to the business judgment rule. Thus, shareholders upset at a corporate failure to bring actions for, say, non-payment of a debt for goods sold and delivered, may not initiate a derivative suit without first making a demand upon the directors to bring the action. Where the directors refuse, and the derivative action challenges that refusal, courts apply the business judgment rule to the action of the directors.

[Judge Winter (who used to teach corporation law at Yale Law School) then acknowledged that situations in which "there is a conflict of interest in the directors' decision not to sue because the directors themselves . . . are named defendants" are treated differently. He rejected the argument that the business judgment rule applies to the recommendations by a special litigation committee composed of directors who are not defendants. We will discuss the use of such committees in derivative litigation in subsection D of this chapter.]

* * *

E. The Present Case * * *

We turn now to the contents of the Special Litigation Committee's Report. We emphasize that this recitation is the Committee's version of the facts. The record suggests that a trial might reveal sharply differing versions of the same events from various witnesses as well as sharply differing inferences drawn from that testimony.

According to the Report, Nelson L. North was Citytrust's Chief Executive Officer and Norman Schaff, Jr. was its Chief Lending Officer during the period in question. The management of Citytrust was completely dominated by North. North also exercised strong control over the activities of the Board of Directors. Board members were given neither materials nor agendas prior to meetings and requests for long range planning documents were left unanswered. * * *

We look first to potential liability generally without regard to which defendants are responsible. As to that liability, we find that plaintiff's chances of success are rather high. The loss to Citytrust resulted from decisions which put the bank in a classic "no win" situation. The Katz venture was risky and increasingly so. By continuing extensions of substantial amounts of credit the bank subjected the principal to those risks although its potential gain was no more than the interest it could have earned in less risky, more diversified loans. In a real sense, there was a low ceiling on profits but only a distant floor for losses. It is so similar to the classic case of *Litwin v. Allen, supra* (bank purchase of bonds with an option in the seller to repurchase at the original price, the bank thus bearing the entire risk of a drop in price with no hope of gain beyond the stipulated interest) that we cannot agree with the Committee's conclusion that only a "possibility of a finding of negligence" exists.

The issue as to which defendants are responsible is less clear. The Committee concluded that there is "no reasonable possibility" of the outside defendants being found liable because they had neither information nor reasonable notice of the problems raised by the Katz transactions. We note first that members of the inside defendants may contradict that version and, if so, a possibility of liability in the outside group exists. Moreover, lack of knowledge is not necessarily a defense, if it is the result of an abdication of directional responsibility. Directors who willingly allow others to make major decisions affecting the future of the corporation wholly without supervision or oversight may not defend on their lack of knowledge, for that ignorance itself is a breach of fiduciary duty. The issue turns in large part upon how and why these defendants were left in the dark. An individual analysis of each outside defendant's role may show that some are blameless or even that they all were justified in not acting before they did, but neither is an inexorable conclusion on the basis of the present record.

The Report concluded as to the inside defendants that there was a "possibility" of liability. This conclusion is a considerable understatement and not entirely consistent with the Report's finding as to the outside defendants. The outsiders' best defense may well be that the inside group actively concealed the Katz problem. Given the fact that exoneration of the outside defendants may show culpability of the insiders and our conclusion that the probability of liability somewhere is high, we think the exposure of the inside group is considerably more than a "possibility." * * *

The grant of summary judgment is reversed, the protective order is vacated, and the case is remanded. * * *

QUESTIONS AND NOTES

1. There was no liability exposure for the directors in *Shlensky*. There was liability exposure for the directors in *Joy v. North*. Are the two cases reconcilable?

2. In *Joy v. North*, the Second Circuit repeatedly refers to the "business judgment rule." Courts, not legislatures, created the business judgment rule. This rule reflects the oft-stated judicial policy that courts will not interfere with business decisions by corporate directors as long as the directors are acting with disinterest, good faith, and due diligence. While courts created the business judgment rule, the MBCA and other corporate codes now contain "guidance as to its application in dealing with director liability claims." Official Comment to § 8.31. Please read MBCA § 8.31 and consider whether *Joy v. North* would have been decided differently under § 8.31. (Note MBCA § 8.31 is limited to directors. *Joy v. North* involved claims against both directors and officers. Should the business judgment rule be limited to directors? *See* MBCA § 8.42, Official Comment.)

3. Professor Booth of the University of Maryland Law School describes *Joy v. North* as "one of those rare cases in which the plaintiff overcomes the business judgment rule. In fact, the plaintiff does it twice." Richard A. Booth, *A Minimalist Approach to Corporate Law*, 34 GA. L. REV. 431, 439 (2000). Do you agree?

4. In an earlier article, Professor Booth summarized *Joy v. North* with the following parenthetical: ("bank directors may be held liable for making loan at inadequate interest rate given risk of project being financed"). Richard A. Booth, *Federalism and the Market for Corporate Control*, 69 WASH. U. L. Q.

411, 443 n. 121 (1991). That footnote ends with a *"See also"* reference to our next case, *Smith v. Van Gorkom.*

Smith v. Van Gorkom involves a sale ("cash merger") of a large, publicly-held company, Trans Union Corporation ("Trans Union"). Van Gorkom, Chief Executive Officer (CEO) of Trans Union and a member of its board of directors, negotiated a deal to sell Trans Union to Pritzker for $55 a share (a total of almost $700,000,000). Only one of the other directors, Trans Union's Chief Operating Officer (COO) Chelberg, was involved in the negotiations; the other directors were not even aware of the negotiations until they attended a special meeting of the board of directors and were asked to approve the sale.

The edited portion of the Delaware Supreme Court opinion set out below involves a "duty of care" challenge to the Trans Union board of directors' approval of the sale at a two-hour meeting, with no prior notice of the purpose of the meeting.* The trial court granted judgment for the defendant directors, holding that they were protected by the business judgment rule. A divided Delaware Supreme Court reversed.

SMITH v. VAN GORKOM

Supreme Court of Delaware, 1985
488 A.2d 858

HORSEY, JUSTICE (for the majority). * * * A class action was brought by shareholders of a corporation, originally seeking rescission of a merger of the corporation into a new corporation. Alternate relief in the form of damages was sought against members of the board of directors, the new corporation, and the owners of the parent of the new corporation. Following trial, the Court of Chancery granted judgment for the directors by an unreported letter opinion. * * *

The Court of Chancery made but one finding; i.e., that the Board's conduct over the entire period from September 20 through January 26, 1981 was not reckless or improvident, but informed. * * *

We conclude that the Court's ultimate finding that the Board's conduct was not "reckless or imprudent" is contrary to the record and not the product of a logical and deductive reasoning process. * * *

Under Delaware law, the business judgment rule is the offspring of the fundamental principle, codified in 8 Del.C. § 141(a), that the business and affairs of a Delaware corporation are managed by or under its board of directors.† [11] Aronson v. Lewis, Del.Supr., 473 A.2d 805, 811 (1984).

---

* If we had not severely edited the facts, you would spend more time trying to understand the deal than the directors of Trans Union did.

† [11] 8 Del.C. § 141 provides, in pertinent part:

In carrying out their managerial roles, directors are charged with an unyielding fiduciary duty to the corporation and its shareholders. The business judgment rule exists to protect and promote the full and free exercise of the managerial power granted to Delaware directors. The rule itself "is a presumption that in making a business decision, the directors of a corporation acted on an informed basis, in good faith and in the honest belief that the action taken was in the best interests of the company." *Aronson, supra* at 812. Thus, the party attacking a board decision as uninformed must rebut the presumption that its business judgment was an informed one.

The determination of whether a business judgment is an informed one turns on whether the directors have informed themselves "prior to making a business decision, of all material information reasonably available to them." * * *

A director's duty to inform himself in preparation for a decision derives from the fiduciary capacity in which he serves the corporation and its stockholders. Since a director is vested with the responsibility for the management of the affairs of the corporation, he must execute that duty with the recognition that he acts on behalf of others. Such obligation does not tolerate faithlessness or self-dealing. But fulfillment of the fiduciary function requires more than the mere absence of bad faith or fraud. Representation of the financial interests of others imposes on a director an affirmative duty to protect those interests and to proceed with a critical eye in assessing information of the type and under the circumstances present here.

Thus, a director's duty to exercise an informed business judgment is in the nature of a duty of care, as distinguished from a duty of loyalty. * * *

The standard of care applicable to a director's duty of care has also been recently restated by this Court. In *Aronson, supra*, we stated:

> While the Delaware cases use a variety of terms to describe the applicable standard of care, our analysis satisfies us that under the business judgment rule director liability is predicated upon concepts of gross negligence. (footnote omitted) * * *

We again confirm that view. We think the concept of gross negligence is also the proper standard for determining whether a business judgment reached by a board of directors was an informed one. * * *

On the record before us, we must conclude that the Board of Directors did not reach an informed business judgment on September 20, 1980 in

---

(a) The business and affairs of every corporation organized under this chapter shall be managed by or under the direction of a board of directors, except as may be otherwise provided in this chapter or in its certificate of incorporation. If any such provision is made in the certificate of incorporation, the powers and duties conferred or imposed upon the board of directors by this chapter shall be exercised or performed to such extent and by such person or persons as shall be provided in the certificate of incorporation.

voting to "sell" the Company for $55 per share pursuant to the Pritzker cash-out merger proposal. * * *

The Board based its September 20 decision to approve the cash-out merger primarily on Van Gorkom's representations. None of the directors, other than Van Gorkom and Chelberg, had any prior knowledge that the purpose of the meeting was to propose a cash-out merger of Trans Union. No members of Senior Management were present, other than Chelberg, Romans [the Chief Financial Officer] and Peterson; and the latter two had only learned of the proposed sale an hour earlier. Both general counsel Moore and former general counsel Browder attended the meeting, but were equally uninformed as to the purpose of the meeting and the documents to be acted upon.

Without any documents before them concerning the proposed transaction, the members of the Board were required to rely entirely upon Van Gorkom's 20–minute oral presentation of the proposal. No written summary of the terms of the merger was presented; the directors were given no documentation to support the adequacy of $55 price per share for sale of the Company; and the Board had before it nothing more than Van Gorkom's statement of his understanding of the substance of an agreement which he admittedly had never read, nor which any member of the Board had ever seen.

Under 8 Del.C. § 141(e),* **[15]** "directors are fully protected in relying in good faith on reports made by officers." The term "report" has been liberally construed to include reports of informal personal investigations by corporate officers. However, there is no evidence that any "report," as defined under § 141(e), concerning the Pritzker proposal, was presented to the Board on September 20. Van Gorkom's oral presentation of his understanding of the terms of the proposed Merger Agreement, which he had not seen, and Romans' brief oral statement of his preliminary study regarding the feasibility of a leveraged buy-out of Trans Union do not qualify as § 141(e) "reports" for these reasons: The former lacked substance because Van Gorkom was basically uninformed as to the essential provisions of the very document about which he was talking. At a minimum for a report to enjoy the status conferred by § 141(e), it must be pertinent to the subject matter upon which a board is called to act, and otherwise be entitled to good faith, not blind, reliance. * * *

We do not say that the Board of Directors was not entitled to give some credence to Van Gorkom's representation that $55 was an adequate or fair price. Under § 141(e), the directors were entitled to rely upon their chairman's opinion of value and adequacy, provided that such opinion was reached on a sound basis. Here, the issue is whether the directors

---

* **[15]** Section 141(e) provides in pertinent part:

A member of the board of directors ... shall, in the performance of his duties, be fully protected in relying in good faith upon the books of accounts or reports made to the corporation by any of its officers, or by an independent certified public accountant, or by an appraiser selected with reasonable care by the board of directors ..., or in relying in good faith upon other records of the corporation

informed themselves as to all information that was reasonably available to them. Had they done so, they would have learned of the source and derivation of the $55 price and could not reasonably have relied thereupon in good faith.

None of the directors, management or outside, were investment bankers or financial analysts. Yet the Board did not consider recessing the meeting until a later hour that day (or requesting an extension of Pritzker's Sunday evening deadline) to give it time to elicit more information as to the sufficiency of the offer, either from inside Management (in particular Romans) or from Trans Union's own investment banker, Salomon Brothers, whose Chicago specialist in merger and acquisitions was known to the Board and familiar with Trans Union's affairs.

Thus, the record compels the conclusion that on September 20 the Board lacked valuation information adequate to reach an informed business judgment as to the fairness of $55 per share for sale of the Company.
* * *

We hold, therefore, that the Trial Court committed reversible error in applying the business judgment rule in favor of the director defendants in this case.

On remand, the Court of Chancery shall conduct an evidentiary hearing to determine the fair value of the shares represented by the plaintiffs' class, based on the intrinsic value of Trans Union on September 20, 1980. * * *

Thereafter, an award of damages may be entered to the extent that the fair value of Trans Union exceeds $55 per share.
* * *

REVERSED and REMANDED for proceedings consistent herewith.
* * * *

McNeilly, Justice, dissenting. The majority opinion reads like an advocate's closing address to a hostile jury. And I say that not lightly. Throughout the opinion great emphasis is directed only to the negative, with nothing more than lip service granted the positive aspects of this case. In my opinion Chancellor Marvel (retired) should have been affirmed. * * *

The majority has spoken and has effectively said that Trans Union's Directors have been the victims of a "fast shuffle" by Van Gorkom and Pritzker. That is the beginning of the majority's comedy of errors. The first and most important error made is the majority's assessment of the directors' knowledge of the affairs of Trans Union and their combined ability to act in this situation under the protection of the business judgment rule.

Trans Union's Board of Directors consisted of ten men, five of whom were "inside" directors and five of whom were "outside" directors. The "inside" directors were Van Gorkom, Chelberg, Bonser, William B. Browder, Senior Vice–President–Law, and Thomas P. O'Boyle, Senior Vice–President–Administration. At the time the merger was proposed the inside five directors had collectively been employed by the Company for 116 years and had 68 years of combined experience as directors. The "outside" directors were A.W. Wallis, William B. Johnson, Joseph B. Lanterman, Graham J. Morgan and Robert W. Reneker. With the exception of Wallis, these were all chief executive officers of Chicago based corporations that were at least as large as Trans Union. The five "outside" directors had 78 years of combined experience as chief executive officers, and 53 years cumulative service as Trans Union directors.

The inside directors wear their badge of expertise in the corporate affairs of Trans Union on their sleeves. But what about the outsiders? Dr. Wallis is or was an economist and math statistician, a professor of economics at Yale University, dean of the graduate school of business at the University of Chicago, and Chancellor of the University of Rochester. Dr. Wallis had been on the Board of Trans Union since 1962. He also was on the Board of Bausch & Lomb, Kodak, Metropolitan Life Insurance Company, Standard Oil and others.

William B. Johnson is a University of Pennsylvania law graduate, President of Railway Express until 1966, Chairman and Chief Executive of I.C. Industries Holding Company, and member of Trans Union's Board since 1968.

Joseph Lanterman, a Certified Public Accountant, is or was President and Chief Executive of American Steel, on the Board of International Harvester, Peoples Energy, Illinois Bell Telephone, Harris Bank and Trust Company, Kemper Insurance Company and a director of Trans Union for four years.

Graham Morgan is a chemist, was Chairman and Chief Executive Officer of U.S. Gypsum, and in the 17 and 18 years prior to the Trans Union transaction had been involved in 31 or 32 corporate takeovers.

Robert Reneker attended University of Chicago and Harvard Business Schools. He was President and Chief Executive of Swift and Company, director of Trans Union since 1971, and member of the Boards of seven other corporations including U.S. Gypsum and the Chicago Tribune.

Directors of this caliber are not ordinarily taken in by a "fast shuffle." I submit they were not taken into this multi-million dollar corporate transaction without being fully informed and aware of the state of the art as it pertained to the entire corporate panorama of Trans Union. True, even directors such as these, with their business acumen, interest and expertise, can go astray. I do not believe that to be the case here. These men knew Trans Union like the back of their hands and were more than well qualified to make on the spot informed business judgments concerning the affairs of Trans Union including a 100% sale of the corporation. Lest we forget, the corporate world of then and now operates on what is so aptly referred to as "the fast track." These men were at the time an integral part of that world, all professional businessmen, not intellectual figureheads. * * *

QUESTIONS AND NOTES

1. Looking back, is *Smith v. Van Gorkom* consistent with *Joy v. North*?

2. Looking back further, is *Smith v. Van Gorkom* consistent with *Shlensky*? Is the court in *Van Gorkom* as deferential to the board of directors as the court was in the *Shlensky* case? Did the court in *Shlensky* review the merits of the board's decision? Did the court in *Van Gorkom* review the merits of the board's decision or merely the process by which the decision was reached?

3. First the court states: "The determination of whether a business judgment is an informed one turns on whether the directors have informed themselves on all material information reasonably available to them." Later in the opinion the court states, "We think the concept of gross negligence is the proper standard for determining whether a business judgment was an informed one." Are these two statements consistent?

4. Would the directors still be grossly negligent if:

a. the $55 a share offer price was almost $18 a share more than what a share of Trans Union was selling for; and

b. under the terms of the deal, the offer would be rescinded if not approved by the board by the end of the next day; and

c. a Trans Union attorney advised the directors that "they might be sued if they failed to accept the deal"; and

d. 69.9% of the outstanding shares of Trans Union were voted in favor of the merger; and only 7.25% were voted against the merger?

5. What if Epstein was a shareholder of Trans Union and did not want to sell his three shares of Trans Union common stock for $55 a share? Reconsider this question when we consider mergers and other corporate combinations.

6. Why didn't Delaware § 141(e) protect the directors? What if Van Gorkom had provided the directors with a written report summarizing the terms of the deals and his reasons for supporting the deal?

7. How would *Smith v. Van Gorkom* have been decided under MBCA §§ 8.30 and 8.31? What language in those statutes is most helpful to the defendants?

8. Professor Fischel of the University of Chicago Law School has described *Smith v. Van Gorkom* as "one of the worst decisions in the history of corporate law." Daniel R. Fischel, *The Business Judgment Rule and the Trans–Union Case*, 40 BUS. LAW. 1437, 1455 (1985).

9. Professor Elson of the University of Delaware puts *Smith v. Van Gorkom* on his list of top ten cases having an impact on corporate law and governance and describes it as having a "major impact on board behavior. It was responsible for the now common use of third-party advisers to provide

expert opinions to boards. And it has led to far more elaborate decisionmaking procedures, involving lengthy meetings, voluminous documentation and the like." Charles M. Elson, *Courts and Boards: The Top Ten Cases,* SD 39 ALI–ABA743 (1998).

10. *Smith v. Van Gorkom* also had an effect on the Delaware legislature. Less than a year after the Delaware Supreme Court's decision in *Smith v. Van Gorkom,* the Delaware legislature decided to permit corporations to limit their directors' liability for money damages for breach of fiduciary duty. Please read Delaware § 102(b)(7). Would *Smith v. Van Gorkom* be decided differently in Delaware today? Would it be decided differently under MBCA § 2.02(b)(4)? Does MBCA § 8.56 add anything relevant? Note that articles drafted according to the statutes cannot protect directors from all liability. Such corporate articles can limit directors' liability to the corporation and its shareholders, but not to outside third parties. In addition, the provisions can eliminate liability only for violations of the duty of care, not for violations of the duty of loyalty or conduct that was in bad faith.

11. Looking ahead, after you read the next case, *Barnes v. Andrews,* consider whether it is consistent with *Smith v. Van Gorkom.*

(ii) Breach of Duty of Care by Board Inaction

Assume that Capel is one of the three directors of Bubba's Burritos, Inc. Capel misses all board meetings and otherwise totally ignores what is happening at the corporation. Propp and Agee, the other two directors, make a series of incredibly dumb and costly decisions. Bubba's Burritos, Inc., files for bankruptcy, and the bankruptcy trustee sues Capel.

Barnes v. Andrews is an early, somewhat subtler version of this story. Consider whether Capel would be held liable under the *Barnes* decision.

BARNES v. ANDREWS
United States District Court, Southern District of New York, 1924
298 F. 614

In Equity. Suit by Earl B. Barnes, as receiver of the Liberty Starters Corporation, against Charles Lee Andrews [who was a director of the corporation]. Decree for defendant.

Final hearing on a bill in equity, under section 91–a of the General Corporation Law of New York (Consol. Laws, c. 23), to hold liable the defendant as director for misprision of office. The corporation was organized under the laws of that state to manufacture starters for Ford motors and aeroplanes. On October 9, 1919, about a year after its organization, the defendant took office as a director, and served until he resigned on June 21, 1920. During that period over $500,000 was raised by the sales of stock of the company, made through an agent working on commission. A force of officers and employees was hired at substantial salaries, and the factory, already erected when the defendant took office, was equipped with machinery. Starter parts were made in quantity, but delays were experienced in the production of starters as a whole, and the funds of the company were steadily depleted by the running charges.

After the defendant resigned, the company continued business until the spring of 1921, when the plaintiff was appointed receiver, found the company without funds, and realized only a small amount on the sale of its assets. During the incumbency of the defendant there had been only two meetings of directors, one of which (i.e., that of October 9, 1919) he attended; the other happening at a day when he was forced to be absent because of his mother's death. He was a friend of the president, who had induced him as the largest stockholder to become a director, and his only attention to the affairs of the company consisted of talks with the president as they met from time to time.

The theory of the bill was that the defendant had failed to give adequate attention to the affairs of the company, which had been conducted incompetently and without regard to the waste in salaries during the period before production was possible. This period was unduly prolonged by the incompetence of the factory manager, and disagreements between him and the engineer, upon whose patents the company depended. The officers were unable to induce these men to compose their differences, and the work languished from incompetence and extravagance. More money was paid the engineer than his royalty contracts justified, and money was spent upon fraudulent circulars to induce the purchase of stock.

* * * *

LEARNED HAND, DISTRICT JUDGE (after stating the facts as above). * * * The first liability must rest upon the defendant's general inattention to his duties as a director. He cannot be charged with neglect in attending directors' meetings, because there were only two during his incumbency, and of these he was present at one and had an adequate excuse for his absence from the other. His liability must therefore depend upon his failure in general to keep advised of the conduct of the corporate affairs. The measure of a director's duties in this regard is uncertain; the courts contenting themselves with vague declarations, such as that a director must give reasonable attention to the corporate business. While directors are collectively the managers of the company, they are not expected to interfere individually in the actual conduct of its affairs. To do so would disturb the authority of the officers and destroy their individual responsibility, without which no proper discipline is possible. To them must be left the initiative and the immediate direction of the business; the directors can act individually only by counsel and advice to them. Yet they have an individual duty to keep themselves informed in some detail, and it is this duty which the defendant in my judgment failed adequately to perform.

All he did was to talk with Maynard [who was the president of the corporation and a friend of Andrews] as they met, while commuting from Flushing, or at their homes. That, indeed, might be enough, because Andrews had no reason to suspect Maynard's candor, nor has any reason to question it been yet disclosed. But it is plain that he did not press him for details, as he should. It is not enough to content oneself with general answers that the business looks promising and that all seems prosperous.

Andrews was bound, certainly as the months wore on, to inform himself of what was going on with some particularity, and, if he had done so, he would have learned that there were delays in getting into production which were putting the enterprise in most serious peril. It is entirely clear from his letters of April 14, 1920, and June 21, 1920, that he had made no effort to keep advised of the actual conduct of the corporate affairs, but had allowed himself to be carried along as a figurehead, in complete reliance upon Maynard. In spite of his own substantial investment in the company, which I must assume was as dear to him as it would be to other men, his position required of him more than this. Having accepted a post of confidence, he was charged with an active duty to learn whether the company was moving to production, and why it was not, and to consider, as best he might, what could be done to avoid the conflicts among the personnel, or their incompetence, which was slowly bleeding it to death.

Therefore I cannot acquit Andrews of misprision in his office, though his integrity is unquestioned. The plaintiff must, however, go further than to show that he should have been more active in his duties. This cause of action rests upon a tort, as much though it be a tort of omission as though it had rested upon a positive act. The plaintiff must accept the burden of showing that the performance of the defendant's duties would have avoided loss, and what loss it would have avoided. I pressed Mr. Alger to show me a case in which the courts have held that a director could be charged generally with the collapse of a business in respect of which he had been inattentive, and I am not aware that he has found one. * * *

The defendant is not subject to the burden of proving that the loss would have happened, whether he had done his duty or not. If he were, it would come to this: That, if a director were once shown slack in his duties, he would stand charged prima facie with the difference between the corporate treasury as it was, and as it would be, judged by a hypothetical standard of success. How could such a standard be determined? How could anyone guess how far a director's skill and judgment would have prevailed upon his fellows, and what would have been the ultimate fate of the business, if they had? How is it possible to set any measure of liability, or to tell what he would have contributed to the event? Men's fortunes may not be subjected to such uncertain and speculative conjectures. It is hard to see how there can be any remedy, except one can put one's finger on a definite loss and say with reasonable assurance that protest would have deterred, or counsel persuaded, the managers who caused it. No men of sense would take the office, if the law imposed upon them a guaranty of the general success of their companies as a penalty for any negligence.

It is, indeed, hard to determine just what went wrong in the management of this company. Any conclusion is little better than a guess. * * *

Suppose I charge Andrews with a complete knowledge of all that we have now learned. What action should he have taken, and how can I say that it would have stopped the losses? The plaintiff gives no definite answer to that question. It is easy to say that he should have done something, but that will not serve to harness upon him the whole loss, nor is it the equivalent of saying that, had he acted, the company would now flourish.

True, he was not very well suited by experience for the job he had undertaken, but I cannot hold him on that account. After all, it is the same corporation that chose him which now seeks to charge him. Directors are not specialists, like lawyers or doctors. They must have good sense, perhaps they must have acquaintance with affairs; but they need not—indeed, perhaps they should not—have any technical talent. They are the general advisers of the business, and if they faithfully give such ability as they have to their charge, it would not be lawful to hold them liable. Must a director guarantee that his judgment is good? Can shareholders call him to account for deficiencies which their votes assured him did not disqualify him for his office? While he may not have been the Cromwell for that Civil War, Andrews did not engage to play any such role.

I conclude, therefore, as to this first claim that there is no evidence that the defendant's neglect caused any losses to the company, and that, if there were, that loss cannot be ascertained. * * *

QUESTIONS AND NOTES

1. Andrews attended one of the two board of directors meetings held while he was a director. Can a director satisfy her duty of care by attending all meetings of the board of directors?

2. Do you agree with Judge Hand's statement that "directors are not specialists, like lawyers or doctors"? What if a director happens to have special expertise relevant to a matter before the board?

3. Is the *Barnes* decision consistent with the MBCA? Please read MBCA §§ 8.30(b), and 8.31(a) and (b)(1).

4. Is the *Barnes* decision consistent with *Meinhard v. Salmon?*

5. In *Francis v. United Jersey Bank*, 432 A.2d 814 (N.J. 1981), Lillian Pritchard inherited 48 percent of the stock in the family reinsurance brokerage business from her husband. The husband had founded and run the corporation, which also employed the couple's sons, Charles, Jr. and William. When the husband died, the two boys (who owned the rest of the stock) took over, and allegedly helped themselves to vast sums of the company's clients' money. Lillian and her two sons were the directors. Lillian knew nothing about the reinsurance business and did nothing to inform herself even of its rudiments. She never read corporate documents. She went to the office only once. Even though her husband had warned her that the sons "would take the shirt off my back," Mrs. Pritchard simply did nothing to fulfill the duties of being a director. To make matters worse, after her husband's death Mrs. Pritchard starting drinking heavily.

The sons allegedly misappropriated so much money that the company filed a bankruptcy petition. The trustee in bankruptcy sued Mrs. Pritchard (actually, her estate, since she had died by then).

The New Jersey Supreme Court held her estate liable for her breach of the duty of care. According to the court, that duty requires one to exercise the degree of diligence, care, and skill that an ordinarily prudent person would use in similar circumstances. A prudent person in Mrs. Pritchard's position would at least have acquired some knowledge of the business and would have kept herself informed by attending meetings and reviewing relevant documents, including financial statements. Clearly, Mrs. Pritchard failed to discharge this duty.

As a further requirement for liability, however, the plaintiff had to show that this dereliction caused harm to the corporation. Causation was clear, the court concluded, because if Mrs. Pritchard had not been asleep at the switch, she would easily have seen that something was terribly amiss and would have investigated, thereby finding the misappropriation.

6. The court in *Barnes v. Andrews* places the burden of proof on the plaintiff to show causation. In other words, the plaintiff must show not only that the defendant breached the duty of care, but that this breach caused a loss to the corporation. The court discusses the practical difficulty of placing the burden regarding causation on the defendant (in the paragraph starting "The defendant is not subject to the burden . . .").

While *Barnes* reflects the majority view on this point, it is not the universal view. Notably, Delaware courts do not make the plaintiff show causation. Rather, lack of causation is an affirmative defense to be pleaded by the defendant. After the plaintiff shows that the defendant breached the duty of care, the burden shifts to the defendant to satisfy the "entire fairness test." *Cede & Co. v. Technicolor*, 634 A.2d 345, 361 (Del. 1993). This requires the defendant to show both that the process used to approve the deal was fair and that the terms of the deal were fair.

We will discuss the entire fairness test in detail in *HMG Courtland* on page 249 and in *Weinberger* on page 494. As we will see, defendants have a tough time satisfying the entire fairness test. Note, then, that Delaware law on burden of proof regarding causation in duty of care cases seems much more "pro-plaintiff" than the majority view.

7. *Barnes v. Andrews* is another of the cases on Professor Elson's top ten list:

> This famed 1924 case, decided by the eminent American jurist, Judge Learned Hand, established the now critical corporate law principle that in an action against an inattentive director, a complaining shareholder must establish some linkage between the director's bad behavior and corporate loss—or in legal terms, "causation."
>
> An inattentive director or directors cannot be held liable for a corporate loss if it is shown that proper attentiveness to corporate affairs by all the directors would still not have prevented the loss complained of. In other words, it must be demonstrated that the accused director's slothfulness was a cause of the company's loss. This notion of causation is thus a critical element in any action brought against a poorly performing board of directors and has had a tremendous impact on the course of modern corporate governance.

Charles M. Elson, *Courts and the Boards: The Top Ten Cases*, SD ALI–ABA 743 (1998).

8. Section 404 of the Sarbanes–Oxley Act (we met SOX in Chapter 1) adds to the duty of care that a corporation's management owes the corporation. All of a corporation's annual financial reports must now include a statement that the corporation has implemented an "adequate internal control structure and procedures for financial reporting." The section is controversial because many assert that the costs of complying with it will be large.

The 1996 Delaware Chancery Court decision in *In re Caremark Int'l, Inc., Derivative Litigation* is widely regarded as the seminal modern case on directors' liability for failure to act. As background, we should know about *Graham v. Allis–Chalmers Mfg. Co.*, 188 A.2d 125 (Del. 1963). In that case, several mid-level employees of a large corporation were indicted and pleaded guilty to violating federal antitrust laws by engaging in price fixing. In a derivative suit, a shareholder argued that the directors of the corporation breached the duty of care by failing to monitor the employees sufficiently to uncover the problem.

The Delaware Supreme Court held that the directors had not breached their duty. According to the court, the fact that the corporation had over 30,000 employees in several states meant that the board could be responsible only for very broad policy issues, and not for the immediate supervision of employees. The plaintiff countered by arguing that the board had a duty to establish some sort of monitoring system to uncover pricing problems. The court, in overly sweeping language, said that the directors were not required to set up a monitoring system until they had some reason to suspect that the employees were not being honest.

No one doubts that the board has the right to rely on subordinates. But such reliance must be reasonable. In *Graham*, the plaintiffs simply failed to produce enough evidence to raise the suspicion of price-fixing by employees (even though the company had engaged in such activity previously). In the *Caremark* case, the Delaware Chancery Court revisits the question of when monitoring systems might be required.

IN RE CAREMARK INT'L, INC., DERIVATIVE LITIGATION

Delaware Chancery Court, 1996
698 A.2d 959

[Caremark is a health care provider. Caremark's settlement of various governmental and private claims of violations of Medicare and Medicaid rules cost the corporation over $250,000,000. A shareholder derivative action was filed (i) alleging that the directors violated their duty of care by failing to supervise the conduct of Caremark employees and (ii) seeking the recovery from the directors of the $250,000,000 paid by Caremark.

The following is an edited version of the opinion approving a settlement of the shareholder derivative suit. Under the settlement, "plaintiffs have been given express assurances that Caremark will have a more centralized, active supervisory system in the future." Plaintiffs' attorneys were given "a fee of $816,000 plus $53,000 of expenses."]

ALLEN, CHANCELLOR. * * * The complaint charges the director defendants with breach of their duty of attention or care in connection with the on-going operation of the corporation's business. The claim is that the directors allowed a situation to develop and continue which exposed the corporation to enormous legal liability and that in so doing they violated a duty to be active monitors of corporate performance. * * *

The theory here advanced is possibly the most difficult theory in corporation law upon which a plaintiff might hope to win a judgment.

1. Potential liability for directoral decisions. Director liability for a breach of the duty to exercise appropriate attention may, in theory, arise in two distinct contexts. First, such liability may be said to follow from a board decision that results in a loss because that decision was ill advised or "negligent." Second, liability to the corporation for a loss may be said to arise from an unconsidered failure of the board to act in circumstances in which due attention would, arguably, have prevented the loss. * * *

What should be understood, but may not widely be understood by courts or commentators who are not often required to face such questions, is that compliance with a director's duty of care can never appropriately be judicially determined by reference to the content of the board decision that leads to a corporate loss, apart from consideration of the good faith or rationality of the process employed. That is, whether a judge or jury considering the matter after the fact, believes a decision substantively wrong, or degrees of wrong extending through "stupid" to "egregious" or "irrational," provides no ground for director liability, so long as the court determines that the process employed was either rational or employed in a good faith effort to advance corporate interests. To employ a different rule—one that permitted an "objective" evaluation of the decision—would expose directors to substantive second guessing by ill-equipped judges or juries, which would, in the long-run, be injurious to investor interests. Thus, the business judgment rule is process oriented and informed by a deep respect for all good faith board decisions.

Indeed, one wonders on what moral basis might shareholders attack a good faith business decision of a director as "unreasonable" or "irrational." Where a director in fact exercises a good faith effort to be informed and to exercise appropriate judgment, he or she should be deemed to satisfy fully the duty of attention. If the shareholders thought themselves entitled to some other quality of judgment than such a director produces in the good faith exercise of the powers of office, then the shareholders should have elected other directors. Judge Learned Hand made the point rather better than can I. In speaking of the passive director defendant Mr.

Andrews in *Barnes v. Andrews*, 298 F. 614 (S.D. N.Y. 1924), Judge Hand said:

> True, he was not very suited by experience for the job he had undertaken, but I cannot hold him on that account. After all it is the same corporation that chose him that now seeks to charge him. . . . Directors are not specialists like lawyers or doctors. . . . They are the general advisors of the business and if they faithfully give such ability as they have to their charge, it would not be lawful to hold them liable. Must a director guarantee that his judgment is good? Can a shareholder call him to account for deficiencies that their votes assured him did not disqualify him for his office? While he may not have been the Cromwell for that Civil War, Andrews did not engage to play any such role.

In this formulation Learned Hand correctly identifies, in my opinion, the core element of any corporate law duty of care inquiry: whether there was good faith effort to be informed and exercise judgment.

2. Liability for failure to monitor. The second class of cases in which director liability for inattention is theoretically possible entail circumstances in which a loss eventuates not from a decision but, from unconsidered inaction. Most of the decisions that a corporation, acting through its human agents, makes are, of course, not the subject of director attention. Legally, the board itself will be required only to authorize the most significant corporate acts or transactions: mergers, changes in capital structure, fundamental changes in business, appointment and compensation of the CEO, etc. As the facts of this case graphically demonstrate, ordinary business decisions that are made by officers and employees deeper in the interior of the organization can, however, vitally affect the welfare of the corporation and its ability to achieve its various strategic and financial goals. * * *

In 1963, the Delaware Supreme Court in *Graham v. Allis–Chalmers Mfg. Co.*, 188 A.2d 125 (Del. 1963), addressed the question of potential liability of board members for losses experienced by the corporation as a result of the corporation having violated the anti-trust laws of the United States. There was no claim in that case that the directors knew about the behavior of subordinate employees of the corporation that had resulted in the liability. Rather, as in this case, the claim asserted was that the directors ought to have known of it and if they had known they would have been under a duty to bring the corporation into compliance with the law and thus save the corporation from the loss. The Delaware Supreme Court concluded that, under the facts as they appeared, there was no basis to find that the directors had breached a duty to be informed of the ongoing operations of the firm. In notably colorful terms, the court stated that "absent cause for suspicion there is no duty upon the directors to install and operate a corporate system of espionage to ferret out wrongdoing which they have no reason to suspect exists." The Court found that there were no grounds for suspicion in that case and, thus, concluded that the directors were blamelessly unaware of the conduct leading to the corporate liability.

How does one generalize this holding today? Can it be said today that, absent some ground giving rise to suspicion of violation of law, that corporate directors have no duty to assure that a corporate information gathering and reporting systems exists which represents a good faith attempt to provide senior management and the Board with information respecting material acts, events or conditions within the corporation, including compliance with applicable statutes and regulations? I certainly do not believe so. I doubt that such a broad generalization of the *Graham* holding would have been accepted by the Supreme Court in 1963. The case can be more narrowly interpreted as standing for the proposition that, absent grounds to suspect deception, neither corporate boards nor senior officers can be charged with wrongdoing simply for assuming the integrity of employees and the honesty of their dealings on the company's behalf.

A broader interpretation of *Graham v. Allis–Chalmers*—that it means that a corporate board has no responsibility to assure that appropriate information and reporting systems are established by management— would not, in any event, be accepted by the Delaware Supreme Court in 1996, in my opinion. In stating the basis for this view, I start with the recognition that in recent years the Delaware Supreme Court has made it clear—especially in its jurisprudence concerning takeovers, from *Smith v. Van Gorkom* through *Paramount Communications v. QVC*, 637 A.2d 34 (Del. 1994)—the seriousness with which the corporation law views the role of the corporate board. Secondly, I note the elementary fact that relevant and timely information is an essential predicate for satisfaction of the board's supervisory and monitoring role under Section 141 of the Delaware General Corporation Law. Thirdly, I note the potential impact of the federal organizational sentencing guidelines on any business organization. Any rational person attempting in good faith to meet an organizational governance responsibility would be bound to take into account this development and the enhanced penalties and the opportunities for reduced sanctions that it offers.

* * * [I]t would, in my opinion, be a mistake to conclude that our Supreme Court's statement in *Graham* concerning "espionage" means that corporate boards may satisfy their obligation to be reasonably informed concerning the corporation, without assuring themselves that information and reporting systems exist in the organization that are reasonably designed to provide to senior management and to the board itself timely, accurate information sufficient to allow management and the board, each within its scope, to reach informed judgments concerning both the corporation's compliance with law and its business performance.

Obviously the level of detail that is appropriate for such an information system is a question of business judgment. And obviously too, no rationally designed information and reporting system will remove the possibility that the corporation will violate laws or regulations, or that senior officers or directors may nevertheless sometimes be misled or otherwise fail reasonably to detect acts material to the corporation's compliance with the law. But it is important that the board exercise a good faith judgment that the corporation's information and reporting system is in concept and design adequate to assure the board that appropriate information will come to its attention in a timely manner as a matter of ordinary operations, so that it may satisfy its responsibility.

Thus, I am of the view that a director's obligation includes a duty to attempt in good faith to assure that a corporate information and reporting system, which the board concludes is adequate, exists, and that failure to do so under some circumstances may, in theory at least, render a director liable for losses caused by non-compliance with applicable legal standards. I now turn to an analysis of the claims asserted with this concept of the directors duty of care, as a duty satisfied in part by assurance of adequate information flows to the board, in mind.

* * * Generally where a claim of directorial liability for corporate loss is predicated upon ignorance of liability creating activities within the corporation in my opinion only a sustained or systematic failure of the board to exercise oversight—such as an utter failure to attempt to assure a reasonable information and reporting system exists—will establish the lack of good faith that is a necessary condition to liability.

Here the record supplies essentially no evidence that the director defendants were guilty of a sustained failure to exercise their oversight function. To the contrary, insofar as I am able to tell on this record, the corporation's information systems appear to have represented a good faith attempt to be informed of relevant facts. If the directors did not know the specifics of the activities that lead to the indictments, they cannot be faulted.

The liability that eventuated in this instance was huge. But the fact that it resulted from a violation of criminal law alone does not create a breach of fiduciary duty by directors. The record at this stage does not support the conclusion that the defendants either lacked good faith in the exercise of their monitoring responsibilities or conscientiously permitted a known violation of law by the corporation to occur. The claims asserted against them must be viewed at this stage as extremely weak.

The proposed settlement provides very modest benefits. Under the settlement agreement, plaintiffs have been given express assurances that Caremark will have a more centralized, active supervisory system in the future. Specifically, the settlement mandates duties to be performed by the newly named Compliance and Ethics Committee on an ongoing basis and increases the responsibility for monitoring compliance with the law at the lower levels of management. In adopting the resolutions required under the settlement, Caremark has further clarified its policies concerning the prohibition of providing remuneration for referrals. These appear to be positive consequences of the settlement of the claims brought by the plaintiffs, even if they are not highly significant. Nonetheless, given the weakness of the plaintiffs' claims the proposed settlement appears to be an adequate, reasonable, and beneficial outcome for all of the parties. Thus, the proposed settlement will be approved. * * *

QUESTIONS

1. What did the directors do wrong?

2. *Caremark* was decided by a Delaware trial court. The high court of that state later adopted its reasoning, however, in *Stone v. Ritter*, 911 A.2d 362, 370 (Del. 2006). There, the court explained:

> We hold that *Caremark* articulates the necessary conditions predicate for director oversight liability: (a) the directors utterly failed to implement any reporting or information system or controls; or (b) having implemented such a system or controls, consciously failed to monitor or oversee its operations thus disabling themselves from being informed of risks or problems requiring their attention. In either case, imposition of liability requires a showing that the directors knew that they were not discharging their fiduciary obligations. Where directors fail to act in the face of a known duty to act, thereby demonstrating a conscious disregard for their responsibilities, they breach their duty of loyalty by failing to discharge that fiduciary obligation in good faith.

3. Is the duty of care as expressed in *Caremark* consistent with the duty of care in MBCA §§ 8.30 and 8.31? Is it consistent with the earlier statement of Delaware law in the *Graham* case discussed by the *Caremark* court? Is it consistent with the later statement of Delaware law in the next case?

McCALL v. SCOTT

United States Court of Appeals, Sixth Circuit, 2001
239 F.3d 808

[McCall is in most respects remarkably similar to *Caremark*: another health care corporation incorporated in Delaware (Columbia/HCA Healthcare Corporation) that sustained significant losses because of health care fraud, and was the subject of a shareholder derivative suit against officers and directors alleging, inter alia, breach of duty of care. The opinion deals with both the law of shareholder derivative suits and the law of directors' duty of care. The district court dismissed the suit for failure to comply with the requirements for a shareholder derivative suit. The Sixth Circuit reverses and remands. We have included portions of the Sixth Circuit decision to give you a better understanding of (i) how courts apply the *Caremark* case and (ii) how courts apply the waiver of liability provision in the Delaware Code.]

RALPH B. GUY, JR., CIRCUIT JUDGE. Columbia/HCA is a Delaware corporation with its headquarters and principal place of business in Nashville, Tennessee. Founded in 1987 by Richard L. Scott, Columbia grew so aggressively that, by 1995, it owned and operated 45% of all for-profit hospitals in the United States. It was three times as large as the next largest for-profit health care management company and was the nation's ninth largest employer. Its strategy for growth was to acquire mid- to large-size general, acute-care hospitals. Plaintiffs alleged that Columbia operated 314 hospitals, 143 outpatient surgery centers, and over 500 home health care centers located in 35 states and 3 foreign countries. Columbia was Medicare's single largest provider and, between 1994 and 1996, received over 40% of its revenues from Medicare and Medicaid. Columbia participated in the Medicare, Medicaid, and CHAMPUS programs, with nearly all of its hospitals certified as providers of benefits under these programs.

Plaintiffs alleged that Columbia's senior management, with Board knowledge, devised schemes to improperly increase revenue and profits, and perpetuated a management philosophy that provided strong incentives for employees to commit fraud. Plaintiffs averred that management set growth targets at 15 to 20%, or three to four times the industry average, which could not reasonably be attained without violating Medicare and Medicaid laws and regulations. Results were monitored using a "score card," and good results were rewarded with cash bonuses. Fraudulent practices allegedly included: (1) "upcoding" by providers, which refers to billing for services under DRG (diagnosis related group) codes for illnesses with a higher degree of complexity and severity than a patient's condition actually warranted; (2) improper cost reporting, such as seeking reimbursement for advertising and marketing costs, "grossing up" outpatient revenues, allocating costs from one division to another, and structuring transactions to disguise acquisition costs as reimbursable management fees; (3) offering financial incentives to physicians to increase referrals of Medicare patients to Columbia's facilities (i.e., equity interests, fees, rents, or other perquisites); and (4) acquisition practices that offered inducements to executives of target companies and interfered with existing physician relationships. Plaintiffs also asserted that some of the defendants engaged in illegal insider trading since they traded while knowing of Columbia's fraudulent activities. Damages were alleged to include, among other things, the consequences of federal and state investigations, stockholder and whistle-blower lawsuits, loss of good will, and declines in the value of Columbia stock.

[After a lengthy review of law, the court concluded that Delaware law relating to shareholder derivative suits requires that the "particularized allegations in the complaint present 'a substantial likelihood' of liability on the part of the directors." The following part of the opinion considers whether there was a substantial likelihood of liability for intentional or reckless breach of the fiduciary duty of care.]

The contours of director liability for breach of the duty to exercise appropriate attention to potentially illegal corporate activities were discussed in *In re Caremark International Inc. Derivative Litigation*, 698 A.2d 959 (Del.Ch.1996). There, the court explained that this was "possibly the most difficult theory in corporation law upon which a plaintiff might hope to win a judgment." Director liability for such a breach may arise (1) from a board decision that resulted in a loss because the decision was ill-advised, or (2) from "an unconsidered failure of the board to act in circumstances in which due attention would, arguably, have prevented the loss." As discussed earlier, the duty of care claims in this case fall into the second category as they arise from the Board's failure to act under the circumstances. The court in *Caremark* held that when director liability is predicated upon ignorance of liability creating activities "only a sustained or systematic failure of the board to exercise oversight—such as an utter failure to attempt to assure a reasonable information and reporting system exists—will establish the lack of good faith that is a necessary condition to liability."

Unconsidered inaction can be the basis for director liability because, even though most corporate decisions are not subject to director attention, ordinary business decisions of officers and employees deeper in the corporation can significantly injure the corporation and make it subject to criminal sanctions. This theory grew out of an earlier decision, in which the Delaware Supreme Court explained that:

> The question of whether a corporate director has become liable for losses to the corporation through neglect of duty is determined by the circumstances. If he has recklessly reposed confidence in an obviously untrustworthy employee, has refused or neglected cavalierly to perform his duty as a director, or has ignored either willfully or through inattention obvious danger signs of employee wrongdoing, the law will cast the burden of liability upon him.

Graham v. Allis–Chalmers Mfg. Co., 188 A.2d 125, 130 (Del.1963). Since then, the Delaware Supreme Court specifically adopted gross negligence as the standard for measuring a director's liability for a breach of the duty of care. *See Smith v. Van Gorkom*, 488 A.2d 858, 872 (Del.1985).

After reviewing the cases, we cannot agree with the district court's conclusion that *Caremark* requires a director to have intentionally acted to harm the corporation. While defendants do not deny that something less than intentional conduct may state a claim under *Caremark*, they argue instead that intentional conduct is required to overcome the waiver of liability adopted by Columbia pursuant to Delaware statute. Columbia's Restated Certificate of Incorporation provides as follows:

> TWELFTH: A director of the Corporation shall not be personally liable to the Corporation or its stockholders for monetary damages for breach of fiduciary duty as a director; provided, however, that the foregoing shall not eliminate or limit the liability of a director (i) for any breach of the director's duty of loyalty to the Corporation or its stockholders, (ii) for acts or omissions not in good faith or which involve intentional misconduct or a knowing violation of law, (iii) under Section 174 of the General Corporation Law of Delaware, or (iv) for any transaction from which the director derived an improper personal benefit.

When the validity of such a provision is not contested and the factual basis for the claims implicates only a breach of the duty of care, the waiver may properly be considered and applied in deciding a motion to dismiss. * * *

Plaintiffs maintain that their duty of care claims are not barred as the second exception excludes protection from director liability for "acts or omissions not in good faith or which involve intentional misconduct or a knowing violation of law." Although plaintiffs urge us to interpret "intentional misconduct" to include "recklessness," we do not believe the Delaware Supreme Court would interpret the provision in this way. Still, it is unclear whether some reckless acts or omissions may be excluded from the protection of provisions adopted pursuant to § 102(b)(7). As one treatise explained:

> Whether the statute would protect a director against reckless acts is not altogether clear. To the extent that recklessness involves a conscious disregard of a known risk, it could be argued that such an approach is not one taken in good faith and thus could not be liability exempted under the new statute. On the other hand, to the extent that the conduct alleged to be reckless is predicated solely on allegations of sustained inattention to the duty it is arguable whether such conduct is "grossly negligent," but not conduct amounting to bad faith.

Balotti & Finkelstein, DELAWARE LAW OF CORPORATIONS AND BUSINESS ORGANIZATIONS § 4.29 at 4–116 to 4–116.1 (3d ed. Supp.2000). Thus, we find the district court erred in concluding that only intentional conduct would escape the protection of the provision adopted in Columbia's Restated Certificate of Incorporation.

We find that the particularized facts, when taken together, are sufficient to present a substantial likelihood of liability on the part of at least five of Columbia's directors, which creates a reasonable doubt as to the disinterestedness of a majority of the Board as of filing of the derivative suit. At the same time, we caution that this conclusion involves only the sufficiency of the pleadings with respect to demand futility and reflects no opinion as to the truth of the allegations or the outcome of the claims on the merits.

A significant factor in our assessment of the factual allegations was the prior experience of a number of the defendants as directors or managers of health care organizations that were acquired by Columbia. * * *

Given their prior experience, plaintiffs maintain that the failure of these directors to act was the result of an intentional or reckless disregard of the "red flags" that warned of the systematic fraudulent practices employed and encouraged by Columbia management. In particular, plaintiffs alleged that intentional or reckless disregard can be inferred from the failure to act in the face of audit information, ongoing acquisition practices, allegations brought against Columbia in a qui tam action, the extensive federal investigation, the New York Times' investigation into Columbia's billing practices, and inaction by the Board prior to July 26, 1997. * * *

Taking the allegations as a whole and drawing the reasonable inferences in plaintiffs' favor, we find that the particularized facts are sufficient to [allege] facts that presented a substantial likelihood of director liability for intentional or reckless breach of the duty of care. * * *

QUESTIONS AND NOTES

1. Do you agree with *McCall's* statement of what "the court in *Caremark* held"?

2. After *McCall*, what should a plaintiff allege in a complaint that asserts a director's neglect of duty? Negligence? Gross negligence? Reckless conduct? Intentional conduct?

3. Is the statement by Judge Guy Cole in *McCall* that "a significant factor in our assessment of the factual allegation was the prior experience of a number of the defendants as directors or managers of healthcare organizations that were acquired by Columbia" consistent with Judge Learned Hand's statement in *Barnes v. Andrews* that "[d]irectors are not specialists, like lawyers or doctors * * * [T]hey need not—indeed, perhaps they should not—have any technical talent"?

4. Why didn't the waiver of liability in Columbia's certificate of incorporation protect the defendants? Would it have protected the defendants if the MBCA, and not Delaware law, controlled? *Compare* MBCA § 2.02(b)(4) *with* Delaware § 102(b)(7).

b. Duty of Loyalty

We move from the duty of care to the duty of loyalty. One hornbook provides this overview and comparison of duty of care and duty of loyalty: "We depart now from cases in which the complaint is that directors and officers breached their duty of care—in other words, they were lazy or dumb. In this section, we consider complaints that directors or officers breached their duty of loyalty—in other words, they were greedy and put their own financial interests ahead of the interests of the corporations and its shareholders." Franklin Gevurtz, CORPORATION LAW 321.

Questions of a director's duty of loyalty generally arise when the director (1) competes with the company, or (2) takes for herself a "corporate opportunity" or (3) has some personal pecuniary interest in a corporation's decision. In dealing with the following cases, remember the Delaware and MBCA provisions regarding a corporation's waiver of directors' duties.

(i) Competing With the Corporation

JONES CO., INC. v. FRANK BURKE, JR.

New York Court of Appeals, 1954
117 N.E.2d 237

[An advertising agency, Duane Jones Co., Inc., began to suffer hard times because of "behavior lapses" by its founder Duane Jones. Several of the company's officers, while still in its employ, began a new competing agency, Scheideler, Beck & Werner, Inc. They lured to the new agency both Jones Co.'s key employees and many of its clients. Once the new agency got on its feet, the disloyal officers resigned from Jones Co. After Jones Co. sued, the court found these former officers liable for breach of fiduciary duty for competing with their employer Jones Co.]

LEWIS, CHIEF JUDGE. In 1942, Duane Jones, a man of experience in the field of advertising, organized the plaintiff corporation. From the date of its formation, Jones has continued to be the dominating personality and the policy maker of plaintiff corporation, which by 1951 had acquired accounts in such number and quality as produced a gross billing of $9,000,000. Plaintiff's income was derived from commissions paid to it in the amount of 15% of the sum spent by plaintiff's customers with advertising media. Plaintiff's service consisted of originating advertising ideas and campaigns satisfactory to its customers, and of arranging for the execution of such campaigns through various media. * * * In July, 1951, plaintiff serviced approximately twenty-five customers or accounts, including the following which the amended complaint alleges were diverted to the defendant Scheideler, Beck & Werner, Inc.: Manhattan Soap Co., Inc., G.F. Heublein & Bro., Inc., International Salt Co., Inc., Wesson Oil & Snowdrift Sales Co., C.F. Mueller Co., The Borden Company, The Marlin Fire Arms Co. and McIlhenny Corp. * * *

During the preceding six months plaintiff had lost three of its accounts—total gross billings of which approximated $6,500,000—and had received resignations from three executives as well as from certain staff members of the organization. It also appears that Duane Jones, the president of plaintiff corporation, had been guilty of certain behavior lapses at his office, at business functions and during interviews with actual and prospective customers. As a result of those occasions of misbehavior, several of plaintiff's officers and directors expressed dissatisfaction with conditions—described as "intolerable"—which existed at the plaintiff agency in the spring and summer of 1951.

On June 28, 1951, a meeting took place at the Park Lane Hotel in Manhattan, which was attended by a number of the plaintiff's officers, directors and employees, including all the individual defendants named in this action except the defendant Burke. * * * There was substantial evidence of record that at the meeting of June 28th, the defendant Scheideler informed the group that he had spoken to several of plaintiff's customers whose accounts he serviced from whom he gained favorable reaction to a proposal that the group either buy out Duane Jones' interest in the plaintiff corporation or that they form a new corporation. It also appears that Scheideler suggested to the others present that they inquire whether the accounts being serviced by them for the plaintiff would favor such a project. Defendants Scheideler and Hayes each admitted that at the June 28th meeting it was decided that Hayes should speak to Duane Jones concerning a possible purchase by the defendants of Jones' interest in the plaintiff corporation.

According to Hayes, he informed Duane Jones on July 3, 1951, that the nine defendants associated with plaintiff were interested in purchasing Jones' stock in the plaintiff agency. Mr. Jones' recital of that conversation was that Hayes told him of the group's intention either to buy him out or to start their own agency, and that if he did not agree to a sale they would resign en masse within forty-eight hours. Duane Jones further testified that Hayes indicated to him that the agency's customers had been "already presold" on the alternative plan and that the group would notify him on July 5th of the price they would pay for the business. According to Jones he said to Hayes: "In other words, you are standing there with a Colt .45, holding it at my forehead, and there is not much I can do except to give up?", to which Hayes replied: "Well, you can call it anything you want, but that is what we are going to do." * * *

However, despite frequent meetings between representatives of Duane Jones and the individual defendants the proposed sale was never consummated. Negotiations terminated on or about August 6, 1951, the claim of both Duane Jones and the defendants being that the failure to agree was the result of the other's increased demands. * * *

On August 22, 1951, the defendants Scheideler, Werner and Beck signed a certificate of incorporation of the defendant Scheideler, Beck & Werner, Inc., which certificate was filed with the Secretary of State on August 23, 1951. A few days later, on August 30th, the corporate defendant executed a lease of office space at 487 Park Avenue, where it opened for business as an advertising agency on September 10, 1951. [The officers of Jones Co. who had started the Scheideler, Beck Company then resigned from Jones Co., effective mid-September 1951.]

Within six weeks after its formal opening, the defendant Scheideler, Beck & Werner, Inc., had in its employ seventy-one of the one hundred thirty-two persons formerly employed by plaintiff, including the defendants Scheideler, Werner, Beck, Hughes, Brooks, Hubbard and Hulshizer. Each of the defendants named above was a stockholder in the corporate defendant, and the defendants Scheideler, Werner, Hulshizer and Beck held the offices of president, vice president, secretary, and treasurer of the corporation respectively. * * *

Upon the question of accounts or customers, it appears that, at the time of its opening or shortly thereafter, defendant Scheideler, Beck & Werner, Inc., had as accounts Manhattan Soap Co., G.F. Heublein, International Salt, Wesson Oil, C.F. Mueller Company, The Borden Company,

Marlin Fire Arms, McIlhenny Corp., Haskins Bros. and Continental Briar Pipe, all of which were customers of plaintiff prior to the formation of defendant Scheideler, Beck & Werner, Inc.

The foregoing evidence has led us to conclude that the conduct of the individual defendants-appellants as officers, directors or employees of the plaintiff corporation " * * * fell below the standard required by the law of one acting as an agent or employee of another." (*Lamdin* v. *Broadway Surface Adv. Corp.*, 272 N.Y. 133, 138.) Each of these defendants was " * * * prohibited from acting in any manner inconsistent with his agency or trust and [was] at all times bound to exercise the utmost good faith and loyalty in the performance of his duties." * * * The inferences reasonably to be drawn from the record justify the conclusion—reached by the jury and by a majority of the Appellate Division—that the individual defendants-appellants, while employees of plaintiff corporation, determined upon a course of conduct which, when subsequently carried out, resulted in benefit to themselves through destruction of plaintiff's business, in violation of the fiduciary duties * * * imposed on defendants by their close relationship with plaintiff corporation. * * *

Nor is it a defense to say that the defendants-appellants did not avail themselves of the benefit of the customers and personnel diverted from plaintiff until after defendants * * * had informed plaintiff of their intention to leave Duane Jones Company. Upon this record the jury might have found that the conspiracy originated in June or July while a fiduciary duty existed, and that the benefits realized when defendant Scheideler, Beck & Werner, Inc., commenced operation in September were merely the results of a predetermined course of action. In view of that circumstance, the individual defendants would not be relieved of liability for advantages secured by them, after termination of their employment, as a result of opportunities gained by reason of their employment relationship.

Questions and Notes

1. Was it important that the defendants were officers of Jones Co., rather than directors? Should it have been? *Cf.* Restatement (Second) of Agency § 393 ("Unless otherwise agreed, an agent is subject to a duty not to compete with the principal concerning the subject matter of his agency.").

2. Is *Jones Co.* consistent with *Meinhard v. Salmon?*

3. Would the plaintiff have prevailed if the New York Court of Appeals followed the American Law Institute Principles of Corporate Governance? It provides:

§ 5.06   Competition With The Corporation

(a) *General Rule.* Directors and senior executives may not advance their pecuniary interests by engaging in competition with the corporation unless either:

(1) Any reasonably foreseeable harm to the corporation from such competition is outweighed by the benefit that the corporation may rea-

sonably be expected to derive from allowing the competition to take place, or there is no reasonably foreseeable harm to the corporation from such competition;

(2) The competition is authorized in advance or ratified, following disclosure concerning the conflict of interest and the competition, by disinterested directors, or in the case of a senior executive who is not a director, is authorized in advance by a disinterested superior . . . ; or

(3) The competition is authorized in advance or ratified, following such disclosure, by disinterested shareholders, and the shareholders' action is not equivalent to a waste of corporate assets

* * *

4. Does a corporation's officer or director improperly compete if she also serves as a director for another corporation? Comment c to § 5.06 of ALI's Principles says no because the person is not pursuing his self interest by serving on the other board.

5. Suppose that a director of Bubba's Burritos wants to open his own restaurant nearby that sells healthful burritos made with hemp and recycled insect carcasses. Is there anything that he can do to reduce the risk of getting sued for competing with Bubba's?

(ii) *"Usurping" a Corporate Opportunity*

We encountered the notion of usurping a business opportunity briefly in connection with partnerships when reading *Meinhard v. Salmon*. In that case, the managing coadventurer took the real estate development opportunity for himself. The following case considers these questions: (1) what is a corporate opportunity? and (2) what does a director have to do when she is offered a corporate opportunity? In reading the case for the answers to these two legal questions, also consider the following:

1. Was Nancy Harris a director? What if she had been a director of the corporation but not its president?

2. How did Harris learn of the opportunity to buy the Gilpin property? The Smallidge parcel?

3. Could the corporation afford to purchase the property? Would that matter?

NORTHEAST HARBOR GOLF CLUB, INC. v. HARRIS
Supreme Court of Maine, 1995
661 A.2d 1146

ROBERTS, JUSTICE. Northeast Harbor Golf Club, Inc., appeals from a judgment entered in the Superior Court (Hancock County, Atwood, J.) following a nonjury trial. The Club maintains that the trial court erred in finding that Nancy Harris did not breach her fiduciary duty as president of the Club by purchasing and developing property abutting the golf course. Because we today adopt principles different from those applied by the trial court in determining that Harris's activities did not constitute a breach of the corporate opportunity doctrine, we vacate the judgment.

Nancy Harris was the president of the Northeast Harbor Golf Club, a Maine corporation, from 1971 until she was asked to resign in 1990. The Club also had a board of directors that was responsible for making or approving significant policy decisions. The Club's only major asset was a golf course in Mount Desert. During Harris's tenure as president, the board occasionally discussed the possibility of developing some of the Club's real estate in order to raise money. Although Harris was generally in favor of tasteful development, the board always "shied away" from that type of activity.

In 1979, Robert Suminsby informed Harris that he was the listing broker for the Gilpin property, which comprised three noncontiguous parcels located among the fairways of the golf course. The property included an unused right-of-way on which the Club's parking lot and clubhouse were located. It was also encumbered by an easement in favor of the Club allowing foot traffic from the green of one hole to the next tee. Suminsby testified that he contacted Harris because she was the president of the Club and he believed that the Club would be interested in buying the property in order to prevent development.

Harris immediately agreed to purchase the Gilpin property in her own name for the asking price of $45,000. She did not disclose her plans to purchase the property to the Club's board prior to the purchase. She informed the board at its annual August meeting that she had purchased the property, that she intended to hold it in her own name, and that the Club would be "protected." The board took no action in response to the Harris purchase. She testified that at the time of the purchase she had no plans to develop the property and that no such plans took shape until 1988.

In 1984, while playing golf with the postmaster of Northeast Harbor, Harris learned that a parcel of land owned by the heirs of the Smallidge family might be available for purchase. The Smallidge parcel was surrounded on three sides by the golf course and on the fourth side by a house lot. It had no access to the road. With the ultimate goal of acquiring the property, Harris instructed her lawyer to locate the Smallidge heirs. At a board meeting in August 1985, Harris formally disclosed to the board that she had purchased the Smallidge property. The minutes of that meeting show that she told the board she had no present plans to develop the Smallidge parcel. Harris testified that at the time of the purchase of the Smallidge property she nonetheless thought it might be nice to have some houses there. Again, the board took no formal action as a result of Harris's purchase. Harris acquired the Smallidge property from ten heirs, paying a total of $60,000. In 1990, Harris paid $275,000 for the lot and building separating the Smallidge parcel from the road in order to gain access to the otherwise landlocked parcel.

The trial court expressly found that the Club would have been unable to purchase either the Gilpin or Smallidge properties for itself, relying on testimony that the Club continually experienced financial difficulties, operated annually at a deficit, and depended on contributions from the directors to pay its bills. On the other hand, there was evidence that the Club had occasionally engaged in successful fund-raising, including a two-year period shortly after the Gilpin purchase during which the Club raised $115,000. The Club had $90,000 in a capital investment fund at the time of the Smallidge purchase.

* * * In 1988, Harris, who was still president of the Club, and her children began the process of obtaining approval for a five-lot subdivision known as Bushwood on the lower Gilpin property. * * *

After Harris's plans to develop Bushwood became apparent, the board grew increasingly divided concerning the propriety of development near the golf course. * * *

In April 1991, after a substantial change in the board's membership, the board authorized the instant lawsuit against Harris for the breach of her fiduciary duty to act in the best interests of the corporation. The board simultaneously resolved that the proposed housing development was contrary to the best interests of the corporation.

The Club filed a complaint against Harris, her sons John and Shepard, and her daughter-in-law Melissa Harris. As amended, the complaint alleged that during her term as president Harris breached her fiduciary duty by purchasing the lots without providing notice and an opportunity for the Club to purchase the property and by subdividing the lots for future development. The Club sought an injunction to prevent development and also sought to impose a constructive trust on the property in question for the benefit of the Club.

The trial court found that Harris had not usurped a corporate opportunity because the acquisition of real estate was not in the Club's line of business. Moreover, it found that the corporation lacked the financial ability to purchase the real estate at issue. Finally, the court placed great emphasis on Harris's good faith. It noted her long and dedicated history of service to the Club, her personal oversight of the Club's growth, and her frequent financial contributions to the Club. The court found that her development activities were "generally * * * compatible with the corporation's business." This appeal followed.

Corporate officers and directors bear a duty of loyalty to the corporations they serve. As Justice Cardozo explained the fiduciary duty in *Meinhard v. Salmon*, 249 N.Y. 458, 164 N.E. 545, 546 (1928):

> A trustee is held to something stricter than the morals of the marketplace. Not honesty alone, but the punctilio of an honor the most sensitive, is then the standard of behavior. As to this there has developed a tradition that is unbending and inveterate. * * *

Despite the general acceptance of the proposition that corporate fiduciaries owe a duty of loyalty to their corporations, there has been much confusion about the specific extent of that duty when, as here, it is contended that a fiduciary takes for herself a corporate opportunity.

Various courts have embraced different versions of the corporate opportunity doctrine. The test applied by the trial court and embraced by Harris is generally known as the "line of business" test. The seminal case applying the line of business test is *Guth v. Loft, Inc.*, 5 A.2d 503 (Del. 1939). In *Guth*, the Delaware Supreme Court adopted an intensely factual test stated in general terms as follows:

> [I]f there is presented to a corporate officer or director a business opportunity which the corporation is financially able to undertake, is, from its nature, in the line of the corporation's business and is of practical advantage to it, is one in which the corporation has an interest or a reasonable expectancy, and, by embracing the opportunity, the self-interest of the officer or director will be brought into conflict with that of his corporation, the law will not permit him to seize the opportunity for himself.

The "real issue" under this test is whether the opportunity "was so closely associated with the existing business activities . . . as to bring the transaction within that class of cases where the acquisition of the property would throw the corporate officer purchasing it into competition with his company." The Delaware court described that inquiry as "a factual question to be decided by reasonable inferences from objective facts."

The line of business test suffers from some significant weaknesses. First, the question whether a particular activity is within a corporation's line of business is conceptually difficult to answer. The facts of the instant case demonstrate that difficulty. The Club is in the business of running a golf course. It is not in the business of developing real estate. In the traditional sense, therefore, the trial court correctly observed that the opportunity in this case was not a corporate opportunity within the meaning of the *Guth* test. Nevertheless, the record would support a finding that the Club had made the policy judgment that development of surrounding real estate was detrimental to the best interests of the Club. The acquisition of land adjacent to the golf course for the purpose of preventing future development would have enhanced the ability of the Club to implement that policy. The record also shows that the Club had occasionally considered reversing that policy and expanding its operations to include the development of surrounding real estate. Harris's activities effectively foreclosed the Club from pursuing that option with respect to prime locations adjacent to the golf course.

Second, the *Guth* test includes as an element the financial ability of the corporation to take advantage of the opportunity. The court in this case relied on the Club's supposed financial incapacity as a basis for excusing Harris's conduct. Often, the injection of financial ability into the equation will unduly favor the inside director or executive who has command of the facts relating to the finances of the corporation. Reliance on financial ability will also act as a disincentive to corporate executives to solve corporate financing and other problems. In addition, the Club could have prevented development without spending $275,000 to acquire the property Harris needed to obtain access to the road. * * *

In an attempt to protect the duty of loyalty while at the same time providing long-needed clarity and guidance for corporate decisionmakers, the American Law Institute has offered the most recently developed version of the corporate opportunity doctrine. PRINCIPLES OF CORPORATE GOVERNANCE § 5.05 (May 13, 1992), provides as follows:

§ 5.05 Taking of Corporate Opportunities by Directors or Senior Executives

(a) *General Rule.* A director or senior executive may not take advantage of a corporate opportunity unless:

(1) The director or senior executive first offers the corporate opportunity to the corporation and makes disclosure concerning the conflict of interest [§ 1.14(a)] and the corporate opportunity [§ 1.14(b)];

(2) The corporate opportunity is rejected by the corporation; and

(3) Either:

(A) The rejection of the opportunity is fair to the corporation;

(B) The opportunity is rejected in advance, following such disclosure, by disinterested directors [§ 1.15], or, in the case of a senior executive who is not a director, by a disinterested superior, in a manner that satisfies the standards of the business judgment rule [§ 4.01(c)]; or

(C) The rejection is authorized in advance or ratified, following such disclosure, by disinterested shareholders [§ 1.16], and the rejection is not equivalent to a waste of corporate assets [§ 1.42].

(b) *Definition of a Corporate Opportunity.* For purposes of this Section, a corporate opportunity means:

(1) Any opportunity to engage in a business activity of which a director or senior executive becomes aware, either:

(A) In connection with the performance of functions as a director or senior executive, or under circumstances that should reasonably lead the director or senior executive to believe that the person offering the opportunity expects it to be offered to the corporation; or

(B) Through the use of corporate information or property, if the resulting opportunity is one that the director or senior executive should reasonably be expected to believe would be of interest to the corporation; or

(2) Any opportunity to engage in a business activity of which a senior executive becomes aware and knows is closely related to a business in which the corporation is engaged or expects to engage.

(c) *Burden of Proof.* A party who challenges the taking of a corporate opportunity has the burden of proof, except that if such party establishes that the requirements of Subsection (a)(3)(B) or (C) are not met, the director or the senior executive has the burden of proving that the rejection and the taking of the opportunity were fair to the corporation.

(d) *Ratification of Defective Disclosure.* A good faith but defective disclosure of the facts concerning the corporate opportunity may be cured if at any time (but no later than a reasonable time after suit is filed challenging the taking of the corporate opportunity) the original rejection of the corporate opportunity is ratified, following the required disclosure, by the board, the shareholders, or the corporate decisionmaker who initially approved the rejection of the corporate opportunity, or such decisionmaker's successor.

(e) *Special Rule Concerning Delayed Offering of Corporate Opportunities.* Relief based solely on failure to first offer an opportunity to the corporation under Subsection (a)(1) is not available if: (1) such failure resulted from a good faith belief that the business activity did not constitute a corporate opportunity, and (2) not later than a reasonable time after suit is filed challenging the taking of the corporate opportunity, the corporate opportunity is to the extent possible offered to the corporation and rejected in a manner that satisfies the standards of Subsection (a).

The central feature of the ALI test is the strict requirement of full disclosure prior to taking advantage of any corporate opportunity. Id., § 5.05(a)(1). "If the opportunity is not offered to the corporation, the director or senior executive will not have satisfied § 5.05(a)." Id., cmt. to § 5.05(a). The corporation must then formally reject the opportunity. Id., § 5.05(a)(2).

The ALI test defines "corporate opportunity" broadly. It includes opportunities "closely related to a business in which the corporation is engaged." Id., § 5.05(b). It also encompasses any opportunities that accrue to the fiduciary as a result of her position within the corporation. This concept is most clearly illustrated by the testimony of Suminsby, the listing broker for the Gilpin property, which, if believed by the factfinder, would support a finding that the Gilpin property was offered to Harris specifically in her capacity as president of the Club. If the factfinder reached that conclusion, then at least the opportunity to acquire the Gilpin property would be a corporate opportunity. The state of the record concerning the Smallidge purchase precludes us from intimating any opinion whether that too would be a corporate opportunity.

Under the ALI standard, once the Club shows that the opportunity is a corporate opportunity, it must show either that Harris did not offer the opportunity to the Club or that the Club did not reject it properly. If the Club shows that the board did not reject the opportunity by a vote of the disinterested directors after full disclosure, then Harris may defend her actions on the basis that the taking of the opportunity was fair to the corporation. *Id.*, § 5.05(c). If Harris failed to offer the opportunity at all, however, then she may not defend on the basis that the failure to offer the opportunity was fair. Id., cmt. to § 5.05(c).

* * * We follow the ALI test. The disclosure-oriented approach provides a clear procedure whereby a corporate officer may insulate herself through prompt and complete disclosure from the possibility of a legal challenge. The requirement of disclosure recognizes the paramount importance of the corporate fiduciary's duty of loyalty. At the same time it protects the fiduciary's ability pursuant to the proper procedure to pursue her own business ventures free from the possibility of a lawsuit.

* * * The question remains how our adoption of the rule affects the result in the instant case. The trial court made a number of factual findings based on an extensive record. The court made those findings, however, in the light of legal principles that are different from the principles that we today announce. Similarly, the parties did not have the opportunity to develop the record in this case with knowledge of the applicable legal standard. In these circumstances, fairness requires that we remand the case for further proceedings. Those further proceedings may include, at the trial court's discretion, the taking of further evidence.

The entry is: Judgment vacated.

Remanded for further proceedings consistent with the opinion herein.

QUESTIONS AND NOTES

1. At the trial, the trial court found that the corporation "would have been unable to purchase either the Gilpin or Smallidge properties for itself." Is that relevant under ALI § 5.05? Should it be?

2. Harris learned of the availability of the Smallidge property independent of her position with the corporation. Is that relevant under ALI § 5.05? Is it determinative?

3. Robert Clark, then a professor at the Harvard Law School (and later Dean there), analogized usurpation of corporate opportunity to theft of corporate property: "At a general level therefore, the reasons for considering a manager's taking a corporate opportunity to be wrong are the same as the reasons for considering outright theft from the corporate treasury to be wrong." Robert C. Clark, CORPORATE LAW 224 (1986). Is *Northeast Harbor* consistent with this analogy?

4. On remand in *Northeast Harbor*, the court found that both land purchases were corporate opportunities but that the corporation's suit against Ms. Harris was barred by the statute of limitations. *See* Northeast Harbor Golf Club, Inc. v. Harris, 725 A.2d 1018 (Me. 1999).

In *Northeast Harbor*, the Maine Supreme Court discusses and criticizes the Delaware corporate opportunity test from *Guth v. Loft*. In the next case, the Delaware Supreme Court discusses and applies the Delaware corporate opportunity test from *Guth v. Loft.*

BROZ v. CELLULAR INFORMATION SYSTEMS, INC.

Supreme Court of Delaware, 1996
673 A.2d 148

[The defendant, Broz, was one of the directors of the plaintiff Cellular Information Systems, Inc. ("CIS"), a Delaware corporation in the business of providing cellular telephone service. Broz was also the sole stockholder and President of RFB Cellular, Inc. ("RFBC"), a competitor of CIS.

Mackinac Cellular Corp. ("Mackinac"), the owner of a Michigan–2 FCC cellular phone license for a portion of Michigan adjacent to an area served by RFBC, approached Broz about the possibility of RFBC's acquiring its license. Mackinac did not even contact CIS. CIS had recently emerged from a lengthy, contentious Chapter 11 bankruptcy case, had sold most of its license areas, and no longer had business operations in the Midwest.

Broz bought the license for RFBC without making formal disclosure to and obtaining the approval of the CIS board. Broz did mention his intentions to the CEO of CIS and to two other members of CIS's board—both of whom indicated that CIS was not interested in acquiring the Michigan–2 license.

An additional complicating (if not important) fact was that, during this time, PriCellular, Inc., ("PriCellular") was engaged in acquiring CIS. And, PriCellular was also interested in acquiring the Michigan–2 license.]

VEASEY, CHIEF JUSTICE. In this appeal, we consider the application of the doctrine of corporate opportunity. The Court of Chancery decided that the defendant, a corporate director, breached his fiduciary duty by not formally presenting to the corporation an opportunity which had come to the director individually and independent of the director's relationship with the corporation. Here the opportunity was not one in which the corporation in its current mode had an interest or which it had the financial ability to acquire, but, under the unique circumstances here, that mode was subject to change by virtue of the impending acquisition of the corporation by another entity.

We conclude that, although a corporate director may be shielded from liability by offering to the corporation an opportunity which has come to the director independently and individually, the failure of the director to present the opportunity does not necessarily result in the improper usurpation of a corporate opportunity. We further conclude that, if the corporation is a target or potential target of an acquisition by another company which has an interest and ability to entertain the opportunity, the director of the target company does not have a fiduciary duty to present the opportunity to the target company. Accordingly, the judgment of the Court of Chancery is REVERSED. * * *

The doctrine of corporate opportunity represents but one species of the broad fiduciary duties assumed by a corporate director or officer. A corporate fiduciary agrees to place the interests of the corporation before his or her own in appropriate circumstances. In light of the diverse and often competing obligations faced by directors and officers, however, the corporate opportunity doctrine arose as a means of defining the parameters of fiduciary duty in instances of potential conflict. The classic statement of the doctrine is derived from the venerable case of *Guth v. Loft, Inc.* [5 A.2d 503 (Del. 1939)]. In *Guth*, this Court held that:

> if there is presented to a corporate officer or director a business opportunity which the corporation is financially able to undertake, is, from its nature, in the line of the corporation's business and is of practical advantage to it, is one in which the corporation has an interest or a reasonable expectancy, and, by embracing the opportunity, the self-interest of the officer or director will be brought into conflict with that of the corporation, the law will not permit him to seize the opportunity for himself.

The corporate opportunity doctrine, as delineated by *Guth* and its progeny, holds that a corporate officer or director may not take a business opportunity for his own if: (1) the corporation is financially able to exploit the opportunity; (2) the opportunity is within the corporation's line of business; (3) the corporation has an interest or expectancy in the opportunity; and (4) by taking the opportunity for his own, the corporate fiduciary will thereby be placed in a position inimical to his duties to the corporation. The Court in *Guth* also derived a corollary which states that a director or officer may take a corporate opportunity if: (1) the opportunity is presented to the director or officer in his individual and not his corporate capacity; (2) the opportunity is not essential to the corporation; (3) the corporation holds no interest or expectancy in the opportunity; and (4) the director or officer has not wrongfully employed the resources of the corporation in pursuing or exploiting the opportunity. *Guth*, 5 A.2d at 509.

Thus, the contours of this doctrine are well established. It is important to note, however, that the tests enunciated in *Guth* and subsequent cases provide guidelines to be considered by a reviewing court in balancing the equities of an individual case. No one factor is dispositive and all factors must be taken into account insofar as they are applicable. Cases involving a claim of usurpation of a corporate opportunity range over a multitude of factual settings. Hard and fast rules are not easily crafted to deal with such an array of complex situations. The determination of "[w]hether or not a director has appropriated for himself something that in fairness should belong to the corporation is 'a factual question to be decided by reasonable inference from objective facts.' " *Guth*, 5 A.2d at 513. In the instant case, we find that the facts do not support the conclusion that Broz misappropriated a corporate opportunity.

We note at the outset that Broz became aware of the Michigan–2 opportunity in his individual and not his corporate capacity. In fact, it is clear from the record that Mackinac did not consider CIS a viable candidate for the acquisition of Michigan–2. Accordingly, Mackinac did not offer the property to CIS. In this factual posture, many of the fundamental concerns undergirding the law of corporate opportunity are not present (e.g., misappropriation of the corporation's proprietary information). The burden imposed upon Broz to show adherence to his fiduciary duties to CIS is thus lessened to some extent. Nevertheless, this fact is not dispositive. The determination of whether a particular fiduciary has usurped a corporate opportunity necessitates a careful examination of the circumstances, giving due credence to the factors enunciated in *Guth* and subsequent cases.

We turn now to an analysis of the factors relied on by the trial court. First, we find that CIS was not financially capable of exploiting the Michigan–2 opportunity. Although the Court of Chancery concluded otherwise, we hold that this finding was not supported by the evidence. The record shows that CIS was in a precarious financial position at the time Mackinac presented the Michigan–2 opportunity to Broz. Having recently emerged from lengthy and contentious bankruptcy proceedings, CIS was not in a position to commit capital to the acquisition of new assets. Further, the loan agreement entered into by CIS and its creditors severely limited the discretion of CIS as to the acquisition of new assets and substantially restricted the ability of CIS to incur new debt.

The Court of Chancery based its contrary finding on the fact that PriCellular had purchased an option to acquire CIS' bank debt. At the time that Broz was required to decide whether to accept the Michigan–2 opportunity, PriCellular had not yet acquired CIS, and any plans to do so were wholly speculative. Thus, contrary to the Court of Chancery's finding, Broz was not obligated to consider the contingency of a PriCellular acquisition of CIS and the related contingency of PriCellular thereafter waiving restrictions on the CIS bank debt. Broz was required to consider the facts only as they existed at the time he determined to accept the Mackinac offer and embark on his efforts to bring the transaction to fruition.

Second, while it may be said with some certainty that the Michigan–2 opportunity was within CIS' line of business, it is not equally clear that CIS had a cognizable interest or expectancy in the license.* **[7]** Under the third factor laid down by this Court in *Guth*, for an opportunity to be

---

* **[7]** The language in the *Guth* opinion relating to "line of business" is less than clear:

Where a corporation is engaged in a certain business, and an opportunity is presented to it embracing an activity as to which it has fundamental knowledge, practical experience and ability to pursue, which, logically and naturally, is adaptable to its business having regard for its financial position, and is consonant with its reasonable needs and aspirations for expansion, it may properly be said that the opportunity is within the corporation's line of business. *Guth*, 5 A.2d at 514. This formulation of the definition of the term "line of business" suggests that the business strategy and financial well-being of the corporation are also relevant to a determination of whether the opportunity is within the corporation's line of business. Since we find that these considerations are decisive under the other factors enunciated by the Court in *Guth*, we do not reach the question of whether they are here relevant to a determination of the corporation's line of business.

deemed to belong to the fiduciary's corporation, the corporation must have an interest or expectancy in that opportunity. Despite the fact that the nature of the Michigan–2 opportunity was historically close to the core operations of CIS, changes were in process. At the time the opportunity was presented, CIS was actively engaged in the process of divesting its cellular license holdings. CIS' articulated business plan did not involve any new acquisitions.

Finally, the corporate opportunity doctrine is implicated only in cases where the fiduciary's seizure of an opportunity results in a conflict between the fiduciary's duties to the corporation and the self-interest of the director as actualized by the exploitation of the opportunity. In the instant case, Broz' interest in acquiring and profiting from Michigan–2 created no duties that were inimical to his obligations to CIS. Broz, at all times relevant to the instant appeal, was the sole party in interest in RFBC, a competitor of CIS. CIS was fully aware of Broz' potentially conflicting duties. Broz, however, comported himself in a manner that was wholly in accord with his obligations to CIS. Broz took care not to usurp any opportunity which CIS was willing and able to pursue.

In concluding that Broz had usurped a corporate opportunity, the Court of Chancery placed great emphasis on the fact that Broz had not formally presented the matter to the CIS board. In so holding, the trial court erroneously grafted a new requirement onto the law of corporate opportunity, viz., the requirement of formal presentation under circumstances where the corporation does not have an interest, expectancy or financial ability.

The teaching of *Guth* and its progeny is that the director or officer must analyze the situation *ex ante* to determine whether the opportunity is one rightfully belonging to the corporation. If the director or officer believes, based on one of the factors articulated above, that the corporation is not entitled to the opportunity, then he may take it for himself. Of course, presenting the opportunity to the board creates a kind of "safe harbor" for the director, which removes the specter of a *post hoc* judicial determination that the director or officer has improperly usurped a corporate opportunity. Thus, presentation avoids the possibility that an error in the fiduciary's assessment of the situation will create future liability for breach of fiduciary duty. It is not the law of Delaware that presentation to the board is a necessary prerequisite to a finding that a corporate opportunity has not been usurped. * * *

The corporate opportunity doctrine represents a judicially crafted effort to harmonize the competing demands placed on corporate fiduciaries in a modern business environment. The doctrine seeks to reduce the possibility of conflict between a director's duties to the corporation and interests unrelated to that role. In the instant case, Broz adhered to his obligations to CIS. We hold that the Court of Chancery erred as a matter of law in concluding that Broz had a duty formally to present the Michigan–2 opportunity to the CIS board. We also hold that the trial court erred in its application of the corporate opportunity doctrine under the unusual facts of this case, where CIS had no interest or financial ability to acquire the opportunity, but the impending acquisition of CIS by PriCellular would or could have caused a change in those circumstances.

Therefore, we hold that Broz did not breach his fiduciary duties to CIS. Accordingly, we REVERSE the judgment of the Court of Chancery holding that Broz diverted a corporate opportunity properly belonging to CIS and imposing a constructive trust.

QUESTIONS

1. In *Meinhard v. Salmon*, it was important that Salmon learned of the opportunity because he was the managing coadventurer. Is it important that Broz's knowledge of the opportunity was not due to his position as a director of CIS? Is it determinative?

2. What could Broz have done differently to avoid this litigation?

3. Would the court have analyzed the case differently if it had applied the ALI approach from *Northeast Harbor*? *See generally* Harvey Gelb, *The Corporate Opportunity Doctrine—Recent Cases and the Elusive Goal of Certainty*, 31 U. Rich. L. Rev. 371 (1997) (discussion and comparison of *Northeast Harbor* and *Broz* cases). Which is the better approach?

4. Would the court have analyzed the *Broz* case differently if RFBC had shareholders other than Broz? Does the corporate opportunity doctrine present special challenges to a person who is the director of two companies in competing businesses? *See* Note, *Venture Capitalist's Corporate Opportunity Problem*, 2001 Colum. Bus. L. Rev. 473 (2001) ("[W]hen a venture capitalist serves on the boards of numerous companies that operate in similar fields of business, the application of these tests is impractical, and as I intend to demonstrate, has the potential to harm capital formation and business development.").

5. What is the relationship between improper competition with a corporation and usurpation of a corporate opportunity? The court in Broz noted that "the corporate opportunity doctrine is implicated only in cases where the fiduciary's seizure of an opportunity results in a conflict between the fiduciary's duties to the corporation and the self-interest of the director as actualized by the exploitation of the opportunity." If an officer or director usurps a corporate opportunity is she necessarily then also improperly competing with the corporation?

(iii) Being on Both Sides of a Deal With the Corporation ("Interested Director Transactions")

Bubba's Burritos, Inc. prospers: more locations, more shareholders. The corporation is now considering leasing a building owned by Capel, who is a director and the majority shareholder. Should a corporation be able to transact business with one of its directors? With the spouse of a director? With its majority shareholder? Should challenges to any such transactions be subject to the business judgment rule?

HMG/COURTLAND PROPERTIES, INC. v. GRAY

Delaware Chancery Court, 1999
749 A.2d 94

[Gray and Fieber were two of the five directors of HMG/Courtland Properties, Inc., ("HMG"), a corporation that bought and sold commercial real estate. Gray was HMG's principal negotiator in these real estate transactions. On behalf of HMG, Gray negotiated a major sale of HMG real estate to NAF Associates ("NAF").

Fieber owned an interest in NAF, disclosed that interest to the other directors and abstained from voting on the proposed sale to NAF at the HMG directors meeting. Gray, through relatives and related business entities, also owned an interest in NAF. Gray did not disclose that interest to the other directors. Gray was one of the four directors of HMG who voted to approve the land sale to NAF. Fieber knew of Gray's interest but did not disclose Gray's interest to the other directors.]

STRINE, VICE CHANCELLOR. This case involves thirteen-year-old real estate sales transactions between HMG/Courtland Properties, Inc. as seller and two of HMG's directors, Lee Gray and Norman Fieber as buyers. While Fieber's self-interest in the transactions was properly disclosed, neither he nor Gray informed their fellow directors that Gray—who took the lead in negotiating the sales for HMG—had a buy-side interest. Gray's interest was concealed from HMG for a decade and was only discovered inadvertently by the company in 1996.

In this post-trial opinion, I find that Fieber and Gray breached their fiduciary duties of loyalty and care and defrauded the company. I award relief to HMG designed to remedy the harm caused by their misconduct.

This case directly implicates both the business judgment rule and § 144. Even though the business judgment rule and § 144 serve somewhat different purposes and cannot be interpreted identically, they are closely related.

In a case where § 144 is directly applicable, compliance with its terms should be a minimum requirement to retain the protection of the business judgment rule. The desirability of doctrinal and statutory coherence, where that can be accomplished without sacrificing public policy interests, also counsels that conclusion. In this case, both the business judgment rule as traditionally interpreted and § 144 point toward the entire fairness standard as the appropriate form of review.

Gray's interest in the * * * NAF Transactions implicates both the primary rationale for the entire fairness standard of review and the core concern of § 144—"self-dealing."

Gray's undisclosed, buy-side interest in the Transactions is a classic case of self-dealing. Proof of such undisclosed self-dealing, in itself, is sufficient to rebut the presumption of the business judgment rule and invoke entire fairness review.

Section 144 of the Delaware General Corporation Law dictates this conclusion. That statute is implicated whenever a corporation and "1 or more of its directors or officers * * * or partnership * * * or other organization in which 1 or more of its directors or officers * * * have a financial interest" engage in a transaction. 8 Del. C. § 144.

The interests of Gray and Fieber in the NAF Transactions trigger the statute. Section 144 provides that a self-dealing transaction will not be "void or voidable solely for this reason" if the transaction is ratified by a majority of the disinterested directors or by a shareholder vote. 8 Del. C. § 144(a)(1), (2). Such ratification is valid, however, only if the "material facts as [to the director's] relationship or interest and as to the contract or transaction are disclosed or are known to the [relevant ratifying authority]. . . ." Id. Neither Fieber nor Gray disclosed Gray's "interest" in the "[T]ransaction[s]" to the HMG Board. Id. In the absence of such disclosure, 8 Del. C. § 144(a)(1), the Transactions can only be rendered non-voidable if they were "fair as to [HMG] as of the time [they were] authorized."* **[24]** 8 Del. C. § 144(a)(3).

For all these reasons, Gray and Fieber must demonstrate the fairness of the NAF Transactions.

It is a well-settled principle of Delaware law that where directors stand on both sides of a transaction, they have "the burden of establishing its entire fairness, sufficient to pass the test of careful scrutiny by the courts." *Weinberger v. UOP, Inc,* Del. Supr., 457 A.2d 701, 710 (1983) ("There is no 'safe harbor' for such divided loyalties in Delaware."). Directors will be found to have acted with entire fairness where they "demonstrate their utmost good faith and the most scrupulous inherent fairness of the bargain." Id.

                    * * *

The concept of entire fairness has two components: fair dealing and fair price. Fair dealing "embraces questions of when the transaction was timed, how it was initiated, structured, negotiated, disclosed to the directors, and how the approvals of the directors and the stockholders were obtained." Id. Fair price "relates to the economic and financial considerations of the proposed merger, including all relevant factors: assets, market value, earnings, future prospects, and any other elements that affect the intrinsic or inherent value of a company's stock." Id. In making a determination as to the entire fairness of a transaction, the Court does not focus on one component over the other, but examines all aspects of the issue as a whole.

---

* **[24]** While non-compliance with §§ 144(a)(1), (2)'s disclosure requirement by definition triggers fairness review rather than business judgment rule review, the satisfaction of §§ 144(a)(1) or (a)(2) alone does not always have the opposite effect of invoking business judgment rule review that one might presume would flow from a literal application of the statute's terms. Rather, satisfaction of §§ 144(a)(1) or (a)(2) simply protects against invalidation of the transaction "solely" because it is an interested one. Id. As such, § 144 is best seen as establishing a floor for board conduct but not a ceiling.

i. Fair Dealing

The defendants have failed to convince me that the NAF Transactions were fairly negotiated or ratified. From the beginning of the negotiations, Gray, the primary negotiator for the seller in the Transactions, was interested in taking a position on the buyer's side. As such, Gray lacked the pure seller-side incentive that should have been applied on behalf of HMG—particularly in Transactions in which one director was already on the other side.

Given the intrinsically unique nature of real estate, the bargaining skills and incentives of HMG's negotiator were likely to be more important than if the negotiator was arranging for the sale of a financial asset. As the defendants' own expert conceded, in the context of a real estate sales transaction negotiation skills are "exceedingly important."

The process was thus anything but fair. Because neither Gray nor Fieber disclosed Gray's interest, the HMG Board unwittingly ratified Transactions in which a conflicted negotiator was relied upon by the Adviser to negotiate already conflicted Transactions.

ii. Fair Price

The defendants attempt to meet their burden of demonstrating fair price by trying to convince me that the prices used in the Transactions were in a range of fairness, as proven by the 1984 Appraisals.

Once again, I believe the defendants misconceive their burden. On the record before me, I obviously cannot conclude that HMG received a shockingly low price in the Transactions or that the prices paid were not within the low end of the range of possible prices that might have been paid in negotiated arm's-length deals. In that narrow sense, the defendants have proven that the price was "fair." But that proof does not necessarily satisfy their burden under the entire fairness standard. As the American Law Institute corporate governance principles point out:

> A contract price might be fair in the sense that it corresponds to market price, and yet the corporation might have refused to make the contract if a given material fact had been disclosed * * *. Furthermore, fairness is often a range, rather than a point, so that a transaction involving a payment by the corporation may be fair even though it is consummated at the high end of the range. If an undisclosed material fact had been disclosed, however, the corporation might have declined to transact at that high price, or might have bargained the price down lower in the range. 1 Principles of Corporate Governance; Analysis and Recommendations Part V at 202 (1994).

The defendants have failed to persuade me that HMG would not have gotten a materially higher value for Wallingford and the Grossman's Portfolio had Gray and Fieber come clean about Gray's interest. That is, they have not convinced me that their misconduct did not taint the price to HMG's disadvantage. I base this conclusion on several factors.

First, the defendants' own expert on value, James Nolan, testified that his opinion that the prices paid in the Transactions were fair was premised on his assumption that Gray was not the leading negotiator from HMG's side. To the extent that Gray was a principal player in discussing terms with Fieber, Nolan said that his conclusion about the fairness of the price might well be different.* [28]

Second, the 1984 Appraisals understated the values of the Wallingford Property and the Portfolio as of early 1986. The Leased Fee Values in the 1984 Appraisals were generated through a discounted cash flow analysis utilizing 1983 actual rents and projected rents for 1984–1986. By 1986, it was clear that the Grossman's stores operating at Portfolio sites were performing better, and thereby generating higher lease payments (because a portion of the lease payments was tied to store sales) than estimated by the appraisers who conducted the 1984 Appraisals. If an update had been done in 1986, it would have produced values well in excess of the 1984 Appraisals. This conclusion is bolstered by appraisals done on six of the Portfolio properties in 1987 at the request of Chemical Bank, which selected the properties to be appraised. The 1987 appraisals indicated values 66% higher than the Leased Fee Values in the 1984 Appraisals. PX 396 (also indicating a 64.5% increase in the Fee Simple Values).

Third, a skilled and properly motivated negotiator could have done better than Leased Fee Value in price negotiations. As the defendants' expert Nolan testified, the skills of a negotiator are "exceedingly important" in a real estate transaction. Even without an updated appraisal, a properly motivated negotiator could have argued from the actual rents in 1984 and 1985 that the Leased Fee Value understated the value of the Portfolio. Furthermore, a properly motivated negotiator would have focused on the Fee Simple Value because of the likelihood that many of the Portfolio properties would come off lease from Grossman's. That eventuality—which came true—justified a higher price than the Leased Fee Value. I have no confidence that Gray negotiated with the Fiebers in any vigorous or skillful way. Since he wanted to participate on the buy-side, he had less than a satisfactory incentive to do so. Since the outcome of a real estate negotiation is often heavily influenced by the skills of the negotiators, this factor undercuts the claim that the price was fair to HMG. *See* 1 Principles of Corporate Governance: Analysis and Recommendations § 5.02 at 220 (1994) (in evaluating the fairness of a transaction, the court should consider the fact that the corporation was not represented by an unconflicted negotiator).

Finally, had Gray disclosed his interest, I believe that HMG would have terminated his involvement in the negotiations and have taken a

---

* [28] Nolan is not a certified appraiser but has extensive experience in the real estate field so I decided to consider his testimony despite a credible challenge to his credentials mounted by HMG. Nolan did not perform a formal valuation of the affected properties as of 1986. While I believe Nolan sincerely attempted to give his honest opinion about the financial fairness of the Transactions, his rather unique "role playing" approach was heavily dependent on assumptions he made about the motivations and roles of the humans involved. Since those assumptions do not comport with my view of the evidence, I give little weight to his testimony.

much more traditional approach to selling the affected properties. To the extent that HMG continued to consider a sales transaction, I believe it would have commissioned new appraisals and would have sought purchasers other than Fieber.

Taken together, these factors lead me to conclude that the defendants have not demonstrated that they paid a fair price in the sense inherent in the entire fairness standard.

For the foregoing reasons, judgment shall be entered for HMG against defendants Gray and Fieber.* * * The parties shall report back to me in three weeks. If an agreed upon order is not presented, each party shall submit its position regarding the outstanding issues and an accompanying form of order.

QUESTIONS

1. What did Fieber do wrong?

2. Would the court have held Fieber and Gray liable if both Fieber and Gray had completely disclosed their interests in NAF and Fieber and Gray had abstained from voting?

    a. Is Delaware § 144(a)(1) exculpatory? Note the phrase "solely for this reason" in the prefatory paragraph of § 144(a).

    b. What is the relationship between § 144 and the business judgment rule?

    c. Under § 144, when is the fairness of the transaction to the corporation an issue?

3. We have omitted portions of the opinion discussing other claims against Fieber and Gray, claims against another defendant, and the measure of recovery. If you were representing HMG, what evidence would you present to establish the measure of recovery against Fieber and Gray for breach of duty of loyalty in connection with HMG's sale of real estate to NAF?

4. Why didn't the Delaware court in *HMG* treat NAF's purchase of land from HMG as a usurpation of a corporate opportunity? What is the difference between "interested director transactions" and "corporate opportunities"? *Shapiro v. Greenfield*, 764 A.2d 270, 277 (Md. 2000), made the following comparison: a director transacting business with the corporation as contrasted with a director taking business transactions away from the corporation. Is that helpful?

5. Looking back, how do the Delaware rules for interested director transactions in the *HMG/Courtland* case differ from the Delaware rules for corporate opportunities in *Broz*? *See generally* Eric G. Orlinsky, *Corporate Opportunity Doctrine and Interested Directors Transactions: A Framework for Analysis in An Attempt to Restore Predictability*, 24 DEL. J. CORP. L. 451 (1999).

6. We have seen that a corporation's top managers may also be directors. How does the board set such a manager's pay and benefits? Isn't the manager/director's negotiation of her compensation with the board an interested director transaction? Often a corporation's board will delegate compen-

sation decisions to a "compensation committee" made up of directors other than those whose compensation is being established. As recent publicity about huge pay packages for some corporate managers have shown, such committees can be ineffective. Why?

———————

Looking ahead, how do the Delaware rules for interested director transactions in the *HMG/Courtland* case differ from the Iowa (an MBCA state) rules in the next case? In reading the *Cookies Food Products* case, consider the following questions:

1. What were the interested director transactions?

2. Who approved the transactions?

3. In this litigation challenging the transactions, who proved what?

COOKIES FOOD PRODUCTS, INC. v. LAKES WAREHOUSE DISTRIBUTING, INC.

Supreme Court of Iowa, 1988
430 N.W.2d 447

Neuman, Justice. This is a shareholders' derivative suit brought by the minority shareholders of a closely held Iowa corporation specializing in barbeque sauce, Cookies Food Products, Inc. (Cookies). The target of the lawsuit is the majority shareholder, Duane "Speed" Herrig and two of his family-owned corporations, Lakes Warehouse Distributing, Inc. (Lakes) and Speed's Automotive Co., Inc. (Speed's). Plaintiffs alleged that Herrig, by acquiring control of Cookies and executing self-dealing contracts, breached his fiduciary duty to the company and fraudulently misappropriated and converted corporate funds. Plaintiffs sought actual and punitive damages. Trial to the court resulted in a verdict for the defendants, the district court finding that Herrig's actions benefited, rather than harmed, Cookies. We affirm.

I. Background.

* * * L.D. Cook of Storm Lake, Iowa, founded Cookies in 1975 to produce and distribute his original barbeque sauce. Searching for a plant site in a community that would provide financial backing, Cook met with business leaders in seventeen Iowa communities, outlining his plans to build a growth-oriented company. He selected Wall Lake, Iowa, persuading thirty-five members of that community, including Herrig and the plaintiffs, to purchase Cookies stock. All of the investors hoped Cookies would improve the local job market and tax base. The record reveals that it has done just that.

Early sales of the product, however, were dismal. After the first year's operation, Cookies was in dire financial straits. At that time, Herrig was one of thirty-five shareholders and held only two hundred shares. He was also the owner of an auto parts business, Speed's Automotive, and Lakes

Warehouse Distributing, Inc., a company that distributed auto parts from Speed's. Cookies' board of directors approached Herrig with the idea of distributing the company's products. It authorized Herrig to purchase Cookies' sauce for twenty percent under wholesale price, which he could then resell at full wholesale price. Under this arrangement, Herrig began to market and distribute the sauce to his auto parts customers and to grocery outlets from Lakes' trucks as they traversed the regular delivery routes for Speed's Automotive.

In May 1977, Cookies formalized this arrangement by executing an exclusive distribution agreement with Lakes. Pursuant to this agreement, Cookies was responsible only for preparing the product; Lakes, for its part, assumed all costs of warehousing, marketing, sales, delivery, promotion, and advertising. Cookies retained the right to fix the sales price of its products and agreed to pay Lakes thirty percent of its gross sales for these services.

Cookies' sales have soared under the exclusive distributorship contract with Lakes. Gross sales in 1976, the year prior to the agreement, totaled only $20,000, less than half of Cookies' expenses that year. By 1985, when this suit was commenced, annual sales reached $2,400,000.

As sales increased, Cookies' board of directors amended and extended the original distributorship agreement. In 1979, the board amended the original agreement to give Lakes an additional two percent of gross sales to cover freight costs for the ever-expanding market for Cookies' sauce. In 1980, the board extended the amended agreement through 1984 to allow Herrig to make long-term advertising commitments. Recognizing the role that Herrig's personal strengths played in the success of their joint endeavor, the board also amended the agreement that year to allow Cookies to cancel the agreement with Lakes if Herrig died or disposed of the corporation's stock.

In 1981, L.D. Cook, the majority shareholder up to this time, decided to sell his interest in Cookies. He first offered the directors an opportunity to buy his stock, but the board declined to purchase any of his 8100 shares. Herrig then offered Cook and all other shareholders $10 per share for their stock, which was twice the original price. Because of the overwhelming response to these offers, Herrig had purchased enough Cookies stock by January 1982 to become the majority shareholder. His investment of $140,000 represented fifty-three percent of the 28,700 outstanding shares.

Shortly after Herrig acquired majority control he replaced four of the five members of the Cookies' board with members he selected. Subsequent changes made in the corporation under Herrig's leadership formed the basis for this lawsuit.

First, under Herrig's leadership, Cookies' board has extended the term of the exclusive distributorship agreement with Lakes and expanded the scope of services for which it compensates Herrig and his companies. In April 1982, when a sales increase of twenty-five percent over the previous year required Cookies to seek additional short-term storage for the peak summer season, the board accepted Herrig's proposal to compensate Lakes at the "going rate" for use of its nearby storage facilities. The board decided to use Lakes' storage facilities because building and staffing its own facilities would have been more expensive.

Second, Herrig moved from his role as director and distributor to take on an additional role in product development. This created a dispute over a royalty Herrig began to receive. Herrig's role in product development began in 1982 when Cookies diversified its product line to include taco sauce. Herrig developed the recipe because he recognized that taco sauce, while requiring many of the same ingredients needed in barbeque sauce, is less expensive to produce. Further, since consumer demand for taco sauce is more consistent throughout the year than the demand for barbeque sauce, this new product line proved to be a profitable method for increasing year-round utilization of production facilities and staff. In August 1982, Cookies' board approved a royalty fee to be paid to Herrig for this taco sauce recipe. This royalty plan was similar to royalties the board paid to L.D. Cook for the barbeque sauce recipe. Although Herrig's rate is equivalent to a sales percentage slightly higher than what Cook receives, it yields greater profit to Cookies because this new product line is cheaper to produce.

Third, since 1982 Cookies' board has twice approved additional compensation for Herrig. In January 1983, the board authorized payment of a $1000 per month "consultant fee" in lieu of salary, because accelerated sales required Herrig to spend extra time managing the company. In August, 1983, the board authorized another increase in Herrig's compensation. Further, at the suggestion of a Cookies director who also served as an accountant for Cookies, Lakes, and Speed's, the Cookies board amended the exclusive distributorship agreement to allow Lakes an additional two percent of gross sales as a promotion allowance to expand the market for Cookies products outside of Iowa. As a direct result of this action, by 1986 Cookies regularly shipped products to several states throughout the country.

As we have previously noted, however, Cookies' growth and success has not pleased all its shareholders. The discontent is motivated by two factors that have effectively precluded shareholders from sharing in Cookies' financial success: the fact that Cookies is a closely held corporation, and the fact that it has not paid dividends. Because Cookies' stock is not publicly traded, shareholders have no ready access to buyers for their stock at current values that reflect the company's success. Without dividends, the shareholders have no ready method of realizing a return on their investment in the company. This is not to say that Cookies has improperly refused to pay dividends. The evidence reveals that Cookies would have violated the terms of its loan with the Small Business Administration had it declared dividends before repaying that debt. That SBA loan was not repaid until the month before the plaintiffs filed this action.

Through the exclusive distributorship agreements, taco sauce royalty, warehousing fees, and consultant fee, plaintiffs claimed that Herrig breached his fiduciary duties to the corporation and its shareholders because he allegedly negotiated for these arrangements without fully disclosing the benefit he would gain.

The court concluded that Herrig had breached no duties owed to Cookies or to its minority shareholders. * * *

On appeal from this ruling, the plaintiffs challenge: (1) the district court's allocation of the burden of proof with regard to the four claims of self-dealing; (2) the standard employed by the court to determine whether Herrig's self-dealing was fair and reasonable to Cookies; (3) the finding that any self-dealing by Herrig was done in good faith, and with honesty and fairness; (4) the finding that Herrig breached no duty to disclose crucial facts to Cookies' board before it completed deliberations on Herrig's self-dealing transactions; and (5) the district court's denial of restitution and other equitable remedies as compensation for Herrig's alleged breach of his duty of loyalty. After a brief review of the nature and source of Herrig's fiduciary duties, we will address the appellants' challenges in turn.

II. Fiduciary Duties.

Herrig, as an officer and director of Cookies, owes a fiduciary duty to the company and its shareholders. Herrig concedes that Iowa law imposed the same fiduciary responsibilities based on his status as majority stockholder.

* * * Appellants claim that Herrig violated his duty of loyalty to Cookies.

* * * The legislature enacted section 496A.34, quoted here in pertinent part, that establishes three sets of circumstances under which a director may engage in self-dealing without clearly violating the duty of loyalty:

No contract or other transaction between a corporation and one or more of its directors or any other corporation, firm, association or entity in which one or more of its directors are directors or officers or are financially interested, shall be either void or voidable because of such relationship or interest * * * if any of the following occur:

1. The fact of such relationship or interest is disclosed or known to the board of directors or committee which authorizes, approves, or ratifies the contract or transaction ... without counting the votes * * * of such interested director.

2. The fact of such relationship or interest is disclosed or known to the shareholders entitled to vote [on the transaction] and they authorize * * * such contract or transaction by vote or written consent.

3. The contract or transaction is fair and reasonable to the corporation.

Some commentators have supported the view that satisfaction of any one of the foregoing statutory alternatives, in and of itself, would prove that a director has fully met the duty of loyalty. We are obliged, however, to interpret statutes in conformity with the common law wherever statutory language does not directly negate it. Because the common law and section 496A.34 require directors to show "good faith, honesty, and fairness" in self-dealing, we are persuaded that satisfaction of any one of these three alternatives under the statute would merely preclude us from rendering the transaction void or voidable outright solely on the basis "of such [director's] relationship or interest." Iowa Code § 496A.34. To the contrary, we are convinced that the legislature did not intend by this statute to enable a court, in a shareholder's derivative suit, to rubber stamp any transaction to which a board of directors or the shareholders of a corporation have consented. Such an interpretation would invite those who stand to gain from such transactions to engage in improprieties to obtain consent. We thus require directors who engage in self-dealing to establish the additional element that they have acted in good faith, honesty, and fairness.

III.   Burden of Proof.

Appellants contend that the district court improperly placed upon them the burden of proving that Herrig's self-dealing was not honest, in good faith, or fair to Cookies. The district court's ruling addressed Herrig's duties of care and loyalty in these circumstances, noting that in duty of care challenges the burden of proof is on plaintiffs because of the business judgment rule which affords directors the presumption that their decisions are informed, made in good faith, and honestly believed by them to be in the best interests of the company. *See Smith v. Van Gorkom*, 488 A.2d 858, 872 (Del.1985). The district court then noted the different burden imposed in challenges under Iowa's duty of loyalty statute, which, in its words "require[s] the director challenged in a self-dealing suit to carry the burden of establishing his good faith, honesty, and fairness."

After reviewing the record in light of the district court's ruling, we are persuaded that the court appropriately recognized the shifting burdens of proof in duty of loyalty cases.

IV.   Standard of Law.

Next, appellants claim the district court applied an inappropriate standard of law to determine whether Herrig's conduct was fair and reasonable to Cookies. Appellants correctly assert that self-dealing transactions must have the earmarks of arms-length transactions before a court can find them to be fair or reasonable. The crux of appellants' claim is that the court should have focused on the fair market value of Herrig's services to Cookies rather than on the success Cookies achieved as a result of Herrig's actions.

We agree with appellants' contention that corporate profitability should not be the sole criteria [sic; should be "sole criterion"] by which to test the fairness and reasonableness of Herrig's fees. Applying such reasoning to the record before us, however, we cannot agree with appellants' assertion that Herrig's services were either unfairly priced or inconsistent with Cookies corporate interest.

There can be no serious dispute that the four agreements in issue— for exclusive distributorship, taco sauce royalty, warehousing, and consulting fees—have all benefited Cookies, as demonstrated by its financial success. Even if we assume Cookies could have procured similar services from other vendors at lower costs, we are not convinced that Herrig's fees were therefore unreasonable or exorbitant. Like the district court, we are not persuaded by appellants' expert testimony that Cookies' sales and profits would have been the same under agreements with other vendors.

V. Denial of Equitable Relief.

* * * While both Iowa's statutes and case law impose a duty of disclosure on interested directors who engage in self-dealing, neither has delineated what information must be disclosed, or to whom. * * *

Examining Herrig's conduct under this duty of disclosure, we find no support for plaintiffs' assertion that Herrig owed the minority shareholders a duty to disclose any information before the board executed the exclusive distributorship, royalty, warehousing, or consultant fee agreements. These actions comprise management activity, and our statutes place the duty of managing the affairs of the corporation on the board of directors, not the shareholders. Because the shareholders had no role in making decisions concerning these agreements, we hold that Herrig owed these shareholders no duty to disclose facts concerning any aspect of these agreements before the board entered or extended them. We also note that plaintiffs did not complain at trial that the financial reports they regularly received concerning the affairs of the company were anything less than adequate.

With regard to the board of directors, the record before us aptly demonstrates that all members of Cookies' board were well aware of Herrig's dual ownership in Lakes and Speed's. We are unaware of any authority supporting plaintiffs' contention that Herrig was obligated to disclose to Cookies' board or shareholders the extent of his profits resulting from these distribution and warehousing agreements. * * *

We concur in the trial court's assessment of the evidence presented and affirm its dismissal of plaintiffs' claims.

AFFIRMED.

SCHULTZ, JUSTICE (*dissenting*). My quarrel with the majority opinion is not with its interpretation of the law, but with its application of the law to the facts. I would reverse the trial court's holding.

The majority opinion correctly stated the common law and statutory principles. When there is self-dealing by a majority stockholder which is challenged, the majority stockholder has the burden to establish that they have acted in good faith, honesty and fairness. This burden of fairness requires not just a showing of profitability, but also a showing of the fairness of the bargain to the interest of the corporation. I would hold that Herrig failed to sustain his burden. * * *

I believe that Herrig failed on his burden of proof by what he did not show. He did not produce evidence of the local going rate for distribution contracts or storage fees outside of a very limited amount of self-serving testimony. He simply did not show the fair market value of his services or expense for freight, advertising and storage cost. He did not show that his taco sauce royalty was fair. This was his burden. He cannot succeed on it by merely showing the success of the company. * * *

QUESTIONS AND NOTE

1. Duane "Speed" Herrig was both a director and the majority shareholder. Would the court have decided this case differently if he had been only a director? Only a majority shareholder?

2. Under the Iowa version of the MBCA, when is fairness of an interested director transaction an issue? Under the current version of the MBCA, when is fairness of an interested director transaction an issue? *See* MBCA § 8.61(b) and Official Comment 2 to § 8.61.

3. Is the approach of the Iowa court in determining the fairness of Cookies' interested director transactions with Herrig's entities consistent with the approach of the Delaware court in determining the fairness of HMG's transaction with Gray's entity?

4. If Cookies were a Delaware corporation, would the court have decided this case differently? MBCA §§ 8.60–8.63 are the MBCA counterparts to Delaware § 144. The MBCA uses the phrase "director's conflicting interest transaction" instead of "interested director transaction." Are there more important substantive differences?

5. For more on Cookies' barbecue and taco sauces, see "Cookies Wild Web Page" at www.cookiesbbq.com.

c. The Requirement of Good Faith

In addition to the duties of care and loyalty, an additional requirement exists: to act in good faith. MBCA §§ 8.30(a) and 831(a)(2)(i). Courts and litigants had paid little attention to this requirement in the corporate context until recently.

Shortly after *Smith vs. Van Gorkum*, many state legislatures, including Delaware's, began to permit companies incorporated in their states to place provisions in the articles that eliminated directors' liability for violations of the duty of care. MBCA § 2.02(b)(4) and Delaware § 102(b)(7).

Plaintiffs began to attempt to evade such exculpatory provisions by pleading claims not as violations of the duty of care, but instead as violations of a duty of good faith. Unlike for the duty of care, the new statutes did not permit liability for failure to act in good faith to be eliminated in the articles. For example, in *Stone v. Ritter*, 911 A. 2d 362 (Del. 2006), the plaintiffs asserted, as in *Caremark*, that the company's directors had failed to provide proper oversight. However, because the company's articles included provisions that eliminated the directors' liability for violation of the duty of care, the plaintiffs instead asserted that the directors were liable because their actions were not in good faith. The court dismissed the complaint, finding that the defendants' conduct was not sufficiently egregious to constitute bad faith. As discussed in the *Disney* opinion in the following section, Delaware courts currently define bad faith as an intentional dereliction of duty, a conscious disregard for one's responsibilities.

d. The Special Case of Executive Compensation

Chief executives of large companies in the U.S. get paid a lot. A whole lot. The average compensation in 2008 for the CEOs of the 500 biggest companies in the U.S. was $11.4 million, including salary, bonus, stock, and stock options. In the past decades, pay has grown steadily, except for a 15% fall in 2007 because of the financial crisis: average CEO pay quadrupled between 1993 and 2008. The gap between CEOs and those who work for them has also increased. In 1993, a CEO of a large company received on average 131 times as much as the average worker. In 2005, they earned 369 times as much.

Activists and the government have tried to control CEO pay in many ways. In the early 1990s, the SEC began requiring greater disclosure of executives' compensation. The hope was that disclosure would shame boards of directors into limiting the amounts. The government also limited the tax deductibility of executive salaries above $1 million. More recently, the government has attempted to limit the pay of the CEOs of companies that have received government bailouts.

The measures have often seemed to backfire. For example, the disclosure requirement tended to increase compensation, not reduce it. Many CEOs demanded and received more pay when they found out how much other CEOs were making.

Similarly, the government attempted to curb "golden parachutes," in which a small number of CEOs had become entitled to receive big bucks if their companies were taken over and they lost their jobs. The purpose was to prevent CEOs from opposing takeover attempts that would benefit shareholders. The new tax that the government imposed on the parachutes caused the number of parachutes to increase, not decrease. The publicity caused jealous CEOs who didn't know about the parachutes to demand them.

But are CEOs overpaid? CEOs argue that their pay is fair. For example, Harvey Golub, CEO of American Express Co., received total compensation of more than $250 million when he was CEO from 1993–2000. However, during his time as CEO, the value of the company's shares increased more than six times, and the company's value increased $55 *billion*, from $10 billion to $65 billion. "I made a lot of money. I became wealthy," he notes. "My shareholders became even wealthier. How much of the $55 billion should I get?" Joann S. Lublin & Scott Thurm, *Behind Soaring Executive Pay, Decades of Failed Restraints*, WALL ST. J., October 12, 2006, at A1.

Opponents respond that huge executive paydays are often the result not of worthy executive performance, but of failed oversight by directors. Suppose that a CEO has demanded that his board of directors grant him a big pay raise. To avoid conflicts if officer-directors were to vote on their own pay, most boards delegate compensation decisions to a "compensation committee." The compensation committee often in turn then hires an outside consultant to advise it.

According to opponents, compensation committees and consultants are poor watchdogs. Subtle conflicts of interests can exist. CEOs often influence who sits on the company's board. A compensation-committee member who opposes the CEO's pay demands may find herself not renominated to the board. A consultant who finds a CEO's pay demands excessive may not be rehired.

At minimum, the class of those who serve as large corporations' officers and directors is often seen as a cozy club whose members have little enthusiasm for opposing each other's demands. It should not be surprising that CEOs tend to believe that the CEO job is a difficult one that deserves big pay, whether it is their own job or that of a fellow CEO on whose board they sit. According to Warren Buffet, the famous investor, compensation committees are "tail-wagging puppy dogs meekly following recommendations by consultants." For a director to oppose such a recommendation "would be like belching at the dinner table." *Id.*

Occasional stunning paydays fuel suspicions that board oversight is weak. Lawrence Ellison, the CEO of Oracle, received $706 million in 2001. Disney's CEO, Michael Eisner, received $203 million in 1993 and $576 million in 1998.

A CEO's mammoth pay can cause special outrage when the CEO's company performs poorly. In the five years after Robert Nardelli joined Home Depot as CEO in 2000, Home Depot's stock price declined 12% while the stock price of its archrival Lowe's rose 175%. During the period, Nardelli received total compensation of $245 million, with the compensation committee giving him several big raises.

As the following case shows, shareholders may sometimes sue derivatively, asserting that directors' approval of massive compensation violated their fiduciary duties. In 1995 Hollywood super agent Michael Ovitz was hired as Disney's CEO. Bad choice. Fourteen months later, Disney fired him. Shareholders then sued derivatively when they discovered that Disney's directors had approved a contract that gave Ovitz $130 million when he left. The resulting nine years of litigation, which concluded with the following opinion, was a nail-biter for the defendant Disney directors (including actor Sidney Poitier). In addition to offering a window into the world of breathtaking CEO salaries, the opinion develops the law concerning directors' duties to be informed and to act in good faith.

IN RE THE WALT DISNEY COMPANY DERIVATIVE LITIGATION

Supreme Court of Delaware, 2006
906 A.2d 27

JACOBS, JUSTICE:

In 1994 Disney lost in a tragic helicopter crash its President and Chief Operating Officer, Frank Wells, who together with Michael Eisner, Disney's Chairman and Chief Executive Officer, had enjoyed remarkable success at the Company's helm. Eisner temporarily assumed Disney's presidency, but only three months later, heart disease required Eisner to undergo quadruple bypass surgery. Those two events persuaded Eisner and Disney's board of directors that the time had come to identify a successor to Eisner.

Eisner's prime candidate for the position was Michael Ovitz, who was the leading partner and one of the founders of Creative Artists Agency ("CAA"), the premier talent agency whose business model had reshaped the entire industry. By 1995, CAA had 550 employees and a roster of about 1400 of Hollywood's top actors, directors, writers, and musicians. That roster generated about $150 million in annual revenues and an annual income of over $20 million for Ovitz, who was regarded as one of the most powerful figures in Hollywood.

Russell [one of Disney's directors and chairman of its compensation committee] assumed the lead in negotiating the financial terms of the Ovitz employment contract. In the course of negotiations, Russell learned * * * that Ovitz owned 55% of CAA and earned approximately $20 to $25 million a year from that company. From the beginning Ovitz made it clear that he would not give up his 55% interest in CAA without "downside protection." Considerable negotiation then ensued over downside protection issues. During the summer of 1995, the parties agreed to a draft version of Ovitz's employment agreement (the "OEA") modeled after Eisner's and the late Mr. Wells' employment contracts.

As the basic terms of the OEA were crystallizing, Russell prepared and gave Ovitz and Eisner a "case study" to explain those terms. In that study, Russell also expressed his concern that the negotiated terms represented an extraordinary level of executive compensation. Russell acknowledged, however, that Ovitz was an "exceptional corporate executive" and "highly successful and unique entrepreneur" who merited "downside protection and upside opportunity." Both would be required to enable Ovitz to adjust to the reduced cash compensation he would receive from a public company, in contrast to the greater cash distributions and other perquisites more typically available from a privately held business. But, Russell did caution that Ovitz's salary would be at the top level for any corporate officer and significantly above that of the Disney CEO. Moreover, the stock options granted under the OEA would exceed the standards applied within Disney and corporate America and would "raise very strong criticism."

To assist in evaluating the financial terms of the OEA, Russell recruited Graef Crystal, an executive compensation consultant * * * Crystal prepared a comprehensive executive compensation database to accept various inputs and to conduct Black–Scholes analyses to output a range of values for the options.* [8] Watson [another board member] also prepared similar computations on spreadsheets, but without using the Black–Scholes method.

[Disney's directors (the "Disney defendants") then approved both Ovitz' hiring and his employment package. Once Ovitz started at Disney, Eisner and the Disney board quickly concluded that Ovitz was a disaster. Disney quickly fired him, but could do so only as a "non-fault termination" ("NFT") because he had not done anything that violated his contract. After Ovitz received his stunning severance package, several shareholders sued the Disney directors derivatively, challenging the board's approval of Ovitz' hiring and his lucrative contract. Among other claims, the plaintiffs asserted, following *Smith vs. Van Gorkum*, that the directors' approvals violated their duty of care because they were insufficiently informed. The plaintiff's also pleaded that the directors were liable because they had acted in bad faith. The Delaware trial court rejected the claims, and the state's supreme court here affirms.]

[T]he appellants' core argument in the trial court was that the Disney defendants' approval of the OEA and election of Ovitz as President were not entitled to business judgment rule protection. * * * This argument is best understood against the backdrop of the presumptions that cloak director action being reviewed under the business judgment standard. Our law presumes that "in making a business decision the directors of a corporation acted on an informed basis, in good faith, and in the honest belief that the action taken was in the best interests of the company." Those presumptions can be rebutted if the plaintiff shows that the directors breached their fiduciary duty of care or of loyalty or acted in bad faith. If that is shown, the burden then shifts to the director defendants to demonstrate that the challenged act or transaction was entirely fair to the corporation and its shareholders.

Because no duty of loyalty claim was asserted against the Disney defendants, the only way to rebut the business judgment rule presumptions would be to show that the Disney defendants had either breached their duty of care or had not acted in good faith. At trial, the plaintiff-appellants attempted to establish both grounds, but the Chancellor determined that the plaintiffs had failed to prove either. * * *

---

* [8] The Black–Scholes method is a formula for option valuation that is widely used and accepted in the industry and by regulators.

1. THE DUE CARE DETERMINATIONS * * *

(d) Holding That The Compensation Committee Members Did Not Fail To Exercise Due Care In Approving The OEA

The appellants next challenge the Chancellor's determination that although the compensation committee's decision-making process fell far short of corporate governance "best practices," the committee members breached no duty of care in considering and approving the NFT terms of the OEA. That conclusion is reversible error, the appellants claim, because the record establishes that the compensation committee members did not properly inform themselves of the material facts and, hence, were grossly negligent in approving the NFT provisions of the OEA. * * *

In our view, a helpful approach is to compare what actually happened here to what would have occurred had the committee followed a "best practices" (or "best case") scenario, from a process standpoint. In a "best case" scenario, all committee members would have received, before or at the committee's first meeting on September 26, 1995, a spreadsheet or similar document prepared by (or with the assistance of) a compensation expert (in this case, Graef Crystal). Making different, alternative assumptions, the spreadsheet would disclose the amounts that Ovitz could receive under the OEA in each circumstance that might foreseeably arise. One variable in that matrix of possibilities would be the cost to Disney of a non-fault termination for each of the five years of the initial term of the OEA. The contents of the spreadsheet would be explained to the committee members, either by the expert who prepared it or by a fellow committee member similarly knowledgeable about the subject. That spreadsheet, which ultimately would become an exhibit to the minutes of the compensation committee meeting, would form the basis of the committee's deliberations and decision.

Had that scenario been followed, there would be no dispute (and no basis for litigation) over what information was furnished to the committee members or when it was furnished. Regrettably, the committee's informational and decisionmaking process used here was not so tidy. That is one reason why the Chancellor found that although the committee's process did not fall below the level required for a proper exercise of due care, it did fall short of what best practices would have counseled.

The Disney compensation committee met twice: on September 26 and October 16, 1995. The minutes of the September 26 meeting reflect that the committee approved the terms of the OEA (at that time embodied in the form of a letter agreement), except for the option grants, which were not approved until October 16—after the Disney stock incentive plan had been amended to provide for those options. At the September 26 meeting, the compensation committee considered a "term sheet" which, in summarizing the material terms of the OEA, relevantly disclosed that in the event of a non-fault termination, Ovitz would receive: (i) the present value of his salary ($1 million per year) for the balance of the contract term, (ii) the present value of his annual bonus payments (computed at $7.5

million) for the balance of the contract term, (iii) a $10 million termination fee, and (iv) the acceleration of his options for 3 million shares, which would become immediately exercisable at market price.

Thus, the compensation committee knew that in the event of an NFT, Ovitz's severance payment alone could be in the range of $40 million cash, plus the value of the accelerated options. Because the actual payout to Ovitz was approximately $130 million, of which roughly $38.5 million was cash, the value of the options at the time of the NFT payout would have been about $91.5 million. Thus, the issue may be framed as whether the compensation committee members knew, at the time they approved the OEA, that the value of the option component of the severance package could reach the $92 million order of magnitude if they terminated Ovitz without cause after one year. The evidentiary record shows that the committee members were so informed.

On this question the documentation is far less than what best practices would have dictated. There is no exhibit to the minutes that discloses, in a single document, the estimated value of the accelerated options in the event of an NFT termination after one year. The information imparted to the committee members on that subject is, however, supported by other evidence, most notably the trial testimony of various witnesses about spreadsheets that were prepared for the compensation committee meetings.

The compensation committee members derived their information about the potential magnitude of an NFT payout from two sources. The first was the value of the "benchmark" options previously granted to Eisner and Wells and the valuations by Watson of the proposed Ovitz options. Ovitz's options were set at 75% of parity with the options previously granted to Eisner and to Frank Wells. Because the compensation committee had established those earlier benchmark option grants to Eisner and Wells and were aware of their value, a simple mathematical calculation would have informed them of the potential value range of Ovitz's options. Also, in August and September 1995, Watson and Russell met with Graef Crystal to determine (among other things) the value of the potential Ovitz options, assuming different scenarios. Crystal valued the options under the Black–Scholes method, while Watson used a different valuation metric. Watson recorded his calculations and the resulting values on a set of spreadsheets that reflected what option profits Ovitz might receive, based upon a range of different assumptions about stock market price increases. Those spreadsheets were shared with, and explained to, the committee members at the September meeting.

The committee's second source of information was the amount of "downside protection" that Ovitz was demanding. Ovitz required financial protection from the risk of leaving a very lucrative and secure position at CAA, of which he was a controlling partner, to join a publicly held corporation to which Ovitz was a stranger, and that had a very different culture and an environment which prevented him from completely controlling his destiny. The committee members knew that by leaving CAA and coming to Disney, Ovitz would be sacrificing "booked" CAA commissions of $150 to $200 million—an amount that Ovitz demanded as protection against the risk that his employment relationship with Disney might not work out. Ovitz wanted at least $50 million of that compensation to take the form of an "up-front" signing bonus. Had the $50 million bonus been paid, the size of the option grant would have been lower. Because it was contrary to Disney policy, the compensation committee rejected the up-front signing bonus demand, and elected instead to compensate Ovitz at the "back end," by awarding him options that would be phased in over the five-year term of the OEA.

It is on this record that the Chancellor found that the compensation committee was informed of the material facts relating to an NFT payout. If measured in terms of the documentation that would have been generated if "best practices" had been followed, that record leaves much to be desired. The Chancellor acknowledged that, and so do we. But, the Chancellor also found that despite its imperfections, the evidentiary record was sufficient to support the conclusion that the compensation committee had adequately informed itself of the potential magnitude of the entire severance package, including the options, that Ovitz would receive in the event of an early NFT.

The OEA was specifically structured to compensate Ovitz for walking away from $150 million to $200 million of anticipated commissions from CAA over the five-year OEA contract term. This meant that if Ovitz was terminated without cause, the earlier in the contract term the termination occurred the larger the severance amount would be to replace the lost commissions. Indeed, because Ovitz was terminated after only one year, the total amount of his severance payment (about $130 million) closely approximated the lower end of the range of Ovitz's forfeited commissions ($150 million), less the compensation Ovitz received during his first and only year as Disney's President. Accordingly, the Court of Chancery had a sufficient evidentiary basis in the record from which to find that, at the time they approved the OEA, the compensation committee members were adequately informed of the potential magnitude of an early NFT severance payout. * * *

(e) Holding That The Remaining Disney Directors Did Not Fail To Exercise Due Care In Approving The Hiring Of Ovitz As the President Of Disney

The appellants' final claim in this category is that the Court of Chancery erroneously held that the remaining members of the old Disney board had not breached their duty of care in electing Ovitz as President of Disney. * * * The Chancellor determined that in electing Ovitz, the directors were informed of all information reasonably available and, thus, were not grossly negligent. We agree.

The Chancellor found and the record shows the following: well in advance of the September 26, 1995 board meeting the directors were fully aware that the Company needed—especially in light of Wells' death and Eisner's medical problems—to hire a "number two" executive and potential successor to Eisner. There had been many discussions about that need and about potential candidates who could fill that role even before Eisner decided to try to recruit Ovitz. Before the September 26 board meeting Eisner had individually discussed with each director the possibility of hiring Ovitz, and Ovitz's background and qualifications. The directors thus knew of Ovitz's skills, reputation and experience, all of which they believed would be highly valuable to the Company. The directors also knew that to accept a position at Disney, Ovitz would have to walk away from a very successful business—a reality that would lead a reasonable person to believe that Ovitz would likely succeed in similar pursuits elsewhere in the industry. The directors also knew of the public's highly positive reaction to the Ovitz announcement, and that Eisner and senior management had supported the Ovitz hiring. Indeed, Eisner, who had long desired to bring Ovitz within the Disney fold, consistently vouched for Ovitz's qualifications and told the directors that he could work well with Ovitz.

The board was also informed of the key terms of the OEA (including Ovitz's salary, bonus and options). Russell reported this information to them at the September 26, 1995 executive session, which was attended by Eisner and all non-executive directors. Russell also reported on the compensation committee meeting that had immediately preceded the executive session. And, both Russell and Watson responded to questions from the board. Relying upon the compensation committee's approval of the OEA and the other information furnished to them, the Disney directors, after further deliberating, unanimously elected Ovitz as President.

Based upon this record, we uphold the Chancellor's conclusion that, when electing Ovitz to the Disney presidency the remaining Disney directors were fully informed of all material facts, and that the appellants failed to establish any lack of due care on the directors' part.

2.   THE GOOD FAITH DETERMINATIONS

The Court of Chancery held that the business judgment rule presumptions protected the decisions of the compensation committee and the remaining Disney directors, not only because they had acted with due care but also because they had not acted in bad faith. * * *

In its Opinion the Court of Chancery defined bad faith as follows:

> Upon long and careful consideration, I am of the opinion that the concept of *intentional dereliction of duty*, a *conscious disregard for one's responsibilities*, is an appropriate (although not the only) standard for determining whether fiduciaries have acted in good faith. Deliberate indifference and inaction *in the face of a duty to act* is, in my mind, conduct that is clearly disloyal to the corporation. It is the epitome of faithless conduct. * * *

[After rejecting the claims of bad faith for technical reasons, the court nonetheless discussed the requirements for a successful bad-faith claim.]

The precise question is whether the Chancellor's articulated standard for bad faith corporate fiduciary conduct—intentional dereliction of duty, a conscious disregard for one's responsibilities—is legally correct. In approaching that question, we note that the Chancellor characterized that definition as *"an* appropriate (*although not the only*) standard for determining whether fiduciaries have acted in good faith." That observation is accurate and helpful, because as a matter of simple logic, at least three different categories of fiduciary behavior are candidates for the "bad faith" pejorative label.

The first category involves so-called "subjective bad faith," that is, fiduciary conduct motivated by an actual intent to do harm. That such conduct constitutes classic, quintessential bad faith is a proposition so well accepted in the liturgy of fiduciary law that it borders on axiomatic. We need not dwell further on this category, because no such conduct is claimed to have occurred, or did occur, in this case.

The second category of conduct, which is at the opposite end of the spectrum, involves lack of due care—that is, fiduciary action taken solely by reason of gross negligence and without any malevolent intent. In this case, appellants assert claims of gross negligence to establish breaches not only of director due care but also of the directors' duty to act in good faith. Although the Chancellor found, and we agree, that the appellants failed to establish gross negligence, to afford guidance we address the issue of whether gross negligence (including a failure to inform one's self of available material facts), without more, can also constitute bad faith. The answer is clearly no. * * * [G]rossly negligent conduct, without more, does not and cannot constitute a breach of the fiduciary duty to act in good faith.... Both our legislative history and our common law jurisprudence distinguish sharply between the duties to exercise due care and to act in good faith, and highly significant consequences flow from that distinction.

The Delaware General Assembly has addressed the distinction between bad faith and a failure to exercise due care (*i.e.*, gross negligence). * * * Section 102(b)(7) of the DGCL * * *authorizes Delaware corporations, by a provision in the certificate of incorporation, to exculpate their directors from monetary damage liability for a breach of the duty of care. That exculpatory provision affords significant protection to directors of Delaware corporations. The statute carves out several exceptions, however, including most relevantly, "for acts or omissions not in good faith...." Thus, a corporation can exculpate its directors from monetary liability for a breach of the duty of care, but not for conduct that is not in good faith. To adopt a definition of bad faith that would cause a violation of the duty of care automatically to become an act or omission "not in good faith," would eviscerate the protections accorded to directors by the General Assembly's adoption of Section 102(b)(7). * * *

Section 102(b)(7) * * * evidences the intent of the Delaware General Assembly to afford significant protections to directors * * * of Delaware corporations. To adopt a definition that conflates the duty of care with the duty to act in good faith by making a violation of the former an automatic violation of the latter, would nullify those legislative protections and defeat the General Assembly's intent. There is no basis in policy, precedent or common sense that would justify dismantling the distinction between gross negligence and bad faith.

That leaves the third category of fiduciary conduct, which falls in between the first two categories of (1) conduct motivated by subjective bad intent and (2) conduct resulting from gross negligence. This third category is what the Chancellor's definition of bad faith—intentional dereliction of duty, a conscious disregard for one's responsibilities—is intended to capture. The question is whether such misconduct is properly treated as a non-exculpable * * * violation of the fiduciary duty to act in good faith. In our view it must be, for at least two reasons.

[T]he universe of fiduciary misconduct is not limited to either disloyalty in the classic sense (*i.e.*, preferring the adverse self-interest of the fiduciary or of a related person to the interest of the corporation) or gross negligence. Cases have arisen where corporate directors have no conflicting self-interest in a decision, yet engage in misconduct that is more culpable than simple inattention or failure to be informed of all facts material to the decision. To protect the interests of the corporation and its shareholders, fiduciary conduct of this kind, which does not involve disloyalty (as traditionally defined) but is qualitatively more culpable than gross negligence, should be proscribed. A vehicle is needed to address such violations doctrinally, and that doctrinal vehicle is the duty to act in good faith. The Chancellor implicitly so recognized in his Opinion, where he identified different examples of bad faith as follows:

The good faith required of a corporate fiduciary includes not simply the duties of care and loyalty, in the narrow sense that I have discussed them above, but all actions required by a true faithfulness and devotion to the interests of the corporation and its shareholders. A failure to act in good faith may be shown, for instance, where the fiduciary intentionally acts with a purpose other than that of advancing the best interests of the corporation, where the fiduciary acts with the intent to violate applicable positive law, or where the fiduciary intentionally fails to act in the face of a known duty to act, demonstrating a conscious disregard for his duties. There may be other examples of bad faith yet to be proven or alleged, but these three are the most salient.

Those articulated examples of bad faith are not new to our jurisprudence. Indeed, they echo pronouncements our courts have made throughout the decades.

D. WHO SUES AND WHO RECOVERS?

1. WHAT ARE DERIVATIVE SUITS AND WHY DO WE HAVE THEM?

As we already know, shareholders are the owners of the corporation. This status carries various rights we address throughout this chapter, such as the right to inspect corporate records, to share in declared distributions, to share in assets upon dissolution, to elect directors and to vote on various fundamental corporate changes. Here, we address one of the most interesting rights held by shareholders: the right to bring a "shareholder's derivative suit."

In a derivative suit, a shareholder sues to vindicate the *corporation's* claim. She stands in the shoes of the corporation in asserting the claim. The suit is "derivative" because the shareholder's right to bring it "derives" from the corporation's right. Some courts refer to these as "secondary" suits, because the shareholder's right to sue is secondary to the corporation's.

On the face of it, it seems odd that the shareholder should be allowed to vindicate a claim belonging to the corporation. After all, the decision whether to sue is a *management* decision. And like management decisions generally, it is vested in the sound discretion of the directors. So if the corporation has a claim, we would expect the directors to authorize the corporation to bring suit.

But in at least two situations, the board might not act to vindicate the corporation's rights. First, suppose Bubba's Burritos, Inc. has entered a contract with Tina's Tofu, which requires Tina's to provide one of the key ingredients for burritos in Bubba's Northern California stores. Tina's fails to deliver, and Bubba's has to cover by getting the ingredient from another supplier at a higher price. Although Bubba's has a contract claim against Tina's, the directors might decide *not* to pursue it. Why? Maybe there was such ambiguity in the contract that Bubba's might not win. Or maybe the cost of litigation might exceed any recovery. Or perhaps Bubba's has had an excellent overall relationship with Tina's, which both parties want to continue. The directors might decide that litigation would strain the relationship unduly, and that Tina's will make things right in the future.

Second, the directors might refuse to have the corporation bring suit for a more questionable motive. Suppose the directors of Bubba's—Capel, Propp, and Agee—want to have Bubba's take advantage of the national craze for eggplant by offering eggplant burritos. Capel tells her fellow directors about an offer from Edith's Eggplant Co., but does not tell them (1) that she owns Edith's Eggplant Co. and (2) that the price charged by Edith's is higher than Bubba's could negotiate with another supplier. The board votes unanimously to enter the deal with Bubba's. The result, of course, is that Bubba's loses money (or doesn't make as much as it would have) because it has to pay too much for eggplant.

If Bubba's Burritos, Inc. has shareholders other than Agee, Capel and Propp, should we allow one or more of the other shareholders to vindicate the corporation's claim in either of these circumstances? In the first situation, allowing the shareholder to proceed would seem to violate the business judgment rule—after all, if the shareholder can assert the corporation's claim when the directors have opted not to, the shareholder would be permitted to second-guess a management decision. In the second situation, though, we are nervous about whether the directors will pursue the corporation's claim against the misbehaving director diligently.* Certainly Capel will not vote in favor of having Bubba's sue her for breaching her duty of loyalty to the corporation.† And we may harbor legitimate doubt that Propp and Agee would want to pursue litigation against their friend and fellow director. For these reasons, it makes sense to allow the shareholder to sue on behalf of the corporation here.

These cases illustrate the tension inherent in permitting shareholders to bring derivative suits. On the one hand, we do not want to permit untoward second-guessing of management. On the other, there may be cases in which we question the directors' ability to make an impartial decision about whether the corporation ought to sue. As a matter of policy, American law permits shareholders to bring derivative suits to vindicate corporate claims, but imposes significant procedural requirements for doing so. We will discuss these requirements in detail below.

Derivative suits must be distinguished from *direct suits*, in which a shareholder seeks to vindicate her own *personal* claim growing out of her ownership of stock. Direct suits are simply regular litigation, to which the procedural restrictions applicable to derivative suits do not apply. One hint that a direct suit is appropriate is that the defendant's conduct injured only some shareholders, rather than all of them. In contrast, suits that injure all shareholders tend to be derivative, although they can also sometimes be direct.

Occasionally, a shareholder will claim that her suit is direct, and the corporation will take the position that the case is derivative. It does so to force the plaintiff shareholder to abide by the burdensome procedural restrictions for derivative suits. Some plaintiffs might find the restrictions so onerous that they will abandon the case rather than pursue a derivative action. The corporation took this tack in the following case. The main point of *Eisenberg* is to learn to distinguish between derivative and direct suits.

---

* By the way, why is this "the corporation's claim" at all? Hint: to whom do the directors owe the duties of care and loyalty?

† This sentence answered the question in the preceding footnote. But why would the deal described be an interested director transaction? Why would (1) the way in which it was approved and (2) its terms not satisfy the MBCA provision for approval of interested director deals?

EISENBERG v. FLYING TIGER LINE, INC.

United States Court of Appeals, Second Circuit, 1971
451 F.2d 267

[These facts are pretty involved. You may want to diagram the various corporate entities and their relationships. Plaintiff, Eisenberg, owned stock in Flying Tiger Line, Inc. ("Flying Tiger"), which operated a freight and charter airline. That corporation formed a wholly-owned subsidiary called Flying Tiger Corporation ("FTC"). FTC, in turn, then formed a wholly-owned subsidiary, called FTL Air Freight Corporation ("FTL"). Then—and here it gets tough, so stick with it—Flying Tiger merged into FTL. That means Flying Tiger ceased to exist as a separate entity, and FTL survived. FTL took over running the airline. But the shareholders of Flying Tiger got stock not in FTL, but in FTC. Thus, Eisenberg and others (who used to own stock in an airline) now own stock in a holding company (FTC), a subsidiary of which (FTL) runs the airline.

Eisenberg sued, arguing that these machinations had deprived him (and other minority shareholders of Flying Tiger) of any vote or influence over the affairs of the corporation that now runs the airline. Rather than the minority owner of a corporation that ran an airline, he was now the minority owner of a corporation that owned another corporation that ran an airline.

The defendants argued that Eisenberg's claim was derivative and thus that he was required to post a bond as "security-for-expenses" under § 627 of the New York Business Corporation Law. The trial court agreed, and ordered Eisenberg to post a bond of $35,000. When he refused to do so, the court dismissed the case. Here, the Court of Appeals reverses. It finds that Eisenberg's case was a direct suit. Therefore, Eisenberg did not have to satisfy a derivative suit's procedural requirements, including posting a bond.]

IRVING KAUFMAN, JUDGE. In this action, Eisenberg is seeking to overturn a reorganization and merger which Flying Tiger effected in 1969. He charges that a series of corporate maneuvers were intended to dilute his voting rights. * * *

* * * Eisenberg contends that the end result of this complex plan was to deprive minority stockholders [of Flying Tiger] of any vote or any influence over the affairs of the newly spawned company [FTL]. Flying Tiger insists the plan was devised to bring about diversification without interference from the Civil Aeronautics Board, which closely regulates air carriers, and to better use available tax benefits. Even if any of these motives prove to be relevant, the alleged illegality is not relevant to the questions before this court. We are called on to decide, assuming Eisenberg's complaint is sufficient on its face, only whether he should have been required to post security for costs as a condition to prosecuting his action.

To resolve this question we look first to *Cohen v. Beneficial Industrial Loan Corp.*, 337 U.S. 541 (1949), which instructs that a federal court with diversity jurisdiction must apply a state statute providing security for costs if the state court would require the security in similar circumstances. [The Court determined that New York law would apply, and that Eisenberg would have to post security in this case if he would be required to do so in a New York state court. The answer to that depended on whether Eisenberg's claim is direct or derivative.]

We are told that if the gravamen of the complaint is injury to the corporation, the suit is derivative, but "if the injury is one to the plaintiff as a stockholder and to him individually and not to the corporation," the suit is individual in nature. * * * This generalization is of little use in our case, which is one of those "borderline cases which are more or less troublesome to classify." * * * The essence of Eisenberg's claimed injury is that the reorganization has deprived him and fellow stockholders of their right to vote on the operating company affairs and that this right in no sense ever belonged to Flying Tiger itself. This right, he says, belonged to the stockholders per se. Flying Tiger notes, however, that the stockholders were harmed, if at all, only because their company was dissolved, and their vote can be restored only if that company is revived. It insists, therefore, that stockholders are affected only secondarily or derivatively because we must first breathe life back into their dissolved corporation before the stockholders can be helped.

Despite a leading New York case which would seem at first glance to support Flying Tiger's position, we find that its contention misses the mark by a wide margin in its failure to distinguish between derivative and non-derivative [cases]. In *Gordon v. Elliman*, 306 N.Y. 456 (1954), by a vote of 4 to 3, the Court of Appeals took an expansive view of the coverage of [the statute requiring plaintiff to post a bond in derivative suits]. The majority held that an action to compel the payment of a dividend was derivative in nature and security for costs could be required. The test formulated by the majority was "whether the object of the lawsuit is to recover upon a *chose in action* belonging directly to the stockholders, or whether it is to compel the performance of corporate acts which good faith requires the directors to take in order to perform a duty which they owe to the corporation, and through it, to its stockholders." 306 N.Y. at 459. Pursuant to this test it is argued that if Flying Tiger's directors had a duty not to merge the corporation, that duty was owed to the corporation and only derivatively to its stockholders.

Both the 4–1 Appellate Division and the 4–3 Court of Appeals opinions [in *Gordon*] evoked the quick and unanimous condemnation of commentators. Moreover, this test, "which appears to sweep away the distinction between a [direct] and a derivative action," in effect classifying all stockholder [cases] as derivative, has been limited strictly to its facts by lower New York courts.* **[5]** * * * In [one such case, *Lazar v. Knolls*

---

* **[5]** In his dissenting opinion [in *Gordon*], Judge Fuld noted "in a very real sense, all suits against corporations * * * involve the actions of the directors or of officers responsible to the directors" so the majority's test would do away with representative actions altogether.

Cooperative Section No. 2, Inc., 130 N.Y.S.2d 407 (Sup. Ct. 1954)], a stockholder sought to force directors to call a stockholders' meeting. The court stated security for costs could not be required where a plaintiff

> does not challenge acts of the management on behalf of the corporation. He challenges the right of the present management to exclude him and other stockholders from proper participation in the affairs of the corporation. He claims that the defendants are interfering with the plaintiff's rights and privileges as stockholders.

130 N.Y.S.2d at 410. In substance, this is similar to what Eisenberg challenges here.

The legislature also was concerned with the sweeping breadth of *Gordon.* In the recodification of corporate statutes completed in 1963, it added three words to the definition of derivative suits contained in § 626. Suits are now derivative only if brought in the right of a corporation to procure a judgment "in its favor." This was to "forestall any such pronouncement in the future as that made by the Court of Appeals in *Gordon v. Elliman.*" Hornstein, "Analysis of Business Corporation Law," 6 McKINNEY'S CONSOLIDATED LAWS OF NEW YORK ANN. 483 (1963).

Other New York cases which have distinguished between derivative and [direct] actions are of some interest. In *Horwitz v. Balaban,* 112 F. Supp. 99 (S.D. N.Y.1949), a stockholder sought to restrain the exercise of conversion rights that the corporation had granted to its president. The court found the action [was direct] and refused to require security, setting forth the test as "where the corporation has no right of action by reason of the transaction complained of, the suit is * * * not derivative." Id. at 101. Similarly, actions to compel the dissolution of a corporation have been held [to be direct], since the corporation could not possibly benefit therefrom. Fontheim v. Walker, 141 N.Y.S.2d 62 (Sup. Ct. 1955). * * * And *Lehrman v. Godchaux Sugars, Inc.,* [138 N.Y.S.2d 163 (Sup. Ct. 1955)] discloses that an action by a stockholder complaining that a proposed recapitalization would unfairly benefit holders of another class of stock was [direct]. These cases and *Lazar* are totally consistent with the postulates of the leading treatises. Professor Moore instructs that "where a shareholder sues on behalf of himself and all others similarly situated to * * * enjoin a proposed merger or consolidation * * * he is not enforcing a derivative right; he is, by an appropriate type of class suit, enforcing a right common to all the shareholders which runs against the corporation."

Eisenberg's position is even stronger than it would be in the ordinary merger case. In routine merger circumstances the stockholders retain a voice in the operation of the company, albeit a corporation other than their original choice. Here, however, the reorganization deprived him and other minority stockholders of any voice in the affairs of their previously existing operating company.

It is thus clear to us that *Gordon* is factually distinguishable from the instant case. Moreover, a close analysis of other New York cases, the amendment to § 626 and the major treatises, lead us to conclude that *Gordon* has lost its viability as stating a broad principle of law.

Furthermore, we view as an objective of a requirement for security for costs the prevention of strike suits and collusive settlements. Where directors are sued for mismanagement, the risk of personal monetary liability is a strong motive for bringing the suit and inducing settlement. Here, no monetary damages are sought, and no individuals will be liable.

* * *

Reversed.

Questions

1. Why was Mr. Eisenberg's claim direct? Could it have been characterized in a way to make it derivative?

2. The court noted that the plaintiff was not seeking monetary recovery from any of the defendants. Why was that fact significant?

3. Even without a monetary claim, wouldn't a baseless suit by Mr. Eisenberg still require the defendants to make out-of-pocket payments for attorneys' fees and litigation costs?

4. In New York *today*, would a suit to force the directors to declare a dividend be derivative or direct?

5. According to the discussion in *Eisenberg*, how would you classify the following cases? Are they derivative or direct suits? Why?

5.1 Roberts sues the directors of Bubba's Burritos, Inc. because they failed to permit him to inspect corporate books and records.

5.2 The articles of Bubba's Burritos, Inc. provide that the corporation will "operate restaurants featuring burritos and related food and beverage products." Shepherd learns that the directors plan to enter a contract with Chad & Associates to go into the voting machine business. He sues to enjoin the corporation for engaging in this ultra vires activity.

5.3 Roberts sues the directors of Bubba's Burritos, Inc. for wasting corporate assets by paying themselves huge bonuses. Why is this a derivative suit?

5.4 Shepherd sues the directors of Bubba's Burritos, Inc. for usurping corporate opportunities.

5.5 Epstein sues the directors of Bubba's Burritos, Inc. for failing to exercise due care because they purchased supplies at a price much higher than could have been negotiated.

5.6 Roberts is the minority shareholder in Bubba's Burritos, Inc., which is a close corporation. He sues the controlling shareholders, alleging that they have breached fiduciary duties by oppressing him. Specifically, he alleges that while they have had the corporation hire them and purchase their stock for cash, they have refused to allow the corporation to do such things for him.

5.7 Suppose that Freer is not only the CEO of Bubba's Burritos, but also works as its bouncer. Shepherd, a Bubba's shareholder, eats at Bubba's, gets boisterous after too many beers, and is pummeled by Freer as Freer tosses him out a window. Whom can Shepherd sue, and what kind of suit (direct or derivative) will it be?

2. PROCEDURAL REQUIREMENTS OF A DERIVATIVE SUIT

a. Stock Ownership and Other Standing Requirements

Study MBCA § 7.41 and the following questions should help you answer the question of who has standing to bring a derivative suit.

QUESTIONS AND NOTE

1. Suppose Roberts hears of some wrongdoing by directors of Bubba's Burritos, Inc. He wants to bring a derivative suit, but did not own stock in Bubba's when the claim arose. He buys one share of Bubba's stock. Clearly, he cannot bring a derivative suit under the "contemporaneous ownership" requirement of MBCA § 7.41(1). But why should this be so? What would be wrong with allowing him to purchase shares and purchase the right to sue at the same time? Has he suffered any loss? A few states would allow him to sue, at least in some circumstances. *See* Cal. Corp. Code § 800(b).

2. Can you think of some examples of how stock could be transferred "by operation of law" so as to allow someone to bring suit even though she did not own stock when the claim arose? Does this rule make sense? Would a transferee by operation of law be any better equipped to bring a derivative suit than Roberts in Question 1? Indeed, since Roberts at least had the desire to bring the suit, wouldn't he be a better candidate for serving as plaintiff than the transferee by operation of law?

3. Does MBCA § 7.41 require that the plaintiff be a shareholder at the outset of the derivative litigation? How about at the entry of judgment of the derivative litigation? If not, should it? Why?

4. Does § 7.41 require that the plaintiff own stock of a particular value? If not, should it? Why?

5. What does the requirement of MBCA § 7.41(2) add to that of contemporaneous ownership?

6. Some courts have strained to uphold shareholder standing under the "continuing wrong" theory. They reason that some defendants' breach of duty do not occur simply at a single moment, but over time. If the shareholder owned stock at any point during this "continuing wrong," such a court will uphold the plaintiff's right to sue. *See, e.g., Palmer v. Morris*, 316 F.2d 649 (5th Cir. 1963) (shareholder buys stock after wrongful transaction was entered, but before all payments thereunder were made). Not all courts have been so solicitous, although some legislatures have endorsed the proposition. *See, e.g.,* Cal. Corp. Code § 800(b)(1) (requiring plaintiff to own stock during the alleged wrong "or any part thereof").

b. Security-for-Expenses

Remember the fight in *Eisenberg*—over whether his was a derivative suit? He wanted the case characterized as direct so he would not have to adhere to the New York requirement that plaintiffs in his position post security to cover the corporation's expenses in the litigation. The New York requirement was the response to a report commissioned by the New York Chamber of Commerce in the 1940s. It concluded that the vast majority of derivative suits brought in New York were filed by shareholders with minor holdings and were lacking in merit. The purpose of most suits, the report found, was to cajole the corporation to pay the shareholder to "go away."

The MBCA and most states do not have security-for-expenses provisions.

c. Demand on Directors

This is the big one. Most states require the shareholder who wants to bring a derivative suit to make a *written demand* on the directors that they assert a claim allegedly existing in favor of the corporation. Some states, however, recognize the possibility that such a demand might be excused.

Why is there a demand requirement and why should it ever be excused? Whether the corporation should bring suit presents a management decision. The most important management decisions, generally, are to be made by the directors. So the demand requirement (sometimes called the requirement to "exhaust intracorporate remedies") places the issue squarely before the people who should be making the decision.

If a demand is such a good idea, why should it ever be excused? One court explains that "[e]quity will not require a useless act. * * * Where demand upon the board would be 'futile,' the demand requirement will be excused." *Heineman v. Datapoint Corp.*, 611 A.2d 950 (Del. 1992).

But what constitutes "futility"? Do the statutory provisions give any hint? Read MBCA § 7.42. Does that provision recognize any exception to its demand requirement? If not, does it, unlike the equity-based approach in Delaware and some other states, "require a useless act?"

What happens if the plaintiff makes a demand? One of two things can then happen. For one, the board can accept the recommendation and authorize the corporation to sue. At that point, the shareholder bows out. Because the corporation brings the case, it is not a derivative suit, and no shareholder involvement is required.

The other possibility, of course, is that the board rejects the demand. At that point, the shareholder can (1) forget the whole thing or (2) continue the fight by asserting that the board erred in its decision not to have the corporation sue.

The latter course will almost always be a loser. Why? Because the shareholder at that point is asserting that the directors violated the business judgment rule. And as we know, it is almost impossible to make such a showing. A plaintiff would have to show either that the directors made their decision without any on-the-record-efforts to look like they were acting seriously, or that the decision was tainted by conflict of interest. *See* MBCA § 7.44(d).

Under Delaware law, it will be impossible to make the latter showing. According to the Delaware Supreme Court, the fact that the plaintiff made the demand constitutes an admission that the directors were disinterested. *Spiegel v. Buntrock*, 571 A.2d 767 (Del. 1990). In other words, making the demand admitted that demand was not futile.

With this state of affairs, why would a plaintiff (at least in Delaware) *ever* make a demand? The answer is that, if she has a competent lawyer, she wouldn't. She almost automatically loses the case if she does.

What happens if the plaintiff brings suit without making a demand? Suppose the plaintiff decides not to make a demand on the directors, and simply files the derivative suit. Then what? The directors will probably seek dismissal of the action on the ground that the plaintiff should have made the demand. The issue in deciding the directors' motion will be whether demand was excused because it would have been futile. If not, then the court dismisses the case. Only if the court finds that demand was excused can the case continue. This motion whether demand was excused then is of life-and-death importance for the plaintiff's case.

The following opinion is the leading discussion of New York law on the subject of when a demand on directors will be excused. It is especially helpful because it also explains the Delaware and MBCA approaches to the topic. Before reading it, use your intuition to consider whether any of the following scenarios would lead you to believe that a demand on directors would be futile. In each, assume that the board consists of five directors. After you read the opinion, we ask you how each scenario would come out under the approaches of New York, Delaware, and the MBCA.

1. Suppose the claim to be asserted is that all five directors breached their duty of loyalty by engaging in competing ventures. Demand excused?

2. Suppose the claim to be asserted is that three of the directors breached their duty of loyalty. Demand excused?

3. Suppose the claim is that two directors breached the duty. Demand excused?

4. Suppose the claim is that one director breached the duty, but that she is the dominant member of the board, and that the other four are under her control. Demand excused?

5. Suppose the claim is that a *former* director breached the duty (while serving as a director), but that she essentially arranged to have all five present directors named to the board. Demand excused?

MARX v. AKERS

New York Court of Appeals, 1996
88 N.Y.2d 189, 666 N.E.2d 1034

SMITH, J. Plaintiff commenced this shareholder derivative action against International Business Machines Corporation (IBM) and IBM's board of directors without first demanding that the board initiate a lawsuit. The amended complaint (complaint) alleges that the board wasted corporate assets by awarding excessive compensation to IBM's executives and outside directors. The issues raised on this appeal are whether the Appellate Division abused its discretion by dismissing plaintiff's complaint for failure to make a demand and whether plaintiff's complaint fails to state a cause of action. We affirm the order of the Appellate Division because we conclude that plaintiff was not excused from making a demand with respect to the executive compensation claim and that plaintiff has failed to state a cause of action for corporate waste in connection with the allegations concerning payments to IBM's outside directors.

Facts and Procedural History

The complaint alleges that during a period of declining profitability at IBM the director defendants engaged in self-dealing by awarding excessive compensation to the 15 outside directors on the 18–member board. Although the complaint identifies only one of the three inside directors as an IBM executive (defendant Akers is identified as a former chief executive officer of IBM),* [1] plaintiff also appears to allege that the director defendants violated their fiduciary duties to IBM by voting for unreasonably high compensation for IBM executives.† [2]

Defendants moved to dismiss the complaint for (1) failure to state a cause of action, and (2) failure to serve a demand on IBM's board to initiate a lawsuit based on the complaint's allegations. The Supreme Court [the trial court in New York] dismissed, holding that plaintiff failed to establish the futility of a demand. [The] Supreme Court concluded that excusing a demand here would render Business Corporation Law § 626(c) "virtually meaningless in any shareholders' derivative action in which all members of a corporate board are named as defendants." Having decided the demand issue in favor of defendants, the court did not reach the issue of whether plaintiff's complaint stated a cause of action.

The Appellate Division affirmed the dismissal, concluding that the complaint did not contain any details from which the futility of a demand could be inferred. The Appellate Division found that plaintiff's objections

---

* [1] The other inside directors, although identified as Employee Directors, are never explicitly identified as executive officers in the complaint. However, the names of these directors appear on a chart disclosing "payments to certain executives."

† [2] Executives at IBM are compensated through a fixed salary and performance incentives. Payouts on the performance incentives are based on IBM's earnings per share, return on equity and cash flow. Plaintiff's complaint criticizes only the performance incentive component of executive compensation as excessive because of certain accounting practices which plaintiff alleges artificially inflate earnings, return on equity and cash flow.

to the level of compensation were not stated with sufficient particularity in light of statutory authority permitting directors to set their own compensation.

Background

A shareholder's derivative action is an action "brought in the right of a domestic or foreign corporation to procure a judgment in its favor, by a holder of shares or of voting trust certificates of the corporation or of a beneficial interest in such shares or certificates" (Business Corporation Law § 626 (a)). "Derivative claims against corporate directors belong to the corporation itself" (*Auerbach v. Bennett*, 47 NY2d 619, 631 [1979]).

> The remedy sought is for wrong done to the corporation; the primary cause of action belongs to the corporation; recovery must enure to the benefit of the corporation. The stockholder brings the action, in behalf of others similarly situated, to vindicate the corporate rights and a judgment on the merits is a binding adjudication of these rights [citations omitted] (*Isaac v. Marcus*, 258 NY 257, 264 [1932]).

Business Corporation Law § 626(c) provides that in any shareholders' derivative action, "the complaint shall set forth with particularity the efforts of the plaintiff to secure the initiation of such action by the board or the reasons for not making such effort." Enacted in 1961 * * * section 626(c) codified a rule of equity developed in early shareholder derivative actions requiring plaintiffs to demand that the corporation initiate an action, unless such demand was futile, before commencing an action on the corporation's behalf (*Barr v. Wackman*, 36 NY2d 371, 377 [1975]). The purposes of the demand requirement are to (1) relieve courts from deciding matters of internal corporate governance by providing corporate directors with opportunities to correct alleged abuses, (2) provide corporate boards with reasonable protection from harassment by litigation on matters clearly within the discretion of directors, and (3) discourage "strike suits" commenced by shareholders for personal gain rather than for the benefit of the corporation (*Barr*, 36 NY2d at 378). "[T]he demand is generally designed to weed out unnecessary or illegitimate shareholder derivative suits" (id.).

By their very nature, shareholder derivative actions infringe upon the managerial discretion of corporate boards. "As with other questions of corporate policy and management, the decision whether and to what extent to explore and prosecute such [derivative] claims lies within the judgment and control of the corporation's board of directors." (*Auerbach*, 47 NY2d at 631) Consequently, we have historically been reluctant to permit shareholder derivative suits, noting that the power of courts to direct the management of a corporation's affairs should be "exercised with restraint." (*Gordon v. Elliman*, 306 N.Y. 456, 462 [1954])

In permitting a shareholder derivative action to proceed because a demand on the corporation's directors would be futile, the object is for the court to chart the course for the corporation which the directors should have selected, and which it is presumed that they would have chosen if they had not been actuated by fraud or bad faith. Due to their misconduct, the court substitutes its judgment ad hoc for that of the directors in the conduct of its business.

Achieving a balance between preserving the discretion of directors to manage a corporation without undue interference, through the demand requirement, and permitting shareholders to bring claims on behalf of the corporation when it is evident that directors will wrongfully refuse to bring such claims, through the demand futility exception, has been accomplished by various jurisdictions in different ways. One widely cited approach to demand futility which attempts to balance these competing concerns has been developed by Delaware courts and applies a two-pronged test to each case to determine whether a failure to serve a demand is justified. At the other end of the spectrum is a universal demand requirement which would abandon particularized determinations in favor of requiring a demand in every case before a shareholder derivative suit may be filed.

The Delaware Approach

Delaware's demand requirement, codified in Delaware Chancery Court Rule 23.1, provides, in relevant part,

> In a derivative action brought by 1 or more shareholders or members to enforce a right of a corporation ... [the complaint shall allege] with particularity the efforts, if any, made by the plaintiff to obtain the action the plaintiff desires from the directors or comparable authority and the reasons for the plaintiff's failure to obtain the action or for not making the effort.

Interpreting Rule 23.1, the Delaware Supreme Court in *Aronson v. Lewis* developed a two-prong test for determining the futility of a demand. Plaintiffs must allege particularized facts which create a reasonable doubt that,

> (1) the directors are disinterested and independent and (2) the challenged transaction was otherwise the product of a valid exercise of business judgment. Hence, the Court of Chancery must make two inquiries, one into the independence and disinterestedness of the directors and the other into the substantive nature of the challenged transaction and the board's approval thereof.

The two branches of the *Aronson* test are disjunctive. Once director interest has been established, the business judgment rule becomes inapplicable and the demand is excused without further inquiry. Similarly, a director whose independence is compromised by undue influence exerted by an interested party cannot properly exercise business judgment and the loss of independence also justifies the excusal of a demand without further inquiry. Whether a board has validly exercised its business judgment must be evaluated by determining whether the directors exercised procedural (informed decision) and substantive (terms of the transaction) due care.

The reasonable doubt threshold of Delaware's two-fold approach to demand futility has been criticized. The use of a standard of proof which is the heart of a jury's determination in a criminal case has raised questions concerning its applicability in the corporate context. The reasonable doubt standard has also been criticized as overly subjective, thereby permitting a wide variance in the application of Delaware law to similar facts (2 American Law Institute, Principles of Corporate Governance: Analysis and Recommendations § 7.03, Comment d, at 57 [1992]).

Universal Demand

A universal demand requirement would dispense with the necessity of making case-specific determinations and impose an easily applied bright line rule. The Business Law Section of the American Bar Association has proposed requiring a demand in all cases, without exception, and [prohibits] the commencement of a derivative proceeding within 90 days of the demand unless the demand is rejected earlier (Model Business Corporation Act § 7.42 [1] [1995 Supp]). However, plaintiffs may file suit before the expiration of 90 days, even if their demand has not been rejected, if the corporation would suffer irreparable injury as a result [of waiting the 90 days] (Model Business Corporation Act § 7.42 [2]).

The American Law Institute (ALI) has also proposed a "universal" demand. Section 7.03 of ALI's Principles of Corporate Governance would require shareholder derivative action plaintiffs to serve a written demand on the corporation unless a demand is excused because "the plaintiff makes a specific showing that irreparable injury to the corporation would otherwise result" (2 ALI, Principles of Corporate Governance: Analysis and Recommendations § 7.03 [b], at 53–54 [1992]). Once a demand has been made and rejected, however, the ALI would subject the board's decision to "an elaborate set of standards that calibrates the deference afforded the decision of the directors to the character of the claim being asserted."

At least 11 States have adopted, by statute, the universal demand requirement proposed in the Model Business Corporation Act. Georgia, Michigan, Wisconsin, Montana, Virginia, New Hampshire, Mississippi, Connecticut, Nebraska and North Carolina require shareholders to wait 90 days after serving a demand before filing a derivative suit unless the demand is rejected before the expiration of the 90 days, or irreparable injury to the corporation would result. * * * Arizona additionally permits shareholders to file suit before the expiration of 90 days if the Statute of Limitations would expire during the 90–day period. * * * Florida also appears to have adopted a universal demand requirement, although the statutory language does not track the Model Business Corporation Act. Florida's statute provides, "A complaint in a proceeding brought in the right of a corporation must be verified and allege with particularity the demand made to obtain action by the board of directors and that the demand was refused or ignored." * * *

New York State has also considered and continues to consider implementing a universal demand requirement. However, even though bills to adopt a universal demand have been presented over three legislative sessions, the Legislature has yet to enact a universal demand requirement. * * *

New York's Approach to Demand Futility

Although instructive, neither the universal demand requirement nor the Delaware approach to demand futility is adopted here. Since New York's demand requirement is codified in Business Corporation Law § 626(c), a universal demand may only be adopted by the Legislature. Delaware's approach, which resembles New York law in some respects, incorporates a "reasonable doubt" standard which, as we have already pointed out, has provoked criticism as confusing and overly subjective. An analysis of the *Barr* decision compels the conclusion that in New York, a demand would be futile if a complaint alleges with particularity that (1) a majority of the directors are interested in the transaction, or (2) the directors failed to inform themselves to a degree reasonably necessary about the transaction, or (3) the directors failed to exercise their business judgment in approving the transaction.

In *Barr v. Wackman, supra,* we considered whether the plaintiff was excused from making a demand where the board of Talcott National Corporation (Talcott), consisting of 13 outside directors, a director affiliated with a related company and four interested inside directors, rejected a merger proposal involving Gulf & Western Industries (Gulf & Western) in favor of another proposal on allegedly less favorable terms for Talcott and its shareholders. The merger proposal, memorialized in a board-approved "agreement in principle," proposed exchanging one share of Talcott common stock for approximately $24 consisting of $17 in cash and 0.6 of a warrant to purchase Gulf & Western stock, worth approximately $7. This proposal was abandoned in favor of a cash tender offer for Talcott shares by Associates First Capital Corporation (a Gulf & Western subsidiary) at $20 per share—$4 less than proposed for the merger.

The plaintiff in *Barr* alleged that Talcott's board discarded the merger proposal after the four "controlling" inside directors received pecuniary and personal benefits from Gulf & Western in exchange for ceding control of Talcott on terms less favorable to Talcott's shareholders. As alleged in the complaint, these benefits included new and favorable employment contracts for nine Talcott officers, including five-year employment contracts for three of the controlling directors. In addition to his annual salary of $125,000 with Talcott, defendant Silverman (a controlling director) would allegedly receive $60,000 a year under a five-year employment contract with Associates First Capital, and an aggregate of $275,000 for the next five years in an arrangement with Associates First Capital to serve as a consultant. This additional compensation would be awarded to

Silverman after control of Talcott passed to Associates First Capital and Gulf & Western. Plaintiff also alleged that Gulf & Western and Associates First Capital paid an excessive "finder's fee" of $340,000 to a company where Silverman's son was an executive vice-president. In addition to alleging that the controlling defendants obtained personal benefits, the complaint also alleged that Talcott's board agreed to sell a Talcott subsidiary at a net loss of $6,100,000 solely to accommodate Gulf & Western.

In *Barr*, we held that insofar as the complaint attacked the controlling directors' acts in causing the corporation to enter into a transaction for their own financial benefit, demand was excused because of the self-dealing, or self-interest of those directors in the challenged transaction. Specifically, we pointed to the allegation that the controlling directors "breached their fiduciary obligations to Talcott in return for personal benefits."

We also held in *Barr*, however, that as to the disinterested outside directors, demand could be excused even in the absence of their receiving any financial benefit from the transaction. That was because the complaint alleged that, by approving the terms of the less advantageous offer, those directors were guilty of a "breach of their duties of due care and diligence to the corporation." Their performance of the duty of care would have "put them on notice of the claimed self-dealing of the affiliated directors." The complaint charged that the outside directors failed "to do more than passively rubber-stamp the decisions of the active managers," resulting in corporate detriment. These allegations, the *Barr* Court concluded, also excused demand as to the charges against the disinterested directors.

Barr also makes clear that "[i]t is not sufficient * * * merely to name a majority of the directors as parties defendant with conclusory allegations of wrongdoing or control by wrongdoers" to justify failure to make a demand. Thus, *Barr* reflects the statutory requirement that the complaint "shall set forth with particularity the * * * reasons for not making such effort" (Business Corporation Law § 626 [c]).

Unfortunately, various courts have overlooked the explicit warning that conclusory allegations of wrongdoing against each member of the board are not sufficient to excuse demand and have misinterpreted *Barr* as excusing demand whenever a majority of the board members who approved the transaction are named as defendants [citations to five cases]. As stated most recently, "[t]he rule is clear in this State that no demand is necessary if 'the complaint alleges acts for which a majority of the directors may be liable and plaintiff reasonably concluded that the board would not be responsive to a demand.'" The problem with such an approach is that it permits plaintiffs to frame their complaint in such a way as to automatically excuse demand, thereby allowing the exception to swallow the rule.

We thus deem it necessary to offer the following elaboration of *Barr's* demand/futility standard. (1) Demand is excused because of futility when a complaint alleges with particularity that a majority of the board of directors is interested in the challenged transaction. Director interest may either be self-interest in the transaction at issue, or a loss of independence because a director with no direct interest in a transaction is "controlled" by a self-interested director. (2) Demand is excused because of futility when a complaint alleges with particularity that the board of directors did not fully inform themselves about the challenged transaction to the extent reasonably appropriate under the circumstances. The "long-standing rule" is that a director "does not exempt himself from liability by failing to do more than passively rubber-stamp the decisions of the active managers." (3) Demand is excused because of futility when a complaint alleges with particularity that the challenged transaction was so egregious on its face that it could not have been the product of sound business judgment of the directors.

The Current Appeal

Plaintiff argues that the demand requirement was excused both because the outside directors awarded themselves generous compensation packages and because of the acquiescence of the disinterested directors in the executive compensation schemes. The complaint states:

> Plaintiff has made no demand upon the directors of IBM to institute this lawsuit because such demand would be futile. As set forth above, each of the directors authorized, approved, participated and/or acquiesced in the acts and transactions complained of herein and are liable therefor. Further, each of the Non–Employee [outside] Directors has received and retained the benefit of his excessive compensation and each of the other directors has received and retained the benefit of the incentive compensation described above. The defendants cannot be expected to vote to prosecute an action against themselves. Demand upon the company to bring [an] action to redress the wrongs herein is therefore unnecessary.

* * *

As in *Barr*, we look to the complaint here to determine whether the allegations are sufficient and establish with particularity that demand would have been futile. Here, the plaintiff alleges that the compensation awarded to IBM's outside directors and certain IBM executives was excessive.

Defendants' motion to dismiss for failure to make a demand as to the allegations concerning the compensation paid to IBM's executive officers was properly granted. A board is not interested "in voting compensation for one of its members as an executive or in some other nondirectorial capacity, such as a consultant to the corporation," although "so-called 'back-scratching' arrangements, pursuant to which all directors vote to approve each other's compensation as officers or employees, do not constitute disinterested directors' action" (1 ALI § 5.03, Comment g, at 250).

Since only three directors are alleged to have received the benefit of the executive compensation scheme, plaintiff has failed to allege that a majority of the board was interested in setting executive compensation. Nor do the allegations that the board used faulty accounting procedures to calculate executive compensation levels move beyond "conclusory allegations of wrongdoing" (*Barr*, 36 NY2d at 379) which are insufficient to excuse demand. The complaint does not allege particular facts in contending that the board failed to deliberate or exercise its business judgment in setting those levels. Consequently, the failure to make a demand regarding the fixing of executive compensation was fatal to that portion of the complaint challenging that transaction.

However, a review of the complaint indicates that plaintiff also alleged that a majority of the board was self-interested in setting the compensation of outside directors because the outside directors comprised a majority of the board.

Directors are self-interested in a challenged transaction where they will receive a direct financial benefit from the transaction which is different from the benefit to shareholders generally * * * A director who votes for a raise in directors' compensation is always "interested" because that person will receive a personal financial benefit from the transaction not shared in by stockholders (see, 1 ALI § 5.03, Comment g, at 250 ["if the board votes directorial compensation for itself, the board is interested"]. Consequently, a demand was excused as to plaintiff's allegations that the compensation set for outside directors was excessive.

Corporate Waste

Our conclusion that demand should have been excused as to the part of the complaint challenging the fixing of directors' compensation does not end our inquiry. We must also determine whether plaintiff has stated a cause of action regarding director compensation, i.e., some wrong to the corporation. We conclude that plaintiff has not, and thus dismiss the complaint in its entirety.

Historically, directors did not receive any compensation for their work as directors. * * *

* * * Thus, a bare allegation that corporate directors voted themselves excessive compensation was sufficient to state a cause of action * * *. Many jurisdictions, including New York, have since changed the common-law rule by statute providing that a corporation's board of directors has the authority to fix director compensation unless the corporation's charter or bylaws provides otherwise. Thus, the allegation that directors have voted themselves compensation is clearly no longer an allegation which gives rise to a cause of action, as the directors are statutorily entitled to set those levels. Nor does a conclusory allegation that the compensation directors have set for themselves is excessive give rise to a cause of action.

The courts will not undertake to review the fairness of official salaries, at the suit of a shareholder attacking them as excessive, unless wrongdoing and oppression or possible abuse of a fiduciary position are shown. However, the courts will take a hand in the matter at the instance of the corporation or of shareholders in extreme cases. A case of fraud is presented where directors increase their collective salaries so as to use up nearly the entire earnings of a company; where directors or officers appropriate the income so as to deprive shareholders of reasonable dividends, or perhaps so reduce the assets as to threaten the corporation with insolvency. [5A (1995 rev. vol.) Fletcher, CYCLOPEDIA OF PRIVATE CORPORATIONS § 2122, at 46–67.]

Thus, a complaint challenging the excessiveness of director compensation must—to survive a dismissal motion—allege compensation rates excessive on their face or other facts which call into question whether the compensation was fair to the corporation when approved, the good faith of the directors setting those rates, or that the decision to set the compensation could not have been a product of valid business judgment.* **[6]**

Applying the foregoing principles to plaintiff's complaint, it is clear that it must be dismissed. The complaint alleges that the directors increased their compensation rates from a base of $20,000 plus $500 for each meeting attended to a retainer of $55,000 plus 100 shares of IBM stock over a five-year period. The complaint also alleges that "[t]his compensation bears little relation to the part-time services rendered by the Non–Employee Directors or to the profitability of IBM. The board's responsibilities have not increased, its performance, measured by the company's earnings and stock price, has been poor yet its compensation has increased far in excess of the cost of living."

These conclusory allegations do not state a cause of action. There are no factually based allegations of wrong-doing or waste which would, if true, sustain a verdict in plaintiff's favor. Plaintiff's bare allegations that the compensation set lacked a relationship to duties performed or to the cost of living are insufficient as a matter of law to state a cause of action.

Accordingly, the order of the Appellate Division should be affirmed, with costs.

QUESTIONS AND NOTE

1. Now, how would the hypotheticals raised before the *Marx* case come out under (A) New York law; (B) Delaware law; and (C) the MBCA?

2. Suppose only two of the five directors would be defendants in the case to be asserted. What in FRCP 23.1 or New York § 626(c) is to stop the

---

* **[6]** There is general agreement that the allocation of the burden of proof differs depending on whether the compensation was approved by disinterested directors or shareholders, or by interested directors. Plaintiffs must prove wrongdoing or waste as to compensation arrangements regarding disinterested directors or shareholders, but directors who approve their own compensation bear the burden of proving that the transaction was fair to the corporation. * * * However, at the pleading stage we are not concerned with burdens of proof.

plaintiff from alleging that all five (or a majority) engaged in the breach of duty (to escape the demand requirement)? After all, aren't those provisions really aimed only at pleading, as opposed to actual findings of fact?

3. And speaking of pleading, note the requirement that the plaintiff plead that the demand was excused "with particularity." You may recall from Civil Procedure that parties usually need plead only enough detail to put the other parties "on notice" of their claims or defenses. Pleading with particularity, obviously, requires a more developed sense of the facts. Yet, precisely because the case is at the pleading stage, it may be difficult to muster the particularized allegations.

What happens if the court denies the directors' motion? Suppose the court finds that demand was excused, and therefore permits the suit to continue. At this point, the case sometimes settles. Or the case can be litigated on the merits.

A third alternative is that the directors might bring a motion to dismiss, arguing that the potential benefits from the corporation's continuing the suit are not worth the costs. For example, the directors might argue that the corporation's litigation costs will exceed any recovery or that the likelihood of success is not great.

It was long considered appropriate for the directors to bring a motion to dismiss the derivative suit, *at least* when the case was against a third party. In such a case, there was no direct conflict of interest for the directors who were making the decision. Because no director was interested directly in the case, the issue of whether the litigation should be pursued involves a business judgment that the court would respect.

But what about a case involving a claim of director wrongdoing? Suppose the directors who were being sued moved to dismiss the suit because it was not in the corporation's best interests. The court would not respect that decision as a valid exercise of the directors' business judgment because of the directors' self interest in having the suit dismissed.

To avoid this problem, smart lawyers then devised the strategy of having the decision to move to dismiss be made not by the whole board, including the interested directors who were being sued. Instead, the decision would be delegated to a "special litigation committee," or "SLC," made up of supposedly disinterested directors who were not accused of wrongdoing. Often the SLC's members would be appointed as directors after the alleged wrongdoing occurred, specifically to serve on the SLC.

In 1976, one court permitted a disinterested committee of directors to bring a motion to dismiss because the case was not in the best interests of the corporation. Gall v. Exxon Corp., 418 F. Supp. 508 (S.D. N.Y. 1976). The court was (properly) concerned with whether that committee was sufficiently independent of the alleged wrongdoers to make an impartial assessment of whether the case should proceed. So it held hearings on whether those committee members in fact were independent of the defendants. *Gall* marked a sea change. Before that case, most people thought a shareholder simply had a right to proceed with litigation against corporate insiders.

Since then, courts have taken varying approaches to attempts of special litigation committees to dismiss derivative suits. The next two cases—*Auerbach* and *Zapata*—reflect the leading competing schools of thought.

In reading each, keep in mind what the problem is: can a committee of directors be expected to make an impartial decision about whether litigation should proceed against one or more of the directors' colleagues?

AUERBACH v. BENNETT

New York Court of Appeals, 1979
47 N.Y.2d 619, 393 N.E.2d 994

JONES, J. * * * As all parties and both courts below recognize, the disposition of this case on the merits turns on the proper application of the business judgment doctrine, in particular to the decision of a specially appointed committee of disinterested directors acting on behalf of the board to terminate a shareholders' derivative action. That doctrine bars judicial inquiry into actions of corporate directors taken in good faith and in the exercise of honest judgment in the lawful and legitimate furtherance of corporate purposes.

* * *

In the present case we confront a special instance of the application of the business judgment rule and inquire whether it applies in its full vigor to shield from judicial scrutiny the decision of a three-person minority committee of the board acting on behalf of the full board not to prosecute a shareholder's derivative action. The record in this case reveals that the board is a 15–member board, and that the derivative suit was brought against four of the directors. Nothing suggests that any of the other directors participated in any of the challenged * * * transactions. Indeed the report of the audit committee on which the complaint is based specifically found that no other directors had any prior knowledge of or were in any way involved in any of these transactions. Other directors had, however, been members of the board in the period during which the transactions occurred. Each of the three director members of the special litigation committee joined the board thereafter.

The business judgment rule does not foreclose inquiry by the courts into the disinterested independence of those members of the board chosen by it to make the corporate decision on its behalf—here the members of the special litigation committee. Indeed the rule shields the deliberations and conclusions of the chosen representatives of the board only if they possess a disinterested independence and do not stand in a dual relation which prevents an unprejudicial exercise of judgment.

We examine then the proof submitted by defendants. It is not disputed that the members of the special litigation committee were not members of the corporation's board of directors at the time of the * * * transactions in question. Howard Blauvelt, chairman of the board of Continental Oil Company, had been elected to the corporation's board of directors on October 9, 1975. Dr. John T. Dunlop, Lamont University professor at the Graduate School of Business Administration of Harvard University had been elected to the board on April 21, 1976. James R. Barker, chairman of the board and chief executive officer of Moore McCormack Resources, Inc., was added as the third member of the committee when he was elected to the board on July 19, 1976. None of the three had had any prior affiliation with the corporation. Notwithstanding the vigorous and imaginative hypothesizing and innuendo of counsel there is nothing in this record to raise a triable issue of fact as to the independence and disinterested status of these three directors.

The contention of [plaintiff] that any committee authorized by the board of which defendant directors were members must be held to be legally infirm and may not be delegated power to terminate a derivative action must be rejected. In the very nature of the corporate organization it was only the existing board of directors which had authority on behalf of the corporation to direct the investigation and to assure the co-operation of corporate employees, and it is only that same board by its own action— or as here pursuant to authority duly delegated by it—which had authority to decide whether to prosecute the claims against defendant directors. The board in this instance, with slight adaptation, followed prudent practice in observing the general policy that when individual members of a board of directors prove to have personal interests which may conflict with the interests of the corporation, such interested directors must be excluded while the remaining members of the board proceed to consideration and action. (*Cf.* Business Corporation Law, § 713, which contemplates such situations and provides that the interested directors may nonetheless be included in the quorum count.) Courts have consistently held that the business judgment rule applies where some directors are charged with wrongdoing, so long as the remaining directors making the decision are disinterested and independent. * * *

To accept the assertions of [plaintiff] and to disqualify the entire board would be to render the corporation powerless to make an effective business judgment with respect to prosecution of the derivative action. The possible risk of hesitancy on the part of the members of any committee, even if composed of outside, independent, disinterested directors, to investigate the activities of fellow members of the board where personal liability is at stake is an inherent, inescapable, given aspect of the corporation's predicament. To assign responsibility of the dimension here involved to individuals wholly separate and apart from the board of directors would, except in the most extraordinary circumstances, itself be an act of default and breach of the nondelegable fiduciary duty owed by the members of the board to the corporation and to its shareholders, employees and creditors. For the courts to preside over such determinations would similarly work an ouster of the board's fundamental responsibility and authority for corporate management.

We turn then to the action of the special litigation committee itself[,] which comprised two components. First, there was the selection of procedures appropriate to the pursuit of its charge, and second, there was the ultimate substantive decision, predicated on the procedures chosen and the data produced thereby, not to pursue the claims advanced in the shareholders' derivative actions. The latter, substantive decision falls squarely within the embrace of the business judgment doctrine, involving as it did the weighing and balancing of legal, ethical, commercial, promotional, public relations, fiscal and other factors familiar to the resolution of many if not most corporate problems. To this extent the conclusion reached by the special litigation committee is outside the scope of our review. Thus, the courts cannot inquire as to which factors were considered by that committee or the relative weight accorded them in reaching that substantive decision—"the reasons for the payments, the advantages or disadvantages accruing to the corporation by reason of the transactions, the extent of the participation or profit by the respondent directors and the loss, if any, of public confidence in the corporation which might be incurred." Inquiry into such matters would go to the very core of the business judgment made by the committee. To permit judicial probing of such issues would be to emasculate the business judgment doctrine as applied to the actions and determinations of the special litigation committee. Its substantive evaluation of the problems posed and its judgment in their resolution are beyond our reach.

As to the other component of the committee's activities, however, the situation is different, and here we agree with the Appellate Division. As to the methodologies and procedures best suited to the conduct of an investigation of facts and the determination of legal liability, the courts are well equipped by long and continuing experience and practice to make determinations. In fact they are better qualified in this regard than are corporate directors in general. Nor do the determinations to be made in the adoption of procedures partake of the nuances or special perceptions or comprehensions of business judgment or corporate activities or interests. The question is solely how appropriately to set about to gather the pertinent data.

While the court may properly inquire as to the adequacy and appropriateness of the committee's investigative procedures and methodologies, it may not under the guise of consideration of such factors trespass in the domain of business judgment. At the same time those responsible for the procedures by which the business judgment is reached may reasonably be required to show that they have pursued their chosen investigative methods in good faith. What evidentiary proof may be required to this end will, of course, depend on the nature of the particular investigation, and the proper reach of disclosure at the instance of the shareholders will in turn relate inversely to the showing made by the corporate representatives themselves. The latter may be expected to show that the areas and subjects to be examined are reasonably complete and that there has been a good-faith pursuit of inquiry into such areas and subjects. What has been uncovered and the relative weight accorded in evaluating and balancing the several factors and considerations are beyond the scope of judicial concern. Proof, however, that the investigation has been so restricted in scope, so shallow in execution, or otherwise so pro forma or halfhearted as to constitute a pretext or sham, consistent with the principles underlying the application of the business judgment doctrine, would raise questions of good faith or conceivably fraud which would never be shielded by that doctrine.

In addition to the issue of the disinterested independence of the special litigation committee, addressed above, the disposition of the present appeal turns, then, on whether plaintiff, on defendants' motions for summary judgment predicated on the investigation and determination of the special litigation committee, * * * has shown facts sufficient to require a trial of any material issue of fact as to the adequacy or appropriateness of the *modus operandi* of that committee or has demonstrated acceptable excuse for failure to make such tender. * * * We conclude that the requisite showing has not been made on this record.

        * * *

On the submissions made by defendants in support of their motions, we do not find either insufficiency or infirmity as to the procedures and methodologies chosen and pursued by the special litigation committee. That committee promptly engaged eminent special counsel to guide its deliberations and to advise it. The committee reviewed the prior work of the audit committee, testing its completeness, accuracy and thoroughness by interviewing representatives of Wilmer, Cutler & Pickering, reviewing transcripts of the testimony of 10 corporate officers and employees before the Securities and Exchange Commission, and studying documents collected by and work papers of the Washington law firm. Individual interviews were conducted with the directors found to have participated in any way in the questioned payments, and with representatives of Arthur Andersen & Co. Questionnaires were sent to and answered by each of the corporation's nonmanagement directors. At the conclusion of its investigation the special litigation committee sought and obtained pertinent legal advice from its special counsel. The selection of appropriate investigative methods must always turn on the nature and characteristics of the particular subject being investigated, but we find nothing in this record that requires a trial of any material issue of fact concerning the sufficiency or appropriateness of the procedures chosen by this special litigation committee. Nor is there anything in this record to raise a triable issue of fact as to the good-faith pursuit of its examination by that committee. * * *

QUESTIONS

1. According to *Auerbach*, what issues may a court properly review? Another court characterized *Auerbach* as having "extended the business

judgment rule to the decisions of special litigations committees, precluding judicial review of the merits of those decisions. Under *Auerbach*, judicial review of committee decisions is limited to the issues of good faith, independence, and sufficiency of the investigation." Alford v. Shaw, 358 S.E.2d 323, 325 (N.C. 1987). Is this an accurate characterization?

2.   According to *Auerbach*, would it ever be proper for a court to inquire into the substantive wisdom of a committee's recommendation that a derivative suit be dismissed? How could such a view be reconciled with the business judgment rule?

3.   Isn't it a realistic concern that the special litigation committee was chosen by a board, four members of which were defendants in the derivative litigation? Can such a board be expected to choose truly independent outside investigators? How does the court address these concerns? Not all courts have agreed on this point.

ZAPATA CORPORATION v. MALDONADO

Supreme Court of Delaware, 1981
430 A.2d 779

Quillen, J. In June, 1975, William Maldonado, a stockholder of Zapata, instituted a derivative action in the Court of Chancery on behalf of Zapata against ten officers and/or directors of Zapata, alleging, essentially, breaches of fiduciary duty. Maldonado did not first demand that the board bring this action, stating instead such demand's futility because all directors were named as defendants and allegedly participated in the acts specified. * * *

By June, 1979, four of the defendant-directors were no longer on the board, and the remaining directors appointed two new outside directors to the board. The board then created an "Independent Investigation Committee" (Committee), composed solely of the two new directors, to investigate Maldonado's actions, as well as a similar derivative action then pending in Texas, and to determine whether the corporation should continue any or all of the litigation. The Committee's determination was stated to be "final, ... not ... subject to review by the Board of Directors and ... in all respects ... binding upon the Corporation."

Following an investigation, the Committee concluded, in September, 1979, that each action should "be dismissed forthwith as their continued maintenance is inimical to the Company's best interests...." Consequently, Zapata moved for dismissal or summary judgment in the * * * derivative actions. * * *

          * * *

We limit our review in this interlocutory appeal to whether the Committee has the power to cause the present action to be dismissed.

We begin with an examination of the carefully considered opinion of the Vice Chancellor which states, in part, that the "business judgment" rule does not confer power "to a corporate board of directors to terminate a derivative suit" * * *. His conclusion is particularly pertinent because several federal courts, applying Delaware law, have held that the business judgment rule enables boards (or their committees) to terminate derivative suits, decisions now in conflict with the holding below.

As the term is most commonly used, and given the disposition below, we can understand the Vice Chancellor's comment that "the business judgment rule is irrelevant to the question of whether the Committee has the authority to compel the dismissal of this suit." * * * Corporations, existing because of legislative grace, possess authority as granted by the legislature. Directors of Delaware corporations derive their managerial decision-making power, which encompasses decisions whether to initiate, or refrain from entering, litigation, from 8 Del.C. § 141 (a). This statute is the fount of directorial powers. The "business judgment" rule is a judicial creation that presumes propriety, under certain circumstances, in a board's decision. Viewed defensively, it does not create authority. In this sense the "business judgment" rule is not relevant in corporate decision making until after a decision is made. It is generally used as a defense to an attack on the decision's soundness. The board's managerial decision making power, however, comes from § 141(a). The judicial creation and legislative grant are related because the "business judgment" rule evolved to give recognition and deference to directors' business expertise when exercising their managerial power under § 141(a).

In the case before us, although the corporation's decision to move to dismiss or for summary judgment was, literally, a decision resulting from an exercise of the directors' (as delegated to the Committee) business judgment, the question of "business judgment," in a defensive sense, would not become relevant until and unless the decision to seek termination of the derivative lawsuit was attacked as improper. * * * This question was not reached by the Vice Chancellor because he determined that the stockholder had an individual right to maintain this derivative action. * * *

Thus, the focus in this case is on the power to speak for the corporation as to whether the lawsuit should be continued or terminated. As we see it, this issue in the current appellate posture of this case has three aspects: the conclusions of the Court below concerning the continuing right of a stockholder to maintain a derivative action; the corporate power under Delaware law of an authorized board committee to cause dismissal of litigation instituted for the benefit of the corporation; and the role of the Court of Chancery in resolving conflicts between the stockholder and the committee.

Accordingly, we turn first to the Court of Chancery's conclusions concerning the right of a plaintiff stockholder in a derivative action. We find that its determination that a stockholder, once demand is made and refused, possesses an independent, individual right to continue a derivative suit for breaches of fiduciary duty over objection by the corporation, * * * as an absolute rule, is erroneous. The Court of Chancery relied principally upon *Sohland v. Baker*, Del.Supr., 141 A. 277 (1927), for this statement of the Delaware rule. *Sohland* is sound law. But *Sohland* cannot be fairly read as supporting the broad proposition which evolved in the opinion below.

In *Sohland,* the complaining stockholder was allowed to file the derivative action in equity after making demand and after the board refused to bring the lawsuit. But the question before us relates to the power of the corporation by motion to terminate a lawsuit properly commenced by a stockholder without prior demand. No Delaware statute or case cited to us directly determines this new question and we do not think that *Sohland* addresses it by implication.

The language in *Sohland* relied on by the Vice Chancellor negates the contention that the case stands for the broad rule of stockholder right which evolved below. This Court therein stated that "a stockholder may sue in his own name for the purpose of enforcing corporate rights . . . in a proper case if the corporation on the demand of the stockholder refuses to bring suit." * * * The Court also stated that "whether ["(t)he right of a stockholder to file a bill to litigate corporate rights"] exists necessarily depends on the facts of each particular case." * * * Thus, the precise language only supports the stockholder's right to initiate the lawsuit. It does not support an absolute right to continue to control it.

* * *

Moreover, *McKee v. Rogers*, Del.Ch., 156 A. 191 (1931), stated "as a general rule" that "a stockholder cannot be permitted . . . to invade the discretionary field committed to the judgment of the directors and sue in the corporation's behalf when the managing body refuses. This rule is a well settled one."

The *McKee* rule, of course, should not be read so broadly that the board's refusal will be determinative in every instance. Board members, owing a well-established fiduciary duty to the corporation, will not be allowed to cause a derivative suit to be dismissed when it would be a breach of their fiduciary duty. Generally disputes pertaining to control of the suit arise in two contexts.

Consistent with the purpose of requiring a demand, a board decision to cause a derivative suit to be dismissed as detrimental to the company, after demand has been made and refused, will be respected unless it was wrongful.* [10] * * * A claim of a wrongful decision not to sue is thus the first exception and the first context of dispute. Absent a wrongful refusal, the stockholder in such a situation simply lacks legal managerial power.

---

* [10] In other words, when stockholders, after making demand and having their suit rejected, attack the board's decision as improper, the board's decision falls under the "business judgment" rule and will be respected if the requirements of the rule are met. * * * That situation should be distinguished from the instant case, where demand was not made, and the power of the board to seek a dismissal, due to disqualification, presents a threshold issue. * * *

But it cannot be implied that, absent a wrongful board refusal, a stockholder can never have an individual right to initiate an action. For, as is stated in *McKee,* a "well settled" exception exists to the general rule.

> [A] stockholder may sue in equity in his derivative right to assert a cause of action in behalf of the corporation, without prior demand upon the directors to sue, when it is apparent that a demand would be futile, that the officers are under an influence that sterilizes discretion and could not be proper persons to conduct the litigation.

156 A. at 193. This exception, the second context for dispute, is consistent with the Court of Chancery's statement below, that "the stockholders' individual right to bring the action does not ripen, however, . . . unless he can show a demand to be futile."

These comments in *McKee* and in the opinion below make obvious sense. A demand, when required and refused (if not wrongful), terminates a stockholder's legal ability to initiate a derivative action. But where demand is properly excused, the stockholder does possess the ability to initiate the action on his corporation's behalf.

These conclusions, however, do not determine the question before us. Rather, they merely bring us to the question to be decided. It is here that we part company with the Court below. Derivative suits enforce corporate rights and any recovery obtained goes to the corporation. * * * "The right of a stockholder to file a bill to litigate corporate rights is, therefore, solely for the purpose of preventing injustice where it is apparent that material corporate rights would not otherwise be protected." *Sohland,* 141 A. at 282. We see no inherent reason why the "two phases" of a derivative suit, the stockholder's suit to compel the corporation to sue and the corporation's suit, should automatically result in the placement in the hands of the litigating stockholder sole control of the corporate right throughout the litigation. To the contrary, it seems to us that such an inflexible rule would recognize the interest of one person or group to the exclusion of all others within the corporate entity. Thus, we reject the view of the Vice Chancellor as to the first aspect of the issue on appeal.

The question to be decided becomes: When, if at all, should an authorized board committee be permitted to cause litigation, properly initiated by a derivative stockholder in his own right, to be dismissed? As noted above, a board has the power to choose not to pursue litigation when demand is made upon it, so long as the decision is not wrongful. If the board determines that a suit would be detrimental to the company, the board's determination prevails. Even when demand is excusable, circumstances may arise when continuation of the litigation would not be in the corporation's best interests. Our inquiry is whether, under such circumstances, there is a permissible procedure under § 141(a) by which a corporation can rid itself of detrimental litigation. If there is not, a single stockholder in an extreme case might control the destiny of the entire corporation. This concern was bluntly expressed by the Ninth Circuit in

Lewis v. Anderson, 9th Cir., 615 F.2d 778, 783 (1979) * * * "To allow one shareholder to incapacitate an entire board of directors merely by leveling charges against them gives too much leverage to dissident shareholders." But, when examining the means, including the committee mechanism examined in this case, potentials for abuse must be recognized. This takes us to the second and third aspects of the issue on appeal.

Before we pass to equitable considerations as to the mechanism at issue here, it must be clear that an independent committee possesses the corporate power to seek the termination of a derivative suit. Section 141(c) allows a board to delegate all of its authority to a committee. Accordingly, a committee with properly delegated authority would have the power to move for dismissal or summary judgment if the entire board did.

Even though demand was not made in this case and the initial decision of whether to litigate was not placed before the board, Zapata's board, it seems to us, retained all of its corporate power concerning litigation decisions. If Maldonado had made demand on the board in this case, it could have refused to bring suit. Maldonado could then have asserted that the decision not to sue was wrongful and, if correct, would have been allowed to maintain the suit. The board, however, never would have lost its statutory managerial authority. The demand requirement itself evidences that the managerial power is retained by the board. When a derivative plaintiff is allowed to bring suit after a wrongful refusal, the board's authority to choose whether to pursue the litigation is not challenged although its conclusion—reached through the exercise of that authority—is not respected since it is wrongful. Similarly, [the relevant rule], by excusing demand in certain instances, does not strip the board of its corporate power. It merely saves the plaintiff the expense and delay of making a futile demand resulting in a probable tainted exercise of that authority in a refusal by the board or in giving control of litigation to the opposing side. But the board entity remains empowered under § 141(a) to make decisions regarding corporate litigation. The problem is one of member disqualification, not the absence of power in the board.

The corporate power inquiry then focuses on whether the board, tainted by the self-interest of a majority of its members, can legally delegate its authority to a committee of two disinterested directors. We find our statute clearly requires an affirmative answer to this question. As has been noted, under an express provision of the statute, § 141(c), a committee can exercise all of the authority of the board to the extent provided in the resolution of the board. Moreover, at least by analogy to our statutory section on interested directors, 8 Del.C. § 141, it seems clear that the Delaware statute is designed to permit disinterested directors to act for the board. * * *

We do not think that the interest taint of the board majority is *per se* a legal bar to the delegation of the board's power to an independent committee composed of disinterested board members. The committee can properly act for the corporation to move to dismiss derivative litigation that is believed to be detrimental to the corporation's best interest.

Our focus now switches to the Court of Chancery which is faced with a stockholder assertion that a derivative suit, properly instituted, should continue for the benefit of the corporation and a corporate assertion, properly made by a board committee acting with board authority, that the same derivative suit should be dismissed as inimical to the best interests of the corporation.

At the risk of stating the obvious, the problem is relatively simple. If, on the one hand, corporations can consistently wrest bona fide derivative actions away from well-meaning derivative plaintiffs through the use of the committee mechanism, the derivative suit will lose much, if not all, of its generally recognized effectiveness as an intra-corporate means of policing boards of directors. * * * If, on the other hand, corporations are unable to rid themselves of meritless or harmful litigation and strike suits, the derivative action, created to benefit the corporation, will produce the opposite, unintended result. * * * It thus appears desirable to us to find a balancing point where bona fide stockholder power to bring corporate causes of action cannot be unfairly trampled on by the board of directors, but the corporation can rid itself of detrimental litigation.

As we noted, the question has been treated by other courts as one of the "business judgment" of the board committee. If a "committee, composed of independent and disinterested directors, conducted a proper review of the matters before it, considered a variety of factors and reached, in good faith, a business judgment that [the] action was not in the best interest of [the corporation]," the action must be dismissed. * * * The issues become solely independence, good faith, and reasonable investigation. The ultimate conclusion of the committee, under that view, is not subject to judicial review.

We are not satisfied, however, that acceptance of the "business judgment" rationale at this stage of derivative litigation is a proper balancing point. While we admit an analogy with a normal case respecting board judgment, it seems to us that there is sufficient risk in the realities of a situation like the one presented in this case to justify caution beyond adherence to the theory of business judgment.

The context here is a suit against directors where demand on the board is excused. We think some tribute must be paid to the fact that the lawsuit was properly initiated. It is not a board refusal case. Moreover, this complaint was filed in June of 1975 and, while the parties undoubtedly would take differing views on the degree of litigation activity, we have to be concerned about the creation of an "Independent Investigation Committee" four years later, after the election of two new outside directors. Situations could develop where such motions could be filed after years of vigorous litigation for reasons unconnected with the merits of the lawsuit.

Moreover, notwithstanding our conviction that Delaware law entrusts the corporate power to a properly authorized committee, we must be mindful that directors are passing judgment on fellow directors in the same corporation and fellow directors, in this instance, who designated them to serve both as directors and committee members. The question naturally arises whether a "there but for the grace of God go I" empathy might not play a role. And the further question arises whether inquiry as to independence, good faith and reasonable investigation is sufficient safeguard against abuse, perhaps subconscious abuse. * * *

Whether the Court of Chancery will be persuaded by the exercise of a committee power resulting in a summary motion for dismissal of a derivative action, where a demand has not been initially made, should rest, in our judgment, in the independent discretion of the Court of Chancery. We thus steer a middle course between those cases which yield to the independent business judgment of a board committee and this case as determined below which would yield to unbridled plaintiff stockholder control. In pursuit of the course, we recognize that "the final substantive judgment whether a particular lawsuit should be maintained requires a balance of many factors—ethical, commercial, promotional, public relations, employee relations, fiscal as well as legal." * * * But we are content that such factors are not "beyond judicial reach" of the Court of Chancery which regularly and competently deals with fiduciary relationships, disposition of trust property, approval of settlements and scores of similar problems. We recognize the danger of judicial overreaching but the alternatives seem to us to be outweighed by the fresh view of a judicial outsider. Moreover, if we failed to balance all the interests involved, we would in the name of practicality and judicial economy foreclose a judicial decision on the merits. At this point, we are not convinced that is necessary or desirable.

After an objective and thorough investigation of a derivative suit, an independent committee may cause its corporation to file a pretrial motion to dismiss in the Court of Chancery. The basis of the motion is the best interests of the corporation, as determined by the committee. The motion should include a thorough written record of the investigation and its findings and recommendations. Under appropriate Court supervision, akin to proceedings on summary judgment, each side should have an opportunity to make a record on the motion. As to the limited issues presented by the motion noted below, the moving party should be prepared to meet the normal burden under [the summary judgment rule] that there is no genuine issue as to any material fact and that the moving party is entitled to dismiss as a matter of law. The Court should apply a two-step test to the motion.

First, the Court should inquire into the independence and good faith of the committee and the bases supporting its conclusions. Limited discovery may be ordered to facilitate such inquiries. The corporation should have the burden of proving independence, good faith and a reasonable investigation, rather than presuming independence, good faith and reasonableness. If the Court determines either that the committee is not independent or has not shown reasonable bases for its conclusions, or, if the Court is not satisfied for other reasons relating to the process, including but not limited to the good faith of the committee, the Court shall deny the corporation's motion. If, however, the Court is satisfied under [the summary judgment rule] standards that the committee was independent and showed reasonable bases for good faith findings and recommendations, the Court may proceed, in its discretion, to the next step.

The second step provides, we believe, the essential key in striking the [proper balance] between legitimate corporate claims as expressed in a derivative stockholder suit and a corporation's best interests as expressed by an independent investigating committee. The Court should determine, applying its own independent business judgment, whether the motion should be granted. This means, of course, that instances could arise where a committee can establish its independence and sound bases for its good faith decisions and still have the corporation's motion denied. The second step is intended to thwart instances where corporate actions meet the criteria of step one, but the result does not appear to satisfy its spirit, or where corporate actions would simply prematurely terminate a stockholder grievance deserving of further consideration in the corporation's interest. The Court of Chancery of course must carefully consider and weigh how compelling the corporate interest in dismissal is when faced with a non-frivolous lawsuit. The Court of Chancery should, when appropriate, give special consideration to matters of law and public policy in addition to the corporation's best interests.

If the Court's independent business judgment is satisfied, the Court may proceed to grant the motion, subject, of course, to any equitable terms or conditions the Court finds necessary or desirable.

The * * * order of the Court of Chancery is reversed and the cause is remanded for further proceedings consistent with this opinion.

QUESTIONS

1. How does the approach in *Zapata* differ from that in *Auerbach*? Which is more intrusive on director discretion? How is the intrusion justified as consistent with the business judgment rule?

2. One court has said this of *Zapata*:

> In *Zapata* the court reasoned that the only legal effect of the self-interest taint is to disable the board from properly exercising its authority in a manner worthy of judicial deference. The court reasoned that such circumstance does not preclude the board from delegating to an independent body the power to exercise that same authority in a manner worthy of judicial deference. As one commentator has suggested, however, this approach leaves unanswered or at least fails to analyze the question of why, if the director interest is a disqualification to participation in the decision to recommend dismissal of a derivative action, is it not also a

disqualification to participation in the selection of the litigation committee empowered to make the same decision. * * *

Delaware law permits a court in some cases ("demand excused" cases) to apply its own business judgment in the review process when deciding to honor the directors' decision to terminate derivative litigation. In our view, this is a defect which could eviscerate the business judgment rule.

Miller v. The Register & Tribune Syndicate, Inc., 336 N.W.2d 709, 717 (1983).

Is the characterization in the first two sentences of this excerpt accurate? Do you agree with the last point made?

3. How does the MBCA treat decisions by special litigation committees? *See* MBCA §§ 7.42 and 7.44. Recall that the MBCA does not provide that a derivative plaintiff's making a demand on directors automatically leads to dismissal. Instead, the corporation decides how to respond to the plaintiff's demand through a vote of disinterested directors, or a committee of them—similar to a SLC. Will a court review the merits of the disinterested directors' decision, as in *Zapata*? *See* § 7.44, Official Comment.

d. Court Approval of Settlement or Dismissal

Read MBCA § 7.45. All states have similar provisions not only about derivative suits but about class actions as well. These provisions reflect the representative nature of such litigation. In routine, non-representative, litigation, the parties may settle at will. No court approval is required. In addition, with some procedural restrictions, the plaintiff may dismiss her case voluntarily.

But with the derivative suit and the class action, other interests are at stake; the named parties are not the only people who can be affected. Thus, in both types of cases, the procedural rules thrust the judge into an unconventional position. She is required to police the terms of the proposed settlement or dismissal to ensure that they are fair to everyone before the court and, more importantly, to those who are not present but who may be affected by the action. It is a reflection of our system's nervousness about the motives of the prime movers behind such cases that we have the judge review the terms of settlements and dismissals. The judge is supposed to review the settlement to make sure that it does not sell out the corporation and its shareholders to the benefit of the lone shareholder bringing the suit or, more importantly, his lawyers.

Suppose that the CEO of Bubba's Burritos becomes the defendant in a derivative suit that asserts that he secretly required the company to substitute asbestos for sugar in its milkshakes, causing the company to incur large tort judgments. Should the judge approve a settlement that requires the CEO to promise never to do it again, and grants the plaintiff's lawyers $10 million in attorneys' fees to be paid by the corporation?

As with class actions, the court may give notice to those who may be affected. The court can thus solicit their input on the wisdom of the proposed settlement or dismissal. The court retains the discretion, of course, to determine whether to allow either of these, and on what terms. It also has the discretion, under the MBCA provision, to determine who should pay for giving notice to the absentees.

3. RECOVERY IN DERIVATIVE SUITS

Because a derivative suit vindicates the *corporation's* claim, it makes sense that the recovery in a successful derivative case goes to the corporation. On the other hand, this may seem odd, because the shareholder (not the corporation) took the initiative and bore the burden of bringing and prosecuting the suit. Most courts will allow the successful shareholder to recover her costs from the losing litigant* and her attorneys' fees from the corporation. After all, by suing and winning, the shareholder has done the corporation a favor, and it should pick up the tab.

What if the shareholder loses the derivative suit? Obviously, she cannot look to the corporation or the defendants to recover her costs or attorneys' fees. (Usually, the shareholder's lawyer will have taken the case on a contingent fee, and thus will not recover here.) Under some statutes, the defendants may be able to recover *their* attorneys' fees from the shareholder if the court finds that she sued "without reasonable cause."

In addition, the shareholder's loss is *res judicata* for other shareholders—they cannot sue to try to vindicate the corporation's claim a second time. So it's not a good idea to bring a derivative suit and lose.

E. WHO REALLY PAYS?

Remember the McDonald's directors—who they are, how much they are being paid for serving as directors of McDonald's, how much other money they probably have. These folks—like their counterparts at smaller corporations such as Bubba's Burritos, Inc.—do not want to have to pay for the honor of serving as a director of a corporation. They want to be protected from liability: from civil damages, from criminal penalties, from litigation costs.

We have previously considered one form of such protection: statutes allowing corporations to limit or eliminate director liability to the corporation of its shareholders for breach of the duty or care. Please review MBCA § 2.02(b)(4) and Delaware § 102(b)(7). Recall the two obvious limitations on the protection from such statutes. First, the statutes affect only claims against directors by the corporation or its shareholders, not by third parties. Second, the statutes do not apply to all claims that might be

---

* This is just basic Civil Procedure. The winning party in litigation routinely recovers its costs from the loser. Costs are said to be "taxed" to the losing party. But "costs" does not include attorney's fees. And attorney's fees will always be the big ticket item.

asserted by such plaintiffs. They exculpate only violations of the duty of care, not violations of the duty of loyalty nor claims based on the directors' having acted in bad faith.

We need to consider two other forms of director protection: indemnification and insurance.

1. INDEMNIFICATION

Directors do not have a common law right to indemnification from the corporation for any judgment or settlement that they have to pay or for the litigation costs they incur in connection with their corporate duties. Under general agency principles, an agent has a right to be indemnified by its principal. But, under the same agency principles, a director is not an agent of the corporation. *See* Restatement (Second) of Agency § 14D.

Accordingly, the legal bases for a corporation's indemnification of a director are found in indemnification statutes, the articles of incorporation, the bylaws of the corporation and contracts between a corporation and its directors.

Relevant statutes typically differentiate between situations in which a corporate is *permitted* to indemnify its directors (*See* MBCA §§ 8.51 and 8.55) and situations in which a corporation is *required* to indemnify its directors (*See* MBCA § 8.52). Please apply the MBCA indemnification provisions to the following questions.

QUESTIONS

1.   Capel, a director of Bubba's Burritos, Inc., is sued for breach of her duty of care. The court finds that Capel is not liable. Does Capel have a right to be indemnified by the corporation for her attorneys' fees? *See* MBCA § 8.52. Would your answer be different if Capel prevailed because of a "legal technicality" such as the statute of limitations?

2.   Agee, a director of Bubba's Burritos, Inc., is sued by the Securities and Exchange Commission for violation of the federal securities laws. The court assesses damages and fines against Agee.

2.1   Does Agee have a right to be indemnified by the corporation for his attorneys' fees? *See* MBCA §§ 8.51 and 8.52.

2.2   Would your answers be different if the articles of Bubba's Burritos contain the following provision regarding indemnification?

ARTICLE VI

INDEMNIFICATION

Section 6.1 <u>Indemnification</u>. The Corporation shall, to the full extent permitted by applicable law, indemnify any person (and the heirs, executors and administrators of such person) who, by reason of the fact that he is or was a director, officer, employee or agent of the Corporation or of a constituent corporation absorbed by the Corporation in a consolidation or merger or is or was serving at the request of the Corporation or such constituent corporation as a director, officer, employee or agent of any other corporation, partnership, joint venture, trust or other enterprise, was or is a party or is threatened to be a party to:

(a) any threatened, pending or completed action, suit or proceeding, whether civil, criminal, administrative or investigative (other than an action by or in the right of the Corporation), against expenses (including attorneys' fees), judgments, fines and amounts paid in settlement actually and reasonably incurred by such person in connection with any such action, suit or proceeding, or,

(b) any threatened, pending or completed action or suit by or in the right of the Corporation to procure a judgment in its favor, against expenses (including attorneys' fees) actually and reasonably incurred by him in connection with the defense or settlement of such action or suit.

Expenses incurred by a director, officer, employee or agent of the Corporation in defending an action, suit or proceeding described in subsections (a) and (b) above may be paid by the Corporation in advance of the final disposition of such action, suit or proceeding upon receipt by the Corporation of an undertaking by or on behalf of the director, officer, employee or agent to repay such amount if and to the extent that it shall ultimately be determined that he is not entitled to be indemnified by the Corporation as authorized in this Section 6.1.

Any indemnification or advancement of expenses by the Corporation pursuant hereto shall be made only in the manner and to the extent authorized by applicable law, and any such indemnification or advancement of expenses shall not be deemed exclusive of any other rights to which those seeking indemnification may otherwise be entitled.

Section 6.2 Indemnification Insurance. The Corporation shall have power to purchase and maintain insurance on behalf of any person who is or was a director, officer, employee or agent of the Corporation, or is or was serving at the request of the Corporation as a director, officer, employee or agent of another corporation, partnership, joint venture, trust or other enterprise against liability asserted against him and incurred by him in any such capacity, or arising out of his status as such, regardless of whether the Corporation would have the power to indemnify him against such liability under applicable law.

2. INSURANCE

MBCA § 8.57 authorizes a corporation to buy liability insurance for its directors and officers. Most states have similar provisions, authorizing corporations to purchase and maintain such "D & O" insurance. Generally, there is no corporate-law question as to whether a corporation has the legal authority to buy D & O insurance; it does. Instead, the common questions are (i) the business questions such as whether to buy D & O insurance and, if so, what kind; (ii) the contract law questions such as what is covered by the policy and who makes what decisions with respect to litigating and settling claims.

The following part of an article by two Chicago lawyers specializing in D & O insurance discusses some of these questions.

Companies may buy D & O insurance for a variety of reasons. Indemnification may be insufficient protection if a company has assets that may not be adequate to allow the corporation to easily satisfy its indemnification obligations. Insurance coverage may also be available in some situations where a director or officer does not meet a standard of "good faith" required for indemnification by the corporation (such as where conduct was opposed to the best interests of the corporation but not intentionally dishonest and thus excluded by the D & O policy). There may also be restrictions on the corporation's ability to indemnify directors and officers in some jurisdictions for derivative judgments and settlements.

In some circumstances (for example, a healthy corporation with strong indemnification provisions and a low risk of claims), corporations may opt not to purchase D & O insurance or to only buy direct coverage for directors and officers where the corporation cannot or does not indemnify its directors and officers.

This direct coverage for directors and officers is often referred to as "Side A" or "last resort" coverage. It is usually much cheaper than traditional D & O insurance because it only comes into play when the corporation cannot (because of insolvency or the failure to meet a standard of care, for example), or does not, indemnify the directors and officers. This is a relatively infrequent occurrence, usually arising where there has been a dispute regarding corporate control.

Given the severity and expense of potential claims, however, many companies, especially public corporations, purchase traditional D & O insurance to cover not only unindemnified claims made against the directors and officers but also to reimburse the company for its costs in providing indemnification. Under this corporate reimbursement, or "Side B" coverage, the insurer agrees to "pay on behalf of" or "reimburse" the corporation for amounts the corporation has paid or is required to pay in indemnifying its directors and officers.

D & O insurance typically covers "loss" arising from claims made against directors and officers (or in some instances against the company or employees) for negligent, rather than intentionally dishonest, conduct causing economic injury. A typical definition of "wrongful act" is "any breach of duty, neglect, error, misstatement, misleading statement, omission or act by the directors or officers in their respective capacities as such, or any matter claimed against them solely by reason of their status as directors or officers of the company." (American International Companies Directors, Officer and Corporate Liability Insurance Policy, Form 62334 (5/95), Section 2(m).)

Most D & O policies generally provide "claims made" coverage. Coverage is triggered and provided by the policy in effect when the claim is made, not when the allegedly wrongful conduct took place.

Because the trigger of coverage under a D & O policy generally is when a claim is made, the definition of "claim" is important. Insureds negotiating coverage should seek a broad definition of "claim" that encompasses written demands for relief, lawsuits, civil, criminal, administrative and regulatory proceedings and investigations.

Most D & O policies allow the insured to select counsel to defend the claim, with the carrier's consent, but the payment of defense costs is charged against the limits of the policy. The defense costs are incurred by the insureds and typically indemnified by the corporation, which then seeks reimbursement from the carrier for the amounts paid.

The policy provisions and issues discussed above are a sampling of the items that can be negotiated. One thing is certain: Negotiating terms at the inception of the policy is infinitely better than discovering policy pitfalls after a claim arises.

Carolyn Rosenberg & Duane Sigleko, *The Armor Plated Board—Yes D & O Coverage Needs to be Negotiated,* BUSINESS LAW TODAY 20 (Oct. 1999).

QUESTIONS AND NOTE

1.   Freer serves as an outside director of Bubba's Burritos, Inc. Does he care whether Bubba's Burritos maintains D & O insurance after he leaves the board?

2.   Professor James D. Cox of the Duke University Law School studied D & O insurance and concluded:

We should understand that both the employee and the corporation face a good deal of uncertainty as to whether the liability arising from the employee's misbehavior and the entity's vicarious responsibility will ultimately be borne by their insurer. First, there are some inconveniences and burdens of such litigation, such as its distractions or any accompanying loss of reputation, for which insurance provides no protection. Of greater concern is whether the misconduct falls within one of the numerous exclusions. Because willful misconduct is beyond the scope of the policy, exclusions have their greatest impact on the willful violator. With insurance unavailable, the only basis for arguing that insurance undercuts the deterrence effects of private liability is if the plaintiff's lawyer drafts the complaint so as to allege misconduct that is not excluded from the policy's coverage. Here, the evidence * * * regarding coverage disputes between carriers and their insureds serves as a sobering reminder to those considering whether to misbehave; they then proceed on less than certain ground. Further uncertainty arises because of the uncertainty that insurance will be available when the claim is asserted. As most D & O insurance is on a claims-made basis and the insurer can be expected to dispute coverage if the application for insurance does not fully disclose the events and the facts that underlie the asserted claim. Moreover, the insurance cycle may rear its historic ugly head so that deductions are raised and coverage amounts lowered from the levels available when the misconduct occurred that gave rise to the claim.

James D. Cox, *Private Litigation and the Deterrence of Corporate Misconduct*, 60 LAW & CONTEMP. PROBS. 1, 36–37 (1997).

3. Capel, a director of Bubba's Burritos, Inc., is sued in a shareholder derivative suit and held liable to the corporation for $400,000 for breach of her duty of care. Under the indemnification agreement in question 2.2 above, will Bubba's Burritos indemnify Capel for the $400,000 or her attorneys' fees? Will Bubba's Burritos D & O insurance cover either the $400,000 or Capel's attorneys' fees?

4. What is the rationale for permitting the corporation's paying for D & O insurance, but prohibiting the corporation's paying for indemnification for certain director actions? What is the rationale for permitting the corporation or its shareholders to sue directors for damages and then, through D & O insurance and indemnity, permit the directors to pay these damages using funds provided directly or indirectly by the corporation and the shareholders? *See generally* Ehud Kamar, *Shareholder Litigation Under Indeterminate Corporate Law*, 66 U. CHI. L. REV. 887 (1999).

CHAPTER SIX

HOW DOES A BUSINESS STRUCTURED AS A CORPORATION GROW?

■ ■ ■

Like those involved with running any business, those running a corporation will want to make the business grow. And, as with any business, this will take money. The basic choices about how to get that money are the same as we saw with other structures: the proprietors can (1) borrow money, (2) sell interests in the corporation, or (3) use earnings. (Of course, you can only use earnings if you have them; getting to that point may well require one of the first two choices).

A. HOW A BUSINESS DECIDES HOW MUCH MONEY IT NEEDS AND HOW TO GET IT

You'll recall that in Chapter 1, we looked at the financial statements of a typical business, using simple examples. In tackling the questions of why a business needs money and how it decides how much money it needs and how to get it, we need again to look at a typical business in a simplified way. In essence, most businesses (1) take money, i.e. "financial capital" which may be in the form of debt or equity (about which we will discuss more later), (2) turn that financial capital into "physical capital," e.g., machines, factories, offices, and (3) use that physical capital in combination with "human capital," i.e., employees, in order to generate revenues, profits and cash flow.

One very important statistic in any business is what is called the return on capital—that is, the rate of return that the business earns on financial capital. For example, if the enterprise is using $1,000,000 of capital and generating $100,000 of annual cash flow, then the business would be earning a 10% return on capital.

1. DEBT AND EQUITY CAPITAL

Remember that this financial capital may be debt, or equity, or (most commonly) a combination. The managers/owners of a business decide on the combination of debt and equity that best serves the needs of that business, i.e., its "capital structure," and then try to raise that combination from lenders or investors.

But, let's dig deeper into these two types of capital.

As you know, debt is money that must be paid back, and is (generally) borrowed at a fixed interest rate. There is no similar obligation to repay equity, nor does equity earn a fixed rate of return. Equity is money that is invested so that, in exchange for their money, the investors become owners of the firm. We'll assume the business is a corporation so that they become shareholders.

When businesses incur debt, they often do so subject to complicated loan agreements or bond "indentures" (which you may one day get to draft yourself) that give the lender not only the right to be repaid but also protections to ensure that it *will* get repaid. For example, loan "covenants" force the borrowing company to keep its business within certain parameters of financial health or be forced to pay the loan back immediately. The loans may require that certain assets of the company be pledged as collateral, so that if the loan is not paid in time, the lender has the right to seize these assets.

Equity comes with no such protections. Instead, investors get stock, which carries with it some measure of control—principally the right to elect the members of the company's board of directors. But, again, an investor, unlike a creditor, has no legal right to recover her investment from the corporation. A shareholder simply has a right to what is left over *after* the company pays off its loans and other obligations. The creditors get paid first; the loan documents will usually prevent the corporation from paying the shareholders a dime if the loan payments are not made in a timely fashion.

So, one obvious question is why someone would invest money without the promise of having it repaid when she could instead lend it as debt and have a legal right to be repaid. The answer is the hope of superior returns. That is, no one would invest equity capital if debt offered a similar financial return. Companies know that to attract equity investors, they must generate a return on equity that is superior to the return they offer their debt holders.

It stands to reason that, because debt is less risky for the lender than equity, the loans should earn a lower return than the equity investment. That is, the holders of debt—bondholders or the bank—should earn less than the holders of equity (on average, over time). Financial historians tell us that, over time, the stocks of large, publicly traded corporations such as McDonald's do generally outperform the debt of such companies. And, for such companies, there is not only a market for buying the company's stock but also a market for buying the company's debt, commonly referred to as bonds.

2. DEBT AND RETURN ON EQUITY CAPITAL

The performance of many companies—and of their stock—has been quite poor during the recent financial crisis, and there's much discussion of the high debt levels that contributed to this problem. So we need to understand why companies use so much debt in their capital structures, and how it can come back to bite them.

Suppose you owned this company we described above, which makes a 10% return on capital. Imagine that *all* that capital is equity, so your return on equity (ROE) is also 10% (the annual cash flow of $100,000 divided by your equity investment of $1,000,000).

Now, let's suppose you could borrow half of the total capital at a 5% interest rate, so you only had to invest $500,000 of your own money (to create a business with $1,000,000 of total capital). Well, the cash flow of the business will drop slightly, because now it has a new expense: interest of 5% on borrowings of $500,000 is $25,000, so the cash flow drops to $75,000. *But* the ROE shoots up because the equity capital invested dropped in half. $75,000 divided by $500,000 in equity is 15%. Your ROE has increased by 5 percentage points, or 50%. As we already discussed briefly in Chapter 2, debt has "levered up" your return (they don't call it "leverage" for nothing).

What if, instead, you borrowed 90% of the $1,000,000 of required capital—$900,000? Now your cash flow drops by the $45,000 in interest expenses ($900,000 × 5%) so cash flow is only $55,000. But, since equity is only $100,000, the ROE is now 55%.

Let's consider an even further extreme. Imagine how fabulous your ROE would be if you borrowed $999,999 and put in just $1 of equity!

3. DEBT AND THE FINANCIAL CRISIS

So how does all this relate to the recent financial crisis? Glad you asked.

Think about what's wrong with the picture we've painted in the preceding paragraphs. We have only discussed the increased return, but have ignored the *risk* of debt. To understand how and why debt increases the risk of a business, just imagine a business, Company 1, with no debt, where investors had invested $1,000,000 in equity. The business has $600,000 of fixed yearly costs, and $1,000,000 of sales revenues, where the cost of goods sold (COGS) is 30% of revenues or $300,000. With $1,000,000 in revenues, the company can pay its $600,000 of fixed costs, $300,000 of COGS, and make $100,000 of net profit, for a ROE of 10%.

Now, suppose we have an identical Company 2, except for one thing. Instead of having no debt, this company had begun its operations with investors putting in only $100,000 of equity and taking out a loan of $900,000 at 5% interest. Its fixed costs go up (by the $45,000 of interest expense) and it now has $645,000 of fixed costs. As long as the economy stays healthy and revenues continue at $1,000,000 per year, then the investors are doing great. Profit is $55,000—$1,000,000 revenues minus $645,000 fixed costs and $300,000 of COGS). Because the investors have invested only $100,000 of their own money, the ROE is much higher: $55,000 divided by $100,000, or 55%. The investors in this highly-leveraged company are doing great when the economy is thriving.

However, look what happens when the economy stops booming. Suppose the economy then goes into a recession and sales revenues drop to $900,000. Unleveraged Company 1 would still be OK. Its fixed costs will remain $600,000, its COGS will fall to $270,000, so that it will still have positive net revenue of $30,000. The investors' return on equity will have fallen to 3%. But the company can still pay its bills.

In contrast, Company 2 is in peril. Its costs will exceed its revenues. Costs will be $915,000 (fixed costs and interest of $645,000 plus COGS of $270,000), compared to $900,000 revenue. Unless it has saved money from earlier years, the company will be unable to pay its bills. The company will be insolvent, and the investors will not only have a return on their equity of zero, they are in danger of losing their $100,000 investment completely.

This is how leveraged companies get into financial trouble, explaining a lot of what happened in the recent financial crisis. Without the added fixed costs of debt, the company would have more flexibility to cushion these fluctuations in the cash flow. (Please note that these simple examples consider just the fixed interest cost, and ignore the additional cash expenditure associated with paying back the principal amount of the loan.)

So now you see the downside of leverage. The examples above show the intimate relationship between risk and return. We can raise our return (when things go well) by bearing more risk. But, that risk means a higher probability of things going wrong, and a worse outcome when they do.

4.   THE BEST CAPITAL STRUCTURE

We've discussed the two main sources for obtaining growth capital for a business: debt and equity. There are entire courses in business school devoted to thinking about how much debt and how much equity should be in a corporation's capital structure. Indeed, this is one of the two or three most significant issues in the entire field of finance. Let's quickly examine the main issues.

We have seen that a corporation's lenders tend to receive a lower return than equity investors. This is the same as saying that the company pays a lower price for debt than for equity. Moreover, once we understand that a corporation can deduct the interest payments from its reported income and thus lower its taxes, we will realize that the federal government subsidizes debt. This all creates a powerful incentive for the company to load up its capital structure with debt.

There are two forces that put the brakes on the inclination to rely exclusively on debt. First, lenders understand this phenomenon, and work hard to lend only what they are sure will be paid back. This is the primary work of bankers—figuring out where that line is and not stepping over it.

Second, the corporation will fear bankruptcy. Every corporation's cash flow varies somewhat from month to month. Well, if you are the owners of a company, you understand these ups-and-downs, and if you borrow too much, then—in the year when the cash flow is low—you may get in trouble with your bank. Your debt-repayment obligations can result in bankruptcy. The use of equity in the capital structure reduces this risk, by lowering the amount of debt and the fixed annual costs associated with that debt.

As you can imagine, companies have different cost structures (i.e., levels of fixed vs. variable costs) as well as different historical levels of exposure to economic risk. For example, resort hotels may be very exposed to downturns in the economy, with utilities and oil companies less so. Skilled business managers carefully weigh the risk of increased debt against the larger returns to the equity holders that debt leverage provides.

5. CALIBRATING RISK

Economists and financial theorists have developed complicated models of the correct way to measure the risk of a particular stock or of stocks in general. Intuitively, we have seen, the riskier a company is, the higher the interest it will have to pay on its debt; lenders demand that they are being compensated for taking the extra risk.

That risk may stem from the fundamental risk of the business. For example, a company that makes hula hoops or gourmet pet food is seen to have higher risk than an electric utility. As we have seen, a company's total level of debt will affect the riskiness of its bonds. A company with $1 million of debt is less risky than the same company with $100 million of debt.

There are also "contingent liabilities" that may present a risk. For example, a pharmaceutical company may face a recall of its product, or it may lose its patent protection and be subject to competition from generics. These contingent liabilities are all things that do not show up on a set of financial statements, but are real risks nonetheless.

Several "rating agencies" help investors assess the riskiness of different companies' bonds. The most well-known of these are Moody's, Standard & Poor's and Fitch. There is an elaborate grading system for debt securities. The table below describes the various rating categories used by Standard & Poor's.

Long-term issuer credit ratings

AAA: An obligor rated 'AAA' has extremely strong capacity to meet its financial commitments. 'AAA' is the highest Issuer credit rating assigned by Standard & Poor's.

AA: An obligor rated 'AA' has very strong capacity to meet its financial commitments. It differs from the highest-rated obligors only to a small degree.

A: An obligor rated 'A' has strong capacity to meet its financial commitments but is somewhat more susceptible to the adverse effects of changes in circumstances and economic conditions than obligors in higher-rated categories.

BBB: An obligor rated 'BBB' has adequate capacity to meet its financial commitments. However, adverse economic conditions or changing circumstances are more likely to lead to a weakened capacity of the obligor to meet its financial commitments. Bonds rated BBB or higher are considered "investment grade."

BB, B, CCC, and CC: Obligors rated 'BB', 'B', 'CCC', and 'CC' are regarded as having significant speculative characteristics. 'BB' indicates the least degree of speculation and 'CC' the highest. While such obligors will likely have some quality and protective characteristics, these may be outweighed by large uncertainties or major exposures to adverse conditions.

BB: An obligor rated 'BB' is less vulnerable in the near term than other lower-rated obligors. However, it faces major ongoing uncertainties and exposure to adverse business, financial, or economic conditions, which could lead to the obligor's inadequate capacity to meet its financial commitments.

B: An obligor rated 'B' is more vulnerable than the obligors rated 'BB', but the obligor currently has the capacity to meet its financial commitments. Adverse business, financial, or economic conditions will likely impair the obligor's capacity or willingness to meet its financial commitments.

CCC: An obligor rated 'CCC' is currently vulnerable, and is dependent upon favorable business, financial, and economic conditions to meet its financial commitments.

CC: An obligor rated 'CC' is currently highly vulnerable.

Note that bonds are rated when they are initially issued, and that the rating may change even after the bonds are sold to the public. Suppose McDonald's sells $100,000,000 worth of 5% bonds this year, and they are rated AA. Next year, there is an oil crisis, gas prices spike, people stop driving, and everyone believes that McDonald's basic business is a lot riskier than it looked a year ago. The rating for the bonds might fall to A or even BBB.

In the secondary market for the bonds, where they are traded after McDonald's initially sells them, the *effective interest rate* on the bonds will rise to reflect the increased risk. McDonald's cannot change the face interest rate on the bonds it has already issued—a 5%, $1,000 bond is still going to pay $50 in interest each year. But potential buyers of these bonds in the marketplace can force a rise in the effective interest rate on these bonds by refusing to pay the face principal amount. That is, if you bought a bond for $1,000 and investors now believe they are entitled to a 10% interest rate for bearing the new *higher* risk of McDonald's debt, than they will simply offer to pay only $500 for a $1,000 McDonald's bond, doubling the effective interest rate on the bond from 5% to 10%. (Note that this is a bit of an oversimplification because it ignores the fact that you will get principal—the original investment—back when the bond matures.)

Let's look at how interest rates for bonds of different risk levels vary. Below is a table that compares the average interest rates, or yield, on bonds of various risk levels on two different dates.

	Yield (effective interest rate)	
Rating	Nov. 28 2008	June 30 2009
AAA	5.96	4.22
AA	7.03	4.81
A	8.69	5.80
BBB	9.99	7.20
BB	15.95	10.47
B	20.59	12.26

Note first that the effective interest rate always increases as the risk increases. The more risk, the higher the interest rate. Note also that the interest rate on the bonds of a particular rating changes over time. This is a function, in part, of the interest rate on government bonds, where that rate, in turn, is set by the Federal Reserve. If the government changes interest rates for government bonds, then this will cause interest rates on all other bonds to change too.

Finally, note that the "spread" between the bonds of various risk levels also varies. In June of 2009, you were paid a premium of roughly 8 percentage points to bear the increased risk of a B bond (compared to an AAA). But earlier in November of 2008, that premium was as high as 14.5 percentage points. These spreads reflect the market's appetite for—or aversion to—risk at any particular time.

6.   THE FINANCIAL CRISIS REVISITED

Not surprisingly, even a basic understanding of the recent financial crisis is less simple. We need to see banks and Wall Street investment firms as different from other business in that they don't buy physical plant and equipment to produce and sell goods. Rather, in addition to making loans to consumers and other businesses, they buy and sell other companies' equity and debt securities (which they hope will rise in value). The risk is not that a bank will experience a decrease in its sales revenues, but rather that some of the financial assets the banks own as investments will decrease in value.

Imagine you are a bank with $1,000,000 of your own equity and $25,000,000 of borrowed money (this is about what the actual ratios of equity to debt were in many financial institutions). You take your $26,000,000 of capital and go out and buy $26,000,000 worth of different kinds of investment securities of other companies.

You believe that you are smart and buying good securities, and you also believe that you have "hedged" your bets. That is, historically, some investments go up when others go down, so if you have a mix of things, then if some of your bets lose money, others will make money to offset it. And the rating agencies have told you that the debt securities you bought have a very low chance of failing to make their required payments to you—that is, of "defaulting." And the bank regulators bless all this and say indeed, your assumptions make sense.

But then, all of a sudden, some of these securities started to look riskier than expected. Homeowners who had obtained risky, or "sub-prime," loans stopped paying their mortgages once the houses they owned were worth less than the amounts they owed on their mortgages. They just walked away from their loans and homes. Because housing prices were dropping all over the country, the hedge of owning mortgages from different parts of the country wasn't proving to provide much insulation from the risk after all.

The rating agencies started to confirm what lots of people already knew—that these were risky investments with a high threat of default. As soon as the bond ratings dropped, investors demanded a higher effective rate of interest to compensate them for that risk, and the prices of these securities had to fall to raise the effective interest rate.

Owners of bonds secured by home mortgages had a strong incentive to sell these already plummeting securities, which further depressed their prices. For example, banks had to book these losses to the value of the securities as losses on their income statements, which in turn, lowered the value of *their* shareholders' equity. So banks had to sell these and other securities to generate cash. As many other banks found themselves in the same position, they were all selling these securities at once, which further depressed the prices of these securities.

What made this a crisis instead of simply requiring a normal market price adjustment was that the number of these subprime mortgages was huge. Residential housing represents a large pool of assets and subprime mortgages had become an important part of that market.

The crisis with subprime mortgages was magnified by the practice known as "securitization," in which pools of these mortgages were bundled together and sold to large financial institutions. Instead of local banks making and then holding these mortgages, large mortgage brokers and originators—like Countrywide and Washington Mutual (WAMU)—made huge numbers of loans but did not hold on to the mortgages. Instead, they sold the mortgages to Wall Street firms that bundled them into complicated new debt instruments that few people really understood.

One especially destructive practice was the technique of creating "derivatives," or securities that were, in turn, derived from other securities. Pools of residential mortgages were sliced into "layers" and each layer (or "tranche") became a separate security. Suppose there was a pool of mortgages that was expected to generate $1,000,000 of repayment per month. A separate security would be created that would have a claim on the first 65% of the money flowing into the pool, then one with a claim on the next 15%, then the next 10%, and so on. The thinking was that these higher tranches were very safe, because many mortgage holders would have to default before the top (or most senior) 65% of the cash flow was impaired. The rating agencies gave these "higher tranche" securities high ratings. These securities were considered so low-risk that regulators did not require banks and other financial institutions to have a capital cushion to protect them from potential losses on these securities.

Decisions about the risk of these securities were largely driven from models based on historical data. A key assumption in these models was the rate of appreciation in housing prices. Because housing prices had risen so steadily for so long, many analytic models simply assumed they would continue to go up. As we know, they did not. The falling housing prices created a downward spiral in which the falling prices of mortgage-related debt securities put financial institutions in a position where they had to sell the debt securities to raise capital. These sales, in turn, further depressed the prices of these securities.

Moreover, that so many banks were affected by this problem led to a further "liquidity crisis." Banks were so harmed by their losses on these debt securities that they did not have money to lend to their usual corporate borrowers. Without the benefit of these loans, business ground to a crawl in a broad range of industries.

A final significant factor in the financial crisis was the sale of so-called "credit default swaps" (CDSs). CDSs are a form of insurance on bonds. Perhaps for $1 per $1,000 of face value of a bond, you could buy a CDS as an insurance policy that would compensate you for your loss if the bond defaulted.

It turned out that these CDSs were unregulated. That is, no one kept track of who was buying and selling CDSs. And there were no capital or collateral requirements to insure that if a bond defaulted and the CDS insurance had to be paid, then the insurer would actually be able to pay off on the insurance. In contrast, on a normal insurance policy, regulators require the insurer to have so many dollars in capital for every $1,000 of policy coverage it is writing. This protects the insurance purchaser so that, if the company does have to pay off on the policy, the money is there from which to make those payments. In this corner of the financial world, however, this was not done.

AIG was a major seller of CDSs to financial institutions and others. When there was a recognized danger of AIG's defaulting on these CDSs, it was like a run on the bank, and AIG almost failed. Everyone feared that if AIG went under, there would be a ripple effect at other major financial institutions.

The underlying cause of the crisis was the drive of banks and other large financial institutions to generate high returns by purchasing securities that paid a high rate of interest. It was particularly tempting because of the perceived low risk of these securities. The institutions attempted to increase their returns further by using borrowed money to purchase the securities. The lax regulatory environment allowed them to do this. Although leverage magnifies gains in an up-market, it magnifies losses in a down-market.

QUESTIONS

1. Two companies in the same industry have dramatically different levels of debt in their capital structures. Company A has debt measuring 10% of total capital and company B's debt is 40% of total capital. How would you think about which company was closer to the right level of debt?

2. A company has $5 million of equity and $5 million of debt, and earns a profit of $1 million. What is its rate of return on total capital? Its rate of return on equity?

3. Same company as above, but the following year-everything plays out exactly the same, *except* that the company has reduced its equity to $3 million and increased it debt to $7 million with a $2 million loan at 7% annual interest. What are its profit, rate of return on capital, and rate of return on equity?

4. Is the company "more profitable" or "less profitable" after this transaction?

5. As shown in the table in part 4, the premium paid for bearing the increased risk of lower rated-debt varies over time. Why might that be?

B. BORROWING MORE MONEY

Lawyers are often involved in a corporation's efforts to grow by borrowing more money. Lawyers, of course, draft the loan documents. Here the problems are primarily contract drafting problems. These deals can be structured in many ways. The loan documents will spell out not only the basic loan payment and repayment terms, but also the parties' other rights and responsibilities.

Lawyers are also often involved in negotiating the loan. Here the problems are primarily the following four business/financial problems.

First (and foremost): who is going to make the loan? Banks and other institutional lenders like to make loans to borrowers who really don't need the money. These borrowers have the assets to be able to assure lenders that they won't default. At the very least, lenders prefer borrowers who have unencumbered assets that can be used as collateral for the loan. In the event of default, the lender can then seize and sell this collateral to collect its debt. So the corporation that would like to borrow must consider what is available to offer as collateral for the loan.

Second: what covenants will the lender require? Lenders reduce their risks by requiring financial and operational commitments from the borrower until the loan has been repaid. Typical loan covenants include limits on large expenditures and restrictions on both distributions to owners and issuance of new debt that would need to be repaid before earlier debt. Such covenants limit the corporation's ability to do things that might make it more difficult for the corporation to meet its obligations.

Third: how is the corporation going to service the debt, i.e., pay the monthly interest and then repay the loan? Can the corporation generate sufficient additional cash to make the loan payments?

Fourth: what happens if the corporation defaults? Lenders often require that major shareholders personally guarantee repayment. By the way, the loan documents will generally define default much more broadly than a single late or missed payment. For example, the documents might provide that the loan defaults, and so must immediately be repaid, if the corporation's cash declines below a certain level.

C. ISSUING MORE STOCK

1. TO WHOM?

a. Preemptive Rights and Other Rights of Existing Shareholders

Assume that Agee, Propp and Capel are the only three shareholders of Bubba's Burritos and that each owns one-third of the outstanding shares. If the corporation subsequently issues 150 new shares to each of the existing three shareholders, then the percentage of ownership remains unchanged. If, however, Bubba's Burritos subsequently issues 300 shares to a new shareholder or to Agee and Propp, then Capel's ownership interest will be decreased, or "diluted." What are the potential harms to Capel from dilution? Are there situations in which dilution would not harm him?

Existing shareholders can be protected from such dilution if they have "preemptive rights." A shareholder with preemptive rights has the right to purchase that number of shares of any new issuance of shares that will enable the shareholder to maintain her percentage of ownership. For example, if Capel owns one-third of the outstanding stock, preemptive rights means that Capel has the right to buy one-third of the new issuance.

Whether a shareholder has preemptive rights depends upon (1) what the state corporation code says about preemptive rights, (2) what the articles of incorporation say about preemptive rights, and (3) what the purpose of the issuance is. Please read MBCA § 6.30 and the following questions.

QUESTIONS

1. What is the practical significance of preemptive rights? Does a shareholder with preemptive rights get the new stock for free? Does she get it at a reduced price?

2. Is a shareholder with preemptive rights *required* to exercise the rights?

3. Bubba's Burritos, Inc. has issued 10,000 shares. Shepherd owns 2,000 of these. Assume Bubba's is planning to issue an additional 5,000 shares, the consideration for which is to be cash. If Shepherd has preemptive rights, how many shares can he purchase of the new issuance?

4. Same facts as in Question 3, except the new issuance of 5,000 shares is to Roberts in exchange for Roberts's sale to the corporation of his racing yacht. Why does Shepherd *not* have preemptive rights as to this issuance under MBCA § 6.30. Does the lack of preemptive rights in this scenario make sense?

5. Capel owns 1000 shares of Bubba's Burritos stock. Agee and Propp each own 200 shares. If Capel agrees to sell all of her 1000 shares to Agee, can Propp assert preemptive rights?

6. Assume that Bubba's Burritos is incorporated in a state in which shareholders have preemptive rights unless the articles otherwise provide, and Bubba's articles do not eliminate preemptive rights. Capel, who owns 80% of the outstanding shares, learns that McDonald's is interested in acquiring Bubba's Burritos. Capel successfully proposes an amendment to the Bubba's articles that eliminates preemptive rights. Capel then causes Bubba's Burritos to issue more stock, all of which she buys at a very low price. As a result of this new stock issuance, Capel owns 99% of the stock of Bubba's Burritos. Is this fair to the other Bubba's Burritos stockholders? Do they have any legal remedy? Consider the following case.

BYELICK v. VIVADELLI

United States District Court, Eastern District of Virginia, 1999
79 F. Supp. 2d 610

[The plaintiff, Byelick, owned 10% of the defendant corporation, VTIC. The defendant Vivadellis owned the other 90%. The court described the underlying facts as follows:

On November 1, 1996, VTIC's Board of Directors—by then comprised of John Vivadelli (referred to by the court as "Vivadelli") and his wife

Stephany Vivadelli—eliminated the shareholders' preemptive rights which were provided for in the company's by-laws. Then, on December 30, 1996, Vivadelli and his wife, as VTIC directors, authorized VTIC's issuance of an additional 50,000 shares to Vivadelli; this issuance is referred to in the pleadings as the "December 1996 Stock Sale." That transaction reduced Byelick's ownership interest in the company from 10% to 1%. Byelick alleged, *inter alia*, that the issuance constituted a breach of fiduciary duty. The defendants moved for summary judgment. In the opinion below, the trial court denied summary judgment on this part of the complaint.]

Byelick also claims that the December 30, 1996 issuance of 50,000 shares, and the sale of those shares to Vivadelli, breached the fiduciary duty owed to Byelick, as a shareholder, by Vivadelli and Stephany Vivadelli. This claim raises several legal questions.

It is well settled that "[a] Virginia corporation's directors and officers owe a duty of loyalty both to the corporation and to the corporation's shareholders." * * *

Although a shareholder challenging an action of the directors of a publicly-held corporation is typically required to sue in a derivative capacity, closely-held corporations raise a different set of concerns.

In *Donahue v. Rodd Electrotype Company of New England, Inc.*, 328 N.E.2d 505 (Mass. 1975), the Supreme Judicial Court of Massachusetts addressed these unique concerns in the context of a minority shareholder's suit against, *inter alia*, the directors and the former director, officer, and controlling shareholder of a closely held corporation. The court first recognized that the close corporation—because it is typified by a small number of stockholders, a limited market for the stock, and significant majority stockholder participation in management—"is often little more than an 'incorporated' or 'chartered' partnership." Because the close corporation functions much like a small partnership, "the relationship among the stockholders must be one of trust, confidence and absolute loyalty if the enterprise is to succeed." And, because the minority shareholder in a close corporation is generally incapable of authorizing dissolution, yet cannot reclaim his capital because there is rarely a market for his shares, minority shareholders are easily "trapped in a disadvantageous situation" and subjected to "freeze-out" schemes by majority shareholders seeking to acquire their shares for inadequate prices. The Supreme Judicial Court of Massachusetts concluded:

> Because of the fundamental resemblance of the close corporation to the partnership, the trust and confidence which are essential to this scale and manner of enterprise, and the inherent danger to minority interests in the close corporation, we hold that stockholders in the close corporation owe one another substantially the same fiduciary duty in the operation of the enterprise that partners owe to one another.

Accordingly, the minority shareholder in *Donahue* was accorded the right to sue individually. This view has found acceptance in numerous jurisdictions. Notably, the American Law Institute has incorporated the views articulated in *Donahue* and the related cases in its recommendations respecting corporate governance:

> 7.01(d) In the case of a closely held corporation [§ 1.06], the court in its discretion may treat an action raising derivative claims as a direct action, exempt it from those restrictions and defenses applicable only to derivative actions, and order an individual recovery, if it finds that to do so will not (i) unfairly expose the corporation or the defendants to a multiplicity of actions, (ii) materially prejudice the interests of creditors of the corporation, or (iii) interfere with a fair distribution of the recovery among all interested persons. A.L.I., Principles of Corporate Governance: Analysis and Recommendations, § 7.01(d) (1994).

Although the issue does not appear to have been decided in Virginia, it appears that the same principles would find acceptance by the Supreme Court of Virginia.

Having concluded that a minority shareholder of a closely held corporation can sue a director/majority shareholder for breach of fiduciary duty in respect of a transaction benefitting the inside director, it is now necessary to assess the substance of Byelick's claim that the December 30, 1996 dilutive sale to Vivadelli constituted such a breach. Before undertaking that task, however, it is necessary to consider an argument asserted repeatedly by the Vivadellis respecting the dilutive transaction.

The Vivadellis characterize Byelick's breach of fiduciary duty claim as an attempt to gain preemptive rights, which rights, according to the Vivadellis, were lawfully eliminated on December 2, 1996 by a properly conducted board meeting. The Vivadellis then argue that "[a]ny right a shareholder has to avoid dilution must be based on [§ 13.1–651, governing] preemptive rights, and Byelick had no preemptive rights." In pressing this position, the Vivadellis argue that to permit Byelick to proceed here would require creation of "an entirely new right and a new cause of action," in disregard of "the only exception to the Virginia Code section that governs preemptive rights, Va. Code. Ann. § 13.1–651."

The Vivadellis' argument is misplaced. First, although they assert that the argument is "unshakeable as a matter of law [and] more than fair as a matter of equity," the Vivadellis cite absolutely no authority for the proposition that Byelick's sole remedy for the allegedly improper dilution presented by the facts of this action is provided by § 13.1–651. That section provides, in pertinent part, that:

> Unless limited or denied in the articles of incorporation ... the shareholders of a corporation have a preemptive right, granted on uniform terms and conditions prescribed by the board of directors to provide a fair and reasonable opportunity to exercise the right, to acquire proportional amounts of the corporation's unissued shares upon the decision of the board of directors to issue them.

The Vivadellis argue that, because preemptive rights were "limited or denied in the amendment to the articles of incorporation" effected pursuant to the Consent of the Board of Directors of December 2, 1996, Byelick has no legal right to challenge the dilution of his interest in VTIC.

In effect, the Vivadellis read § 13.1–651 to preempt all other law, statutory or decisional, bearing on the dilution of interests in a corporation—including the law that a director owes a fiduciary duty to a corporation's shareholders. Nothing in the text of Section 13.1–651 suggests that the statute was intended to swallow whole the Virginia common law respecting the duty of a fiduciary. Nor would such an interpretation be consistent with the general principles controlling the elimination of preemptive rights. In that respect, a leading treatise explains the requirements for a lawful amendment of a corporation's articles of incorporation to eliminate preemptive rights:

> If preemptive rights exist in a particular corporation, their elimination by amendment of the articles of incorporation is possible if such amendment is authorized by the laws of the jurisdiction of incorporation, no violation of fiduciary duties is involved, and procedures required to effectuate such amendment are followed.

Harry G. Henn & John R. Alexander, LAW OF CORPORATIONS, 444 (1983). Indeed, even where preemptive rights are not provided to shareholders in the articles of incorporation, a director's fiduciary duty nonetheless constrains the issuance of shares:

> Whether or not preemptive rights are elected, however, the director's fiduciary duty extends to the issuance of shares. Issuance of shares at favorable prices to directors (but excluding other shareholders) or the issuance of shares on a non-proportional basis for the purpose of affecting control rather than raising capital may violate that duty. 1 Model Bus. Corp. Act Ann., 6–168 (1997 Supp.).

The Vivadellis' error of law is equally visible in the backwards assertion that "Byelick never suggests why the concepts of fiduciary duty or interested party provide him with some kind of common law preemptive rights...." In fact, Byelick never made such an assertion. Quite to the contrary, Byelick's contention is that the common law of fiduciaries prohibits the Vivadellis from amending the articles of incorporation to eliminate preemptive rights in derogation of their fiduciary duty (as they allegedly did on December 2, 1996), and then, barely a month later, approving (by Consent of the Board of Directors of December 30, 1996) the sale by VTIC to John Vivadelli of an additional 50,000 shares, which reduced Byelick's ownership interest from 10% to less than 1%, again, allegedly in violation of his fiduciary duty.

The Vivadellis' argument would give the statute on which it is based an effect not apparent on the face of the statute by eviscerating Virginia's common law respecting the fiduciary duties of directors. That can be done, of course, but only in clear terms not yet used by Virginia's legislature or her courts.

Having concluded that a dilutive transaction can be challenged under the Virginia common law of fiduciaries, it becomes necessary to ascertain how an individual shareholder can seek redress by reference to this law.

In the context of this action, the burden is on the Vivadellis to show: (1) the fairness to the corporation of the Consent of the Board of Directors of December 30, 1996, approving the sale by VTIC to John Vivadelli of an additional 50,000 shares, as well as (2) the fairness of the actual sale itself. This is a disputed issue of material fact, and therefore cannot be decided on summary judgment. Accordingly, the motions for summary judgment on Count IV filed by both Byelick and the Vivadellis must be denied, and the issue must be decided at trial.

QUESTIONS

1. Who did what wrong in *Byelick*?

2. Is the case about preemptive rights? Would the court have decided the case differently if the shareholders of VTIC never had preemptive rights?

3. There was some confusion in the *Byelick* opinion about whether the corporation addressed preemptive rights in its articles or in its bylaws. The norm is to address them in the articles. The default provision of the Virginia statute in *Byelick* (§ 13.1–651) is that preemptive rights exist unless the articles provide otherwise. As you saw before reading the case, MBCA § 6.30 provides the opposite default rule: preemptive rights do not exist unless the articles provide for them.

4. Do preemptive rights make sense in a publicly-traded corporation?

b. Selling to Venture Capitalists

There is no separate law regarding venture capital. There is, however, a lore regarding venture capitalists. As Bob Zider, an entrepreneur and observer of venture capitalists in Silicon Valley, noted in the Harvard Business Review: "[T]he entrepreneur is the modern day cowboy, roaming new industrial frontiers much the same way the earlier Americans explored the West. At his [or her] side stands the venture capitalist, a trail-wise sidekick ready to help the hero through all the tight spots—in exchange of course for a piece of the action." Bob Zider, *How Venture Capital Works*, HARVARD BUSINESS REVIEW 131 (Nov.-Dec. 1998).

Professor Dent of the Case Western Reserve Law School provides a less picturesque but clearer picture of venture capital:

I. WHAT AND WHY IS VENTURE CAPITAL?

Venture capital is a substantial equity investment in a non-public enterprise that does not involve active control of the firm. It is often associated with the financing of high technology start-up companies, where it has achieved its most spectacular successes. But, many companies financed with venture capital are neither high technology nor start-up companies. Indeed, companies past the start-up stage often raise additional venture capital when they are unable to finance through more conventional sources. These later round financings are often called "second tier," or "mezzanine" financings. Furthermore, once-successful companies that have fallen on hard times may also obtain financing from venture capitalists; these investors are often called "angels."

Entrepreneurs usually seek venture capital when they need capital but are unable to raise it elsewhere. Retained earnings are a manager's favorite source of funding. However, this source of funding is unavailable for start-up companies since they have not yet produced earnings to retain; and even after the start-up, a growing company usually requires more capital than its cash flow provides. Debt is often the managers' second choice for capital. Debt financing is generally preferred over equity because equity investors demand a higher return on their investment than lenders. Moreover, sales of stock dilute managers' equity interest and voting power. However, loans are unavailable to most start-up and growth companies because of the high risk of loss. In theory, lenders can offset increased risk by charging a high interest rate. In practice, however, usury laws, as well as regulations that require institutional lenders (such as banks and insurance companies) to be conservative, preclude such high interest loans. Moreover, few start-up companies generate sufficient cash flow to service high interest charges. For these companies such a loan would rapidly lead to insolvency. Even more established firms may need more capital than they can borrow.

Most companies that seek venture capital are unstable and risky. In fact, one-third of venture capital-financed companies wind up in bankruptcy. Another one-third end up in "limbo" or as "living dead"—limping along, able to pay expenses (including managers' salaries), but unable to go public or pay significant dividends. Only one-third of the companies that use venture capital financing succeed. Venture capitalists demand high returns because the successful one-third of their investments must cover the losses generated by the other two-thirds, as well as the high transactions costs that venture capitalists pay in seeking, monitoring, and evaluating their investments.

Venture capitalists also demand high returns because they cannot reduce risks by diversifying. Although modern portfolio theory advises investors not to put all their eggs in one basket, venture capitalists are forced to ignore this advice. High transaction costs of choosing, monitoring, and evaluating private equity investments limit the venture capitalist to a few major purchases rather than many small investments.

Illiquidity also requires venture capitalists to demand a higher return on their investment. The inability of venture capitalists to sell their stock at a fair price whenever they choose is a burden for which they must be compensated. Thus, venture capitalists demand higher returns than the yield typically paid on debt or even on other types of equity investments.

II. HOW VENTURE CAPITALISTS PROTECT THEIR INVESTMENTS

Venture capitalists usually obtain a significant voice in the control of the firm. Venture capitalists also demand protective covenants.

Although contracts are quite standardized in many areas, the varied business contexts of venture capital discourage uniformity. For example, an investor who has the power to choose a majority of the board of directors has needs far different from an investor who lacks even a veto power over the board's decisions. The variety of terms in venture capital contracts also mirrors the diverse preferences of the parties involved. Venture capitalists range from pension funds and other huge financial institutions to individual investors of modest means. In addition, managers have varied preferences, such as differing levels of risk aversion. Another factor is the parties' level of sophistication. Unusual terms may reflect either mutual ignorance or overreaching by a more sophisticated party.

George W. Dent, Jr., *Venture Capital and the Future of Corporate Finance*, 70 WASH. U.L.Q. 1029, 1031 et seq. (1992).

Looking at venture capital in traditional business structure terms, a venture capitalist is a shareholder, but a shareholder with special rights including (1) "downside protection" such as a liquidation preference that requires the venture capitalist to be paid first if the company's assets are sold off and (2) "upside opportunities" such as the right to acquire additional stock at a predetermined price and (3) voting and veto rights and (4) "exit opportunities," such as a "redemption" right to sell the shares back to the corporation.*

c. Selling to a Person (or a Few People) or to the Public

A corporation can sell stock to a few people or to thousands. The issuance of the stock to a venture capital firm is usually a "private placement." This means that the sale is exempt from the dangerously complicated "registration" requirements that federal and state laws impose on some stock sales. Any "public offering" of stock generally will require registration.* Dangerously complicated law also determines what types of stock issuances are exempt from registration. Put generally, federal and state securities laws tend to treat a corporation's offering of a limited amount of its stock to a limited number of investors differently

---

* We have already seen an example of such provisions in the discussion of Silicon Gaming's preferred stock in Chapter 4 § (B)(4).

* A corporation's first public offering is called an "initial public offering," or "IPO."

than they do a corporation's offering of a substantial amount of its stock to the public.

While registration and exemptions from registration are a substantial part of the law school course in Securities Regulation, every lawyer who works on matters involving corporations needs a general understanding of the registration process and its perils.[†] So we now turn to an overview of the business and legal considerations relating to a public offering.

2. WHAT ARE THE LEGAL CONSTRAINTS ON HOW A CORPORATION ISSUES ITS STOCK?

a. Registration Requirements for Public Offerings

(i) Some of What Your Clients Might Have Learned About Securities Registration in B–School

This section focuses on why and how a business structured as a corporation "goes public."

Why "Go Public"? The reason to go public is to raise money. Most growing companies require the continued investment of capital, and the public markets are viewed as the largest and least expensive source of capital. Typically, firms that desire to go public have a record of sales and earnings that allows prospective investors—purchasers of the shares—to have some confidence in the long run profitability of the company, and thus, the value of their shares. Often, it takes several years—and successive rounds of private financing, perhaps venture capital—to reach this point. The private financing is expensive for the firm's owners; they have to give up a relatively large fraction of their ownership—or equity—to obtain that funding.

Thus, when the firm has reached a stage in its evolution where it believes it has proven its business model, a public offering can be an attractive means of funding business growth. The question then arises: how much money to raise?

How much money to raise? In part, this is a function of the amount of capital the firm will need to finance its growth. A very rapidly growing firm in a capital-intensive business will need more capital than a more slowly growing company. Because the fixed costs of going public, such as legal and accounting fees, can be significant (costs often reach more than 10% of the amount raised), it can be in the firm's interest to seek as much money as possible.

In deciding how much money to raise, the company will balance fear against greed. First, the greed. Suppose that the company is a big success after its initial public offering. If the company accomplishes what it hopes

---

[†] "[S]ecurities law is a highly technical, demanding area of the law that has ruined the career of many young lawyers who practiced in the area without proper preparation and experience." Arthur Pinto & Douglas Branson, UNDERSTANDING CORPORATE LAW 157 (2d ed. 2004).

to, it will grow, become more profitable, and its value will increase. If this hugely successful corporation later needs more money to grow, it will be able to get that financing by giving up less ownership to the new investors. Greed then argues for raising as little money as possible to get to the next milestone.

Now, the fear. What if, after the first public offering, the company is not as successful as anticipated? If the company falters after the IPO, it will wish it had raised as much money as it could have in the first public offering. The extra cash is money in the bank that buys time to try new things to get the business back on track.

How does this balancing of greed and fear generally resolve itself? Companies tend to use a public offering to raise enough money to meet anticipated needs for at least two years.

How many additional shares to sell? To raise its chosen amount, the company will need to think carefully about how many shares it will attempt to sell, and at what price.

The company will first calculate what it is currently worth. For a corporation whose shares are traded publicly, it's easy to see what the consensus is about the firm's value. The company's market value—the market capitalization or "market cap"—is simply the price per share at which the shares trade times the number of shares outstanding. The price per share is printed in the newspaper each day and available immediately online.

The price per share is a reflection of the "voting" that takes place every day in the stock market on these relative values. Of course, the number of shares sold has to equal the number bought. If the price is such that many people think the stock is a good deal, then the price has to rise to coax out the shares required to clear the market. If the number of willing sellers is high for the opposite reason, then the price falls to coax out the buyers.

In contrast, before a corporation's stock is freely tradable (i.e., before an initial public offering while it is still a private company), the valuation is harder to calculate. The firm will need to estimate its future earnings as best it can. This is a science and an art. Note that the firm's value depends on its *future* earnings, not its earnings in the past. Even companies that have never had any earnings can be worth lots of money if people expect them to have large earnings in the future. Examples would be a company that is developing a drug that promises to cure cancer, or an internet start-up with a great idea that is not yet developed. However, in estimating future earnings, past earnings are not irrelevant. They often are the best evidence of what earnings will be in the future.

Based on this estimate of future earnings, the firm will then calculate its *current* value. One way for a company to do this is to look at comparables—businesses like theirs—that are publicly traded, and determine the market value of these enterprises. If several fast food chains sell for about 20 times the past year's earnings, then, the logic goes, Bubba's Burritos, Inc., should be worth about 20 times *its* expected future earnings. If Bubba's expects to earn $10 million per year into the future, then it should be valued at $200 million.*

Once the company has estimated what its entire business is worth, it will then divide that sum by the number of shares outstanding. This results in the value per share. Suppose that it already has issued eight million total shares, to the company's founders and to a venture capital firm. Then the value per share is $200 million divided by eight million, or $25 per share.† This is the price at which the firm can sell more shares.

The company can then easily calculate how many additional shares it should sell. Suppose that it has decided to raise an additional $30 million. At $25 per share, it will need to sell 1.2 million more shares.

In pricing the shares, the company will try to ensure that it doesn't price them too high or too low. If it prices them at more than they are worth, people won't buy them, and the offering will fail. In contrast, if it sets the price too low, then it won't raise as much money as it could have. The shares' buyers will be delighted to have received a bargain. But the company will have thrown away money.

How does a corporation make a public offering? In part, a public offering is about a "registration process"—involving documents such as a registration statement and prospectus prepared by lawyers and accountants and filed with and approved by the Securities and Exchange Commission (SEC). We will consider that part later. In part a public offering is also a sales process—involving the marketing of the stock by an underwriter.

When a company starts down the road to an IPO, one of the first tasks is selecting an underwriter. The underwriter is typically an investment bank—Morgan Stanley or Goldman Sachs or one of their brethren. The process of selecting an underwriter is generally driven by the company's sense of who can get it the best price for its stock, particularly if market conditions sour—who has the relationships and reputation to get a deal done.

The underwriter manages the process of drawing up the offering memorandum that is filed with the SEC. More important, the underwriter is responsible for advice on structuring the offering, pricing the securities,

---

* Another, more sophisticated way to calculate the firm's value is to calculate the present discounted value of the firm's expected future earnings. You can learn how to do this in a course in Corporate Finance, either at the law school or business school.

† Companies like for their stock to trade at around $25 or $30 per share. Any higher, and investors with few funds may be unable to purchase even one share. Any lower, and the price is so cheap that the public's perception of the company itself is cheapened. There are techniques that the company can use to adjust the price into the sweet spot. If the market-clearing price is too high—say $50—the company can perform a "stock split" in which it exchanges each share for two shares. This will cut the market price of each share in half, to $25. If the price is too low, the company uses a "reverse stock split." For example, the company will swap two old shares for one new share. How do stock splits and reverse stock splits affect the underlying value of each shareholder's investment in the company?

and maintaining a market for the securities after the offering. The underwriter and the company executives go on a "road show" where they speak with the likely buyers of the shares—people who run mutual funds or otherwise manage large pools of money. Buyers provide an indication of their interest in buying the stock at the various prices within the range that the firm is considering offering its shares. All of this sales effort comes to a head when the SEC approves the registration materials (sometimes after several rounds of comments and responses) and the offering is said to be "effective."

The shares of stock hit the market the next morning at a price set the night before. That is, the price at which the stock will be publicly offered is set only just before the offering actually begins. It is not set earlier at the time the corporation decided to make the public offering. It is also not set at the time that the corporation selected its underwriter. It is not set before the corporation has spent hundreds of thousands of dollars on attorneys and accountants. It will take at least three or four months from the time a company makes the decision to go public to the time that the SEC makes the decision that the registration is effective. The company must wait to set the price because the market—and the best price for the offering—may change dramatically during that time.

Earlier, all companies that went public had earnings, and most fit within some well-established group. So, if a new pharmaceutical company was conducting an IPO, it was a straightforward matter to look at comparable companies, see the kind of P/E (price-to-earnings ratio) at which they traded, and price the new company's offering at a similar level. Recently, however, companies have been going public far earlier in their life cycle, before they even have earnings. This makes the problem of valuing the company's stock much more difficult. Faced with this uncertainty, to make sure that the shares sell, the company and its underwriters may set the price relatively low. Thus, it is not uncommon for the stock price to rise quickly after the IPO when they are resold on the secondary market. Can you see why a soaring stock price directly after an IPO should cause the company's managers to weep, not cheer?

However, underpricing may also occur for a more sinister reason. Occasional unscrupulous underwriters may have an incentive to underprice the shares for their own selfish purposes. Recent financial scandals have shown that they might hope to funnel the bargain shares to their other clients to create loyalty and future business for themselves.

One factor that corporations use to select an underwriter is who has a reputation for bringing good companies public in the particular industry. This, in turn, is often a function of the firm's research analysts. So, if an underwriter is known to have a very strong research analyst in the optical communications industry, then an optical communications company that wants to go public might choose that underwriter so that the underwriter's analyst will follow the stock, thus marketing it to investment professionals. While it is tempting to think of the analysts as neutral, objective reporters on a company's prospects, it is widely believed that they act as part of the underwriter's marketing force, attracting clients and then supporting their shares with favorable reports.

Where does the money come from? Underwriting activities are conducted on either a "firm commitment" or a "best efforts" basis. In a firm commitment underwriting, the money comes from the underwriter. The underwriter actually buys all of the shares in the public offering from the issuing company at the public offering price, less a negotiated discount. The underwriter then resells the shares to other investment bankers and the public.

In a firm commitment offering, the underwriter bears the risk that the shares cannot be resold at the offering price. The underwriter reduces this risk by ensuring that the offering price is not set until very late in the offering process.

In a "best efforts underwriting," the money comes from the public, not the underwriter. Rather than buying the stock itself and then reselling it, the underwriter instead uses its best efforts to help the issuer to find buyers for the stock. The corporation, not the underwriter, bears the risk that shares cannot be sold at the offering price. Most underwritings are on a best efforts basis.

Where does the money go? Now, for the interesting question—what happens to the money that is raised in the IPO? Let's take an example where 10 million shares are sold to the public at $10 per share—this would result in $100 million. Once we subtract the 7.5% that the investment bank gets for its underwriting fee plus fees for other professionals such as lawyers and accountants, there is a transfer of $90 million or so from the public to someone. Who gets the money?

The answer depends on who is selling the shares. If the company itself is selling shares, then the company gets the money. If the existing owners of the company are selling shares that they own, then these people get the money, and the company does not. The prospectus* will always have a table that describes in great detail where the shares are coming from, so you will always know—at least for the offering as a whole.

You might ask whether the potential buyer of the stock—the public—cares about any of this. If a share of stock represents a proportional claim of the company's value, does it matter whether you bought it from an original owner or the company itself?

There are two components to answering this question. First, in the above example, suppose all 10 million shares were shares that other shareholders already owned. Then after the offering, the company would have the same amount of money in the bank as it did before the offering; all of the money goes to shareholders who owned the shares, not the

---

* The prospectus is a document an issuer provides to potential purchasers, describing the security being sold, the issuing company, and the risk characteristic of the security. As we will see below, the prospectus is an important part of a registration statement under federal securities laws.

company. If instead the offering sold only new shares, then the company would have $100 million more in the bank the day after the offering than the day before. So, part of the answer is that the company might benefit more if the money went into the company, where it could be invested to generate earnings, rather than merely go to the old shareholders to make them rich.

A second part of the answer depends on which shareholders are selling. If, for example, a company was backed by a venture capital (VC) firm, and that firm is selling some or all of its shares, then that needn't worry the new shareholders. The VC firm has investors of its own and they expect to get their money back. On the other hand, suppose the company's CEO is selling a large percentage of her shares. Presumably, this person knows a lot more about the company than you do. Do you want to be buying if she is selling?

Of course, there are sound reasons why an executive should sell some stock—to diversify her own financial situation, for instance. But, many investors look unfavorably on a company's prospects when an executive sells a significant fraction of her shares.

Although a corporation going public gets money only at the time of the public offering, the offering will require the company to continue to spend money. It will continue spending money on attorneys and accountants to comply with various SEC reporting requirements that will now extend indefinitely.

There are other, less direct costs. Once you are a public company, the world changes. Investors attempt to gauge the value of the stock as a function of forecast earnings. Analysts develop earnings models and tweak them quarterly as the company publicly discloses its actual performance. Missing the analysts' estimates can quickly cause investors to sour on a company. If these professional investors abandon the stock, it can become relatively illiquid, allowing relatively small sales or purchases to produce large swings in the stock's price. Employees—especially those with stock options—begin to pay a great deal of attention to the price of the stock, and its gyrations can have a significant effect on employee morale, and on the job prospects of the company's managers.

QUESTIONS AND NOTE

1. At what point in the public offering process,

    - does the issuing corporation make money?

    - does the underwriter make money?

    - do the attorneys and accountants make money?

2. Bubba's Burritos, Inc. decides to make a public offering. Propp, an existing shareholder, wants to know how she is affected by this public

offering. What can you tell her? What else do you need to learn about federal securities law?*

3. *See generally* Howard H. Stevenson, Michael J. Roberts, H. Irving Grousbeck, & Amar V. Bhide, New Business Ventures and the Entrepreneur (5th ed. 1999).

Now that you understand what an underwriter is and part of what your client might have learned from B–School, let's look at what the federal securities laws are and what you can learn from the SEC website.

(ii) Some of the Legal Issues in Securities Regulation

Federal securities law is very much a product of the stock market crash of the 1920s and the New Deal of the 1930s. The two most significant federal statutes are the Securities Act of 1933 (the " '33 Act") and the Securities Exchange Act of 1934 (you guessed it, the " '34 Act").

In general, the '33 Act governs the issuance of securities by the corporation itself. In contrast, the '34 Act provides information to the markets for new securities and resales by requiring many corporations continually to provide detailed public reports about their operations. The securities that the acts cover include not only stock, but also securities such as bonds by which investors lend the company money. This book provides only a very general introduction to the disclosure requirements of the '33 Act.

The '33 Act contemplates that a corporation issuing securities will first file a detailed and extensive "registration statement" with the SEC and will provide a copy of the main part of that registration statement (the "prospectus") to all people to whom the securities are offered. Only after the SEC staff reviews the registration statement carefully will it permit the statement to be effective.

The federal system is based on disclosure. As long as full disclosure is made, the government will not prevent a security from being sold because of its underlying merits. This differs from the system in some other countries.

The '33 Act also provides for a series of exemptions from these disclosure requirements. Although we will not study these exemptions in detail in this course, securities lawyers study the exemptions in detail in their practices. "Because SEC registration is expensive and intrusive, many securities lawyers devote a big part of their practice to helping clients gain an exemption from registration." Alan R. Palmiter, Corporations—Examples and Explanations 92 (6th ed. 2009).

---

* "[S]ecurities law is a highly technical, demanding area of law that has ruined the careers of many young lawyers who practiced in the area without proper preparation and experience." Arthur Pinto & Douglas Branson, Understanding Corporate Law 157 (2d ed. 2004). Note from your authors: we understand that this footnote is exactly the same as an earlier footnote.

In addition to the requirements under the federal securities laws, the issuer must be careful to comply with various state-law requirements—the so-called state "blue-sky" laws—the name comes from early attempts by hucksters to sell pieces of the blue sky.

QUESTIONS AND NOTES

1. What is the reason for the SEC's requiring and reviewing registration statements? Who is protected? From what?

2. One professor has speculated about the problems the Wright brothers would have encountered if they had needed to raise money to pursue their dreams of manned flight under today's federal securities laws. He imagines that the brothers' lawyer, Horace, would give the following advice:

"Boys," he started, "I have to tell you that these new securities laws are not helpful. They're supposed to protect the public against fraudulent schemes, but it looks to me like they mostly hurt young inventors like you."

"We're not doing anything fraudulent," responded Wilbur, "so we should have no worries about that."

"You'd think so," Horace replied, "but these registration provisions are so time-consuming and costly that they make it near-impossible for young entrepreneurs like you to raise money. Here's what I've found. First, for federal law purposes, you have to file a registration statement unless you can qualify for an exemption. Preparing a registration statement will probably take a couple of months, then the SEC will have to review it. And meanwhile, you can't sell a single share of stock. You're stuck in a long timetable and running up expenses with no way to pay for them. Once you've got the SEC go-ahead, the questions become how much can you raise, and how quickly? Who knows? You're a new and untested company. What's more, registration entails potential liabilities that might not be imposed in unregistered offerings. In a nutshell, registration involves huge problems in terms of time, costs, and potential liabilities, all the while not knowing whether an offering will even be successful."

"Anything that takes several months won't work," Orville noted. "We've got to have money in hand within a month to prepare for our North Carolina experiments."

"That's why I've abandoned the registration idea. We need to fit the offering into a registration exemption. Some registration exemptions are in the statute,* [37] and others have been created by the SEC. Stuart R. Cohn, *The Impact of Securities Laws on Developing Companies: Would*

---

* [37] Statutory exemptions in the 1933 Act are as follows: section 3(a)(11) (the intrastate exemption); section 4(2) (the private offering exemption); and section 4(6) (the accredited investor exemption). The SEC has used its rulemaking authority to create administrative exemptions under both the intrastate, Rule 147, and private offering, Rule 506, exemptions. Rules 147 and 506 do not necessarily mirror their statutory counterparts. Compliance with either the statutory or administrative provisions suffices for exemption purposes.

the Wright Brothers Have Gotten Off the Ground? 3 J. SMALL & EMERGING BUS. L. 315, 326–28 (1999).

3. Reconsider your answer to Question 1 regarding the reason for the registration process. Professor Choi suggests that the registration exemptions are inconsistent with the reasons for the registration requirements:

> Although the exemptions for small businesses reduce the expense for businesses seeking to raise capital, the exemptions are not without costs. Paradoxically those companies where investors require the greatest protection—small, unknown business—are also those companies with the greatest ability to skirt securities regulatory protections.

Stephen J. Choi, *Gatekeepers and the Internet: Rethinking the Regulation of Small Business Capital Formation,* 2 J. SMALL & EMERGING BUS. L. 27, 33 (1998).

b. Common Law Fraud and Misrepresentation and Rule 10b–5 Constraints on Any Stock Issuance

While many issuances of stock are exempt from federal and state registration requirements, no issuance of stock is exempt from the common law of fraud and misrepresentation. A person who buys stock from a corporation as a result of that corporation's false or misleading statement can either invoke the contract law of misrepresentation to avoid her contract to buy the stock or invoke the tort law of fraud or deceit to recover damages from the corporation. The contract law of misrepresentation was (supposed to be) covered in your contracts course; the law of fraud or deceit was (supposed to be) covered in your torts course.

No issuance of stock is exempt from Rule 10b–5, the securities antifraud rule promulgated by the SEC under section 10 of the '34 Act. Rule 10b–5 has been described as "a bedrock of protection for those who purchase and sell securities. Every securities transaction lives under its protective shade and menacing shadow." Alan R. Palmiter, CORPORATIONS—EXAMPLES AND EXPLANATIONS 413 (6th ed. 2009).

Rule 10b–5 was promulgated in 1948 and provides:

It shall be unlawful for any person, directly or indirectly, by the use of any means or instrumentality of interstate commerce, or the mails or of any facility of any national securities exchange,

> (a) To employ any device, scheme, or artifice to defraud,

> (b) To make any untrue statement of a material fact or to omit to state a material fact necessary in order to make the statements made, in the light of the circumstances under which they were made, not misleading, or

> (c) To engage in any act, practice, or course of business which operates or would operate as a fraud or deceit upon any person

in connection with the purchase or sale of any security.

Most of the content of Rule 10b–5 is the result of decades of case law.* Most of those cases involve fraud, misrepresentations, or omissions in connection with *re*sales of stock or corporate combinations such as mergers—and not fraud, misrepresentation or omissions by corporations in connection with their initial issuance of stock. And we will consider some of those cases later in the parts of the book dealing with resales of stock and corporate combinations.†

For now, apply Rule 10b–5 and common sense to the following easy (we hope) issuance problems.

PROBLEMS: APPLICATION OF 10B–5 TO STOCK ISSUANCE

1. Agee, Capel and Propp are the only three shareholders of Bubba's Burritos, Inc. Each owns 1,000 shares. Roberts is considering buying 1,000 shares from Bubba's for $100,000. Agee, the CEO of Bubba's, tells Roberts that Bubba's has never received a Health Department rating lower than "VG" (Very Good). In reliance on that representation, Roberts buys the 1,000 shares from Bubba's. Roberts later learns that Bubba's had received seven Health Department ratings of UB—Unbelievably Bad. Advise Roberts as to possible recourse.

2. Same facts as Problem 1 except that Bubba's had not received a Health Department rating lower than VG. However, the day before Agee told Roberts that Bubba's had never received a Health Department rating lower that VG, the Health Department had inspected Bubba's and the inspector had met with Agee and told Agee that there were major problems and that it was almost certain that the company would receive the lowest possible rating. While Agee tells Roberts about Bubba's history of good Health Department ratings, he does not mention this conversation with the inspector. After Roberts buys the stock from Bubba's, the Health Department announces Bubba's UB (Unbelievably Bad) rating and Roberts learns of the inspector's conversation with Agee. Advise Roberts as to possible recourse.

3. Same facts as Problem 2 except that Agee does not say anything about Health Department ratings. He does not say that past ratings have been good and he does not disclose that a bad rating is coming. Roberts buys the stock from Bubba's. Later he learns of the bad Health Department rating. Advise Roberts as to possible recourse. (Let's reconsider Problems 1–3 after you have read *EP Medsystems, Inc. v. Echocath, Inc.*, which is in Chapter 7. Then let's re-reconsider them after you have read *Jordan v. Duff & Phelps, Inc.* and *Berreman v. West Publishing Co.*, which appear in Chapter 7.)

4. Now, man bites dog. Bubba's is considering acquiring a building from Epstein in exchange for 1,000 shares of Bubba's stock. Epstein tells Agee, Bubba's CEO, that the building has never had any termite problems. In reliance on Epstein's representation, Bubba's issues 1,000 shares of its stock

---

* The Supreme Court has described 10b–5 law as "a judicial oak which has grown from little more than a legislative acorn." Blue Chip Stamps v. Manor Drug Stores, 421 U.S. 723, 737 (1975).

† And you can cover still more of those 10b–5 cases by taking your law school's course in securities regulation. (We put this statement in the footnotes because (i) it is not that important and (ii) we did not want to begin another sentence in the text with "And.")

to Epstein and takes title to the building. Bubba's later learns that Epstein's representation was a lie—that Epstein was aware of the building's past and present termite problems. Advise Bubba's as to possible recourse. Note from this Problem that Rule 10b–5 does not require that the issuer be the bad guy.

D. USING EARNINGS

A business structured as a corporation can grow by using its earnings. If Bubba's Burritos, Inc. earns $100,000 in 2011, that $100,000 can be used to increase the size of the business—to advertise, to buy new equipment, to hire an additional employee, to improve the building, etc.

But if that $100,000 is used in these ways, it cannot be distributed to shareholders as dividends. How would a well-managed business decide whether to distribute earnings to shareholders or to retain them? How do the shareholders of a business structured as a corporation make money?

CHAPTER SEVEN

HOW DO THE OWNERS OF A CORPORATION MAKE MONEY?

■ ■ ■

The owners of Bubba's Burritos, Inc., i.e., the Bubba's Burritos, Inc. stockholders, would probably answer this question differently than the owners of McDonald's. Recall that an owner of a business usually makes money either because she receives all or part of the money that a business earns or because she sells her ownership interest.

It is relatively easy to sell shares in McDonald's or some other large, publicly-held corporation. A phone call to your broker or a couple of clicks on your mouse will do the trick. In contrast, it is usually difficult to find a buyer of your stock in a small, closely held corporation such as Bubba's Burritos. If a shareholder is not able easily to sell her ownership interest in the corporation, then the corporation's paying her dividends or salary becomes even more important. It becomes the only way that she can make money from her investment in the business.

Assume, for example, that Agee, Propp, and Capel each own 1/3 of the outstanding stock of Bubba's Burritos, Inc., and that the corporation earned $150,000 last year. Agee needs money to pay for her sister's hospital bills and so she wants Bubba's Burritos to pay as much dividends as legally permitted. Propp and Capel do not need money; they want Bubba's Burritos to retain the $150,000 and use it to expand. Who decides how the corporation will use the $150,000?

As another example of how the three might disagree on how to use the earnings, assume that Propp and Capel work for the business and Agee does not. Propp and Capel want Bubba's Burritos, Inc. to use the $150,000 to pay them higher salaries. Agee again wants the $150,000 to be distributed as dividends. Who decides whether the $150,000 is to be paid only to Propp and Capel as salary or to Agee, Propp and Capel as dividends?

If Agee does receive dividends or salary from Bubba's Burritos, Inc., is she more likely or less likely to be willing to sell his stock? Would he be more likely or less likely to be willing to sell his stock at a lower price? Who are the most likely buyers of Agee's stock?

Questions such as these both prompted Professor Douglas Moll to write the article excerpted below about shareholder "oppression" in a closely held corporation and prompted judges to write opinions such as *Hollis v. Hill,* which follows the excerpt.

A close corporation is a business entity typified by a small number of stockholders, *the absence of a market for the corporation's stock,* and substantial shareholder participation in the management of the corporation. In the traditional public corporation, the typical shareholder is an investor who neither contributes labor to the corporation nor takes part in the responsibilities of management. In contrast, within a close corporation, "a more intimate and intense relationship exists between capital and labor." Close corporation shareholders "usually expect employment and a meaningful role in management, as well as a return on the money paid for [their] shares." In addition, the close corporation investor typically looks to salary rather than dividends for the principal return on investment because "[e]arnings of a close corporation often are distributed in major part in salaries, bonuses and retirement benefits."

Traditional corporate law norms of majority rule and centralized control can place the close corporation minority shareholder in a serious predicament. Under the traditional norms, most corporate power is centralized in the hands of a board of directors. Ordinarily, "the board of a close corporation is dominated by the shareholder or shareholders holding a majority of the voting power." With this control of the board, the majority shareholder has the ability to take various actions that threaten the minority shareholder. Such tactics are often referred to as "squeeze-out" or "freeze-out" techniques that "oppress" the close corporation minority shareholder. Common squeeze-out techniques include the termination of a minority shareholder's employment, the refusal to declare dividends, the removal of a minority shareholder from a position of management, and the siphoning off of corporate earnings through high compensation to the majority shareholder.

In the typical public corporation, the minority shareholders can escape these abuses of power by simply selling their shares in the market. This market exit, however, is not available to the close corporation minority shareholder because, by definition, there is no ready market for the stock of a close corporation. Thus, when a close corporation shareholder is treated unfairly through termination or otherwise, the investor "cannot escape the unfairness simply by selling out at a fair price."

Over the years, both legislative and judicial efforts have been made to ease the plight of the "oppressed" close corporation shareholder. Two significant avenues of relief have developed. First, many state legislatures have amended their dissolution statutes to include "oppression" (or a similar term) by the controlling shareholder as a ground for involuntary dissolution of the corporation. Moreover, when oppression is established, actual dissolution is not the only remedy at the court's disposal. Both state statutes and judicial precedents have authorized alternative remedies that are less drastic than dissolution. As the legislative and judicial remedies have broadened over the years, an order of actual dissolution has become less likely. Thus, "oppression" has evolved from a ground for involuntary dissolution to a ground for a wide variety of relief. Where statutes include "oppression" or similar language as a ground for dissolution or other remedy, the close corporation shareholder's ability to petition for relief has been referred to as "the statutory cause of action for oppression."

Particularly in states without an oppression-triggered dissolution statute, a second avenue of relief has developed for close corporation shareholders. Some courts have imposed an enhanced fiduciary duty between close corporation shareholders and have allowed an oppressed shareholder to bring a direct cause of action for breach of this duty. In the seminal decision of *Donahue v. Rodd Electrotype Co.*, 328 N.E.2d 505 (1975), the Massachusetts Supreme Judicial Court adopted such a standard.

Douglas K. Moll, *Shareholder Oppression v. Employment At Will in the Close Corporation: The Investment Model Solution*, 1999 U. Ill. L. Rev. 517 (quotations, citations, and footnotes omitted; emphasis original).

By the way, we will study the *Donahue* case later in this chapter.

A. RECEIVING SALARIES FROM THE CORPORATION

If Propp, Agee, and Capel own and operate Bubba's Burritos, Inc. as a corporation, one way for them to make money is have the corporation pay them salaries. This raises three questions: (1) Who decides which shareholders get salaries? (2) Who decides how much the salaries will be? And (3) what are the legal limitations, if any, on such salary decisions?

None of the three questions is expressly answered by the MBCA. Section 6.40 deals with "distributions" to shareholders. But a salary for services to the corporation is not a "distribution" as defined in § 1.40(6) ("transfer of money or other property * * * in respect of any of its shares").

More relevant to the question of who decides what salaries a corporation pays to its shareholders is § 8.01, which generally authorizes the board of directors to manage "the business and affairs of the corporation." Please read §§ 8.01 and 7.32.

1. WHO DECIDES WHICH SHAREHOLDERS GET SALARIES?

"A guaranty of employment may have been one of the basic reasons why a minority owner has invested capital in the firm. The minority shareholder typically depends on his salary as the principal return on his investment since the earnings of a close corporation * * * are distributed in major part in salaries, bonus and retirement benefits." Wilkes v. Springside Nursing Home, Inc., 353 N.E.2d 657 (Mass. 1976).

In that case, Wilkes was one of four shareholders of a corporation that owned and operated a nursing home. Initially, all of the shareholders worked at the nursing home and were paid salaries for their work. After a falling out with his fellow shareholders, Wilkes was forced out of his nursing home job and salary by his fellow shareholders.

Wilkes sued the other shareholders, alleging a breach of the fiduciary duty owed to him by the majority shareholders. The Massachusetts court held for Wilkes because the majority had not shown a "legitimate business purpose" in firing Wilkes.

The next case, *Hollis v. Hill*, also involves a shareholder (Hollis) who lost his job and salary with the corporation and who relies on *Wilkes* in suing the shareholder (Hill) who, he argued, oppressed him. In reading the Fifth Circuit's decision, please consider these questions:

1. When he became a shareholder in FFUSA, did the plaintiff Hollis expect that he would have a job with the corporation and receive a salary from FFUSA?

2. Do we know whether Hollis had a contract either with FFUSA or with Hill that provided for such a job and salary?

3. Do we know whether FFUSA needed Hollis to work at the Florida office? Do we know whether FFUSA needed a Florida office? Do we know whether FFUSA needed Hollis to work with Hill at the Texas office? Do we know whether FFUSA needed Hollis to work?

4. What did Hill do wrong?

HOLLIS v. HILL

United States Court of Appeals, Fifth Circuit, 2000
232 F.3d 460

POLITZ, CIRCUIT JUDGE. James P. Hollis seeks a court-ordered buy-out of his 50% interest in a Nevada corporation. The district court found that Dan Hill, holder of the other 50% interest, breached the fiduciary duty he owed to Hollis and ordered a buy-out of Hollis' shares based on the corporation's value more than one year prior to the date of judgment. Hill timely appeals. For the reasons assigned, we affirm in part and vacate and remand in part.

BACKGROUND

In early 1995, Hill and Hollis jointly founded First Financial USA, Inc. (FFUSA), a Nevada corporation which marketed first lien mortgage notes and other non-security financial products. All of the whole mortgage notes placed by FFUSA were obtained from and serviced by South Central

Mortgage.* **[1]** Hill and Hollis also owned equal shares of First Financial United Investments, Ltd., L.L.P. (FFUI), a Texas limited liability partnership organized in June 1996 to sell securities products as a broker/dealer. This action focuses on the parties' rights and obligations respecting FFUSA.

Hill was a 50% owner of FFUSA, was a director and served as its president, and operated its Houston office. He testified his duties were "to set up the company, set up all the administration, hire the personnel, set up the tracking systems, support reps, recruit reps, and generally help in the strategizing of the company's direction." Hollis owned the other 50% interest in FFUSA, was a director and served as its vice president. Hollis operated its Melbourne, Florida office, with duties including recruiting, training and supporting representatives in their marketing efforts, seeking out new revenue sources, and participating in management. Their wives completed the board of directors and were employed by the firm.

From its inception through 1997, FFUSA did very well financially and paid substantial salaries to Hill and Hollis. In early December 1997, however, Hill began to complain that Hollis was not carrying an equal share of the firm's workload and made known his belief that Hollis was getting more money than he deserved. He stopped paying Hollis' salary. Hollis proposed several ways to resolve the dispute, including mediation, relocating to Houston, placing a disinterested person on the board to break the deadlock, or exchanging his interest in FFUI for Hill's interest in FFUSA. Hill rejected all of the proposals. In March 1998, Hill proposed to buy Hollis' interest in FFUSA in exchange for a ten-year, $1.5 million consultant agreement.* **[2]** When Hollis rejected the proposal, Hill threatened to close FFUI and establish his own broker/dealer business.

Meanwhile, Hill took FFUSA's annuity business and, without Hollis' knowledge, placed it into a sole proprietorship called "Dan Hill d.b.a. First Financial U.S.A." Hill explained that this move was in response to a cease and desist letter FFUSA received from the State of Texas prohibiting it, as a corporation not licensed in Texas, from marketing insurance products. Hill, a resident of Texas, created the sole proprietorship so that FFUSA could continue the marketing of insurance products and executed a contemporaneous assignment transferring all accounts of the sole proprietorship back to FFUSA. Hill charged the corporation a fee for providing this "service." He later split this fee with Hollis.

---

* **[1]** Hill explained that FFUSA relied heavily on South Central Mortgage for two reasons: Hill's experience with South Central and his relationship with its president, Todd Etter, persuaded him that the company could be relied upon to service the notes properly. This was particularly important in the event that a note was defaulted. In addition, South Central was among the few firms outsourcing the marketing of its notes. Most other mortgage companies preferred to keep the entire operation in-house by maintaining their own sales forces. As FFUSA was strictly a marketing company, few other firms would complement its business as well as South Central.

* **[2]** A valuation report by Dixon & Company dated December 17, 1997, estimated the company's value to be between $1.3 million and $3.5 million.

Hill also stopped sending FFUSA financial reports to Hollis. On May 11, 1998, Hollis visited the Houston office of FFUSA and FFUI and requested copies of financial reports and other documents. Hill refused, claiming that he and the key Houston office employees had appointments that day and that they did not have time to go over the books with Hollis. Hollis later, through his attorney, asserted his right as a shareholder of FFUSA and limited partner of FFUI to inspect the books and records of the two firms. On the eve of the inspection, Hill and Hollis agreed to negotiate. Hollis testified that the result was an agreement under which Hill would acquire Hollis' interest in FFUI and would draw a salary of $200,000 from FFUSA, and Hollis would draw an annual salary of $120,000 therefrom for encouraging FFUSA's representatives to produce business and for supplying them with the necessary paperwork. Under the agreement, both men retained a 50% interest in FFUSA.

By August 1998, the tension between Hollis and Hill resurfaced. Hill stopped sending company reports to Hollis and unilaterally undertook a number of measures he claims were intended to lower the firm's costs, including reducing officer salaries by 50%. On October 16, 1998, he informed Hollis that he had decided to reduce his own annual salary to $80,000 and would reduce Hollis' salary to zero dollars. In a November 1998 letter, Hill told Hollis that: "[his] position as an inactive officer commands no salary;" phone service in the Florida office would be canceled; and the lease for the Florida office would be terminated. Hollis was informed that he was no longer authorized to use the company cellular phone and that FFUSA would no longer pay the expense of his leased vehicle. Hill terminated the employment of Hollis' wife. Hill significantly reduced costs in the Houston office, as well. He testified that cost cutting measures were necessary because he had received word from Etter that South Central Mortgage would likely not be able to provide FFUSA the steady stream of business it had in the past. He conceded, however, that he had made very little effort to produce new lines of business for FFUSA.

Hollis filed the instant action on December 8, 1998, alleging shareholder oppression. A few weeks later Hill terminated Hollis as vice-president and eliminated all of his company benefits. Hollis continued as corporate secretary, board member, and 50% shareholder. The financial condition of FFUSA worsened and, according to Hill's expert, the firm had decreased in value to $100,000 by May 11, 1999. On April 30, 1999, Hill, acting through his attorney, made an unsuccessful "capital call" on Hollis. [A capital call requires principals to contribute more capital to the business.]

The district court, applying Nevada law, concluded that Hill's conduct was oppressive and ordered him to buy Hollis' shares in FFUSA. The court cited the capital call and the firing of Hollis as the "easiest objective data" supporting the claim of oppression, and added that the "more egregious" act of moving the annuity business to the Hill-sole-proprietorship should not have occurred without the approval of the board of directors. The court also suggested that Hill's interference with the flow of information to Hollis and his threat to start a business that competed with FFUI were oppressive acts.* **[3]** The court ordered Hill to purchase Hollis' shares for $667,950, which represented the value of the corporation on February 28, 1998, the date the court found that the oppression began. Adding attorney's and expert's fees, the total award to Hollis was $792,915. This appeal followed.

ANALYSIS

We apply Texas law in this diversity action. Texas, like most other states, follows the "internal affairs doctrine." That is, the internal affairs of the foreign corporation, "including but not limited to the rights, powers, and duties of its board of directors and shareholders and matters relating to its shares," are governed by the laws of the jurisdiction of incorporation. Nevada corporate law therefore determines the existence and scope of duties between Hollis and Hill. "In order to determine state law, federal courts look to final decisions of the highest court of the state. When there is no ruling by the state's highest court, it is the duty of the federal court to determine as best it can, what the highest court of the state would decide."

Generally, in determining what a state's highest court would hold with respect to a particular issue, "we may consider relevant state precedent, analogous decisions, considered dicta, scholarly works and any other reliable data." In the present situation, however, the most reliable source of assistance, namely dispositive decisions from the Nevada courts, are non-existent. In addition, the corporate law of Nevada gives limited guidance, and determining where the Nevada Supreme Court would look for such guidance on the issues presented herein presents a challenge. We therefore must resolve the questions posed by evaluating the available Nevada case law addressing similar factual scenarios and by looking to other jurisdictions when necessary.

Nearly every state statutorily permits holders of a certain percentage of corporate shares to petition the courts for dissolution under particular enumerated circumstances. Thirty-six states list the oppression of minority shareholders by controlling shareholders as grounds for dissolution. Nevada does not. Hollis, however, has not sought dissolution of FFUSA under Nev.Rev.Stat. § 78.650. Instead, he contended, and the district court found, that Hill's actions amount to a breach of fiduciary duty owed him and that equitable relief is therefore available. Before us, then, is the question whether a duty of loyalty was breached by Hill and, if so, whether the district court erred in granting a retroactive buy-out remedy.

---

* **[3]** In ruling from the bench, the district court opined that the absence of a non-compete agreement was of no consequence and that Hill's actions were subject to the corporate opportunity doctrine. Any finding of the breach of duty of loyalty based on usurpation of a corporate opportunity necessarily related to opportunities available to FFUI. Hollis has made no claims as an FFUI shareholder and has not claimed that Hill usurped a corporate opportunity. The trial court appropriately did not specifically find a violation of the corporate opportunity doctrine. We assume that the district court intended this discussion to support its finding of oppression.

A. *Existence of a Fiduciary Duty*

We find that a fiduciary duty existed between Hollis and Hill. The facts reveal that they agreed to begin a business together, incorporating it under the name FFUSA. They retained equal ownership in the corporation, and became officers and directors, agreeing to the work obligations and salary of the other. With only two shareholders and management responsibilities divided between them, a fiduciary relationship was created not unlike that in a partnership.

We find this case analogous to *Clark v. Lubritz*, [944 P.2d 861 (Nev. 1997)], where five doctors agreed to join their practices to form a preferred provider organization called Nevada Preferred Professionals (NPP). They agreed orally that each would contribute $15,000, and that they would share profits and losses equally. Soon after the agreement, they decided to incorporate.* **[12]** After a dispute over NPP's benefit plan sales, Lubritz resigned as president and director, intending to relegate himself to "just being a stockholder." Over the next four years, he continued to perform limited services for NPP and continued to receive an equal share of the firm's proceeds. In the fifth year, however, the other doctors voted, unbeknownst to Lubritz, to reduce the portion of proceeds distributed to Lubritz while increasing their distributions. When Lubritz learned that he was receiving a lesser share of the firm's profits, he sued. The court found for Lubritz, both on a breach of contract theory, based on the doctors' original oral agreement, and for breach of fiduciary duty, based on the four shareholders' concealment of the unequal distribution of profits.

In *Clark*, despite the incorporation of NPP, the court imposed fiduciary duties between the shareholders akin to [those] of a partnership. The evidence revealed that the doctors continued to treat each other as partners; no actual stock was issued, no annual shareholder meetings were held, officers and directors were not actually elected, and the bylaws were not used in operating NPP. In the case at bar only two shareholders existed, and there appear to have been no shareholder meetings, election of directors, or adherence to by-laws. Thus, the analogy to a partnership seems perhaps even stronger here, and we see no reason why the Nevada Supreme Court would not treat the agreement between Hollis and Hill in the same manner as the agreement in *Clark*.† **[16]**

---

* **[12]** It is unclear from the opinion whether the doctors elected to incorporate as a statutory close corporation under Nev.Rev.Stat. § 78A.020. Nevada, not unlike many other states, allows corporations held by fewer than thirty persons to select a set of special governance rules. It matters not in our analysis of this case, however, because these rules do not alter the fiduciary duties running between corporate participants.

† **[16]** We note that both parties argue over the relevance of Hollis' status as an "equal" rather than "minority" shareholder. We find this distinction immaterial to the present dispute. While we acknowledge that in *Clark* the plaintiff truly was a "minority" shareholder, in the sense that he owned only one-fifth of the stock, we find this difference insignificant in light of Hill's virtually unfettered control of FFUSA. Further, the court in *Clark* never spoke of "minority" shareholder status, partially because it treated the organization as a de facto partnership, but also because the partners who decreased his salary clearly controlled the organization, much like Hill controlled FFUSA in the case at bar. Furthermore, other jurisdictions have agreed that the question of minority versus majority should not focus on mechanical mathematical calculations, but instead,

We find our decision buttressed by the legal authority dealing with close corporations.* **[17]** We concede that many of Hill's alleged "oppressive" acts, including the diminution and eventual termination of salary, the failure to deliver financial information, the closing of one of the company's offices, termination of employment, and the cessation of benefits, are classic examples of acts typically shielded from judicial scrutiny under the business judgment rule. Generally, employees who are adversely affected by such officer and director decisions may not claim oppression by those in control of the corporation, even if they are also shareholders of the corporation.† **[18]** Certain actions by a director, however, receive much different treatment when the corporation only has a few shareholders, including that director.

[handwritten margin note: not consistent with → BJR]

In the context of a closely held corporation, many classic business judgment decisions can also have a substantial and adverse effect on the "minority's" interest as shareholder. Close corporations present unique opportunities for abuse because the expectations of shareholders in closely held corporations ‡ **[19]** are usually different from those of share-holders in public corporations. As a leading commentator has noted:

> Unlike the typical shareholder in a publicly-held corporation, who may be simply an investor or a speculator and does not desire to assume the responsibilities of management, the shareholder in a close corporation considers himself or herself as a co-owner of the business and wants the privileges and powers that go with ownership. Employment by the corporation is often the shareholder's principal or sole source of income. Providing employment may have been the principal reason why the shareholder participated in organizing the corporation. Even if shareholders in a close corporation anticipate an ultimate profit from the sale of shares, they usually expect (or perhaps should expect) to receive an immediate return in the form of salaries as officers or employees of the corporation, rather than in the form of dividends on their stock. Earnings of a close corporation are distributed in major part in salaries, bonuses and retirement benefits.... * **[20]**

"The question is whether they have the power to work their will on others—and whether they have done so improperly."

* **[17]** FFUSA was not incorporated as a close corporation, but, * * * this does not affect our analysis in the instant action. Relevant references herein to "close corporation" also mean "closely held" corporation.

† **[18]** As one court has observed, "a 'fiduciary' duty to every baggage handler at United Airlines just because the employee owns a share of stock would put employee-owned firms at such a competitive disadvantage that they would soon collapse." *Nagy v. Riblet Products Corp.*, 79 F.3d 572, 577 (7th Cir.1996).

‡ **[19]** Closely held corporations are characterized by a small number of stockholders, the absence of a ready market for the corporate stock, and substantial majority stockholder participation in the management, direction, and operation of the company. *Donahue v. Rodd Electrotype Co.*, 367 Mass. 578, 328 N.E.2d 505 (1975).

* **[20]** F. Hodge O'Neal & Robert B. Thompson, 1 O'Neal's Close Corporations § 1:08, at 31–32 (3d ed. 1998).

In this setting, it is not difficult for a controlling stockholder to frustrate such expectations and deny a return on investment through means that would otherwise be legitimate.† **[21]**

For this reason, a number of jurisdictions, including Massachusetts in the landmark case *Donahue v. Rodd Electrotype Co.*, have held that the duty existing between controlling and minority shareholders in close corporations is the same as the duty existing between partners.‡ **[23]** In *Donahue*, the court required a majority shareholder, whose shares were purchased by the corporation, to make available to the minority an equal opportunity to sell a ratable number of shares to the corporation at an identical price. While *Donahue's* equal opportunity principle has been rejected by some courts, its recognition of special rules of fiduciary duty applicable to close corporations has gained widespread acceptance.

We find that because FFUSA bore all the traditional characteristics of a close corporation, although not formally incorporated as such, the reasoning behind placing a fiduciary duty on controlling shareholders applies to these facts. Both Hill and Hollis began the organization in order to participate personally in its management, and made money principally through salaries as officers. There is no evidence that either received large dividends or sought to benefit from the sale of his interest. We thus find close corporation jurisprudence an equally persuasive basis for imposing a fiduciary duty on Hill and for finding that he breached that duty. Further, as noted above, in *Clark* the Nevada Supreme Court applied to the doctor shareholders the fiduciary duty applicable to partners rather than the duty of loyalty that applies to corporate actors. Whether couched in terms of a de facto partnership or a close corporation, *Clark* provides a strong indication that the Nevada Supreme Court would find fiduciary obligations between shareholders in a corporation such as FFUSA operated by shareholder-directors. * * *

We * * * decline Hill's invitation to apply the law of Delaware. While mindful of the cases cited by Hill where courts applying Nevada law have looked to Delaware on unrelated issues of corporate law, we conclude that cases such as *Clark* remain a better indication of the Nevada court's position with respect to issues involving close and closely held corporations. The opinions of the Delaware courts are often influential in matters of corporate law, but no more so in Nevada than any of the other states that have followed *Donahue*.* **[28]**

---

† **[21]** It is not critical that Hill and Hollis each owned 50% of FFUSA and therefore neither was a majority shareholder. A fiduciary duty exists between shareholders by virtue of the fact that one of the shareholders has control over the corporation's assets. Indeed, a duty has been found to run from the minority to the majority where the minority shareholder had veto power over corporate action. Hill acknowledges that he had control over FFUSA.

‡ **[23]** The Massachusetts court borrowed this oft-quoted statement from then-Chief Judge Cardozo: "Joint adventurers, like copartners, owe to one another, while the enterprise continues, the duty of the finest loyalty. Many forms of conduct permissible in a workaday world for those acting at arm's length, are forbidden to those bound by fiduciary ties ... Not honesty alone, but the punctilio of an honor the most sensitive, is then the standard of behavior." Id. at 516 (quoting *Meinhard v. Salmon*, 164 N.E. 545 (N.Y. 1928)).

* **[28]** While it is true that some of the Delaware opinions, most notably *Nixon v. Blackwell*, 626 A.2d 1366 (Del.1993), contain very forceful dicta indicating that Delaware is likely not to

Nor do we accept Hill's suggestion that our analysis should reflect Nevada's desire to provide management-friendly corporate law. If indeed that is Nevada's desire, it would not necessarily be furthered in the context of the close or closely held corporation where disputes typically pit manager/share-holder against manager/shareholder.

B.   Breach of Fiduciary Duty

Convinced of the existence of a fiduciary duty between shareholders in a close corporation, we turn to the scope of that duty and examine whether Hill breached his duty in the case at bar. As previously noted, the scope of this fiduciary duty has varied among the jurisdictions which have adopted *Donahue*. One context in which the scope has been frequently litigated has been with regard to salary and employment decisions. Again, Nevada has not addressed this issue and we must look to the law of other jurisdictions for guidance.

In another landmark Massachusetts case, *Wilkes v. Springside Nursing Home*, four associates formed a corporation in 1951 for the purpose of operating a nursing home. Each paid in $100 with the understanding that each of them would be a director and would participate in the management of the corporation. The corporation paid no dividends, but by 1955 each was receiving $100 per week as salary. When relations became strained between Wilkes and one of the other investors, Wilkes declared his intention to sell his shares. The other three board members met, eliminated Wilkes' salary, declined to reelect him as director, and terminated his employment with the corporation.

The Massachusetts court reiterated that, under *Donahue*, shareholders in close corporations owe each other a duty of utmost good faith and loyalty. It curtailed *Donahue's* equal opportunity rule by holding that the duty was not breached if the majority acted pursuant to a legitimate business purpose. In order to avoid hampering management's effectiveness in operating the corporation, the court reasoned, such a rule was necessary in order to preserve management's discretion in declaring dividends, negotiating mergers, establishing the salaries of officers, dismissing directors, and hiring and firing of employees. The court also held that when a legitimate business purpose exists, the minority shareholder must be given an opportunity to demonstrate that the purpose could have been achieved through means less disruptive to its shareholder interests. The court found that the majority shareholders of Springside lacked a legitimate business purpose for ousting Wilkes, and found that the duty they owed Wilkes had been breached for several reasons. The company had a longstanding policy that each investor would be a director in the corporation and that employment would go hand-in-hand with stock ownership. Wilkes was one of the company's four founders and had invested time and capital with the expectation that he would continue to

___

apply heightened fiduciary duties to participants in close corporations, the Delaware Supreme Court has yet to consider the precise issue in this case, namely whether a controlling shareholder is liable for actions taken with the purpose and effect of freezing out another shareholder.

participate in its management. Perhaps most importantly, eliminating Wilkes' salary, in combination with the fact that the corporation never declared a dividend, guaranteed that he would not obtain a return on his investment. These facts led the court to infer a design to pressure Wilkes to sell his shares at a price below their value.

That a controlling shareholder cannot, consistent with his fiduciary duty, effectively deprive a minority shareholder of his interest as a shareholder by terminating the latter's employment or salary has been widely accepted. The states considering the issue directly essentially have adopted the approach of *Wilkes*. In addition, shareholder oppression under the dissolution statutes, which is often defined in the same terms as the fiduciary duty between shareholders, frequently has been found under circumstances similar to those described in *Wilkes*. The opinions make clear, however, that shareholders do not enjoy fiduciary-rooted entitlements to their jobs. Such a result would clearly interfere with the doctrine of employment-at-will. Rather, the courts have limited relief to instances in which the shareholder has been harmed as a shareholder. The fiduciary duty in the close corporation context, as in the context of public corporations, appropriately is viewed as a protection of the shareholder's investment. The precise nature of an investment in a close corporation often is not clear, particularly when the shareholder is also an employee. It is therefore important to distinguish investors who obtain their return on investment through benefits provided to them as employees from employees who happen also to be investors. To that end, courts may consider the following non-exclusive factors: whether the corporation typically distributes its profits in the form of salaries; whether the shareholder/employee owns a significant percentage of the firm's shares; whether the shareholder/employee is a founder of the business; whether the shares were received as compensation for services; whether the shareholder/employee expects the value of the shares to increase; whether the share-holder/employee has made a significant capital contribution; whether the shareholder/employee has otherwise demonstrated a reasonable expectation that the returns from the investment will be obtained through continued employment; and whether stock ownership is a requirement of employment. The minority's shareholder interest is not injured, however, if the corporation redeems shares at a fair price or a price determined by prior contract or the shareholder is otherwise able to obtain a fair price.

Overlaying these factors to the relevant facts at bar, we conclude that Hollis demonstrated an injury as a shareholder. He was a founder and 50% shareholder of FFUSA. His positions as vice president and director clearly resulted therefrom. He had no reason to expect he would be able to sell his FFUSA shares for a higher price, meaning that the value of his investment was tied directly to his employment. The benefits he received from his investment were distributed in the form of salary and certain perquisites; the firm never declared a dividend and paid no salary to its directors. Hill totally deprived Hollis of those benefits by terminating his employment and salary, closing the Florida office, and cutting him off from company benefits. As a result, Hollis' shares in FFUSA were rendered worthless. No offer was made by the corporation to purchase Hollis' shares at a fair price upon termination, and Hollis did not have the option of selling his shares to another buyer.

C. Remedy

The district court found Hill liable for breach of his fiduciary duty and ordered a buy-out of Hollis' shares. The court determined that Hill began his oppressive conduct on February 28, 1998, and thus ordered the buy-out as of that date, calculating the value of the shares at $667,950. While we essentially agree with the district court's remedial approach, we conclude that its decision to backdate the buy-out to February 28 is clear error. * * *

Although Hollis' relationship with Hill began to decline significantly in February 1998, many of the actions upon which we base our finding of oppression occurred after this date. Hollis continued to receive his agreed upon salary until September of 1998, when it was reduced by 50%. His salary was not reduced to zero until October of 1998. Hill's unilateral decision to close the Florida office, discontinue the car lease payments, and terminate phone service was not communicated to Hollis until November of 1998. Hollis' original complaint was filed in the district court in December of 1998. As an equal shareholder, [Hollis] commanded as much authority to assert control over the corporation as did [Hill]. His failure to act on this authority until December of 1998 was his choice. The presumptive valuation date for other states allowing buy-out remedies is the date of filing unless exceptional circumstances exist which require an earlier or later date to be chosen. No such circumstances exist in this case. Therefore, we conclude that the date of valuation for the court ordered buy-out should be the date suit was filed herein. Use of this date will take into consideration all of Hill and Hollis' actions, inactions, and prudent and imprudent business decisions which affected the value of the business during the intervening period.

We therefore vacate the calculation of the value of Hollis' shares by the district court and remand for further proceedings to determine the proper valuation of Hollis' shares consistent herewith. We likewise vacate the award of attorneys' fees and the fees of expert witnesses, and remand for reconsideration of those settings in light of relevant Nevada law. In all other respects, the decision appealed is affirmed.

* * * * *

E. Grady Jolly, Circuit Judge, dissenting. Because I find that the cause of action and remedy here would not be adopted by Nevada courts, I respectfully dissent.

The question that needs to be answered in this case, whether framed as a breach of fiduciary duty or a statutory right, is whether Nevada recognizes a cause of action for oppression of minority shareholders. I find no basis to conclude that it does. The Nevada dissolution statute, Nev.Rev.

Stat. § 78.650, sets out a statutory basis for the remedy effectively imposed here, and the statute does not allow dissolution for the oppression of minority stockholders. The Nevada case cited to justify the extension of fiduciary duty to cover shareholder oppression, *Clark v. Lubritz*, treated the business as a partnership because the parties treated the corporation as a partnership. To follow *Clark* here, where there is nothing in the past history* or present arrangement indicating that the parties have treated the business as anything other than a corporation, effectively finds that Nevada will ignore corporate structure, when, on a case-by-case basis, equity justifies it.

Furthermore, all indications are that Nevada attempts to pattern its corporate law after the management-friendly approach of Delaware, a state that clearly prohibits a cause of action for oppression of minority shareholders. *See Nixon v. Blackwell*, 626 A.2d 1366, 1380–81 (Del.1993) (finding that majority shareholders owe no special fiduciary duties to minority shareholders). Even if Nevada is not as friendly to corporate structures and management as Delaware, there is no basis to find that Nevada would adopt the law of Massachusetts, which seems to be at the other end of the spectrum respecting corporate formalities. In sum, I am convinced that, given the general acknowledgment that Nevada is corporate friendly, as shown through its statutory dissolution provision and its tendency to follow Delaware law, the cause of action and remedy here would not be recognized. I therefore respectfully dissent.

QUESTIONS AND NOTE

1.   At the time of the litigation, FFUSA's only office was in Houston. FFUSA was incorporated in Nevada. Why was FFUSA incorporated in Nevada? Why does Judge Politz, who is from Louisiana, rely on Massachusetts law? Why does Judge Jolly, who is from Mississippi, rely on Delaware law?

2.   The plaintiff Hollis was a 50% shareholder. The defendant Hill was a 50% shareholder. Hill, Hollis, and their wives were the four directors of FFUSA. Why was Hill able to make decisions for FFUSA?

3.   Did Hollis have a legal right to receive the same salary from FFUSA as Hill? Would Hollis be able to compel Hill to buy his stock if Hollis's salary was $200,000 and Hill's salary was only $120,000? What if Hollis's salary was $100,000 and Hill's salary was $20,000? [handwritten: > Salary does not matter]

4.   Is this decision consistent with the business judgment rule? With the "legitimate business purpose" rule of *Donahue* and *Wilkes*?

5.   If you were representing the defendant in the appeal to the Fifth Circuit, how would you have distinguished *Clark* (the doctors' case)? How about *Wilkes* (the nursing home case)?

6.   Two professors are critical of the decision in the *Wilkes* nursing home case:

---

* Note from your authors: Why do people say "past history?" What other kind of history is there? Think carefully about the words you use; they are your most important tool as a lawyer.

Could the other shareholders in Wilkes have been behaving opportunistically? Could they have terminated Wilkes' relationship with the firm in order to expropriate his investment, considering that he had already committed whatever special skills and knowledge he possessed? Absolutely. Opportunistic behavior is clearly possible in such circumstances. Yet that alone is not sufficient to justify the court's response, which was namely a case-by-case analysis of terminations to determine if the firm acted with a "legitimate business purpose" and with no "less harmful alternatives." That is the same as stating that because opportunistic behavior is possible in the employment relationship, a court should scrutinize each termination to see if it was for just cause.

The *Wilkes* case is a good example of the difficulties courts have with the employment issues that frequently overlay close corporation cases. For example, was the court correct in saying that there was no legitimate business purpose in terminating Wilkes' employment? On the one hand, we are told that there was no misconduct and that Wilkes "had always accomplished his assigned share of the duties competently." The court, however, made no attempt to determine whether Wilkes' services were still needed. Apparently he was not replaced, suggesting overstaffing. By not appreciating the norms of the employment relation, the court stumbled badly, inferring a right to continued employment, subject only to proof of misconduct. Such a right is so far at variance with employment practice anywhere that its insertion in the case undermines the logical application of the legitimate business purpose standard.

Edward B. Rock & Michael L. Wachter, *Waiting for the Omelet To Set: Match–Specific Assets and Minority Oppression in Close Corporations,* 24 J.CORP.L. 913, 933–34 (1999).

2.   WHAT ARE THE LEGAL LIMITATIONS ON SALARIES?

The MBCA and other state corporate codes do not set limits on the salaries that a corporation pays its officers or directors. Federal income tax law, however, does limit the amount of salary payment that a corporation can deduct as an ordinary and necessary business expense.

Recall that a corporation is a separate taxpayer. It must pay taxes on its income after deducting its ordinary and necessary business expenses.* Salaries can be a reasonable and necessary business expense. In contrast, dividends and other distributions to shareholders cannot be claimed as an ordinary and necessary business expense tax deduction.

Accordingly, there can be a strong tax incentive for corporations to set salaries to shareholders as high as possible. So the Internal Revenue Service has a strong incentive to review the reasonableness of salaries that corporations pay to shareholders. With regard to the next case, consider the following:

---

* An exception to this rule is the S Corporation, mentioned briefly in Chapter 1, which enjoys flow-through taxation, like a partnership.

1. Whose money is being used to pay Heitz's salary?

2. Who approved Heitz's salary?

3. Are any of the shareholders receiving a salary from the corporation?

4. Are the shareholders receiving dividends from the corporation?

EXACTO SPRING CORP. v. COMMISSIONER OF INTERNAL REVENUE

United States Court of Appeals, Seventh Circuit, 1999
196 F.3d 833

POSNER, CHIEF JUDGE. This appeal from a judgment by the Tax Court requires us to interpret and apply 26 U.S.C. § 162(a)(1), which allows a business to deduct from its income its "ordinary and necessary" business expenses, including a "reasonable allowance for salaries or other compensation for personal services actually rendered." In 1993 and 1994, Exacto Spring Corporation, a closely held corporation engaged in the manufacture of precision springs, paid its cofounder, chief executive, and principal owner, William Heitz, $1.3 and $1.0 million, respectively, in salary. The Internal Revenue Service thought this amount excessive, that Heitz should not have been paid more than $381,000 in 1993 or $400,000 in 1994, with the difference added to the corporation's income, and it assessed a deficiency accordingly, which Exacto challenged in the Tax Court. That court found that the maximum reasonable compensation for Heitz would have been $900,000 in the earlier year and $700,000 in the later one—figures roughly midway between his actual compensation and the IRS's determination—and Heitz has appealed.

In reaching its conclusion, the Tax Court applied a test that requires the consideration of seven factors, none entitled to any specified weight relative to another. The factors are, in the court's words, "(1) the type and extent of the services rendered; (2) the scarcity of qualified employees; (3) the qualifications and prior earning capacity of the employee; (4) the contributions of the employee to the business venture; (5) the net earnings of the employer; (6) the prevailing compensation paid to employees with comparable jobs; and (7) the peculiar characteristics of the employer's business." 75 T.C.M. at 2525. It is apparent that this test, though it or variants of it (one of which has the astonishing total of 21 factors) are encountered in many cases, leaves much to be desired—being, like many other multi-factor tests, "redundant, incomplete, and unclear."

To begin with, it is nondirective. No indication is given of how the factors are to be weighed in the event they don't all line up on one side. And many of the factors, such as the type and extent of services rendered, the scarcity of qualified employees, and the peculiar characteristics of the employer's business, are vague.

Second, the factors do not bear a clear relation either to each other or to the primary purpose of section 162(a)(1), which is to prevent dividends (or in some cases gifts), which are not deductible from corporate income, from being disguised as salary, which is. Suppose that an employee who let us say was, like Heitz, a founder and the chief executive officer and principal owner of the taxpayer rendered no services at all but received a huge salary. It would be absurd to allow the whole or for that matter any part of his salary to be deducted as an ordinary and necessary business expense even if he were well qualified to be CEO of the company, the company had substantial net earnings, CEOs of similar companies were paid a lot, and it was a business in which high salaries are common. The multifactor test would not prevent the Tax Court from allowing a deduction in such a case even though the corporation obviously was seeking to reduce its taxable income by disguising earnings as salary. The court would not allow the deduction, but not because of anything in the multifactor test; rather because it would be apparent that the payment to the employee was not in fact for his services to the company.

Third, the seven-factor test invites the Tax Court to set itself up as a superpersonnel department for closely held corporations, a role unsuitable for courts. The judges of the Tax Court are not equipped by training or experience to determine the salaries of corporate officers; no judges are.

Fourth, since the test cannot itself determine the outcome of a dispute because of its nondirective character, it invites the making of arbitrary decisions based on uncanalized discretion or unprincipled rules of thumb. The Tax Court in this case essentially added the IRS's determination of the maximum that Mr. Heitz should have been paid in 1993 and 1994 to what he was in fact paid, and divided the sum by two. It cut the baby in half. One would have to be awfully naive to believe that the seven-factor test generated this pleasing symmetry.

Fifth, because the reaction of the Tax Court to a challenge to the deduction of executive compensation is unpredictable, corporations run unavoidable legal risks in determining a level of compensation that may be indispensable to the success of their business. * * *

Finally, under factor (7) ("peculiar characteristics"), the court first and rightly brushed aside the IRS's argument that the low level of dividends paid by Exacto (zero in the two years at issue, but never very high) was evidence that the corporation was paying Heitz dividends in the form of salary. The court pointed out that shareholders may not want dividends. They may prefer the corporation to retain its earnings, causing the value of the corporation to rise and thus enabling the shareholders to obtain corporate earnings in the form of capital gains taxed at a lower rate than ordinary income. The court also noted that while Heitz, as the owner of 55 percent of Exacto's common stock, obviously was in a position to influence his salary, the corporation's two other major shareholders, each with 20 percent of the stock, had approved it. They had not themselves been paid a salary or other compensation, and are not relatives of Heitz; they had no financial or other incentive to allow Heitz to siphon off dividends in the form of salary. * * *

* * * The Internal Revenue Code limits the amount of salary that a corporation can deduct from its income primarily in order to prevent the corporation from eluding the corporate income tax by paying dividends but calling them salary because salary is deductible and dividends are not. (Perhaps they should be, to avoid double taxation of corporate earnings, but that is not the law.) In the case of a publicly-held company, where the salaries of the highest executives are fixed by a board of directors that those executives do not control, the danger of siphoning corporate earnings to executives in the form of salary is not acute. The danger is much greater in the case of a closely held corporation, in which ownership and management tend to coincide; unfortunately, as the opinion of the Tax Court in this case illustrates, judges are not competent to decide what business executives are worth.

There is, fortunately, an indirect market test, as recognized by the Internal Revenue Service's expert witness. A corporation can be conceptualized as a contract in which the owner of assets hires a person to manage them. The owner pays the manager a salary and in exchange the manager works to increase the value of the assets that have been entrusted to his management; that increase can be expressed as a rate of return to the owner's investment. The higher the rate of return (adjusted for risk) that a manager can generate, the greater the salary he can command. If the rate of return is extremely high, it will be difficult to prove that the manager is being overpaid, for it will be implausible that if he quit if his salary was cut, and he was replaced by a lower-paid manager, the owner would be better off; it would be killing the goose that lays the golden egg. The Service's expert believed that investors in a firm like Exacto would expect a 13 percent return on their investment. Presumably they would be delighted with more. They would be overjoyed to receive a return more than 50 percent greater than they expected—and 20 percent, the return that the Tax Court found that investors in Exacto had obtained, is more than 50 percent greater than the benchmark return of 13 percent.

When, notwithstanding the CEO's "exorbitant" salary (as it might appear to a judge or other modestly paid official), the investors in his company are obtaining a far higher return than they had any reason to expect, his salary is presumptively reasonable. We say "presumptively" because we can imagine cases in which the return, though very high, is not due to the CEO's exertions. Suppose Exacto had been an unprofitable company that suddenly learned that its factory was sitting on an oil field, and when oil revenues started to pour in its owner raised his salary from $50,000 a year to $1.3 million. The presumption of reasonableness would be rebutted. There is no suggestion of anything of that sort here and likewise no suggestion that Mr. Heitz was merely the titular chief executive and the company was actually run by someone else, which would be another basis for rebuttal.

The government could still have prevailed by showing that while Heitz's salary may have been no greater than would be reasonable in the circumstances, the company did not in fact intend to pay him that amount as salary, that his salary really did include a concealed dividend though it need not have. This is material (and the "independent investor" test, like the multifactor test that it replaces, thus incomplete, though invaluable) because any business expense to be deductible must be, as we noted earlier, a bona fide expense as well as reasonable in amount. The fact that Heitz's salary was approved by the other owners of the corporation, who had no incentive to disguise a dividend as salary, goes far to rebut any inference of bad faith here, which in any event the Tax Court did not draw and the government does not ask us to draw.

The judgment is reversed with directions to enter judgment for the taxpayer.

QUESTIONS

1.   What is the "danger that is much greater in the case of a closely held corporation in which ownership and management tend to coincide"?

2.   If the other shareholders of Exacto Spring Corporation are not receiving salaries or dividends from the corporation, how are they making money from their ownership of the business?

3.   How did the Internal Revenue Service's expert witness determine that 13% is a reasonable return for Exacto's investors? How did the Court determine that Exacto's stockholders had received a 20% return on their investment? How important are such determinations in applying the holding in this case?

———

One can understand why shareholders of a closely held corporation who do not have jobs with the corporation might object if high salaries are paid to other shareholders. We also understand that these shareholders would prefer that the same sum be distributed in the form of a dividend to all shareholders (even though the tax obligations of the corporation might thereby be higher). The next case involves such an objection. In reading the case, consider the following:

1.   Who set the salaries that the corporation paid the defendants?

2.   Were the defendants both officers and directors?

3.   What did the plaintiffs ask the court to do?

4.   Who made money as a result of the court's ruling in this case?

GIANNOTTI v. HAMWAY

Supreme Court of Virginia, 1990
387 S.E.2d 725

COMPTON, JUSTICE. In this intracorporate dispute arising in a close corporation, we examine the correctness of the trial court's decision to order liquidation of the corporate assets and business.

Because this suit was filed in 1980, former Code § 13.1–94 (Repl.Vol. 1978) (now Code § 13.1–747) applies. As pertinent to the controversy, the statute provided:

> Any court of record, with general equity jurisdiction ..., shall have full power to liquidate the assets and business of [a] corporation ...:
>
> (a) In an action by a stockholder when it is established:
> * * *
>
> (2) That the acts of the directors or those in control of the corporation are illegal, oppressive or fraudulent; or * * *
>
> (4) That the corporate assets are being misapplied or wasted.

In September 1980, appellees Alexander Hamway, Leroy Steiner, and Louis Adelman filed a bill of complaint against Libbie Rehabilitation Center, Inc. (Libbie), Frank R. Giannotti, Alex Grossman, Henry C. Miller, Ernest H. Dervishian, and Lewis T. Cowardin (defendants). The plaintiffs asserted that Libbie was a duly organized Virginia corporation and that the defendants were directors of Libbie holding the following offices: Giannotti–Chairman of the Board and Chief Executive Officer; Grossman–President; Miller–Vice President; Dervishian–Secretary and Corporate Attorney; and, Cowardin–Treasurer. The corporation was engaged in the development and operation of nursing homes.

The plaintiffs also asserted that the defendants, either individually or through corporations they controlled, owned or controlled a majority of the 209,054 shares of the then outstanding Libbie common stock. The plaintiffs also alleged that they were minority stockholders owning a total of approximately 74,500 shares of Libbie common stock. * * *

The plaintiffs specifically charged defendants with authorizing and making payments from corporate funds to themselves for directors' fees and officers' salaries "grossly in excess of the value of the services they have rendered to Libbie." * * *

Plaintiffs also charged that defendants, acting in bad faith, had "refused to declare dividends on Libbie common stock which, with due regard to the condition of the property and affairs of Libbie, should have been declared." * * *

Asserting that they were "unable to prevent the continuing oppression, * * * mismanagement, waste and self-dealing practiced by the defendants," plaintiffs asked the court, pursuant to Code §§ 13.1–94 and –95, to appoint a receiver pending the suit, to require defendants, "jointly and severally to restore to Libbie such funds as have been misspent or lost by Libbie as a result of their oppressive acts, and mismanagement, breach of fiduciary duty and improper self-dealing," and to "order the liquidation of the assets and business of Libbie."

The defendants filed a demurrer and answer to the bill, generally contending that the plaintiffs had not alleged any facts which would support their prayer for relief and specifically denying the allegations of wrongful conduct. [The court overruled the demurrer and the litigation continued.]

The trial eventually was held and the chancellor heard evidence *ore tenus* [that's what Virginia courts say when they want to tell us that the witnesses testified orally (rather than having their depositions read by the judge)] for 20 days from November 1985 to February 1986. The parties submitted proposed findings of fact and conclusions of law to the trial court in April 1986. The plaintiffs filed 265 proposals; the defendants filed 153. In November 1987, the chancellor announced his decision by letter opinion, finding in favor of the plaintiffs and ordering dissolution of the corporation. The trial court refused plaintiffs' request to order the defendants to restore certain assets to the corporation. These rulings were incorporated in a February 1988 final decree in which the court appointed a receiver to liquidate the corporate assets. * * *

The evidence relating to excessive compensation focused on officers' salaries, directors' fees, bonuses, expense allowances, and other payments, all authorized by the recipients. * * *

The plaintiffs' evidence of inadequate dividends showed that from June 1975 through September 30, 1985, defendants' compensation totalled $2,799,006 while during the same period the plaintiffs received $50,000 of $132,000 in common stock dividends. The plaintiffs showed that after-tax profits during the period amounted to $1,042,350, which, according to plaintiffs, meant that for every dollar of profit earned, defendants received $2.67 in compensation. This comparison, the plaintiffs urged, did not take into account an additional $1.4 million attributable to unnecessary loan and interest costs incurred in order to enable those payments to be made to defendants. The plaintiffs claimed that when profits are compared to the total cost of compensation, the ratio of compensation to profits is 4 to 1. * * *

The trial court found "that plaintiffs have borne their burden as to the substance of their claims," relying principally on the testimony of the administrators of each of the three Libbie facilities "as most telling regarding the lack of sufficient work and supervision to justify officer salaries, fees and other benefits." * * *

Finally, the chancellor made the specific finding "that defendants by their actions have been oppressive to the minority plaintiff shareholders in breach of their fiduciary duties in their capacity as majority controllers of the corporation by effectively freezing out plaintiffs from a reasonable opportunity to receive a reasonable return on their investment given the financial condition of the corporation during the period." * * *

As used in § 13.1–94, "oppressive" means conduct by corporate managers toward stockholders which departs from the standards of fair dealing and violates the principles of fair play on which persons who entrust their funds to a corporation are entitled to rely. The term does not mean that a corporate disaster may be imminent and does not necessarily mean fraudulent conduct. Indeed, "oppressive" is not synonymous with the statutory terms "illegal" or "fraudulent." The term can contemplate a continuous course of conduct and includes a lack of probity in corporate affairs to the prejudice of some of its shareholders.

A corporate officer has the same duties of fidelity in dealing with the corporation that arise in dealings between a trustee and a beneficiary of the trust. Thus, "a director of a private corporation cannot directly or indirectly, in any transaction in which he is under a duty to guard the interests of the corporation, acquire any personal advantage, or make any profit for himself, and if he does so, he may be compelled to account therefor to the corporation." * * *

Courts are hesitant to question the reasonableness of a corporate officer's compensation when it is set by a disinterested board. However, as in this case, where the directors of a close corporation elect themselves as officers and set their own salaries, and they are all accused of combining to fix excessive salaries for each other, it is impossible to have a "disinterested board."

Further, when a plaintiff "demonstrates that a director had an interest in the transaction at issue, the burden shifts to the director to prove that the transaction was fair and reasonable to the corporation." In defendants' words, they "have not contested in this appeal that the ultimate burden of proof lies with them on the issue of the reasonableness of compensation."

Against the background of these settled principles, our study of this record convinces us that the chancellor's findings of fact are neither plainly wrong nor without evidence to support them. Indeed, there is abundant, credible evidence to support the trial court's conclusions that defendants engaged in oppressive conduct and that they misapplied and wasted corporate assets. * * *

The defendants came to the Libbie enterprise with few qualifications to operate a nursing home. Giannotti had been a carpet and tile retailer, Grossman a pharmacist, Miller a retired real estate developer, Dervishian a lawyer, and Cowardin a retail jeweler. While Giannotti and Dervishian had operated a small nursing home in the city of Richmond for a while before becoming associated with Libbie, none of the defendants, either by education or training, had any expertise in the operation of nursing homes.

The nature, extent, and scope of defendants' work in attending to corporate affairs were very limited. Giannotti was the main actor in directing the affairs of Libbie, although he principally was involved in approving administrators' decisions regarding the day-to-day operation of the facilities. While Grossman received compensation from all three facilities, his activities were limited almost exclusively to Libbie Convalescent. Miller had few work responsibilities. Dervishian's role was limited. He was a friend and advisor of Giannotti, but his corporate responsibilities were duplicated by his assignments as general counsel. Cowardin, Libbie's finance officer, demonstrated no knowledge of the Medicare and Medicaid programs, the principal sources of Libbie's income. While he claimed to have spent 20–25 hours per week on his corporate duties, about 50 percent of a normal 40–hour work week, Cowardin reported on tax returns for his jewelry business that he spent 90 percent of his working time in that business for its fiscal years ending in 1978 and 1979; 80 percent of his time during fiscal 1980, 1981, and 1983; 75 percent of his time during fiscal 1984; and 40 percent of his time in 1985. From the standpoint of hours worked for Libbie, defendants were part-time employees with significant outside business interests.

The difficulties of the business can justify officers' and directors' compensation. But, the complexities of nursing home operation were handled by the administrators of Libbie's facilities. The respective parties offered expert testimony on the reasonableness of the compensation, which included comparisons with amounts paid to officers in similar businesses. The credibility of defendants' main expert was challenged, and the trial court accepted the opinion of one of plaintiffs' experts that "the work that was performed was not of sufficient scope and complexity to justify the salary, bonuses, fringe benefits and other compensation which was paid to these individuals." According to another plaintiffs' expert, five men were performing management functions that could have been per-formed by one individual.

Defendants rely heavily on Libbie's purported success in attempting to convince us that they sustained their burden of proving that the compensation was reasonable. The defendants offered evidence comparing their salary and efforts with two other nursing homes in Central Virginia. The comparison showed, however, that Libbie has not been operated profitably by the standards of the other homes upon which defendants relied. During the period of 1980 to 1985, the average, before-tax profit per bed was $2,009 in one case and $2,975 in another. During the same period, Libbie's profits were $1,107 per bed. The trial court was justified in finding, under the evidence as a whole, that Libbie would have been more profitable except for the excessive compensation extracted from the corporation by defendants. * * *

Having concluded that the chancellor did not err in finding defendants guilty of oppressive conduct, which involved misapplication and waste of corporate funds, including failure to pay adequate dividends, we turn to the correctness of the relief awarded below. Defendants argue that the "corporate death penalty" should not be imposed on a viable, solvent corporation.

As the trial court recognized, courts generally should be reluctant to order liquidation of a functioning corporation at the instance of minority stockholders. However, the General Assembly has cloaked courts of equity with, in the words of the statute, "full power" to liquidate in a proper case where oppressive conduct has been established. The remedy specified by the legislature, while discretionary, is "exclusive," and does not permit the trial court to fashion other, apparently equitable remedies. Because the trial court's finding of oppression in this case is not plainly wrong or without evidence to support it, we cannot say, under these circumstances, that the court abused its discretion in decreeing dissolution. * * *

This brings us to the assignments of cross-error. Plaintiffs contend that the trial court erred in refusing to require defendants to restore corporate funds which the court found the defendants had misapplied or wasted. * * *

We hold that the trial court did not err in refusing to require restoration of funds at this stage of the proceeding. Former Code § 13.1–95 (1978 Repl.Vol.) (now, in substance, § 13.1–748) prescribes the procedure to be employed after dissolution has been decreed under the judicial dissolution statute and allows the liquidating receiver to maintain suits in his name as receiver of the corporation. Indeed, the final decree in this case empowers the receiver "to institute and prosecute all suits as may be necessary ... to collect the ... obligations due to Libbie." And, defendants represent on brief that this receiver, relying on the trial court's findings of excessive compensation and improper related party transactions, instituted an action against them in May 1988 seeking to recover certain sums. * * *

Accordingly, we hold that the assignments of cross-error have no merit. For these reasons, the final decree of the trial court will be affirmed and the cause will be remanded for the court to supervise the liquidation as provided in its decree.

     * * * * *

GORDON, JUSTICE (RETIRED), dissenting. To liquidate the corporation is to kill the goose that laid the golden egg. The history, as shown by the record, since the individual defendants assumed control proves the point:

Financial Data	1975	1985	Percentage Increase
Total Assets	$1,720,076	$6,392,997	272%
Current Ratio	1.31	2.64	
Total Operating Revenues	1,514,686	6,807,902	349%
Retained Earnings	181,984	922,473	406%
Common Stockholders Equity	602,363	1,274,851	112%
Book Value of Common Stock	2.41	5.85	143%
Net Income Before Taxes	150,000	330,000	220%
Net Income After Taxes	89,473	191,407	114%

During the period, the corporation opened additional facilities, requiring the expenditure of substantial sums. Bed capacity increased from 195 to 443.

Neither the corporation nor the plaintiff-stockholders have suffered from oppressive actions by the defendants. The record discloses that the plaintiff-stockholders have suffered only the usual and legal burdens borne by minority stockholders.

The complainants rely on the individual defendants' failure to declare dividends as a ground for liquidation. In *Penn v. Pemberton & Penn*, 53 S.E.2d 823 ([Va.] 1949) (affirming the trial court's refusal to order liquidation under a statute then in force), the Court said:

> The general rule is that in the absence of a special contract or statute the board of directors, in its discretion, determines whether to declare dividends on the stock, or to apply the earnings and surplus to operating capital, or to some other corporate purpose. If the directors act in good faith, a court of equity usually will not interfere with the exercise of their discretion. However, if the action of the board in refusing to declare a dividend when there are sufficient earnings or surplus not necessarily needed in the business, is so arbitrary, or so unreasonable, as to amount to a breach of trust, such action is subject to judicial review. * * *

The complainants' remedy here (if any) is the enforced declaration of a dividend, not liquidation. But in view of the expanded corporate business and finances, the record does not support even that remedy.

I would reverse the decree and dismiss the bill of complaint.

QUESTIONS AND NOTES

1. Why did the defendants have the burden of proof? How could the defendants have satisfied that burden of proof?

2. Why didn't the plaintiffs sue for money damages instead of dissolution?

3. Why didn't the plaintiffs simply sell their stock?

B. RECEIVING DIVIDENDS FROM THE CORPORATION

1. WHAT IS A DIVIDEND?

Easy question. We have already seen dividends in *Giannotti* and in several of the other cases we have considered. A dividend is a "special type of distribution, a payment to shareholders by the corporation out of its current or retained earnings in proportion to the number of shares owned by the shareholder." Robert W. Hamilton, BUSINESS ORGANIZATIONS: ESSENTIAL TERMS AND CONCEPTS 434 (1996).

Now let's consider a couple more difficult questions about dividends.

2. WHY DO CORPORATIONS PAY DIVIDENDS? WHY DO INVESTORS PAY ATTENTION TO DIVIDENDS?

Whether to pay dividends is a management decision, to be made (like other management decisions) by the board of directors. Most corporations do not pay dividends. Some do. What message does a corporation send to the investing public if it pays dividends? Why don't more pay dividends?

It might be appropriate to think of dividends as a return to the investor who put his money at risk in the corporation. In this view, dividends reward existing shareholders and may encourage others to buy the corporation's stock. So maybe investors pay attention to dividends because they might make the stock more attractive to others so that the price of the stock will increase.

On the other hand, a corporation that pays no dividends might be demonstrating confidence that it has attractive investment opportunities that might be missed if it paid dividends. If it makes these investments (instead of paying dividends), it may increase the value of the shares by more than the amount of the lost dividends. If that happens, its shareholders may be doubly better off. They end up with capital appreciation greater than the dividends they missed out on. Moreover, this capital appreciation has been taxed at lower effective rates than dividends—although legislation in 2003 has changed this substantially.

After ruminating about these and other aspects of dividends, one scholar concludes: "The harder we look at the dividend picture, the more it seems like a puzzle, with pieces that just don't fit together." F. Black, *The Dividend Puzzle*, 2 J. OF PORTFOLIO MGT. 5, 7 (1976). For a more complete study of share valuation as a function of dividend policy, see Roland Lease, Kose John, Avner Kalay, Uri Lowenstein & Oded Sarig, DIVIDEND POLICY (2000).

Professor Black's article and the book by Professor Lease and the other business school professors focus on the dividend policies of large, publicly-held corporations. Public corporations such as McDonald's regularly declare dividends. For such corporations, decisions about dividends are important aspects of business policy. Each such company must ask what dividend policies will cause investors to buy its stock, to hold its stock, etc.

In contrast, closely held corporations such as Bubba's Burritos, Inc. generally do not pay dividends. For them, as the next two cases illustrate, the dividend questions can often be legal questions.

3. WHAT IS THE LAW ON WHEN A DIVIDEND *MAY* BE PAID? WHAT IS THE LAW ON WHEN A DIVIDEND *MUST* BE PAID?

Bubba's Burritos, Inc. has done well. It had a positive cash flow of $200,000 last year. It now has $300,000 in cash, $400,000 in other assets, and only $500,000 in debt.

What is the amount of equity? Can the corporation pay that amount in dividends? Can the corporation pay $300,000 in dividends? Who decides? What if they decide not to pay any dividends?

A   L   E
700   500   200

The MBCA is not much more helpful on dividend questions than it was on salary questions. Generally, the MBCA uses the term "distribution" rather than the term "dividend" and the definition of "distribution"* includes a "dividend." *See* MBCA § 1.40.

MBCA § 6.40(c) spells out when a corporation *cannot* declare a dividend and § 8.33(b) imposes liability on directors for making distributions in violation of § 6.40(c). Please read §§ 6.40(c) and 8.33 and consider the following related questions:

- Why does a state's corporate code limit directors' discretion in declaring dividends?
- Who will complain if the directors distribute too much to shareholders? ~Investors, Employees~
- How can directors determine if the corporation will be able to "pay its debts as they come due in the usual course of business"? Is the ~ALE~ balance sheet helpful? The income statement? ~R E NI~

As the cited statutes make clear, under the MBCA a distribution is proper so long as the corporation is not insolvent and as long as the distribution does not render the corporation insolvent. This approach is the modern view, but it is not the universal view.

The traditional approach to the propriety of distributions, which is still followed in several states, including important corporate states such as Delaware and New York, requires reference to different funds or accounts that the corporate codes in such states require the corporation to keep. (We introduced these funds in Chapter 4, Part B, § 3, when we discussed issuing stock.)

~R.E.~ One account is "earned surplus" (also known as "retained earnings"), which consists of money generated by the business itself. It consists of all earnings minus all losses minus distributions previously paid. If Bubba's Burritos, Inc. has earned surplus, it is making money in the real world by selling lots of burritos and other products. Earned surplus may be used to pay a distribution; under the traditional approach, it is a proper source from which such a payment to a stockholder can be made.

The other accounts relate to raising capital not by selling burritos (or widgets or doing whatever our corporation does), but by issuing stock. Proceeds received from the corporation's sale of stock (which is the definition of issuance, you will recall) are generally divided into two accounts under the traditional approach to the propriety of distributions.

~Stated capital~ "Stated capital" consists of the par value of a par issuance plus the amount allocated to stated capital on a no-par issuance. At this point you might be tempted to say "huh?" Remember from Chapter 4 that "par"

---

* Distributions are payments by the corporation to a shareholder. The three most common types of distributions are dividends, repurchases (in which the corporation enters a deal with a shareholder to purchase her stock), and redemptions (in which certain shareholders have obtained a contractual right that, under specified circumstances, the corporation must repurchase their shares at a specified price). Although the payment to the shareholders in any distribution can be made in money or property, usually they are made in money.

means "minimum issuance price." So if Bubba's Burritos, Inc. is selling 10,000 shares of $2 par stock, it must receive at least $2 per share for each of those shares, for a total of $20,000. That $20,000 would be allocated to stated capital. Why does this matter? Because under the traditional approach, stated capital cannot be used for a distribution. Stated capital was a cushion to provide protection for the corporation's creditors. In practice, however, corporations in these states can set par at miniscule amounts, like one-tenth of one cent.

But what if Bubba's Burritos, Inc. issued the 10,000 shares of $2 par stock for $100,000? (After all, par just means minimum issuance price. The corporation is free to sell at a higher price if it can get it.) In this hypothetical, $20,000 would be allocated to stated capital (as discussed in the previous paragraph). The other $80,000 would go into another fund, called "capital surplus." Why does this matter? Because capital surplus (like earned surplus) can be used to pay a distribution. Some states impose restrictions, such as a requirement that the shareholders receiving a distribution from capital surplus must be given notice that it is coming from that source and not from earned surplus.

Capital Surplus

Under the traditional approach, then, every cent generated from the issuance of stock is allocated either to stated capital or capital surplus. We just saw how this allocation is effected in a par issuance. What about a no-par sale of stock by the corporation? Recall that "no-par" simply means that there is no minimum issuance price. The board is free to determine the appropriate amount of consideration for such an issuance. On a no-par issuance, the directors are usually free to allocate the funds received between stated capital and capital surplus. But, perhaps counterintuitively, if the directors do nothing, the funds go into stated capital, not capital surplus, and so they are not available for a distribution.

So when it comes to whether a corporation *may* pay a distribution, such as a dividend, there are two general approaches. The traditional view requires us to know the three accounts just described. The modern approach, typified by the MBCA, does not. Instead, it simply imposes insolvency limitations; distributions cannot be paid if the corporation is insolvent or would be rendered insolvent by the distribution. (The modern approach reflects the decline in the importance of the concept of par stock.) As the dissent in *Giannotti* points out, the "general rule is * * * the board of directors in its discretion determines whether to declare dividends on the stock." Under the modern approach, the only exception is when the corporation is about to go broke.

The following case, *Zidell v. Zidell*, shows how much discretion courts afford directors on dividend questions. In reading the case, please consider the following:

1. Is the plaintiff in *Zidell* contending that the salaries paid by the corporations to his brother and nephew are too high?

2. Do we know the dollar amount of dividends paid by the corporations in 1973 and 1974?

3.   Do we know the dollar amount of additional dividends the trial court ordered the corporations to declare?

ZIDELL v. ZIDELL

Supreme Court of Oregon, 1977
560 P.2d 1086

Howell, Justice. These four suits were filed by Arnold Zidell, a minority shareholder of four related, closely held corporations, seeking to compel the directors of those corporations to declare dividends. Plaintiff's complaints alleged that defendants "arbitrarily, unreasonably and in bad faith" refused to declare more than a modest dividend in 1973. The trial court ordered each of the defendant corporations to declare additional dividends out of its earnings for 1973 and 1974. * * *

Defendants have appealed, contending that the court was not justified in ordering the declaration of any additional dividends. * * *

[Arnold Zidell owned 3/8 of the issued and outstanding stock of four affiliated different corporations that bought and sold scrap metal. The other 5/8 of the stock of each of the corporations was owned by his brother Emery Zidell, and Emery Zidell's son, Jay Zidell. (Emery held 3/8 of the corporation's stock and Jay had 1/4 (or 2/8) of the stock.) Until 1973, Arnold, Emery and Jay were the directors of all four corporations. Also, until 1973, all three were employed by the four corporations. In May of 1973, the board refused Arnold's demand that his salary be raised from $30,000 to $50,000. Arnold resigned his employment with the corporations, and his salary from the corporations ended.]

* * * Prior to Arnold's resignation, the customary practice had been to retain all earnings in the business rather than to distribute profits as dividends. Arnold had agreed with this policy, since all significant stockholders were active in the business and received salaries adequate for their needs. Following his resignation, however, Arnold demanded that the corporations begin declaring reasonable dividends. Thereafter, a dividend was declared and paid on the 1973 earnings of each corporation.

Arnold contends that these dividends are unreasonably small and were not set in good faith. He notes that at about the same time, corporate salaries and bonuses were increased substantially. Arnold does not contend that these salaries are excessive in his briefs on appeal. He does argue, however, that the change in compensation policy, coinciding as it did with his departure from active involvement in the business, is evidence of a concerted effort by the other shareholders to wrongfully deprive him of his right to a fair proportion of the profits of the business. He points out that each corporation had substantial retained earnings at the end of 1973, and he argues that he was entitled to a larger return on his equity.

The trial court specifically declined to rule that defendants acted in bad faith but held that larger dividends should have been declared in order to allow plaintiff a reasonable return. The court then ordered the declaration of a much larger dividend than that which had been set by the board of directors in each case.

We have recognized that those in control of corporate affairs have fiduciary duties of good faith and fair dealing toward the minority shareholders. Insofar as dividend policy is concerned, however, that duty is discharged if the decision is made in good faith and reflects legitimate business purposes rather than the private interests of those in control. * * *

Plaintiff had the burden of proving bad faith on the part of the directors in determining the amount of corporate dividends. In the present case, plaintiff has shown that the corporations could afford to pay additional dividends, that he has left the corporate payroll, that those stockholders who are working for the corporations are receiving generous salaries and bonuses, and that there is hostility between him and the other major stockholders. We agree with plaintiff that these factors are often present in cases of oppression or attempted squeeze-out by majority shareholders. They are not, however, invariably signs of improper behavior by the majority. *See Gottfried v. Gottfried,* [73 N.Y.S. 2d 692, 695 (1947)]:

> There are no infallible distinguishing earmarks of bad faith. The following facts are relevant to the issue of bad faith and are admissible in evidence: Intense hostility of the controlling faction against the minority; exclusion of the minority from employment by the corporation; high salaries, or bonuses or corporate loans made to the officers in control; the fact that the majority group may be subject to high personal income taxes if substantial dividends are paid; the existence of a desire by the controlling directors to acquire the minority stock interests as cheaply as possible. But if they are not motivating causes they do not constitute "bad faith" as a matter of law.

Defendants introduced a considerable amount of credible evidence to explain their conservative dividend policy. There was testimony that the directors took into consideration a future need for expensive physical improvements, and possibly even the relocation of a major plant; the need for cash to pay for large inventory orders; the need for renovation of a nearly obsolescent dock; and the need for continued short-term financing through bank loans which could be "called" if the corporations' financial position became insecure. There was also evidence that earnings for 1973 and 1974 were abnormally high because of unusual economic conditions that could not be expected to continue.

In rebuttal, plaintiff contends that the directors did not really make their decisions on the basis of these factors, pointing to testimony that they did not rely on any documented financial analysis to support their dividend declarations. This is a matter for consideration, but it is certainly not determinative. All of the directors of these corporations were active in the business on a day-to-day basis and had intimate first-hand knowledge of financial conditions and present and projected business needs. In order to substantiate their testimony that the above factors were taken into consideration, it was not necessary that they provide documentary evidence or show that formal studies were conducted. Their testimony is believable, and the burden of proof on this issue is on the plaintiff, not the defendants.

Nor are we convinced by plaintiff's arguments that we should approve the forced declaration of additional dividends in order to prevent a deliberate squeeze-out. Plaintiff left his corporate employment voluntarily. He was not forced out. Although the dividends he has since received are modest when viewed as a rate of return on his investment, they are not unreasonable in light of the corporations' projected financial needs. Moreover, having considered the evidence presented by both sides, we are not persuaded that the directors are employing starvation tactics to force the sale of plaintiff's stock at an unreasonably low price.

Since we have determined that plaintiff has not carried his burden of proving a lack of good faith, we must conclude that the trial court erred in decreeing the distribution of additional dividends.

Reversed and remanded with directions to enter decrees of dismissal.

QUESTIONS AND NOTE

1. Do you agree with the court's conclusion that "Plaintiff had the burden of proving bad faith on the part of the directors in determining the amount of corporate dividends"? Would the court in the *Giannotti* case agree? Is this case distinguishable from *Giannotti*?

2. Do you agree with the Oregon court's conclusion that the plaintiff did not satisfy his burden of proof? Would the court have reached a different decision if:

- the board of directors had not declared any dividend in 1973?
- the plaintiff had not resigned as an employee but instead had been fired?

3. Reconsider the court's statement: "We have recognized that those in control of corporate affairs have fiduciary duties of good faith and fair dealing toward the minority shareholder." Professor Mitchell is critical of the *Zidell* approach to fiduciary duty: "The clear import is that actions of controlling interests in close corporations will not result in liability so long as those actions are not intended to harm minority shareholders. This reduces fiduciary analysis to nothing more than the avoidance of unfair treatment of the minority, rather than exclusive pursuit of the minority's interests." Lawrence E. Mitchell, *The Death of Fiduciary Duty in Close Corporations*, 138 U. PA. L. REV. 1675, 1715–16 (1990). Do you agree with Professor Mitchell's view of *Zidell*? With his view of fiduciary duty?

4. The leading (and somewhat lonely) case requiring a corporation to pay a dividend to shareholders is *Dodge v. Ford Motor Co.*, 170 N.W. 668

(Mich. 1919). At that time, Ford Motor Company had relatively few shareholders. Two of the shareholders were the brothers Dodge (who formed their own automobile manufacturing business (which became a division of Chrysler)). Ford Motor Company had paid extraordinarily high dividends, which the Dodge Boys used to get their company rolling (so to speak). Presumably, Henry Ford was not pleased with this potential competition. At any rate, Ford Motor Company then refused to pay dividends, and the Dodges sued.

Henry Ford had legitimate reasons to use earnings for purposes other than paying dividends. He wanted to expand production facilities of Ford Motor. In addition, Ford paid his workers more than twice the going wage, and wanted to use some of the money to continue that practice as well. Although some people thought paying such high wages was a mistake, in fact it was brilliant, because it gave Ford a loyal, stable workforce. Once on the Ford line, a worker was not going to give up his job, because he was making twice as much as other auto workers. Ford knew that the new plant would enable the company to build cars far less expensively and, thus, to drive the price of the cars down. Again, some people thought this was a mistake—they asked "why not make cars more expensive?" But again, Henry Ford was brilliant. He understood that his company would make far more money by making cheaper cars and selling many more of them.

In the Dodge brothers' lawsuit, Ford could simply have testified at trial that he wanted to use earnings to make cars less expensive and to pay the higher wages to improve his workforce, both of which would increase profits. Had he done so, no court would have overruled his decision to plow the money into the new plant and not into dividends. Instead, however, Ford testified at great length about how he wanted to make sure that everyone could afford a car—that the goal of his company was not so much to make money as to provide the public with cheap cars and his workers with high wages. The Michigan Supreme Court found his stated reasons so imprudent as not to be protected by the business judgment rule. In light of the huge cash surpluses and the history of declaring dividends, the court concluded that the directors had "a duty to distribute * * * a very large sum of money to stockholders." *Id.* at 685.

Professor Charles M. Elson of the Stetson University Law School has included this case in his list of "ten top cases" that "shaped the nature of discourse on corporate governance." Charles M. Elson, *Courts and Boards: the Top Ten Cases*, SD 39 ALI–ABA 743 (1998). Nonetheless, the decision is unique. We are not aware of any other reported decision in which a court required directors to pay dividends because the corporation had a large surplus.

For an interesting treatment of the success of Henry Ford, *see* Douglas Brinkley, WHEELS FOR THE WORLD: HENRY FORD, HIS COMPANY, AND A CENTURY OF PROGRESS (2003).

We are aware of at least one reported "man bites dog" case on payment of dividends, *Sinclair Oil Corporation v. Levien*. In this case, the minority shareholder is complaining that the corporation paid too much in dividends, not too little. Please consider the following questions.

1.   Who is the plaintiff?

2   Who is the defendant?

3.   What does the plaintiff minority shareholder claim that the defendant majority shareholder did wrong? What does the plaintiff want the defendant to do differently? If Sinven's earnings had not been paid to shareholders in the form of dividends, what would have happened to the earnings?

SINCLAIR OIL CORPORATION v. LEVIEN

Supreme Court of Delaware, 1971
280 A.2d 717

WOLCOTT, CHIEF JUSTICE. This is an appeal by the defendant, Sinclair Oil Corporation (hereafter Sinclair), from an order of the Court of Chancery, in a derivative action requiring Sinclair to account for damages sustained by its subsidiary, Sinclair Venezuelan Oil Company (hereafter Sinven), organized by Sinclair for the purpose of operating in Venezuela, as a result of dividends paid by Sinven.

Sinclair, operating primarily as a holding company, is in the business of exploring for oil and of producing and marketing crude oil and oil products. At all times relevant to this litigation, it owned about 97% of Sinven's stock. The plaintiff owns about 3000 of 120,000 publicly-held shares of Sinven. Sinven, incorporated in 1922, has been engaged in petroleum operations primarily in Venezuela and since 1959 has operated exclusively in Venezuela.

Sinclair nominates all members of Sinven's board of directors. The Chancellor found as a fact that the directors were not independent of Sinclair. Almost without exception, they were officers, directors, or employees of corporations in the Sinclair complex. By reason of Sinclair's domination, it is clear that Sinclair owed Sinven a fiduciary duty. Sinclair concedes this.

The Chancellor held that because of Sinclair's fiduciary duty and its control over Sinven, its relationship with Sinven must meet the test of intrinsic fairness. The standard of intrinsic fairness involves both a high degree of fairness and a shift in the burden of proof. Under this standard the burden is on Sinclair to prove, subject to careful judicial scrutiny, that its transactions with Sinven were objectively fair.

Sinclair argues that the transactions between it and Sinven should be tested, not by the test of intrinsic fairness with the accompanying shift of the burden of proof, but by the business judgment rule under which a court will not interfere with the judgment of a board of directors unless there is a showing of gross and palpable overreaching. * * *

A parent does indeed owe a fiduciary duty to its subsidiary when there are parent-subsidiary dealings. However, this alone will not evoke the intrinsic fairness standard. This standard will be applied only when the fiduciary duty is accompanied by self-dealing—the situation when a parent is on both sides of a transaction with its subsidiary. Self-dealing occurs when the parent, by virtue of its domination of the subsidiary, causes the subsidiary to act in such a way that the parent receives something from the subsidiary to the exclusion of, and detriment to, the minority stockholders of the subsidiary.

We turn now to the facts. The plaintiff argues that, from 1960 through 1966, Sinclair caused Sinven to pay out such excessive dividends that the industrial development of Sinven was effectively prevented, and it became in reality a corporation in dissolution.

From 1960 through 1966, Sinven paid out $108,000,000 in dividends ($38,000,000 in excess of Sinven's earnings during the same period). The Chancellor held that Sinclair caused these dividends to be paid during a period when it had a need for large amounts of cash. Although the dividends paid exceeded earnings, the plaintiff concedes that the payments were made in compliance with 8 Del.C. § 170, authorizing payment of dividends out of surplus or net profits. However, the plaintiff attacks these dividends on the ground that they resulted from an improper motive– Sinclair's need for cash. The Chancellor, applying the intrinsic fairness standard, held that Sinclair did not sustain its burden of proving that these dividends were intrinsically fair to the minority stockholders of Sinven.

Since it is admitted that the dividends were paid in strict compliance with 8 Del.C. § 170, the alleged excessiveness of the payments alone would not state a cause of action. Nevertheless, compliance with the applicable statute may not, under all circumstances, justify all dividend payments. If a plaintiff can meet his burden of proving that a dividend cannot be grounded on any reasonable business objective, then the courts can and will interfere with the board's decision to pay the dividend.

Sinclair contends that it is improper to apply the intrinsic fairness standard to dividend payments even when the board which voted for the dividends is completely dominated. * * *

We do not accept the argument that the intrinsic fairness test can never be applied to a dividend declaration by a dominated board, although a dividend declaration by a dominated board will not inevitably demand the application of the intrinsic fairness standard. If such a dividend is in essence self-dealing by the parent, then the intrinsic fairness standard is the proper standard. For example, suppose a parent dominates a subsidiary and its board of directors. The subsidiary has outstanding two classes of stock, X and Y. Class X is owned by the parent and Class Y is owned by minority stockholders of the subsidiary. If the subsidiary, at the direction of the parent, declares a dividend on its Class X stock only, this might well be self-dealing by the parent. It would be receiving something from the subsidiary to the exclusion of and detrimental to its minority stockholders. This self-dealing, coupled with the parent's fiduciary duty, would make intrinsic fairness the proper standard by which to evaluate the dividend payments.

Consequently it must be determined whether the dividend payments by Sinven were, in essence, self-dealing by Sinclair. The dividends resulted in great sums of money being transferred from Sinven to Sinclair. However, a proportionate share of this money was received by the minority shareholders of Sinven. Sinclair received nothing from Sinven to the exclusion of its minority stockholders. As such, these dividends were not self-dealing. We hold therefore that the Chancellor erred in applying the intrinsic fairness test as to these dividend payments. The business judgment standard should have been applied.

We conclude that the facts demonstrate that the dividend payments complied with the business judgment standard and with 8 Del.C. § 170. The motives for causing the declaration of dividends are immaterial unless the plaintiff can show that the dividend payments resulted from improper motives and amounted to waste. The plaintiff contends only that the dividend payments drained Sinven of cash to such an extent that it was prevented from expanding.

* * * However, the plaintiff could point to no opportunities which came to Sinven. * * *

We will therefore reverse that part of the Chancellor's order that requires Sinclair to account to Sinven for damages sustained as a result of dividends paid between 1960 and 1966. * * *

QUESTIONS AND NOTE

1. How could Sinven pay dividends from 1960 through 1966 "in excess of Sinven's earnings during the same period"?

2. Which party had the burden of proof? What did that party have to prove? Did that party satisfy its burden of proof?

3. According to Professor Siegel, more recent Delaware cases have significantly limited the precedential impact of *Sinclair v. Levien*:

> *Sinclair's* attempt to effectively identify at the threshold those controlling-shareholder transactions that warrant the demanding fairness review, however, has largely been dissipated. Three lines of cases have coalesced to cause this result: one has ignored the *Sinclair* test; a second has diluted it by omitting its "detriment" prong; a third has applied the test mechanically, without any meaningful evaluation at the threshold. As a result, *Sinclair* currently does little more than relegate pure pro-rata transactions to the business judgment rule. The undermining of *Sinclair* has relegated the bulk of transactions involving controlling shareholders for review under the entire fairness standard, thereby making it the dominant standard of review in Delaware to monitor these transactions. As this significant shift in the law has occurred *sub rosa*, there has been

little appreciation that this shift has occurred, no explanation for what may have motivated the shift, no explicit examination of the implications of this change, and no analysis of whether this change is beneficial.

Mary Siegel, *The Erosion of the Law of Controlling Shareholders*, 24 DEL. J. CORP. L. 27, 31 (1999).

4. Did we put this case in the right place in the book? Other casebooks include the *Sinclair* case in the part of the book dealing with duty of loyalty.

4. TO WHOM ARE DIVIDENDS PAID: PREFERRED, PARTICIPATING, CUMULATIVE?

The answer to the question of to whom a corporation pays dividends is generally found in that corporation's articles of incorporation. To understand the answer that you find in the articles, it is necessary to understand the following terms:

(1) classes of stock;

(2) common stock;

(3) preferred stock;

(4) preferred participating stock; and

(5) preferred cumulative stock.

Recall that state corporate codes authorize a corporation, in its articles of incorporation, to create different classes or types of stock. MBCA § 6.01(a) is a representative statutory provision. Please re-read (read?) MBCA § 6.01(a) and the documents that establish Silicon Gaming, Inc.'s class D stock in Chapter 4, Part B, § 3.

Although all of the shares in a particular class must have identical rights, one class can have greater rights, or "preferences," than another. A class with such a preference is generally referred to as "preferred." The class without such a preference is generally referred to as "common."

A typical preference for a class of stock is priority in the receipt of dividends. Assume, for example, that Bubba's Burritos, Inc. has two classes of stock: Class 1 and Class 2 and that Class 2 stock must receive a payment of $2 per share before the Class 1 common stock can receive any dividend. Assume further that there are 10,000 outstanding shares of Class 1 and 2,000 shares of Class 2. If the directors of Bubba's Burritos, Inc. declare a total dividend of only $4,000, only Class 2 stock would receive a dividend ($2 × 2,000); there would be nothing left for the Class 1 shares. Preferred means "pay first."

(1) What if the directors declare a $40,000 dividend instead of a $4,000 dividend? Again, the 2,000 shares of Class 2 preferred stock would first be paid the $2 a share dividend preference for a total of $4,000. The remaining $36,000 would be paid to the 10,000 shares of Class 1 common stock. In sum, each preferred share would be paid a $2 dividend while

each common share would be paid a $3.60 dividend. Class 2's preference was as to priority of payment, not amount of payment.

"Preferred participating" stock not only gets paid first (because it is preferred), but also gets paid again. "Participating" thus means that these shares also get paid, along with the common shares, in what is left over after payment of the preference. So they get paid twice!

(2) For example, take the same basic facts as above. Bubba's Burritos, Inc. declares a total dividend of $40,000. As before, there are 10,000 shares of common stock. However, the 2,000 shares of preferred stock not only have a $2 preference, but they are also participating. The preferred aspect of this stock is handled the same as in (1). Thus, the 2,000 preferred shares receive their $2 preference first, meaning they get a total of $4000. That leaves $36,000, just as in (1). But here, that $36,000 does not go only to the 10,000 common shares. Instead, that stock has to share that money with the 2,000 preferred participating shares. So the $36,000 gets divided here among a total of 12,000 shares (the 10,000 common and the 2,000 preferred participating shares). This works out to $3 per share. So the common get $3 per share. The preferred participating get $5 per share—$2 because of their dividend preference and $3 because they are participating.

Recall that there is no statutory requirement that dividends be paid. Generally, there is no right to a dividend until the board of directors declares one. And, generally, dividends do not accrue from year to year. If, for example, the board of directors of Bubba's Burritos, Inc. declares a dividend in 2008, after having paid no dividends in 2007, the holders of Class 2 stock with a $2 dividend preference would still get only $2 a share, *unless* their stock was not only preferred but preferred and *cumulative*. Cumulative dividends do accrue—do carry over from year-to-year. All omitted cumulative dividends must be paid before any dividend is paid on common stock.

(3) To take another variation of the facts, suppose Bubba's Burritos, Inc. declares a total dividend of $40,000. There are 2,000 shares of class 2 cumulative preferred stock with a $2 preference (but not participating) and 10,000 shares of class 1 common stock. Now suppose the board has not declared a dividend in any of the last three years. The cumulative preferred dividend of $2 has been accruing year-to-year over that period. So when the corporation declares any dividend, it owes each preferred share $2 for each of the three previous years as well as for this year. So they get four years' worth of a $2 preference, or $8 per share. There are 2,000 such shares, so they get a total of $16,000. That sum is paid first, because it is preferred. After paying the preferred cumulative shares their total of $16,000, that leaves $24,000 to be distributed among the common shares. There are 10,000 of those, so each common share gets $2.40 per share.

C. BUYING AND SELLING STOCK AT A PROFIT

1. HOW DOES SOMEONE KNOW WHAT SHARES OF A CORPORATION'S STOCK ARE WORTH?

a. Available Information

If you are considering buying or selling McDonald's stock, it is relatively easy to learn what McDonald's stock is worth—or at least the market price for McDonald's shares. Go to the "Business" section of any newspaper (even THE TUSCALOOSA NEWS). Or go on-line to any of a variety of sources providing stock quotes (e.g., www.schwab.com). One important internet source for a wide variety of information about publicly-traded corporations is EDGAR, which provides online access to the reports that public corporations file with the SEC (Securities & Exchange Commission). Such publicly traded corporations are "registered," as we discussed in Chapter 6, Part B, § 2(a).*

We are used to hearing about the major stock exchanges, such as the New York Stock Exchange and NASDAQ. These exchanges set prices for publicly-traded stocks each trading day. For some smaller corporations, there may be something of a market, recorded on what are called the "pink sheets." Wikipedia provides this helpful description:

> Pink Sheets is an electronic system, published by Pink Sheets LLC, to display bid and ask quotation prices. The name "Pink Sheets" stems itself from an earlier paper-based system, which was printed on pink paper. It is mainly used by stock brokers trading OTC securities [OTC or over-the-counter securities are those that are not traded on a public exchange.]

> Pink Sheets LLC is neither an NASD broker-dealer, nor registered with the U.S. Securities and Exchange Commission; it is not a stock exchange, the companies listed do not need to fulfill any requirements. With the exception of a few foreign issuers, the companies quoted in the Pink Sheets tend to be closely held, extremely small and/or thinly traded. Most do not meet the minimum listing requirements for trading on a national securities exchange, such as the New York Stock Exchange or the NASDAQ Stock Market. Many of these companies do not file periodic reports or audited financial statements with the SEC, making it very difficult for investors to find reliable, unbiased information about those companies. For these reasons, the SEC sees companies listed on Pink Sheets as "among the most risky investments" and advises potential investors to heavily research the companies they plan to invest in.

---

* Corporations that have filed registration statements to sell securities must thereafter file annual reports (Form 10–K), quarterly reports (Form 10–Q), and reports of current material developments (Form 8–K).

http://en.wikipedia.org/wiki/Pink_Sheets (17 July 2006).

Not all close corporations are traded on the pink sheets. For smaller close corporations such as Bubba's Burritos, whose securities are not traded on formal exchanges or in the pink sheets, how does one get information about appropriate pricing? Recall the earlier consideration of the information provided by financial statements and the earlier consideration of the statutory rights of an existing shareholder to look at the books and records.

Can you rely on what you find in the books and records of a corporation? Consider the following answer by an "experienced chancery practitioner" and a "qualified forensic accountant":

> There exist no definitive guidelines regarding the form and content of "books and records of account" that are required to be maintained by a corporation under the statute (the New Jersey counterpart to MBCA § 2.20). The Internal Revenue Code offers some guidance, but only of a general nature.

> Although a company may maintain what appears to be accurate books and records, those records may be a product of manipulation and fraud. An experienced chancery practitioner, assisted by a qualified forensic accountant, is essential in effectively representing the interests of a minority shareholder who wishes to exercise his or her statutory inspection rights and protect his or her overall financial interests in the corporation.

Michael J. Faul, Jr. and Robert Dipasquale, *A Minority Shareholder's Inspection Rights Under N.J.S.A. 14A:5–28*, NEW JERSEY LAWYER, 2004–Aug NJLAW 8.

b. Reliability of Information—Common Law and 10b–5 Protection From Fraud

Although Freer was born there, most of what your authors know about New Jersey has been learned from watching reruns of *The Sopranos*. Still, we would like to think that even in New Jersey it is obvious that a corporation with books and records that are the "product of manipulation and fraud" can be sued for common law fraud. Less obvious examples of fraud involve statements by corporations that are misleading or incomplete.

The next case involves the application of Rule 10b–5 to such statements. We were introduced to Rule 10b–5 in Chapter 6. In reading the case, please consider the following:

1. Were Basic's statements in footnote 4 untrue?

2. Who are the plaintiffs? Did the plaintiffs read the October 21, 1977 edition of the *Cleveland Plain Dealer*?

3. Did Max Muller, the President of Basic, act with "scienter"? Could he spell "scienter"? Can you pronounce "scienter"? Is Scienter the name of a trendy perfume?

BASIC INC. v. LEVINSON

United States Supreme Court, 1988
485 U.S. 224

BLACKMUN, *J.* Prior to December 20, 1978, Basic Incorporated was a publicly traded company primarily engaged in the business of manufacturing chemical refractories for the steel industry. As early as 1965 or 1966, Combustion Engineering, Inc., a company producing mostly alumina-based refractories, expressed some interest in acquiring Basic. * * *

Beginning in September 1976, Combustion representatives had meetings and telephone conversations with Basic officers and directors, including petitioners here, concerning the possibility of a merger. During 1977 and 1978, Basic made three public statements denying that it was engaged in merger negotiations.* **[4]** On December 18, 1978, Basic asked the New York Stock Exchange to suspend trading in its shares and issued a release stating that it had been "approached" by another company concerning a merger. On December 19, Basic's board endorsed Combustion's offer of $46 per share for its common stock, and on the following day publicly announced its approval of Combustion's tender offer for all outstanding shares.

Respondents are former Basic shareholders who sold their stock after Basic's first public statement of October 21, 1977, and before the suspension of trading in December 1978. Respondents brought a class action against Basic and its directors, asserting that the defendants issued three false or misleading public statements and thereby were in violation of § 10(b) of the 1934 Act and of Rule 10b–5. Respondents alleged that they were injured by selling Basic shares at artificially depressed prices in a market affected by petitioners' misleading statements and in reliance thereon.

The District Court adopted a presumption of reliance by members of the plaintiff class upon petitioners' public statements that enabled the court to conclude that common questions of fact or law predominated over particular questions pertaining to individual plaintiffs.* The District

---

* **[4]** On October 21, 1977, after heavy trading and a new high in Basic stock, the following news item appeared in the *Cleveland Plain Dealer*:

"[Basic] President Max Muller said the company knew no reason for the stock's activity and that no negotiations were under way with any company for a merger. He said Flintkote recently denied Wall Street rumors that it would make a tender offer of $25 a share for control of the Cleveland-based maker of refractories for the steel industry."

On September 25, 1978, in reply to an inquiry from the New York Stock Exchange, Basic issued a release concerning increased activity in its stock and stated that: "management is unaware of any present or pending company development that would result in the abnormally heavy trading activity and price fluctuation in company shares that have experienced in the past few days."

On November 6, 1978, Basic issued to its shareholders a "Nine Months Report 1978." This Report stated:

With regard to the open stock market activity in the Company's shares, we remain unaware of any present or pending developments which would account for the high volume of trading and price fluctuations in recent months.

* [Note from your authors: To certify a class action under Federal Rule 23 (b)(3), as plaintiffs sought here, one must show that common questions predominate over individual questions.]

Court therefore certified respondents' class. On the merits, however, the District Court granted summary judgment for the defendants. It held that, as a matter of law, any misstatements were immaterial: there were no negotiations ongoing at the time of the first statement, and although negotiations were taking place when the second and third statements were issued, those negotiations were not "destined, with reasonable certainty, to become a merger agreement in principle."

The United States Court of Appeals for the Sixth Circuit affirmed the class certification, but reversed the District Court's summary judgment, and remanded the case. The court reasoned that while petitioners were under no general duty to disclose their discussions with Combustion, any statement the company voluntarily released could not be "so incomplete as to mislead." In the Court of Appeals' view, Basic's statements that no negotiations where taking place, and that it knew of no corporate developments to account for the heavy trading activity, were misleading. With respect to materiality, the court rejected the argument that preliminary merger discussions are immaterial as a matter of law, and held that "once a statement is made denying the existence of any discussions, even discussions that might not have been material in absence of the denial are material because they make the statement made untrue."

The Court of Appeals joined a number of other Circuits in accepting the "fraud-on-the-market theory" to create a rebuttable presumption that respondents relied on petitioners' material misrepresentations, noting that without the presumption it would be impractical to certify a class under Federal Rule of Civil Procedure 23(b)(3).

We granted certiorari to resolve the split among the Courts of Appeals as to the standard of materiality applicable to preliminary merger discussions, and to determine whether the courts below properly applied a presumption of reliance in certifying the class, rather than requiring each class member to show direct reliance on Basic's statements.

II

The 1934 Act was designed to protect investors against manipulation of stock prices. Underlying the adoption of extensive disclosure requirements was a legislative philosophy: "There cannot be honest markets without honest publicity. Manipulation and dishonest practices of the market place thrive upon mystery and secrecy." * * *

Pursuant to its authority under § 10(b) of the 1934 Act, the Securities and Exchange Commission promulgated Rule 10b–5.* **[6]** Judicial interpretation and application, legislative acquiescence, and the passage of

---

* **[6]** In relevant part, Rule 10b–5 provides:

"It shall be unlawful for any person, directly or indirectly, by the use of any means or instrumentality of interstate commerce, or of the mails or of any facility of any national securities exchange,

(b) To make any untrue statement of a material fact or to omit to state a material fact necessary in order to make the statements made, in the light of the circumstances under which they were made, not misleading . . . "in connection with the purchase or sale of any security."

time have removed any doubt that a private cause of action exists for a violation of § 10(b) and Rule 10b–5, and constitutes an essential tool for enforcement of the 1934 Act's requirements.

The Court previously has addressed various positive and common-law requirements for a violation of § 10(b) or of Rule 10b–5. *See, e.g., Blue Chip Stamps v. Manor Drug Stores*, ("in connection with the purchase or sale" requirement of the Rule); *Dirks v. SEC*, (duty to disclose); *Ernst & Ernst v. Hochfelder*, (scienter); *see TSC Industries, Inc. v. Northway, Inc.*, concluding in the proxy-solicitation context that "[a]n omitted fact is material if there is a substantial likelihood that a reasonable shareholder would consider it important in deciding how to vote." The Court was careful not to set too low a standard of materiality; it was concerned that a minimal standard might bring an overabundance of information within its reach, and lead management "simply to bury the shareholders in an avalanche of trivial information—a result that is hardly conducive to informed decisionmaking." It further explained that to fulfill the materiality requirement "there must be a substantial likelihood that the disclosure of the omitted fact would have been viewed by the reasonable investor as having significantly altered the 'total mix' of information made available." * * *

III

The application of this materiality standard to preliminary merger discussions is not self-evident. Where the impact of the corporate development on the target's fortune is certain and clear, the *TSC Industries* materiality definition admits straightforward application. Where, on the other hand, the event is contingent or speculative in nature, it is difficult to ascertain whether the "reasonable investor" would have considered the omitted information significant at the time. Merger negotiations, because of the ever-present possibility that the contemplated transaction will not be effectuated, fall into the latter category. * * *

This case does not concern the timing of a disclosure; it concerns only its accuracy and completeness. We face here the narrow question whether information concerning the existence and status of preliminary merger discussions is significant to the reasonable investor's trading decision. Arguments based on the premise that some disclosure would be "premature" in a sense are more properly considered under the rubric of an issuer's duty to disclose. The "secrecy" rationale is simply inapposite to the definition of materiality. * * *

Even before this Court's decision in *TSC Industries*, the Second Circuit had explained the role of the materiality requirement of Rule 10b–5, with respect to contingent or speculative information or events, in a manner that gave that term meaning that is independent of the other provisions of the Rule. Under such circumstances, materiality "will depend at any given time upon a balancing of both the indicated probability that the event will occur and the anticipated magnitude of the event in light of the totality of the company activity." *SEC v. Texas Gulf Sulphur*

Co., 401 F.2d [833, 849 (2d Cir. 1968)]. Interestingly, neither the Third Circuit decision adopting the agreement-in-principle test nor petitioners here take issue with this general standard. Rather, they suggest that with respect to preliminary merger discussions, there are good reasons to draw a line at agreement on price and structure.

In a subsequent decision, the late Judge Friendly, writing for a Second Circuit panel, applied the *Texas Gulf Sulphur* probability/magnitude approach in the specific context of preliminary merger negotiations. After acknowledging that materiality is something to be determined on the basis of the particular facts of each case, he stated: "Since a merger in which it is bought out is the most important event that can occur in a small corporation's life, to wit, its death, we think that inside information, as regards a merger of this sort, can become material at an earlier stage than would be the case as regards lesser transactions–and this even though the mortality rate of mergers in such formative stages is doubtless high."

We agree with that analysis.

Whether merger discussions in any particular case are material therefore depends on the facts. Generally, in order to assess the probability that the event will occur, a factfinder will need to look to indicia of interest in the transaction at the highest corporate levels. Without attempting to catalog all such possible factors, we note by way of example that board resolutions, instructions to investment bankers, and actual negotiations between principals or their intermediaries may serve as indicia of interest. To assess the magnitude of the transaction to the issuer of the securities allegedly manipulated, a factfinder will need to consider such facts as the size of the two corporate entities and of the potential premiums over market value. No particular event or factor short of closing the transaction need be either necessary or sufficient by itself to render merger discussions material.* **[17]**

As we clarify today, materiality depends on the significance the reasonable investor would place on the withheld or misrepresented information. Because the standard of materiality we have adopted differs from that used by both courts below, we remand the case for reconsideration of the question whether a grant of summary judgment is appropriate on this record.

---

* **[17]** To be actionable, of course, a statement must also be misleading. Silence, absent a duty to disclose, is not misleading under Rule 10b–5. "No comment" statements are generally the functional equivalent of silence. It has been suggested that given current market practices, a "no comment" statement is tantamount to an admission that merger discussions are underway. That may well hold true to the extent that issuers adopt a policy of truthfully denying merger rumors when no discussions are underway, and of issuing "no comment" statements when they are in the midst of negotiations. There are, of course, other statement policies firms could adopt; we need not now advise issuers as to what kind of practice to follow, within the range permitted by law. Perhaps more importantly, we think that creating an exception to a regulatory scheme founded on a prodisclosure legislative philosophy, because complying with the regulation might be "bad for business," is a role for Congress, not this Court.

IV

A

We turn to the question of reliance and the fraud-on-the-market theory. Succinctly put:

> The fraud on the market theory is based on the hypothesis that, in an open and developed securities market, the price of a company's stock is determined by the available material information regarding the company and its business.... Misleading statements will therefore defraud purchasers of stock even if the purchasers do not directly rely on the misstatements.... The causal connection between the defendants' fraud and the plaintiffs' purchase of stock in such a case is no less significant than in a case of direct reliance on misrepresentations.

Our task, of course, is not to assess the general validity of the theory, but to consider whether it was proper for the courts below to apply a rebuttable presumption of reliance, supported in part by the fraud-on-the-market theory.

This case required resolution of several common questions of law and fact concerning the falsity or misleading nature of the three public statements made by Basic, the presence or absence of scienter, and the materiality of the misrepresentations, if any. In their amended complaint, the named plaintiffs alleged that in reliance on Basic's statements they sold their shares of Basic stock in the depressed market created by petitioners. Requiring proof of individualized reliance from each member of the proposed plaintiff class effectively would have prevented respondents from proceeding with a class action, since individual issues then would have overwhelmed the common ones. The District Court found that the presumption of reliance created by the fraud-on-the-market theory provided "a practical resolution to the problem of balancing the substantive requirement of proof of reliance in securities cases against the procedural requisites of [Federal Rules of Civil Procedure, Rule] 23." The District Court thus concluded that with reference to each public statement and its impact upon the open market for Basic shares, common questions predominated over individual questions, as required by Federal Rules of Civil Procedure 23(a)(2) and (b)(3).

Petitioners and their amici complain that the fraud-on-the-market theory effectively eliminates the requirement that a plaintiff asserting a claim under Rule 10b–5 prove reliance. * * *

We agree that reliance is an element of a Rule 10b–5 cause of action. Reliance provides the requisite causal connection between a defendant's misrepresentation and a plaintiff's injury. There is, however, more than one way to demonstrate the causal connection. * * *

The modern securities markets, literally involving millions of shares changing hands daily, differ from the face-to-face transactions contemplated by early fraud cases, and our understanding of Rule 10b–5's reliance requirement must encompass these differences.

* * * The courts below accepted a presumption, created by the fraud-on-the-market theory and subject to rebuttal by petitioners, that persons who had traded Basic shares had done so in reliance on the integrity of the price set by the market, but because of petitioners' material misrepresentations that price had been fraudulently depressed. Requiring a plaintiff to show a speculative state of facts, i.e., how he would have acted if omitted material information had been disclosed, or if the misrepresentation had not been made, would place an unnecessarily unrealistic evidentiary burden on the Rule 10b–5 plaintiff who has traded on an impersonal market. * * *

The presumption is also supported by common sense and probability. Recent empirical studies have tended to confirm Congress' premise that the market price of shares traded on well-developed markets reflects all publicly available information, and, hence, any material misrepresentations. Because most publicly available information is reflected in market price, an investor's reliance on any public material misrepresentations, therefore, may be presumed for purposes of a Rule 10b–5 action.

The Court of Appeals found that petitioners "made public, material misrepresentations and [respondents] sold Basic stock in an impersonal, efficient market. Thus the class, as defined by the district court, has established the threshold facts for proving their loss." The court acknowledged that petitioners may rebut proof of the elements giving rise to the presumption, or show that the misrepresentation in fact did not lead to a distortion of price or that an individual plaintiff traded or would have traded despite his knowing the statement was false.

Any showing that severs the link between the alleged misrepresentation and either the price received (or paid) by the plaintiff, or his decision to trade at a fair market price, will be sufficient to rebut the presumption of reliance. For example, if petitioners could show that the "market makers" were privy to the truth about the merger discussions here with Combustion, and thus that the market price would not have been affected by their misrepresentations, the causal connection could be broken: the basis for finding that the fraud had been transmitted through market price would be gone. Similarly, if, despite petitioners' allegedly fraudulent attempt to manipulate market price, news of the merger discussions credibly entered the market and dissipated the effects of the misstatements, those who traded Basic shares after the corrective statements would have no direct or indirect connection with the fraud. Petitioners also could rebut the presumption of reliance as to plaintiffs who would have divested themselves of their Basic shares without relying on the integrity of the market. For example, a plaintiff who believed that Basic's statements were false and that Basic was indeed engaged in merger discussions, and who consequently believed that Basic stock was artificially underpriced, but sold his shares nevertheless because of other unrelated concerns, e.g., potential antitrust problems, or political pressures to divest from shares of certain businesses, could not be said to have relied on the integrity of a price he knew had been manipulated.

In summary:

* * *

Materiality in the merger context depends on the probability that the transaction will be consummated, and its significance to the issuer of the securities. Materiality depends on the facts and thus is to be determined on a case-by-case basis.

It is not inappropriate to apply a presumption of reliance supported by the fraud-on-the-market theory.

That presumption, however, is rebuttable.

The judgment of the Court of Appeals is vacated, and the case is remanded to that court for further proceedings consistent with this opinion.

QUESTIONS AND NOTE

1. What do the plaintiffs have to prove on remand?

2. "Petitioners and their amici complain that the fraud on the market theory effectively eliminates the requirement that a plaintiff asserting a claim under Rule 10b–5 prove reliance." Do you agree with this assertion? Did the Court?

3. Your client T (for "target"), a publicly traded corporation, is involved in preliminary, secret merger discussions with A ("acquirer"), which is also a publicly traded company. A has repeatedly told T that if news of their merger discussion is disclosed prematurely, A will "walk away from the deal." T's CEO gets a telephone message from the business reporter of the local newspaper that he has heard rumors that T and A are negotiating a merger. The reporter wants to talk with the CEO about T and A. On the basis of *Basic*, how would you advise T's CEO?

4. Professors Arlen and Carney use economic analysis to criticize the fraud on the market theory. They find that most fraud on the market cases simply transfer wealth from one set of stockholders to another, while incurring enormous transactions costs. Jennifer Arlen and William Carney, *Vicarious Liability for Fraud on the Securities Markets*, 1992 U. ILL. L. REV. 691.

———

You, of course, would not rely solely on *Basic* to advise a real client.* In the years since the *Basic* decision, both Congress and the courts have made changes in the securities laws. The next case considers two of the

———

* One more time: "[S]ecurities law is a highly technical, demanding area of the law that has ruined the careers of many young lawyers who practiced in the area without proper preparation and experience." Arthur R. Pinto & Douglas Branson, UNDERSTANDING CORPORATE LAW 157 (2d ed. 2004).

changes: The Private Securities Litigation Reform Act of 1995 and the judicially created principle of "bespeaks caution."

EP MEDSYSTEMS, INC. v. ECHOCATH, INC.

United States Court of Appeals, Third Circuit, 2000
235 F.3d 865

SLOVITER, CIRCUIT JUDGE. EP MedSystems, Inc. appeals the dismissal with prejudice of its securities action against EchoCath, Inc. According to the complaint, the Chief Executive Officer of EchoCath enticed MedSystems into investing $1.4 million in EchoCath by assuring MedSystems that lengthy negotiations had already taken place with four prominent companies to market certain new EchoCath products and that contracts with these companies were "imminent." Relying on cautionary language contained in several public documents filed by EchoCath with the Securities Exchange Commission, the District Court held that these representations, as well as other related representations, were immaterial as a matter of law under the "bespeaks caution" doctrine and the general test for materiality. It also held that MedSystems failed to adequately plead scienter, reasonable reliance, and loss causation and could not do so. It accordingly dismissed the complaint without leave to amend.

Our review of a decision granting a motion to dismiss is plenary.

BACKGROUND

The following facts are drawn largely from the amended complaint and the documents attached to the pleadings by the parties, including several EchoCath public filings with the Securities Exchange Commission (SEC).

EchoCath is a small New Jersey research and development company engaged in developing, manufacturing, and marketing medical devices to enhance and expand the use of ultrasound technology for medical applications and procedures. Among the products that EchoCath has developed with the company's proprietary ultrasound technology are ColorMark, which highlights metallic objects such as needles and other interventional instruments in color to permit them to be seen on existing ultrasound imaging screens, and EchoMark, which electronically marks and displays the position of non-metallic objects such as catheters within the body. The parties refer to these two products as the "women's health products." EchoCath describes its women's health products as enabling physicians to perform procedures such as needle biopsies, catheterizations, and intravascular imaging more safely and efficiently.

EchoCath consummated its initial public offering on January 17, 1996 and issued a lengthy Prospectus that included details of the company's technologies, future plans, capitalization, collaborative agreements, and selected financial data. The Prospectus also included the caution that "[a]n investment in the securities offered ... is speculative in nature and involves a high degree of risk," and set forth several pages of risk factors.

In particular, EchoCath cautioned investors that the company "intend[ed] to pursue licensing, joint development and other collaborative arrangements with other strategic partners ... [but] [t]here can be no assurance ... that the Company will be able to successfully reach agreements with any strategic partners, or that other strategic partners will ever devote sufficient resources to the Company's technologies."

More than six months after the public offering, MedSystems began consideration of a sizable investment in EchoCath. * * *

Frank DeBernardis, the Chief Executive Officer (CEO) of EchoCath, made a lengthy presentation during the August meeting to David Jenkins, MedSystems President and CEO, James Caruso, its Chief Financial Officer (CFO), and Anthony Varrichio, a Director. DeBernardis represented that EchoCath had engaged in lengthy negotiations to license its products and was on the verge of signing contracts with a number of prominent medical companies, which he identified as including UroHealth, Johnson & Johnson, Medtronic, and C.R. Bard, Inc., to develop and market EchoCath's women's health products.

* * * Throughout the negotiations and until the closing in February 1997, EchoCath's CEO continued to represent to MedSystems officials that EchoCath was actively moving forward with the line of women's health products described in the August meeting, and that the contracts with UroHealth, Johnson & Johnson, Medtronic and C.R. Bard to develop these products were "imminent." * * *

* * * On February 27, 1997, MedSystems entered into a subscription agreement with EchoCath to purchase 280,000 shares of preferred Echo-Cath stock for $1,400,000. In the agreement, MedSystems specified that it "ha[d] not relied upon any representation or other information (oral or written) other than as contained in documents or answers to questions so furnished to [MedSystems] by [EchoCath]," that it had "relied on the advice of, or has consulted with, only its own Advisors," and acknowledged that "an investment in the Shares involves a number of very significant risks and [MedSystems was] able to bear the loss of its entire investment." Nonetheless, MedSystems alleges in the complaint that it relied on the representations from EchoCath's CEO of imminent contracts. * * *

In the fifteen months after MedSystems made its investment, Echo-Cath failed to enter into a single contract or to receive any income in connection with the marketing and development of the women's health products. * * *

MedSystems filed suit in the United States District Court for the District of New Jersey, alleging that EchoCath intentionally or recklessly made misrepresentations to MedSystems in connection with the sale of securities in an effort to induce MedSystems to purchase its securities, in violation of Section 10 of the Securities Exchange Act of 1934, 15 U.S.C. S 78j, and Rule 10b–5. MedSystems also alleged a supplemental state law fraud claim. * * *

EchoCath moved to dismiss the complaint. It attached to its motion: (1) the January 17, 1996 Prospectus; (2) the February 27, 1997 Subscription Agreement between EchoCath and MedSystems for the purchase of the stock; (3) its annual 10–KSB report filed with the SEC on December 12, 1996 for the 1996 fiscal year ending August 31, 1996 ("Annual Report"), which reported, inter alia, that as of August 31, 1996, Echo-Cath's operations had not generated significant revenues and which contained substantial cautionary language;* **[1]** (4) EchoCath's quarterly update filed with the SEC on January 21, 1997 for the three months ending on November 30, 1996 ("Quarterly Report"), which reported that EchoCath anticipated additional cash resources that would be provided by the completion of unspecified licensing agreements and strategic alliances, but that there "can be no assurances that the Company will be able to complete the aforementioned license agreements and strategic alliances on acceptable terms." EchoCath took the position that these documents established that any alleged misrepresentations were immaterial under the "bespeaks caution" doctrine because they contained sufficient cautionary language.

* * * There is no indication that MedSystems ever received a copy of these documents, but they were readily available to the public. * * *

The District Court then dismissed the complaint with prejudice. In an exhaustive and lengthy opinion, the court concluded that the representations were immaterial as a matter of law under the "bespeaks caution" doctrine because of the cautionary language accompanying these alleged misrepresentations. The court also stated that MedSystems had failed to plead scienter with sufficient particularity as required by 15 U.S.C. § 78u–4(b)(2). Next, the court found that MedSystems could not have reasonably relied on EchoCath's optimistic financial projections. Finally, the court concluded that MedSystems failed to plead loss causation. Having dismissed the federal securities claim, the District Court declined to retain jurisdiction over the remaining state law fraud claim. * * *

DISCUSSION

* * * Rule 10b–5 makes it unlawful for a person to "make any untrue statement of a material fact or to omit to state a material fact necessary in order to make the statements made, in the light of the circumstances under which they were made, not misleading ... in connection with the purchase or sale of any security." * * *

Under the legal principles governing actions alleging securities fraud, MedSystems must prove that EchoCath (1) made misstatements or omissions of material fact; (2) with scienter; (3) in connection with the

---

* **[1]** Among the cautions contained in the Annual Report were statements that "[n]o assurance can be given that the Company will successfully commercialize any of its products or achieve profitable operations," that the report contained "forward-looking statements" within the meaning of the Private Securities Litigation Reform Act of 1995, and that many known and unknown risks may cause the actual results to be materially different from the company's future predictions.

purchase or sale of securities; (4) upon which MedSystems relied; and (5) that MedSystems' reliance was the proximate cause of its injury. The District Court relied on these principles, and the precedents applying them, in dismissing MedSystems' complaint as a matter of law.

At the outset, it is important to recognize that there are important distinctions between this case and the usual securities actions for which these principles were developed. Although EchoCath, like the companies sued in those cases, sought to sell its securities in the market by an offering accompanied by the January 1996 Prospectus, MedSystems does not base its claim on public misrepresentations or omissions that affected the price of the stock it purchased. Instead, it contends that it was induced to make the substantial $1.4 million investment as a result of personal representations directly made to its executives by EchoCath's executives and that those representations were false and misleading.

In one sense, this action is more akin to a contract action than a securities action, and that may be the claim encompassed in its state law fraud count that the District Court did not consider. The distinction between the fact pattern alleged here and that in the typical securities cases explains why it is difficult to apply the precedent from those cases to many of the issues. It is like the proverbial difficulty of fitting a square peg in a round hole. While the question whether EchoCath's alleged misrepresentations are immaterial as a matter of law can be readily considered under the precedent, it is far more difficult to do so with the subsequent issues, such as whether MedSystems pled scienter with sufficient particularity, failed to plead reasonable reliance, and failed to plead loss causation. We consider each of these issues hereafter, keeping in mind throughout not only this distinction but also that the District Court dismissed the complaint without leave to amend.

A. *General Principles of Materiality*

That materiality is a prerequisite to a viable securities action based on a misrepresentation is too well established to require citation. Nor can there be any disagreement as to the general definition of materiality under the securities laws. As the Supreme Court has defined it, a misrepresentation or omitted fact "is material if there is a substantial likelihood that a reasonable shareholder would consider it important in deciding how to [act]." *TSC Industries, Inc. v. Northway, Inc.*, [426 U.S. 438 (1976)]. Although the *TSC Industries* case involved a proxy solicitation dispute, the *TSC Industries* standard of materiality was expressly applied by the Court to Rule 10b–5 in *Basic Inc. v. Levinson*, [485 U.S. 224 (1988)]. According to the Court, for a misrepresentation or omission to be material "there must be a substantial likelihood that the disclosure of the omitted fact [or misrepresentation] would have been viewed by the reasonable investor as having significantly altered the 'total mix' of information made available." * * *

The materiality requirement has been further refined in recent years. In 1995, Congress enacted the Private Securities Litigation Reform Act (the "Reform Act") because of significant evidence of abuse in private securities litigation, particularly the filing of frivolous suits alleging securities violations designed solely to coerce companies to settle quickly and avoid the expense of litigation. The Reform Act contains, inter alia, a statutory safe harbor for forward-looking written or oral statements.* **[2]** Under that provision, an issuer is not liable for a forward-looking statement if it is "identified as a forward-looking statement, and is accompanied by meaningful cautionary statements identifying important factors that could cause actual results to differ materially from those in the forward-looking statement." The safe harbor is also available for oral forward-looking statements under certain conditions.

In this case, the District Court did not rely on, nor did EchoCath cite, the safe harbor provision as a basis for finding the representations at issue immaterial as a matter of law. This may be because the oral misrepresentations on which MedSystems brought suit were not identified as forward-looking as required by the safe harbor provision. Instead, the District Court found that the misrepresentations were immaterial under the "bespeaks caution" doctrine as adopted by this court in *In re Donald J. Trump Casino Sec. Litig.*, 7 F.3d 357 (3d Cir.1993).

Under the "bespeaks caution" doctrine, "cautionary language, if sufficient, renders the alleged omissions or misrepresentations immaterial as a matter of law." In *In re Trump Casino Sec. Litig.*, we held that a suit brought by a class of investors who purchased bonds to provide funding for the acquisition and completion of the Taj Mahal, a lavish casino/hotel on the boardwalk of Atlantic City, could not be maintained because the alleged misrepresentations and omissions in the prospectus were accompanied by warning signals in the text of the prospectus that conveyed to potential investors the extreme risks inherent in the venture and the variety of obstacles the venture would face. We stated that "bespeaks caution" represents new nomenclature, but it "is essentially shorthand for the well-established principle that a statement or omission must be considered in context, so that accompanying statements may render it immaterial as a matter of law." * * *

---

* **[2]** The Act defines "forward-looking statement" to include:

(A) a statement containing a projection of revenues, income (including income loss), earnings (including earnings loss) per share, capital expenditures, dividends, capital structure, or other financial items;

(B) a statement of the plans and objectives of management for future operations, including plans or objectives relating to the products or services of the issuer;

(C) a statement of future economic performance, including any such statement contained in a discussion and analysis of financial condition by the management or in the results of operations included pursuant to the rules and regulations of the Commission;

(D) any statement of the assumptions underlying or relating to any statement described in subparagraph (A), (B), or (C);

(E) any report issued by an outside reviewer retained by an issuer, to the extent that the report assesses a forward-looking statement made by the issuer; or

(F) a statement containing a projection or estimate of such other items as may be specified by rule or regulation of the Commission.

15 U.S.C.A. § 78u–5(i)(1) (West Supp. 2000).

By its terms, the "bespeaks caution" doctrine, like the safe harbor provision in the Reform Act, is directed only to forward-looking statements. * * *

We have also recognized that for the "bespeaks caution" doctrine to apply, the cautionary language must be directly related to the alleged misrepresentations or omissions. * * *

We turn to consideration of the misrepresentations alleged by MedSystems in light of these general principles to determine if dismissal at the pleading stage should be upheld.

B. *Alleged Misrepresentations*

The principal allegation of MedSystems is that EchoCath repeatedly misrepresented the existence of imminent contracts for its women's health products. The complaint alleges that EchoCath's CEO represented that it "had engaged in lengthy negotiations with and was on the verge of signing contracts with a number of companies including UroHealth, Johnson & Johnson, Medtronic and C.R. Bard, Inc. to develop and market [Echo-Cath's] women's health products." MedSystems also alleges that "[t]hroughout the negotiations and until the closing in February, 1997," EchoCath "continued to represent . . . that EchoCath was actively moving forward with the line of women's health products. . . ." * * *

As we noted earlier, the "bespeaks caution" doctrine applies only to forward-looking statements. On review, we cannot say as a matter of law that the representation was not a present statement of fact. EchoCath's CEO had told MedSystems that lengthy negotiations with the four companies had already taken place and that the contracts were "imminent." An event is "imminent" if it is "ready to take place." WEBSTER'S THIRD NEW INTERNATIONAL DICTIONARY 1130 (1976). A statement by the CEO of Echo-Cath that contracts with four companies were "ready to take place" may reasonably be construed as a representation about the current state of negotiations between EchoCath and the four companies it had identified. As such, the representation could be reasonably construed by a trier of fact to be a statement of fact rather than a prediction of future events. * * *

There is also a question whether the cautionary language cited by the District Court was sufficiently proximate to the imminent contracts representations to meet the relatedness test established by our precedent. The representations were not accompanied by any cautionary language. * * *

C. *Scienter*

EchoCath argues on appeal that the District Court correctly held that dismissal of the complaint was also warranted on the ground that MedSystems failed to meet the heightened pleading required for the scienter element in securities fraud cases. Rule 9(b) of the Federal Rules of Civil Procedure, which applies to all complaints filed in federal court, provides that "[i]n all averments of fraud or mistake, the circumstances constituting fraud or mistake shall be stated with particularity." Fed.R.Civ.P. 9(b). The 1995 Reform Act requires, inter alia, that a "complaint shall, with respect to each act or omission alleged to violate [the Securities Exchange Act], state with particularity facts giving rise to a strong inference that the defendant acted with the required state of mind." 15 U.S.C.A. § 78u–4(b)(2) (West Supp.2000). * * *

MedSystems' complaint alleges that "[c]ontrary to EchoCath's repeated representations to EP MedSystems, EchoCath was not on the verge of signing contracts with UroHealth, Johnson & Johnson, Medtronic, C.R. Bard, Inc. or any other company to market and develop a line of women's health products in September, 1996 or at any other time up to the closing of February 27, 1997." Moreover, "EchoCath knew at all times relevant hereto that it had no reasonable prospects of entering into the contracts it had identified to EP MedSystems." The complaint then notes that "Echo-Cath has failed to entered [sic] into a single contract and has yet to receive any income from the sale of women's health products" since September 1996.

* * * The District Court, on the other hand, viewed the complaint as merely alleging fraud by hindsight. It is, of course, true that we generally require more than a showing that a predicted event did not occur in order to sustain a claim of fraud. * * *

As we noted earlier, this case presents a factual situation unlike that in our prior precedent and, indeed, unlike those that were the basis for the 1995 Reform Act. The legislative history of the Reform Act makes clear that it was primarily directed at the abuse and misuse of securities class action lawsuits where defendant companies "choose to settle rather than face the enormous expense of discovery and trial." As the Senate Report states: The fact that many of these lawsuits are filed as class actions has had an in terrorem effect on Corporate America. A whole stable of "professional plaintiffs," who own shares—or sometimes fractions of shares—in many companies, stand ready to lend their names to class action complaints.

* * *

The "victims" on whose behalf these lawsuits are allegedly brought often receive only pennies on the dollar in damages. Even worse, long-term investors ultimately end up paying the costs associated with the lawsuits. As the Council for Institutional Investors advised: "We are * * * hurt if a system allows someone to force us to spend huge sums of money in legal costs by merely paying ten dollars and filing a meritless cookie cutter complaint against a company or its accountants when that plaintiff is disappointed in his or her investment."

MedSystems stands in contrast to the professional plaintiffs who were the focus of the statute. MedSystems invested the substantial sum of $1.4 million in EchoCath. It did so on the basis of personal representations by EchoCath executives to MedSystems officers concerning negotiations that had occurred and the imminent results expected of those negotiations.

MedSystems' complaint is not a "cookie cutter complaint" or a class action brought by shareholders with an insignificant interest in the company; it is an individual action, based on a transaction arising from direct negotiations between the parties to the action.

It is difficult to see how MedSystems could have pled fraud or scienter with more specificity without having been given the opportunity to conduct any discovery. Here, the necessary information as to the status of EchoCath's negotiations with the four companies lies in the defendant's hands. We acknowledge the Reform Act's heightened pleading requirement for the defendant's state of mind, but we believe that MedSystems' allegations are sufficient under the particular facts of this case, which is not the typical class action that Congress intended to target. * * *

D. Reliance

It is undisputed that a plaintiff seeking relief under Rule 10b–5 must show reasonable reliance on a false statement or omission of material fact. MedSystems' complaint alleges that its executives believed the "representations concerning EchoCath's line of women's health products were true and would not have made its substantial investment in EchoCath if it had known these representations were false." The District Court treated the imminent contracts representation as involving future predictions by EchoCath that contained no guarantee that the contracts would be consummated. The court repeated its position that the representation was contradicted by disclaimers and cautionary language in the 1996 Prospectus, the Annual Report, and the Quarterly Report filed with the SEC. Thus, the court found that any reliance by MedSystems on the representation was unreasonable as a matter of law.

Our consideration of the District Court's analysis leads us to a conclusion similar to that we reached in our discussion on materiality where we concluded that none of the documents containing cautionary language sufficiently neutralized the materiality of the imminent contracts representation. It follows that reliance on the repeated oral representations by EchoCath's CEO was not unreasonable as a matter of law because of those documents. * * *

E. Loss Causation

Finally, we turn to EchoCath's contention that dismissal was appropriate because the complaint fails to plead loss causation. The Reform Act provides that in a securities law action, "the plaintiff shall have the burden of proving that the act or omission of the defendant ... caused the loss for which the plaintiff seeks to recover damages." 15 U.S.C.A. § 78u–4(b)(4) (West Supp.2000). Although this provision does not deal with pleading, the District Court concluded that MedSystems failed to plead loss causation. The court stated that the plaintiff must show that the misrepresentations "caused the decline in value rather than merely inducing the transaction." * * *

In considering loss causation, it is important to recognize once again how this case differs from the usual securities action. In the usual securities action, plaintiffs complain because some announcement emanating from the company, whether regarding a tender offer, earnings, projected earnings, or the company's financial condition, fraudulently represented the actual state of affairs. Plaintiffs claim that, as a result, they purchased the securities at a price that was artificially inflated, only to suffer a loss when the true situation was made known.

This case differs. In this case, MedSystems claims that as a result of fraudulent misrepresentations made in personal communications by Echo-Cath executives, it was induced to make an investment of $1.4 million which turned out to be worthless. * * *

The causation issue becomes most critical at the proof stage. Whether the plaintiff has proven causation is usually reserved for the trier of fact. MedSystems' complaint was dismissed at the pleading stage. Although, as noted above, the allegation that it "sustained substantial financial losses as a direct result of the aforementioned misrepresentations and omissions on the part of EchoCath" could have more specifically connected the misrepresentation to the alleged loss, i.e., investment in a company with little prospects, when we draw all reasonable inferences in plaintiff's favor, we conclude that MedSystems has adequately alleged loss causation. * * *

CONCLUSION

* * * Specifically, we have concluded that MedSystems' central allegation, that EchoCath's CEO gave MedSystems executives assurances that, after lengthy negotiations, contracts with four identified companies were "imminent" and provided sales projections that were an integral part of these assurances, should not have been dismissed. This was a statement of fact in the context in which presented by MedSystems' complaint that could be found to meet the requirement of materiality. The allegation that EchoCath knew or had reason to know that this was not the case adequately met the requirement of pleading scienter. A trier of fact could find that reliance was reasonable and that there was the requisite causal connection between the assurances and MedSystems' loss, i.e., its investment.

* * * It follows that we will reverse the dismissal of the complaint, and also direct reinstatement of the state fraud count. * * *

QUESTIONS

1. Are there any differences between the "forward-looking statement" safe harbor in the Private Securities Litigation Reform Act and the judicially created "bespeaks caution" principle?

2. Would the Third Circuit have decided the case differently if, after each of his statements about EchoCath's being "on the verge of signing

contracts with a number of prominent medical companies," DeBernardis had added the statement "Of course, that is just my opinion. I could be wrong."?

3.   Recall that the Third Circuit merely reversed and remanded the case for trial. If you were representing EchoCath, what would you recommend that your client offer in settlement?

4.   The Private Securities Litigation Reform Act imposes "loss causation" as a requirement in addition to regular but-for causation. But-for causation simply requires that the plaintiff would not have entered the transaction if it were not for the defendant's fraudulent behavior. In essence, the plaintiff must be able to say "I bought this stock *because* defendant lied to me." In contrast, loss causation requires the plaintiff to show that the lie caused the plaintiff not only to buy the stock, but also to suffer a loss.

For example, suppose D tells P that the corporation will do very well because it has just perfected a new method for marketing widgets. It is a lie. The corporation does not have a new method for anything. P buys stock in the corporation because of this misrepresentation. Now suppose the stock plummets in value for reasons wholly unrelated to D's lie. For example, suppose the market for widgets simply dries up because of macroeconomic forces.

In this case, P can show but-for causation, because she would not have bought the stock but for D's misrepresentation. But she cannot show loss causation; the stock lost value for reasons unrelated to D's misrepresentation. Thus, under the Private Securities Litigation Reform Act, P cannot recover. As *EP Medsystems* makes clear, the plaintiff has the burden of proving loss causation.

5.   Now, having read *EP Medsystems*, reconsider Questions 1 through 3 on page 336.

Recall that Rule 10b–5 ends with the phrase "in connection with the purchase or sale of any security" and that the plaintiffs in *EchoCath* had bought EchoCath stock and the plaintiffs in *Basic* had sold their Basic stock. What protects the shareholder who decides *not to sell* because of a false or misleading statement?

In *Birnbaum v. Newport Steel Corp.*, 193 F.2d 461 (2d Cir. 1952), the court held that only those who bought or sold in reliance on a false or misleading statement may bring a private claim for damages. The Supreme Court adopted this interpretation of "in connection with the purchase or sale of any security" in *Blue Chip Stamps v. Manor Drug Stores*, 421 U.S. 723 (1975). (Still, many refer to this as the "*Birnbaum* rule.") Thus folks who sit on the sidelines and do not buy or sell in the face of a false or misleading statement may not bring a private case for damages under Rule 10b–5.

Perhaps the courts are restrictive in this area because Rule 10b–5 does not expressly provide for a private right of action. Rule 10b–5 simply provides that various misstatements or omissions are "unlawful." Clearly, the SEC can enforce the rule through civil actions or administrative enforcement proceedings. The SEC can also refer suspected violations to the Department of Justice for criminal prosecution. Nonetheless lower courts inferred from the existence of the rule that a private right of action should be recognized, allowing suits for damages by those defrauded. *See* Kardon v. National Gypsum Co., 73 F.Supp. 798 (E.D. Pa. 1947). The Supreme Court finally embraced this position expressly in *Herman & MacLean v. Huddleston*, 459 U.S. 375 (1983). According to the Court, the fact that lower courts had long recognized the private right to sue, coupled with the fact that neither Congress nor the SEC had attempted to change that understanding, indicated that such an action was consistent with Congress's intent.

In the next case, shareholders allege that the corporation's overstatement of its earnings caused them to retain (and not sell) their shares. Note that a claim was possible, despite the *Birnbaum* rule, because the plaintiffs invoked only state law, not Rule 10b–5. The alleged misstatement by the corporation was made in a document that was unrelated to any required shareholder action.

In reading the case, please consider the following:

1.   Did the directors tell lies? If so, to whom?

2.   How did the lies hurt the plaintiff shareholders?

3.   How much do the defendants now have to pay the plaintiffs?

MALONE v. BRINCAT

Supreme Court of Delaware, 1998
722 A.2d 5

Holland, Justice. [Mercury Finance Company ("Mercury") is in the automobile finance business. It is publicly traded, with thousands of shareholders. Because it is publicly-traded, federal securities laws require Mercury to make public various information about its earnings and financial performance. It does so by filing that information with the Securities and Exchange Commission. In 1997, Mercury's accountants discovered that Mercury's reports of earnings during the years 1993 through 1996 were substantially overstated. The overstatement was significant. When the corrected numbers were used, Mercury's stock price plunged, reducing Mercury's market capitalization (the number of shares multiplied by the market price of each share) by more than two billion dollars. Dozens of cases were filed; this case was brought under Delaware law.]

Doran Malone, Joseph P. Danielle, and Adrienne M. Danielle, the plaintiffs-appellants, filed this individual and class action in the Court of Chancery. The complaint alleged that the directors of Mercury Finance Company ("Mercury"), a Delaware corporation, breached their fiduciary duty of disclosure. The individual defendant-appellee directors are John N. Brincat, Dennis H. Chookaszian, William C. Croft, Clifford R. Johnson,

Andrew McNally IV, Bruce I. McPhee, Fred G. Steingraber, and Phillip J. Wicklander. The Court of Chancery dismissed the complaint with prejudice pursuant to Chancery Rule 12(b)(6) for failure to state a claim upon which relief may be granted.

The complaint alleged that the director defendants intentionally overstated the financial condition of Mercury on repeated occasions throughout a four-year period in disclosures to Mercury's shareholders. Plaintiffs contend that the complaint states a claim upon which relief can be granted for a breach of the fiduciary duty of disclosure. * * *

This Court has concluded that the Court of Chancery properly granted the defendants' motions to dismiss the complaint. That dismissal, however, should have been without prejudice. Plaintiffs are entitled to file an amended complaint. Therefore, the judgment of the Court of Chancery is affirmed in part, reversed in part, and remanded for further proceedings consistent with this opinion.

* * * The Court of Chancery held that directors have no fiduciary duty of disclosure under Delaware law in the absence of a request for shareholder action. In so holding, the Court stated:

> The federal securities laws ensure the timely release of accurate information into the marketplace. The federal power to regulate should not be duplicated or impliedly usurped by Delaware. When a shareholder is damaged merely as a result of the release of inaccurate information into the marketplace, unconnected with any Delaware corporate governance issue, that shareholder must seek a remedy under federal law.

We disagree, and although we hold that the Complaint as drafted should have been dismissed, our rationale is different. * * *

This Court has held that a board of directors is under a fiduciary duty to disclose material information when seeking shareholder action. It is well established that the duty of disclosure "represents nothing more than the well-recognized proposition that directors of Delaware corporations are under a fiduciary duty to disclose fully and fairly all material information within the board's control when it seeks shareholder action."

* * * The present appeal requires this Court to decide whether a director's fiduciary duty arising out of misdisclosure is implicated in the absence of a request for shareholder action. We hold that directors who knowingly disseminate false information that results in corporate injury or damage to an individual stockholder violate their fiduciary duty, and may be held accountable in a manner appropriate to the circumstances.

Fiduciary Duty
Delaware Corporate Directors

An underlying premise for the imposition of fiduciary duties is a separation of legal control from beneficial ownership. Equitable principles act in those circumstances to protect the beneficiaries who are not in a position to protect themselves. One of the fundamental tenets of Delaware corporate law provides for a separation of control and ownership. The board of directors has the legal responsibility to manage the business of a corporation for the benefit of its shareholder owners. Accordingly, fiduciary duties are imposed on the directors of Delaware corporations to regulate their conduct when they discharge that function.

The directors of Delaware corporations stand in a fiduciary relationship not only to the stockholders but also to the corporations upon whose boards they serve. The director's fiduciary duty to both the corporation and its shareholders has been characterized by this Court as a triad: due care, good faith, and loyalty. That triparte fiduciary duty does not operate intermittently but is the constant compass by which all director actions for the corporation and interactions with its shareholders must be guided.

Although the fiduciary duty of a Delaware director is unremitting, the exact course of conduct that must be charted to properly discharge that responsibility will change in the specific context of the action the director is taking with regard to either the corporation or its shareholders. This Court has endeavored to provide the directors with clear signal beacons and brightly lined-channel markers as they navigate with due care, good faith, and loyalty on behalf of a Delaware corporation and its shareholders. This Court has also endeavored to mark the safe harbors clearly.

Director Communications
Shareholder Reliance Justified

The shareholder constituents of a Delaware corporation are entitled to rely upon their elected directors to discharge their fiduciary duties at all times. Whenever directors communicate publicly or directly with shareholders about the corporation's affairs, with or without a request for shareholder action, directors have a fiduciary duty to shareholders to exercise due care, good faith and loyalty. It follows *a fortiori* that when directors communicate publicly or directly with shareholders about corporate matters the *sine qua non* of directors' fiduciary duty to shareholders is honesty.

According to the appellants, the focus of the fiduciary duty of disclosure is to protect shareholders as the "beneficiaries" of all material information disseminated by the directors. The duty of disclosure is, and always has been, a specific application of the general fiduciary duty owed by directors. The duty of disclosure obligates directors to provide the stockholders with accurate and complete information material to a transaction or other corporate event that is being presented to them for action.

The issue in this case is not whether Mercury's directors breached their duty of disclosure. It is whether they breached their more general fiduciary duty of loyalty and good faith by knowingly disseminating to the stockholders false information about the financial condition of the company. The directors' fiduciary duties include the duty to deal with their stockholders honestly.

Shareholders are entitled to rely upon the truthfulness of all information disseminated to them by the directors they elect to manage the corporate enterprise. Delaware directors disseminate information in at least three contexts: public statements made to the market, including shareholders; statements informing shareholders about the affairs of the corporation without a request for shareholder action; and, statements to shareholders in conjunction with a request for shareholder action. Inaccurate information in these contexts may be the result of a violation of the fiduciary duties of care, loyalty or good faith. We will examine the remedies that are available to shareholders for misrepresentations in each of these three contexts by the directors of a Delaware corporation.

State Fiduciary Disclosure Duty
Shareholder Remedy In Action Requested Context

In the absence of a request for stockholder action, the Delaware General Corporation Law does not require directors to provide shareholders with information concerning the finances or affairs of the corporation. Even when shareholder action is sought, the provisions in the General Corporation Law requiring notice to the shareholders of the proposed action do not require the directors to convey substantive information beyond a statutory minimum. Consequently, in the context of a request for shareholder action, the protection afforded by Delaware law is a judicially recognized equitable cause of action by shareholders against directors. * * *

The duty of directors to observe proper disclosure requirements derives from the combination of the fiduciary duties of care, loyalty and good faith. The plaintiffs contend that, because directors' fiduciary responsibilities are not "intermittent duties," there is no reason why the duty of disclosure should not be implicated in every public communication by a corporate board of directors. The directors of a Delaware corporation are required to disclose fully and fairly all material information within the board's control when it seeks shareholder action. When the directors disseminate information to stockholders when no stockholder action is sought, the fiduciary duties of care, loyalty and good faith apply. Dissemination of false information could violate one or more of those duties.

An action for a breach of fiduciary duty arising out of disclosure violations in connection with a request for stockholder action does not include the elements of reliance, causation and actual quantifiable monetary damages. Instead, such actions require the challenged disclosure to have a connection to the request for shareholder action. The essential inquiry in such an action is whether the alleged omission or misrepresentation is material. Materiality is determined with respect to the shareholder action being sought.

The directors' duty to disclose all available material information in connection with a request for shareholder action must be balanced against its concomitant duty to protect the corporate enterprise, in particular, by keeping certain financial information confidential. Directors are required to provide shareholders with all information that is material to the action being requested and to provide a balanced, truthful account of all matters disclosed in the communications with shareholders. Accordingly, directors have definitive guidance in discharging their fiduciary duty by an analysis of the factual circumstances relating to the specific shareholder action being requested and an inquiry into the potential for deception or misinformation.

Fraud On Market
Regulated by Federal Law

When corporate directors impart information they must comport with the obligations imposed by both the Delaware law and the federal statutes and regulations of the United States Securities and Exchange Commission ("SEC"). Historically, federal law has regulated disclosures by corporate directors into the general interstate market. This Court has noted that "in observing its congressional mandate the SEC has adopted a 'basic philosophy of disclosure.'" Accordingly, this Court has held that there is "no legitimate basis to create a new cause of action which would replicate, by state decisional law, the provisions of . . . the 1934 Act." In deference to the panoply of federal protections that are available to investors in connection with the purchase or sale of securities of Delaware corporations, this Court has decided not to recognize a state common law cause of action against the directors of Delaware corporations for "fraud on the market." Here, it is to be noted, the claim appears to be made by those who did not sell and, therefore, would not implicate federal securities laws which relate to the purchase or sale of securities. * * *

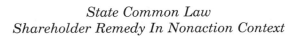

State Common Law
Shareholder Remedy In Nonaction Context

Delaware law also protects shareholders who receive false communications from directors even in the absence of a request for shareholder action. When the directors are not seeking shareholder action, but are deliberately misinforming shareholders about the business of the corporation, either directly or by a public statement, there is a violation of fiduciary duty. That violation may result in a derivative claim on behalf of the corporation or a cause of action for damages. There may also be a basis for equitable relief to remedy the violation.

Complaint Properly Dismissed
No Shareholder Action Requested

Here the complaint alleges (if true) an egregious violation of fiduciary duty by the directors in knowingly disseminating materially false information. Then it alleges that the corporation lost about $2 billion in value as a result. Then it merely claims that the action is brought on behalf of the named plaintiffs and the putative class. It is a *non sequitur* rather than a syllogism.

The allegation in paragraph 3 that the false disclosures resulted in the corporation losing virtually all its equity seems obliquely to claim an injury to the corporation. The plaintiffs, however, never expressly assert a derivative claim on behalf of the corporation or allege compliance with Court of Chancery Rule 23.1, which requires pre-suit demand or cognizable and particularized allegations that demand is excused. If the plaintiffs intend to assert a derivative claim, they should be permitted to replead to assert such a claim and any damage or equitable remedy sought on behalf of the corporation. Likewise, the plaintiffs should have the opportunity to replead to assert any individual cause of action and articulate a remedy that is appropriate on behalf of the named plaintiffs individually, or a properly recognizable class consistent with Court of Chancery Rule 23. * * *

The Court of Chancery properly dismissed the complaint before it against the individual director defendants, in the absence of well-pleaded allegations stating a derivative, class or individual cause of action and properly assertable remedy. * * *

Nevertheless, we disagree with the Court of Chancery's holding that such a claim cannot be articulated on these facts. The plaintiffs should have been permitted to amend their complaint, if possible, to state a properly cognizable cause of action. * * * Consequently, the Court of Chancery should have dismissed the complaint without prejudice.

The judgment of the Court of Chancery to dismiss the complaint is affirmed. The judgment to dismiss the complaint with prejudice is reversed. This matter is remanded for further proceedings in accordance with this opinion.

QUESTIONS

1.   Did the defendant directors breach their duty of disclosure? What did the court mean when it said: "The issue in this case is not whether Mercury's directors breached their duty of disclosure. It is whether they breached their more general fiduciary duty of loyalty and good faith by knowingly disseminating false information to the shareholders about the financial condition of the company"?

2.   Were the claims asserted in *Malone* direct or derivative?

3.   The Delaware court seems to be blowing its own horn. Does this case provide "clear signal beacons and brightly lined channel markers"? *See generally* Mark Klock, *Lighthouse or Hidden Reef? Navigating the Fiduciary Duty of Delaware Corporations' Directors in the Wake of Malone*, 6 STAN. J. L. & BUS. & FIN. 1 (2000).

4.   On remand, what will the plaintiffs have to prove? Will the plaintiffs have to prove they relied on the misrepresentation? That the misrepresentation caused them quantifiable money damages?

5.   *Malone v. Brincat* has been described as a case that "significantly broadened the fiduciary disclosure duties of corporate directors under Dela-

ware law." Nicole M. Kim, *Malone v. Brincat: The Fiduciary Disclosure Duty of Corporate Directors Under Delaware Law,* 74 WASH. L. REV. 1151 (1999). Do you agree?

6. Could the plaintiffs (or the court) have relied upon § 552 of the RESTATEMENT (SECOND) OF TORTS? It provides:

> (1) One who, in the course of his business, profession or employment, or in any other transaction in which he has a pecuniary interest, supplies false information for the guidance of others in their business transactions, is subject to liability for pecuniary loss caused to them by their justifiable reliance upon the information, if he fails to exercise reasonable care or competence in obtaining or communicating the information.

> (2) Except as stated in Subsection (3), the liability stated in Subsection (1) is limited to loss suffered (a) by the person or one of a limited group of persons for whose benefit and guidance he intends to supply the information or knows that the recipient intends to supply it; and (b) through reliance upon it in a transaction that he intends the information to influence or knows that the recipient so intends or in a substantially similar transaction.

> (3) The liability of one who is under a public duty to give the information extends to loss suffered by any of the class of persons for whose benefit the duty is created, in any of the transactions in which it is intended to protect them.

2. WHAT ARE THE LEGAL DUTIES APPLICABLE TO BUYING OR SELLING STOCK?

a. 10b–5 Again and Buying or Selling With Inside Information

Remember 10b–5? Always remember Rule 10b–5 whenever anyone is buying or selling securities, including stock. We have seen Rule 10b–5 applied when there was an alleged misrepresentation upon which someone relied in buying or selling securities. There, Rule 10b–5 complements common law fraud in providing a remedy for an aggrieved buyer or seller.

Rule 10b–5 has had an even greater impact, however, with regard to insider trading—that is, where there is no misrepresentation, but instead someone privy to confidential business information (an "insider") uses it (or perhaps passes it along to another) to trade in securities of that business (or perhaps another business). As we will see, Rule 10b–5 goes beyond what would have been actionable as insider trading under common law fraud.

But before we dive into the insider-trading cases, we need to explore the range of *jurisdiction* for Rule 10b–5. Recall that Rule 10b–5 was promulgated pursuant to § 10 of the '34 Act. To ensure that this regulation fell within power properly exercised by the federal government, both § 10 and Rule 10b–5 require an interstate commerce nexus. Specifically, Rule 10b–5 provides that it is unlawful to do certain things (like misrepresent or to trade on inside information) through "use of any means or instrumentality of interstate commerce or of the mails, or of any facility of any national securities exchange." The following case demonstrates how easily this jurisdictional nexus can be satisfied.

DUPUY v. DUPUY

United States Court of Appeals, Fifth Circuit, 1975
511 F.2d 641

DYER, CIRCUIT JUDGE: This appeal presents a narrow question of law— Does the making of intrastate telephone calls satisfy the jurisdictional requirement of "use of any means or instrumentality of interstate commerce" found in § 10 of the Securities Exchange Act of 1934, and Securities and Exchange Commission Rule 10b–5? The district court held that it did not, and granted the defendant's motion for summary judgment on a complaint which alleged intrastate calls as the only basis for federal jurisdiction. We reverse and remand for further proceedings.

Plaintiff Milton Dupuy (Milton) and defendant Clarence Dupuy (Clarence) are brothers living in the same apartment complex in New Orleans, Louisiana. Together with their mother, they had engaged in a number of joint commercial ventures, including in 1971 the formation of the Lori Corporation for the purpose of building, owning, and operating a hotel in the French Quarter of New Orleans. Initially, each brother owned 47% of the Lori Corporation shares, with their mother owning the remaining 6%. However, Milton's subsequent illness necessitated both his withdrawal from active participation in the management of the corporation and, ultimately, the sale of his shares to Clarence.

The gist of Milton's lawsuit, which is grounded both on a Rule 10b–5 violation and a pendent fraud claim under state law, is that during the negotiations for the sale of his shares, Clarence misrepresented certain material facts and concealed others in order to induce Milton to part with his interest for only a small fraction of its true value. For example, he alleged that Clarence told him the hotel project was stalled when in fact it was not, and also that he failed to disclose that the corporation had entered into a partnership agreement whereby its chief asset, the ground lease for the hotel site, had been assigned to the partnership at a valuation of $1,000,000.

As a basis of federal jurisdiction, Milton further alleged that the sale negotiations had in large measure been conducted through intrastate telephone conversations between his brother and himself. Clarence, while denying that such conversations occurred, moved for summary judgment on the ground that, even if held, intrastate telephone conversations were legally insufficient to confer federal jurisdiction over a 10b–5 claim. The district court granted the motion, and Milton appealed.

In determining whether intrastate telephone calls may confer federal jurisdiction under § 10 of the Securities Exchange Act, we are of course dealing exclusively with a question of Congressional intent, not Congressional power. * * *

The primary thrust of the Securities Exchange Act is of course clear. It and its companion acts embrace [a] fundamental purpose ... to substitute a philosophy of full disclosure for the philosophy of *caveat emptor* and thus to achieve a high standard of ethics in the securities industry.* **[2]** *S.E.C. v. Capital Research Bureau*, 1963, 375 U.S. 180, 186. * * *

Appellee has not advanced, nor do we perceive, any reasoned justification for treating the Rule's jurisdiction phrase, "use of any means or instrumentality of interstate commerce," in a [narrow] manner. Indeed, it seems somewhat anomalous to assume, in the absence of express indication of such an intent, that on the one hand, Congress and the S.E.C. meant to erect a comprehensive statutory scheme for the prevention of securities fraud, and on the other, intended to narrowly circumscribe its scope of operation. Therefore, we align ourselves with the great majority of courts which have considered this issue, and hold that intrastate use of the telephone may confer federal jurisdiction over a private action alleging violation of § 10 of the Securities Exchange Act of 1934 and S.E.C. Rule 10b–5.

Reversed and Remanded.

QUESTIONS

1. Clearly, a transaction does not have to cross state lines to satisfy the interstate nexus for Rule 10b–5. Why, as a matter of policy, does the court embrace a liberal reading of this requirement?

2. Freer misrepresents facts about the value of his stock in Bubba's Burritos, Inc. to Shepherd in a face-to-face meeting. As a result of those misrepresentations, Shepherd agrees to buy Freer's stock. He pays for it with a check. Freer endorses the stock certificates to Shepherd. Clearly, Shepherd can sue Freer for common law fraud. Can he sue Freer under Rule 10b–5?

3. Agee, who is a director of Bubba's Burritos, Inc., misrepresents facts about the future value of Bubba's stock in a face-to-face meeting with Epstein. In reliance on those misrepresentations, Epstein goes to an online brokerage service and purchases stock in Bubba's through a national exchange. The stock craters in value. Can Epstein sue Agee under Rule 10b–5?

4. In *Dupuy*, the defendant was a buyer. Is Rule 10b–5 limited to situations in which the defendant bought stock?

5. In *Dupuy*, the defendant shareholder was the manager of the corporation. Is Rule 10b–5 limited to situations where the buying or selling shareholder is involved in the management of the corporation?

6. In *Dupuy*, the defendant "misrepresented certain material facts." Is Rule 10b–5 limited to situations in which the defendant makes material

---

* **[2]** The "securities industry" encompasses more than the organized securities market. We read § 10(b) to mean that Congress meant to bar deceptive devices and contrivances in the purchase or sale of securities whether conducted in the organized markets or face to face.

misrepresentations? After all, if Rule 10b–5 is limited to cases involving misrepresentations, it is not much of an advance over common law fraud. What about nondisclosure? Common sense tells us that most insider trading is done by someone who knows material inside information which she does not disclose to the other side in a securities transaction. Such activity is not common law fraud, because it does not involve a misrepresentation.

We now turn from jurisdictional issues to the substantive law of insider trading. The next case is a famous state-law treatment of nondisclosure. Although the decision does not represent current federal law on insider trading, some states still employ a similar approach. After it, we will look at leading Rule 10b–5 cases in the area.

GOODWIN v. AGASSIZ

Supreme Judicial Court of Massachusetts, 1933
186 N.E. 659

RUGG, J. [Plaintiff owned 700 shares of stock in Cliff Mining Company. He sold this stock on a public exchange—the Boston Stock Exchange. Although it was not clear at the time, the two defendants (MacNaughton and Agassiz) bought those very shares on the same exchange. The trial court lacked personal jurisdiction over MacNaughton, so the case proceeded against Agassiz. Agassiz was the president and a director of Cliff Mining Company and, because of that inside position, was aware that "an experienced geologist" had formulated a theory that a particular area of Michigan was rich with copper deposits. Cliff Mining Company had begun securing mineral and other rights to land in that area.

Because of this favorable information, the defendants bought as much Cliff Mining stock as they could. Plaintiff was not aware of the favorable information, and asserts that he would not have sold his 700 shares had he known of the geologist's theory. Because he sold his stock, and the defendants bought it, on a stock exchange, there was no communication between plaintiff and defendants. The trial court expressly found that Agassiz had not committed common law fraud and that he had not breached a duty to Cliff Mining Company in engaging in this classic example of insider trading.

Nonetheless, plaintiff asserted a theory that Agassiz's purchasing plaintiff's stock without disclosing the material inside information constituted an actionable common law wrong for which he could sue.]

The trial judge ruled that conditions may exist which would make it the duty of an officer of a corporation purchasing its stock from a stockholder to inform him as to knowledge possessed by the buyer and not by the seller, but found, on all the circumstances [of this case] that there was no fiduciary relation requiring such disclosure by the defendants to the plaintiff before buying his stock in the manner in which they did. * * *

The directors of a commercial corporation stand in a relation of trust to the corporation and are bound to exercise the strictest good faith in respect to its property and business. * * * The contention that directors also occupy the position of trustee toward individual stockholders in the corporation is plainly contrary to repeated decisions of this court and cannot be supported. * * * The directors are not the bailees, the factors, agents or trustees of such individual stockholders. * * * In *Blabon v. Hay*, 269 Mass. 401, 407 [1929], occurs this language with reference to sale of stock in a corporation by a stockholder to two of its directors: "The fact that the defendants were directors created no fiduciary relation between them and the plaintiff in the matter of the sale of his stock." * * *

While the general principle is as stated, circumstances may exist requiring that transactions between a director and a stockholder as to stock in the corporation be set aside. The knowledge naturally in the possession of a director as to the condition of a corporation places upon him a peculiar obligation to observe every requirement of fair dealing when directly buying or selling its stock. Mere silence does not usually amount to a breach of duty, but parties may stand in such relation to each other that an equitable responsibility arises to communicate facts. * * * Purchases and sales of stock dealt in on the stock exchange are commonly impersonal affairs. An honest director would be in a difficult situation if he could neither buy nor sell on the stock exchange shares of stock in his corporation without first seeking out the other actual ultimate party to the transaction and disclosing to him everything which a court or jury might later find that he then knew affecting the real or speculative value of such shares. Business of that nature is a matter to be governed by practical rules. Fiduciary obligations of directors ought not to be made so onerous that men of experience and ability will be deterred from accepting such office. Law in its sanctions is not coextensive with morality. It cannot undertake to put all parties to every contract on an equality as to knowledge, experience, skill and shrewdness. It cannot undertake to relieve against hard bargains made between competent parties without fraud. On the other hand, directors cannot rightly be allowed to indulge with impunity in practices which do violence to prevailing standards of upright business men. Therefore, where a director personally seeks a stockholder for the purpose of buying his shares without making disclosure of material facts within his peculiar knowledge and not within reach of the stockholder, the transaction will be closely scrutinized and relief may be granted in appropriate instances. *Strong v. Repide*, 213 U.S. 419 [1909]. * * * The applicable legal principles "have almost always been the fundamental ethical rules of right and wrong." *Robinson v. Mollett*, L.R. 7 H.L. 802, 817 [English & Irish Appeals 1875].

The precise question to be decided in the case at bar is whether on the facts found the defendants as directors had a right to buy stock of the plaintiff, a stockholder. * * * The facts found afford no ground for inferring fraud or conspiracy. The only knowledge possessed by the defendants not open to the plaintiff was the existence of a theory formulated in a thesis by a geologist as to the possible existence of copper deposits where certain geological conditions existed. * * * This thesis did not express an opinion that copper deposits would be found at any particular spot or on property of any specified owner. Whether that theory was sound or fallacious, no one knew, and so far as appears has never been demonstrated. The defendants made no representations to anybody about the theory. No facts found placed upon them any obligation to disclose the theory. A few days after the thesis expounding the theory was brought to the attention of the defendants, the annual report by the directors of the Cliff Mining Company for the calendar year 1925, signed by Agassiz for the directors, was issued. It did not cover the time when the theory was formulated. The report described the status of the operations under exploration which had been begun in 1925. At the annual meeting of the stockholders of the company held early in April, 1926, no reference was made to the theory. It was then at most a hope, possibly an expectation. It had not passed the nebulous stage. No disclosure was made of it. The Cliff Mining Company was not harmed by the nondisclosure. There would have been no advantage to it, so far as appears, from a disclosure. * * * In the circumstances there was no duty on the part of the defendants to set forth to the stockholders at the annual meeting their faith, aspirations and plans for the future. Events as they developed might render advisable radical changes in such views. Disclosure of the theory, if it ultimately was proved to be erroneous or without foundation in fact, might involve the defendants in litigation with those who might act on the hypothesis that it was correct. The stock of the Cliff Mining Company was bought and sold on the stock exchange. The identity of buyers and seller of the stock in question in fact was not known to the parties and perhaps could not readily have been ascertained. The defendants caused the shares to be bought through brokers on the stock exchange. They said nothing to anybody as to the reasons actuating them. The plaintiff was no novice. He was a member of the Boston stock exchange and had kept a record of sales of Cliff Mining Company stock. He acted upon his own judgment in selling his stock. He made no inquiries of the defendants or of other officers of the company. The result is that the plaintiff cannot prevail.

Decree dismissing bill affirmed with costs.

QUESTIONS AND NOTES

1. As *Goodwin* recognized, for starters, a director or officer who has obtained nonpublic information by virtue of her office is not generally under a common law duty to disclose that information in buying or selling stock. Courts further recognize, however, that there are situations in which they will go beyond the starting point and impose precisely such a duty. They usually do so under what is called the "special facts" or "special circumstances" doctrine. The theory is that a fiduciary of the corporation has a duty to

disclose "special facts" when engaging in a stock transaction with a stockholder of the corporation. What are such "special facts"? It's an elastic concept, but generally covers any facts that a reasonable investor would consider important in making a decision on whether to buy or sell shares.

2.   The existence of the geologist's theory about the copper deposits in *Goodwin* would seem to be a "special fact." Obviously, plaintiff in *Goodwin* wishes he had known about the theory; if he had, he would not have sold his shares. So why did the court conclude in *Goodwin* that the plaintiff could not recover? There seem to be two reasons. First, the court is not sure the "fact" was a fact at all—it considered the geologist's theory as too ephemeral, too speculative to require disclosure. Second, the court seems to hold that there is no common law duty on directors or other insiders to disclose inside information when trading *on an exchange*. The court notes that such transactions are "impersonal affairs" and that an insider would be at a disadvantage if he had to seek out the other party in the transaction and make disclosure to that person. Such a rule would be unworkable.

3.   There is also a minority view, rejected in *Goodwin*, that a director who obtains inside information in his role as a director holds the information in trust for stockholders. Under this view, such a director has a common-law duty to disclose the information before purchasing from a stockholder. This is usually called the "Kansas rule," after cases such as *Hotchkiss v. Fischer*, 16 P.2d 531, 534 (1932), in which the Kansas Supreme Court held that a director has a duty to shareholders "to communicate . . . all material facts in connection with the transaction which the director knows or should know."

4.   According to *Goodwin*, what is the source of the duty to disclose? Would it be imposed upon someone who, although not an "insider," accidentally became aware of inside information, e.g., by overhearing Agassiz discuss the geological theory in an elevator?

5.   Also according to *Goodwin*, under what circumstances would a court impose a duty to disclose? Reread the (overly long) paragraph starting "While the general principle is as stated, . . ." and address these questions.

5.1. Agee is a director of Bubba's Burritos, Inc. and in that capacity has learned that Bubba's may well be taken over by McDonald's (a fact that will make Bubba's stock rise in value). The public does not yet know this information. Roberts owns 50 shares of Bubba's and thinks the company is doing poorly. At a stockholders' meeting, he complains to Agee and says "I wish I had never bought this stock." Agee then offers to purchase Roberts's stock. Roberts sells, after which the announcement of the McDonald's takeover is made. Would the *Goodwin* court permit suit by Roberts against Agee?

5.2   Agee is a director of Bubba's Burritos, Inc. and in that capacity has learned some devastating information that will cause the price of Bubba's stock to plummet. The public does not yet know this information. Epstein is not a Bubba's stockholder, but thinks the company is interesting. Epstein knows Agee socially and one day, while playing golf, asks her if she would sell Epstein some of Agee's Bubba's stock. Agee says nothing except "O.K." After Epstein buys and the stock craters, would the *Goodwin* court permit suit by Epstein against Agee? *See Joseph v. Farnsworth Radio & Television Corp.*, 99 F.Supp. 701 (S.D. N.Y.1951).

6. At least one court has held that insider trading on the open stock market violates a fiduciary duty to the corporation and thus opens the offending insider to a derivative suit. In *Diamond v. Oreamuno*, 248 N.E.2d 910 (N.Y. 1969), a director and an officer of a corporation knew of some impending bad news for the corporation. They unloaded their stock in a market transaction before the bad news was made public, selling at $28 per share. After the bad news hit the streets, the price of the stock dropped to $11 per share. The New York Court of Appeals held that the two defendants breached a fiduciary duty to their corporation *even though the corporation did not suffer a loss as a result of their actions.* The court also noted that what the defendants did harmed the corporation's reputation.

Because the defendants breached a duty to the corporation, a derivative suit was proper and the defendants were forced to give their "profits" (presumably the losses they avoided by selling at $28 per share) to the corporation. The case might be seen as saying that the insiders misappropriated corporate "property" (the confidential information) for their own benefit. It is a simple step from there to say that the corporation ought to recover the profit.

We've just had a detour through the common law. Now, does Rule 10b–5 impose a duty to disclose? Look carefully at the language of the Rule. It contains three subsections listing inappropriate behavior. The first and third subsections seem to be exercises in finding different ways to say "fraud is inappropriate." Only the second of the three seems even remotely to refer to nondisclosure, as it makes it unlawful to "omit" a material fact. But look again. This language imposes a requirement to disclose *only* to correct a statement already made. So it would not seem to impose a general analog to the "special facts" doctrine.

The next case is one of the most famous Rule 10b–5 opinions. It has been cited by the courts more than 2,000 times and countless times in law review commentary. It is a lengthy opinion, one part of which deals with misrepresentation by the corporation in a press release. In our edited version of the opinion, we have removed that discussion (because it doesn't add to what we already learned in *Basic Inc. v. Levinson* and *EP Medsystems*). Instead, we present that part of the opinion addressing "insider trading" under Rule 10b–5. In reading it, note what part of Rule 10b–5 is involved.

SECURITIES AND EXCHANGE COMMISSION v. TEXAS GULF SULPHUR CO.

United States Court of Appeals, Second Circuit, 1968
401 F.2d 833

WATERMAN, CIRCUIT JUDGE [The Texas Gulf Sulphur Company ("TGS") was looking for mineral sites in Canada. In October of 1963, aerial surveys indicated that the K–55 site near Timmons, Ontario was promising. TGS drilled a test hole in November and, when it appeared favorable, started buying land in the area. TGS also decided to refrain from further drilling and to keep the test results secret so it could buy the land around the drill site as cheaply as possible. TGS bought enough land to resume drilling in March of 1964. TGS did not issue a press release with facts about its major mineral discovery until April 1964.

From October 1963 until April 1964, Francis G. Coates (a TGS director) and various TGS insiders (including Fogarty, Murray, Holyk, and Darke) and their "tippees" purchased TGS stock in the open market for as little as $18 a share. On April 16, the day of the official announcement, the price of TGS stock had climbed to $37 a share. The price had climbed steadily as rumors circulated that TGS had discovered something big in Timmons.

The SEC filed an action under 10b–5 against both TGS and the [individual] defendants. The portion of the opinion excerpted below deals only with the SEC's allegations that the individual defendants violated Rule 10b–5 in these ways: (1) defendants had either personally or through agents purchased TGS's stock or "calls"* thereon from November 12, 1963 through April 16, 1964 on the basis of material inside information concerning the results of TGS drilling in Timmons, while such information remained undisclosed to the investing public generally or to the particular sellers; (2) defendants Darke and Coates had divulged such information to others for use in purchasing TGS stock or calls or recommended its purchase while the information was undisclosed to the public or to the sellers.]

I. THE INDIVIDUAL DEFENDANTS

A. Introductory

Rule 10b–5, 17 CFR 240.10b–5, on which this action is predicated, provides: It shall be unlawful for any person, directly or indirectly, by the use of any means or instrumentality of interstate commerce, or of the mails, or of any facility of any national securities exchange,

> (1) to employ any device, scheme, or artifice to defraud,
>
> (2) to make any untrue statement of a material fact or to omit to state a material fact necessary in order to make the statements made, in the light of the circumstances under which they were made, not misleading, or
>
> (3) to engage in any act, practice, or course of business which operates or would operate as a fraud or deceit upon any person,
>
> in connection with the purchase or sale of any security.

---

* A "call" option is a contractual right to purchase stock at a specified price in the future. It is a bet that the stock's price will rise. If the price of the stock increases, then the option's owner can buy the stock at the agreed "exercise" or "strike" price, and then immediately resell it for a profit at the higher market price.

* * * The essence of the Rule is that anyone who, trading for his own account in the securities of a corporation, has "access, directly or indirectly, to information intended to be available only for a corporate purpose and not for the personal benefit of anyone" may not take "advantage of such information knowing it is unavailable to those with whom he is dealing," i.e., the investing public. *Matter of Cady, Roberts & Co.*, 40 SEC 907, 912 (1961). Insiders, as directors or management officers are, of course, by this Rule, precluded from so unfairly dealing, but the Rule is also applicable to one possessing the information who may not be strictly termed an "insider" within the meaning of Sec. 16(b) of the Act.* *Cady, Roberts,* supra. Thus, anyone in possession of material inside information must either disclose it to the investing public, or, if he is disabled from disclosing it in order to protect a corporate confidence, or he chooses not to do so, must abstain from trading in or recommending the securities concerned while such inside information remains undisclosed. So, it is here no justification for insider activity that disclosure was forbidden by the legitimate corporate objective of acquiring options to purchase the land surrounding the exploration site; if the information was, as the SEC contends, material, its possessors should have kept out of the market until disclosure was accomplished. *Cady, Roberts, supra,* at 911.

B. *Material Inside Information*

An insider is not, of course, always foreclosed from investing in his own company merely because he may be more familiar with company operations than are outside investors. An insider's duty to disclose information or his duty to abstain from dealing in his company's securities arises only in "those situations which are essentially extraordinary in nature and which are reasonably certain to have a substantial effect on the market price of the security if (the extraordinary situation is) disclosed."

Nor is an insider obligated to confer upon outside investors the benefit of his superior financial or other expert analysis by disclosing his educated guesses or predictions. The only regulatory objective is that access to material information be enjoyed equally, but this objective requires nothing more than the disclosure of basic facts so that outsiders may draw upon their own evaluative expertise in reaching their own investment decisions with knowledge equal to that of the insiders.

This is not to suggest, however, the "the test of materiality must necessarily be a conservative one, particularly since many actions under Section 10(b) are brought on the basis of hindsight," in the sense that the materiality of facts is to be assessed solely by measuring the effect the knowledge of the facts would have upon prudent or conservative investors. The basic test of materiality * * * is whether a reasonable man would attach importance * * * in determining his choice of action in the transaction in question.

---

* Note from your authors: We will see later that § 16(b), inapplicable here, defines insiders very narrowly—as officers, directors, or holders of more than ten percent of a corporation's stock.

In each case, then, whether facts are material within Rule 10b–5 when the facts relate to a particular event and are undisclosed by those persons who are knowledgeable thereof will depend at any given time upon a balancing of both the indicated probability that the event will occur and the anticipated magnitude of the event in light of the totality of the company activity.

Our survey of the facts found below conclusively establishes that knowledge of the results of the discovery hole, K–55–1, would have been important to a reasonable investor and might have affected the price of the stock. Here, a valuable corporate purpose was served by delaying the publication of the K–55–1 discovery. Where a corporate purpose is thus served by withholding the news of a material fact, those persons who are thus quite properly true to their corporate trust must not during the period of non-disclosure deal personally in the corporation's securities or give to outsiders confidential information not generally available to all the corporations' stockholders and to the public at large.

Finally, a major factor in determining whether the K–55–1 discovery was a material fact is the importance attached to the drilling results by those who knew about it. From November 12, 1963 to April 6, 1964 Fogarty, Murray, Holyk and Darke spent more than $100,000 in purchasing TGS stock and calls on that stock. No reason appears why outside investors, perhaps better acquainted with speculative modes of investment and with, in many cases, perhaps more capital at their disposal for intelligent speculation, would have been less influenced, and would not have been similarly motivated to invest if they had known what the insider investors knew about the K–55–1 discovery.

Our decision is not at all shaken by fears that the elimination of insider trading benefits will deplete the ranks of capable corporate managers by taking away an incentive to accept such employment. Such benefits, in essence, are forms of secret corporate compensation, derived at the expense of the uninformed investing public and not at the expense of the corporation which receives the sole benefit from insider incentives. Moreover, adequate incentives for corporate officers may be provided by properly administered stock options and employee purchase plans of which there are many in existence. In any event, the normal motivation induced by stock ownership, i.e., the identification of an individual with corporate progress, is ill-promoted by condoning the sort of speculative insider activity which occurred here; for example, some of the corporation's stock was sold at market in order to purchase short-term calls upon that stock, calls which would never be exercised to increase a stockholder equity in TGS unless the market price of that stock rose sharply.

The core of Rule 10b–5 is the implementation of the Congressional purpose that all investors should have equal access to the rewards of participation in securities transactions. It was the intent of Congress that all members of the investing public should be subject to identical market risks, which market risks include, of course, the risk that one's evaluative capacity or one's capital available to put at risk may exceed another's capacity or capital. The insiders here were not trading on an equal footing with the outside investors. They alone were in a position to evaluate the probability and magnitude of what seemed from the outset to be a major ore strike; they alone could invest safely, secure in the expectation that the price of TGS stock would rise substantially in the event such a major strike should materialize, but would decline little, if at all, in the event of failure, for the public, ignorant at the outset of the favorable probabilities would likewise be unaware of the unproductive exploration, and the additional exploration costs would not significantly affect TGS market prices. Such inequities based upon unequal access to knowledge should not be shrugged off as inevitable in our way of life, or, in view of the congressional concern in the area, remain uncorrected.

We hold, therefore, that all transactions in TGS stock or calls by individuals apprised of the drilling results of K–55–1 were made in violation of Rule 10b–5.

As it is our holding that the information acquired after the drilling of K–55–1 was material, we hold that Darke violated Rule 10b–5(3) and Section 10(b) by "tipping" and we remand, pursuant to the agreement of the parties, for a determination of the appropriate remedy. As Darke's "tippees" are not defendants in this action, we need not decide whether, if they acted with actual or constructive knowledge that the material information was undisclosed, their conduct is as equally violative of the Rule as the conduct of their insider source, though we note that it certainly could be equally reprehensible.

[Those portions of the opinion applying Rule 10b–5 to stock options and to the TGS press release (which was designed to deflect rumors that TGS had hit a major mineral strike) are omitted.]

QUESTIONS

1. Did any of the individual defendants "make an untrue statement of a material fact"? Did any make any statement at all?

2. What part of Rule 10b–5 did the defendants violate: Rule 10b–5(1) or (2) or (3)? Would the behavior of the defendants in *Texas Gulf Sulphur* have constituted common law fraud? Would it have been actionable under *Goodwin?* Is Rule 10b–5 broader than the common law on insider trading?

In Part I(A) of the opinion, the court said: "The essence of the Rule is that anyone who, trading for his own account in the securities of a corporation, has 'access, directly or indirectly, to information intended to be available only for a corporate purpose and not for the personal benefit of anyone' may not take 'advantage of such information knowing it is unavailable to those with whom he is dealing,' i.e., the investing public." Where does Rule 10b–5 express any such concern?

For the quoted proposition, the *Texas Gulf Sulphur* court cited the opinion from an SEC enforcement action called *In re Matter of Cady, Roberts.*

This opinion of the SEC has played a major role in making Rule 10b–5 an effective tool against insider trading. The Supreme Court will embrace *Cady, Roberts* in the next case we read.

3.   Recall that the United States Supreme Court in the *Basic* case referred to the Second Circuit's decision in *Texas Gulf Sulphur*. Is the *Texas Gulf Sulphur* analysis of 10b–5 consistent with the analysis of 10b–5 in the *Basic* case?

4.   In *Leitch Gold Mines, Ltd. v. Texas Gulf Sulphur Co.*, 1 O.R. 469, 492–493 (1968), the Ontario High Court of Justice ruled that TGS was under no obligation to disclose its mineral discovery information to the owner of the land before purchasing the land at a price far below its true value. Is the *Texas Gulf Sulphur* opinion we read consistent with *Leitch*? (Did anybody from TGS violate Rule 10b–5 by buying land without disclosing its potential mineral content?)

5.   In the *Texas Gulf Sulphur* opinion that we read, Judge Waterman rejects the idea that insider trading should be permitted as an incentive to corporate officers. Since 1966, Dean Henry Manne has argued that insider trading would be an efficient way to compensate insiders without harming investors. Indeed, Manne and others have argued that permitting corporate officers to make money by using confidential inside information could increase the value of the corporation for which the insider works: the opportunity to reap trading profits because good things had happened for the corporation that the public did not yet know about would motivate these insiders to make such good things happen. *See generally* Henry G. Manne, INSIDER TRADING AND THE STOCK MARKET 138–41 (1996); Symposium, *The Legacy of Henry G. Manne—Pioneer in Law & Economics and Innovator in Legal Education*, 50 CASE W. RES. L. REV. 1 (1999). Are there ways other than insider trading that an officer can be compensated if she improves her corporation's performance?

Manne also pointed out that shareholders who just randomly happen to sell their shares during the period when insiders are purchasing shares based on inside information actually *benefit* from the insider trading. Can you see why?

6.   Recall the Second Circuit's mention, in the last substantive paragraph of *Texas Gulf Sulphur*, of "tippees" and "tipping." Some TGS defendants violated Rule 10b–5 not only by insider trading (buying TGS stock on the basis of inside information), but also by "tipping" others about the information. (For now, our tip is to limit your tipping to 20% of the check—25% for especially good service.)

The American Lawyer published an article about lawyer tipping from which the following is an excerpt. It reminds us of the posters from World War II: "Loose lips sink ships."

In January, Julie Freese was one of the young associates at San Francisco's Brobeck, Phleger & Harrison we wrote about in "Still Golden." Freese, we noted, was running her own deals, characteristic of the responsibility given to Brobeck associates during the dot-com boom.

Like the stock market itself, Freese has since fallen to earth. The second-year M & A associate resigned from the firm's Palo Alto office in

March in the wake of an insider trading investigation of Joel Mesplou, a Palo Alto stock trader.

Mesplou made more than $400,000 after he learned privileged information from Freese about Sun Microsystems, Inc.'s acquisition of Cobalt Networks.

Freese—who is simply referred to as an associate at Brobeck in the court papers—has not been charged with anything. Her lawyer, Nanci Clarence, says Mesplou was already familiar with the possibility of the pending transaction when Freese unintentionally mentioned something about it. "She made an inadvertent statement while talking about the nature of her work," says Clarence.

Clarence explains that her client had met Mesplou at a "very crowded party" last September. A couple of weeks later—after working grueling hours on the deal—Freese ran into Mesplou a second time and indirectly mentioned what was keeping her so busy, Clarence says.

James Burns, Jr., Brobeck's managing partner, says that the firm learned of the investigation and Freese's connection to it in mid-January, when Freese told the lead partner on the Sun–Cobalt transaction that she had been questioned by authorities. Soon afterward, when Freese was questioned further, she was placed on administrative leave according to firm policy. In March she voluntarily resigned.

Amy Fantini, *Youthful Indiscretions,* THE AMERICAN LAWYER (May 2001).

———————

Texas Gulf Sulphur was a Second Circuit opinion about trading on inside information. The Supreme Court became especially active in this area of Rule 10b–5 in the 1980s. In the first of those cases, which we read next, the Court held that the person trading on the basis of nonpublic information did not violate Rule 10b–5. In reading it, pay especial attention to how the Court reconciles its holding with the result in *Texas Gulf Sulphur* and with the SEC opinion in *Cady, Roberts*, which we discussed in Note 2 above.

CHIARELLA v. UNITED STATES

United States Supreme Court, 1980
445 U.S. 222

POWELL, J. The question in this case is whether a person who learns from the confidential documents of one corporation that it is planning an attempt to secure control of a second corporation violates § 10 (b) of the Securities Exchange Act of 1934 if he fails to disclose the impending takeover before trading in the target company's securities.

I

Petitioner is a printer by trade. In 1975 and 1976, he worked as a "markup man" in the New York composing room of Pandick Press, a financial printer. Among documents that petitioner handled were five announcements of corporate takeover bids. When these documents were delivered to the printer, the identities of the acquiring and target corporations were concealed by blank spaces or false names. The true names were sent to the printer on the night of the final printing.

The petitioner, however, was able to deduce the names of the target companies before the final printing from other information contained in the documents. Without disclosing his knowledge, petitioner purchased stock in the target companies and sold the shares immediately after the takeover attempts were made public. By this method, petitioner realized a gain of slightly more than $30,000 in the course of 14 months. Subsequently, the Securities and Exchange Commission (Commission or SEC) began an investigation of his trading activities. In May 1977, petitioner entered into a consent decree with the Commission in which he agreed to return his profits to the sellers of the shares. On the same day, he was discharged by Pandick Press.

In January 1978, petitioner was indicted on 17 counts of violating § 10 (b) of the Securities Exchange Act of 1934 (1934 Act) and SEC Rule 10b–5. After petitioner unsuccessfully moved to dismiss the indictment, he was brought to trial and convicted on all counts.

The Court of Appeals for the Second Circuit affirmed petitioner's conviction. We granted certiorari, and we now reverse.

II

* * *

This case concerns the legal effect of the petitioner's silence. The District Court's charge permitted the jury to convict the petitioner if it found that he willfully failed to inform sellers of target company securities that he knew of a forthcoming takeover bid that would make their shares more valuable. In order to decide whether silence in such circumstances violates § 10(b), it is necessary to review the language and legislative history of that statute as well as its interpretation by the Commission and the federal courts.

Although the starting point of our inquiry is the language of the statute, § 10(b) does not state whether silence may constitute a manipulative or deceptive device. Section 10(b) was designed as a catchall clause to prevent fraudulent practices. But neither the legislative history nor the statute itself affords specific guidance for the resolution of this case. When Rule 10b–5 was promulgated in 1942, the SEC did not discuss the possibility that failure to provide information might run afoul of § 10(b).

The SEC took an important step in the development of § 10(b) when it held that a broker-dealer and his firm violated that section by selling securities on the basis of undisclosed information obtained from a director of the issuer corporation who was also a registered representative of the brokerage firm. In *Cady, Roberts & Co.*, 40 S.E.C. 907 (1961), the Commission decided that a corporate insider must abstain from trading in the shares of his corporation unless he has first disclosed all material inside information known to him. The obligation to disclose or abstain derives from "[an] affirmative duty to disclose material information, [which] has been traditionally imposed on corporate 'insiders,' particularly officers, directors, or controlling stockholders. We and the courts have consistently held that insiders must disclose material facts which are known to them by virtue of their position but which are not known to persons with whom they deal and which, if known, would affect their investment judgment." *Id.*, at 911.

The Commission emphasized that the duty arose from (i) the existence of a relationship affording access to inside information intended to be available only for a corporate purpose, and (ii) the unfairness of allowing a corporate insider to take advantage of that information by trading without disclosure.

That the relationship between a corporate insider and the stockholders of his corporation gives rise to a disclosure obligation is not a novel twist of the law. At common law, misrepresentation made for the purpose of inducing reliance upon the false statement is fraudulent. But one who fails to disclose material information prior to the consummation of a transaction commits fraud only when he is under a duty to do so. And the duty to disclose arises when one party has information "that the other [party] is entitled to know because of a fiduciary or other similar relation of trust and confidence between them."* **[10]** In its *Cady, Roberts* decision, the Commission recognized a relationship of trust and confidence between the shareholders of a corporation and those insiders who have obtained confidential information by reason of their position with that corporation. This relationship gives rise to a duty to disclose because of the "necessity of preventing a corporate insider from ... [taking] unfair advantage of the uninformed minority stockholders."

> The federal courts have found violations of § 10(b) where corporate insiders used undisclosed information for their own benefit. E.g., *SEC v. Texas Gulf Sulphur Co.*, 401 F.2d 833 (CA2 1968). The cases also have emphasized, in accordance with the common-law rule, that "[the] party charged with failing to disclose market information must be under a duty to disclose it." *Frigitemp Corp. v. Financial Dynamics Fund, Inc.*, 524 F.2d 275, 282 (CA2 1975). Accordingly, a purchaser of stock who has no duty to a prospective seller because he is neither an insider nor a fiduciary has been held to have no obligation to reveal material facts.

* * *

---

* **[10]** * * * Mr. Justice Blackmun [in his dissent in this case, which we do not include in the casebook] suggests that the "special facts" doctrine may be applied to find that silence constitutes fraud where one party has superior information to another. This Court has never so held. In *Strong v. Repide*, 213 U.S. 419, 431–434 (1909), this Court applied the special-facts doctrine to conclude that a corporate insider had a duty to disclose to a shareholder. In that case, the majority shareholder of a corporation secretly purchased the stock of another shareholder without revealing that the corporation, under the insider's direction, was about to sell corporate assets at a price that would greatly enhance the value of the stock. The decision in *Strong v. Repide* was premised upon the fiduciary duty between the corporate insider and the shareholder.

Thus, administrative and judicial interpretations have established that silence in connection with the purchase or sale of securities may operate as a fraud actionable under § 10(b) despite the absence of statutory language or legislative history specifically addressing the legality of nondisclosure. But such liability is premised upon a duty to disclose arising from a relationship of trust and confidence between parties to a transaction. Application of a duty to disclose prior to trading guarantees that corporate insiders, who have an obligation to place the shareholder's welfare before their own, will not benefit personally through fraudulent use of material, nonpublic information.

In this case, the petitioner was convicted of violating § 10(b) although he was not a corporate insider and he received no confidential information from the target company. Moreover, the "market information" upon which he relied did not concern the earning power or operations of the target company, but only the plans of the acquiring company. Petitioner's use of that information was not a fraud under § 10(b) unless he was subject to an affirmative duty to disclose it before trading. In this case, the jury instructions failed to specify any such duty. In effect, the trial court instructed the jury that petitioner owed a duty to everyone; to all sellers, indeed, to the market as a whole. The jury simply was told to decide whether petitioner used material, nonpublic information at a time when "he knew other people trading in the securities market did not have access to the same information."

The Court of Appeals affirmed the conviction by holding that "[anyone]—corporate insider or not—who regularly receives material nonpublic information may not use that information to trade in securities without incurring an affirmative duty to disclose." Although the court said that its test would include only persons who regularly receive material, nonpublic information, its rationale for that limitation is unrelated to the existence of a duty to disclose. The Court of Appeals, like the trial court, failed to identify a relationship between petitioner and the sellers that could give rise to a duty. Its decision thus rested solely upon its belief that the federal securities laws have "created a system providing equal access to information necessary for reasoned and intelligent investment decisions." The use by anyone of material information not generally available is fraudulent, this theory suggests, because such information gives certain buyers or sellers an unfair advantage over less informed buyers and sellers.

This reasoning suffers from two defects. First, not every instance of financial unfairness constitutes fraudulent activity under § 10(b). Second, the element required to make silence fraudulent—a duty to disclose—is absent in this case. No duty could arise from petitioner's relationship with the sellers of the target company's securities, for petitioner had no prior dealings with them. He was not their agent, he was not a fiduciary, he was not a person in whom the sellers had placed their trust and confidence. He was, in fact, a complete stranger who dealt with the sellers only through impersonal market transactions.

We cannot affirm petitioner's conviction without recognizing a general duty between all participants in market transactions to forgo actions based on material, nonpublic information. Formulation of such a broad duty, which departs radically from the established doctrine that duty arises from a specific relationship between two parties, should not be undertaken absent some explicit evidence of congressional intent.

As we have seen, no such evidence emerges from the language or legislative history of § 10(b). * * *

We see no basis for applying * * * a new and different theory of liability in this case. * * * Section 10(b) is aptly described as a catchall provision, but what it catches must be fraud. When an allegation of fraud is based upon nondisclosure, there can be no fraud absent a duty to speak. We hold that a duty to disclose under § 10(b) does not arise from the mere possession of nonpublic market information. * * *

IV

* * *

The jury instructions demonstrate that petitioner was convicted merely because of his failure to disclose material, non-public information to sellers from whom he bought the stock of target corporations. The jury was not instructed on the nature or elements of a duty owed by petitioner to anyone other than the sellers. Because we cannot affirm a criminal conviction on the basis of a theory not presented to the jury, we will not speculate upon whether such a duty exists, whether it has been breached, or whether such a breach constitutes a violation of § 10(b)* **[21]** petitioner was charged. Thus, we do not believe that a "misappropriation" theory was included in the jury instructions. * * *

The judgment of the Court of Appeals is reversed.

Concurring opinions of JUSTICE STEVENS and JUSTICE BRENNAN are omitted.

* * * * *

BURGER, CHIEF JUSTICE, dissenting.

I believe that the jury instructions in this case properly charged a violation of § 10(b) and Rule 10b–5, and I would affirm the conviction.

---

* [21] The dissent of THE CHIEF JUSTICE relies upon a single phrase from the jury instructions, which states that the petitioner held a "confidential position" at Pandick Press, to argue that the jury was properly instructed on the theory "that a person who has misappropriated nonpublic information has an absolute duty to disclose that information or to refrain from trading." The few words upon which this thesis is based do not explain to the jury the nature and scope of the petitioner's duty to his employer, the nature and scope of petitioner's duty, if any, to the acquiring corporation, or the elements of the tort of misappropriation. Nor do the jury instructions suggest that a "confidential position" is a necessary element of the offense for which petitioner was charged. Thus, we do not believe that a "misappropriation" theory was included in the jury instructions. The conviction would have to be reversed even if the jury had been instructed that it could convict the petitioner either (1) because of his failure to disclose material, nonpublic information to sellers or (2) because of a breach of a duty to the acquiring corporation. We may not uphold a criminal conviction if it is impossible to ascertain whether the defendant has been punished for noncriminal conduct.

I

As a general rule, neither party to an arm's-length business transaction has an obligation to disclose information to the other unless the parties stand in some confidential or fiduciary relation. This rule permits a businessman to capitalize on his experience and skill in securing and evaluating relevant information; it provides incentive for hard work, careful analysis, and astute forecasting. But the policies that underlie the rule also should limit its scope. In particular, the rule should give way when an informational advantage is obtained, not by superior experience, foresight, or industry, but by some unlawful means. One commentator has written:

> "[The] way in which the buyer acquires the information which he conceals from the vendor should be a material circumstance. The information might have been acquired as the result of his bringing to bear a superior knowledge, intelligence, skill or technical judgment; it might have been acquired by mere chance; or it might have been acquired by means of some tortious action on his part.... Any time information is acquired by an illegal act it would seem that there should be a duty to disclose that information." Keeton, *Fraud—Concealment and Non–Disclosure*, 15 Texas L. Rev. 1, 25–26 (1936).

I would read § 10(b) and Rule 10b–5 to encompass and build on this principle: to mean that a person who has misappropriated nonpublic information has an absolute duty to disclose that information or to refrain from trading.

The language of § 10(b) and of Rule 10b–5 plainly supports such a reading. By their terms, these provisions reach any person engaged in any fraudulent scheme. This broad language negates the suggestion that congressional concern was limited to trading by "corporate insiders" or to deceptive practices related to "corporate information." Just as surely Congress cannot have intended one standard of fair dealing for "white collar" insiders and another for the "blue collar" level. The very language of § 10(b) and Rule 10b–5 "by repeated use of the word 'any' [was] obviously meant to be inclusive." * * *

The history of the statute and of the Rule also supports this reading. The antifraud provisions were designed in large measure "to assure that dealing in securities is fair and without undue preferences or advantages among investors." H. R. Conf. Rep. No. 94–229, p. 91 (1975). These provisions prohibit "those manipulative and deceptive practices which have been demonstrated to fulfill no useful function." S. Rep. No. 792, 73d Cong., 2d Sess., 6 (1934). An investor who purchases securities on the basis of misappropriated nonpublic information possesses just such an "undue" trading advantage; his conduct quite clearly serves no useful function except his own enrichment at the expense of others.

This interpretation of § 10(b) and Rule 10b–5 is in no sense novel. It follows naturally from legal principles enunciated by the Securities and

Exchange Commission in its seminal *Cady, Roberts* decision. 40 S.E.C. 907 (1961). There, the Commission relied upon two factors to impose a duty to disclose on corporate insiders: (1) "... access ... to information intended to be available only for a corporate purpose and not for the personal benefit of anyone"; and (2) the unfairness inherent in trading on such information when it is inaccessible to those with whom one is dealing. Both of these factors are present whenever a party gains an informational advantage by unlawful means. * * *

* * *

Dissenting opinions of JUSTICE MARSHALL and JUSTICE BLACKMUN are omitted.

QUESTIONS AND NOTE

1. In a later case (which we will see below), the Supreme Court referred to *Chiarella* as having espoused the "classical" or "traditional" theory of insider trading. Where does this theory come from?

2. Could the *Chiarella* theory have come from *Texas Gulf Sulphur* and *Cady, Roberts*? If so, why did those cases impose liability while *Chiarella* did not?

3. Is *Chiarella* consistent with the "special facts" doctrine? Recall that that doctrine relied at least in part on a fiduciary relationship between a corporation's insiders and its stockholders. Arguably, then, it would not apply to a transaction in which an insider—knowing negative, nonpublic information about the corporation—sells his stock to an unsuspecting buyer. Because that buyer is not yet a shareholder, is there a fiduciary relationship between buyer and seller? Could there be Rule 10b–5 liability according to *Chiarella*?

4. Are *Texas Gulf Sulphur* and *Cady, Roberts* more consistent with Justice Burger's dissent in *Chiarella* than with the majority opinion? Keep the "misappropriation" theory in mind, because the Supreme Court will come back to it in a case we will see below.

5. Why did the majority not address Justice Burger's "misappropriation" theory?

6. The fact that you might not be liable under Rule 10b–5 does not mean that you are home free. There are many other securities laws that might impose liability, as well as other federal statutes such as those involving mail fraud. You can study the entire panoply of such potential traps in a course on securities regulation or white collar crime.

7. Did it matter that the defendant purchased shares not in the *acquiring* company about which he had inside information, but in the *target* company? Here, we note that § 14(e) of the '34 Act (added in the Williams Act) is aimed at fraud in connection with tender offers. Under this statute, the SEC promulgated Rule 14e–3(a), which makes it unlawful to trade on material nonpublic information concerning a tender offer. Under that Rule, the information might come from the acquiring company or the target or insiders or others working for either the acquiring or target company—just so

the defendant knows or should know that the information is nonpublic. Thus, a person in Mr. Chiarella's position would violate Rule 14e–3(a) even though he did not violate Rule 10b–5.

8.   Would the Court have found that Mr. Chiarella violated Rule 10b–5 if a director of the acquiring company had told him who the target corporation was? Would that director also have violated Rule 10b–5? Consider this question in light of the next case.

9.   In *Cady, Roberts*, the person trading on nonpublic information was not a corporate official. Yet he was held to have violated Rule 10b–5. How? Keep that one in mind, too, while reading the next case.

DIRKS v. SECURITIES & EXCHANGE COMMISSION

United States Supreme Court, 1983
463 U.S. 646

POWELL, J. Petitioner Raymond Dirks received material nonpublic information from "insiders" of a corporation with which he had no connection. He disclosed this information to investors who relied on it in trading in the shares of the corporation. The question is whether Dirks violated the antifraud provisions of the federal securities laws by this disclosure.

I

In 1973, Dirks was an officer of a New York broker-dealer firm who specialized in providing investment analysis of insurance company securities to institutional investors. On March 6, Dirks received information from Ronald Secrist, a former officer of Equity Funding of America. Secrist alleged that the assets of Equity Funding, a diversified corporation primarily engaged in selling life insurance and mutual funds, were vastly overstated as the result of fraudulent corporate practices. Secrist also stated that various regulatory agencies had failed to act on similar charges made by Equity Funding employees. He urged Dirks to verify the fraud and disclose it publicly.

Dirks decided to investigate the allegations. He visited Equity Funding's headquarters in Los Angeles and interviewed several officers and employees of the corporation. The senior management denied any wrongdoing, but certain corporation employees corroborated the charges of fraud. Neither Dirks nor his firm owned or traded any Equity Funding stock, but throughout his investigation he openly discussed the information he had obtained with a number of clients and investors. Some of these persons sold their holdings of Equity Funding securities, including five investment advisers who liquidated holdings of more than $16 million.

While Dirks was in Los Angeles, he was in touch regularly with William Blundell, the Wall Street Journal's Los Angeles bureau chief. Dirks urged Blundell to write a story on the fraud allegations. Blundell did not believe, however, that such a massive fraud could go undetected and declined to write the story. He feared that publishing such damaging hearsay might be libelous.

During the two-week period in which Dirks pursued his investigation and spread word of Secrist's charges, the price of Equity Funding stock fell from $26 per share to less than $15 per share. This led the New York Stock Exchange to halt trading on March 27. Shortly thereafter California insurance authorities impounded Equity Funding's records and uncovered evidence of the fraud. Only then did the Securities and Exchange Commission (SEC) file a complaint against Equity Funding and only then, on April 2, did the Wall Street Journal publish a front-page story based largely on information assembled by Dirks. Equity Funding immediately went into receivership.

The SEC began an investigation into Dirks' role in the exposure of the fraud. After a hearing by an Administrative Law Judge, the SEC found that Dirks had aided and abetted violations of [other federal securities provisions and] SEC Rule 10b–5 by repeating the allegations of fraud to members of the investment community who later sold their Equity Funding stock. The SEC concluded: "Where 'tippees'—regardless of their motivation or occupation—come into possession of material 'corporate information that they know is confidential and know or should know came from a corporate insider,' they must either publicly disclose that information or refrain from trading." 21 S.E.C. Docket 1401, 1407 (1981) (quoting Chiarella v. United States, 445 U.S. 222, 230, n. 12 (1980)). Recognizing, however, that Dirks "played an important role in bringing [Equity Funding's] massive fraud to light," * * * the SEC only censured him.

Dirks sought review in the Court of Appeals for the District of Columbia Circuit. The court entered judgment against Dirks * * *.

In view of the importance to the SEC and to the securities industry of the question presented by this case, we granted a writ of certiorari. * * * We now reverse.

II

In the seminal case of *In re Cady, Roberts & Co.*, 40 S.E.C. 907 (1961), the SEC recognized that the common law in some jurisdictions imposes on "corporate 'insiders,' particularly officers, directors, or controlling stockholders" an "affirmative duty of disclosure ... when dealing in securities." The SEC found that not only did breach of this common-law duty also establish the elements of a Rule 10b–5 violation, but that individuals other than corporate insiders could be obligated either to disclose material nonpublic information before trading or to abstain from trading altogether. In *Chiarella*, we accepted the two elements set out in *Cady, Roberts* for establishing a Rule 10b–5 violation: "(i) the existence of a relationship affording access to inside information intended to be available only for a corporate purpose, and (ii) the unfairness of allowing a corporate insider to take advantage of that information by trading without disclosure." In examining whether Chiarella had an obligation to disclose or abstain, the

Court found that there is no general duty to disclose before trading on material nonpublic information, and held that "a duty to disclose under § 10(b) does not arise from the mere possession of nonpublic market information." Such a duty arises rather from the existence of a fiduciary relationship.

Not "all breaches of fiduciary duty in connection with a securities transaction," however, come within the ambit of Rule 10b–5. Santa Fe Industries, Inc. v. Green, 430 U.S. 462, 472 (1977). There must also be "manipulation or deception." In an inside-trading case this fraud derives from the "inherent unfairness involved where one takes advantage" of "information intended to be available only for a corporate purpose and not for the personal benefit of anyone." In re Merrill Lynch, Pierce, Fenner & Smith, Inc., 43 S.E.C. 933, 936 (1968). Thus, an insider will be liable under Rule 10b–5 for inside trading only where he fails to disclose material nonpublic information before trading on it and thus makes "secret profits."

III

We were explicit in *Chiarella* in saying that there can be no duty to disclose where the person who has traded on inside information "was not [the corporation's] agent, . . . was not a fiduciary, [or] was not a person in whom the sellers [of the securities] had placed their trust and confidence." Not to require such a fiduciary relationship, we recognized, would "[depart] radically from the established doctrine that duty arises from a specific relationship between two parties" and would amount to "recognizing a general duty between all participants in market transactions to forgo actions based on material, nonpublic information." This requirement of a specific relationship between the shareholders and the individual trading on inside information has created analytical difficulties for the SEC and courts in policing tippees who trade on inside information. Unlike insiders who have independent fiduciary duties to both the corporation and its shareholders, the typical tippee has no such relationships.* **[14]** In view of this absence, it has been unclear how a tippee acquires the *Cady, Roberts* duty to refrain from trading on inside information.

A

The SEC's position, as stated in its opinion in this case, is that a tippee "inherits" the *Cady, Roberts* obligation to shareholders whenever he receives inside information from an insider:

---

* **[14]** Under certain circumstances, such as where corporate information is revealed legitimately to an underwriter, accountant, lawyer, or consultant working for the corporation, these outsiders may become fiduciaries of the shareholders. The basis for recognizing this fiduciary duty is not simply that such persons acquired nonpublic corporate information, but rather that they have entered into a special confidential relationship in the conduct of the business of the enterprise and are given access to information solely for corporate purposes. * * * When such a person breaches his fiduciary relationship, he may be treated more properly as a tipper than a tippee. *See* Shapiro v. Merrill Lynch, Pierce, Fenner & Smith, Inc., 495 F.2d 228, 237 (CA2 1974) (investment banker had access to material information when working on a proposed public offering for the corporation). For such a duty to be imposed, however, the corporation must expect the outsider to keep the disclosed nonpublic information confidential, and the relationship at least must imply such a duty.

> In tipping potential traders, Dirks breached a duty which he had assumed as a result of knowingly receiving confidential information from [Equity Funding] insiders. Tippees such as Dirks who receive non-public, material information from insiders become "subject to the same duty as [the] insiders." Such a tippee breaches the fiduciary duty which he assumes from the insider when the tippee knowingly transmits the information to someone who will probably trade on the basis thereof.... Presumably, Dirks' informants were entitled to disclose the [Equity Funding] fraud in order to bring it to light and its perpetrators to justice. However, Dirks—standing in their shoes—committed a breach of the fiduciary duty which he had assumed in dealing with them, when he passed the information on to traders.

This view differs little from the view that we rejected as inconsistent with congressional intent in *Chiarella*. In that case, the Court of Appeals agreed with the SEC and affirmed Chiarella's conviction, holding that "[anyone]—corporate insider or not—who regularly receives material non-public information may not use that information to trade in securities without incurring an affirmative duty to disclose." United States v. Chiarella, 588 F.2d 1358, 1365 (CA2 1978). Here, the SEC maintains that anyone who knowingly receives nonpublic material information from an insider has a fiduciary duty to disclose before trading.* **[15]**

In effect, the SEC's theory of tippee liability in both cases appears rooted in the idea that the antifraud provisions require equal information among all traders.* **[16]** This conflicts with the principle set forth in *Chiarella* that only some persons, under some circumstances, will be barred from trading while in possession of material nonpublic information. Judge Wright [in the Court of Appeals' consideration of this case] correctly read our opinion in *Chiarella* as repudiating any notion that all traders must enjoy equal information before trading: "[The] 'information' theory is rejected. Because the disclose-or-refrain duty is extraordinary, it attaches only when a party has legal obligations other than a mere duty to comply with the general antifraud proscriptions in the federal securities laws." We reaffirm today that "[a] duty [to disclose] arises from the

---

* **[15]** Apparently, the SEC believes this case differs from *Chiarella* in that Dirks' receipt of inside information from Secrist, an insider, carried Secrist's duties with it, while Chiarella received the information without the direct involvement of an insider and thus inherited no duty to disclose or abstain. The SEC fails to explain, however, why the receipt of non-public information from an insider automatically carries with it the fiduciary duty of the insider. As we emphasized in *Chiarella*, mere possession of nonpublic information does not give rise to a duty to disclose or abstain; only a specific relationship does that. And we do not believe that the mere receipt of information from an insider creates such a special relationship between the tippee and the corporation's shareholders.

Apparently recognizing the weakness of its argument in light of *Chiarella*, the SEC attempts to distinguish that case factually as involving not "inside" information, but rather "market" information, i. e., "information originating outside the company and usually about the supply and demand for the company's securities." This Court drew no such distinction in *Chiarella* and, as THE CHIEF JUSTICE noted, "[it] is clear that § 10(b) and Rule 10b–5 by their terms and by their history make no such distinction."

* **[16]** In *Chiarella*, we noted that formulation of an absolute equal information rule "should not be undertaken absent some explicit evidence of congressional intent." * * *

relationship between parties ... and not merely from one's ability to acquire information because of his position in the market."

Imposing a duty to disclose or abstain solely because a person knowingly receives material nonpublic information from an insider and trades on it could have an inhibiting influence on the role of market analysts, which the SEC itself recognizes is necessary to the preservation of a healthy market. It is commonplace for analysts to "ferret out and analyze information," and this often is done by meeting with and questioning corporate officers and others who are insiders. And information that the analysts obtain normally may be the basis for judgments as to the market worth of a corporation's securities. The analyst's judgment in this respect is made available in market letters or otherwise to clients of the firm. It is the nature of this type of information, and indeed of the markets themselves, that such information cannot be made simultaneously available to all of the corporation's stockholders or the public generally.

B

The conclusion that recipients of inside information do not invariably acquire a duty to disclose or abstain does not mean that such tippees always are free to trade on the information. The need for a ban on some tippee trading is clear. Not only are insiders forbidden by their fiduciary relationship from personally using undisclosed corporate information to their advantage, but they also may not give such information to an outsider for the same improper purpose of exploiting the information for their personal gain. * * * Thus, the tippee's duty to disclose or abstain is derivative from that of the insider's duty. As we noted in Chiarella, "[the] tippee's obligation has been viewed as arising from his role as a participant after the fact in the insider's breach of a fiduciary duty."

Thus, some tippees must assume an insider's duty to the shareholders not because they receive inside information, but rather because it has been made available to them improperly. And for Rule 10b–5 purposes, the insider's disclosure is improper only where it would violate his Cady, Roberts duty. Thus, a tippee assumes a fiduciary duty to the shareholders of a corporation not to trade on material nonpublic information only when the insider has breached his fiduciary duty to the shareholders by disclosing the information to the tippee and the tippee knows or should know that there has been a breach. As Commissioner Smith perceptively observed in In re Investors Management Co., 44 S.E.C. 633 (1971): "[Tippee] responsibility must be related back to insider responsibility by a necessary finding that the tippee knew the information was given to him in breach of a duty by a person having a special relationship to the issuer not to disclose the information...." Tipping thus properly is viewed only as a means of indirectly violating the *Cady, Roberts* disclose-or-abstain rule.

C

In determining whether a tippee is under an obligation to disclose or abstain, it thus is necessary to determine whether the insider's "tip" constituted a breach of the insider's fiduciary duty. All disclosures of confidential corporate information are not inconsistent with the duty insiders owe to shareholders. In contrast to the extraordinary facts of this case, the more typical situation in which there will be a question whether disclosure violates the insider's *Cady, Roberts* duty is when insiders disclose information to analysts. * * * In some situations, the insider will act consistently with his fiduciary duty to shareholders, and yet release of the information may affect the market. For example, it may not be clear— either to the corporate insider or to the recipient analyst—whether the information will be viewed as material nonpublic information. Corporate officials may mistakenly think the information already has been disclosed or that it is not material enough to affect the market. Whether disclosure is a breach of duty therefore depends in large part on the purpose of the disclosure. This standard was identified by the SEC itself in *Cady, Roberts*: a purpose of the securities laws was to eliminate "use of inside information for personal advantage." Thus, the test is whether the insider personally will benefit, directly or indirectly, from his disclosure. Absent some personal gain, there has been no breach of duty to stockholders. And absent a breach by the insider, there is no derivative breach. As Commissioner Smith stated in *Investors Management Co.*: "It is important in this type of case to focus on policing insiders and what they do . . . rather than on policing information *per se* and its possession. . . ."

The SEC argues that, if inside-trading liability does not exist when the information is transmitted for a proper purpose but is used for trading, it would be a rare situation when the parties could not fabricate some ostensibly legitimate business justification for transmitting the information. We think the SEC is unduly concerned. In determining whether the insider's purpose in making a particular disclosure is fraudulent, the SEC and the courts are not required to read the parties' minds. Scienter in some cases is relevant in determining whether the tipper has violated his *Cady, Roberts* duty. But to determine whether the disclosure itself "[deceives], [manipulates], or [defrauds]" shareholders, *Aaron v. SEC*, 446 U.S. 680, 686 (1980), the initial inquiry is whether there has been a breach of duty by the insider. This requires courts to focus on objective criteria, i. e., whether the insider receives a direct or indirect personal benefit from the disclosure, such as a pecuniary gain or a reputational benefit that will translate into future earnings. * * * There are objective facts and circumstances that often justify such an inference. For example, there may be a relationship between the insider and the recipient that suggests a *quid pro quo* from the latter, or an intention to benefit the particular recipient. The elements of fiduciary duty and exploitation of nonpublic information also exist when an insider makes a gift of confidential information to a trading relative or friend. The tip and trade resemble trading by the insider himself followed by a gift of the profits to the recipient.

Determining whether an insider personally benefits from a particular disclosure, a question of fact, will not always be easy for courts. But it is essential, we think, to have a guiding principle for those whose daily activities must be limited and instructed by the SEC's inside-trading rules, and we believe that there must be a breach of the insider's fiduciary duty before the tippee inherits the duty to disclose or abstain. In contrast, the rule adopted by the SEC in this case would have no limiting principle.

IV

Under the inside-trading and tipping rules set forth above, we find that there was no actionable violation by Dirks. It is undisputed that Dirks himself was a stranger to Equity Funding, with no pre-existing fiduciary duty to its shareholders. He took no action, directly or indirectly, that induced the shareholders or officers of Equity Funding to repose trust or confidence in him. There was no expectation by Dirks' sources that he would keep their information in confidence. Nor did Dirks misappropriate or illegally obtain the information about Equity Funding. Unless the insiders breached their *Cady, Roberts* duty to shareholders in disclosing the nonpublic information to Dirks, he breached no duty when he passed it on to investors as well as to the *Wall Street Journal.*

It is clear that neither Secrist nor the other Equity Funding employees violated their *Cady, Roberts* duty to the corporation's shareholders by providing information to Dirks. The tippers received no monetary or personal benefit for revealing Equity Funding's secrets, nor was their purpose to make a gift of valuable information to Dirks. As the facts of this case clearly indicate, the tippers were motivated by a desire to expose the fraud. In the absence of a breach of duty to shareholders by the insiders, there was no derivative breach by Dirks. Dirks therefore could not have been "a participant after the fact in [an] insider's breach of a fiduciary duty." *Chiarella*, 445 U.S. at 230, n. 12.

V

We conclude that Dirks, in the circumstances of this case, had no duty to abstain from use of the inside information that he obtained. The judgment of the Court of Appeals therefore is Reversed.

* * *

Blackmun, J., with whom Brennan and Marshall, J.J. join, dissenting.

The Court today takes still another step to limit the protections provided investors by § 10(b) of the Securities Exchange Act of 1934. *See* Chiarella v. United States, 445 U.S. 222, 246 (1980)(dissenting opinion). The device employed in this case engrafts a special motivational requirement on the fiduciary duty doctrine. This innovation excuses a knowing and intentional violation of an insider's duty to shareholders if the insider does not act from a motive of personal gain. Even on the extraordinary facts of this case, such an innovation is not justified. * * *

QUESTIONS AND NOTES

1. What did Dirks do wrong? Did he deserve punishment, or a reward?

2. According to the Court in *Dirks*, what must be shown to impose liability on someone as a tipper?

3. What must be shown to impose liability on someone as a tippee?

4. If a tipper tips a tippee, but the tippee does not act on the tip, has anyone violated Rule 10b–5?

5. Why can there be no tippee liability under Rule 10b–5 if there is no tipper?

6. Note that when the case was filed, Secrist was a *former* officer of Equity Funding. This fact could not help him under Rule 10b–5, however, because he allegedly obtained the information while serving as an officer.

7. Footnote 14 discusses the possibility of "temporary insiders," also described by those familiar with *Dirks* as "footnote 14 insiders." What is required to charge someone with such status for Rule 10b–5 purposes?

8. One important question is whether "secondary" violators can be held liable under the disclosure requirements of Rule 10b–5. For example, suppose a corporation violated Rule 10b–5 in issuing its stock. Obviously, defrauded investors can sue the corporation. Often, however, the business has no assets. So plaintiffs routinely joined "secondary" or "collateral" participants—such as the corporation's accountants, bankers, directors, and officers—for aiding and abetting the corporation's violation of Rule 10b–5.

The Supreme Court rejected the effort in *Central Bank of Denver, N.A. v. First Interstate Bank of Denver, N.A.*, 511 U.S. 164 (1994), by holding that there can be no liability—at least in a civil case—for aiding and abetting a violation of Rule 10b–5.

We note two reactions to the holding in *Central Bank of Denver*. First, Congress, in the Private Securities Litigation Reform Act of 1995, expressly embraced liability for "aiding and abetting" violations of the securities laws (including, obviously, Rule 10b–5). The provision does so, however, only for cases brought by the Securities and Exchange Commission; so aiding and abetting is not a viable theory in private actions.

Second, enterprising plaintiffs' lawyers attempted to find ways around the holding in *Central Bank of Denver*. *See, e.g.,* In re Enron Corporation Securities, Derivative & ERISA Litig., 235 F.Supp.2d 549 (S.D. Tex. 2002) (concerning potential liability of such secondary actors as law and accounting firms and banks in the collapse of Enron). One such effort was something called "scheme liability," essentially arguing that secondary players are part of the same scheme as the primary violator of Rule 10b–5.

The Supreme Court rejected the effort and reaffirmed its holding from *Central Bank of Denver* in *Stoneridge Investment Partners, LLC v. Scientific–Atlanta, Inc.*, 552 U.S. 148 (2008). In that case, the operator of a cable television system agreed to pay two companies (Motorola and Scientific–Atlanta) additional funds for cable boxes; those companies then returned a portion of the money to the cable operator, as part of an effort to make its books look better, in violation of Rule 10b–5. The Court held that Motorola and Scientific–Atlanta could not be held liable because they had neither made statements to investors nor participated in the cable operator's statements to investors. Accordingly, investors in the cable operator could not have relied upon anything Motorola or Scientific–Atlanta said. Without reliance, there could be no Rule 10b–5 violation.

———————

Recall that in his dissent in *Chiarella*, Chief Justice Burger raised the possibility of liability under Rule 10b–5 for "misappropriation" of information. The Supreme Court finally addressed the "misappropriation theory" definitively in the following case, which involves the very sad story of a badly-behaved lawyer in Minnesota.

UNITED STATES v. O'HAGAN

United States Supreme Court, 1997
521 U.S. 642

Ginsburg, J. [O'Hagan was a partner in the Minneapolis law firm of Dorsey & Whitney. In July 1988, an English company (Grand Metropolitan PLC, or "Grand Met") retained the firm concerning a potential tender offer to acquire Pillsbury Company, which was headquartered in Minneapolis. The tender offer was announced publicly on October 4, 1988. Although O'Hagan was not working on the Grand Met–Pillsbury transaction, he learned of it. In August and September 1988, he bought Pillsbury stock and options to acquire Pillsbury stock. After the tender offer was announced and the price of Pillsbury stock rose, O'Hagan sold the stock for a profit of $4,300,000.

He was charged in a 57–count federal indictment, which included 17 counts of securities fraud in violation of Rule 10b–5. According to the indictment, by the way, O'Hagan used the profits from the alleged insider trading to replenish client trust funds from which he had converted money. O'Hagan was convicted on this point in state court and was, not surprisingly, disbarred. A jury convicted O'Hagan of all 57 federal counts, and O'Hagan appealed to the United States Court of Appeals for the Eighth Circuit.

That court reversed the convictions on all counts. The Supreme Court agreed to hear the case. In the portion of the opinion set forth below, the Supreme Court addresses whether O'Hagan should be convicted under Rule 10b–5. The Court concludes that he should, and adopts a version of the "misappropriation theory" of Rule 10b–5.]

* * *

II

We address first the Court of Appeals' reversal of O'Hagan's convictions under § 10(b) and Rule 10b–5. Following the Fourth Circuit's lead, the Eighth Circuit rejected the misappropriation theory as a basis for § 10(b) liability. We hold, in accord with several other Courts of Appeals, that criminal liability under § 10(b) may be predicated on the misappropriation theory.* **[4]**

A

* * *

Under the "traditional" or "classical theory" of insider trading liability, § 10(b) and Rule 10b–5 are violated when a corporate insider trades in the securities of his corporation on the basis of material, nonpublic information. Trading on such information qualifies as a "deceptive device" under § 10(b), we have affirmed, because "a relationship of trust and confidence [exists] between the shareholders of a corporation and those insiders who have obtained confidential information by reason of their position with that corporation." Chiarella v. United States, 445 U.S. 222, 228 (1980). That relationship, we recognized, "gives rise to a duty to disclose [or to abstain from trading] because of the 'necessity of preventing a corporate insider from ... taking unfair advantage of ... uninformed ... stockholders.' " The classical theory applies not only to officers, directors, and other permanent insiders of a corporation, but also to attorneys, accountants, consultants, and others who temporarily become fiduciaries of a corporation. *See* Dirks v. SEC, 463 U.S. 646, 655, n. 14 (1983).

The "misappropriation theory" holds that a person commits fraud "in connection with" a securities transaction, and thereby violates § 10(b) and Rule 10b–5, when he misappropriates confidential information for securities trading purposes, in breach of a duty owed to the source of the information. * * * Under this theory, a fiduciary's undisclosed, self-serving use of a principal's information to purchase or sell securities, in breach of a duty of loyalty and confidentiality, defrauds the principal of the exclusive use of that information. In lieu of premising liability on a fiduciary relationship between company insider and purchaser or seller of the company's stock, the misappropriation theory premises liability on a fiduciary-turned-trader's deception of those who entrusted him with access to confidential information.

The two theories are complementary, each addressing efforts to capitalize on nonpublic information through the purchase or sale of securities. The classical theory targets a corporate insider's breach of duty to shareholders with whom the insider transacts; the misappropriation theory outlaws trading on the basis of nonpublic information by a corporate "outsider" in breach of a duty owed not to a trading party, but to the

---

* **[4]** Twice before we have been presented with the question whether criminal liability for violation of § 10(b) may be based on a misappropriation theory. In *Chiarella v. United States*, 445 U.S. 222, 235–237 (1980), the jury had received no misappropriation theory instructions, so we declined to address the question. In Carpenter v. United States, 484 U.S. 19, 24 (1987), the Court divided evenly on whether, under the circumstances of that case, convictions resting on the misappropriation theory should be affirmed. * * *

source of the information. The misappropriation theory is thus designed to "protect the integrity of the securities markets against abuses by 'outsiders' to a corporation who have access to confidential information that will affect the corporation's security price when revealed, but who owe no fiduciary or other duty to that corporation's shareholders."

In this case, the indictment alleged that O'Hagan, in breach of a duty of trust and confidence he owed to his law firm, Dorsey & Whitney, and to its client, Grand Met, traded on the basis of nonpublic information regarding Grand Met's planned tender offer for Pillsbury common stock. This conduct, the Government charged, constituted a fraudulent device in connection with the purchase and sale of securities.* **[5]**

B

We agree with the Government that misappropriation, as just defined, satisfies § 10(b)'s requirement that chargeable conduct involve a "deceptive device or contrivance" used "in connection with" the purchase or sale of securities. We observe, first, that misappropriators, as the Government describes them, deal in deception. A fiduciary who "[pretends] loyalty to the principal while secretly converting the principal's information for personal gain," * * * "dupes" or defrauds the principal. * * *

We addressed fraud of the same species in *Carpenter v. United States*, 484 U.S. 19 (1987), which involved the mail fraud statute's proscription of "any scheme or artifice to defraud," 18 U.S.C. § 1341. Affirming convictions under that statute, we said in *Carpenter* that an employee's undertaking not to reveal his employer's confidential information "became a sham" when the employee provided the information to his co-conspirators in a scheme to obtain trading profits. A company's confidential information, we recognized in *Carpenter*, qualifies as property to which the company has a right of exclusive use. The undisclosed misappropriation of such information, in violation of a fiduciary duty, the Court said in *Carpenter*, constitutes fraud akin to embezzlement—"the fraudulent appropriation to one's own use of the money or goods entrusted to one's care by another." *Carpenter's* discussion of the fraudulent misuse of confidential information, the Government notes, "is a particularly apt source of guidance here, because [the mail fraud statute] (like Section 10(b)) has long been held to require deception, not merely the breach of a fiduciary duty." * * *

Deception through nondisclosure is central to the theory of liability for which the Government seeks recognition. As counsel for the Government stated in explanation of the theory at oral argument: "To satisfy the common law rule that a trustee may not use the property that [has] been

---

* **[5]** The Government could not have prosecuted O'Hagan under the classical theory, for O'Hagan was not an "insider" of Pillsbury, the corporation in whose stock he traded. Although an "outsider" with respect to Pillsbury, O'Hagan had an intimate association with, and was found to have traded on confidential information from, Dorsey & Whitney, counsel to tender offeror Grand Met. Under the misappropriation theory, O'Hagan's securities trading does not escape Exchange Act sanction, as it would under the dissent's reasoning, simply because he was associated with, and gained nonpublic information from, the bidder, rather than the target.

entrusted [to] him, there would have to be consent. To satisfy the requirement of the Securities Act that there be no deception, there would only have to be disclosure." * **[6]**

The misappropriation theory advanced by the Government is consistent with *Santa Fe Industries, Inc. v. Green*, 430 U.S. 462 (1977), a decision underscoring that § 10(b) is not an all-purpose breach of fiduciary duty ban; rather, it trains on conduct involving manipulation or deception. In contrast to the Government's allegations in this case, in *Santa Fe Industries*, all pertinent facts were disclosed by the persons charged with violating § 10(b) and Rule 10b–5, therefore, there was no deception through nondisclosure to which liability under those provisions could attach. Similarly, full disclosure forecloses liability under the misappropriation theory: Because the deception essential to the misappropriation theory involves feigning fidelity to the source of information, if the fiduciary discloses to the source that he plans to trade on the nonpublic information, there is no "deceptive device" and thus no § 10(b) violation—although the fiduciary-turned-trader may remain liable under state law for breach of a duty of loyalty. * **[7]**

We turn next to the § 10(b) requirement that the misappropriator's deceptive use of information be "in connection with the purchase or sale of [a] security." This element is satisfied because the fiduciary's fraud is consummated, not when the fiduciary gains the confidential information, but when, without disclosure to his principal, he uses the information to purchase or sell securities. The securities transaction and the breach of duty thus coincide. This is so even though the person or entity defrauded is not the other party to the trade, but is, instead, the source of the nonpublic information. * * * A misappropriator who trades on the basis of material, nonpublic information, in short, gains his advantageous market position through deception; he deceives the source of the information and simultaneously harms members of the investing public.

The misappropriation theory targets information of a sort that misappropriators ordinarily capitalize upon to gain no-risk profits through the purchase or sale of securities. Should a misappropriator put such information to other use, the statute's prohibition would not be implicated. The theory does not catch all conceivable forms of fraud involving confidential information; rather, it catches fraudulent means of capitalizing on such information through securities transactions.

     * * *

---

* **[6]** Under the misappropriation theory urged in this case, the disclosure obligation runs to the source of the information, here, Dorsey & Whitney and Grand Met. Chief Justice Burger, dissenting in *Chiarella*, advanced a broader reading of § 10(b) and Rule 10b–5; the disclosure obligation, as he envisioned it, ran to those with whom the misappropriator trades. 445 U.S. at 240 ("a person who has misappropriated nonpublic information has an absolute duty to disclose that information or to refrain from trading"). * * * The Government does not propose that we adopt a misappropriation theory of that breadth.

* **[7]** Where, however, a person trading on the basis of material, nonpublic information owes a duty of loyalty and confidentiality to two entities or persons—for example, a law firm and its client—but makes disclosure to only one, the trader may still be liable under the misappropriation theory.

The misappropriation theory comports with § 10(b)'s language, which requires deception "in connection with the purchase or sale of any security," not deception of an identifiable purchaser or seller. The theory is also well-tuned to an animating purpose of the Exchange Act: to insure honest securities markets and thereby promote investor confidence. * * * Although informational disparity is inevitable in the securities markets, investors likely would hesitate to venture their capital in a market where trading based on misappropriated nonpublic information is unchecked by law. An investor's informational disadvantage vis-a-vis a misappropriator with material, nonpublic information stems from contrivance, not luck; it is a disadvantage that cannot be overcome with research or skill. * * *

In sum, considering the inhibiting impact on market participation of trading on misappropriated information, and the congressional purposes underlying § 10(b), it makes scant sense to hold a lawyer like O'Hagan a § 10(b) violator if he works for a law firm representing the target of a tender offer, but not if he works for a law firm representing the bidder. The text of the statute requires no such result. The misappropriation at issue here was properly made the subject of a § 10(b) charge because it meets the statutory requirement that there be "deceptive" conduct "in connection with" securities transactions.

C

The Court of Appeals rejected the misappropriation theory primarily on two grounds. First, as the Eighth Circuit comprehended the theory, it requires neither misrepresentation nor nondisclosure. As just explained, however, deceptive nondisclosure is essential to the § 10(b) liability at issue. Concretely, in this case, "it [was O'Hagan's] failure to disclose his personal trading to Grand Met and Dorsey, in breach of his duty to do so, that made his conduct 'deceptive' within the meaning of [§]10(b)."

Second and "more obvious," the Court of Appeals said, the misappropriation theory is not moored to § 10(b)'s requirement that "the fraud be 'in connection with the purchase or sale of any security.'" According to the Eighth Circuit, [*Chiarella* and other] of our decisions reveal that § 10(b) liability cannot be predicated on a duty owed to the source of nonpublic information * * *.

* * *

The Court did not hold in *Chiarella* that the only relationship prompting liability for trading on undisclosed information is the relationship between a corporation's insiders and shareholders. That is evident from our response to the Government's argument before this Court that the printer's misappropriation of information from his employer for purposes of securities trading—in violation of a duty of confidentiality owed to the acquiring companies—constituted fraud in connection with the purchase or sale of a security, and thereby satisfied the terms of § 10(b). The Court declined to reach that potential basis for the printer's liability, because the theory had not been submitted to the jury. But four Justices found merit in it. * * *

Chiarella thus expressly left open the misappropriation theory before us today. * * *

Dirks, too, left room for application of the misappropriation theory in cases like the one we confront. * * *

III

[The Court here upheld the SEC's authority to promulgate Rule 14e–3(a), discussed in Note 7 after the *Chiarella* case.]

QUESTIONS AND NOTE

1. After *O'Hagan*, would Mr. Chiarella be held to have violated Rule 10b–5?

2. How does the misappropriation theory adopted in *O'Hagan* differ from the misappropriation theory proposed by Chief Justice Burger in *Chiarella*?

3. Does *O'Hagan* apply in private damages cases brought for violations of Rule 10b–5?

4. Could O'Hagan have been charged as a temporary insider, as defined in footnote 14 of *Dirks?*

5. What if, before purchasing the Pillsbury stock, O'Hagan had told his law firm about his intentions to do that?

6. Could Grand Met have sued Whitney & Dorsey for misappropriation by O'Hagan? Could Grand Met have sued the other partners of the law firm? Interestingly, that firm did not become a limited liability partnership until 1996. Recall from Chapter 3 that in a limited liability partnership, individual partners are not on the hook for business debts. Do you think the *O'Hagan* case might have been a reason for adopting LLP status?

7. It appears that Osama Bin Laden and his terrorist network, knowing in advance of the September 11, 2001 attacks on the World Trade Center, may have sold short stocks of various U.S. airlines and purchased put options on them. Short sales and put options are both financial bets that the stocks will decline in price. Because the prices of the airline stocks declined sharply after 9/11, the short sales and puts earned profits of approximately $2.5 million. Christian Berthelsen, et al., *Suspicious Profits Sit Uncollected*, SAN FRANCISCO CHRONICLE, p. A–1, (September 29, 2001). Was Osama Bin Laden guilty of insider trading under Rule 10b–5?

8. Again, Rule 10b–5 is only one of many federal securities and related provisions. Mr. O'Hagan was convicted not only under Rule 10b–5, but under Rule 14e–3(a), and money laundering provisions. While most of these (other than Rule 10b–5) are the focus of other courses, there is one other major federal securities regulation we must address here. It's next.

b. Section 16(b) and Short–Swing Trading

Read §§ 16 (a) and 16 (b) of the '34 Act.

RELIANCE ELECTRIC CO. v. EMERSON ELECTRIC CO.

United States Supreme Court, 1972
404 U.S. 418

STEWART, J. Section 16(b) of the Securities Exchange Act of 1934 provides, among other things, that a corporation may recover for itself the profits realized by an owner of more than 10% of its shares from a purchase and sale of its stock within any six-month period, provided that the owner held more than 10% "both at the time of the purchase and sale."* [1] In this case, the respondent, the owner of 13.2% of a corporation's shares, disposed of its entire holdings in two sales, both of them within six months of purchase. The first sale reduced the respondent's holdings to 9.96%, and the second disposed of the remainder. The question presented is whether the profits derived from the second sale are recoverable by the Corporation under § 16(b). We hold that they are not.

On June 16, 1967, the respondent, Emerson Electric Co., acquired 13.2% of the outstanding common stock of Dodge Manufacturing Co., pursuant to a tender offer made in an unsuccessful attempt to take over Dodge. The purchase price for this stock was $63 per share. Shortly thereafter, the shareholders of Dodge approved a merger with the petitioner, Reliance Electric Co. Faced with the certain failure of any further attempt to take over Dodge, and with the prospect of being forced to exchange its Dodge shares for stock in the merged corporation in the near future, Emerson, following a plan outlined by its general counsel, decided to dispose of enough shares to bring its holdings below 10%, in order to immunize the disposal of the remainder of its shares from liability under § 16(b). Pursuant to counsel's recommendation, Emerson on August 28 sold 37,000 shares of Dodge common stock to a brokerage house at $68 per share. This sale reduced Emerson's holdings in Dodge to 9.96% of the outstanding common stock. The remaining shares were then sold to Dodge at $69 per share on September 11.

---

* [1] Section 16(b) provides:

For the purpose of preventing the unfair use of information which may have been obtained by such beneficial owner, director, or officer by reason of his relationship to the issuer, any profit realized by him from any purchase and sale, or any sale and purchase, of any equity security of such issuer (other than an exempted security) within any period of less than six months ... shall inure to and be recoverable by the issuer, irrespective of any intention on the part of such beneficial owner, director, or officer in entering into such transaction of holding the security purchased or of not repurchasing the security sold for a period exceeding six months ... This subsection shall not be construed to cover any transaction where such beneficial owner was not such both at the time of the purchase and sale, or the sale and purchase, of the security involved, or any transaction or transactions which the Commission by rules and regulations may exempt as not comprehended within the purpose of this subsection. 15 U.S.C. § 78p(b). The term "such beneficial owner" refers to one who owns "more than 10 per centum of any class of any equity security (other than an exempted security) which is registered pursuant to section (12) of this title." Securities Exchange Act of 1934, § 16(a), 15 U.S.C. § 78p(a).

After a demand on it by Reliance for the profits realized on both sales, Emerson filed this action seeking a declaratory judgment as to its liability under § 16(b). Emerson first claimed that it was not liable at all, because it was not a 10% owner at the time of the purchase of the Dodge shares. The District Court disagreed, holding that a purchase of stock falls within § 16(b) where the purchaser becomes a 10% owner by virtue of the purchase. The Court of Appeals affirmed this holding, and Emerson did not cross-petition for certiorari. Thus that question is not before us.

Emerson alternatively argued to the District Court that, assuming it was a 10% stockholder at the time of the purchase, it was liable only for the profits on the August 28 sale of 37,000 shares, because after that time it was no longer a 10% owner within the meaning of § 16(b). After trial on the issue of liability alone, the District Court held Emerson liable for the entire amount of its profits. The court found that Emerson's sales of Dodge stock were "effected pursuant to a single predetermined plan of disposition with the overall intent and purpose of avoiding Section 16(b) liability," and construed the term "time of . . . sale" to include "the entire period during which a series of related transactions take place pursuant to a plan by which a 10% beneficial owner disposes of his stock, holdings."

On an interlocutory appeal under 28 U.S.C. § 1292(b), the Court of Appeals upheld the finding that Emerson "split" its sale of Dodge stock simply in order to avoid most of its potential liability under § 16(b), but it held this fact irrelevant under the statute so long as the two sales are "not legally tied to each other and (are) made at different times to different buyers. . . ." Accordingly, the Court of Appeals reversed the District Court's judgment as to Emerson's liability for its profits on the September 11 sale, and remanded for a determination of the amount of Emerson's liability on the August 28 sale. Reliance filed a petition for certiorari, which we granted in order to consider an unresolved question under an important federal statute.

The history and purpose of § 16(b) have been exhaustively reviewed by federal courts on several occasions since its enactment in 1934. Those courts have recognized that the only method Congress deemed effective to curb the evils of insider trading was a flat rule taking the profits out of a class of transactions in which the possibility of abuse was believed to be intolerably great.

Thus Congress did not reach every transaction in which an investor actually relies on inside information. A person avoids liability if he does not meet the statutory definition of an "insider," or if he sells more than six months after purchase. Liability cannot be imposed simply because the investor structured his transaction with the intent of avoiding liability under § 16(b). The question is, rather, whether the method used to "avoid" liability is one permitted by the statute.

Among the "objective standards" contained in § 16(b) is the requirement that a 10% owner be such "both at the time of the purchase and sale . . . of the security involved." Read literally, this language clearly contemplates that a statutory insider might sell enough shares to bring his holdings below 10%, and later—but still within six months—sell additional shares free from liability under the statute. Indeed, commentators on the securities laws have recommended this exact procedure for a 10% owner who, like Emerson, wishes to dispose of his holdings within six months of their purchase.

Under the approach urged by Reliance, and adopted by the District Court, the apparent immunity of profits derived from Emerson's second sale is lost where the two sales, though independent in every other respect, are "interrelated parts of a single plan." But a "plan" to sell that is conceived within six months of purchase clearly would not fall within § 16(b) if the sale were made after the six months had expired, and we see no basis in the statute for a different result where the 10% requirement is involved rather than the six-month limitation. * * *

The judgment is affirmed.

QUESTIONS AND NOTES

1. The seller in *Reliance Electric* was correct that the sale of stock that took it from owning 9.96 percent to zero was not covered by § 16(b). Note, however, that it abandoned the argument that its original purchase—the one that took it from zero to owning 13.2 percent—should not be covered. Bad move. In a later case, the Supreme Court held that such a purchase is not covered under the provision of § 16(b) relating to shareholders. Foremost–McKesson, Inc. v. Provident Securities Co., 423 U.S. 232 (1976).

So to determine whether one qualifies as one who owns more than ten percent of the stock under § 16(b), one takes a snap shot of the level of ownership immediately *before* both the buy and the sell. To qualify, one must own more than 10% at both times.

Roberts owns no stock in Bubba's Burritos, Inc. He then purchases 15 percent of the company's stock. That purchase is not covered under § 16(b), *because* immediately before the purchase, his ownership was zero. Now Roberts buys an additional five percent of the Bubba's stock. That purchase is covered, because he was above ten percent when he made this purchase. Now Roberts sells all 20 percent of the Bubba's stock. That sale is covered, because he was above ten percent when he made the sale. The profit on the purchase and sale would be calculated in the method explored in the Problems below.

Don't get so focused on the percentage of ownership that you forget who else falls within § 16(b). If Roberts were an officer or director of Bubba's either when he bought or sold, he would be covered by the statute—regardless of how much Bubba's stock he owned. If the reason for this is not clear, look at the language of § 16(b) again. It clearly applies its (very mechanical) rule to three types of corporate big-shots: officers, directors and shareholders with more than ten percent of the corporation's stock. We will do more with this with some Problems at the end of these notes.

2. Section 16(b) applies only to large corporations—those which are required to register under § 12 of the '34 Act. So the statute basically creates problems only for the "big machers" of publicly traded corporations. This is different from Rule 10b–5, which has no such size limitation.

3. Compare § 16(b) and Rule 10b–5. Why didn't the plaintiff in *Dupuy* bring an action under § 16(b)? Why didn't someone bring an action under Rule 10b–5 in *Reliance*?

4. The policy behind § 16(b) was to deter transactions that have a high potential for fraud. However, Congress determined that it was not practical to require proof of improper intent or scienter in cases of insider trading, and thus, § 16(b) was written to impose strict liability.

The statute does not require proof that the trading information was improperly obtained. It is enough to prove an insider relationship that gives rise to the potential that improper information "may have been obtained" and utilized in the trade. We find a "clear congressional intent to provide a catch-all, prophylactic remedy, not requiring proof of actual misconduct." First Golden Bancorporation v. Weiszmann, 942 F.2d 726, 729 (10th Cir. 1991).

5. The *Reliance Electric* case was a declaratory judgment action by the seller of corporate stock to determine its possible liability under § 16(b). Who is usually the plaintiff in a § 16(b) action? How does that plaintiff discover that it has a § 16(b) cause of action? *See* § 16(a) of the '34 Act. Notice how § 16(a) requires disclosure that would make a § 16(b) case easy.

6. "In general, insiders may plan their transactions to avoid the literal language of the statute (§ 16(b)) and thus escape or reduce liability." Peter G. Samuels, *Liability for Short–Swing Profits and Reporting Obligations Under Section 16(b) of the Securities Exchange Act of 1934*, in PLI Securities Filing 2000, 1205 PLI/Corp 603 (October 5, 2000). Do you agree? You will be in a better position to understand § 16(b) and this statement when you take the Securities Regulation course or, if your professor insists, after you work through the following problems.

7. Section 16(b) creates a claim for the corporation. Accordingly, if the corporation does not bring the suit, a shareholder may do so through the device of the shareholder derivative suit, which we studied in Chapter 5, § D. Unlike the regular derivative suit, however, under § 16(b), a shareholder need not make demand on the directors to bring the suit. In addition, the shareholder-plaintiff need not have owned stock when the claim arose; owning it at the time the case is filed is sufficient. Why would § 16(b) suits be subject to these different rules?

PROBLEMS: § 16(b) SUITS

1. Bubba's Burritos, Inc. is registered under the '34 Act with 1,000,000 shares outstanding. Roberts is not a director or an officer. He buys 200,000 shares of Bubba's at $10 a share on January 20. What is his § 16(b) liability if:

(a) On May 1, he sells all 200,000 shares for $30 a share?

(b) On May 1, he sells 110,000 shares for $30 a share. On May 10, he sells the other 90,000 shares for $40 a share.

2.   Same facts as Problem 1 except that Roberts was also a director of Bubba's.

3.   Freer is an officer of Bubba's Burritos, Inc., which is registered under the '34 Act. He owns 200,000 of the 1,000,000 outstanding shares of Bubba's. He bought the stock two years ago for $70 a share. On January 15, Freer sells 100,000 shares for $30 a share. On March 1, Freer buys 110,000 shares for $20 a share. Who can sue whom for what under § 16(b)?

4.   Same facts as Problem 3 except that in addition Freer sells 110,000 shares on April 5 for $10 a share.

c.   Common Law Duty of Selling Shareholder

Assume that Capel owns 51% of the outstanding stock of Bubba's Burritos, Inc. and he has received an offer from Epstein Equine and Epicurean Endustries, Inc. for her stock. Capel knows that Propp, one of the other shareholders, would also like to sell his stock. Does Capel have any legal obligation to condition the sale of her stock on the sale of Propp's stock?

Assume also that Epstein has a reputation as a corporate looter—one who acquires control and then steals the corporation's assets and otherwise runs the corporation into the ground. Capel also has an offer for her shares from Freer Fajitas, Inc., an exemplary corporate citizen. The Freer offer is significantly lower than Epstein's offer. Does Capel have any legal obligation to accept the lower Freer offer for her shares?

Nothing in the MBCA or other corporate codes answers these questions. As a starting point, obviously, someone who owns enough stock to exercise control over the corporation (for example, because she can elect a majority of the directors) can sell her stock for more than the sheer value of the stock. A buyer will be willing to pay an extra amount—over the bare value of the stock—because ownership of this block of stock carries with it the power to control the direction of the corporation. This extra amount is usually called a "control premium." Although some people argue that any such premium should be seen as an asset of the corporation, to be shared with other shareholders, to our knowledge no court has imposed liability on a controlling shareholder for getting a control premium in selling her stock. But the controlling shareholder must be careful to whom she sells, as the next case demonstrates.

DeBAUN v. FIRST WESTERN BANK & TRUST CO.

California Court of Appeal, 1975
120 Cal.Rptr. 354

THOMPSON, ASSOCIATE JUSTICE. [Alfred Johnson founded Alfred S. Johnson Incorporated ("Corporation") in 1955. The company processed color photography. DeBaun and Stephens worked for the corporation and soon were permitted to buy stock. One hundred shares were issued. Johnson held 70 shares, DeBaun held 20 shares, and Stephens held 10 shares. The three got along well and the company thrived, making handsome net profits each year. Johnson died in 1965. First Western Bank & Trust ("Bank") was the executor and took title to Johnson's 70 shares. Without telling DeBaun or Stephens, Bank took bids from potential buyers of the 70 shares.]

On May 15 and 20, 1968, Bank received successive offers for the 70 shares from Raymond J. Mattison, acting in the name of S.O.F. Fund, an *inter vivos* revocable trust of which he was both settlor and trustee. A sketchy balance sheet of S.O.F. Fund was submitted with the second offer. The offers were rejected. Anticipating a further offer from Mattison and his trust, [Bank] ordered a Dun & Bradstreet report on Mattison and the fund.

* * * It noted pending litigation, bankruptcies, and tax liens against corporate entities in which Mattison had been a principal, and suggested that S.O.F. Fund no longer existed.

As of May 24, * * * Earl Funk, a vice-president of Bank, had personal knowledge that: (1) on October 24, 1957, the Los Angeles Superior Court had entered a judgment against Mattison in favor of Bank's predecessor in interest for compensatory and punitive damages as the result of Mattison's fraudulent misrepresentations and a fraudulent financial statement to obtain a loan; and (2) the judgment remained unsatisfied in 1968 and was an asset of Bank acquired from its predecessor in an acquisition of 65 branch banks.

[Mattison made a third proposal. It was conveyed to Bank by Mattison's counsel, McCarrol, who previously worked for a predecessor of Bank and knew several of the officers at Bank. This offer proposed a sales price of $250,000, of which $200,000 would come from the corporation's ongoing revenues.] Troubled by the Dun & Bradstreet report, personnel of Bank met with Mattison and McCarrol. * * * Mattison explained that it had been his practice to take over failing companies so that the existence of the litigation and tax liens noted in the Dun & Bradstreet report was not due to his fault. Not entirely satisfied, [a Bank officer] wrote to McCarrol requesting a written report on the status of all pending litigation in which Mattison was involved. McCarrol telephoned his response, declining to represent the status of the litigation but noting that the information was publicly available. Partly because [another Bank officer] knew McCarrol as a former trust officer of Bank's predecessor in interest, and partly because during a luncheon with Mattison at the Jonathan Club * * * Mattison was warmly received * * * by [members of the Jonathan Club],* Bank did not pursue its investigation into the public records of Los Angeles County where a mass of derogatory information lay.

---

* [Note from your authors: the Jonathan Club is a very nice private club in downtown Los Angeles. It also has a great beach facility in Santa Monica.]

As of July 1, 1968, the public records of Los Angeles County revealed 38 unsatisfied judgments against Mattison or his entities totalling $330,886.27, and 54 pending actions claiming a total of $373,588.67 from them. The record also contained 22 recorded abstracts of judgments against Mattison or his entities totalling $285,704.11, and 18 tax liens aggregating $20,327.97. Bank did not investigate the public record and hence was unaware of Mattison's financial track record.

While failing to pursue the investigation of the known information adverse to Mattison, Bank's employees knew or should have known that if his proposal through McCarrol were accepted the payment of the $200,000 balance of the purchase price would necessarily come from Corporation. They assumed that the payments would be made by Mattison from distributions of the Corporation which he would cause it to make after assuming control. They were aware that Corporation would not generate a sufficient after-tax cash flow to pay dividends in a sufficient amount to permit the payments of interest and principal on the $200,000 balance as scheduled in the McCarrol proposal, and knew that Mattison could make those payments only by resorting to distribution of "pre-sale" retained earnings and assets of Corporation.

On July 11, 1968, Bank accepted the McCarrol modification by entering into an exchange agreement with S.O.F. Fund. * * *

[Mattison called a special meeting of the board of directors, was elected to the board, and was elected president. DeBaun and Stephens also remained on the board.]

At the moment of Bank's sale of the controlling shares to Mattison, Corporation was an eminently successful going business with a bright future. It had cash of $76,126.15 and other liquid assets of over $122,000. Its remaining assets were worth $60,000. Its excess of current assets over current liabilities and reserve for bad debts was $233,391.94, and its net worth about $220,000. Corporation's earnings indicated a pattern of growth. Mattison immediately proceeded to change that situation. Beginning with the date that he acquired control, Mattison implemented a systematic scheme to loot Corporation of its assets. His first step was to divert $73,144 in corporate cash to himself and to MICO, a shell company owned by Mattison. The transfer was made in exchange for unsecured noninterest bearing notes but for no other consideration. On August 2, 1968, Mattison caused Corporation to assign to MICO all of Corporation's assets, including its receivables in exchange for a fictitious agreement for management services. He diverted all corporate mail to a post office box from which he took the mail, opened it, and extracted all incoming checks to the corporation before forwarding the mail on. He ceased paying trade creditors promptly, as had been Corporation's practice, delaying payment of trade creditors to the last possible moment and, to the extent he could, not paying some at all. He delayed shipments on new orders. To cover his activities, Mattison removed the corporate books and records.

In September 1968, DeBaun left Corporation's employ as a salesman because of Mattison's policy of not filling orders and because Mattison had drastically reduced DeBaun's compensation. Acting as an independent salesman, DeBaun obtained business for Corporation for which Mattison refused to compensate him, causing DeBaun to broker the business for a competitor. Mattison continued to loot the corporation, although at a reduced pace by reason of its depleted assets. He collected payments from employees to pay premiums on a voluntary health insurance plan although the policy covering the plan was terminated in September for failure to pay premiums. He issued payroll checks without sufficient funds and continued not to pay trade creditors. Mattison did not supply Bank with the financial reports required by the [purchase] agreement.

While Bank was not aware of the initial transfer of cash to MICO, it did learn of the other misconduct of Mattison as it occurred. Although the conduct was a breach of the [purchase] agreement, Bank took no action beyond seeking an oral explanation from Mattison. In December 1968, Stephens also left Corporation's employ.

Bank took no action in the matter until April 25, 1969. On that date, it filed an action in the superior court seeking the appointment of a receiver. * * * By that time, Corporation was hopelessly insolvent. Its debts exceeded its assets by over $200,000, excluding its contingent liability to Bank, as a result of the fraudulently obtained hypothecation of corporate assets to secure Mattison's debt. Both the federal Internal Revenue Service and California State Board of Equalization had filed liens upon corporate assets and notices to withhold funds. A trade creditor had placed a keeper on the corporate premises.

On July 10, 1969, Bank, pursuant to the security agreement [part of the purchase agreement], sold all of Corporation's then remaining assets for $60,000. $25,000 of the proceeds of sale was paid to release the federal tax lien while the remaining $35,000 was retained by Bank. After the sale, Corporation had no assets and owed $218,426 to creditors.

[DeBaun and Stephens] filed two related actions against Bank. One asserted their right to recover, as shareholders, for damage caused by Bank. The other was a stockholders' derivative action brought on behalf of Corporation * * *. The two cases were consolidated. Bank demurred to both complaints. In the demurrer to the first action, it contended that [plaintiffs] DeBaun and Stephens, as shareholders, lacked capacity to pursue their claim. In the demurrer to the second complaint, Bank took the opposite tack, contending that its liability did not run to Corporation. The demurrer to the first complaint was sustained without leave to amend, and the demurrer to the second complaint was overruled. The case at bench proceeded to trial before a judge as a derivative action. The trial court held for [plaintiffs], finding that Bank had breached duties it owed as a majority controlling shareholder to the corporation it controlled. It assessed monetary damages in the amount of $473,836, computed by adding to $220,000, the net asset value of the corporation as the date of transfer of the shares to Mattison, an amount equal to anticipated after-tax earnings of the corporation for the ensuing 10–year period, taking into account an 8 percent growth factor. The court additionally awarded Corporation an amount equal to the sum it would be required to pay and the cost of defending valid claims existing against it when it became defunct. Pursuant to Fletcher v. A. J. Industries, Inc., 266 Cal.App.2d 313, 320–321, the trial court awarded [plaintiffs] attorneys' fees payable from the fund recovered for Corporation's benefit. It denied [plaintiffs'] claim for punitive damages. This appeal from the resulting judgment followed.

Contentions on Appeal

In a variety of ways, * * * Bank contends: (1) as a majority shareholder, it owed no duty to Corporation in selling its shares; * * * and (4) the measure of damages is excessive. The contentions are not supported by the record or applicable law.

Breach of Duty

Early case law held that a controlling shareholder owed no duty to minority shareholders or to the controlled corporation in the sale of his stock. Decisional law, however, has since recognized the fact of financial life that corporate control by ownership of a majority of shares may be misused. Thus the applicable proposition now is that "[i]n any transaction where the control of the corporation is material," the controlling majority shareholder must exercise good faith and fairness "from the viewpoint of the corporation and those interested therein." (*Remillard Brick Co. v. Remillard–Dandini*, 109 Cal.App.2d 405, 420 *quoted in Jones v. H. F. Ahmanson & Co.*, 1 Cal.3d 93, 110). That duty of good faith and fairness encompasses an obligation of the controlling shareholder in possession of facts "[such] as to awaken suspicion and put a prudent man on his guard [that a potential buyer of his shares] may loot the corporation of its assets to pay for the shares purchased . . . to conduct a reasonable and adequate investigation [of the buyer]."

Here Bank was the controlling majority shareholder of Corporation. As it was negotiating with Mattison, it became directly aware of facts that would have alerted a prudent person that Mattison was likely to loot the corporation. Bank knew from the Dun & Bradstreet report that Mattison's financial record was notable by the failure of entities controlled by him. Bank knew that the only source of funds available to Mattison to pay it for the shares he was purchasing lay in the assets of the corporation. The after-tax net income from the date of the sale would not be sufficient to permit the payment of dividends to him which would permit the making of payments. An officer of Bank possessed personal knowledge that Mattison, on at least one occasion, had been guilty of a fraud perpetrated on Bank's predecessor in interest and had not satisfied a judgment Bank held against him for damages flowing from that conduct.

Armed with knowledge of those facts, Bank owed a duty to Corporation and its minority shareholders to act reasonably with respect to its dealings in the controlling shares with Mattison. It breached that duty. Knowing of McCarrol's refusal to express an opinion on litigation against Mattison and his entities, and that the information could be obtained from the public records, Bank closed its eyes to that obvious source. Rather, it relied upon Mattison's friendly reception by fellow members of the Jonathan Club and the fact that he was represented by a lawyer who had been a trust officer of Bank's predecessor in interest to conclude that indicators that Mattison was a financial bandit should be ignored. Membership in a club, whether it be the Jonathan or the informal group of ex-trust officers of Bank, does not excuse investigation. Nor can Bank be justified in accepting Mattison's uncorroborated statement that the past financial disasters of his entities reported by Dun & Bradstreet were due to his practice of acquiring failing companies. Only one who loots a failed company at the expense of its creditors can profit from its acquisition.

Mattison's constantly repeated entry into the transactions without ever pulling a company from the morass was a strong indication that he was milking the companies profitably. Had Bank investigated, as any prudent man would have done, it would have discovered from the public records the additional detail of Mattison's long, long trail of financial failure that would have precluded its dealings with him except under circumstances where his obligation was secured beyond question and his ability to loot Corporation precluded.

Bank, however, elected to deal with Mattison in a fashion that invited rather than tended to prevent his looting of Corporation's assets. It agreed to a payment schedule that virtually required Mattison to do so. By fraudulently concealing its nature from DeBaun and Stephens, Bank obtained corporate approval of a security agreement which hypothecated corporate assets to secure Mattison's obligation to it. Thus, to permit it to sell its majority shares to Mattison, Bank placed the assets and business of Corporation in peril. Not content with so doing, Bank used its control for still another purpose of its own by requiring Mattison to agree to cause Corporation to give its major banking business to Bank.

Thus the record establishes the duty of Bank and its breach. * * * Bank seeks to avoid responsibility for its action by reversing the position taken by it in its demurrer to the complaint filed by DeBaun and Stephens individually for injury to their minority stock position by now claiming that its duty ran only to the minority shareholders and not to the controlled corporation. California precedent is to the contrary, holding that the duty runs to both.

    * * *

Measure of Damages

[Bank] contends finally that the trial court improperly multiplied the measure of damages by adding to net asset value on the date of Bank's tortious conduct an estimate for future net profit and an obligation that

Bank discharge the valid existing obligations of Corporation. The record refutes the contention.

The trial judge arrived at a value of the corporation as a going concern at the time of [Bank's] breach by adding to the value of Corporation's tangible assets a goodwill factor computed on the basis of future net income reasonably to be anticipated from the Corporation's past record. This the trial court was authorized to do in determining "the amount which will compensate for all the detriment proximately caused ..." by [defendant]'s breach of duty. Bank's breach damaged Corporation not only in the loss of its assets but also in the loss of its earning power. Since the trial court's determination of loss of earning power was based upon a past record of earnings and not speculation, it is supported by substantial evidence.

The trial court's order requiring Bank to pay all valid claims of creditors against Corporation is also proper as necessary to restore Corporation to the condition in which it existed prior to the time that Bank contributed to its destruction. Prior to Bank's action, Corporation was a going concern with substantial net assets. As a proximate result of Bank's dereliction of duty, Corporation acquired a negative net worth of about $218,000. Total damage to Corporation is thus the sum necessary to restore the negative net worth, plus the value of its tangible assets, plus its going business value determined with reference to its future profits reasonably estimated. That is the measure which the trial court applied. Since the derivative action is equitable in nature, the court properly framed part of its judgment in terms of an obligation dependent upon future contingencies rather than at a fixed dollar amount.

The judgment is affirmed. The matter is, however, remanded to the trial court with directions to hold a hearing to determine the additional amount payable to [plaintiffs] from the fund recovered by them for benefit of Corporation for counsel fees due for services on this appeal.

QUESTIONS AND NOTE

1. When Mattison harmed the corporation for his own benefit, wasn't he also harming himself because he owned 70% of the company? Why?

2. The plaintiffs in *DeBaun* sued both directly (for harm done to them) and derivatively (for harm done to the corporation). The trial court dismissed the direct claim and the plaintiffs did not raise that issue on appeal. In light of what the Court of Appeal says in this opinion, how would it have ruled if the plaintiffs had appealed on the question of whether they had direct claims against Bank?

3. Because this case proceeded to trial and appeal as a derivative suit, who will recover the judgment against Bank? Will such a recovery reward Mattison? Would that be fair? Does that mean the claims were direct after all?

4. Review the elements of damages awarded by the court. Would the recovery have been the same had the claims been direct rather than derivative?

5. Both plaintiffs—DeBaun and Stephens—had left the employ of Corporation by the time they brought suit. Would this fact affect their standing to bring either direct or derivative claims?

6. Suppose McCarrol had responded to Bank's inquiry about the status of litigation against Mattison by listing two or three cases. Would Bank be charged with notice of what was in the public records concerning litigation against Mattison?

7. *DeBaun* is not included in most casebooks. We include it because it gives an excellent example of what looting is (and because Freer used to live in Los Angeles and wanted to reminisce about the Jonathan Club (not that he was ever a member)).

The next case is far more well-known than *DeBaun*. It is in all the casebooks. What does it add to *DeBaun*?

PERLMAN v. FELDMANN

United States Court of Appeals, Second Circuit, 1955
219 F.2d 173

CLARK, CHIEF JUDGE. This is a derivative action brought by minority stockholders of Newport Steel Corporation to compel accounting for, and restitution of, allegedly illegal gains which accrued to defendants as a result of the sale in August, 1950, of their controlling interest in the corporation. The principal defendant, C. Russell Feldmann, who represented and acted for the others, members of his family,* [1] was at that time not only the dominant stockholder, but also the chairman of the board of directors and the president of the corporation. Newport, an Indiana corporation, operated mills for the production of steel sheets for sale to manufacturers of steel products, first at Newport, Kentucky, and later also at other places in Kentucky and Ohio. The buyers, a syndicate organized as Wilport Company, a Delaware corporation, consisted of end-users of steel who were interested in securing a source of supply in a market becoming ever tighter in the Korean War. Plaintiffs contend that the consideration paid for the stock included compensation for the sale of a corporate asset, a power held in trust for the corporation by Feldmann as its fiduciary. This power was the ability to control the allocation of the corporate product in a time of short supply, through control of the board of directors; and it was effectively transferred in this sale by having Feldmann procure the resignation of his own board and the election of Wilport's nominees immediately upon consummation of the sale.

---

* [1] The stock was not held personally by Feldmann in his own name, but was held by the members of his family and by personal corporations. The aggregate of stock thus had amounted to 33% of the outstanding Newport stock and gave working control to the holder. The actual sale included 55,552 additional shares held by friends and associates of Feldmann, so that a total of 37% of the Newport stock was transferred.

Plaintiffs argue here, as they did in the court below, that in the situation here disclosed the vendors must account to the non-participating minority stockholders for that share of their profit which is attributable to the sale of the corporate power. Judge Hincks denied the validity of the premise, holding that the rights involved in the sale were only those normally incident to the possession of a controlling block of shares, with which a dominant stockholder, in the absence of fraud or foreseeable looting, was entitled to deal according to his own best interests. Furthermore, he held that plaintiffs had failed to satisfy their burden of proving that the sales price was not a fair price for the stock *per se*. Plaintiffs appeal from these rulings of law which resulted in the dismissal of their complaint.

The essential facts found by the trial judge are not in dispute. Newport was a relative newcomer in the steel industry with predominantly old installations which were in the process of being supplemented by more modern facilities. Except in times of extreme shortage Newport was not in a position to compete profitably with other steel mills for customers not in its immediate geographical area. Wilport, the purchasing syndicate, consisted of geographically remote end-users of steel who were interested in buying more steel from Newport than they had been able to obtain during recent periods of tight supply. The price of $20 per share was found by Judge Hincks to be a fair one for a control block of stock, although the over-the-counter market price had not exceeded $12 and the book value per share was $17.03. But this finding was limited by Judge Hincks' statement that "what value the block would have had if shorn of its appurtenant power to control distribution of the corporate product, the evidence does not show." It was also conditioned by his earlier ruling that the burden was on plaintiffs to prove a lesser value for the stock.

Both as director and as dominant stockholder, Feldmann stood in a fiduciary relationship to the corporation and to the minority stockholders as beneficiaries thereof. His fiduciary obligation must in the first instance be measured by the law of Indiana, the state of incorporation of Newport. Directors of a business corporation act in a strictly fiduciary capacity. Their office is a trust. When a director deals with his corporation, his acts will be closely scrutinized. Directors of a corporation are its agents, and they are governed by the rules of law applicable to other agents, and, as between themselves and their principal, the rules relating to honesty and fair dealing in the management of the affairs of their principal are applicable. They must not, in any degree, allow their official conduct to be swayed by their private interest, which must yield to official duty.

The responsibility of the fiduciary is not limited to a proper regard for the tangible balance sheet assets of the corporation, but included the dedication of his uncorrupted business judgment for the sole benefit of the corporation, in any dealings which may adversely affect it. The same rule should apply to his fiduciary duties as majority stockholder, for in that capacity he chooses and controls the directors, and thus is held to have assumed their liability. This, therefore, is the standard to which Feldmann was by law required to conform in his activities here under scrutiny.

It is true, as defendants have been at pains to point out, that this is not the ordinary case of breach of fiduciary duty. We have here no fraud, no misuse of confidential information, no outright looting of a helpless corporation. But on the other hand, we do not find compliance with that high standard which we have just stated and which we and other courts have come to expect and demand of corporate fiduciaries. In the often-quoted words of Judge Cardozo: "Many forms of conduct permissible in a workaday world for those acting at arm's length, are forbidden to those bound by fiduciary ties. A trustee is held to something stricter than the morals of the market place. Not honesty alone, but the punctilio of an honor the most sensitive, is then the standard of behavior. As to this, there has developed a tradition that is unbending and inveterate. Uncompromising rigidity has been the attitude of courts of equity when petitioned to undermine the rule of undivided loyalty by the 'disintegrating erosion' of particular exceptions." *Meinhard v. Salmon*, 249 N.Y. 458, 464, 164 N.E. 545, 546 [1948]. The actions of defendants in siphoning off for personal gain corporate advantages to be derived from a favorable market situation do not betoken the necessary undivided loyalty owed by the fiduciary to his principal.

The corporate opportunities of whose misappropriation the minority stockholders complain need not have been an absolute certainty in order to support this action against Feldmann. If there was possibility of corporate gain, they are entitled to recover.

In the past Newport had used and profited by its market leverage by operation of what the industry had come to call the "Feldmann Plan." This consisted of securing interest-free advances from prospective purchasers of steel in return for firm commitments to them from future production. The funds thus acquired were used to finance improvements in existing plants and to acquire new installations. In the summer of 1950 Newport had been negotiating for cold-rolling facilities which it needed for a more fully integrated operation and a more marketable product, and Feldmann plan funds might well have been used toward this end.

Further, as plaintiffs alternatively suggest, Newport might have used the period of short supply to build up patronage in the geographical area in which it could compete profitably even when steel was more abundant. Either of these opportunities was Newport's, to be used to its advantage only. Only if defendants had been able to negate completely any possibility of gain by Newport could they have prevailed. It is true that a trial court finding states: "Whether or not, in August, 1950, Newport's position was such that it could have entered into Feldmann Plan-type transactions to procure funds and financing for the further expansion and integration of its steel facilities and whether such expansion would have been desirable for Newport, the evidence does not show." This, however, cannot avail the defendants, who—contrary to the ruling below—had the burden of proof on this issue, since fiduciaries always have the burden of proof in establishing the fairness of their dealings with trust property.

Defendants seek to categorize the corporate opportunities which might have accrued to Newport as too unethical to warrant further consideration. It is true that reputable steel producers were not participating in the gray market brought about by the Korean War and were refraining from advancing their prices, although to do so would not have been illegal. But Feldmann plan transactions were not considered within this self-imposed interdiction; the trial court found that around the time of the Feldmann sale Jones & Laughlin Steel Corporation, Republic Steel Company, and Pittsburgh Steel Corporation were all participating in such arrangements. In any event, it ill becomes the defendants to disparage as unethical the market advantages from which they themselves reaped rich benefits.

We do not mean to suggest that a majority stockholder cannot dispose of his controlling block of stock to outsiders without having to account to his corporation for profits or even never do this with impunity when the buyer is an interested customer, actual or potential, for the corporation's product. But when the sale necessarily results in a sacrifice of this element of corporate good will and consequent unusual profit to the fiduciary who has caused the sacrifice, he should account for his gains. So in a time of market shortage, where a call on a corporation's product commands an unusually large premium, in one form or another, we think it sound law that a fiduciary may not appropriate to himself the value of this premium. Such personal gain at the expense of his coventurers seems particularly reprehensible when made by the trusted president and director of his company. In this case the violation of duty seems to be all the clearer because of this triple role in which Feldmann appears, though we are unwilling to say, and are not to be understood as saying, that we should accept a lesser obligation for any one of his roles alone.

Hence to the extent that the price received by Feldmann and his codefendants included such a bonus, he is accountable to the minority stockholders who sue here. And plaintiffs, as they contend, are entitled to a recovery in their own right, instead of in right of the corporation (as in the usual derivative actions), since neither Wilport nor their successors in interest should share in any judgment which may be rendered. Defendants cannot well object to this form of recovery, since the only alternative, recovery for the corporation as a whole, would subject them to a greater total liability.

The case will therefore be remanded to the district court for a determination of the question expressly left open below, namely, the value of defendants' stock without the appurtenant control over the corporation's output of steel. We reiterate that on this issue, as on all others relating to a breach of fiduciary duty, the burden of proof must rest on the defendants. Judgment should go to these plaintiffs and those whom they represent for any premium value so shown to the extent of their respective stock interests.

The judgment is therefore reversed and the action remanded for further proceedings pursuant to this opinion.

* * *

SWAN, CIRCUIT JUDGE (dissenting).

With the general principles enunciated in the majority opinion as to the duties of fiduciaries I am, of course, in thorough accord. But, as Mr. Justice Frankfurter stated in *Securities and Exchange Comm. v. Chenery Corp.*, 318 U.S. 80, 85, "to say that a man is a fiduciary only begins analysis; it gives direction to further inquiry. To whom is he a fiduciary? What obligations does he owe as a fiduciary? In what respect has he failed to discharge these obligations?" My brothers' opinion does not specify precisely what fiduciary duty Feldmann is held to have violated or whether it was a duty imposed upon him as the dominant stockholder or as a director of Newport. Without such specification I think that both the legal profession and the business world will find the decision confusing and will be unable to foretell the extent of its impact upon customary practices in the sale of stock.

The power to control the management of a corporation, that is, to elect directors to manage its affairs, is an inseparable incident to the ownership of a majority of its stock, or sometimes, as in the present instance, to the ownership of enough shares, less than a majority, to control an election. Concededly a majority or dominant shareholder is ordinarily privileged to sell his stock at the best price obtainable from the purchaser. In so doing he acts on his own behalf, not as an agent of the corporation. If he knows or has reason to believe that the purchaser intends to exercise to the detriment of the corporation the power of management acquired by the purchase, such knowledge or reasonable suspicion will terminate the dominant shareholder's privilege to sell and will create a duty not to transfer the power of management to such purchaser. The duty seems to me to resemble the obligation which everyone is under not to assist another to commit a tort rather than the obligation of a fiduciary. But whatever the nature of the duty, a violation of it will subject the violator to liability for damages sustained by the corporation. Judge Hincks found that Feldmann had no reason to think that Wilport would use the power of management it would acquire by the purchase to injure Newport, and that there was no proof that it ever was so used. Feldmann did know, it is true, that the reason Wilport wanted the stock was to put in a board of directors who would be likely to permit Wilport's members to purchase more of Newport's steel than they might otherwise be able to get. But there is nothing illegal in a dominant shareholder purchasing from his own corporation at the same prices it offers to other customers. That is what the members of Wilport did, and there is no proof that Newport suffered any detriment therefrom.

My brothers say that "the consideration paid for the stock included compensation for the sale of a corporate asset," which they describe as "the ability to control the allocation of the corporate product in a time of short supply, through control of the board of directors; and it was effectively transferred in this sale by having Feldmann procure the resignation of his own board and the election of Wilport's nominees immediately upon consummation of the sale." The implications of this are not clear to me. If it means that when market conditions are such as to induce users of a corporation's product to wish to buy a controlling block of stock in order to be able to purchase part of the corporation's output at the same mill list prices as are offered to other customers, the dominant stockholder is under a fiduciary duty not to sell his stock, I cannot agree. For reasons already stated, in my opinion Feldmann was not proved to be under any fiduciary duty as a stockholder not to sell the stock he controlled.

Judge Hincks went into the matter of valuation of the stock with his customary care and thoroughness. He made no error of law in applying the principles relating to valuation of stock. Concededly a controlling block of stock has greater sale value than a small lot. While the spread between $10 per share for small lots and $20 per share for the controlling block seems rather extraordinarily wide, the $20 valuation was supported by the expert testimony of Dr. Badger, whom the district judge said he could not find to be wrong. I see no justification for upsetting the valuation as clearly erroneous.

The final conclusion of my brothers is that the plaintiffs are entitled to recover in their own right instead of in the right of the corporation. This appears to be completely inconsistent with the theory advanced at the outset of the opinion, namely, that the price of the stock "included compensation for the sale of a corporate asset." If a corporate asset was sold, surely the corporation should recover the compensation received for it by the defendants. Moreover, if the plaintiffs were suing in their own right, Newport was not a proper party.

I would affirm the judgment on appeal.

QUESTIONS AND NOTES

1. Does this case belong in a section of the book entitled "common law duty of selling shareholders"?

2. Was Feldmann the majority shareholder?

3. Was it important that Feldmann was a director? Would Judge Clark have ruled differently if Feldmann was only the "dominant shareholder" but not a director or officer?

4. Was the identity of the buyer relevant? What if the buyer had been an investor rather than an end-user of steel? What if the buyer had been an investor with a reputation for buying and looting companies? Before the sale of the stock, what did Feldmann do to circumvent the informal price controls

that President Truman had placed on steel during the Korean war? What were the objectives of the buyers in purchasing the stock?

5. Is *Perlman* a looting case like *DeBaun*? Is it a direct or derivative action? What was the measure of damages? Who would benefit from a judgment for the plaintiffs? Would the judgment benefit the buyers of Feldmann's shares?

6. What effect did Feldmann's sale to Wilport have on the value of the other shareholders' shares? Was that relevant? Should it have been? Judge (then Professor) Easterbrook and Professor Fischel argued that it was relevant:

> The Second Circuit held in *Perlman* that the seller of the control block had a duty to share the control premium with other shareholders. The court's holding that Feldmann could not accept the premium paid by Wilport without violating his fiduciary duty was based on a belief that the steel shortage allowed Newport to finance needed expansion via the "Plan," and that the premium represented an attempt by Wilport to divert a corporate opportunity—to secure for itself the benefits resulting from the shortage. The court stated that "[o]nly if defendants had been able to negate completely any possibility of gain by Newport could they have prevailed."
>
> There are several problems with this treatment. Foremost is its assumption that the gain resulting from the "Plan" was not reflected in the price of Newport's stock. Newport stock was widely traded, and the existence of the Feldmann Plan was known to investors. The going price of Newport shares prior to the transaction therefore reflected the full value of Newport, including the value of advances under the Feldmann Plan. The Wilport syndicate paid some two-thirds more than the going price and thus could not profit from the deal unless (a) the sale of control resulted in an increase in the value of Newport, or (b) Wilport's control of Newport was the equivalent of looting. To see the implications of the latter possibility, consider the following simplified representation of the transaction. Newport has only 100 shares, and Wilport pays $20 for each of 37 shares. The market price of shares is $12, and hence the premium over the market price is $8 \times 37 = 296. Wilport must extract more than $296 from Newport in order to gain from the deal; the extraction comes at the expense of the other 63 shares, which must drop approximately $4.75 each, to $7.25.
>
> Hence, the court's proposition that Wilport extracted a corporate opportunity from Newport—the functional equivalent of looting—has testable implications. Unless the price of Newport's outstanding shares plummeted, the Wilport syndicate could not be extracting enough to profit. In fact, however, the value of Newport's shares rose substantially after the transaction. Part of this increase may have been attributable to the rising market for steel companies at the time, but even holding this factor constant, Newport's shares appreciated in price.*

---

* **[43]** Charles Cope has computed changes in the price of Newport shares using the market model, well developed in the finance literature, under which the rate of return on a firm's shares is a function of the market rate of return, the volatility of the firm's price in the past, a constant,

[43] Frank H. Easterbrook & Daniel R. Fischel, *Corporate Control Transactions*, 91 YALE L.J. 698, 717–18 (1982).

7. *Perlman v. Feldmann* is one of several famous corporations cases that, while included in all of the casebooks and often cited by law review articles, have inspired no following in the courts.† This may be in part because the case's facts and holding are so murky. The facts of *Perlman* are unique and quite complicated. It is not clear that the triggering facts of *Perlman* can be replicated. It is also not clear what facts come close enough to fall within its holding. Not only that, its holding is not all that clear. *Cf.* Elliott J. Weiss & Lawrence J. White, *Of Econometrics and Indeterminancy: A Study of Investors' Reactions to "Changes" in Corporate Law*, 75 CALIF. L. REV. 551, 607, n. 195 (1987) ("Many classic corporate law decisions deal with unique fact situations and are notable for the opacity of their doctrinal statements. *See, e.g., Perlman v. Feldmann.*").

NOTE: "SELLING" FIDUCIARY OFFICES WITH THE CONTROLLING INTEREST

It is not uncommon for the sale of a controlling block of stock to be accompanied by an agreement that directors friendly to the seller will resign. This practice—sometimes called delivering a "stacked" board to the buyer—allows the buyer, who is the new controlling shareholder, to have her people take control of the board of directors. A famous example is *Essex Universal Corp. v. Yates*, 305 F.2d 572 (2d Cir. 1962). In that case, Herbert J. Yates, the chairman of the board of directors of Republic Pictures Corp., agreed to sell his stock in the company to Essex Universal Corp. Yates owned over 28 percent of the Republic stock. Because the rest of the shares were owned by thousands of widely dispersed stockholders (Republic was publicly traded), Yates was the controlling shareholder. Part of the sales agreement provided that "Seller [Yates] will deliver to Buyer the resignations of the majority of the directors of Republic." Moreover, "Seller will cause a special meeting of the board of directors of Republic * * * and simultaneously with the acceptance of the directors' resignations * * * will cause nominees of Buyer to be elected directors * * * in place of the resigned directors." 305 F.2d at 574.

---

and a residual component that represents the consequences of unanticipated events. Increases in this residual reflect good news for the firm. Cope found a significant positive residual for Newport in the month of the sale to Wilport. *See* Charles Cope, Is the Control Premium Really a Corporate Asset? (April 1981) (unpublished paper on file with Yale Law Journal). The raw price data are no less telling. The $12 price to which the *Perlman* court referred was the highest price at which shares changed hands before the sale of control. The average monthly bid prices for Newport stock during 1950 were:

July: 6 3/4

August: 8 1/2

September: 10 7/8

October: 12 1/2

November: 12 3/8

December: 12

The sale to the Wilport syndicate took place on August 31, 1950. This pattern of prices certainly does not suggest that the 63% interest excluded from the premium perceived any damage to Newport.

† Recall that *Dodge v. Ford Motor Co.*, in Chapter 7, Part B, § 3 (the case ordering the payment of a dividend to shareholders), is another such case.

The problem with such a deal is that it looks as though the resigning directors are being paid to relinquish their seats on the board. The control premium might be seen as a bonus for the sale of directorships. Because directorships are fiduciary positions, and directors owe duties to the corporation, many have argued that such deals are invalid—void as against public policy.

Realistically, though, is there any problem with these deals? After all, when the sale goes through, Essex will be the controlling shareholder and can call a special meeting of the shareholders to remove Yates's directors and install its own. (Although, interestingly, the *Essex Universal* case was governed by New York law, which allows shareholders to remove directors without cause *only* if the certificate (articles) provides. *See* New York § 706.) Insisting in these circumstances that Essex actually remove the old directors and elect new ones might be elevating form over substance.

So what do the courts do? In *Essex Universal*, Yates backed out of the agreement* and the buyer sued to enforce it. Yates claimed that the deal was void, and the trial court entered summary judgment in his favor.

On appeal, the three judges on the Second Circuit panel took different positions. Two of them held that the judgment should be reversed, but for different reasons. Judge Lumbard was willing to say that a sale of 28 percent of the stock in a publicly traded company was sufficient to constitute control and to uphold the deal. He put the burden on Yates to show that Essex would not have sufficient shareholder voting power to replace the majority of directors. Judge Clark agreed only that the case should be remanded for trial, since these things ought to be decided on their facts and not on summary judgment. Judge Friendly dissented, asserting that such deals concerning replacement of directors are valid only if they involve a true majority of the corporation's stock.

So everyone seems to agree that a sale involving a true majority of the corporation's stock can legitimately carry with it a deal to deliver a stacked board to the buyer. (Even here, though, what if the board served multi-year, staggered terms? If we make the buyer actually elect new directors, that route might take several years to gain a majority of the board.) What if the controlling shareholder does not own a majority of the outstanding stock? "Many courts have been willing to go below the fifty percent threshold if the court is convinced that the buyer purchased sufficient stock to give working control in view of the high dispersion of the remaining shareholdings." Franklin Gevurtz, CORPORATION LAW 636.

3.   TO WHOM CAN A SHAREHOLDER SELL HER SHARES?

This is not a hard question for a shareholder of a large, public corporation like Mercury Finance Corporation or McDonald's. There is a public market for such shares.

What about the shareholder of a small, closely held corporation? To whom will she be able to sell her shares? If Propp, one of three sharehold-

---

* Evidently, the stock had appreciated considerably since the deal was entered.

ers of Bubba's Burritos, Inc. wants to sell his shares, who are the likely buyers?* If Propp is unable to find any other buyer, is the corporation legally obligated to repurchase Propp's shares? Recall partnership law and the RUPA concept of dissociation.

a.   Redemption and the "Equal Access" Rule

There is no MBCA counterpart to dissociation in partnership law. Corporate codes do not obligate a corporation to repurchase stock from its shareholders. And there is no direct case law corporate counterpart to partnership dissociation. We are not aware of any case that imposes a general obligation on a corporation to buy stock back from any of its shareholders.

There is, however, a line of cases that establishes an "equal access rule." The next case is the leading opinion of that line. In reading it, please consider the following.

1.   Who decided that the corporation would buy Harry Rodd's stock?

2.   Who decided the price that the corporation would pay for Harry Rodd's stock? Was there any evidence that the price paid for the stock was excessive?

3.   Was there any allegation that the corporation or any of its directors or shareholders violated any provisions of Massachusetts law?

4.   Make sure that you understand the difference between a redemption right, under which a shareholder is entitled to *sell* her shares to the corporation, and preemptive right (which we've already discussed), under which the shareholder is entitled to *buy* additional shares.

DONAHUE v. RODD ELECTROTYPE COMPANY OF NEW ENGLAND, INC.

Supreme Judicial Court of Massachusetts, 1975
328 N.E.2d 505

TAURO, CHIEF JUSTICE. The plaintiff, Euphemia Donahue, a minority stockholder in the Rodd Electrotype Company of New England, Inc. (Rodd Electrotype), a Massachusetts corporation, brings this suit against the directors of Rodd Electrotype, Charles H. Rodd, Frederick I. Rodd and Mr. Harold E. Magnuson, against Harry C. Rodd, a former director, officer, and controlling stockholder of Rodd Electrotype and against Rodd Electrotype (hereinafter called defendants). The plaintiff seeks to rescind Rodd Electrotype's purchase of Harry Rodd's shares in Rodd Electrotype and to compel Harry Rodd "to repay to the corporation the purchase price of said

---

* "Savorers of political fare recall with glee the tale of two brothers: one who went off to sea, the other who became Vice–President of the United States and neither was ever heard of again. If there had been a third sibling of this dubious duo who had suffered the same fate, it could only be because he was a minority shareholder in a closely held Alabama corporation. Simply put, no buyer in his right mind would pay cash for paper stock carrying no rights, including the right to income therefrom." Andrew P. Campbell, *Litigating Minority Shareholder Rights and the New Tort of Oppression*, 53 ALA. LAWYER 108 (1992).

shares, $36,000, together with interest from the date of purchase." The plaintiff alleges that the defendants caused the corporation to purchase the shares in violation of their fiduciary duty to her, a minority stockholder of Rodd Electrotype.* [4]

The trial judge, after hearing oral testimony, dismissed the plaintiff's bill on the merits. He found that the purchase was without prejudice to the plaintiff and implicitly found that the transaction had been carried out in good faith and with inherent fairness. The Appeals Court affirmed with costs.

[Plaintiff owned 45 shares of Rodd Electrotype. Harry Rodd and his children owned the remaining 189 outstanding shares. More specifically, Harry Rodd owned 81 shares and each of his three children owned 36 shares].

* * * We come now to the events of 1970 which form the grounds for the plaintiff's complaint. In May of 1970, Harry Rodd was seventy-seven years old. The record indicates that for some time he had not enjoyed the best of health and that he had undergone a number of operations. His sons wished him to retire. Mr. Rodd was not averse to this suggestion. However, he insisted that some financial arrangements be made with respect to his remaining eighty-one shares of stock. A number of conferences ensued. Harry Rodd and Charles Rodd (representing the company) negotiated terms of purchase for forty-five shares which, Charles Rodd testified, would reflect the book value and liquidating value of the shares.

A special board meeting convened on July 13, 1970. As the first order of business, Harry Rodd resigned his directorship of Rodd Electrotype. The remaining incumbent directors, Charles Rodd and Mr. Harold E. Magnuson (clerk of the company [what most states call the corporate "secretary"] and a defendant and defense attorney in the instant suit), elected Frederick Rodd to replace his father. The three directors then authorized Rodd Electrotype's president (Charles Rodd) to execute an agreement between Harry Rodd and the company in which the company would purchase forty-five shares for $800 a share ($36,000). * * *

A few weeks after the meeting, the Donahues, acting through their attorney, offered their shares to the corporation on the same terms given to Harry Rodd. Mr. Harold E. Magnuson replied by letter that the corporation would not purchase the shares and was not in a financial position to do so. This suit followed.

In her argument before this court, the plaintiff has characterized the corporate purchase of Harry Rodd's shares as an unlawful distribution of corporate assets to controlling stockholders. She urges that the distribu-

---

* [4] In form, the plaintiff's bill of complaint presents, at least in part, a derivative action, brought on behalf of the corporation, and, in the words of the bill, 'on behalf of ... (the) stockholders' of Rodd Electrotype. Yet, the plaintiff's bill, in substance, was one seeking redress because of alleged breaches of the fiduciary duty owed to her, a minority stockholder, by the controlling stockholders.

We treat that bill of complaint (as have the parties) as presenting a proper cause of suit in the personal right of the plaintiff.

tion constitutes a breach of the fiduciary duty owed by the Rodds, as controlling stockholders, to her, a minority stockholder in the enterprise, because the Rodds failed to accord her an equal opportunity to sell her shares to the corporation. The defendants reply that the stock purchase was within the powers of the corporation and met the requirements of good faith and inherent fairness imposed on a fiduciary in his dealings with the corporation. They assert that there is no right to equal opportunity in corporate stock purchases for the corporate treasury. For the reasons hereinafter noted, we agree with the plaintiff and reverse the decree of the Superior Court. However, we limit the applicability of our holding to "close corporations," as hereinafter defined. Whether the holding should apply to other corporations is left for decision in another case, on a proper record.

In previous opinions, we have alluded to the distinctive nature of the close corporation, but have never defined precisely what is meant by a close corporation. There is no single, generally accepted definition. Some commentators emphasize an "integration of ownership and management" in which the stockholders occupy most management positions. Others focus on the number of stockholders and the nature of the market for the stock. In this view, close corporations have a few stockholders; there is little market for corporate stock. The Supreme Court of Illinois adopted this latter view in *Galler v. Galler*, 32 Ill.2d 16, 203 N.E.2d 577 (1964): "For our purposes, a close corporation is one in which the stock is held in a few hands, or in a few families, and wherein it is not at all, or only rarely, dealt in by buying or selling." *See, generally*, F. H. O'Neal, Close Corporations: Law and Practice, § 1.02 (1971).* **[11]** We accept aspects of both definitions. We deem a close corporation to be typified by: (1) a small number of stockholders; (2) no ready market for the corporate stock; and (3) substantial majority stockholder participation in the management, direction and operations of the corporation.

As thus defined, the close corporation bears striking resemblance to a partnership. Commentators and courts have noted that the close corporation is often a little more than an "incorporated" or "chartered" partnership. The stockholders "clothe" their partnership "with the benefits peculiar to a corporation, of limited liability, perpetuity and the like. In essence, though, the enterprise remains one in which ownership is limited to the original parties or transferees of their stock to whom the other stockholders have agreed, in which ownership and management are in the same hands, and in which the owners are quite dependent on one another for the success of the enterprise. Many close corporations are 'really partnerships, between two or three people who contribute their capital, skills, experience and labor.'" Just as in a partnership, the relationship among the stockholders must be one of trust, confidence and absolute loyalty if the enterprise is to succeed. Close corporations with substantial

---

* **[11]** O'Neal restricts his definition of the close corporation to those corporations whose shares are not generally traded in securities markets. F.H. O'Neal, Close Corporations: Law and Practice, § 1.02 (1971).

assets and with more numerous stockholders are no different from smaller close corporations in this regard. All participants rely on the fidelity and abilities of those stockholders who hold office. Disloyalty and self-seeking conduct on the part of any stockholder will engender bickering, corporate stalemates, and, perhaps, efforts to achieve dissolution.

In *Helms v. Duckworth*, 249 F.2d 482 (1957), the United States Court of Appeals for the District of Columbia Circuit had before it a stockholders' agreement providing for the purchase of the shares of a deceased stockholder by the surviving stockholder in a small "two-man" close corporation. The court held the surviving stockholder to a duty "to deal fairly, honestly, and openly with ... [his] fellow stockholders." Judge Burger, now Chief Justice Burger, writing for the court, emphasized the resemblance of the two-man close corporation to a partnership: "In an intimate business venture such as this, stockholders of a close corporation occupy a position similar to that of joint adventurers and partners. While courts have sometimes declared stockholders 'do not bear toward each other that same relation of trust and confidence which prevails in partnerships,' this view ignores the practical realities of the organization and functioning of a small 'two-man' corporation organized to carry on a small business enterprise in which the stockholders, directors, and managers are the same persons" (footnotes omitted).

Although the corporate form provides the above-mentioned advantages for the stockholders (limited liability, perpetuity, and so forth), it also supplies an opportunity for the majority stockholders to oppress or disadvantage minority stockholders. The minority is vulnerable to a variety of oppressive devices, termed "freeze-outs," which the majority may employ. An authoritative study of such "freeze-outs" enumerates some of the possibilities: "The squeezers (those who employ the freeze-out techniques) may refuse to declare dividends; they may drain off the corporation's earnings in the form of exorbitant salaries and bonuses to the majority shareholder-officers and perhaps to their relatives, or in the form of high rent by the corporation for property leased from majority shareholders ... ; they may deprive minority share-holders of corporate offices and of employment by the company; they may cause the corporation to sell its assets at an inadequate price to the majority shareholders...." F. H. O'Neal and J. Derwin, EXPULSION OR OPPRESSION OF BUSINESS ASSOCIATES 42 (1961). In particular, the power of the board of directors, controlled by the majority, to declare or withhold dividends and to deny the minority employment is easily converted to a device to disadvantage minority stockholders.

The minority can, of course, initiate suit against the majority and their directors. Self-serving conduct by directors is proscribed by the director's fiduciary obligation to the corporation. However, in practice, the plaintiff will find difficulty in challenging dividend or employment policies. Such policies are considered to be within the judgment of the directors. This court has said: "The courts prefer not to interfere ... with the sound financial management of the corporation by its directors, but declare as a general rule that the declaration of dividends rests within the sound discretion of the directors, refusing to interfere with their determination unless a plain abuse of discretion is made to appear." Judicial reluctance to interfere combines with the difficulty of proof when the standard is "plain abuse of discretion" or bad faith to limit the possibilities for relief. * * *

Thus, when these types of "freeze-outs" are attempted by the majority stockholders, the minority stockholders, cut off from all corporation-related revenues, must either suffer their losses or seek a buyer for their shares. Many minority stockholders will be unwilling or unable to wait for an alteration in majority policy. * * *

At this point, the true plight of the minority stockholder in a close corporation becomes manifest. He cannot easily reclaim his capital. In a large public corporation, the oppressed or dissident minority stockholder could sell his stock in order to extricate some of his invested capital. By definition, this market is not available for shares in the close corporation. In a partnership, a partner who feels abused by his fellow partners may cause dissolution by his "express will ... at any time" and recover his share of partnership assets and accumulated profits. If dissolution results in a breach of the partnership articles, the culpable partner will be liable in damages. By contrast, the stockholder in the close corporation or "incorporated partnership" may achieve dissolution and recovery of his share of the enterprise assets only by compliance with the rigorous terms of the applicable chapter of the General Laws. "The dissolution of a corporation which is a creature of the Legislature is primarily a legislative function, and the only authority courts have to deal with this subject is the power conferred upon them by the Legislature." To secure dissolution of the ordinary close corporation the stockholder, in the absence of corporate deadlock, must own at least fifty per cent of the shares or have the advantage of a favorable provision in the articles of organization. The minority stockholder, by definition lacking fifty per cent of the corporate shares, can never "authorize" the corporation to file a petition for dissolution. He will seldom have at his disposal the requisite favorable provision in the articles of organization.

Thus, in a close corporation, the minority stockholders may be trapped in a disadvantageous situation. No outsider would knowingly assume the position of the disadvantaged minority. The outsider would have the same difficulties. To cut losses, the minority stockholder may be compelled to deal with the majority. This is the capstone of the majority plan. Majority "freeze-out" schemes which withhold dividends are designed to compel the minority to relinquish stock at inadequate prices. When the minority stockholder agrees to sell out at less than fair value, the majority has won.

Because of the fundamental resemblance of the close corporation to the partnership, the trust and confidence which are essential to this scale and manner of enterprise, and the inherent danger to minority interests in the close corporation, we hold that stockholders* [17] in the close corporation owe one another substantially the same fiduciary duty in the operation of the enterprise that partners owe to one another. In our previous decisions, we have defined the standard of duty owed by partners to one another as the "utmost good faith and loyalty." Stockholders in close corporations must discharge their management and stockholder responsibilities in conformity with this strict good faith standard. They may not act out of avarice, expediency or self-interest in derogation of their duty of loyalty to the other stockholders and to the corporation.

We contrast this strict good faith standard with the somewhat less stringent standard of fiduciary duty to which directors and stockholders of all corporations must adhere in the discharge of their corporate responsibilities. Corporate directors are held to a good faith and inherent fairness standard of conduct and are not "permitted to serve two masters whose interests are antagonistic." "Their paramount duty is to the corporation, and their personal pecuniary interests are subordinate to that duty."

The more rigorous duty of partners and participants in a joint adventure,* [21] here extended to stockholders in a close corporation, was described by then Chief Judge Cardozo of the New York Court of Appeals in *Meinhard v. Salmon*, 249 N.Y. 458, 164 N.E. 545 (1928): "Joint adventurers, like copartners, owe to one another, while the enterprise continues, the duty of the finest loyalty. Many forms of conduct permissible in a workaday world for those acting at arm's length, are forbidden to those bound by fiduciary ties.... Not honesty alone, but the punctilio of an honor the most sensitive, is then the standard of behavior."† [22] * * *

Under settled Massachusetts law, a domestic corporation, unless forbidden by statute, has the power to purchase its own shares. An agreement to reacquire stock "(is) enforceable, subject, at least, to the limitations that the purchase must be made in good faith and without prejudice to creditors and stockholders." When the corporation reacquiring its own stock is a close corporation, the purchase is subject to the additional requirement, in the light of our holding in this opinion, that the stockholders, who, as directors or controlling stockholders, caused the corporation to enter into the stock purchase agreement, must have acted with the utmost good faith and loyalty to the other stockholders.

To meet this test, if the stockholder whose shares were purchased was a member of the controlling group, the controlling stockholders must cause the corporation to offer each stockholder an equal opportunity to sell a ratable number of his shares to the corporation at an identical price.

---

* [17] We do not limit our holding to majority stockholders. In the close corporation, the minority may do equal damage through unscrupulous and improper "sharp dealings" with an unsuspecting majority.

* [21] We have indicated previously that the duty owed by partners *inter sese* and that owed by coadventurers *inter sese* are substantially identical.

† [22] These pages of the *Meinhard* case are cited with approval as authority for the standard of duty applicable to joint adventurers and partners and as authority for "the special liabilities of joint venturers."

Purchase by the corporation confers substantial benefits on the members of the controlling group whose shares were purchased. These benefits are not available to the minority stockholders if the corporation does not also offer them an opportunity to sell their shares. The controlling group may not, consistent with its strict duty to the minority, utilize its control of the corporation to obtain special advantages and disproportionate benefit from its share ownership.

The benefits conferred by the purchase are twofold: (1) provision of a market for shares; (2) access to corporate assets for personal use. By definition, there is no ready market for shares of a close corporation. The purchase creates a market for shares which previously had been unmarketable. It transforms a previously illiquid investment into a liquid one. If the close corporation purchases shares only from a member of the controlling group, the controlling stockholder can convert his shares into cash at a time when none of the other stockholders can. Consistent with its strict fiduciary duty, the controlling group may not utilize its control of the corporation to establish an exclusive market in previously unmarketable shares from which the minority stockholders are excluded.

The purchase also distributes corporate assets to the stockholder whose shares were purchased. Unless an equal opportunity is given to all stockholders, the purchase of shares from a member of the controlling group operates as a preferential distribution of assets. In exchange for his shares, he receives a percentage of the contributed capital and accumulated profits of the enterprise. The funds he so receives are available for his personal use. The other stockholders benefit from no such access to corporate property and cannot withdraw their shares of the corporate profits and capital in this manner unless the controlling group acquiesces. Although the purchase price for the controlling stockholder's shares may seem fair to the corporation and other stockholders under the tests established in the prior case law, the controlling stockholder whose stock has been purchased has still received a relative advantage over his fellow stockholders, inconsistent with his strict fiduciary duty—an opportunity to turn corporate funds to personal use.

The rule of equal opportunity in stock purchases by close corporations provides equal access to these benefits for all stockholders. We hold that, in any case in which the controlling stockholders have exercised their power over the corporation to deny the minority such equal opportunity, the minority shall be entitled to appropriate relief. * * *

We turn now to the application of the learning set forth above to the facts of the instant case. The strict standard of duty is plainly applicable to the stockholders in Rodd Electrotype. Rodd Electrotype is a close corporation. Members of the Rodd and Donahue families are the sole owners of the corporation's stock. * * * We reject the defendants' contention that the Rodd family cannot be treated as a unit for this purpose. From the evidence, it is clear that the Rodd family was a close-knit one with strong community of interest. Harry Rodd had hired his sons to work in the family business, Rodd Electrotype. As he aged, he transferred portions of his stock holdings to his children. Charles Rodd and Frederick Rodd were given positions of responsibility in the business as he withdrew from active management. In these circumstances, it is realistic to assume that appreciation, gratitude, and filial devotion would prevent the younger Rodds from opposing a plan which would provide funds for their father's retirement.

Moreover, a strong motive of interest requires that the Rodds be considered a controlling group. When Charles Rodd and Frederick Rodd were called on to represent the corporation in its dealings with their father, they must have known that further advancement within the corporation and benefits would follow their father's retirement and the purchase of his stock. * * *

On its face, then, the purchase of Harry Rodd's shares by the corporation is a breach of the duty which the controlling stockholders, the Rodds, owed to the minority stockholders, the plaintiff and her son. The purchase distributed a portion of the corporate assets to Harry Rodd, a member of the controlling group, in exchange for his shares. The plaintiff and her son were not offered an equal opportunity to sell their shares to the corporation. In fact, their efforts to obtain an equal opportunity were rebuffed by the corporate representative. As the trial judge found, they did not, in any manner, ratify the transaction with Harry Rodd.

Because of the foregoing, we hold that the plaintiff is entitled to relief. Two forms of suitable relief are set out hereinafter. The judge below is to enter an appropriate judgment. The judgment may require Harry Rodd to remit $36,000 with interest at the legal rate from July 15, 1970, to Rodd Electrotype in exchange for forty-five shares of Rodd Electrotype treasury stock. This, in substance, is the specific relief requested in the plaintiff's bill of complaint. In the alternative, the judgment may require Rodd Electrotype to purchase all of the plaintiff's shares for $36,000 without interest. In the circumstances of this case, we view this as the equal opportunity which the plaintiff should have received. Harry Rodd's retention of thirty-six shares, which were to be sold and given to his children within a year of the Rodd Electrotype purchase, cannot disguise the fact that the corporation acquired one hundred per cent of that portion of his holdings (forty-five shares) which he did not intend his children to own. The plaintiff is entitled to have one hundred per cent of her forty-five shares similarly purchased.

The final decree, in so far as it dismissed the bill as to Harry C. Rodd, Frederick I. Rodd, Charles J. Rodd, Mr. Harold E. Magnuson and Rodd Electrotype Company of New England, Inc., and awarded costs, is reversed. The case is remanded to the Superior Court for entry of judgment in conformity with this opinion. * * *

WILKINS, JUSTICE (concurring).

I agree with much of what the Chief Justice says in support of granting relief to the plaintiff. However, I do not join in any implication that the rule concerning a close corporation's purchase of a controlling stockholder's shares applies to all operations of the corporation as they affect minority stockholders. That broader issue, which is apt to arise in connection with salaries and dividend policy, is not involved in this case. The analogy to partnerships may not be a complete one.

QUESTIONS

1. The equal access rule, as espoused in *Donahue,* requires a close corporation not to discriminate in repurchasing shares. To do so breaches a fiduciary obligation owed to the minority shareholders. The equal access rule is not accepted universally. Where it is accepted, as in Massachusetts, it is limited to the close corporation. Why would a court limit the equal access rule to close corporations? In the states that reject the equal access rule even for close corporations, is there any way that minority shareholders can protect themselves? Take another look at the redemption rights in the Silicon Gaming document in Chapter 4, Part B, § 4.

2. Is a claim under *Donahue* direct or derivative?

3. Comparisons

3.1 The court compares close corporations with partnerships and suggests that one of the "benefits peculiar to a corporation" is "perpetuity." What is the importance of attributing "perpetuity" to corporations but not to partnerships? Are corporations in an MBCA state any more permanent than partnerships in a Revised Uniform Partnership Act state? *Cf.* MBCA §§ 14.02, 14.05, *Cf.* RUPA §§ 801, 802(b). *See also* the *Giannotti* case.

3.2 The court also compares the stockholders of close corporations with partners of partnerships. What are the similarities? The differences? Does *Donahue* blur the line between close corporations and partnerships?

3.3 The court also compares the fiduciary duties of directors of corporations with the fiduciary duties of shareholders of close corporations. What are the differences? To whom does the director of a corporation owe a fiduciary duty? To whom does the shareholder of a close corporation owe a fiduciary duty? For whom is a "punctilio of any honor the most sensitive" the standard of behavior? Recall the statement from the *Zidell* case in Chapter 7, Part B, § 3: "Those in control of corporate affairs have fiduciary duties of good faith and fair dealing to minority shareholders." Is that statement from *Zidell* consistent with the statements in *Donahue*?

3.4 Here is one final comparison of different ways in which a corporation can get money to its shareholders. Compare a corporation's decision to redeem stock with a corporation's decision to declare dividends. How did the $36,000 stock redemption affect Rodd Electrotype's balance sheet? How would $36,000 in dividends affect Rodd Electrotype's balance sheet? *Cf.* MBCA § 14.06 ("A distribution may be in the form of a declaration or payment of a dividend; a purchase, redemption or other acquisition of shares; a distribution of indebtedness; or otherwise.")

4. Would the court have decided this case differently if there had been a bylaw provision that the corporation may purchase shares from one share-

holder without offering the other shareholders an equal opportunity to sell their shares to the corporation?

5.   Would the court have decided this case differently if none of the shareholders was a relative? One article emphasizes that the control group in *Donahue* was a family group: "One may worry that the payment to Dad is disguised self-dealing, the more Dad gets for his shares the less the children in the business will have to contribute to buy him an apartment in Miami." Edward B. Rock & Michael L. Wachter, *Waiting for the Omelet to Set: Match–Specific Assets and Minority Oppression in Close Corporations*, 24 J. CORP. L. 913 (1999).

6.   What is "book value"? "Liquidating value"? Are the two the same?

7.   Recall that the court treated this case as a direct, rather than a derivative, action. Why? Do you agree with attorneys and judges who read *Donahue* as "converting all intracorporate disputes that would normally be characterized as derivative actions into direct actions whenever the case involves a closely held corporation"? *Cf.* AMERICAN LAW INSTITUTE PRINCIPLES OF CORPORATE GOVERNACE § 7.01, comment (e); Brown v. Brown, 731 A.2d 1212, 1214–18 (N.J. Sup. Ct. App. Div. 1999) (which misspells and discusses the ALI "Principals").

8.   A couple cases that we have already studied rely on *Donahue*. Can you remember which ones? We can.

b.   Buy–Sell Agreements

Many of the problems that minority shareholders in close corporations might face can be eliminated if the shareholders plan ahead. In many instances, the majority shareholders will benefit by protecting minority shareholders; if the minority shareholders are protected, then investors will be willing to pay more for minority shares.

One of the important planning tools is the "buy-sell agreement." Buy-sell agreements are common because (i) a shareholder in a close corporation is often concerned about finding a buyer for her shares when she wants to sell and (ii) all shareholders of a close corporation are often concerned that a shareholder/co-owner whom they know and trust might sell her shares to an unknown stranger. As the label suggests, a buy-sell agreement is simply a contract that requires the corporation or the majority shareholder of the corporation to purchase shares in specified situations at a specified price. If there is a buy-sell agreement and it is properly drafted, it should establish (1) what triggers an obligation to sell and buy stock, (2) the purchase price, and (3) where the money comes from. The following article addresses these questions.

A buy-sell agreement ensures the orderly and systematic continuation of a business. Such a contract usually obligates one party to sell and another party to buy some or all of the ownership interest in a business in the event of the death, disability or retirement of an owner ("triggering event").

Unless there is a funded buy-sell agreement in place at the time of a triggering event, the continuing business owners may find themselves in business with the heirs of the deceased owner or may be forced to sell the business to compensate the departed owner or his or her heirs. In the case of a sole proprietorship or closely held corporation, there may not be a ready market for the business, leaving the heirs with an essentially valueless entity or the retiring or disabled owner with no source of income.

This article provides an overview of buy-sell agreements and discusses several varieties of such an agreement. A means to fund the buy-sell agreement must be established, and the business must be accurately valued to support the terms of the contract.

Funding Considerations

To be effective, buy-sell agreements must include a means to ensure that funds are available to comply with the terms of the contract. There are two primary ways to fund obligations: a "sinking fund" to which regular contributions are made by each owner, or some form of life insurance covering the owners.

A sinking fund is viable only if the owners have access to sufficient cash on an ongoing basis to ensure that money is available to meet the buy-sell contract terms. In most cases, this approach either ties up too much capital or the cash simply is not available.

Life insurance is available in many forms and generally can be obtained at a cost acceptable to most business owners. The variations available include term, convertible term, universal, variable universal, whole life, first-to-die and second-to-die life insurance. Because the costs and features vary widely among policy types, it is essential to analyze both the business needs of the company and the features of each insurance plan.

There are several elements necessary to a buy-sell agreement. The contract may ensure that a transfer of ownership will occur as planned. However, unless there is a sinking fund or life insurance in place, there is no means to fund the obligation.

Types of Buy–Sell Agreements

The four major types of buy-sell agreements are: "one-way" agreements, cross-purchase agreements, entity (or stock) redemption agreements and "wait and see" agreements. There are diverse tax, legal and funding implications associated with each of these agreements. The heirs of the deceased owner, or the departing owner in the case of retirement or disability, also must agree to and comply with the terms of the buy-sell agreement.

One–Way Agreements

A one-way agreement enables a third party to acquire a deceased or departing owner's interest in the business. This agreement is usually used to provide a market for a closely held corporation or individual ownership interest. In many cases, the third parties are key employees.

This type of buy-sell agreement is simple to fund. The third party can either establish a fund for the purchase or buy a life insurance policy on the owner. In order to demonstrate an "insurable interest" in the owner's life, the third party must be named as a future purchaser in the buy-sell agreement. Life insurance premium payments are not deductible to the purchaser, but the insurance death proceeds are generally received free of income tax. The sale of a sole proprietorship by an estate will normally involve both ordinary income tax and capital gains. The estate of the decedent receives a "step up in basis" when the business is sold. If the amount received by the estate equals the fair market value of the business, no capital gains result because the basis equals the purchase price. When payments include assets such as goodwill, appreciated inventory and unrealized inventory, they are subject to ordinary income tax.

Although the business owner may wish to own the policy on his or her life, there are two potentially adverse tax consequences. First, the IRS may seek to include both the insurance proceeds and the business interest in the decedent's estate. Because the insurance proceeds will pass to the designated purchaser, who is generally not the decedent's spouse, the marital deduction will not apply. Including the proceeds and the business interest in the estate of the deceased may result in additional and unnecessary estate tax costs. Second, the IRS may contend that the beneficiary's promise to use the insurance proceeds to purchase the business in exchange for being named the policy beneficiary constitutes a transfer-for-value and thus subjects the proceeds to income tax.

Cross–Purchase Agreements

A cross-purchase agreement usually obligates surviving owners of a business to purchase a deceased owner's interest directly from the decedent's heirs. If the owner becomes disabled or retires, the surviving owners also may be obligated to purchase the interest of the departing owner directly. The business is not a party to such an agreement.

Normally, each remaining owner purchases enough of the deceased or departed owner's interest to maintain his proportionate interest in the business. To illustrate, if there are four owners (A, B, C, D), and A leaves or dies, B, C and D each would buy one-third of A's interest, retaining the original ratios. The monies paid would go to A or A's estate.

Proportionate purchases are not required, however. It is possible for B and C to have a buy-sell agreement which excludes D. In this case, B and C would each purchase a specified percentage of A's share (to total 100 percent), bringing their combined ownership share to 75 percent of the business. This would effectively prevent D from having any decision-making authority. It is therefore critical to look at ownership implications when designing the buy-sell agreement.

Once each participant has accepted the agreement, the participants are bound by its terms. Each owner can either purchase a life insurance policy on the other owners or agree to purchase a portion of the others' interest using some other source of cash. For example, in the case of a business valued at $1.2 million with four equal owners, each owner could purchase life insurance policies in the amount of $100,000 on the other owners' lives, for a total of twelve policies. When cross-purchase agreements are used with more than two owners, multiple policies are needed.

It is sometimes feasible to use more sophisticated buy-sell techniques (such as a trusteeship) to reduce the number of life insurance policies required, if the buy-sell agreement is to be funded by insurance proceeds. In the preceding example, a trusteeship could be used to reduce the number of policies involved to four from twelve because the trust buys one policy on each owner. The trust distributes the proceeds to each owner in accordance with the trust agreement.

Entity or Stock Redemption Agreements

An entity or stock redemption agreement is entered into by both the owners and the business entity itself. Generally, each owner agrees to sell his or her interest in the business back to the business entity upon a triggering event, and the business agrees to purchase such interest. This provides the deceased owner's heirs with cash in lieu of an interest in the business, or the departing owner with cash payments for disability or retirement.

Under the terms of an entity redemption agreement, because the entity is obligated to purchase the deceased or departing owner's stock, each remaining owner's relative share of the business stays the same with respect to each other owner. However, control over the business may shift.

For example, consider a business with four owners (A, B, C, D), in which A, B and C each own 20 percent of the business and D owns 40 percent. If A dies or departs, B and C will then each have a 25 percent interest. Meanwhile, D has a 50 percent interest. Thus, D effectively gains control of the company. Where previously A, B and C voting together could overrule D, the entity purchase buy-sell agreement changes the result. Again, it is critical to look at possible ownership outcomes when structuring a buy-sell agreement.

Because the obligation to purchase the departing owner's interest would rest with the business and not the remaining owners, any funding vehicle used must be for the benefit of the business rather than the owners. If life insurance is the funding mechanism, the number of policies required can be drastically reduced compared to a standard cross-purchase agreement. The business would own one policy for each owner, with the face amount reflecting that owner's proportionate share of the business. In the earlier example, only four policies would be required, instead of twelve.

Wait and See Agreement

Nothing about a business remains constant for long. Therefore, a hybrid of the preceding two buy-sell options may be appropriate. Wait and see buy-sell agreements are flexible, giving the business entity the option of redeeming any ownership interest upon a triggering event. Under these agreements, the owner or his or her estate is obligated to sell, but the business entity is not obligated to buy, the deceased or departing owner's interest.

The arrangement is usually established and funded immediately with appropriate types and amounts of life insurance. The agreement provides the amount that is to be paid to any deceased stockholder but does not identify the purchaser. The corporation has the first option to purchase all or a part of the decedent's stock and, to the extent the corporation chooses not to exercise its option, the surviving shareholders are given an option to purchase. If any stock remains after the corporation and shareholders have had the opportunity to exercise their options, the corporation is required to purchase the remaining shares.

This form of agreement is funded in the same way as a cross-purchase agreement and has the same general tax implications. The proceeds from the funding vehicle are paid to the remaining business owners, who would then either lend the proceeds to the business or use the money to purchase the shares.

Valuing a Business

A properly structured and implemented buy-sell agreement should include a means of establishing the value of the business which is acceptable to both the owners and the IRS. There are six generally accepted ways to value a business: the "goodwill" multiplier; rate of return on assets; last five years' average earnings; use of a capitalization factor; and two versions of the book value method—combination and capitalization of net earnings.

The one most commonly used by taxing authorities is the combination method book value approach. This method establishes a value for the business based on its past and present financial position, general economic conditions, book value and earnings.

The most reliable means of determining book value is to use the services of a certified appraiser, particularly for closely held corporations, sole proprietorships and partnerships. Proper valuation is critical to the estate tax determination process. The buy-sell agreement also should provide for periodic reviews and updates of both the funding vehicle and business valuation. Serious problems may arise if the IRS is not satisfied with the value established for the business or the valuation method used.

Tailoring Agreement to Entity

In the case of a closely held corporation or sole proprietorship, the owner may have no heirs, the heirs may not wish to inherit or run the business or they may be unsuited to management. In these situations, a "one-way" agreement may be appropriate, enabling and obligating a key employee or some other person to buy the business and providing the departing owner or his or her heirs with cash.

Partnerships often implement a cross-purchase agreement. In the absence of a buy-sell agreement, the partnership may have to be liquidated or run in conjunction with the decedent's heirs. Liquidation is generally disfavored because physical assets may be sold for much less than their actual value, and goodwill is often entirely lost. The deceased partner's heirs may not be of age or may not have the necessary knowledge, desire or experience to run the business. The heirs also may sell their interest to someone else without consulting the remaining partners.

When a partner becomes disabled and is no longer able to contribute to the business, a properly structured and funded buy-sell agreement can both enable and obligate the remaining partners to provide payments over a period of time to the disabled partner and obligate the disabled partner to leave the business. The same situation applies when one or more partners retire.

Corporations also may use any of the buy-sell options but generally will implement an entity redemption or wait and see agreement, unless the number of shareholders is small. If there are few shareholders overall, corporations that lack buy-sell agreements encounter the same problems as do partnerships that lack agreements.

Janet C. Arrowood, *The Buy–Sell Agreement: Alternative Forms*, 22 Colorado Lawyer 2381 (1993).

As Ms. Arrowood's article emphasizes, a buy-sell *agreement* is just that—an agreement. Accordingly most of the law relating to buy-sell agreements comes from the common law of contracts.

Under most corporation codes, to the extent that a buy-sell agreement restricts the right of a shareholder to sell her shares to third parties, the restriction is effective only if either (i) the buyer knows of the restriction or (ii) the restriction is "noted conspicuously" on the stock certificate or contained in the information required for shares without certificates. *See* MBCA § 6.27(b).

And, as the next two cases illustrate, there is a body of law, under both Rule 10b–5 and the common law, on the disclosure obligations of a corporation that is repurchasing its shares under a buy-sell agreement.

JORDAN v. DUFF & PHELPS, INC.

United States Court of Appeals, Seventh Circuit, 1987
815 F.2d 429

EASTERBROOK, CIRCUIT JUDGE. [This case involves a buy-sell agreement and Rule 10b–5. The plaintiff, Jordan, was an employee of the defendant, Duff & Phelps, Inc., a closely held corporation. He was offered the opportunity to buy stock in the defendant pursuant to a buy-sell agreement which required him to sell the stock back to the corporation at book value when his employment ended. Jordan quit and sold his stock back pursuant to the terms of the buy/sell agreement. He then learned that Duff & Phelps, Inc. was negotiating a merger with another company and that the price for his shares would have been much higher if he had delayed his decision to end his Duff & Phelps, Inc. employment. Jordan sued Duff & Phelps, Inc. under Rule 10b–5. The trial court granted summary judgment for the defendant. A divided Seventh Circuit reversed and remanded.]

Duff and Phelps, Inc. evaluates the risk and worth of firms and their securities. It sells credit ratings, investment research, and financial consulting services to both the firms under scrutiny and potential investors in them. Jordan started work at Duff & Phelps in May 1977 and was viewed as a successful securities analyst. In 1981 the firm offered Jordan the opportunity to buy some stock. By November 1983 Jordan had purchased 188 of the 20,100 shares outstanding. He was making installment payments on another 62 shares. Forty people other than Jordan held stock in Duff & Phelps.

Jordan purchased his stock at its "book value" (the accounting net worth of Duff & Phelps, divided by the number of shares outstanding). Before selling him any stock, Duff & Phelps required Jordan to sign a "Stock Restriction and Purchase Agreement" (the Agreement). This provided in part:

> Upon the termination of any employment with the Corporation … for any reason, including resignation, discharge, death, disability or retirement, the individual whose employment is terminated or his estate shall sell to the Corporation, and the Corporation shall buy, all Shares of the Corporation then owned by such individual or his estate. The price to be paid for such Shares shall be equal to the adjusted book value (as hereinafter defined) of the Shares on the December 31 which coincides with, or immediately precedes, the date of termination of such individual's employment.

Duff & Phelps enforced this restriction with but a single exception. During 1983 the board of directors of Duff & Phelps adopted a resolution–of which Jordan did not learn until 1984—allowing employees fired by the firm to keep their stock for five years. The resolution followed the discharge of Carol Franchik, with whom Claire Hansen, the (married) chairman of the board, had been having an affair. When Franchik threatened suit, the board allowed her to keep her stock.

While Jordan was accumulating stock, Hansen, the chairman of the board, was exploring the possibility of selling the firm. Between May and August 1983 Hansen and Francis Jeffries, another officer of Duff & Phelps, negotiated with Security Pacific Corp., a bank holding company. The negotiators reached agreement on a merger, in which Duff & Phelps would be valued at $50 million, but a higher official within Security Pacific vetoed the deal on August 11, 1983. As of that date, Duff & Phelps had no irons in the fire.

Jordan, however, was conducting a search of his own—for a new job. Jordan's family lived near Chicago, the headquarters of Duff & Phelps, and Jordan's wife did not get along with Jordan's mother. The strain between the two occasionally left his wife in tears. He asked Duff & Phelps about the possibility of a transfer to the firm's only branch office, in Cleveland, but the firm did not need Jordan's services there. Concluding that it was time to choose between his job and his wife, Jordan chose his wife and started looking for employment far away from Chicago. His search took him to Houston, where Underwood Neuhaus & Co., a broker-dealer in securities, offered him a job at a salary ($110,000 per year) substantially greater than his compensation ($67,000) at Duff & Phelps. Jordan took the offer on the spot during an interview in Houston, but Underwood would have allowed Jordan to withdraw this oral acceptance.

On November 16, 1983, Jordan told Hansen that he was going to resign and accept employment with Underwood. Jordan did not ask Hansen about potential mergers; Hansen did not volunteer anything. Jordan delivered a letter of resignation, which Duff & Phelps accepted the same day. By mutual agreement, Jordan worked the rest of the year for Duff & Phelps even though his loyalties had shifted. He did this so that he could receive the book value of the stock as of December 31, 1983–for under the Agreement a departure in November would have meant valuation as of December 31, 1982. Jordan delivered his certificates on December 30, 1983, and the firm mailed him a check for $23,225, the book value (at $123.54 per share) of the 188 shares of stock. Jordan surrendered, as worthless under the circumstances, the right to buy the remaining 62 shares.

Before Jordan cashed the check, however, he was startled by the announcement on January 10, 1984, of a merger between Duff & Phelps and a subsidiary of Security Pacific. Under the terms of the merger Duff & Phelps would be valued at $50 million. If Jordan had been an employee on January 10, had quickly paid for the other 62 shares, and the merger had closed that day, he would have received $452,000 in cash and the opportunity to obtain as much as $194,000 more in "earn out" (a percentage of Duff & Phelps's profits to be paid to the former investors—an arrangement that keeps the employees' interest in the firm keen and reduces the buyer's risk if profits fall short). Jordan refused to cash the check and demanded his stock back; Duff & Phelps told him to get lost. He filed this suit in March 1984, asking for damages measured by the value his stock would have had under the terms of the acquisition.

The public announcement on January 10 explained that the boards of the two firms had reached an agreement in principle on January 6. The definitive agreement was signed on March 23. Because Security Pacific is a bank holding company, the acquisition required the approval of the Board of Governors of the Federal Reserve. The Fed granted approval, but with a condition so onerous that the firms abandoned the transaction. Duff & Phelps quickly asked the district court to dismiss Jordan's suit, on the ground that he could not establish damages. Jordan responded by amending his complaint, with Judge Hart's permission, to ask for rescission rather than damages.

Throughout 1985 Duff & Phelps continued looking for a partner; finding none, it decided to dance with itself. The firm's management formed an "Employee Stock Ownership Trust," which was able to borrow $40 million against the security of the firm's assets and business. The Trust acquired Duff & Phelps through a new firm, Duff Research, Inc. This transaction occurred in December 1985. The employees at the time, together with Carol Franchik, received cash, notes, and beneficial interests in the Trust. Jordan asserts that the package was worth almost $2,000 per share, or $497,000 if he had held 250 shares in December 1985.

Defendants' second motion for summary judgment maintained that information about negotiations looking toward a merger is immaterial as a matter of law. The information Jordan says should have been disclosed before he departed includes: (1) the negotiations through August 11, 1983, with Security Pacific; (2) the decision by the board of Duff & Phelps on November 14, 1983, to seek bids for the firm; (3) miscellaneous conversations between Hansen and employees of Security Pacific during the fall of 1983, which Jordan says may have been renewed overtures; (4) the serious negotiations during December 1983 between Duff & Phelps and Security Pacific, after the manager who nixed the deal on August 11 changed his mind; (5) the board's decision to allow Franchik to keep her stock; and (6) the formal settlement agreement signed by Franchik on December 21, 1983. Duff & Phelps, on the other hand, believes that Jordan quit on November 16, 1983, that nothing after that date matters, and that nothing before that date needed to be revealed. * * *

A jury could find that the information withheld on November 16 is "material." A jury also could find that December 30, rather than November 16, is the date of the "sale" of the stock. If December 30 is the date of sale, the information withheld then was "material" under *Michaels* and *TSC Industries* as a matter of law. By then the negotiating teams for Duff & Phelps and Security Pacific had negotiated the price and structure of the deal. (We need not decide whether, had Duff & Phelps been a public firm, it could have withheld notice to the market at large until the boards approved this agreement in January.) So there are two linked materiality questions for the jury: whether the information withheld on November 16 was material, and whether the sale took place on November 16 or December 30.

Duff & Phelps insists that nothing after November 16 matters. A person who sells stock through a broker has several business days to deliver the certificates; the sale is nonetheless final—with price and disclosure obligations fixed forever—on the date of the deal rather than the date of delivery. Duff & Phelps treats the letter of resignation on November 16 as an irrevocable sale with deferred delivery. Yet if the "sale" occurred on November 16, then under the Agreement the stock would have been valued as of December 31, 1982. That Duff & Phelps valued the stock as of December 31, 1983, may persuade a jury that it treated the "sale" as made on that date. Moreover, Jordan insists that other employees were allowed to withdraw their resignations, and that he could have done so as late as December 31—if, say, his wife and his mother had reconciled. A cabinet officer who resigns (and has the resignation accepted by the President) is out of office and cannot stick around without being nominated and confirmed again; but private parties may decide to give less finality to resignations. The terms on which resignations may be withdrawn may be implicit parts of the relations between Duff & Phelps and its employees, and Jordan is entitled to an opportunity to demonstrate that he could have remained at the firm. If he can prove this, then December 30 rather than November 16 is the date on which the materiality of the firm's omissions must be assessed.

All of this supposes that Duff & Phelps had a duty to disclose anything to Jordan. Most people are free to buy and sell stock on the basis of valuable private knowledge without informing their trading partners. Strangers transact in markets all the time using private information that might be called "material" and, unless one has a duty to disclose, both may keep their counsel. The ability to make profits from the possession of information is the principal spur to create the information, which the parties and the market as a whole may find valuable. The absence of a duty to disclose may not justify a lie about a material fact, but Duff & Phelps did not lie to Jordan. It simply remained silent when Jordan quit and tendered the stock, and it offered the payment required by the Agreement. Duff & Phelps maintains that it was entitled to be silent even though it could not have lied in response to the questions Jordan should (in retrospect) have asked but did not.

This argument is unavailing on the facts as we know them. The "duty" in question is the fiduciary duty of corporate law. Close corporations buying their own stock, like knowledgeable insiders of closely held firms buying from outsiders, have a fiduciary duty to disclose material facts. *Kohler* and *Michaels* rest on this duty, as do some of the earliest cases of trading by insiders on material information. The "special facts" doctrine developed by several courts at the turn of the century is based on the principle that insiders in closely held firms may not buy stock from outsiders in person-to-person transactions without informing them of new events that substantially affect the value of the stock.

Because the fiduciary duty is a standby or off-the-rack guess about what parties would agree to if they dickered about the subject explicitly, parties may contract with greater specificity for other arrangements. It is a violation of duty to steal from the corporate treasury; it is not a violation to write oneself a check that the board has approved as a bonus. We may assume that duties concerning the timing of disclosure by an otherwise-silent firm also may be the subject of contract. Section 29(a) of the Securities Exchange Act of 1934, forbids waivers of the provisions of the Act, and here the critical provision is § 10(b), and the SEC's Rule 10b–5. But a provision must be applicable to be "waived," and the existence of a requirement to speak is a condition of the application of § 10(b) to a person's silence during a securities trade. The obligation to break silence is itself based on state law, and so may be redefined to the extent state law permits. But we need not decide how far contracts can redefine obligations to disclose. Jordan was an employee at will; he signed no contract. * * * So the possibility that a firm could negotiate around the fiduciary duty does not assist Duff & Phelps; it did not obtain such an agreement, express or implied.

* * * Jordan * * * exercised choice about the date on which the formula would be triggered. He could have remained at Duff & Phelps; his decision to depart was affected by his wife's distress, his salary, his working conditions, the enjoyment he received from the job, and the value of his stock. The departure of such an employee is an investment decision as much as it is an employment decision. It is not fanciful to suppose that Mrs. Jordan would have found her mother-in-law a whole lot more tolerable if she had known that Jordan's stock might shortly be worth 20 times book value.

The securities acts apply to investment decisions, even those made indirectly or bound up with other decisions, such as employment or entrepreneurship. * * *

There must be an "investment" decision, to be sure, but Jordan unavoidably made one. That he took the value of stock into account is evident from the timing of his departure. A few thousand dollars' increase in book value led the Jordans to stay in Chicago an extra six weeks. How long would they have stayed for the prospect of another $620,000? * * *

The timing of the sale and the materiality of the information Duff & Phelps withheld on November 16 are for the jury to determine. Jordan may have trouble establishing that Duff & Phelps acted with intent to defraud, a necessary element of a case under Rule 10b–5. Duff & Phelps did not seek summary judgment on the ground that it would be impossible to establish scienter, and arguments about the expectations and intent of the parties are for the jury. * * *

Reversed and remanded.

QUESTIONS

1.   Did Duff & Phelps make any misrepresentations to Jordan? If not, what did the defendant do wrong? Did Duff & Phelps engage in illegal insider trading?

2.   What should Duff & Phelps have done differently?

2.1   Suppose the buy-sell agreement provided "As part of the consideration for Corporation's agreeing to buy the individual's shares on termination of employment, the individual agrees that the transaction will not be a 'purchase or sale of securities' for purposes of the federal securities laws, including, without limitation, Rule 10b–5." Would this make a difference?

2.2   What if the buy-sell agreement had provided that "Termination of employment and the purchase of Shares pursuant to this agreement does not create a legal obligation to provide any information about Corporation's business activities or business plans"?

———————

The next case, *Berreman v. West Publishing Company*, also involves a buy-sell agreement and nondisclosure by the buying corporation. The Minnesota Court of Appeals, however, does not look to Rule 10b–5. Instead, the court cites *Rodd Electrotype*, a "leading case on fiduciary duty in a close corporation." In *Berreman*, West was more than willing to redeem its shares from shareholder Berreman at $2,088.90 a share. West was unwilling to tell Berreman that, in the language of the South, it was "fixing to" sell the company. Berreman sued the corporation and three of its directors (who were also shareholders), alleging, inter alia, breach of fiduciary duty. The following is a portion of the Minnesota Court of Appeals' decision affirming summary judgment for the defendants.

BERREMAN v. WEST PUBLISHING COMPANY

Minnesota Court of Appeals, 2000
615 N.W.2d 362

LANSING, JUDGE. Thomas Berreman appeals from summary judgment dismissing his action against West Publishing Company and three West directors (collectively "West"). Berreman's claims were based on his assertion that West had a duty to disclose to him, before Berreman retired from West and sold his stock back to the company in June 1995, that three of West's directors had begun to consider the sale of West and had engaged an investment-banking firm to explore West's options. On cross-motions for summary judgment, the district court granted summary judgment to West on all of Berreman's claims. We affirm.

FACTS

The facts are undisputed. In April 1995, Thomas Berreman, a 25–year employee of West Publishing Company, told West's Chief Executive Officer, Dwight Opperman, that he intended to retire effective June 1, 1995. Berreman had worked for West's lawschool division since 1970. West promoted him to assistant manager of the division in 1977 and to division head in 1992.

Beginning in 1974, Berreman bought West stock through a stock-option program for high-level managers and sales representatives that granted options at Dwight Opperman's discretion. Berreman bought his stock subject to a written agreement for purchase, sale, and resale, which provided that if he decided to sell his stock or in the event of his death, incompetency, or termination of employment, West could exercise an option to repurchase the stock at book value. * * *

Berreman's last day at West was May 31, 1995. On June 1, 1995, with Berreman's authorization, West redeemed Berreman's stock at the current book value of $2,088.90 per share and paid off a bank loan secured by the stock. On June 15, 1995, Chief Financial Officer Grant Nelson gave Berreman a check for approximately $2.8 million.

As of May 31, 1995, West had about 200 employee shareholders, 25 non-employee shareholders, and 328,908 shares outstanding. Dwight Opperman, Nelson, and board president Vance Opperman, in addition to being directors, were each shareholders. Together they held 23 percent of West's outstanding shares. Until its sale to Thomson Corporation in 1996, West was a privately held corporation. And until West announced the possibility of a sale in August 1995, West directors had publicly expressed their commitment to remaining privately held.

During 1994 and 1995, West was facing an increasingly competitive legal publications market. Two of West's competitors, Mead Data, owner of Lexis–Nexis, and Prentice Hall Law & Business, merged into international publishing companies in 1994. That same year West received unsolicited materials on possible mergers from investment-banking firms Goldman–Sachs and A.G. Edwards, which included information about Thomson Corporation. In response to the increasingly competitive conditions, West's board increased its acquisition fund from $70 million to $300 million in October 1994.

During the second week of May 1995, while on vacation, Nelson reflected on the future of West in light of the changing legal-publications market. Nelson was concerned about West's future given increasing competition, changing technology, and pending antitrust investigations. Nelson concluded that rather than making an acquisition, West should consider being acquired or entering into a joint venture.

On May 15, 1995, Nelson met with Dwight Opperman, who listened to Nelson's concerns and told him, "I think you may be right." Nelson and Dwight Opperman met with Vance Opperman the next day, and the three decided to engage A.G. Edwards to explore West's options. Nelson called Ray Kalinowski at A.G. Edwards the same day and told him that West wanted advice on the company's future financial options, including a possible sale of the company. On May 17, 1995, A.G. Edwards representatives met with the West directors. The directors authorized A.G. Edwards to retain another investment-banking firm if necessary.

The West board met on May 23, 1995. During that meeting, the board again addressed its potential acquisitions and authorized A.G. Edwards to explore financing options beyond West's local bank. The board did not discuss the possibility of selling the company. This meeting was the last board meeting before Berreman's June 1 retirement.

On August 28, 1995, A.G. Edwards made a presentation to the West board outlining four options: recapitalization, public offering, status quo, and sale. The board engaged A.G. Edwards and Goldman–Sachs to advise and assist West in evaluating its options and authorized West management to take necessary steps, including contacting potential buyers and developing acquisition proposals.

On August 29, 1995, West announced to its employees and to the public that it had engaged investment bankers and was considering alternative financial options including public offering, entering into a joint venture, joining a strategic partner, recapitalization, sale, or any other available option. In September 1995, West sent invitations for bids to 45 potential purchasers. The bids were due by February 1996, and West eventually received four bids, including one from Thomson Corporation. West accepted Thomson Corporation's bid, and the companies entered into a merger agreement on February 25, 1996. After a shareholder vote and review by the Department of Justice, West concluded the sale to Thomson in June 1996. Thomson paid $10,445 per share to acquire West, about five times the amount Berreman received when he sold his stock back to the company in June 1995. Berreman's action against West followed. * * *

Common Law Fiduciary Duty

At common law, the shareholders in a close corporation owe one another a fiduciary duty. Courts impose the fiduciary duty because they find that close corporations are really more like "partnership[s] in corporate guise." *Donahue v. Rodd Electrotype Co.*, 367 Mass. 578, 328 N.E.2d 505, 512 (1975) ("Commentators and courts have noted that the close corporation is often little more than an 'incorporated' or 'chartered' partnership.").

Attributes of Close Corporation

Courts generally identify common law close corporations by three characteristics: (1) a small number of shareholders; (2) no ready market for corporate stock; and (3) active shareholder participation in the business. In addition, dividends are rarely distributed in a close corporation. Rather, "shareholders derive their income mainly from salaries and perquisites." Id.

In May 1995, West exhibited characteristics of a close corporation. First, West was not publicly traded; thus, there was no ready public market for its stock. This court has recognized the lack of a public market as the dominant characteristic of a common law close corporation. Additionally, West offered its stock only to high-level managers and sales people at Dwight Opperman's discretion. The lack of a public market for West stock, combined with the managerial role West's shareholders occupied, supports the characterization of West as a common-law close corporation.

Second, the rationale for distinguishing close corporations from other corporations supports the characterization of West as a close corporation. Courts have recognized that because majority shareholders of a close corporation can deny minority shareholders income from their investment, minority shareholders are in a vulnerable position. That West's corporate structure would have allowed this type of "freeze out" supports its characterization as a close corporation.

On the other hand, West's 200 shareholders far exceed the number of shareholders in any corporation that Minnesota courts have recognized as a close corporation. To categorize West as a close corporation under Minnesota common law would substantially extend the definition's numerical boundaries. Berreman argues that because 94% of the stock was held by employees and subject to repurchase agreements, West's decision-making was concentrated in only a few individuals, and West's numerical structure should be analyzed from that viewpoint. These arguments have persuasive force and a fact-finder could draw inferences that would credit Berreman's arguments. Because we are reviewing a summary judgment against Berreman's claims, he is entitled to review in a light most favorable to the evidence supporting his claims, and thus we assume for purposes of our analysis that West may be categorized as a close corporation. * * *

Scope of Common Law Fiduciary Duty

We turn next to the scope of the common law fiduciary duty. While it is well established that shareholders in a close corporation owe a fiduciary duty to one another, the scope of the duty has never been well defined. In *Donahue v. Rodd Electrotype Co.*—often cited as a leading case on fiduciary duty in the close corporation context—the Massachusetts Supreme Court held that "stockholders in a close corporation owe[d] one another substantially the same fiduciary duty in the operation of the enterprise that partners owe one another." 328 N.E.2d at 515 (footnote omitted). The court described the duty as one of "utmost good faith and loyalty" and went on to hold that a corporation that buys shares from one shareholder must offer to buy shares from all other shareholders at the same rate. This has since been called the equal-opportunity rule. *Donahue* is probably the broadest statement of the fiduciary duty in the close corporation context. Even the Massachusetts Supreme Court later qualified its holding by recognizing that there may be legitimate business reasons for treating shareholders differently. *Wilkes v. Springside Nursing Home, Inc.*, 370 Mass. 842, 353 N.E.2d 657, 663 (1976) (establishing that when corporation demonstrates legitimate business interest, plaintiff, to succeed on fiduciary claim, must show less harmful alternative to achieve that interest). * * *

The Minnesota cases have not addressed whether the fiduciary duty in [the] close corporation context includes a duty to disclose. The [state] supreme court has, however, ruled that "[o]ne who stands in a confidential or fiduciary relation to the other party to a transaction must disclose material facts." And this court has applied the duty to disclose material facts in the analogous partnership context.

Relying on the principles expressed in the Minnesota cases addressing disclosure, we conclude that the fiduciary duties of shareholders in a close corporation include the duty to disclose material information about the corporation. Our holding is consistent with federal cases recognizing the duty to disclose material facts as within the fiduciary duties of shareholders in a close corporation. Jordan v. Duff & Phelps, Inc., 815 F.2d 429, 435 (7th Cir.1987) (stating that "[c]lose corporations buying their own stock, like knowledgeable insiders of closely held firms buying from outsiders, have a fiduciary duty to disclose material facts").

Materiality of Undisclosed Facts

The recognition that shareholders in a close corporation have a duty to disclose material facts leads us to the second part of the question: What facts are material and thus fall within the scope of that duty? In the context of the federal securities laws, the U.S. Supreme Court has held that an omitted fact is material "if there is a substantial likelihood that a reasonable shareholder would consider it important in deciding how to vote." *Basic Inc. v. Levinson*, 485 U.S. 224, 231, 108 S.Ct. 978, 983 (1988) (citation omitted). * * *

In *Basic v. Levinson*, the Supreme Court adopted the probability-magnitude approach for determining whether preliminary merger discussions are material. Under that test, materiality "will depend at any time upon a balancing of both the indicated probability that the event will occur and the anticipated magnitude of the event in light of the totality of the company activity." Probability should be assessed by evaluating the "indicia of interest in the transaction at the highest corporate levels." Magnitude should be assessed by considering "such facts as the size of the two corporate entities and of the potential premiums over market value." * * *

Application of Probability–Magnitude Test to Undisclosed Facts

Applying the probability-magnitude test to this case, we hold that the facts known to West at the time Berreman resigned were immaterial as a matter of law. By the end of May 1995, Nelson, Dwight Opperman, and Vance Opperman had decided to explore options for the future of West including a possible sale, and they had hired an investment-banking firm to investigate West's options. West, however, had made no decision to solicit bids for the sale of West, much less initiated discussions with any potential buyers. The federal courts have been reluctant to find materiality in the absence of evidence that the corporation engaged in discussions with potential buyers. Even in the close-corporation context, the Seventh Circuit has gone no further than to say that a corporation's decision to seek a buyer may be material. We agree that tentative, speculative discussions about merger are not material.

Berreman urges that the early discussions among the West directors about the possibility of merger should be found material because the magnitude of any potential merger was substantial. West had always been a privately held corporation, and until August 1995, its directors were vocally committed to being privately held. That any merger would have been such a sharp departure from West's long history of being privately held supports the magnitude of the merger discussions. But the magnitude of the discussions does not overcome the low probability that the merger would ever occur. The initial discussions were among West's top directors, which supports probability. But even these three directors had decided only to explore West's financial options. Thus, the discussions were not material. * * *

As a matter of law, West did not breach a fiduciary duty * * * to Berreman. * * * Accordingly, we affirm summary judgment for West.

QUESTIONS

1. Why did the court discuss the fiduciary duty of shareholders instead of the fiduciary duty of directors? Why did it not discuss Rule 10b–5? Can a plaintiff in state court rely on Rule 10b–5?

2. Was West Publishing Company a close corporation?

3. What could West's CEO have told Berreman in June of 1995? Why didn't West's CEO tell Berreman that "three of West's directors had begun to consider the sale of West and had engaged an investment banking firm to explore West's options"?

4. Do you think Berreman would have done better had he sued in federal court under Rule 10b–5?

5. Now, having read *Jordan v. Duff & Phelps* and *Berreman*, reconsider (yet again) Questions 1 through 3 on page 336.

Chapter Eight

What Are the Various "Endgames" for the Corporation, Its Shareholders, Its Managers?

■ ■ ■

A. INTRODUCTION ABOUT FUNDAMENTAL CORPORATE CHANGES

Some changes in the life of the corporation are so fundamental that the law does not permit the board of directors to pursue them alone. These differ from ordinary management decisions, which, as we have seen, are made by the board of directors with no input from stockholders. But when an act will fundamentally alter the corporation, corporate law generally requires not only director approval, but also approval by the shareholders. So shareholders have an important, direct voice in whether a fundamental change will occur.

Which corporate changes are fundamental? As we mentioned in Chapter 5, in most states, they include (1) amendment of the articles of incorporation, (2) dissolution, (3) merger, and (4) sale of substantially all of the corporation's assets. The procedure for each of these is generally the same, and consists of five steps.

First, the board of directors must approve the fundamental change. This is done the same way the board takes any act, as we saw in Chapter 5.

Second, the board must notify the shareholders of its recommendation that the fundamental change be approved.

Third, a special meeting of the shareholders must be held, at which they vote on the change. If it is approved, the corporation will go through with the change. If the shareholders reject the proposal, however, the corporation will not effect the fundamental change.

Fourth, if the change is approved, shareholders who opposed the proposed change might have a right to force the corporation to buy them out. We will explore this "dissenting shareholder's right of appraisal" in Part C of this chapter.

Fifth, the corporation is usually required to inform the state of the fundamental change by filing a document with the secretary of state.

Shareholder voting in this area differs from that in others. To see this, let's review shareholder voting, which we studied in Chapter 5. For a shareholders' meeting, we always need a quorum. Unless the articles or bylaws can and do provide otherwise, a quorum will be a majority of the shares entitled to vote. So Bubba's Burritos, Inc. has 6,000 outstanding voting shares, at least 3,001 would have to be represented at the shareholders' meeting. Without a quorum, the shareholders cannot act. *See, e.g.,* MBCA § 7.25(a); Delaware § 216(i).

Assume we have a quorum. What vote is required now? It depends upon what the shareholders are considering. If they are electing directors, as we discussed in Chapter 5, Part B, all that is required is for a candidate to receive a "plurality" of the votes cast for that particular seat on the board. That is, the candidate who gets more votes than anyone else is elected, even if she does not garner a majority of the votes cast.* *See, e.g.,* MBCA § 7.28(a). (Remember too that in electing directors we might use cumulative voting, which we saw in Chapter 5, Part B(3).)

In addition to electing directors, the only other vote generally required by the law is the approval of fundamental changes. Shareholders are not entitled to vote on other, nonfundamental matters *unless* the board asks them to do so. Boards do this rarely. When it does happen, the modern view is that, if a quorum exists, a measure must receive a majority of the votes *cast*.† *See* MBCA § 7.25(c). The older view—still followed in some states—is that a measure passes only if it garners a majority of the shares *present* at the meeting. *See* Delaware § 217(ii). In practice, this means the newer view ignores abstentions, while the old view counts them as votes against the proposal.

Let's say the shareholders are voting on some nonfundamental substantive measure. There are 6,000 shares entitled to vote. Say 3,600 of them are represented at the meeting (so we have a quorum). Say only 2,000 of the 3,600 of the shares present actually vote on that measure. Under the modern view, the measure would pass if at least 1,001 shares voted for it. Why? Because all we need is a majority of the shares that actually voted (2,000). Under the older view, however, at least 1,801 shares would have to vote in favor for it to pass. Why? Because under that view, we need a majority of the shares *present* at the meeting. There were 3,600 present.

Now let's focus on the big issue: requirements for shareholder voting on fundamental changes. States generally fall into one of three categories on this.

---

* *See* MBCA § 7.28(a) (unless the articles provide otherwise, "directors are elected by a plurality of the votes cast by the shares entitled to vote . . . .").

† *See* MBCA § 7.25(c) (unless the articles provide otherwise, action "is approved if the votes cast within the voting group favoring the action exceed the votes cast opposing the action . . . .").

First, in many states, voting requirements for fundamental issues are the same as for the nonfundamental issues. *See* MBCA §§ 7.25(c), 10.03(e). In other words, a majority of those actually voting or a majority of those present can approve the fundamental change.

Second, in other states, including Delaware, the fundamental change must be approved by a majority of the shares *entitled to vote.** *See* Delaware §§ 242(b)(1) (amending certificate); 251(c) (merger). Based upon the numbers immediately above, we would need at least 3,001 shares to vote in favor of the fundamental change. Why? Because there are 6,000 shares *entitled to vote* and we need a majority of that number. In effect, both an abstention and a no-show are treated as votes of no.

The third approach is even tougher. It is the traditional view, still followed in a few states, including Texas and Massachusetts. It requires approval by *two-thirds of the shares entitled to vote. See, e.g.,* Texas Business Organization Act § 21.455 (2006). So if there were 6,000 shares entitled to vote, at least 4,000 would have to vote yes to approve the fundamental change. So in our hypo above, where 3,600 shares were represented at the meeting, the shareholders simply could not approve the fundamental change under this view—even if all 3,600 shares at the meeting voted yes.

Most of this chapter is devoted to fundamental changes that constitute an endgame for the corporation. That is, the change actually ends the corporation's existence or prepares the way to end that existence. In contrast, amendment of the corporation's articles of incorporation does not kill the corporation. It is a fundamental corporate change, however, because it alters the charter that created the entity. There may be any number of reasons the corporation may wish to amend its articles. For instance, because a corporation has issued all of the stock it was authorized to sell in the original articles, it may wish to amend its charter to permit the issuance of more stock. Like all fundamental corporate changes, the amendment of the articles must be approved by the board of directors and by the shareholders (in accordance with the special voting rules we just saw).

Now we turn to those fundamental changes that actually are the end—or at least the beginning of the end—of the corporation.

B. DISSOLUTION

One obvious endgame for a corporation is dissolution.

The *Giannotti* case, which we studied in Chapter 7, Part A, § 2, showed us that statutes may allow a court to order dissolution of a corporation because of an intracorporate dispute. Most corporation statutes provide for judicial dissolution in a proceeding brought by a share-

---

* *See, e.g.,* Delaware § 242(b)(1) (amending articles requires "majority of the outstanding stock entitled to vote. . . ."); § 251(c) (same for approving a merger).

holder who establishes that "those in control of the corporation have acted . . . in a manner that is illegal, oppressive, or fraudulent." *See, e.g.,* MBCA § 14.30(2).

Corporation statutes also generally provide for voluntary dissolution, which is effected as we discussed in Part A above. Specifically, the board of directors approves the dissolution, and then shareholders vote on the proposal. As we noted, some states require approval merely by a majority of the votes cast. Other states require approval by a majority of the shares entitled to vote. Some still require two-thirds of the shares entitled to vote. Compare MBCA § 14.02(e) (majority of votes cast) with Delaware § 275(b)(majority of shares entitled to vote) with Texas Business Organization Act § 21.502 (2006) (two-thirds of shares entitled to vote).

In both judicial dissolution and voluntary dissolution, it is important that

- the corporation continues after dissolution for the limited purpose of "winding up," *Cf.* MBCA § 14.05;
- winding up activities include collecting and liquidating the assets of the corporation and using the proceeds from the liquidation of the corporation's assets to pay creditors, *Id*;
- these creditors must be paid in full before the shareholders get anything from their corporation's dissolution;
- creditors who are not paid during dissolution may seek to recover later from shareholders, to the extent that the shareholders have received payments from the corporation when it was dissolved. MBCA § 14.07(d);
- notice of the dissolution is to be filed in the same public records that contain the articles of incorporation, *cf.* MBCA §§ 14.03, 14.33;
- additionally, written notice "shall" be provided to "known claimants" and notice by publication "may" be used to reach unknown claimants, *cf.* MBCA §§ 14.06, 14.07.

QUESTIONS

1. For the last 11 weeks, Bubba's Burritos, Inc.'s operating costs have exceeded its gross receipts. The corporation owes more than $100,000. A sale of the corporation's assets would yield less than $90,000. The corporation's three shareholders and directors, Agee, Propp and Capel, have agreed to close the business permanently at the end of this week. They want to know how much it will cost them to dissolve the corporation and how they benefit by spending this money to dissolve. How do you answer their questions?

2. Propp and Capel want to operate Bubba's Burritos without Agee. They come to you with the question of whether they could (i) vote for the dissolution of Bubba's Burritos and then (ii) form a two-person partnership that would buy the assets of Bubba's Burritos during the winding up of Bubba's Burritos, Inc. How do you answer their question?

C. MERGER

Merger is another possible endgame for a corporation as a business structure. In a merger, two or more business entities combine into one business entity—for example, Bubba's Burritos, Inc. merges into McDonald's. In this example, McDonald's would be referred to as the "surviving corporation," and Bubba's Burrtios, Inc. would be referred to as the "disappearing corporation" because it would in fact and in law disappear. MBCA § 11.07(a)(2) is typical of corporate codes in providing that "When a merger becomes effective * * * the separate existence of every corporation * * * that is merged into the survivor ceases."

1. EFFECTS OF A MERGER ON THE CREDITORS AND THE SHAREHOLDERS OF THE DISAPPEARING CORPORATION

Section 11.07 of the MBCA sets out the effects of a merger.* Please apply § 11.07 to the following problems on a merger's impacts.

PROBLEMS: THE EFFECT OF A MERGER

1. Bubba's Burritos, Inc. merges into McDonald's. At the time of the merger, S is a secured creditor of Bubba's. Bubba's owes S $300,000 and S has a first mortgage on Bubba's real estate. U is an unsecured creditor—Bubba's owes U $40,000. Capel is a shareholder of Bubba's, and owns 51% of the outstanding stock. What effect does the merger have on the rights of S, U, and Capel?

2. What if the Bubba's and McDonald's merger is structured as a "triangular merger?" For example, McDonald's might establish a new wholly owned subsidiary, Newco, and transfer McDonald's stock to Newco in exchange for all of Newco's stock. Bubba's and McDonald's could then agree to merge Bubba's into Newco. The shareholders of Bubba's would receive the McDonald's stock that had previously been transferred by McDonald's to Newco. In exchange, Newco would receive all of the Bubba's stock. Because McDonald's owned Newco, McDonalds would indirectly own all of the Bubba's stock. Why is this called a "triangular merger"? What are the possible business and legal reasons to structure a business combination as a triangular merger?

2. SHAREHOLDER PROTECTION

Because of the effect of a merger on shareholders of both the surviving and the disappearing corporations, shareholders of both corporations by case law and by statute have four potential forms of legal protection: (1) sue the directors who approved the merger alleging breach of common

---

* More precisely, § 11.07(a) sets out the effects of a merger that you need to know about for this course. If you do mergers and acquisition ("M & A") work in the "real world," you will also need to know about the tax effects of a merger and the securities-law effects of a merger.

law or statutory duty of care; (2) vote against the merger; (3) assert the dissenting shareholder's right of appraisal; or (4) sue the directors who approved the merger alleging a breach of common law or statutory duty of loyalty.

a. Sue the Directors Who Approved the Merger for Breach of Duty of Care

The MBCA, like other corporation codes, contemplates that the board of directors of each of the merging corporations will agree on a plan of merger. *See* MBCA § 11.01(a). This agreement is (of course) generally referred to as a "merger agreement" or "a plan of merger" and sets out the terms and conditions of the merger, including (i) which corporation survives and (ii) what the shareholders of the disappearing corporation receive. *Cf.* MBCA § 11.01(b). *See generally* James C. Freund, ANATOMY OF A MERGER (1975). And, as we have seen from our consideration of cases such as *Smith v. Van Gorkom* in Chapter 5, shareholders who are dissatisfied with what they receive from a merger sometimes sue the directors who approved the merger, alleging breach of duty of care in approving the merger.

b. Vote Against the Merger

Subject to limited exceptions, a merger requires not only approval by the board of directors of each of the merging companies, but also the approval of the shareholders. Corporation statutes vary as to what level of approval is required and what the exceptions for shareholder approval are. Apply the MBCA provisions, §§ 11.04(a), (e) and (g), and 6.21(f), to the following problem.

PROBLEM: SHAREHOLDER APPROVAL OF A MERGER

Bubba's Burritos, Inc. is merging into McDonald's. Bubba's has 10 shareholders and 10,000 outstanding shares. McDonald's has millions of shareholders and more than a billion outstanding shares. What shareholder approval is required?

c. Assert Dissenting Shareholders' Right of Appraisal

An individual shareholder's vote against a merger will not prevent the merger from happening. While state corporation statutes vary as to what level of approval is required, no state still* requires unanimous approval of a merger by all of the shareholders. Instead of providing a veto to shareholders who oppose the merger, corporations statutes today provide "appraisal rights" to shareholders who dissent from it.† *E.g.*, Delaware § 262.

_____

* Originally, mergers required unanimous shareholder approval.

† Appraisal rights are not limited to mergers. MBCA § 13.02. We will consider appraisal rights again when we consider sale of all or substantially all of the property or a corporation.

The phrase "appraisal rights" is incomplete and maybe even misleading. A shareholder who opposes a merger and complies with the detailed statutory requirements in Delaware § 262 (or MBCA Chapter 13 or whatever the relevant state corporation statute is) has more than the right to have her shares "appraised" or valued. Rather, a shareholder who properly asserts her dissenting shareholder's right of appraisal can compel the corporation to pay her in cash the fair value of her shares as determined by a judicial appraisal process.

To illustrate, S is a 10% shareholder of T Co., which merges into A, Inc. The effect of the merger, of course, is that T Co. and its shares both cease to exist. The merger agreement values T Co. at $3,000,000 and provides that T Co. shareholders will receive consideration that has a value of $3,000,000. This consideration can be A, Inc. stock, or other stock, or other property or cash. *Cf.* MBCA § 11.02. As a 10% shareholder, S would get consideration with a value of $300,000. S instead "complies with the detailed statutory requirements" and properly asserts her dissenting shareholder's right of appraisal. What if the court decides that the fair value of T Co. was $5,000,000, and not $3,000,000? Then S, as a dissenting shareholder who "complies with the detailed statutory requirements," has a right to be paid $500,000 in cash from T Co.

Note the limiting phrase in the preceding paragraphs:

The merger must comply "with the detailed statutory requirements." As Professor Franklin Gevurtz observed, "One problem is that the statutory appraisal rights commonly require shareholders wishing to assert the rights to comply with exacting requirements which can trip up many persons." Franklin Gevurtz, CORPORATION LAW 648. What are the "exacting requirements" in Delaware § 262 (or MBCA Chapter 13) that might trip up your clients?

While there are detailed statutory provisions governing how a shareholder asserts her right to be paid the fair value of her shares by her corporation, there are virtually no statutory provisions governing how a court is to determine that fair value. Rather, both lawyers advising clients and courts deciding cases look to reported decisions that use various standards for determining the fair value of the dissenting shares. We will study two such opinions. In reading the first, please consider the following:

1. Who merged with whom?

2. Which is the surviving corporation?

3. What did the shareholders of the disappearing corporation receive?

HMO–W INC. v. SSM HEALTH CARE SYSTEM

Wisconsin Supreme Court, 2000
611 N.W.2d 250

ANN WALSH BRADLEY, J. HMO–Wisconsin (HMO–W) seeks review of that part of a published court of appeals decision that reversed a circuit court judgment and order applying a minority discount in this dissenters' rights action. HMO–W contends that the court of appeals erred when it precluded the application of minority discounts in determining the fair value of dissenters' shares. We agree with the court of appeals and conclude that minority discounts may not be applied to determine the fair value of dissenters' shares in an appraisal proceeding. * * *

The appraisal action at the center of this review represents the culmination of a relationship between HMO–W and SSM that spanned more than a decade. In 1983, SSM and a number of other health care providers formed HMO–W as a provider-owned health care system. All shareholders assumed minority status in this closely held corporation. SSM and the Neillsville Clinic, another shareholder, together owned approximately twenty percent of HMO–W's shares.

By the early 1990's, competitive pressures from within the health care business led HMO–W to explore the possibility of merging with another health care system. SSM recommended DeanCare Health Plan (Dean-Care), a company with which SSM had close connections, as a potential merger partner. HMO–W later eliminated DeanCare from consideration after having met with company representatives numerous times to discuss a partnership deal. HMO–W instead proposed a joint venture with United Wisconsin Services (United).

Before shareholder approval of the merger, HMO–W retained Valuation Research Corporation (VR) to value HMO–W's net assets both prior to and upon the merger. VR prepared a final valuation report that HMO–W accepted and which estimated the company's net value to fall within the range of $16.5 to $18 million.

Subsequently, HMO–W's board of directors voted to approve the proposed merger with United and to submit the merger to a shareholder vote. In addition to the VR report, the proxy materials sent to the shareholders informed them of their statutory right to dissent to the merger. At the shareholder meeting, both SSM and the Neillsville Clinic voted against the proposed merger. The merger was nevertheless approved.

Both SSM and the Neillsville Clinic then perfected a demand for the payment of their dissenting shares. Abandoning the VR report, HMO–W hired a new appraiser to value its assets. The appraiser arrived at a valuation of approximately $7.4 million, and based upon this valuation, HMO–W sent SSM a check for almost $1.5 million as the value of SSM's shares. Disputing HMO–W's valuation of the shares, SSM informed the company that SSM's fair value calculation of its shares yielded a figure of approximately $4.7 million. * * *

HMO–W instituted a special proceeding to determine the fair value of the dissenting shares. In response, SSM asserted that HMO–W was estopped from claiming a company value that was lower than the $16.5 to $18 million value it had represented to the shareholders prior to the merger vote.

At trial, several experts testified as to the net value of HMO–W. HMO–W's expert testified that the company's value immediately prior to the merger was $10,544,000. SSM's expert submitted the value as $19,250,000. The circuit court accepted the valuation offered by HMO–W's expert, noting various flaws in the earlier VR report that called into question the accuracy of that report.

Upon accepting HMO–W's valuation and observing the dissenters' minority status, the circuit court applied a minority discount of 30% to the value of the dissenting shares but refrained from applying a lack of marketability discount.* [3] The circuit court concluded that it was required to apply the minority discount as a matter of law. The court then ordered SSM and the Neillsville Clinic to repay with interest the amount by which HMO–W's initial payment exceeded the court's fair value determination.

* * *

The court of appeals affirmed in part and reversed in part, remanding the case for a fair value determination without the application of a minority discount. It held as a matter of law that the Wisconsin statutes governing dissenters' rights do not allow minority discounts to be applied in determining the fair value of a dissenter's shares.

The court reasoned that minority discounts frustrate the purpose of dissenters' rights statutes, which protect the rights of shareholders to voice objection to corporate actions and to receive an equitable value for their minority shares. However, the court of appeals affirmed the circuit court's determination as to HMO–W's net asset value. It concluded that SSM had failed to prove harm in reliance on the VR report that initially valued HMO–W's net assets at $16.5–$18 million.

Two issues are currently presented for review, and both are issues of first impression for this court. Initially we address the issue of whether a minority discount may apply in determining the fair value of a dissenter's shares. This inquiry involves statutory interpretation and presents a question of law. Second, we address whether a court in making its fair value determination may consider evidence of unfair dealing relating to the value of the dissenter's shares. This also presents a question of law.

* * *

Tracing the evolution of dissenters' appraisal rights provides a context for the discussion of the two issues presently before this court. At common law, unanimous shareholder consent was required to achieve fundamental corporate changes. Courts and legislatures questioned the wisdom of allowing one shareholder to frustrate changes deemed desirable

---

* [3] A minority discount addresses the lack of control over a business entity on the theory that non-controlling shares of stock are not worth their proportionate share of the firm's value because they lack voting power to control corporate actions. A lack of marketability discount adjusts for a lack of liquidity in one's interests in a firm, on the theory that there is a limited supply of potential buyers in closely held corporations. The type of discount at issue in this case is the minority discount, and thus we do not address the applicability of a lack of marketability discount under the statute.

and profitable by the majority and thus modified tradition by authorizing majority consent.

Although permitting the majority to approve fundamental changes was viewed as a solution to the potential stalemate attendant to a requirement of corporate unanimity, majority consent nevertheless opened the door to victimization of the minority. In response, legislatures widely adopted statutes to address minority victimization by affording dissenters appraisal rights for their shares.

The appraisal remedy has its roots in equity and serves as a *quid pro quo*: minority shareholders may dissent and receive a fair value for their shares in exchange for relinquishing their veto power. Appraisal thus grants protection to the minority from forced participation in corporate actions approved by the majority.

Wisconsin law currently allows a minority shareholder to dissent from a fundamental corporate action, such as a merger, and to receive the fair value of those minority shares. Wisconsin Stat. § 180.1302(1) states that except in certain statutorily defined circumstances, "a shareholder or beneficial shareholder may dissent from, and obtain payment of the fair value of his or her shares in the event of [a merger or other enumerated corporate actions]." If the shareholder expresses dissatisfaction with the payment of shares offered by the corporate entity and complies with the appropriate procedures, a corporation may institute a special proceeding and petition the court to make a binding determination as to the fair value of the shares.

We turn now to address the first issue: whether a minority discount may apply in determining the fair value of a dissenter's shares. * * *

Appraisal rights represent a legislative response to the minority's lack of corporate veto power and the consequential vulnerability to majority oppression. To compensate for nominal control, the legislature granted minority shareholders the right to receive fair value for their shares if they objected to a particular corporate action.

Consistent with the statutory purpose in granting dissenters' rights, an involuntary corporate change approved by the majority requires as a matter of fairness that a dissenting shareholder be compensated for the loss of the shareholder's proportionate interest in the business as an entity. Otherwise, the majority may "squeeze out" minority shareholders to the economic advantage of the majority.

As the Delaware Supreme Court observed in the seminal case of *Cavalier Oil Corp. v. Harnett*, 564 A.2d 1137, 1145 (Del.1989):

> Where there is no objective market data available, the appraisal process is not intended to reconstruct a pro forma sale but to assume that the shareholder was willing to maintain his investment position, however slight, had the merger not occurred.... [T]o fail to accord to a minority shareholder the full proportionate value of his shares imposes a penalty for lack of control, and

unfairly enriches the majority shareholders who may reap a windfall from the appraisal process by cashing out a dissenting shareholder, a clearly undesirable result.

A minority discount based on valuing only the minority block of shares injects into the appraisal process speculation as to the myriad factors that may affect the market price of the block of shares. Examining the purpose of dissenters' rights statutes, we conclude that the application of a minority discount in determining the fair value of a dissenter's shares frustrates the equitable purpose to protect minority shareholders.

A dissenting stockholder is thus entitled to the proportionate interest of his or her minority shares in the going concern of the entire company. *Weinberger v. UOP, Inc.*, 457 A.2d 701, 713 (Del.1983). Although Wis. Stat. § 180.1301(4) defines "fair value" as "the value of the shares" immediately before the corporate action, the focus of fair valuation is not the stock as a commodity but rather the stock only as it represents a proportionate part of the enterprise as a whole. * * *

In rejecting the application of a minority discount, we join a significant number of jurisdictions that have likewise disavowed the minority discount. These courts have also concluded that a minority discount thwarts the purpose of dissenters' rights statutes to protect shareholders subjected to an involuntary corporate change.

Reasoning against a minority discount, courts have recognized that to apply such a discount inflicts a double penalty upon the minority shareholder and upsets the *quid pro quo* underlying dissenters' appraisal rights. The shareholder not only lacks control over corporate decision making, but also upon the application of a minority discount receives less than proportional value for loss of that control. * * *

Having concluded that a minority discount may not apply in determining the fair value of a dissenter's shares, we turn next to the second issue: whether a fair value determination of a dissenter's shares may include consideration of unfair dealing in the valuation of those shares. SSM contends that in this appraisal proceeding, the circuit court should have considered HMO–W's unfair dealing in initially setting the company's net value at $16.5–$18 million and subsequently representing significantly lower values. According to SSM, the court should have bound HMO–W to its initial represented value.

We note at the outset that SSM has not pled breach of fiduciary duty or sought damages based on such a breach. Rather, it states that the issue of unfair dealing is raised as an affirmative defense. SSM has relied on general principles of fiduciary duty to support its contention that HMO–W's unfair dealing should be considered in the valuation of SSM's shares. SSM has also maintained from the initial stage of this action that HMO–W should be estopped from claiming a lower value in this appraisal proceeding than the value established in the initial VR report that was submitted to the shareholders. * * *

Wisconsin law has established that in the absence of fraud or breach of fiduciary duty, appraisal represents the exclusive remedy for a shareholder objecting to the valuation of shares under a plan of corporate merger. Appraisal is a limited remedy, and the dissenter in an appraisal proceeding may assert only a right to the fair value of the dissenter's shares.

However, Wisconsin law has not shed light on whether evidence of unfair dealing and other misconduct in the valuation of a dissenter's shares may be presented in an appraisal proceeding. Furthermore, cases in this state have not addressed whether actions for fraud or breach of fiduciary duty must be brought as separate actions or may be consolidated with an appraisal proceeding.

Delaware appears to represent the jurisdiction that has most frequently addressed whether claims of misconduct and wrongdoing may be submitted in an appraisal action. Recognizing the limited scope of an appraisal proceeding, in which the only issue to be litigated remains the valuation of a dissenter's shares, Delaware has established that claims for fraud and breach of fiduciary duty must be instituted separately.

The ALI, however, observes that no apparent reason exists as to why such actions may not be consolidated with an appraisal proceeding in the discretion of the court. ALI PRINCIPLES, Comment e to § 7.22 at 326. Endorsing the position that courts should not foster a separate and unnecessary damages forum, the ALI suggests that courts entertain claims of fraud or breach of fiduciary duty in the appraisal proceeding. Because we determine that the allegation of unfair dealing in this case directly relates to the issue of fair value, we need not answer the unresolved issue of consolidation. * * *

A court determining the fair value of shares subject to appraisal must consider "all relevant factors." These factors may include evidence of unfair dealing affecting the value of a dissenter's shares. Additionally, courts may examine wrongful actions in gauging or impeaching the credibility of majority shareholders with respect to their valuation contentions.

In this case, SSM's assertion of unfair dealing concerns the value of its shares. SSM neither disputes the legitimacy of the business purpose to be served by HMO–W's merger with United nor contends that the merger should be invalidated. Rather, SSM contends that HMO–W's unfair dealing directly reduced the fair value of shares owned by SSM and that the appropriate remedy for HMO–W's unfair dealing should involve valuing the entity at the original net value advanced by HMO–W: $16.5–$18 million. Because the assertion of unfair dealing relates to the value of SSM's shares, we determine that it is a proper subject for consideration in this appraisal proceeding.

Having determined that SSM's allegation of unfair dealing may be raised in this appraisal action, we now conclude that the circuit court adequately considered the evidence of unfair dealing in rendering its fair value determination. A fair value determination is necessarily a fact-specific process. We will not upset a circuit court's findings of fact unless they are against the great weight and clear preponderance of the evidence.

SSM invokes principles of fiduciary duty and estoppel to assert that HMO–W should be bound to the initial representation of its net asset value. Because HMO–W endorsed the VR report that it submitted as part of its proxy materials to shareholders, and as a result secured shareholder approval for the United merger, SSM contends that HMO–W cannot now subvert the appraisal process by disavowing the VR report. If HMO–W had reservations about the validity of the report, SSM claims that HMO–W was under a duty to inform its shareholders of potential flaws, particularly in light of the significance of the report in influencing shareholder approval.

According to SSM, HMO–W's actions in asserting lower values in the subsequent appraisal proceedings are evidence of unfair dealing because these actions reduced the fair value of SSM's shares. SSM claims that HMO–W's unfair dealing was reflected in its decision to hire a new appraiser for the purposes of maligning the VR report and consequently offering to SSM a significantly depressed value for its dissenting shares. In remedying HMO–W's unfair dealing, SSM urges this court to bind HMO–W to the initial representation of the company's value, thereby altering the fair value of SSM's dissenting shares.

We note that the circuit court addressed SSM's arguments of unfair dealing in the valuation of HMO–W. The record reflects that the court examined all of the relevant evidence, including the allegations of corporate misconduct. The court determined that HMO–W had not made a material misrepresentation to its shareholders and that the initial VR report contained several flaws.

Upon hearing testimony from three experts and the corporate officers of HMO–W, SSM, and United, the court rendered a decision accepting the valuation of HMO–W's second appraiser. We perceive no reason for the court to have relied solely on the value and methodology of the first appraiser or to have accepted a valuation it deemed inaccurate. The circuit court is in the best position to gauge the credibility of witnesses and the relative weight to be given to their testimony. Furthermore, the court decides fair value and is not required to accept any one party's represented valuation.

As the circuit court apparently concluded, SSM has failed to establish that it relied to its detriment on the initial VR report or that but for the report, HMO–W's shareholders would not have approved the United merger that forced SSM to sell its shares. In this appraisal proceeding, the circuit court properly considered SSM's assertion of unfair dealing as it affected the fair value of the shares owned by SSM. The court then made a determination of HMO–W's net value that is not against the great weight and clear preponderance of the evidence.

In sum, we conclude that a minority discount may not be applied to determine the fair value of a dissenter's shares in an appraisal action. This discount unfairly penalizes dissenting shareholders for exercising their legal right to dissent and does not protect them from oppression by the majority. We further conclude that in an appraisal proceeding, the court may entertain assertions of misconduct that relate to the value of a dissenter's shares. In this case, the circuit court properly considered SSM's evidence of unfair dealing and rendered a determination of HMO–W's net value that is supported by the record. Accordingly, we affirm the court of appeals.

QUESTIONS

1.   What is a "minority discount"? What is a "marketability discount"?

2.   When HMO–W sent SSM a check for $1.5 million, what did it send to its other shareholders? Where did the $1.5 million come from?

3.   Do we know how HMO–W's expert determined that the value of HMO–W was $10,544,000? Do we know how SSM's expert determined that the value was $19,250,000? Do we know why the court accepted the valuation of the HMO–W expert? Do we need to know any of this stuff?

4.   Was the claim asserted in this case direct or a derivative? Who pays the costs of litigation over fair value of a dissenting shareholder's stock? Is it expensive litigation?

5.   Note HMO–W is a small, closely held corporation. What if it were a large public corporation whose stock was traded on the New York Stock Exchange? Would there still be litigable issues as to value of HMO–W?

d.   Sue the Directors Who Approved the Merger for Breach of a Duty of Loyalty

Recall how corporation statutes (and this casebook) recognize a director's duty of loyalty. *See* MBCA § 8.31 and Delaware § 144 and Chapter 5, Part C.

Duty-of-loyalty issues arise when a director engages in self-dealing or is in other ways on both sides of the deal. Assume, for example, that Bubba's Burritos, Inc. is discussing a potential merger with both McDonald's and Wendy's and that the Wendy's deal includes lucrative consulting contracts for Bubba's Burritos' present directors. Are there any duty-of-loyalty problems if the directors approve and recommend that the shareholders approve the Wendy's merger agreement?

Or, assume that The Signal Companies, Inc., ("Signal") owns 50.5% of the outstanding stock of UOP, Inc. and that a majority of UOP's directors are also officers or directors of Signal or connected to Signal in some other way. The board of directors of UOP recommends a merger of UOP and Signal that will result in the shareholders of UOP other than Signal receiving $21 per share. The Signal-affiliated directors of UOP know that a study by two Signal officers concluded that the merger would be a good investment for Signal for as high as $24 a share. However, neither the other UOP directors nor the UOP shareholders know of the study at the time that they approve the merger. When the UOP shareholders later learn of the study, what are their rights and remedies?

The next case considered these facts and similar questions. As you read it, please consider the following:

1.   Who is the plaintiff—which corporation's shares did he own?

2.   Which corporation(s) is a defendant? What did the various defendants do wrong?

3.   When did the plaintiff file this suit? We know that the "merger became effective on May 26, 1978." Do we know when the lawsuit was commenced?

4.   What is the plaintiff asking the court to do?

WEINBERGER v. UOP, INC.

Delaware Supreme Court, 1983
457 A.2d 701

MOORE, JUSTICE. This post-trial appeal was reheard *en banc* from a decision of the Court of Chancery. It was brought by the class action plaintiff below, a former shareholder of UOP, Inc., who challenged the elimination of UOP's minority shareholders by a cash-out merger between UOP and its majority owner, The Signal Companies, Inc. Originally, the defendants in this action were Signal, UOP, certain officers and directors of those companies, and UOP's investment banker, Lehman Brothers Kuhn Loeb, Inc. The * * * Chancellor held that the terms of the merger were fair to the plaintiff and the other minority shareholders of UOP. Accordingly, he entered judgment in favor of the defendants. * * *

Signal is a diversified, technically based company operating through various subsidiaries. Its stock is publicly traded on the New York, Philadelphia and Pacific Stock Exchanges. UOP, formerly known as Universal Oil Products Company, was a diversified industrial company engaged in various lines of business, including petroleum and petro-chemical services and related products, construction, fabricated metal products, transportation equipment products, chemicals and plastics, and other products and services including land development, lumber products and waste disposal. Its stock was publicly held and listed on the New York Stock Exchange.

In 1974 Signal became interested in UOP as a possible acquisition. Friendly negotiations ensued. * * *

Signal achieved its goal of becoming a 50.5% shareholder of UOP.

Although UOP's board consisted of thirteen directors, Signal nominated and elected only six. Of these, five were either directors or employees of Signal. * * *

However, the president and chief executive officer of UOP retired during 1975, and Signal caused him to be replaced by James V. Crawford, a long-time employee and senior executive vice president of one of Signal's wholly-owned subsidiaries. Crawford succeeded his predecessor on UOP's board of directors and also was made a director of Signal. * * *

At the instigation of certain Signal management personnel, including William W. Walkup, its board chairman, and Forrest N. Shumway, its president, a feasibility study was made concerning the possible acquisition of the balance of UOP's outstanding shares. This study was performed by two Signal officers, Charles S. Arledge, vice president (director of planning), and Andrew J. Chitiea, senior vice president (chief financial officer). Messrs. Walkup, Shumway, Arledge and Chitiea were all directors of UOP in addition to their membership on the Signal board.

Arledge and Chitiea concluded that it would be a good investment for Signal to acquire the remaining 49.5% of UOP shares at any price up to $24 each. Their report was discussed between Walkup and Shumway who, along with Arledge, Chitiea and Brewster L. Arms, internal counsel for Signal, constituted Signal's senior management. In particular, they talked about the proper price to be paid if the acquisition was pursued, purportedly keeping in mind that as UOP's majority shareholder, Signal owed a fiduciary responsibility to both its own stockholders as well as to UOP's minority. It was ultimately agreed that a meeting of Signal's executive committee would be called to propose that Signal acquire the remaining outstanding stock of UOP through a cash-out merger in the range of $20 to $21 per share.

The executive committee meeting was set for February 28, 1978. As a courtesy, UOP's president, Crawford, was invited to attend, although he was not a member of Signal's executive committee. On his arrival, and prior to the meeting, Crawford was told of Signal's plan to acquire full ownership of UOP and was asked for his reaction to the proposed price range of $20 to $21 per share. Crawford said he thought such a price would be "generous," and that it was certainly one which should be submitted to UOP's minority shareholders for their ultimate consideration. * * *

Signal's executive committee authorized its management "to negotiate" with UOP "for a cash acquisition of the minority ownership in UOP, Inc., with the intention of presenting a proposal to [Signal's] board of directors . . . on March 6, 1978." Immediately after this February 28, 1978 meeting, Signal issued a press release stating:

> The Signal Companies, Inc. and UOP, Inc. are conducting negotiations for the acquisition for cash by Signal of the 49.5 per cent of UOP which it does not presently own, announced Forrest N. Shumway, president and chief executive officer of Signal, and James V. Crawford, UOP president.

> Price and other terms of the proposed transaction have not yet been finalized and would be subject to approval of the boards of directors of Signal and UOP, scheduled to meet early next week, the stockholders of UOP and certain federal agencies.

The announcement also referred to the fact that the closing price of UOP's common stock on that day was $14.50 per share.

Between Tuesday, February 28, 1978 and Monday, March 6, 1978, a total of four business days, Crawford spoke by telephone with all of UOP's non-Signal, i.e., outside, directors. Also during that period, Crawford retained Lehman Brothers to render a fairness opinion as to the price offered the minority for its stock. Second, James W. Glanville, a long-time director of UOP and a partner in Lehman Brothers, had acted as a financial advisor to UOP for many years. Crawford believed that Glanville's familiarity with UOP, as a member of its board, would also be of assistance in enabling Lehman Brothers to render a fairness opinion within the existing time constraints.

* * * The Lehman Brothers team concluded that "the price of either $20 or $21 would be a fair price for the remaining shares of UOP."

On * * * March 6, 1978, both the Signal and UOP boards were convened to consider the proposed merger. Telephone communications were maintained between the two meetings. Walkup, Signal's board chairman, and also a UOP director, attended UOP's meeting with Crawford in order to present Signal's position and answer any questions that UOP's non-Signal directors might have. Arledge and Chitiea, along with Signal's other designees on UOP's board, participated by conference telephone. All of UOP's outside directors attended the meeting either in person or by conference telephone.

First, Signal's board unanimously adopted a resolution authorizing Signal to propose to UOP a cash merger of $21 per share as outlined in a certain merger agreement and other supporting documents. This proposal required that the merger be approved by a majority of UOP's outstanding minority shares voting at the stockholders meeting at which the merger would be considered, and that the minority shares voting in favor of the merger, when coupled with Signal's 50.5% interest would have to comprise at least two-thirds of all UOP shares. Otherwise the proposed merger would be deemed disapproved.

UOP's board then considered the proposal. Copies of the agreement were delivered to the directors in attendance, and other copies had been forwarded earlier to the directors participating by telephone. They also had before them UOP financial data for 1974–1977, UOP's most recent financial statements, market price information, and budget projections for 1978. In addition they had Lehman Brothers' hurriedly prepared fairness opinion letter finding the price of $21 to be fair. * * *

While Signal's men on UOP's board participated in various aspects of the meeting, they abstained from voting. However, the minutes show that each of them "if voting would have voted yes." * * *

Despite the swift board action of the two companies, the merger was not submitted to UOP's shareholders until their annual meeting on May 26, 1978. In the notice of that meeting and proxy statement sent to shareholders in May, UOP's management and board urged that the merger be approved. The proxy statement also advised:

> The price was determined after discussions between James V. Crawford, a director of Signal and Chief Executive Officer of UOP, and officers of Signal which took place during meetings on February 28, 1978, and in the course of several subsequent telephone conversations.

In the original draft of the proxy statement the word "negotiations" had been used rather than "discussions." However, when the Securities and Exchange Commission sought details of the "negotiations" as part of its review of these materials, the term was deleted and the word "discussions" was substituted. The proxy statement indicated that the vote of UOP's board in approving the merger had been unanimous. It also advised the shareholders that Lehman Brothers had given its opinion that the merger price of $21 per share was fair to UOP's minority. However, it did not disclose the hurried method by which this conclusion was reached.

As of the record date of UOP's annual meeting, there were 11,488,302 shares of UOP common stock outstanding, 5,688,302 of which were owned by the minority. At the meeting only 56%, or 3,208,652, of the minority shares were voted. Of these, 2,953,812, or 51.9% of the total minority, voted for the merger, and 254,840 voted against it. When Signal's stock was added to the minority shares voting in favor, a total of 76.2% of UOP's outstanding shares approved the merger while only 2.2% opposed it.

By its terms the merger became effective on May 26, 1978, and each share of UOP's stock held by the minority was automatically converted into a right to receive $21 cash.

II.

A.

A primary issue mandating reversal is the preparation by two UOP directors, Arledge and Chitiea, of their feasibility study for the exclusive use and benefit of Signal. This document was of obvious significance to both Signal and UOP. Using UOP data, it described the advantages to Signal of ousting the minority at a price range of $21–$24 per share. * * *

The Arledge–Chitiea report speaks for itself in supporting the Chancellor's finding that a price of up to $24 was a "good investment" for Signal. It shows that a return on the investment at $21 would be 15.7% versus 15.5% at $24 per share. This was a difference of only two-tenths of one percent, while it meant over $17,000,000 to the minority. Under such circumstances, paying UOP's minority shareholders $24 would have had relatively little long-term effect on Signal, and the Chancellor's findings concerning the benefit to Signal, even at a price of $24, were obviously correct.

Certainly, this was a matter of material significance to UOP and its shareholders. Since the study was prepared by two UOP directors, using UOP information for the exclusive benefit of Signal, and nothing whatever was done to disclose it to the outside UOP directors or the minority shareholders, a question of breach of fiduciary duty arises. This problem occurs because there were common Signal–UOP directors participating, at least to some extent, in the UOP board's decision-making processes without full disclosure of the conflicts they faced.* [7] * * *

C.

The concept of fairness has two basic aspects: fair dealing and fair price. The former embraces questions of when the transaction was timed, how it was initiated, structured, negotiated, disclosed to the directors, and how the approvals of the directors and the stockholders were obtained. The latter aspect of fairness relates to the economic and financial considerations of the proposed merger, including all relevant factors: assets, market value, earnings, future prospects, and any other elements that affect the intrinsic or inherent value of a company's stock. * * *

The Arledge–Chitiea report is but one aspect of the element of fair dealing. How did this merger evolve? It is clear that it was entirely initiated by Signal. The serious time constraints under which the principals acted were all set by Signal. It had not found a suitable outlet for its excess cash and considered UOP a desirable investment, particularly since it was now in a position to acquire the whole company for itself. For whatever reasons, and they were only Signal's, the entire transaction was presented to and approved by UOP's board within four business days. Standing alone, this is not necessarily indicative of any lack of fairness by a majority shareholder. It was what occurred, or more properly, what did not occur, during this brief period that makes the time constraints imposed by Signal relevant to the issue of fairness.

The structure of the transaction, again, was Signal's doing. So far as negotiations were concerned, it is clear that they were modest at best. Crawford, Signal's man at UOP, never really talked price with Signal, except to accede to its management's statements on the subject, and to convey to Signal the UOP outside directors' view that as between the $20–$21 range under consideration, it would have to be $21. The latter is not a surprising outcome, but hardly arm's length negotiations. * * *

This cannot but undermine a conclusion that this merger meets any reasonable test of fairness. The outside UOP directors lacked one material piece of information generated by two of their colleagues, but shared only

---

* [7] Although perfection is not possible, or expected, the result here could have been entirely different if UOP had appointed an independent negotiating committee of its outside directors to deal with Signal at arm's length. Since fairness in this context can be equated to conduct by a theoretical, wholly independent, board of directors acting upon the matter before them, it is unfortunate that this course apparently was neither considered nor pursued. Particularly in a parent-subsidiary context, a showing that the action taken was as though each of the contending parties had in fact exerted its bargaining power against the other at arm's length is strong evidence that the transaction meets the test of fairness.

with Signal. True, the UOP board had the Lehman Brothers' fairness opinion, but that firm has been blamed by the plaintiff for the hurried task it performed, when more properly the responsibility for this lies with Signal. There was no disclosure of the circumstances surrounding the rather cursory preparation of the Lehman Brothers' fairness opinion. Instead, the impression was given UOP's minority that a careful study had been made, when in fact speed was the hallmark. * * *

Finally, the minority stockholders were denied the critical information that Signal considered a price of $24 to be a good investment. Since this would have meant over $17,000,000 more to the minority, we cannot conclude that the shareholder vote was an informed one. Under the circumstances, an approval by a majority of the minority was meaningless. * * *

E.

Turning to the matter of price, plaintiff also challenges its fairness. His evidence was that on the date the merger was approved the stock was worth at least $26 per share. In support, he offered the testimony of a chartered investment analyst who used two basic approaches to valuation: a comparative analysis of the premium paid over market in ten other tender offer-merger combinations, and a discounted cash flow analysis.

In this breach of fiduciary duty case, the Chancellor perceived that the approach to valuation was the same as that in an appraisal proceeding. Consistent with precedent, he rejected plaintiff's method of proof and accepted defendants' evidence of value as being in accord with practice under prior case law. This means that the so-called "Delaware block" or weighted average method was employed wherein the elements of value, i.e., assets, market price, earnings, etc., were assigned a particular weight and the resulting amounts added to determine the value per share. This procedure has been in use for decades. However, to the extent it excludes other generally accepted techniques used in the financial community and the courts, it is now clearly outmoded. It is time we recognize this in appraisal and other stock valuation proceedings and bring our law current on the subject.

While the Chancellor rejected plaintiff's discounted cash flow method of valuing UOP's stock, as not corresponding with "either logic or the existing law," it is significant that this was essentially the focus, i.e., earnings potential of UOP, of Messrs. Arledge and Chitiea in their evaluation of the merger. Accordingly, the standard "Delaware block" or weighted average method of valuation, formerly employed in appraisal and other stock valuation cases, shall no longer exclusively control such proceedings. We believe that a more liberal approach must include proof of value by any techniques or methods which are generally considered acceptable in the financial community and otherwise admissible in court, subject only to our interpretation of 8 Del.C. § 262(h), infra. This will obviate the very structured and mechanistic procedure that has heretofore governed such matters. * * *

The plaintiff has not sought an appraisal, but rescissory damages of the type contemplated by *Lynch v. Vickers Energy Corp.*, Del.Supr., 429 A.2d 497, 505–06 (1981) (*Lynch II*). In view of the approach to valuation that we announce today, we see no basis in our law for *Lynch II's* exclusive monetary formula for relief. On remand the plaintiff will be permitted to test the fairness of the $21 price by the standards we herein establish, in conformity with the principle applicable to an appraisal—that fair value be determined by taking "into account all relevant factors." In our view this includes the elements of rescissory damages if the Chancellor considers them susceptible of proof and a remedy appropriate to all the issues of fairness before him. * * *

While a plaintiff's monetary remedy ordinarily should be confined to the more liberalized appraisal proceeding herein established, we do not intend any limitation on the historic powers of the Chancellor to grant such other relief as the facts of a particular case may dictate. The appraisal remedy we approve may not be adequate in certain cases, particularly where fraud, misrepresentation, self-dealing, deliberate waste of corporate assets, or gross and palpable overreaching are involved. Under such circumstances, the Chancellor's powers are complete to fashion any form of equitable and monetary relief as may be appropriate, including rescissory damages. Since it is apparent that this long completed transaction is too involved to undo, and in view of the Chancellor's discretion, the award, if any, should be in the form of monetary damages based upon entire fairness standards, i.e., fair dealing and fair price.

Obviously, there are other litigants, like the plaintiff, who abjured an appraisal and whose rights to challenge the element of fair value must be preserved. Accordingly, the quasi-appraisal remedy we grant the plaintiff here will apply only to: * * * (2) any case now pending. * * * Thereafter, the provisions of 8 Del.C. § 262, as herein construed, respecting the scope of an appraisal and the means for perfecting the same, shall govern the financial remedy available to minority shareholders in a cash-out merger. * * *

III.

Finally, we address the matter of business purpose. The defendants contend that the purpose of this merger was not a proper subject of inquiry by the trial court. The plaintiff says that no valid purpose existed—the entire transaction was a mere subterfuge designed to eliminate the minority. * * *

The requirement of a business purpose is new to our law of mergers and was a departure from prior case law.

In view of the fairness test which has long been applicable to parent—subsidiary mergers, the expanded appraisal remedy now available to shareholders, and the broad discretion of the Chancellor to fashion such relief as the facts of a given case may dictate, we do not believe that any additional meaningful protection is afforded minority shareholders by the business purpose requirement. * * *

The judgment of the Court of Chancery, finding both the circumstances of the merger and the price paid the minority shareholders to be fair, is reversed. The matter is remanded for further proceedings consistent herewith. Upon remand the plaintiff's post-trial motion to enlarge the class should be granted.

QUESTIONS AND NOTES

1. On remand, the Delaware Court of Chancery awarded Weinberger an additional $1 per share. *See Weinberger v. UOP, Inc.,* 1985 WL 11546 (Del. Ch. 1985).

2. The court describes the transaction by which Signal acquires the remaining UOP stock as a "cash-out merger." Why? Was the transaction a "merger"? *Cf.* MBCA § 11.06. Did the "separate existence" of UOP cease?

3. Law professors have described the transaction by which Signal acquires the remaining UOP stock as a "freeze-out merger." Why? Is every "cash-out merger" also a "freeze-out merger"?

4. The court noted that "[t]he plaintiff has not sought an appraisal but rescissory damages." What are "rescissory" damages? Why didn't the plaintiff assert his right to dissent and obtain payment of the fair value of his shares? Why isn't statutory appraisal the exclusive remedy of a shareholder who disagrees with a merger decision approved by the board of directors and a majority of the shareholders? Did the *HMO–W* case consider this question?

5. The *Weinberger* case rejects the Delaware Block Method. More accurately, the court states that the Delaware Block Method shall no longer "exclusively control." A student law review note criticizes valuation methods:

> A gap exists between statutory language and legal reality in the context of appraisal rights: all fifty states give minority shareholders the right to fair value for their shares when they dissent from certain fundamental transactions, but courts' current valuation methods are incapable, at both a theoretical and a practical level, of providing fair value. This result is inequitable to minority shareholders and inefficient for the corporate takeover market overall. Capital cash flow (CCF) valuation better satisfies these equity and efficiency objectives for appraisal rights. Although CCF valuation was foreshadowed as early as 1986, its formal appearance in the corporate finance literature has been recent and somewhat oblique. Its most detailed exposition appears in a 1995 Harvard Business School Note. CCF valuation is slowly gaining acceptance on Wall Street, and as it does it will no doubt be promulgated in appraisal proceedings as well. However, the considerable lag-time from business schools to Wall Street to the Delaware courts has made it an unknown technique in appraisal proceedings to date. This delay is unfortunate because CCF valuation has desirable properties from the appraisal perspective. CCF valuation would provide more equitable terms for dis-

senting shareholders and would promote a more efficient market for corporate control.

Note, Using Capital Cash Flows to Value Dissenters' Shares in Appraisal Proceedings, 111 HARV. L. REV. 2099–100 (1998).

Professor Grossfield sums up the techniques that courts use for calculating the value of dissenting shareholders' stock: "the answer is left to the 'financial community, where—probably—accountants [and not lawyers] have the upper hand." Bernhard Grossfield, *Lawyers and Accountants: A Semiotic Competition*, 36 WAKE FOREST L. REV. 167, 174 (2001).

6.   Suppose that a corporation's controlling shareholder admits that she had no business purpose for causing the corporation to eliminate its single minority shareholder through a cash-out merger. Instead, she just found the shareholder annoying because he wore his hair in a mullet. Would this affect the outcome of a Delaware court's review of the merger?

7.   What did the defendants do wrong? What should the defendants have done differently? Assume that Signal had (i) made a full disclosure to the UOP directors and shareholders and (ii) had changed the terms of the merger so each share of UOP stock was exchanged for $24 and (iii) had provided ample time for the UOP board and shareholders to consider the deal. What would be the legal rights of P, a UOP shareholder who did not want to sell her shares? The next case provides the Massachusetts answer to this question (and an answer to Question 4 above).

COGGINS v. NEW ENGLAND PATRIOTS FOOTBALL CLUB, INC.

Massachusetts Supreme Judicial Court, 1986
492 N.E.2d 1112

LIACOS, JUSTICE. On November 18, 1959, William H. Sullivan, Jr. (Sullivan), purchased an American Football League (AFL) franchise for a professional football team. Four months later, Sullivan organized a corporation, the American League Professional Football Team of Boston, Inc. Sullivan contributed his AFL franchise; nine other persons each contributed $25,000. In return, each of the ten investors received 10,000 shares of voting common stock in the corporation. Another four months later, in July 1960, the corporation sold 120,000 shares of nonvoting common stock to the public at $5 a share.

Sullivan had effective control of the corporation from its inception until 1974. In 1974 the other voting stockholders ousted him from the presidency and from operating control of the corporation. He then began the effort to regain control of the corporation—an effort which culminated in this and other lawsuits.

In November, 1975, Sullivan succeeded in obtaining ownership or control of all 100,000 of the voting shares, at a price of approximately $102 a share (adjusted cash value), of the corporation, by that time renamed the New England Patriots Football Club, Inc. (Old Patriots). In order to finance this coup, Sullivan borrowed approximately $5,348,000 from the Rhode Island Hospital National Bank and the Lasalle National Bank of Chicago. As a condition of these loans, Sullivan was to use his best efforts to reorganize the Patriots so that the income of the corporation could be devoted to the payment of these personal loans and the assets of the corporation pledged to secure them. At this point they were secured by all of the voting shares held by Sullivan. * * *

In order to accomplish in effect the assumption by the corporation of Sullivan's personal obligations, it was necessary, as a matter of corporate law, to eliminate the interest of the nonvoting shares.

On October 20, 1976, Sullivan organized a new corporation called the New Patriots Football Club, Inc. (New Patriots). The board of directors of the Old Patriots and the board of directors of the New Patriots executed an agreement of merger of the two corporations providing that, after the merger, the voting stock of the Old Patriots would be extinguished, the nonvoting stock would be exchanged for cash at the rate of $15 a share, and the name of the New Patriots would be changed to the name formerly used by the Old Patriots.* [6] As part of this plan, Sullivan gave the New Patriots his 100,000 voting shares of the Old Patriots in return for 100% of the New Patriots stock.

General Laws c. 156B, § 78(c)(1)(iii), as amended through St. 1976, c. 327, required approval of the merger agreement by a majority vote of each class of affected stock. Approval by the voting class, entirely controlled by Sullivan, was assured. The merger was approved by the class of nonvoting stockholders at a special meeting on December 8, 1976.* [7] On January 31, 1977, the merger of the New Patriots and the Old Patriots was consummated.

David A. Coggins (Coggins) was the owner of ten shares of nonvoting stock in the Old Patriots. Coggins, a fan of the Patriots from the time of their formation, was serving in Vietnam in 1967 when he purchased the shares through his brother. Over the years, he followed the fortunes of the team, taking special pride in his status as an owner.[†] [8] When he heard of

---

* [6] Additional findings as to the purpose of this merger * * * as adopted by the trial judge, are: "Purported reasons for the merger [were] stated in the [proxy materials]. Three reasons are given: (1) the policy of the [National Football League] to discourage public ownership of member football teams, (2) the difficulty in reconciling management's obligations to the NFL with its obligations to public stockholders, and (3) the cost and possible revelation of confidential information resulting from the obligations of publicly owned corporations to file reports with various public bodies.... I find, however, that while some of the stated reasons may have been useful by-products of the merger, the true reason for the merger was to enable Sullivan to satisfy his $5,348,000 personal obligation to the banks. The merger would not have occurred for the considerations stated as reasons in the Proxy Statement.... The Proxy Statement is an artful attempt to minimize the future profitability of the Patriots and to put a wash of corporate respectability over Sullivan's diversion of the corporation's income for his own purposes."

* [7] On the date of the meeting, 139,800 shares of nonvoting stock were outstanding, held by approximately 2,400 stockholders. The Sullivan family owned 10,826 shares. Of the remaining 128,974, a total of 71,644 voted in favor of the merger, 22,795 did not vote, and 34,535 voted against. The plaintiffs in this case are stockholders of 2,291 of the 34,535 voting against the merger.

† [8] It was, in part, the goal of the Old Patriots, in offering stock to the public, to generate loyal fans.

the proposed merger, Coggins was upset that he could be forced to sell. Coggins voted against the merger and commenced this suit on behalf of those stockholders, who, like himself, believed the transaction to be unfair and illegal. A judge of the Superior Court certified the class as "stockholders of New England Patriots Football Club, Inc. who have voted against the merger ... but who have neither turned in their shares nor perfected their appraisal rights ... [and who] desire only to void the merger."

The trial judge found in favor of the Coggins class but determined that the merger should not be undone. Instead, he ruled that the plaintiffs are entitled to rescissory damages, and he ordered that further hearings be held to determine the amount of damages. * * *

We conclude that the trial judge was correct in ruling that the merger was illegal and that the plaintiffs have been wronged. Ordinarily, rescission of the merger would be the appropriate remedy. This merger, however, is now nearly ten years old, and, because an effective and orderly rescission of the merger now is not feasible, we remand the case for proceedings to determine the appropriate monetary damages to compensate the plaintiffs. * * *

Scope of Judicial Review. In deciding this case, we address an important corporate law question: What approach will a Massachusetts court reviewing a cash freeze-out merger employ?

The parties have urged us to consider the views of a court with great experience in such matters, the Supreme Court of Delaware. We note that the Delaware court announced one test in 1977, but recently has changed to another.* **[10]** In *Singer v. Magnavox Co.*, 380 A.2d 969, 980 (Del. 1977), the Delaware court established the so-called "business-purpose" test, holding that controlling stockholders violate their fiduciary duties when they "cause a merger to be made for the sole purpose of eliminating a minority on a cash-out basis." *Id.* at 978. In 1983, Delaware jettisoned the business-purpose test, satisfied that the "fairness" test "long ... applicable to parent-subsidiary mergers, the expanded appraisal remedy now available to stockholders, and the broad discretion of the Chancellor to fashion such relief as the facts of a given case may dictate" provided sufficient protection to the frozen-out minority. *Weinberger v. UOP, Inc.*, 457 A.2d 701, 715 (Del.1983). "The requirement of fairness is unflinching in its demand that where one stands on both sides of a transaction, he has the burden of establishing its entire fairness, sufficient to pass the test of careful scrutiny by the courts. The concept of fairness has two basic aspects: fair dealing and fair price." We note that the "fairness" test to which the Delaware court now has adhered is, as we later show, closely related to the views expressed in our decisions. Unlike the Delaware court, however, we believe that the "business-purpose" test is an additional useful means under our statutes and case law for examining a transaction

---

* **[10]** We are not bound, of course, in our interpretation of Massachusetts law by decisions of the courts of our sister States interpreting their laws. We have said before, however, that we consider such decisions instructive.

in which a controlling stockholder eliminates the minority interest in a corporation. *Cf. Wilkes v. Springside Nursing Home, Inc.*, 370 Mass. 842, 851, 353 N.E.2d 657 (1976). This concept of fair dealing is not limited to close corporations but applies to judicial review of cash freeze-out mergers.

The defendants argue that judicial review of a merger cannot be invoked by disgruntled stockholders, absent illegal or fraudulent conduct. They rely on G.L. c. 156B, § 98 (1984 ed.).* **[12]** In the defendants' view, "the Superior Court's finding of liability was premised solely on the claimed inadequacy of the offering price." Any dispute over offering price, they urge, must be resolved solely through the statutory remedy of appraisal.

We have held in regard to so called "close corporations" that the statute does not divest the courts of their equitable jurisdiction to assure that the conduct of controlling stockholders does not violate the fiduciary principles governing the relationship between majority and minority stockholders.† **[13]** "Where the director's duty of loyalty to the corporation is in conflict with his self-interest the court will vigorously scrutinize the situation." The court is justified in exercising its equitable power when a violation of fiduciary duty is claimed.

The dangers of self-dealing and abuse of fiduciary duty are greatest in freeze-out situations like the Patriots merger, where a controlling stockholder and corporate director chooses to eliminate public ownership. It is in these cases that a judge should examine with closest scrutiny the motives and the behavior of the controlling stockholder. A showing of compliance with statutory procedures is an insufficient substitute for the inquiry of the courts when a minority stockholder claims that the corporate action "will be or is illegal or fraudulent as to him."

A controlling stockholder who is also a director standing on both sides of the transaction bears the burden of showing that the transaction does not violate fiduciary obligations. Judicial inquiry into a freeze-out merger in technical compliance with the statute may be appropriate, and the dissenting stockholders are not limited to the statutory remedy of judicial appraisal where violations of fiduciary duties are found.

Factors in Judicial Review. Judicial scrutiny should begin with recognition of the basic principle that the duty of a corporate director must be to further the legitimate goals of the corporation. The result of a freeze-out merger is the elimination of public ownership in the corporation. The

---

* **[12]** "The enforcement by a stockholder of his right to receive payment for his shares in the manner provided in this chapter shall be an exclusive remedy except that this chapter shall not exclude the right of such stockholder to bring or maintain an appropriate proceeding to obtain relief on the ground that such corporate action will be or is illegal or fraudulent as to him." G.L. c. 156B, § 98.

† **[13]** We discussed the nature of a close corporation at some length in *Donahue v. Rodd Electrotype Co. of New England, Inc.*, 367 Mass. 578, 328 N.E.2d 505 (1975). We need not apply the stricter principle of good faith applied to a close corporation in *Donahue* to controlling stockholders in a public corporation to conclude, nevertheless, that the "less stringent standard of fiduciary duty to which directors and stockholders of all corporations must adhere" may warrant judicial scrutiny beyond the specified statutory appraisal right.

controlling faction increases its equity from a majority to 100%, using corporate processes and corporate assets. The corporate directors who benefit from this transfer of ownership must demonstrate how the legitimate goals of the corporation are furthered. A director of a corporation violates his fiduciary duty when he uses the corporation for his or his family's personal benefit in a manner detrimental to the corporation. Because the danger of abuse of fiduciary duty is especially great in a freeze-out merger, the court must be satisfied that the freeze-out was for the advancement of a legitimate corporate purpose. If satisfied that elimination of public ownership is in furtherance of a business purpose, the court should then proceed to determine if the transaction was fair by examining the totality of the circumstances. * * *

The plaintiffs here adequately alleged that the merger of the Old Patriots and New Patriots was a freeze-out merger undertaken for no legitimate business purpose, but merely for the personal benefit of Sullivan. While we have recognized the right to "selfish ownership" in a corporation, such a right must be balanced against the concept of the majority stockholder's fiduciary obligation to the minority stockholders. Consequently, the defendants bear the burden of proving, first, that the merger was for a legitimate business purpose, and, second, that, considering totality of circumstances, it was fair to the minority.

The decision of the Superior Court judge includes a finding that "the defendants have failed to demonstrate that the merger served any valid corporate objective unrelated to the personal interests of the majority shareholders. It thus appears that the sole reason for the merger was to effectuate a restructuring of the Patriots that would enable the repayment of the [personal] indebtedness incurred by Sullivan...." The trial judge considered the defendants' claims that the policy of the National Football League (NFL) requiring majority ownership by a single individual or family made it necessary to eliminate public ownership. He found that "the stock ownership of the Patriots as it existed just prior to the merger fully satisfied the rationale underlying the policy as expressed by NFL Commissioner Pete Rozelle. Having acquired 100% control of the voting common stock of the Patriots, Sullivan possessed unquestionable authority to act on behalf of the franchise at League meetings and effectively foreclosed the possible recurrence of the internal management disputes that had existed in 1974. Moreover, as the proxy statement itself notes, the Old Patriots were under no legal compulsion to eliminate public ownership." Likewise, the defendants did not succeed in showing a conflict between the interests of the league owners and the Old Patriots' stockholders. We perceive no error in these findings. They are fully supported by the evidence. Under the approach we set forth above, there is no need to consider further the elements of fairness of a transaction that is not related to a valid corporate purpose.

Remedy. The plaintiffs are entitled to relief. They argue that the appropriate relief is rescission of the merger and restoration of the parties to their positions of 1976. We agree that the normally appropriate remedy for an impermissible freeze-out merger is rescission. Because Massachusetts statutes do not bar a cash freeze-out, however, numerous third parties relied in good faith on the outcome of the merger. The trial judge concluded that the expectations of those parties should not be upset, and so chose to award damages rather than rescission.

We recognize that, because rescission is an equitable remedy, the circumstances of a particular case may not favor its employment. The goals of a remedy instituted after a finding that a merger did not serve the corporate purpose should include furthering the interests of the corporation. Ordinarily, we would remand with instructions for the trial judge to determine whether rescission would be in the corporation's best interests, but such a remedy does not appear to be equitable at this time. This litigation has gone on for many years. There is yet at least another related case pending (in the Federal District Court). Furthermore, other factors weigh against rescission. The passage of time has made the 1976 position of the parties difficult, if not impossible, to restore. A substantial number of former stockholders have chosen other courses and should not be forced back into the Patriots corporation. In these circumstances the interests of the corporation and of the plaintiffs will be furthered best by limiting the plaintiffs' remedy to an assessment of damages.

We do not think it appropriate, however, to award damages based on a 1976 appraisal value. To do so would make this suit a nullity, leaving the plaintiffs with no effective remedy except appraisal, a position we have already rejected. Rescissory damages must be determined based on the present value of the Patriots, that is, what the stockholders would have if the merger were rescinded. On remand, the judge is to take further evidence on the present value of the Old Patriots on the theory that the merger had not taken place. Each share of the Coggins class is to receive, as rescissory damages, its aliquot share of the present assets. * * *

Summary. The freeze-out merger accomplished by William H. Sullivan, Jr., was designed for his own personal benefit to eliminate the interests of the Patriots' minority stockholders. The merger did not further the interests of the corporation and therefore was a violation of Sullivan's fiduciary duty to the minority stockholders, and so was impermissible. In most cases we would turn to rescission as the appropriate remedy. In the circumstances of this case, however, rescission would be an inequitable solution. Therefore, we remand for a determination of the present value of the non-voting stock, as though the merger were rescinded. The claim for waste of corporate assets brought against the individual defendants is reinstated. Those stockholders who voted against the merger, who did not turn in their shares, who did not perfect their appraisal rights, but who are part of the Coggins class, are to receive damages in the amount their stock would be worth today, plus interest at the statutory rate. * * *

The case is remanded to the Superior Court for further proceedings consistent with this opinion.

QUESTIONS

1. What did the defendant do wrong? What should Sullivan have done differently?

2. What if Sullivan had established that his reasons for the cash-out merger were that (i) he wanted to use all Old Patriots' earnings to acquire better players and build a winning team and (ii) the other shareholders of Old Patriots wanted all Old Patriots' earnings to be distributed to them as dividends?

3. Was the Old Patriots a public company? Was the New Patriots a public company? Should that matter?

4. Was the *Coggins* case direct or derivative? Which should it have been?

PROBLEM: CASH OUT MERGERS

S, an individual, owns approximately 20% of the outstanding stock of T. A, another corporation, owns just under 49% of the outstanding stock of T. T and A have entered into a cash-out merger agreement whereby A will acquire the remaining 51% of the outstanding stock of T for $30 a share. S believes that the $30 price is inadequate. She wants your advice as to whether she can obtain an injunction to bar completion of the cash-out merger. Does it matter whether Massachusetts law or Delaware law controls?

D. SALE OF SUBSTANTIALLY ALL THE ASSETS

Sale of substantially all the corporation's assets is another possible endgame for a corporation. For instance, assume that Bubba's Burritos, Inc. sells all of its assets to McDonald's Inc., instead of merging into McDonald's. Such a sale is a fundamental corporate change, which (like the others) requires approval by the board of directors and by the shareholders, as we saw in Part A of this chapter. *See* MBCA §§ 12.01, 12.02.

1. EFFECT OF SALE OF ASSETS ON THE CREDITORS OF THE SELLING CORPORATION

There are significant differences in the effect on the creditors of Bubba's Burritos, Inc. between a merger of Bubba's Burritos, Inc. into McDonald's and sale of assets to McDonald's.* Recall that if Bubba's Burritos, Inc. merges into McDonald's, the merger provisions of the relevant state corporate law make the creditors of Bubba's Burritos, Inc. creditors of McDonald's.

There are no comparable statutory provisions making a buyer of the assets of a corporation liable to that corporation's creditors. And, the

---

* There are also significant accounting and tax differences, which we leave to your tax professors.

general common-law rule is that the buyer of a corporation's assets is not liable for the selling corporation's debts.

Accordingly, if Bubba's Burritos, Inc. sold its assets to McDonald's, creditors of Bubba's Burritos, Inc. could not collect from McDonald's. Rather, Bubba's Burritos, Inc.'s creditors would be limited to collecting their claims from Bubba's Burritos, Inc.

And Bubba's Burritos, Inc. will still exist, from which the plaintiff may hope to collect. By selling all of its assets, Bubba's Burritos, Inc. may be going out of the burrito business, but it does not go out of legal existence. A corporation's sale of assets does not automatically terminate its legal existence. Indeed, it still has assets: lots of cash.

Often, however, sale of all of a corporation's assets is followed by that corporation's dissolution, which does terminate its legal existence. We have already considered dissolution. Remember that any corporation that is considering dissolution and distribution to shareholders will have to pay off its creditors. A corporation's failure to do so can make its shareholders personally liable to these creditors.

What about claims concerning defective products or environmental damages—claims that were unknown at the time of the sale of assets and dissolution of the selling corporation? Assume, for example, that 20 years after Bubba's Burritos, Inc.'s sale of assets to McDonald's and Bubba's dissolution, P, who worked for Bubba's prior to the sale, has now become sick because of Bubba's smoke-filled working conditions (Bubba's had saved money by turning off the ventilation fan over the stove). Can P now sue McDonald's? The next case deals with such a question. In reading it, please consider the following questions:

1.   Which corporation allegedly wronged Jeanette Franklin?

2.   Would Con Cal be liable to the creditors of WPS? Why/why not? Why didn't the plaintiff sue Con Cal?

FRANKLIN v. USX CORP.

California Court of Appeal, 2001
105 Cal.Rptr.2d 11

WALKER, J. Jeannette Franklin, now deceased, and her husband, Darrel Franklin (respondents), filed an action for personal injury, premises liability and loss of consortium against several defendants including appellant USX Corporation (USX). Respondents contended that Jeannette had contracted mesothelioma, an asbestos-caused cancer, as a result of childhood exposure to secondhand asbestos carried home by her parents, who worked at the Western Pipe & Steel Shipyard (WPS) in South San Francisco during World War II. Respondents sought to hold USX liable for their injuries on the theory that it was the successor in interest to WPS. * * * The trial court concluded that USX was the successor in interest to WPS, and was therefore liable for any damages caused by WPS. In a bifurcated proceeding, a jury decided the issues of liability and damages, and returned a verdict against USX in excess of $5 million.

USX appeals the trial court's conclusion that it was the successor in interest to WPS. It also appeals the jury verdict on several grounds. We hold that the trial court erred in finding USX liable as the successor in interest to WPS. Accordingly, we do not address the issues pertaining to the jury verdict.

Prior to the beginning of World War II, WPS owned a steel fabrication plant in South San Francisco, which had been used to build ships during World War I. When World War II broke out, WPS entered into a contract with the United States Maritime Commission to * * * build ships for use in the war. The contract required the use of ship-building materials containing asbestos.

Jeannette Franklin was a child during World War II. Both of her parents worked at WPS from 1942 to 1945. Neither of her parents worked directly with asbestos-containing materials, but they both worked in areas where asbestos was present. At times, they were exposed to airborne dust during the mixing of mud, during insulation work, and when workers swept up debris. Franklin alleged that she was exposed to this asbestos-containing dust because her parents brought it home on their clothing and in their car. In 1996, Franklin was diagnosed with peritoneal mesothelioma, which she maintained was caused by her childhood secondhand exposure to asbestos.

In December 1945, the assets of WPS were purchased by Consolidated Steel Corporation of California (Con Cal) for over $6.2 million in cash. In connection with the sale, Con Cal agreed to assume all of the liabilities, obligations and commitments of WPS.

* * *

On August 31, 1948, Con Cal sold the transfer assets to Con Del for almost $8.3 million in cash, plus additional consideration that brought the total purchase price to over $17 million. Con Del was later merged into U.S. Steel, which thereafter changed its name to USX, the appellant here. After August 31, 1948, Con Cal changed its name to Consolidated Liquidating Corporation, which dissolved on February 29, 1952. Alden G. Roach was Con Cal's president and chairman of the board at the time of the sale; after the sale he continued as president of Con Del * * *.

* * * In a statement of decision issued March 1, 2000, the trial court found * * * that the transaction between Con Cal [and Con Del] constituted a *de facto* merger * * * [so Con Del assumed the liabilities of Con Cal, which USX then took over after Con Del merged into it].

* * * It has been generally stated that "where one corporation sells or transfers all of its assets to another corporation, the latter is not liable for the debts and liabilities of the former unless (1) the purchaser expressly or impliedly agrees to such assumption, (2) the transaction amounts to a consolidation or merger of the two corporations, (3) the purchasing corporation is merely a continuation of the selling corporation, or (4) the transaction is entered into fraudulently to escape liability for

debts." (*Ortiz v. South Bend Lathe* (1975) 46 Cal.App.3d 842, 846 *disapproved on other grounds in Ray v. Alad Corp.* (1977) 19 Cal.3d 22, 34.
* * *

The trial court also found that USX could be deemed to have assumed the liabilities of Con Cal/WPS under the *de facto* merger theory and under the theory that USX was a "mere continuation" of Con Cal. Although these two theories have been traditionally considered as separate bases for imposing liability on an successor corporation, we perceive the second to be merely a subset of the first. The crucial factor in determining whether a corporate acquisition constitutes either a *de facto* merger or a mere continuation is the same: whether adequate cash consideration was paid for the predecessor corporation's assets.

No California case we have found has imposed successor liability for personal injuries on a corporation that paid adequate cash consideration for the predecessor's assets. The trial court recognized this limitation to its holding, but found "no logical reason why the fact that the consideration for a purchase of corporate assets is cash (with an agreement to liquidate) rather than stock should in itself bar victims from recovering from the purchaser for the seller's tortious conduct." We, however, perceive a very sound reason for the rule of nonliability in adequate cash sales: predictability. "Predictability is vital in the corporate field. Unforeseeable alterations in successor liability principles complicate transfers and necessarily increase transaction costs. Major economic decisions, critical to society, are best made in a climate of relative certainty and reasonable predictability. The imposition of successor liability on a purchasing company long after the transfer of assets defeats the legitimate expectations the parties held during negotiation and sale. Another consequence that must be faced is that few opportunities would exist for the financially troubled company that wishes to cease business but has had its assets devalued by the extension of successor liability."

In addition, of course, a sale for adequate cash consideration ensures that at the time of sale there are adequate means to satisfy any claims made against the predecessor corporation.

In reaching its conclusion that the sale of Con Cal's assets to USX constituted a *de facto* merger, the trial court relied on *Marks v. Minnesota Mining & Manufacturing Co.* (1986) 187 Cal.App.3d 1429. In *Marks*, the court held that the corporate successor's acquisition of the predecessor's assets in exchange for stock constituted a *de facto* merger, rendering the successor liable for the plaintiff's product liability claim. The *Marks* court set forth five often-quoted factors that indicate whether a purported asset sale is the legal equivalent of a merger: "(1) was the consideration paid for the assets solely stock of the purchaser of its parent; (2) did the purchaser continue the same enterprise after the sale; (3) did the shareholders of the seller become the shareholders of the purchaser; (4) did the seller liquidate; and (5) did the buyer assume the liabilities necessary to carry on the business of the seller?" *Marks* held that the transaction before it satisfied all five factors, resulting in a *de facto* merger. In reaching its conclusion, the *Marks* court noted: "The critical fact is that while there was more than one merger or reorganization, an analysis of each transaction discloses to us that its intrinsic structure and nature, unlike a sale of assets for cash, was of a type in which the corporate entity was continued and all liability was transferred."

Marks is not alone in recognizing the overriding significance of the type and adequacy of consideration paid in a corporate asset sale. * * *

In discussing the mere continuation exception to the general rule of successor non-liability, the court in *Ray v. Alad* stated that liability has been imposed on a successor corporation "only upon a showing of one or both of the following factual elements: (1) no adequate consideration was given for the predecessor corporation's assets and made available for meeting the claims of its unsecured creditors; (2) one or more persons were officers, directors, or stockholders of both corporations." Respondents make much of the second prong enunciated by *Ray v. Alad*, asserting that the trial court properly found USX to be a mere continuation of Con Cal because Alden Roach was president and a board member of both the predecessor and the successor corporations. However, a review of the cases cited by the *Ray v. Alad* court to support its statement reveals that all of the cases involved the payment of inadequate cash consideration, and some also involved near complete identity of ownership, management or directorship after the transfer. * * * None of these cases involved a situation such as the one before us, where the consideration paid was undisputedly adequate, and only a single person with minimal ownership interest in either entity remained as an officer and director.

[A]lthough other factors are relevant to both the *de facto* merger and mere continuation exceptions, the common denominator, which must be present in order to avoid the general rule of successor non-liability, is the payment of inadequate consideration. The evidence presented showed that in 1948 Con Cal was paid in excess of $17 million for its business assets. As was the case in *Ray v. Alad*, no claim has been made that this consideration was inadequate, or that there were insufficient assets available at the time of the predecessor's dissolution to meet the claims of its creditors. Lacking the essential factor of inadequate consideration, there was no *de facto* merger [between Con Cal and Con Del], nor could USX be deemed a mere continuation of Con Cal.

QUESTIONS

1. Would USX be legally obligated to WPS's creditors if it had merged with WPS?

2. Why did the court mention that Alden Roach, president of the corporation that sold the assets, Con Cal, was the president of the corporation that bought the assets, Con Del, after the sale? Was that important?

3. Would the court have decided this case differently if Con Del had purchased the assets of Con Cal with stock instead of cash?

4. "The rationale behind the *de facto* merger exception is that when the end result of a transaction is substantially the same as a merger between two corporations * * * the court should treat the transaction as a merger for all purposes, including the automatic assumption by the purchasing corporation of all the debts of the selling corporation. An obvious problem with the *de facto* merger exception is figuring out when the sale of assets transaction looks enough like a merger to demand that the buyer assume all of the debts of the seller." Franklin Gevurtz, CORPORATION LAW 667. Does the California Court of Appeal have a problem in figuring out when a sale of assets transaction looks "enough like a merger"?

5. Suppose that you are the general counsel for McDonald's when McDonald's is considering merging with Bubba's Burritos, Inc. You have learned that Bubba's Burritos inadvertently used asbestos powder rather than flour in a substantial number of the tortillas that it served. If McDonald's still wants to proceed with joining up with Bubba's Burritos, how should the deal be structured?

2. EFFECT OF THE SALE OF ALL OR SUBSTANTIALLY ALL OF A CORPORATION'S ASSETS ON THE SHAREHOLDERS OF THE SELLING CORPORATION AND THE SHAREHOLDERS OF THE BUYING CORPORATION

The economic consequences to Bubba's Burritos, Inc. shareholders and McDonald's shareholders of a sale of assets are basically the same as the economic consequences of a merger. If Bubba's Burritos, Inc. merges into McDonald's, the shareholders of Bubba's Burritos, Inc. will receive McDonald's stock (or cash from McDonald's if it is a cash merger). Similarly, if Bubba's Burritos, Inc. sells all of its assets to McDonald's, Bubba's will receive McDonald's stock or cash from McDonald's which can be distributed to its shareholders.* Will the amount of cash or stock that shareholders receive be larger for a merger or a sale of assets?

The legal rights of Bubba's Burritos, Inc. shareholders and McDonald's shareholders in a sale of assets, however, are, in non-MBCA states, different from the legal rights of the shareholders in a merger. While corporation statutes require a corporation to obtain the approval of its shareholders to sell all or substantially all of its assets, Delaware and some other states do not provide appraisal rights for the shareholders of the selling corporation. More significantly, in Delaware and some other states, the shareholders of the buying corporation have neither appraisal rights nor the right to vote on their corporation's buying the assets. The

---

* We understand that Bubba's Burritos, Inc.'s creditors must be paid before any distribution to shareholders on dissolution. We also understand that the amount of any McDonald's stock that will be received by shareholders of Bubba's Burritos, Inc. as a result of a merger would reflect the liabilities to Bubba's Burritos, Inc.'s creditors that McDonald's assumes.

reason for this is simple: a sale of substantially all the assets is generally a fundamental change *only* for the selling corporation, and not for the buying corporation. Consequently, the shareholders of the buying corporation do not have a voice in whether the deal ought to be approved.

PROBLEM: A SALE OF ASSETS THAT ARGUABLY LOOKS LIKE A MERGER

Sellco and Buyco are Delaware corporations in the electronics business. Sellco agrees to (i) sell all of its assets to Buyco in exchange for 283,000 shares of Buyco, (ii) distribute these Buyco shares to Sellco's stockholders, and (iii) dissolve Sellco. You represent Capel, who owns 140,000 of the 280,000 outstanding shares of Buyco, and is opposed to Buyco's issuing an additional 283,000 shares and using the shares to acquire the assets of Sellco. Advise Capel. Does your advice differ depending on whether Buyco is incorporated in Delaware or in a state that has adopted the MBCA?

E. HOSTILE TAKEOVER

1. WHAT IS A HOSTILE TAKEOVER?

As we saw earlier in Chapter 7, Part C, a shareholder's selling her shares is the end of the game for that shareholder but not the corporation. If that selling shareholder is selling a majority of the outstanding shares or a controlling block of the outstanding shares, the sale can be the end of the game not only for the selling shareholder but also for the management of the corporation. The new controlling shareholder may install new directors who will then fire the corporation's existing managers. The hope is that the new managers will be able to run the company better, increasing its value for the new shareholders. Recall, for example, *Perlman v. Feldmann*, in which Wilport Company was able to obtain control over Newport Steel by buying the Feldmann family's Newport stock.

Compare Wilport's takeover of Newport by buying stock from the Feldmanns with the mergers and sales of assets that we considered earlier in this chapter. Unlike a merger or a sale of assets, the purchase of stock transaction did not require any agreement between the board of directors of Wilport and the board of directors of Newport: the only contract was between the purchasing company and the individual stockholders. Wilport could have acquired control over Newport even if the board of directors of Newport opposed the transaction.

The term "hostile takeover" is used to describe such an acquisition—gaining control over a corporation over the objection of that corporation's board of directors.* The acquiring company or individual is politely described as the "bidder," more colorfully described as the "raider" or the

---

* The phrase "hostile takeover" is also used to describe a proxy or consent solicitation of the target company's shareholders. It seeks their support of an effort to replace incumbent directors. An example is Sam Wyly's Computer Associates' proxy contest, which we discussed in Chapter 5, Part B (7)(a).

"shark." The company whose stock is targeted for acquisition is the "target company."

If the target company is a public company, the usual process for acquiring the shares is a "tender offer." In a tender offer, the bidder makes a public offer of cash or securities of the bidder (or a package of cash and securities) to the target stockholders who tender their stock. The tender offer will typically be conditioned on a sufficient number of the target's shares being tendered to ensure that the bidder gains control of the target company. The tender offer by Chesapeake Corporation to the shareholders of Shorewood Packaging described in the following press release is illustrative.

FOR IMMEDIATE RELEASE

CHESAPEAKE COMMENCES $17.25 PER SHARE CASH TENDER OFFER FOR SHOREWOOD Intends To Conduct Consent Solicitation To Remove Shorewood Board (Richmond, VA—December 3, 1999)

Chesapeake Corporation (NYSE: CSK) today announced that it has commenced a tender offer to acquire all outstanding shares of Shorewood Packaging Corporation (NYSE: SWD) for $17.25 in cash per share, or approximately $500 million. The tender offer would be followed by a second step merger at the same cash price paid in the tender offer. Upon completion of the transaction, Chesapeake would also assume approximately $270 million in Shorewood debt. The transaction can be effected by Chesapeake with cash on hand and a committed credit facility from First Union National Bank, and is not subject to a financing condition. Chesapeake's tender offer represents an approximate 45% premium to Shorewood's closing stock price on November 9, 1999, the day prior to Chesapeake's initial proposal to Shorewood's board of directors. The acquisition of Shorewood is expected to be accretive to Chesapeake's earnings per share in the first year of the combination. Based on available public information, Chesapeake anticipates annual synergies of at least $20 million from the combination of corporate and administrative functions, purchasing savings, and multiple cross-selling opportunities. * * * Thomas H. Johnson, president and chief executive officer of Chesapeake, said, "We believe Chesapeake's acquisition of Shorewood will be beneficial to shareholders, employees and customers. Chesapeake's strategy is to expand its international network of specialty packaging and merchandising services. The acquisition of Shorewood, under Chesapeake's leadership, will allow Chesapeake to provide our customers with an even larger, synergistic array of products and services. Members of our senior management team have the proven expertise to run large-scale global packaging operations. We look forward to working with Shorewood to provide value for shareholders, opportunity for employees, and excellent services and products for customers. It is our continued hope to meet with Shorewood's board to discuss this unique opportunity," concluded Mr. Johnson. The tender offer is open to all holders of common stock. The offer and withdrawal rights will expire at midnight, New York time on Monday, January 3, 2000, unless extended.

The tender offer is conditioned upon, among other things, there being validly tendered and not withdrawn before the expiration date, a number of shares which, when added to the number of shares beneficially owned by Chesapeake and its affiliates, represents a majority of Shorewood's outstanding shares on a fully diluted basis. www.sec.gov/Archives/ edgar/data/19731/0000950109–99–0 04321.txt

———————

While taking over control of a company by acquiring a majority of that target company's outstanding stock does not require action by the management of the target company's board of directors, it usually triggers such action. A target company's management often takes action to prevent a takeover. When the Shorewood board learned of Chesapeake's plans, it enacted bylaws to "better enable the Board to defend the Company against a hostile takeover."

And when the target company's board acts to prevent the takeover, the action is generally challenged in the courts. Like Chesapeake, the bidder will already own some of the target's outstanding shares. As a shareholder of the target, the bidder can challenge the actions taken by the target's board "to defend the Company against a hostile takeover" as violative of the board's fiduciary duties to its shareholders. *Chesapeake Corp. v. Shore*, 771 A.2d 293 (Del. Ch. 2000), held that the Shorewood directors breached their fiduciary duties in their response to the Chesapeake takeover threat.

Lawyers have been creative in developing (and naming) responses to takeover threats: "poison pills," "golden parachutes," "shark repellents," and "white knights." And the courts, particularly the Delaware courts, have created a body of case law on the standards to apply in reviewing challenges to these defenses.

Lawyers at the Linklaters & Alliance law firm have been even more creative in developing a comic book, "Hostile Takeover Bid," which is used as course materials for European law students. A page from this epic *Largo Winch* adventure is set out below:

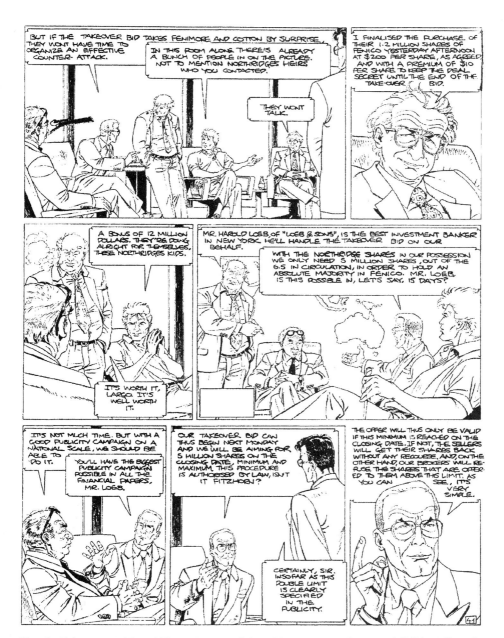

Hostile Takeover Bid by Philippe Franq and Jean Van Hamme, Franq and Editions Dupuis, 1992, p. 41.

2. TAKEOVER DEFENSES

UNOCAL CORP. v. MESA PETROLEUM CO.

Delaware Supreme Court, 1985
493 A.2d 946

MOORE, JUSTICE. We confront an issue of first impression in Delaware—the validity of a corporation's self-tender for its own shares which excludes from participation a stockholder making a hostile tender offer for the company's stock.

* * *

[Unocal Corporation ("Unocal") was the target of a takeover bid by a group of related corporations ("Mesa") controlled by T. Boone Pickens. Mesa already owned approximately 13% of Unocal's outstanding stock. Under Mesa's "two-tiered," "front loaded" tender offer, it would pay $54 per share in cash for 64,000,000 shares (approximately 37% of Unocal's outstanding stock) and then would buy the remaining Unocal stock with high risk debt securities described as "junk bonds" and valued at $54 a share. In response, the Unocal board decided to "self-tender," i.e., to offer its shareholders (or at least some of its shareholders) the opportunity to exchange their Unocal stock for debt.]

* * * The board's decisions were made in reliance on the advice of its investment bankers, including the terms and conditions upon which the securities were to be issued. Based upon this advice, and the board's own deliberations, the directors unanimously approved the exchange offer. Their resolution provided that if Mesa acquired 64 million shares of Unocal stock through its own offer (the Mesa Purchase Condition), Unocal would buy the remaining 49% outstanding for an exchange of debt securities having an aggregate par value of $72 per share. The board resolution also stated that the offer would be subject to other conditions that had been described to the board at the meeting, or which were deemed necessary by Unocal's officers, including the exclusion of Mesa from the proposal (the Mesa exclusion). * * *

Unocal's exchange offer was commenced on April 17, 1985, and Mesa promptly challenged it by filing this suit in the Court of Chancery. * * *

Another focus of the board was the Mesa exclusion. Legal counsel advised that under Delaware law Mesa could only be excluded for what the directors reasonably believed to be a valid corporate purpose. The directors' discussion centered on the objective of adequately compensating shareholders at the "back-end" of Mesa's proposal, which the latter would finance with "junk bonds". To include Mesa would defeat that goal, because under the proration aspect of the exchange offer (49%) every Mesa share accepted by Unocal would displace one held by another stockholder. Further, if Mesa were permitted to tender to Unocal, the latter would in effect be financing Mesa's own inadequate proposal. * * *

On April 29, 1985, the Vice Chancellor temporarily restrained Unocal from proceeding with the exchange offer unless it included Mesa. The trial court recognized that directors could oppose, and attempt to defeat, a hostile takeover which they considered adverse to the best interests of the corporation. However, the Vice Chancellor decided that in a selective purchase of the company's stock, the corporation bears the burden of showing: (1) a valid corporate purpose, and (2) that the transaction was fair to all of the stockholders, including those excluded.

* * *

The issues we address involve these fundamental questions: Did the Unocal board have the power and duty to oppose a takeover threat it reasonably perceived to be harmful to the corporate enterprise, and if so, is its action here entitled to the protection of the business judgment rule?

Mesa contends that the discriminatory exchange offer violates the fiduciary duties Unocal owes it. Mesa argues that because of the Mesa exclusion the business judgment rule is inapplicable, because the directors by tendering their own shares will derive a financial benefit that is not available to all Unocal stockholders. Thus, it is Mesa's ultimate contention that Unocal cannot establish that the exchange offer is fair to all shareholders, and argues that the Court of Chancery was correct in concluding that Unocal was unable to meet this burden.

Unocal answers that it does not owe a duty of "fairness" to Mesa, given the facts here. Specifically, Unocal contends that its board of directors reasonably and in good faith concluded that Mesa's $54 two-tier tender offer was coercive and inadequate, and that Mesa sought selective treatment for itself. Furthermore, Unocal argues that the board's approval of the exchange offer was made in good faith, on an informed basis, and in the exercise of due care. Under these circumstances, Unocal contends that its directors properly employed this device to protect the company and its stockholders from Mesa's harmful tactics.

* * *

When a board addresses a pending takeover bid it has an obligation to determine whether the offer is in the best interests of the corporation and its shareholders. In that respect a board's duty is no different from any other responsibility it shoulders, and its decisions should be no less entitled to the respect they otherwise would be accorded in the realm of business judgment. There are, however, certain caveats to a proper exercise of this function. Because of the omnipresent specter that a board may be acting primarily in its own interests, rather than those of the corporation and its shareholders, there is an enhanced duty which calls for judicial examination at the threshold before the protections of the business judgment rule may be conferred.

This Court has long recognized that:

We must bear in mind the inherent danger in the purchase of shares with corporate funds to remove a threat to corporate policy when a threat to control is involved. The directors are of necessity confronted with a conflict of interest, and an objective decision is difficult. In the face of this inherent conflict directors must show that they had reasonable grounds for believing that a danger to corporate policy and effectiveness existed because of another person's stock ownership. However, they satisfy that burden "by showing good faith and reasonable investigation . . . ." Furthermore, such proof is materially enhanced, as here, by the approval of a board comprised of a majority of outside independent directors who have acted in accordance with the foregoing standards.

In the board's exercise of corporate power to forestall a takeover bid our analysis begins with the basic principle that corporate directors have a fiduciary duty to act in the best interests of the corporation's stockholders. As we have noted, their duty of care extends to protecting the corporation and its owners from perceived harm whether a threat originates from third parties or other shareholders. But such powers are not absolute. A corporation does not have unbridled discretion to defeat any perceived threat by any Draconian means available.

The restriction placed upon a selective stock repurchase is that the directors may not have acted solely or primarily out of a desire to perpetuate themselves in office. Of course, to this is added the further caveat that inequitable action may not be taken under the guise of law. * * * However, this does not end the inquiry.

A further aspect is the element of balance. If a defensive measure is to come within the ambit of the business judgment rule, it must be reasonable in relation to the threat posed. This entails an analysis by the directors of the nature of the takeover bid and its effect on the corporate enterprise. Examples of such concerns may include: inadequacy of the price offered, nature and timing of the offer, questions of illegality, the impact on "constituencies" other than shareholders (i.e., creditors, customers, employees, and perhaps even the community generally), the risk of nonconsummation, and the quality of securities being offered in the exchange. While not a controlling factor, it also seems to us that a board may reasonably consider the basic stockholder interests at stake, including those of short-term speculators, whose actions may have fueled the coercive aspect of the offer at the expense of the long term investor. Here, the threat posed was viewed by the Unocal board as a grossly inadequate two-tier coercive tender offer coupled with the threat of greenmail.

Specifically, the Unocal directors had concluded that the value of Unocal was substantially above the $54 per share offered in cash at the front end. Furthermore, they determined that the subordinated securities to be exchanged in Mesa's announced squeeze out of the remaining shareholders in the "back-end" merger were "junk bonds" worth far less than $54. It is now well recognized that such offers are a classic coercive measure designed to stampede shareholders into tendering at the first tier, even if the price is inadequate, out of fear of what they will receive at the back end of the transaction. Wholly beyond the coercive aspect of an inadequate two-tier tender offer, the threat was posed by a corporate raider with a national reputation as a "greenmailer".* [13]

In adopting the selective exchange offer, the board stated that its objective was either to defeat the inadequate Mesa offer or, should the offer still succeed, provide the 49% of its stockholders, who would otherwise be forced to accept "junk bonds", with $72 worth of senior debt. We find that both purposes are valid.

However, such efforts would have been thwarted by Mesa's participation in the exchange offer. First, if Mesa could tender its shares, Unocal would effectively be subsidizing the former's continuing effort to buy Unocal stock at $54 per share. Second, Mesa could not, by definition, fit within the class of shareholders being protected from its own coercive and inadequate tender offer.

Thus, we are satisfied that the selective exchange offer is reasonably related to the threats posed. It is consistent with the principle that "the minority stockholder shall receive the substantial equivalent in value of what he had before." This concept of fairness, while stated in the merger context, is also relevant in the area of tender offer law. Thus, the board's decision to offer what it determined to be the fair value of the corporation to the 49% of its shareholders, who would otherwise be forced to accept highly subordinated "junk bonds", is reasonable and consistent with the directors' duty to ensure that the minority stockholders receive equal value for their shares.

Mesa contends that it is unlawful, and the trial court agreed, for a corporation to discriminate in this fashion against one shareholder. It argues correctly that no case has ever sanctioned a device that precludes a raider from sharing in a benefit available to all other stockholders. * * *

However, our corporate law is not static. It must grow and develop in response to, indeed in anticipation of, evolving concepts and needs. Merely because the General Corporation Law is silent as to a specific matter does not mean that it is prohibited.

More recently, as the sophistication of both raiders and targets has developed, a host of other defensive measures to counter such ever-mounting threats has evolved and received judicial sanction. These include defensive charter amendments and other devices bearing some rather exotic, but apt, names: Crown Jewel, White Knight, Pac Man, and Golden Parachute. Each has highly selective features, the object of which is to deter or defeat the raider.

Thus, while the exchange offer is a form of selective treatment, given the nature of the threat posed here the response is neither unlawful nor

---

* [13] The term "greenmail" refers to the practice of buying out a takeover bidder's stock at a premium that is not available to other shareholders in order to prevent the takeover. The Chancery Court noted that "Mesa has made tremendous profits from its takeover activities although in the past few years it has not been successful in acquiring any of the target companies on an unfriendly basis." Moreover, the trial court specifically found that the actions of the Unocal board were taken in good faith to eliminate both the inadequacies of the tender offer and to forestall the payment of "greenmail".

unreasonable. If the board of directors is disinterested, has acted in good faith and with due care, its decision in the absence of an abuse of discretion will be upheld as a proper exercise of business judgment.

To this Mesa responds that the board is not disinterested, because the directors are receiving a benefit from the tender of their own shares, which because of the Mesa exclusion, does not devolve upon all stockholders equally. However, Mesa concedes that if the exclusion is valid, then the directors and all other stockholders share the same benefit. The answer of course is that the exclusion is valid, and the directors' participation in the exchange offer does not rise to the level of a disqualifying interest.

Nor does this become an "interested" director transaction merely because certain board members are large stockholders. As this Court has previously noted, that fact alone does not create a disqualifying "personal pecuniary interest" to defeat the operation of the business judgment rule.

Mesa also argues that the exclusion permits the directors to abdicate the fiduciary duties they owe it. However, that is not so. The board continues to owe Mesa the duties of due care and loyalty. But in the face of the destructive threat Mesa's tender offer was perceived to pose, the board had a supervening duty to protect the corporate enterprise, which includes the other shareholders, from threatened harm.

Mesa contends that the basis of this action is punitive, and solely in response to the exercise of its rights of corporate democracy. Nothing precludes Mesa, as a stockholder, from acting in its own self-interest. However, Mesa, while pursuing its own interests, has acted in a manner which a board consisting of a majority of independent directors has reasonably determined to be contrary to the best interests of Unocal and its other shareholders. In this situation, there is no support in Delaware law for the proposition that, when responding to a perceived harm, a corporation must guarantee a benefit to a stockholder who is deliberately provoking the danger being addressed. There is no obligation of self-sacrifice by a corporation and its shareholders in the face of such a challenge.

* * *

Here, the Court of Chancery specifically found that the "directors' decision [to oppose the Mesa tender offer] was made in the good faith belief that the Mesa tender offer is inadequate." We are satisfied that Unocal's board has met its burden of proof.

In conclusion, there was directorial power to oppose the Mesa tender offer, and to undertake a selective stock exchange made in good faith and upon a reasonable investigation pursuant to a clear duty to protect the corporate enterprise. Further, the selective stock repurchase plan chosen by Unocal is reasonable in relation to the threat that the board rationally and reasonably believed was posed by Mesa's inadequate and coercive two-tier tender offer.

Under those circumstances the board's action is entitled to be measured by the standards of the business judgment rule. Thus, unless it is shown by a preponderance of the evidence that the directors' decisions were primarily based on perpetuating themselves in office, or some other breach of fiduciary duty such as fraud, overreaching, lack of good faith, or being uninformed, a Court will not substitute its judgment for that of the board.

In this case that protection is not lost merely because Unocal's directors have tendered their shares in the exchange offer. Given the validity of the Mesa exclusion, they are receiving a benefit shared generally by all other stockholders except Mesa. If the stockholders are displeased with the action of their elected representatives, the powers of corporate democracy are at their disposal to turn the board out.

With the Court of Chancery's findings that the exchange offer was based on the board's good faith belief that the Mesa offer was inadequate, that the board's action was informed and taken with due care, that Mesa's prior activities justify a reasonable inference that its principle objective was greenmail, and implicitly, that the substance of the offer itself was reasonable and fair to the corporation and its stockholders if Mesa were included, we cannot say that the Unocal directors have acted in such a manner as to have passed an "unintelligent and unadvised judgment". The decision of the Court of Chancery is therefore REVERSED, and the preliminary injunction is VACATED.

QUESTIONS AND NOTES

1. Questions about the facts

1.1 If you were a Unocal shareholder, would you have tendered your shares? To whom?

1.2 How did the Unocal board's action adversely affect Mesa?

2. Questions about the law

2.1 Is the *Unocal* two-part test to determine the validity of takeover defenses test different from the business judgment rule?

2.2 Is the Delaware court's approach to takeover defenses in *Unocal* different from the American Law Institute's approach to takeover defenses in the ALI PRINCIPLES OF CORPORATE GOVERNANCE § 6.02.

§ 6.02 Action of Directors That Has the Foreseeable Effect of Blocking Unsolicited Tender Offers

(a) The board of directors may take an action that has the foreseeable effect of blocking an unsolicited tender offer, if the action is a reasonable response to the offer.

(b) In considering whether its action is a reasonable response to the offer:

(1) The board may take into account all factors relevant to the best interests of the corporation and shareholders, including, among other

things, questions of legality and whether the offer, if successful, would threaten the corporation's essential economic prospects; and

(2) The board may * * * have regard for interests or groups (other than shareholders) with respect to which the corporation has a legitimate concern if to do so would not significantly disfavor the long-term interests of shareholders.

(c) A person who challenges an action of the board on the ground that it fails to satisfy the standards of Subsection (a) has he burden of proof that the board's action is an unreasonable response to the offer.

(d) An action that does not meet the standards of Subsection (a) may be enjoined or set aside, but directors who authorize such an action are not subject to liability for damages if their conduct meets the standard of the business judgment rule.

2.3   Would the court have ruled differently if Mesa had simply made a tender offer of $73 per share in cash for 64 million shares? Would the court have ruled differently if Mesa had made a tender offer of $54 in cash for any and all shares tendered so long as least 64 million shares are tendered?

2.4   We edited out the fact that "Unocal's board consists of eight independent outside directors and six insiders." Should we have edited out that fact?

3. Notes

3.1   Recall that a bond is a form of debt. A "junk bond" is a high risk/high yield form of debt.

3.2   The SEC has in effect nullified the ruling of *Unocal*. After the *Unocal* decision, the SEC prohibited issuer tender offers that are not made to all shareholders. *See* Rule 13e–4(f)(8).

3.3   Notwithstanding the later SEC rule on discriminatory self-tenders, courts continue to look to the reasoning of *Unocal* in ruling on takeover defenses.

In the *Chesapeake* case in February 2000, the Delaware Chancery Court relied in part on *Unocal*. Recall that Chesapeake made an unsolicited tender offer for Shorewood stock. The Shorewood board then implemented a package of takeover defenses, including a supermajority bylaw provision requiring a two-thirds stockholder vote to amend its bylaws. Chesapeake then increased its offer for Shorewood shares, initiated a consent solicitation to unseat Shorewood's then-current board, and filed suit challenging the supermajority bylaw as a violation of the Shorewood board's fiduciary duties.

The Delaware Chancery Court stated, "[A] board's unilateral decision to adopt a defensive measure ... is strongly suspect under Unocal, and cannot be sustained without a compelling justification." And, after applying the two-step *Unocal* test, the court found that the supermajority bylaw was a wholly inappropriate response to Chesapeake's takeover attempt.

Shorewood argued that the offer constituted a legitimate threat because (1) the offer was coercive as it created substantial stockholder confusion and (2) the price of the offer was inadequate. The court rejected Shorewood's assertion that substantial stockholder confusion was a threat as a "post hoc, litigation-inspired rationale." Because Shorewood's stock was largely held by institutional investors, Shorewood's stock was covered by analysts from major brokerage houses so that Shorewood's management had ample opportunity to address any purported confusion through public disclosure. However, the court did find merit in Shorewood's argument that the inadequate price of Chesapeake's offer posed a threat, although the court characterized this threat as "mild."

The court then compared this "mild threat" to the board's response of the supermajority bylaw. The court held that, compared to the mild threat, the board's actions were too aggressive and unduly preclusive: "[T]he board could have selected a level within the realm of reason understandable by citizens of a republican democracy." Chesapeake Corp. v. Shore, 771 A.2d 293, 344 (Del Ch. 2000). *See generally* Dennis J. Block & Jonathan M. Hoff, *Judicial Review of Interference with Shareholder Franchise*, New York Law Journal, May 4, 2000.

3.4 In both *Unocal* and *Chesapeake*, the target board was making decisions with respect to dealing with a hostile bidder. In the next three cases, the target boards are making decisions with respect to competing bids or strategic combinations.

REVLON, INC. v. MacANDREWS & FORBES HOLDINGS, INC.

Delaware Supreme Court, 1986
506 A.2d 173

Moore, Justice. [The story starts in summer 1985, with a "bear hug," an uninvited (and unwelcome) overture by Pantry Pride Inc.'s chief executive officer, Ronald O. Perlman, to Revlon, Inc.'s chief executive officer concerning Pantry's Pride's acquiring Revlon for a price in the range of $40 to $45 a share. The Revlon board of directors* [3] met with the company's investment banker, Felix Rohatyn, who advised them that $45 a share was a "grossly inadequate price" and the company's special counsel, Martin Lipton, who recommended, inter alia,† [4] that Revlon purchase stock in exchange for notes.

On August 23, Pantry Pride made its tender offer. On August 29, Revlon commenced its own tender offer.

During September, the Revlon shareholders had tender offers from Pantry Pride at $47.50 in cash for each share and from Revlon for Senior Subordinated Notes ("Notes") with a face value of $47.50 and 1/10th of a

---

* [3] There were 14 directors on the Revlon board. Six of them held senior management positions with the company, and two others held significant blocks of its stock. Four of the remaining six directors were associated at some point with entities that had various business relationships with Revlon. On the basis of this limited record, however, we cannot conclude that this board is entitled to certain presumptions that generally attach to the decisions of a board whose majority consists of truly outside independent directors."

† [4] Mr. Lipton also recommended a "poison pill." A "poison pill," also known as a Rights Plan, is action by the target's board that creates rights in the target's existing shareholders, other than the bidder, to acquire debt or stock of the target at bargain price upon the occurrence of specified events such as the bidder's acquisition of a specified percentage of the target's stock.

share of preferred stock with a stated value of $100 per share for each share. The Notes contained covenants restricting Revlon's ability to incur additional debt, to sell assets, or to pay dividends unless approved by Revlon's "independent directors."

While Pantry Pride and Revlon were increasing their bids to the Revlon shareholders, other bidders were also making bids to the Revlon board. On October 3, Revlon agreed to a leveraged buyout‡ with Forstmann Little & Co. at $56 per share in cash. Under the terms of the buyout, Fortsmann Little would assume Revlon's debt incurred in the issuance of the Notes and Revlon would waive the restrictive covenants in the Notes for Fortsmann.

When Revlon announced the leveraged buyout, it also announced that it would eliminate the Note covenants to facilitate the leveraged buyout and would do the same for any other offer which provided more than $56 per share to Revlon shareholders. After this announcement, the value of the Notes plummeted and people who had tendered their Revlon stock to Revlon in exchange for the Notes threatened to sue Revlon and its board.

Pantry Pride revised its offer to $56.25 per share conditioned on the same elimination of the subordinated note covenants. Forstmann Little responded by increasing its bid to $57.25, and by offering to support the market price of the Notes by making an exchange offer for them.

To end the auction, Forstmann Little said it would withdraw this new offer if it were not immediately accepted and imposed conditions on this new offer, including:

> (1) a "no-shop clause", i.e., Revlon would not shop around for a more attractive deal, and
>
> (2) a "break-up fee", i.e., Revlon would pay Fortsmann Little $25,000,000 if the deal fell through, and
>
> (3) a "lock up" of the "crown jewels", i.e., Fortsmann had an option to buy two divisions of Revlon, Vision Care and National Health Laboratories, exercisable for $525 million when any other person or group acquired 40% of Revlon's shares.

Revlon accepted Forstmann Little's offer, and Pantry Pride sued.]

In this battle for corporate control of Revlon, Inc. (Revlon), the Court of Chancery enjoined certain transactions designed to thwart the efforts of Pantry Pride, Inc. (Pantry Pride) to acquire Revlon. The defendants are Revlon, its board of directors, and Forstmann Little & Co. and the latter's affiliated limited partnership (collectively, Forstmann). The injunction barred consummation of an option granted Forstmann to purchase certain Revlon assets (the lock-up option), a promise by Revlon to deal exclusively with Forstmann in the face of a takeover (the no-shop provision), and the payment of a $25 million cancellation fee to Forstmann if the transaction was aborted. The Court of Chancery found that the Revlon directors had

---

‡ Authors' note: In the typical "leveraged buyout," the acquiring entity uses borrowed funds to acquire another entity, using the assets of the acquired entity as collateral for that borrowing.

breached their duty of care by entering into the foregoing transactions and effectively ending an active auction for the company. The trial court ruled that such arrangements are not illegal per se under Delaware law, but that their use under the circumstances here was impermissible. We agree. Thus, we granted this expedited interlocutory appeal to consider for the first time the validity of such defensive measures in the face of an active bidding contest for corporate control. Additionally, we address for the first time the extent to which a corporation may consider the impact of a takeover threat on constituencies other than shareholders. *See Unocal Corp. v. Mesa Petroleum Co.*, Del.Supr., 493 A.2d 946, 955 (1985).

In our view, lock-ups and related agreements are permitted under Delaware law where their adoption is untainted by director interest or other breaches of fiduciary duty. The actions taken by the Revlon directors, however, did not meet this standard. Moreover, while concern for various corporate constituencies is proper when addressing a takeover threat, that principle is limited by the requirement that there be some rationally related benefit accruing to the stockholders. We find no such benefit here.

Thus, under all the circumstances we must agree with the Court of Chancery that the enjoined Revlon defensive measures were inconsistent with the directors' duties to the stockholders. Accordingly, we affirm.

* * * While the business judgment rule may be applicable to the actions of corporate directors responding to takeover threats, the principles upon which it is founded—care, loyalty and independence—must first be satisfied.

If the business judgment rule applies, there is a "presumption that in making a business decision the directors of a corporation acted on an informed basis, in good faith and in the honest belief that the action taken was in the best interests of the company." However, when a board implements anti-takeover measures there arises "the omnipresent specter that a board may be acting primarily in its own interests, rather than those of the corporation and its shareholders...." This potential for conflict places upon the directors the burden of proving that they had reasonable grounds for believing there was a danger to corporate policy and effectiveness, a burden satisfied by a showing of good faith and reasonable investigation. In addition, the directors must analyze the nature of the takeover and its effect on the corporation in order to ensure balance—that the responsive action taken is reasonable in relation to the threat posed.

* * *

[A] defensive measure adopted by Revlon to thwart a Pantry Pride takeover was the company's own exchange offer for 10 million of its shares. The directors' general broad powers to manage the business and affairs of the corporation are augmented by the specific authority conferred under 8 Del.C. § 160(a), permitting the company to deal in its own stock. However, when exercising that power in an effort to forestall a hostile takeover, the board's actions are strictly held to the fiduciary standards outlined in Unocal. These standards require the directors to determine the best interests of the corporation and its stockholders, and impose an enhanced duty to abjure any action that is motivated by considerations other than a good faith concern for such interests.

The Revlon directors concluded that Pantry Pride's $47.50 offer was grossly inadequate. In that regard the board acted in good faith, and on an informed basis, with reasonable grounds to believe that there existed a harmful threat to the corporate enterprise. The adoption of a defensive measure, reasonable in relation to the threat posed, was proper and fully accorded with the powers, duties, and responsibilities conferred upon directors under our law.

However, when Pantry Pride increased its offer to $50 per share, and then to $53, it became apparent to all that the break-up of the company was inevitable. The Revlon board's authorization permitting management to negotiate a merger or buyout with a third party was a recognition that the company was for sale. The duty of the board had thus changed from the preservation of Revlon as a corporate entity to the maximization of the company's value at a sale for the stockholders' benefit. This significantly altered the board's responsibilities under the Unocal standards. It no longer faced threats to corporate policy and effectiveness, or to the stockholders' interests, from a grossly inadequate bid. The whole question of defensive measures became moot. The directors' role changed from defenders of the corporate bastion to auctioneers charged with getting the best price for the stockholders at a sale of the company.

This brings us to the lock-up with Forstmann and its emphasis on shoring up the sagging market value of the Notes in the face of threatened litigation by their holders. Such a focus was inconsistent with the changed concept of the directors' responsibilities at this stage of the developments. The impending waiver of the Notes covenants had caused the value of the Notes to fall, and the board was aware of the noteholders' ire as well as their subsequent threats of suit. The directors thus made support of the Notes an integral part of the company's dealings with Forstmann, even though their primary responsibility at this stage was to the equity owners.

The original threat posed by Pantry Pride—the break-up of the company—had become a reality which even the directors embraced. Selective dealing to fend off a hostile but determined bidder was no longer a proper objective. Instead, obtaining the highest price for the benefit of the stockholders should have been the central theme guiding director action. Thus, the Revlon board could not make the requisite showing of good faith by preferring the noteholders and ignoring its duty of loyalty to the shareholders. The rights of the former already were fixed by contract. The noteholders required no further protection, and when the Revlon board entered into an auction-ending lock-up agreement with Forstmann on the basis of impermissible considerations at the expense of the shareholders, the directors breached their primary duty of loyalty.

The Revlon board argued that it acted in good faith in protecting the noteholders because Unocal permits consideration of other corporate constituencies. Although such considerations may be permissible, there are fundamental limitations upon that prerogative. A board may have regard for various constituencies in discharging its responsibilities, provided there are rationally related benefits accruing to the stockholders. However, such concern for non-stockholder interests is inappropriate when an auction among active bidders is in progress, and the object no longer is to protect or maintain the corporate enterprise but to sell it to the highest bidder.

Revlon also contended that it had contractual and good faith obligations to consider the noteholders. However, any such duties are limited to the principle that one may not interfere with contractual relationships by improper actions. Here, the rights of the noteholders were fixed by agreement, and there is nothing of substance to suggest that any of those terms were violated. The Notes covenants specifically contemplated a waiver to permit sale of the company at a fair price. The Notes were accepted by the holders on that basis, including the risk of an adverse market effect stemming from a waiver. Thus, nothing remained for Revlon to legitimately protect, and no rationally related benefit thereby accrued to the stockholders. Under such circumstances we must conclude that the merger agreement with Forstmann was unreasonable in relation to the threat posed.

A lock-up is not per se illegal under Delaware law. Such options can entice other bidders to enter a contest for control of the corporation, creating an auction for the company and maximizing shareholder profit. Current economic conditions in the takeover market are such that a "white knight" like Forstmann might only enter the bidding for the target company if it receives some form of compensation to cover the risks and costs involved. However, while those lock-ups which draw bidders into the battle benefit shareholders, similar measures which end an active auction and foreclose further bidding operate to the shareholders' detriment.
* * *

The Forstmann option had a destructive effect on the auction process. Forstmann had already been drawn into the contest on a preferred basis, so the result of the lock-up was not to foster bidding, but to destroy it. The board's stated reasons for approving the transactions were: (1) better financing, (2) noteholder protection, and (3) higher price. As the Court of Chancery found, and we agree, any distinctions between the rival bidders' methods of financing the proposal were nominal at best, and such a consideration has little or no significance in a cash offer for any and all shares. The principal object, contrary to the board's duty of care, appears to have been protection of the noteholders over the shareholders' interests.

While Forstmann's $57.25 offer was objectively higher than Pantry Pride's $56.25 bid, the margin of superiority is less when the Forstmann price is adjusted for the time value of money. In reality, the Revlon board ended the auction in return for very little actual improvement in the final bid. The principal benefit went to the directors, who avoided personal liability to a class of creditors to whom the board owed no further duty under the circumstances. Thus, when a board ends an intense bidding contest on an insubstantial basis, and where a significant by-product of that action is to protect the directors against a perceived threat of personal liability for consequences stemming from the adoption of previous defensive measures, the action cannot withstand the enhanced scrutiny which Unocal requires of director conduct.

In addition to the lock-up option, the Court of Chancery enjoined the no-shop provision as part of the attempt to foreclose further bidding by Pantry Pride. The no-shop provision, like the lock-up option, while not per se illegal, is impermissible under the Unocal standards when a board's primary duty becomes that of an auctioneer responsible for selling the company to the highest bidder. The agreement to negotiate only with Forstmann ended rather than intensified the board's involvement in the bidding contest.

It is ironic that the parties even considered a no-shop agreement when Revlon had dealt preferentially, and almost exclusively, with Forstmann throughout the contest. After the directors authorized management to negotiate with other parties, Forstmann was given every negotiating advantage that Pantry Pride had been denied: cooperation from management, access to financial data, and the exclusive opportunity to present merger proposals directly to the board of directors. Favoritism for a white knight to the total exclusion of a hostile bidder might be justifiable when the latter's offer adversely affects shareholder interests, but when bidders make relatively similar offers, or dissolution of the company becomes inevitable, the directors cannot fulfill their enhanced Unocal duties by playing favorites with the contending factions. Market forces must be allowed to operate freely to bring the target's shareholders the best price available for their equity. Thus, as the trial court ruled, the shareholders' interests necessitated that the board remain free to negotiate in the fulfillment of that duty.

The court below similarly enjoined the payment of the cancellation fee, pending a resolution of the merits, because the fee was part of the overall plan to thwart Pantry Pride's efforts. We find no abuse of discretion in that ruling. * * *

In conclusion, the Revlon board was confronted with a situation not uncommon in the current wave of corporate takeovers. A hostile and determined bidder sought the company at a price the board was convinced was inadequate. The initial defensive tactics worked to the benefit of the shareholders, and thus the board was able to sustain its Unocal burdens in justifying those measures. However, in granting an asset option lock-up to Forstmann, we must conclude that under all the circumstances the directors allowed considerations other than the maximization of shareholder profit to affect their judgment, and followed a course that ended the auction for Revlon, absent court intervention, to the ultimate detriment of its shareholders. In that context the board's action is not entitled to the deference accorded it by the business judgment rule. The measures were properly enjoined. The decision of the Court of Chancery, therefore, is AFFIRMED.

QUESTIONS AND NOTES

1. Did any members of the Revlon board realize a personal benefit from the board's approval of the Fortsmann proposal instead of the Pantry Pride tender offer? Was the Fortsmann proposal more favorable to the former shareholders who now held Notes?

2. Did the court apply the business judgment rule? Did the court apply the *Unocal* decision?

3. In a well-known economic study, two professors concluded that greenmail actually creates benefit for stockholders. Jonathan Macey and Fred McChesney, *A Theoretical Analysis of Corporate Greenmail*, 95 YALE L.J. 13 (1985).

4. In a business deal closely followed by some, Frederick's of Hollywood, Inc. became a target in a bidding contest. A group of Frederick's shareholders sued Frederick's directors, alleging breach of fiduciary duty and duty of care. In affirming the dismissal of the complaint, the Delaware Supreme Court offered the following "explanation" of *Revlon*:

> The central claim in the amended complaint is that the sale of Frederick's to Knightsbridge "constituted a breach of [the Frederick's board's] fiduciary obligation to maximize shareholder value" because the board did not "conduct an auction with a "level playing field" as required by Revlon, Inc. v. MacAndrews & Forbes Holdings. The plaintiffs contend that this sort of allegation cannot be neatly divided into duty of care claims and duty of loyalty claims.
>
> In our view, Revlon neither creates a new type of fiduciary duty in the sale-of-control context nor alters the nature of the fiduciary duties that generally apply. Rather, Revlon emphasizes that the board must perform its fiduciary duties in the service of a specific objective: maximizing the sale price of the enterprise. Although the Revlon doctrine imposes enhanced judicial scrutiny of certain transactions involving a sale of control, it does not eliminate the requirement that plaintiffs plead sufficient facts to support the underlying claims for a breach of fiduciary duties in conducting the sale. * * *
>
> The complaint alleges that "Frederick's representatives expressed concern that if Frederick's approved the [June 15, 1997] Merger Agreement in favor of a transaction with Veritas, Knightsbridge would sue Frederick's and its directors." The plaintiffs argue that this allegation supports a reasonable inference that the directors' individual interests in avoiding personal liability to Knightsbridge influenced their decision to approve the Knightsbridge merger.

Except in egregious cases, the threat of personal liability for approving a merger transaction does not in itself provide a sufficient basis to question the disinterestedness of directors because the risk of litigation is present whenever a board decides to sell the company. * * * We therefore conclude that the facts alleged in the complaint do not state a cognizable claim that the directors acted in their own personal interests rather than in the best interests of the stockholders when they approved the Knightsbridge merger.

Malpiede v. Townson, 2001 WL 995264 (Del. 2001).

5. Under *Revlon*, do the directors of a corporation owe any fiduciary duty to the corporation's creditors?

6. At what point does a director's role change "from defenders of the corporate bastion" to auctioneers charged with getting the best price for the stockholders at a sale of the company? Reconsider your answer after considering each of the next two cases.

PARAMOUNT COMMUNICATIONS, INC. v. TIME, INC.

Delaware Supreme Court, 1989
571 A.2d 1140

HORSEY, JUSTICE. Paramount Communications, Inc. ("Paramount") and two other groups of plaintiffs ("Shareholder Plaintiffs"), shareholders of Time Incorporated ("Time"), a Delaware corporation, separately filed suits in the Delaware Court of Chancery seeking a preliminary injunction to halt Time's tender offer for 51% of Warner Communication, Inc.'s ("Warner") outstanding shares at $70 cash per share. * * * [T]he Chancellor refused to enjoin Time's consummation of its tender offer, concluding that the plaintiffs were unlikely to prevail on the merits.

* * * The principal ground for reversal, asserted by all plaintiffs, is that Paramount's June 7, 1989 uninvited all-cash, all-shares, "fully negotiable" (though conditional) tender offer for Time triggered duties under *Unocal Corp. v. Mesa Petroleum Co.*, Del.Supr., 493 A.2d 946 (1985), and that Time's board of directors, in responding to Paramount's offer, breached those duties. As a consequence, plaintiffs argue that in our review of the Time board's decision of June 16, 1989 to enter into a revised merger agreement with Warner, Time is not entitled to the benefit and protection of the business judgment rule.

Shareholder Plaintiffs also assert a claim based on *Revlon v. MacAndrews & Forbes Holdings, Inc.*, Del.Supr., 506 A.2d 173 (1986). They argue that the original Time–Warner merger agreement of March 4, 1989 resulted in a change of control which effectively put Time up for sale, thereby triggering Revlon duties. Those plaintiffs argue that Time's board breached its Revlon duties by failing, in the face of the change of control, to maximize shareholder value in the immediate term.

* * * [W]e affirm the Chancellor's ultimate finding and conclusion under *Unocal*. We find that Paramount's tender offer was reasonably perceived by Time's board to pose a threat to Time and that the Time

board's "response" to that threat was, under the circumstances, reasonable and proportionate. Applying *Unocal*, we reject the argument that the only corporate threat posed by an all-shares, all-cash tender offer is the possibility of inadequate value.

We also find that Time's board did not by entering into its initial merger agreement with Warner come under a Revlon duty either to auction the company or to maximize short-term shareholder value, notwithstanding the unequal share exchange. Therefore, the Time board's original plan of merger with Warner was subject only to a business judgment rule analysis. Time is a Delaware corporation. During the relevant time period, Time's board consisted of sixteen directors. Twelve of the directors were "outside," nonemployee directors.

* * * As early as 1983 and 1984, Time's executive board began considering expanding Time's operations into the entertainment industry. In 1987, Time established a special committee of executives to consider and propose corporate strategies for the 1990s. The consensus of the committee was that Time should move ahead in the area of ownership and creation of video programming. [Time met with several companies in the communications industry and decided that Warner was the best candidate.]

* * * From the outset, Time's board favored an all-cash or cash and securities acquisition of Warner as the basis for consolidation. Warner insisted on a stock swap in order to preserve its shareholders' equity in the resulting corporation. Time's officers, on the other hand, made it abundantly clear that Time would be the acquiring corporation and that Time would control the resulting board. Time refused to permit itself to be cast as the "acquired" company.

Eventually Time acquiesced in Warner's insistence on a stock-for-stock deal, but talks broke down over corporate governance issues. Ross, however, refused to set a time for his retirement and viewed Time's proposal as indicating a lack of confidence in his leadership. Warner considered it vital that their executives and creative staff not perceive Warner as selling out to Time. Time's request of a guarantee that Time would dominate the CEO succession was objected to as inconsistent with the concept of a Time–Warner merger "of equals." Negotiations ended when the parties reached an impasse. Time's board refused to compromise on its position on corporate governance. Time, and particularly its outside directors, viewed the corporate governance provisions as critical for preserving the "Time Culture" through a pro-Time management at the top. Throughout the fall of 1988 Time pursued its plan of expansion into the entertainment field; Time held informal discussions with several companies, including Paramount. Capital Cities/ABC approached Time to propose a merger. Talks terminated, however, when Capital Cities/ABC suggested that it was interested in purchasing Time or in controlling the resulting board. Time steadfastly maintained it was not placing itself up for sale. Warner and Time resumed negotiations in January 1989. * * *

Time insider directors Levin and Nicholas met with Warner's financial advisors to decide upon a stock exchange ratio. Time's board had recognized the potential need to pay a premium in the stock ratio in exchange for dictating the governing arrangement of the new Time–Warner. * * * The parties ultimately agreed upon an exchange rate favoring Warner of .465. On that basis, Warner stockholders would have owned approximately 62% of the common stock of Time–Warner.

On March 3, 1989, Time's board, with all but one director in attendance, met and unanimously approved the stock-for-stock merger with Warner. Warner's board likewise approved the merger. The agreement called for Warner to be merged into a wholly-owned Time subsidiary with Warner becoming the surviving corporation. The common stock of Warner would then be converted into common stock of Time at the agreed upon ratio. Thereafter, the name of Time would be changed to Time–Warner, Inc.

The rules of the New York Stock Exchange required that Time's issuance of shares to effectuate the merger be approved by a vote of Time's stockholders. The Delaware General Corporation Law required approval of the merger by a majority of the Warner stockholders. Delaware law did not require any vote by Time stockholders. The Chancellor concluded that the agreement was the product of "an arms-length negotiation between two parties seeking individual advantage through mutual action."

The resulting company would have a 24–member board, with 12 members representing each corporation. The company would have co-CEO's, after Ross' retirement, by Nicholas alone. * * *

At its March 3, 1989 meeting, Time's board adopted several defensive tactics. Time entered an automatic share exchange agreement with Warner. Time would receive 17,292,747 shares of Warner's outstanding common stock (9.4%) and Warner would receive 7,080,016 shares of Time's outstanding common stock (11.1%). Either party could trigger the exchange. Time sought out and paid for "confidence" letters from various banks with which it did business. In these letters, the banks promised not to finance any third-party attempt to acquire Time. Time argues these agreements served only to preserve the confidential relationship between itself and the banks. The Chancellor found these agreements to be inconsequential and futile attempts to "dry up" money for a hostile takeover. Time also agreed to a "no-shop" clause, preventing Time from considering any other consolidation proposal, thus relinquishing its power to consider other proposals, regardless of their merits. Time did so at Warner's insistence. Warner did not want to be left "on the auction block" for an unfriendly suitor, if Time were to withdraw from the deal.

Time's board simultaneously established a special committee of outside directors, Finkelstein, Kearns, and Opel, to oversee the merger. The committee's assignment was to resolve any impediments that might arise in the course of working out the details of the merger and its consummation.

* * * Time's board was unanimously in favor of the proposed merger with Warner; and, by the end of May, the Time–Warner merger appeared to be an accomplished fact. On June 7, 1989, these wishful assumptions were shattered by Paramount's surprising announcement of its all-cash offer to purchase all outstanding shares of Time for $175 per share. The following day, June 8, the trading price of Time's stock rose from $126 to $170 per share.

* * *

[The Time board of directors met several times and

- concluded that Paramount's $175 offer was "inadequate" and that "Paramount's bid posed a threat to Time's control of its own destiny and retention of the "Time Culture"";

- expressed concern that "Time stockholders would not comprehend the long-term benefits of the Warner merger" and that Paramount's "cash premium would be a tempting prospect" to the institutional investors who held large quantities of Time stock.]

At the same meeting, Time's board decided to recast its consolidation with Warner into an outright cash and securities acquisition of Warner by Time; and Time so informed Warner. Time accordingly restructured its proposal to acquire Warner as follows: Time would make an immediate all-cash offer for 51% of Warner's outstanding stock at $70 per share. The remaining 49% would be purchased at some later date for a mixture of cash and securities worth $70 per share. To provide the funds required for its outright acquisition of Warner, Time would assume 7–10 billion dollars worth of debt, thus eliminating one of the principal transaction-related benefits of the original merger agreement. Nine billion dollars of the total purchase price would be allocated to the purchase of Warner's goodwill.

Warner agreed but insisted on certain terms. Warner sought a control premium and guarantees that the governance provisions found in the original merger agreement would remain intact. * * * For its part, Time was assured of its ability to extend its efforts into production areas and international markets, all the while maintaining the Time identity and culture. The Chancellor found the initial Time–Warner transaction to have been negotiated at arm's-length and the restructured Time–Warner transaction to have resulted from Paramount's offer and its expected effect on a Time shareholder vote.

On June 23, 1989, Paramount raised its all-cash offer to buy Time's outstanding stock to $200 per share. Paramount still professed that all aspects of the offer were negotiable. Time's board met on June 26, 1989 and formally rejected Paramount's $200 per share second offer. The board reiterated its belief that, despite the $25 increase, the offer was still inadequate. The Time board maintained that the Warner transaction offered a greater long-term value for the stockholders and, unlike Paramount's offer, did not pose a threat to Time's survival and its "culture." Paramount then filed this action in the Court of Chancery.

The Shareholder Plaintiffs first assert a *Revlon* claim. They contend that the March 4 Time–Warner agreement effectively put Time up for sale, triggering *Revlon* duties, requiring Time's board to enhance short-term shareholder value and to treat all other interested acquirors on an equal basis. The Shareholder Plaintiffs base this argument on two facts: (i) the ultimate Time–Warner exchange ratio of .465 favoring Warner, resulting in Warner shareholders' receipt of 62% of the combined company; and (ii) the subjective intent of Time's directors as evidenced in their statements that the market might perceive the Time–Warner merger as putting Time up "for sale" and their adoption of various defensive measures.

The Shareholder Plaintiffs further contend that Time's directors, in structuring the original merger transaction to be "takeover-proof," triggered *Revlon* duties by foreclosing their shareholders from any prospect of obtaining a control premium. In short, plaintiffs argue that Time's board's decision to merge with Warner imposed a fiduciary duty to maximize immediate share value and not erect unreasonable barriers to further bids. * * *

Paramount asserts only a *Unocal* claim in which the shareholder plaintiffs join. Paramount contends that the Chancellor, in applying the first part of the *Unocal* test, erred in finding that Time's board had reasonable grounds to believe that Paramount posed both a legally cognizable threat to Time shareholders and a danger to Time's corporate policy and effectiveness. Paramount also contests the court's finding that Time's board made a reasonable and objective investigation of Paramount's offer so as to be informed before rejecting it. Paramount further claims that the court erred in applying *Unocal*'s second part in finding Time's response to be "reasonable." Paramount points primarily to the preclusive effect of the revised agreement which denied Time shareholders the opportunity both to vote on the agreement and to respond to Paramount's tender offer. Paramount argues that the underlying motivation of Time's board in adopting these defensive measures was management's desire to perpetuate itself in office.

The Court of Chancery posed the pivotal question presented by this case to be: Under what circumstances must a board of directors abandon an in-place plan of corporate development in order to provide its shareholders with the option to elect and realize an immediate control premium? As applied to this case, the question becomes: Did Time's board, having developed a strategic plan of global expansion to be launched through a business combination with Warner, come under a fiduciary duty to jettison its plan and put the corporation's future in the hands of its shareholders?

While we affirm the result reached by the Chancellor, we think it unwise to place undue emphasis upon long-term versus short-term corporate strategy. Two key predicates underpin our analysis. First, Delaware law imposes on a board of directors the duty to manage the business and affairs of the corporation. This broad mandate includes a conferred authority to set a corporate course of action, including time frame, designed to enhance corporate profitability. Thus, the question of "long-term" versus "short-term" values is largely irrelevant because directors, generally, are obliged to chart a course for a corporation which is in its best interests without regard to a fixed investment horizon. Second, absent a limited set of circumstances as defined under *Revlon*, a board of directors, while always required to act in an informed manner, is not under any per se duty to maximize shareholder value in the short term, even in the context of a takeover. In our view, the pivotal question presented by this case is: "Did Time, by entering into the proposed merger with Warner, put itself up for sale?" A resolution of that issue through application of *Revlon* has a significant bearing upon the resolution of the derivative *Unocal* issue.

We first take up plaintiffs' principal *Revlon* argument, summarized above. In rejecting this argument, the Chancellor found the original Time–Warner merger agreement not to constitute a "change of control" and concluded that the transaction did not trigger *Revlon* duties. The Chancellor's conclusion is premised on a finding that "[b]efore the merger agreement was signed, control of the corporation existed in a fluid aggregation of unaffiliated shareholders representing a voting majority—in other words, in the market." The Chancellor's findings of fact are supported by the record and his conclusion is correct as a matter of law. However, we premise our rejection of plaintiffs' *Revlon* claim on different grounds, namely, the absence of any substantial evidence to conclude that Time's board, in negotiating with Warner, made the dissolution or break-up of the corporate entity inevitable, as was the case in *Revlon*.

Under Delaware law there are, generally speaking and without excluding other possibilities, two circumstances which may implicate *Revlon* duties. The first, and clearer one, is when a corporation initiates an active bidding process seeking to sell itself or to effect a business reorganization involving a clear break-up of the company. However, *Revlon* duties may also be triggered where, in response to a bidder's offer, a target abandons its long-term strategy and seeks an alternative transaction involving the breakup of the company. Thus, in *Revlon*, when the board responded to Pantry Pride's offer by contemplating a "bust-up" sale of assets in a leveraged acquisition, we imposed upon the board a duty to maximize immediate shareholder value and an obligation to auction the company fairly. If, however, the board's reaction to a hostile tender offer is found to constitute only a defensive response and not an abandonment of the corporation's continued existence, *Revlon* duties are not triggered, though *Unocal* duties attach.

The plaintiffs insist that even though the original Time–Warner agreement may not have worked "an objective change of control," the transaction made a "sale" of Time inevitable. Plaintiffs rely on the subjective intent of Time's board of directors and principally upon certain board members' expressions of concern that the Warner transaction might be viewed as effectively putting Time up for sale. Plaintiffs argue that the use of a lock-up agreement, a no-shop clause, and so-called "dry-up" agreements prevented shareholders from obtaining a control premium in the immediate future and thus violated *Revlon*.

We agree with the Chancellor that such evidence is entirely insufficient to invoke *Revlon* duties; and we decline to extend *Revlon*'s application to corporate transactions simply because they might be construed as putting a corporation either "in play" or "up for sale." The adoption of structural safety devices alone does not trigger *Revlon*. Rather, as the Chancellor stated, such devices are properly subject to a *Unocal* analysis.
* * *

We turn now to plaintiffs' *Unocal* claim. We begin by noting, as did the Chancellor, that our decision does not require us to pass on the wisdom of the board's decision to enter into the original Time–Warner agreement. That is not a court's task. Our task is simply to review the record to determine whether there is sufficient evidence to support the Chancellor's conclusion that the initial Time–Warner agreement was the product of a proper exercise of business judgment.

We have purposely detailed the evidence of the Time board's deliberative approach, beginning in 1983–84, to expand itself. Time's decision in 1988 to combine with Warner was made only after what could be fairly characterized as an exhaustive appraisal of Time's future as a corporation. After concluding in 1983–84 that the corporation must expand to survive, and beyond journalism into entertainment, the board combed the field of available entertainment companies. By 1987 Time had focused upon Warner; by late July 1988 Time's board was convinced that Warner would provide the best "fit" for Time to achieve its strategic objectives. The record attests to the zealousness of Time's executives, fully supported by their directors, in seeing to the preservation of Time's "culture," i.e., its perceived editorial integrity in journalism. We find ample evidence in the record to support the Chancellor's conclusion that the Time board's decision to expand the business of the company through its March 3 merger with Warner was entitled to the protection of the business judgment rule.

The Chancellor reached a different conclusion in addressing the Time–Warner transaction as revised three months later. He found that the revised agreement was defense-motivated and designed to avoid the potentially disruptive effect that Paramount's offer would have had on consummation of the proposed merger were it put to a shareholder vote. Thus, the court declined to apply the traditional business judgment rule to the revised transaction and instead analyzed the Time board's June 16 decision under *Unocal*. The court ruled that *Unocal* applied to all director actions taken, following receipt of Paramount's hostile tender offer, that were reasonably determined to be defensive. Clearly that was a correct ruling and no party disputes that ruling.

In *Unocal*, we held that before the business judgment rule is applied to a board's adoption of a defensive measure, the burden will lie with the board to prove (a) reasonable grounds for believing that a danger to corporate policy and effectiveness existed; and (b) that the defensive measure adopted was reasonable in relation to the threat posed. Directors satisfy the first part of the *Unocal* test by demonstrating good faith and reasonable investigation. We have repeatedly stated that the refusal to entertain an offer may comport with a valid exercise of a board's business judgment.

Unocal involved a two-tier, highly coercive tender offer. In such a case, the threat is obvious: shareholders may be compelled to tender to avoid being treated adversely in the second stage of the transaction. In subsequent cases, the Court of Chancery has suggested that an all-cash, all-shares offer, falling within a range of values that a shareholder might reasonably prefer, cannot constitute a legally recognized "threat" to shareholder interests sufficient to withstand a *Unocal* analysis. In those cases, the Court of Chancery determined that whatever threat existed related only to the shareholders and only to price and not to the corporation.

From those decisions by our Court of Chancery, Paramount and the individual plaintiffs extrapolate a rule of law that an all-cash, all-shares offer with values reasonably in the range of acceptable price cannot pose any objective threat to a corporation or its shareholders. Thus, Paramount would have us hold that only if the value of Paramount's offer were determined to be clearly inferior to the value created by management's plan to merge with Warner could the offer be viewed—objectively—as a threat.

Implicit in the plaintiffs' argument is the view that a hostile tender offer can pose only two types of threats: the threat of coercion that results from a two-tier offer promising unequal treatment for nontendering shareholders; and the threat of inadequate value from an all-shares, all-cash offer at a price below what a target board in good faith deems to be the present value of its shares. Since Paramount's offer was all-cash, the only conceivable "threat," plaintiffs argue, was inadequate value. We disapprove of such a narrow and rigid construction of *Unocal*, for the reasons which follow.

Plaintiffs' position represents a fundamental misconception of our standard of review under *Unocal* principally because it would involve the court in substituting its judgment as to what is a "better" deal for that of a corporation's board of directors.

The usefulness of *Unocal* as an analytical tool is precisely its flexibility in the face of a variety of fact scenarios. *Unocal* is not intended as an abstract standard; neither is it a structured and mechanistic procedure of appraisal. Thus, we have said that directors may consider, when evaluating the threat posed by a takeover bid, the "inadequacy of the price offered, nature and timing of the offer, questions of illegality, the impact on 'constituencies' other than shareholders ... the risk of nonconsummation, and the quality of securities being offered in the exchange." The open-ended analysis mandated by *Unocal* is not intended to lead to a simple mathematical exercise: that is, of comparing the discounted value of Time–Warner's expected trading price at some future date with Paramount's offer and determining which is the higher. Indeed, in our view, precepts underlying the business judgment rule militate against a court's engaging in the process of attempting to appraise and evaluate the relative merits of a long-term versus a short-term investment goal for shareholders. To engage in such an exercise is a distortion of the *Unocal* process and, in particular, the application of the second part of *Unocal*'s test, discussed below.

In this case, the Time board reasonably determined that inadequate value was not the only legally cognizable threat that Paramount's all-cash, all-shares offer could present. Time's board concluded that Paramount's eleventh hour offer posed other threats. One concern was that Time shareholders might elect to tender into Paramount's cash offer in ignorance or a mistaken belief of the strategic benefit which a business combination with Warner might produce. Moreover, Time viewed the conditions attached to Paramount's offer as introducing a degree of uncertainty that skewed a comparative analysis. Further, the timing of Paramount's offer to follow issuance of Time's proxy notice was viewed as arguably designed to upset, if not confuse, the Time stockholders' vote. Given this record evidence, we cannot conclude that the Time board's decision of June 6 that Paramount's offer posed a threat to corporate policy and effectiveness was lacking in good faith or dominated by motives of either entrenchment or self-interest.

Paramount also contends that the Time board had not duly investigated Paramount's offer. Therefore, Paramount argues, Time was unable to make an informed decision that the offer posed a threat to Time's corporate policy. Although the Chancellor did not address this issue directly, his findings of fact do detail Time's exploration of the available entertainment companies, including Paramount, before determining that Warner provided the best strategic "fit." In addition, the court found that Time's board rejected Paramount's offer because Paramount did not serve Time's objectives or meet Time's needs. Thus, the record does, in our judgment, demonstrate that Time's board was adequately informed of the potential benefits of a transaction with Paramount. We agree with the Chancellor that the Time board's lengthy pre-June investigation of potential merger candidates, including Paramount, mooted any obligation on Time's part to halt its merger process with Warner to reconsider Paramount. Time's board was under no obligation to negotiate with Paramount. Time's failure to negotiate cannot be fairly found to have been uninformed. The evidence supporting this finding is materially enhanced by the fact that twelve of Time's sixteen board members were outside independent directors.

We turn to the second part of the *Unocal* analysis. The obvious requisite to determining the reasonableness of a defensive action is a clear identification of the nature of the threat. It is not until both parts of the *Unocal* inquiry have been satisfied that the business judgment rule attaches to defensive actions of a board of directors.* [18] As applied to the facts of this case, the question is whether the record evidence supports the Court of Chancery's conclusion that the restructuring of the Time–Warner transaction, including the adoption of several preclusive defensive measures, was a reasonable response in relation to a perceived threat.

Paramount argues that, assuming its tender offer posed a threat, Time's response was unreasonable in precluding Time's shareholders from accepting the tender offer or receiving a control premium in the immediately foreseeable future. Once again, the contention stems, we believe, from a fundamental misunderstanding of where the power of corporate governance lies. Delaware law confers the management of the corporate enterprise to the stockholders' duly elected board representatives. The fiduciary duty to manage a corporate enterprise includes the selection of a time frame for achievement of corporate goals. That duty may not be delegated to the stockholders. Directors are not obliged to abandon a deliberately conceived corporate plan for a short-term shareholder profit unless there is clearly no basis to sustain the corporate strategy. * * *

Here, on the record facts, the Chancellor found that Time's responsive action to Paramount's tender offer was not aimed at "cramming down" on its shareholders a management-sponsored alternative, but rather had as its goal the carrying forward of a pre-existing transaction in an altered form. Thus, the response was reasonably related to the threat. The Chancellor noted that the revised agreement and its accompanying safety devices did not preclude Paramount from making an offer for the combined Time–Warner company or from changing the conditions of its offer so as not to make the offer dependent upon the nullification of the Time–Warner agreement. Thus, the response was proportionate. We affirm the Chancellor's rulings as clearly supported by the record. Finally, we note that although Time was required, as a result of Paramount's hostile offer, to incur a heavy debt to finance its acquisition of Warner, that fact alone does not render the board's decision unreasonable so long as the directors could reasonably perceive the debt load not to be so injurious to the corporation as to jeopardize its well being.

Applying the test for grant or denial of preliminary injunctive relief, we find plaintiffs failed to establish a reasonable likelihood of ultimate success on the merits. Therefore, we affirm.

---

* [18] Some commentators have criticized *Unocal* by arguing that once the board's deliberative process has been analyzed and found not to be wanting in objectivity, good faith or deliberateness, the so-called "enhanced" business judgment rule has been satisfied and no further inquiry is undertaken. We reject such views.

QUESTIONS

1. Why did the Time board restructure its deal with Warner so that Warner stockholders received cash instead of Time, Inc. stock?

2. What "danger to corporate policy and effectiveness" was presented by the Paramount offer?

3. Do you think that the people who own Time, Inc. stock are stupid? Did the Time board? The Delaware Supreme Court? Professor Gevurtz describes the *Time* decision as "the high point for 'board knows best' rationale for takeover defenses." Franklin Gevurtz, CORPORATION LAW 689.

PARAMOUNT COMMUNICATIONS, INC. v. QVC NETWORK, INC.

Delaware Supreme Court, 1994
637 A.2d 34

VEASEY, CHIEF JUSTICE. In this appeal we review an order of the Court of Chancery dated November 24, 1993 (the "November 24 Order"), preliminarily enjoining certain defensive measures designed to facilitate a so-called strategic alliance between Viacom Inc. ("Viacom") and Paramount Communications Inc. ("Paramount") approved by the board of directors of Paramount (the "Paramount Board" or the "Paramount directors") and to thwart an unsolicited, more valuable, tender offer by QVC Network Inc. ("QVC"). In affirming, we hold that the sale of control in this case, which is at the heart of the proposed strategic alliance, implicates enhanced judicial scrutiny of the conduct of the Paramount Board under *Unocal Corp. v. Mesa Petroleum Co.*, Del.Supr., 493 A.2d 946 (1985), and *Revlon, Inc. v. MacAndrews & Forbes Holdings, Inc.*, Del. Supr., 506 A.2d 173 (1986). We further hold that the conduct of the Paramount Board was not reasonable as to process or result.

* * * This action arises out of a proposed acquisition of Paramount by Viacom through a tender offer followed by a second-step merger (the "Paramount–Viacom transaction"), and a competing unsolicited tender offer by QVC. The Court of Chancery granted a preliminary injunction. * * *

Paramount is a Delaware corporation with its principal offices in New York City. Approximately 118 million shares of Paramount's common stock are outstanding and traded on the New York Stock Exchange. The majority of Paramount's stock is publicly held by numerous unaffiliated investors. Paramount owns and operates a diverse group of entertainment businesses, including motion picture and television studios, book publishers, professional sports teams, and amusement parks.

There are 15 persons serving on the Paramount Board. Four directors are officer-employees of Paramount: Martin S. Davis ("Davis"), Paramount's Chairman and Chief Executive Officer since 1983; Donald Oresman ("Oresman"), Executive Vice-President, Chief Administrative Officer, and General Counsel; Stanley R. Jaffe, President and Chief Operating Officer; and Ronald L. Nelson, Executive Vice President and Chief Financial Officer. Paramount's 11 outside directors are distinguished and experienced business persons who are present or former senior executives of public corporations or financial institutions.

Viacom is a Delaware corporation with its headquarters in Massachusetts. Viacom is controlled by Sumner M. Redstone ("Redstone"), its Chairman and Chief Executive Officer, who owns indirectly approximately 85.2 percent of Viacom's voting Class A stock and approximately 69.2 percent of Viacom's nonvoting Class B stock through National Amusements, Inc. ("NAI"), an entity 91.7 percent owned by Redstone. Viacom has a wide range of entertainment operations, including a number of well-known cable television channels such as MTV, Nickelodeon, Showtime, and The Movie Channel. Viacom's equity co-investors in the Paramount–Viacom transaction include NYNEX Corporation and Blockbuster Entertainment Corporation.

QVC is a Delaware corporation with its headquarters in West Chester, Pennsylvania. QVC has several large stockholders, including Liberty Media Corporation, Comcast Corporation, Advance Publications, Inc., and Cox Enterprises Inc. Barry Diller ("Diller"), the Chairman and Chief Executive Officer of QVC, is also a substantial stockholder. QVC sells a variety of merchandise through a televised shopping channel. QVC has several equity co-investors in its proposed combination with Paramount including BellSouth Corporation and Comcast Corporation.

Beginning in the late 1980s, Paramount investigated the possibility of acquiring or merging with other companies in the entertainment, media, or communications industry. Paramount considered such transactions to be desirable, and perhaps necessary, in order to keep pace with competitors in the rapidly evolving field of entertainment and communications. Consistent with its goal of strategic expansion, Paramount made a tender offer for Time Inc. in 1989, but was ultimately unsuccessful. *See* Paramount Communications, Inc. v. Time Inc., Del.Supr., 571 A.2d 1140 (1989) ("Time–Warner").

Although Paramount had considered a possible combination of Paramount and Viacom as early as 1990, recent efforts to explore such a transaction began at a dinner meeting between Redstone and Davis on April 20, 1993. Robert Greenhill ("Greenhill"), Chairman of Smith Barney Shearson Inc. ("Smith Barney"), attended and helped facilitate this meeting. After several more meetings between Redstone and Davis, serious negotiations began taking place in early July.

It was tentatively agreed that Davis would be the chief executive officer and Redstone would be the controlling stockholder of the combined company, but the parties could not reach agreement on the merger price and the terms of a stock option to be granted to Viacom. With respect to price, Viacom offered a package of cash and stock (primarily Viacom Class

B nonvoting stock) with a market value of approximately $61 per share, but Paramount wanted at least $70 per share.

Shortly after negotiations broke down in July 1993, two notable events occurred. First, Davis apparently learned of QVC's potential interest in Paramount, and told Diller over lunch on July 21, 1993, that Paramount was not for sale. Second, the market value of Viacom's Class B nonvoting stock increased from $46.875 on July 6 to $57.25 on August 20. QVC claims (and Viacom disputes) that this price increase was caused by open market purchases of such stock by Redstone or entities controlled by him.

On August 20, 1993, discussions between Paramount and Viacom resumed when Greenhill arranged another meeting between Davis and Redstone. After a short hiatus, the parties negotiated in earnest in early September, and performed due diligence with the assistance of their financial advisors, Lazard Freres & Co. ("Lazard") for Paramount and Smith Barney for Viacom. On September 9, 1993, the Paramount Board was informed about the status of the negotiations and was provided information by Lazard, including an analysis of the proposed transaction.

On September 12, 1993, the Paramount Board met again and unanimously approved the Original Merger Agreement whereby Paramount would merge with and into Viacom. The terms of the merger provided that each share of Paramount common stock would be converted into 0.10 shares of Viacom Class A voting stock, 0.90 shares of Viacom Class B nonvoting stock, and $9.10 in cash. In addition, the Paramount Board agreed to amend its "poison pill" Rights Agreement to exempt the proposed merger with Viacom. The Original Merger Agreement also contained several provisions designed to make it more difficult for a potential competing bid to succeed. We focus, as did the Court of Chancery, on three of these defensive provisions: a "no-shop" provision (the "No–Shop Provision"), the Termination Fee, and the Stock Option Agreement.

First, under the No–Shop Provision, the Paramount Board agreed that Paramount would not solicit, encourage, discuss, negotiate, or endorse any competing transaction unless: (a) a third party "makes an unsolicited written, bona fide proposal, which is not subject to any material contingencies relating to financing"; and (b) the Paramount Board determines that discussions or negotiations with the third party are necessary for the Paramount Board to comply with its fiduciary duties.

Second, under the Termination Fee provision, Viacom would receive a $100 million termination fee if: (a) Paramount terminated the Original Merger Agreement because of a competing transaction; (b) Paramount's stockholders did not approve the merger; or (c) the Paramount Board recommended a competing transaction.

The third and most significant deterrent device was the Stock Option Agreement, which granted to Viacom an option to purchase approximately 19.9 percent (23,699,000 shares) of Paramount's outstanding common stock at $69.14 per share if any of the triggering events for the Termination Fee occurred. In addition to the customary terms that are normally associated with a stock option, the Stock Option Agreement contained two provisions that were both unusual and highly beneficial to Viacom: (a) Viacom was permitted to pay for the shares with a senior subordinated note of questionable marketability instead of cash, thereby avoiding the need to raise the $1.6 billion purchase price (the "Note Feature"); and (b) Viacom could elect to require Paramount to pay Viacom in cash a sum equal to the difference between the purchase price and the market price of Paramount's stock (the "Put Feature"). Because the Stock Option Agreement was not "capped" to limit its maximum dollar value, it had the potential to reach (and in this case did reach) unreasonable levels.

After the execution of the Original Merger Agreement and the Stock Option Agreement on September 12, 1993, Paramount and Viacom announced their proposed merger. In a number of public statements, the parties indicated that the pending transaction was a virtual certainty. Redstone described it as a "marriage" that would "never be torn asunder" and stated that only a "nuclear attack" could break the deal. Redstone also called Diller and John Malone of Tele–Communications Inc., a major stockholder of QVC, to dissuade them from making a competing bid.

Despite these attempts to discourage a competing bid, Diller sent a letter to Davis on September 20, 1993, proposing a merger in which QVC would acquire Paramount for approximately $80 per share, consisting of 0.893 shares of QVC common stock and $30 in cash. QVC also expressed its eagerness to meet with Paramount to negotiate the details of a transaction. When the Paramount Board met on September 27, it was advised by Davis that the Original Merger Agreement prohibited Paramount from having discussions with QVC (or anyone else) unless certain conditions were satisfied. In particular, QVC had to supply evidence that its proposal was not subject to financing contingencies. The Paramount Board was also provided information from Lazard describing QVC and its proposal.

On October 5, 1993, QVC provided Paramount with evidence of QVC's financing. The Paramount Board then held another meeting on October 11, and decided to authorize management to meet with QVC. Davis also informed the Paramount Board that Booz–Allen & Hamilton ("Booz–Allen"), a management consulting firm, had been retained to assess, inter alia, the incremental earnings potential from a Paramount–Viacom merger and a Paramount–QVC merger. Discussions proceeded slowly, however, due to a delay in Paramount signing a confidentiality agreement. In response to Paramount's request for information, QVC provided two binders of documents to Paramount on October 20.

On October 21, 1993, QVC filed this action and publicly announced an $80 cash tender offer for 51 percent of Paramount's outstanding shares (the "QVC tender offer"). Each remaining share of Paramount common stock would be converted into 1.42857 shares of QVC common stock in a second-step merger. The tender offer was conditioned on, among other things, the invalidation of the Stock Option Agreement, which was worth over $200 million by that point.* **[5]** QVC contends that it had to commence a tender offer because of the slow pace of the merger discussions and the need to begin seeking clearance under federal antitrust laws.

Confronted by QVC's hostile bid, which on its face offered over $10 per share more than the consideration provided by the Original Merger Agreement, Viacom realized that it would need to raise its bid in order to remain competitive. Within hours after QVC's tender offer was announced, Viacom entered into discussions with Paramount concerning a revised transaction. These discussions led to serious negotiations concerning a comprehensive amendment to the original Paramount–Viacom transaction. In effect, the opportunity for a "new deal" with Viacom was at hand for the Paramount Board. With the QVC hostile bid offering greater value to the Paramount stockholders, the Paramount Board had considerable leverage with Viacom.

At a special meeting on October 24, 1993, the Paramount Board approved the Amended Merger Agreement and an amendment to the Stock Option Agreement. The Amended Merger Agreement was, however, essentially the same as the Original Merger Agreement, except that it included a few new provisions. * * *

Although the Amended Merger Agreement offered more consideration to the Paramount stockholders and somewhat more flexibility to the Paramount Board than did the Original Merger Agreement, the defensive measures designed to make a competing bid more difficult were not removed or modified. In particular, there is no evidence in the record that Paramount sought to use its newly-acquired leverage to eliminate or modify the No–Shop Provision, the Termination Fee, or the Stock Option Agreement when the subject of amending the Original Merger Agreement was on the table.

Viacom's tender offer commenced on October 25, 1993, and QVC's tender offer was formally launched on October 27, 1993. Diller sent a letter to the Paramount Board on October 28 requesting an opportunity to negotiate with Paramount, and Oresman responded the following day by agreeing to meet. The meeting, held on November 1, was not very fruitful, however, after QVC's proposed guidelines for a "fair bidding process" were rejected by Paramount on the ground that "auction procedures" were inappropriate and contrary to Paramount's contractual obligations to Viacom.

On November 6, 1993, Viacom unilaterally raised its tender offer price to $85 per share in cash and offered a comparable increase in the value of the securities being proposed in the second-step merger. At a telephonic

---

* **[5]** By November 15, 1993, the value of the Stock Option Agreement had increased to nearly $500 million based on the $90 QVC bid.

meeting held later that day, the Paramount Board agreed to recommend Viacom's higher bid to Paramount's stockholders.

QVC responded to Viacom's higher bid on November 12 by increasing its tender offer to $90 per share and by increasing the securities for its second-step merger by a similar amount. In response to QVC's latest offer, the Paramount Board scheduled a meeting for November 15, 1993. Prior to the meeting, Oresman sent the members of the Paramount Board a document summarizing the "conditions and uncertainties" of QVC's offer. One director testified that this document gave him a very negative impression of the QVC bid.

At its meeting on November 15, 1993, the Paramount Board determined that the new QVC offer was not in the best interests of the stockholders. The purported basis for this conclusion was that QVC's bid was excessively conditional. The Paramount Board did not communicate with QVC regarding the status of the conditions because it believed that the No–Shop Provision prevented such communication in the absence of firm financing. Several Paramount directors also testified that they believed the Viacom transaction would be more advantageous to Paramount's future business prospects than a QVC transaction. Although a number of materials were distributed to the Paramount Board describing the Viacom and QVC transactions, the only quantitative analysis of the consideration to be received by the stockholders under each proposal was based on then-current market prices of the securities involved, not on the anticipated value of such securities at the time when the stockholders would receive them.

The preliminary injunction hearing in this case took place on November 16, 1993. On November 19, Diller wrote to the Paramount Board to inform it that QVC had obtained financing commitments for its tender offer and that there was no antitrust obstacle to the offer. On November 24, 1993, the Court of Chancery issued its decision granting a preliminary injunction in favor of QVC and the plaintiff stockholders. This appeal followed.

The General Corporation Law of the State of Delaware (the "General Corporation Law") and the decisions of this Court have repeatedly recognized the fundamental principle that the management of the business and affairs of a Delaware corporation is entrusted to its directors, who are the duly elected and authorized representatives of the stockholders. Under normal circumstances, neither the courts nor the stockholders should interfere with the managerial decisions of the directors. The business judgment rule embodies the deference to which such decisions are entitled.

Nevertheless, there are rare situations which mandate that a court take a more direct and active role in overseeing the decisions made and actions taken by directors. In these situations, a court subjects the

directors' conduct to enhanced scrutiny to ensure that it is reasonable.*
[9] The decisions of this Court have clearly established the circumstances
where such enhanced scrutiny will be applied. E.g., *Unocal*, 493 A.2d 946;
Revlon, 506 A.2d 173. The case at bar implicates two such circumstances:
(1) the approval of a transaction resulting in a sale of control, and (2) the
adoption of defensive measures in response to a threat to corporate
control.

* * *

In the case before us, the public stockholders (in the aggregate)
currently own a majority of Paramount's voting stock. Control of the
corporation is not vested in a single person, entity, or group, but vested in
the fluid aggregation of unaffiliated stockholders. In the event the Paramount–Viacom transaction is consummated, the public stockholders will
receive cash and a minority equity voting position in the surviving
corporation. Following such consummation, there will be a controlling
stockholder who will have the voting power to: (a) elect directors; (b)
cause a break-up of the corporation; (c) merge it with another company;
(d) cash-out the public stockholders; (e) amend the certificate of incorporation; (f) sell all or substantially all of the corporate assets; or (g)
otherwise alter materially the nature of the corporation and the public
stockholders' interests. Irrespective of the present Paramount Board's
vision of a long-term strategic alliance with Viacom, the proposed sale of
control would provide the new controlling stockholder with the power to
alter that vision.

Because of the intended sale of control, the Paramount–Viacom transaction has economic consequences of considerable significance to the
Paramount stockholders. Once control has shifted, the current Paramount
stockholders will have no leverage in the future to demand another
control premium. As a result, the Paramount stockholders are entitled to
receive, and should receive, a control premium and/or protective devices of
significant value. There being no such protective provisions in the Viacom–Paramount transaction, the Paramount directors had an obligation
to take the maximum advantage of the current opportunity to realize for
the stockholders the best value reasonably available.

The consequences of a sale of control impose special obligations on the
directors of a corporation. In particular, they have the obligation of acting
reasonably to seek the transaction offering the best value reasonably
available to the stockholders. The courts will apply enhanced scrutiny to
ensure that the directors have acted reasonably. * * *

In the sale of control context, the directors must focus on one primary
objective—to secure the transaction offering the best value reasonably

---

* **[9]** Where actual self-interest is present and affects a majority of the directors approving a
transaction, a court will apply even more exacting scrutiny to determine whether the transaction
is entirely fair to the stockholders. *E.g.*, *Weinberger v. UOP, Inc.*, Del.Supr., 457 A.2d 701, 710–11
(1983).

available for the stockholders—and they must exercise their fiduciary duties to further that end.

* * * [S]ome of the methods by which a board can fulfill its obligation to seek the best value reasonably available to the stockholders * * * include conducting an auction, canvassing the market, etc. Delaware law recognizes that there is "no single blueprint" that directors must follow.

In determining which alternative provides the best value for the stockholders, a board of directors is not limited to considering only the amount of cash involved, and is not required to ignore totally its view of the future value of a strategic alliance. Instead, the directors should analyze the entire situation and evaluate in a disciplined manner the consideration being offered. Where stock or other non-cash consideration is involved, the board should try to quantify its value, if feasible, to achieve an objective comparison of the alternatives. In addition, the board may assess a variety of practical considerations relating to each alternative, including:

> [An offer's] fairness and feasibility; the proposed or actual financing for the offer, and the consequences of that financing; questions of illegality; . . . the risk of non-consum[m]ation; . . . the bidder's identity, prior background and other business venture experiences; and the bidder's business plans for the corporation and their effects on stockholder interests.

These considerations are important because the selection of one alternative may permanently foreclose other opportunities. While the assessment of these factors may be complex, the board's goal is straightforward: Having informed themselves of all material information reasonably available, the directors must decide which alternative is most likely to offer the best value reasonably available to the stockholders.

Board action in the circumstances presented here is subject to enhanced scrutiny. Such scrutiny is mandated by: (a) the threatened diminution of the current stockholders' voting power; (b) the fact that an asset belonging to public stockholders (a control premium) is being sold and may never be available again; and (c) the traditional concern of Delaware courts for actions which impair or impede stockholder voting rights.

The key features of an enhanced scrutiny test are: (a) a judicial determination regarding the adequacy of the decisionmaking process employed by the directors, including the information on which the directors based their decision; and (b) a judicial examination of the reasonableness of the directors' action in light of the circumstances then existing. The directors have the burden of proving that they were adequately informed and acted reasonably.

Although an enhanced scrutiny test involves a review of the reasonableness of the substantive merits of a board's actions, a court should not ignore the complexity of the directors' task in a sale of control. There are many business and financial considerations implicated in investigating and selecting the best value reasonably available. The board of directors is the corporate decisionmaking body best equipped to make these judgments. Accordingly, a court applying enhanced judicial scrutiny should be deciding whether the directors made a reasonable decision, not a perfect decision. If a board selected one of several reasonable alternatives, a court should not second-guess that choice even though it might have decided otherwise or subsequent events may have cast doubt on the board's determination. Thus, courts will not substitute their business judgment for that of the directors, but will determine if the directors' decision was, on balance, within a range of reasonableness.

The Paramount defendants and Viacom assert that the fiduciary obligations and the enhanced judicial scrutiny discussed above are not implicated in this case in the absence of a "break-up" of the corporation, and that the order granting the preliminary injunction should be reversed. This argument is based on their erroneous interpretation of our decisions in Revlon and Time–Warner.

In *Revlon*, we reviewed the actions of the board of directors of Revlon, Inc. ("Revlon"), which had rebuffed the overtures of Pantry Pride, Inc. and had instead entered into an agreement with Forstmann Little & Co. ("Forstmann") providing for the acquisition of 100 percent of Revlon's outstanding stock by Forstmann and the subsequent break-up of Revlon. Based on the facts and circumstances present in *Revlon*, we held that "[t]he directors' role changed from defenders of the corporate bastion to auctioneers charged with getting the best price for the stockholders at a sale of the company." We further held that "when a board ends an intense bidding contest on an insubstantial basis, ... [that] action cannot withstand the enhanced scrutiny which *Unocal* requires of director conduct."

It is true that one of the circumstances bearing on these holdings was the fact that "the break-up of the company ... had become a reality which even the directors embraced." It does not follow, however, that a "break-up" must be present and "inevitable" before directors are subject to enhanced judicial scrutiny and are required to pursue a transaction that is calculated to produce the best value reasonably available to the stockholders. In fact, we stated in *Revlon* that "when bidders make relatively similar offers, or dissolution of the company becomes inevitable, the directors cannot fulfill their enhanced *Unocal* duties by playing favorites with the contending factions." *Revlon* thus does not hold that an inevitable dissolution or "break-up" is necessary.

The decisions of this Court following *Revlon* reinforced the applicability of enhanced scrutiny and the directors' obligation to seek the best value reasonably available for the stockholders where there is a pending sale of control, regardless of whether or not there is to be a break-up of the corporation.

* * * The Paramount defendants have interpreted our decision in *Time–Warner* as requiring a corporate break-up in order for that obligation to apply. The facts in *Time–Warner*, however, were quite different

from the facts of this case, and refute Paramount's position here. In *Time–Warner*, the Chancellor held that there was no change of control in the original stock-for-stock merger between Time and Warner because Time would be owned by a fluid aggregation of unaffiliated stockholders both before and after the merger: * * *

Moreover, the transaction actually consummated in *Time–Warner* was not a merger, as originally planned, but a sale of Warner's stock to Time.

* * * Nevertheless, the Paramount defendants here have argued that a break-up is a requirement and have focused on the following language in our *Time–Warner* decision:

However, we premise our rejection of plaintiffs' Revlon claim on different grounds, namely, the absence of any substantial evidence to conclude that Time's board, in negotiating with Warner, made the dissolution or break-up of the corporate entity inevitable, as was the case in Revlon.

Under Delaware law there are, generally speaking and without excluding other possibilities, two circumstances which may implicate *Revlon* duties. The first, and clearer one, is when a corporation initiates an active bidding process seeking to sell itself or to effect a business reorganization involving a clear break-up of the company. However, *Revlon* duties may also be triggered where, in response to a bidder's offer, a target abandons its long-term strategy and seeks an alternative transaction involving the breakup of the company.

The Paramount defendants have misread the holding of *Time–Warner*. Contrary to their argument, our decision in *Time–Warner* expressly states that the two general scenarios discussed in the above-quoted paragraph are not the only instances where "*Revlon* duties" may be implicated. The Paramount defendants' argument totally ignores the phrase "without excluding other possibilities." Moreover, the instant case is clearly within the first general scenario set forth in *Time–Warner*. The Paramount Board, albeit unintentionally, had "initiate[d] an active bidding process seeking to sell itself" by agreeing to sell control of the corporation to Viacom in circumstances where another potential acquiror (QVC) was equally interested in being a bidder.

The Paramount defendants' position that both a change of control and a break-up are required must be rejected. Such a holding would unduly restrict the application of *Revlon*, is inconsistent with this Court's decisions in *Barkan and Macmillan*, and has no basis in policy. There are few events that have a more significant impact on the stockholders than a sale of control or a corporate break-up. Each event represents a fundamental (and perhaps irrevocable) change in the nature of the corporate enterprise from a practical standpoint. It is the significance of each of these events that justifies: (a) focusing on the directors' obligation to seek the best value reasonably available to the stockholders; and (b) requiring a close scrutiny of board action which could be contrary to the stockholders' interests.

Accordingly, when a corporation undertakes a transaction which will cause: (a) a change in corporate control; or (b) a break-up of the corporate entity, the directors' obligation is to seek the best value reasonably available to the stockholders. This obligation arises because the effect of the Viacom–Paramount transaction, if consummated, is to shift control of Paramount from the public stockholders to a controlling stockholder, Viacom. Neither *Time-Warner* nor any other decision of this Court holds that a "break-up" of the company is essential to give rise to this obligation where there is a sale of control.

We now turn to duties of the Paramount Board under the facts of this case and our conclusions as to the breaches of those duties which warrant injunctive relief.

Under the facts of this case, the Paramount directors had the obligation: (a) to be diligent and vigilant in examining critically the Paramount–Viacom transaction and the QVC tender offers; (b) to act in good faith; (c) to obtain, and act with due care on, all material information reasonably available, including information necessary to compare the two offers to determine which of these transactions, or an alternative course of action, would provide the best value reasonably available to the stockholders; and (d) to negotiate actively and in good faith with both Viacom and QVC to that end.

Having decided to sell control of the corporation, the Paramount directors were required to evaluate critically whether or not all material aspects of the Paramount–Viacom transaction (separately and in the aggregate) were reasonable and in the best interests of the Paramount stockholders in light of current circumstances, including: the change of control premium, the Stock Option Agreement, the Termination Fee, the coercive nature of both the Viacom and QVC tender offers,* [18] the No–Shop Provision, and the proposed disparate use of the Rights Agreement as to the Viacom and QVC tender offers, respectively.

These obligations necessarily implicated various issues, including the questions of whether or not those provisions and other aspects of the Paramount-Viacom transaction (separately and in the aggregate): (a) adversely affected the value provided to the Paramount stockholders; (b) inhibited or encouraged alternative bids; (c) were enforceable contractual obligations in light of the directors' fiduciary duties; and (d) in the end would advance or retard the Paramount directors' obligation to secure for the Paramount stockholders the best value reasonably available under the circumstances.

The Paramount defendants contend that they were precluded by certain contractual provisions, including the No–Shop Provision, from negotiating with QVC or seeking alternatives. Such provisions, whether or

---

* [18] Both the Viacom and the QVC tender offers were for 51 percent cash and a "back-end" of various securities, the value of each of which depended on the fluctuating value of Viacom and QVC stock at any given time. Thus, both tender offers were two-tiered, front-end loaded, and coercive. Such coercive offers are inherently problematic and should be expected to receive particularly careful analysis by a target board.

not they are presumptively valid in the abstract, may not validly define or limit the directors' fiduciary duties under Delaware law or prevent the Paramount directors from carrying out their fiduciary duties under Delaware law. To the extent such provisions are inconsistent with those duties, they are invalid and unenforceable. *See Revlon*, 506 A.2d at 184–85.

Since the Paramount directors had already decided to sell control, they had an obligation to continue their search for the best value reasonably available to the stockholders. This continuing obligation included the responsibility, at the October 24 board meeting and thereafter, to evaluate critically both the QVC tender offers and the Paramount–Viacom transaction to determine if: (a) the QVC tender offer was, or would continue to be, conditional; (b) the QVC tender offer could be improved; (c) the Viacom tender offer or other aspects of the Paramount–Viacom transaction could be improved; (d) each of the respective offers would be reasonably likely to come to closure, and under what circumstances; (e) other material information was reasonably available for consideration by the Paramount directors; (f) there were viable and realistic alternative courses of action; and (g) the timing constraints could be managed so the directors could consider these matters carefully and deliberately.

The Paramount directors made the decision on September 12, 1993, that, in their judgment, a strategic merger with Viacom on the economic terms of the Original Merger Agreement was in the best interests of Paramount and its stockholders. Those terms provided a modest change of control premium to the stockholders. The directors also decided at that time that it was appropriate to agree to certain defensive measures (the Stock Option Agreement, the Termination Fee, and the No–Shop Provision) insisted upon by Viacom as part of that economic transaction. Those defensive measures, coupled with the sale of control and subsequent disparate treatment of competing bidders, implicated the judicial scrutiny of *Unocal, Revlon, Macmillan*, and their progeny. We conclude that the Paramount directors' process was not reasonable, and the result achieved for the stockholders was not reasonable under the circumstances.

When entering into the Original Merger Agreement, and thereafter, the Paramount Board clearly gave insufficient attention to the potential consequences of the defensive measures demanded by Viacom. The Stock Option Agreement had a number of unusual and potentially "draconian" provisions, including the Note Feature and the Put Feature. Furthermore, the Termination Fee, whether or not unreasonable by itself, clearly made Paramount less attractive to other bidders, when coupled with the Stock Option Agreement. Finally, the No–Shop Provision inhibited the Paramount Board's ability to negotiate with other potential bidders, particularly QVC which had already expressed an interest in Paramount.

Throughout the applicable time period, and especially from the first QVC merger proposal on September 20 through the Paramount Board meeting on November 15, QVC's interest in Paramount provided the opportunity for the Paramount Board to seek significantly higher value for the Paramount stockholders than that being offered by Viacom. QVC persistently demonstrated its intention to meet and exceed the Viacom offers, and frequently expressed its willingness to negotiate possible further increases.

The Paramount directors had the opportunity in the October 23–24 time frame, when the Original Merger Agreement was renegotiated, to take appropriate action to modify the improper defensive measures as well as to improve the economic terms of the Paramount–Viacom transaction. Under the circumstances existing at that time, it should have been clear to the Paramount Board that the Stock Option Agreement, coupled with the Termination Fee and the No–Shop Clause, were impeding the realization of the best value reasonably available to the Paramount stockholders. Nevertheless, the Paramount Board made no effort to eliminate or modify these counterproductive devices, and instead continued to cling to its vision of a strategic alliance with Viacom. Moreover, based on advice from the Paramount management, the Paramount directors considered the QVC offer to be "conditional" and asserted that they were precluded by the No–Shop Provision from seeking more information from, or negotiating with, QVC.

By November 12, 1993, the value of the revised QVC offer on its face exceeded that of the Viacom offer by over $1 billion at then current values. This significant disparity of value cannot be justified on the basis of the directors' vision of future strategy, primarily because the change of control would supplant the authority of the current Paramount Board to continue to hold and implement their strategic vision in any meaningful way. Moreover, their uninformed process had deprived their strategic vision of much of its credibility.

When the Paramount directors met on November 15 to consider QVC's increased tender offer, they remained prisoners of their own misconceptions and missed opportunities to eliminate the restrictions they had imposed on themselves. Yet, it was not "too late" to reconsider negotiating with QVC. The circumstances existing on November 15 made it clear that the defensive measures, taken as a whole, were problematic: (a) the No–Shop Provision could not define or limit their fiduciary duties; (b) the Stock Option Agreement had become "draconian"; and (c) the Termination Fee, in context with all the circumstances, was similarly deterring the realization of possibly higher bids. Nevertheless, the Paramount directors remained paralyzed by their uninformed belief that the QVC offer was "illusory." This final opportunity to negotiate on the stockholders' behalf and to fulfill their obligation to seek the best value reasonably available was thereby squandered.

Viacom argues that it had certain "vested" contract rights with respect to the No–Shop Provision and the Stock Option Agreement. In effect, Viacom's argument is that the Paramount directors could enter into an agreement in violation of their fiduciary duties and then render Paramount, and ultimately its stockholders, liable for failing to carry out an agreement in violation of those duties. Viacom's protestations about vested rights are without merit. This Court has found that those defensive measures were improperly designed to deter potential bidders, and that such measures do not meet the reasonableness test to which they must be subjected. They are consequently invalid and unenforceable under the facts of this case.

* * * Viacom, a sophisticated party with experienced legal and financial advisors, knew of (and in fact demanded) the unreasonable features of the Stock Option Agreement. It cannot be now heard to argue that it obtained vested contract rights by negotiating and obtaining contractual provisions from a board acting in violation of its fiduciary duties. As the Nebraska Supreme Court said in rejecting a similar argument, "To so hold, it would seem, would be to get the shareholders coming and going." Likewise, we reject Viacom's arguments and hold that its fate must rise or fall, and in this instance fall, with the determination that the actions of the Paramount Board were invalid.

The realization of the best value reasonably available to the stockholders became the Paramount directors' primary obligation under these facts in light of the change of control. That obligation was not satisfied, and the Paramount Board's process was deficient. The directors' initial hope and expectation for a strategic alliance with Viacom was allowed to dominate their decisionmaking process to the point where the arsenal of defensive measures established at the outset was perpetuated (not modified or eliminated) when the situation was dramatically altered. QVC's unsolicited bid presented the opportunity for significantly greater value for the stockholders and enhanced negotiating leverage for the directors. Rather than seizing those opportunities, the Paramount directors chose to wall themselves off from material information which was reasonably available and to hide behind the defensive measures as a rationalization for refusing to negotiate with QVC or seeking other alternatives. Their view of the strategic alliance likewise became an empty rationalization as the opportunities for higher value for the stockholders continued to develop.

It is the nature of the judicial process that we decide only the case before us—a case which, on its facts, is clearly controlled by established Delaware law. Here, the proposed change of control and the implications thereof were crystal clear. In other cases they may be less clear. The holding of this case on its facts, coupled with the holdings of the principal cases discussed herein where the issue of sale of control is implicated, should provide a workable precedent against which to measure future cases.

For the reasons set forth herein, the November 24, 1993, Order of the Court of Chancery has been AFFIRMED, and this matter has been REMANDED for proceedings consistent herewith, as set forth in the December 9, 1993, Order of this Court.

QUESTIONS AND NOTE

1. Comparing the *Time* and *QVC* decisions, Professor Gevurtz suggested "the rule appears to be the greater the conflict of interest by the target's board (as far as retaining the current directors' and managers' power) the less the scrutiny of the board's action." Franklin Gevurtz, CORPORATION LAW 684. Do you agree?

2. Professor Taylor of Georgia State University has criticized QVC, concluding that the court improperly substituted its business judgment to trump the managers' business judgment. Ellen Taylor, *New and Unjustified Restrictions on Delaware Directors' Authority*, 21 DEL. J. CORP.L.837 (1996). Do you agree?

3. Bubba's Burritos, Inc., a publicly-traded corporation owning and operating 100 restaurants in the South, discussed merger with several comparably sized restaurant corporations. Bubba's CEO then learns from McDonald's CEO that McDonald's will make an offer to buy Bubba's Burritos at a significant premium if, and only if, Bubba's agrees to (i) a no-shop clause and (ii) a substantial break-up fee including an option to purchase the ten most profitable Bubba's Burritos restaurants at a very favorable price. Are *Unocal*, *Revlon*, *Time*, and *QVC* helpful to you in advising Bubba's directors as to what they should do?

4. According to William T. Allen, former Chancellor of the Delaware Court of Chancery, and Jack B. Jacobs and Leo E, Strine, Jr., Vice Chancellors:

> The difficulties with the common law case-by-case form of fiduciary regulation are several. By its nature fiduciary duty law is an imperfect tool to forge rules to regulate a phenomenon as complex and policy-laden as corporate takeovers. Being highly general, prospective statements of the content of fiduciary duties offer limited guidance to transaction planners who seek legal certainty from authoritative judicial decisions. Moreover, as applied in specific cases, the articulated fiduciary duty is often so highly particularized that it becomes difficult to generalize ex ante rules from those judicial holdings. To express it differently, the almost infinite potential variation in the fact patterns calling for director decisions, the disparate time frames within which different boards may be required to act, and the divergent skills and information needed to make particular business decisions, usually make it impossible for courts to articulate ex ante precise guidelines for appropriate fiduciary action in future cases. Given the blunt nature of the fiduciary doctrine tool, judges must instead describe fiduciary duties in general terms that can (it is hoped) be sensibly and fairly applied in future diverse circumstances in which directors are called upon to act. In discharging this task, judges also face the difficulty of bringing legal expertise to bear in reviewing the decisions of business professionals, an exercise inherently fraught with risks of error.

William T. Allen, Jack B. Jacobs, Leo E. Strine, Jr., *Function Over Form: A Reassessment of Standards of Review and Delaware Corporation Law*, 56 BUS. LAW. 1287, 1293–94 (2001).

LYONDELL CHEMICAL CO. v. RYAN

Supreme Court of Delaware, 2009
970 A.2d 235

BERGER, J. We accepted this interlocutory appeal to consider a claim that directors failed to act in good faith in conducting the sale of their company. The Court of Chancery decided that "unexplained inaction" permits a reasonable inference that the directors may have consciously disregarded their fiduciary duties. The trial court expressed concern about the speed with which the transaction was consummated; the directors' failure to negotiate better terms; and their failure to seek potentially superior deals. But the record establishes that the directors were disinterested and independent; that they were generally aware of the company's value and its prospects; and that they considered the offer, under the time constraints imposed by the buyer, with the assistance of financial and legal advisors. At most, this record creates a triable issue of fact on the question of whether the directors exercised due care. There is no evidence, however, from which to infer that the directors knowingly ignored their responsibilities, thereby breaching their duty of loyalty. Accordingly, the directors are entitled to the entry of summary judgment.

Factual and Procedural Background

Before the merger at issue, Lyondell Chemical Company ("Lyondell") was the third largest independent, publicly traded chemical company in North America. Dan Smith ("Smith") was Lyondell's Chairman and CEO. Lyondell's other ten directors were independent and many were, or had been, CEOs of other large, publicly traded companies. Basell AF ("Basell") is a privately held Luxembourg company owned by Leonard Blavatnik ("Blavatnik") through his ownership of Access Industries. Basell is in the business of polyolefin technology, production and marketing.

In April 2006, Blavatnik told Smith that Basell was interested in acquiring Lyondell. A few months later, Basell sent a letter to Lyondell's board offering $26.50–$28.50 per share. Lyondell determined that the price was inadequate and that it was not interested in selling. During the next year, Lyondell prospered and no potential acquirors expressed interest in the company. In May 2007, an Access affiliate filed a Schedule 13D with the Securities and Exchange Commission disclosing its right to acquire an 8.3% block of Lyondell stock owned by Occidental Petroleum Corporation. The Schedule 13D also disclosed Blavatnik's interest in possible transactions with Lyondell.

In response to the Schedule 13D, the Lyondell board immediately convened a special meeting. The board recognized that the 13D signaled to the market that the company was "in play,"* [1] but the directors decided to take a "wait and see" approach. A few days later, Apollo Management,

---

* [1] On the day that the 13D was made public, Lyondell's stock went from $33 to $37 per share.

L.P. contacted Smith to suggest a management-led LBO, but Smith rejected that proposal. In late June 2007, Basell announced that it had entered into a $9.6 billion merger agreement with Huntsman Corporation ("Huntsman"), a specialty chemical company. Basell apparently reconsidered, however, after Hexion Specialty Chemicals, Inc. made a topping bid for Huntsman. Faced with competition for Huntsman, Blavatnik returned his attention to Lyondell.

On July 9, 2007, Blavatnik met with Smith to discuss an all-cash deal at $40 per share. Smith responded that $40 was too low, and Blavatnik raised his offer to $44–$45 per share. Smith told Blavatnik that he would present the proposal to the board, but that he thought the board would reject it. Smith advised Blavatnik to give Lyondell his best offer, since Lyondell really was not on the market. The meeting ended at that point, but Blavatnik asked Smith to call him later in the day. When Smith called, Blavatnik offered to pay $48 per share. Under Blavatnik's proposal, Basell would require no financing contingency, but Lyondell would have to agree to a $400 million break-up fee and sign a merger agreement by July 16, 2007.

Smith called a special meeting of the Lyondell board on July 10, 2007 to review and consider Basell's offer. The meeting lasted slightly less than one hour, during which time the board reviewed valuation material that had been prepared by Lyondell management for presentation at the regular board meeting, which was scheduled for the following day. The board also discussed the Basell offer, the status of the Huntsman merger, and the likelihood that another party might be interested in Lyondell. The board instructed Smith to obtain a written offer from Basell and more details about Basell's financing.

Blavatnik agreed to the board's request, but also made an additional demand. Basell had until July 11 to make a higher bid for Huntsman, so Blavatnik asked Smith to find out whether the Lyondell board would provide a firm indication of interest in his proposal by the end of that day. The Lyondell board met on July 11, again for less than one hour, to consider the Basell proposal and how it compared to the benefits of remaining independent. The board decided that it was interested, authorized the retention of Deutsche Bank Securities, Inc. ("Deutsche Bank") as its financial advisor, and instructed Smith to negotiate with Blavatnik.

Basell then announced that it would not raise its offer for Huntsman, and Huntsman terminated the Basell merger agreement. From July 12–July 15 the parties negotiated the terms of a Lyondell merger agreement; Basell conducted due diligence; Deutsche Bank prepared a "fairness" opinion; and Lyondell conducted its regularly scheduled board meeting. The Lyondell board discussed the Basell proposal again on July 12, and later instructed Smith to try to negotiate better terms. Specifically, the board wanted a higher price, a go-shop provision, and a reduced break-up fee. As the trial court noted, Blavatnik was "incredulous." He had offered his best price, which was a substantial premium, and the deal had to be concluded on his schedule. As a sign of good faith, however, Blavatnik agreed to reduce the break-up fee from $400 million to $385 million.

On July 16, 2007, the board met to consider the Basell merger agreement. Lyondell's management, as well as its financial and legal advisers, presented reports analyzing the merits of the deal. The advisors explained that, notwithstanding the no-shop provision in the merger agreement, Lyondell would be able to consider any superior proposals that might be made because of the "fiduciary out" provision. In addition, Deutsche Bank reviewed valuation models derived from "bullish" and more conservative financial projections. Several of those valuations yielded a range that did not even reach $48 per share, and Deutsche Bank opined that the proposed merger price was fair. Indeed, the bank's managing director described the merger price as "an absolute home run." Deutsche Bank also identified other possible acquirors and explained why it believed no other entity would top Basell's offer. After considering the presentations, the Lyondell board voted to approve the merger and recommend it to the stockholders. At a special stockholders' meeting held on November 20, 2007, the merger was approved by more than 99% of the voted shares.

The first stockholders to litigate this merger filed suit in Texas on July 23, 2007. Walter E. Ryan, Jr., the plaintiff in this action, participated in the Texas litigation and filed suit in Delaware on August 20, 2007. The Texas court denied an application for a preliminary injunction on November 13, 2007, while the defendants in Delaware were briefing their motion for summary judgment. The Court of Chancery issued its opinion on July 29, 2008, denying summary judgment as to the *"Revlon"* and the "deal protection" claims. This Court accepted the Lyondell directors' application for certification of an interlocutory appeal on September 15, 2008.

Discussion

The class action complaint challenging this $13 billion cash merger alleges that the Lyondell directors breached their "fiduciary duties of care, loyalty and candor ... and ... put their personal interests ahead of the interests of the Lyondell shareholders." Specifically, the complaint alleges that: 1) the merger price was grossly insufficient; 2) the directors were motivated to approve the merger for their own self-interest;* [5] 3) the process by which the merger was negotiated was flawed; 4) the directors agreed to unreasonable deal protection provisions; and 5) the preliminary proxy statement omitted numerous material facts. The trial court rejected all claims except those directed at the process by which the directors sold the company and the deal protection provisions in the merger agreement.

The remaining claims are but two aspects of a single claim, under *Revlon v. MacAndrews & Forbes Holdings, Inc.,* that the directors failed to obtain the best available price in selling the company. As the trial court correctly noted, *Revlon* did not create any new fiduciary duties. It simply held that the "board must perform its fiduciary duties in the service of a

---

* [5] The directors' alleged financial interest is the fact that they would receive cash for their stock options.

specific objective: maximizing the sale price of the enterprise." The trial court reviewed the record, and found that Ryan might be able to prevail at trial on a claim that the Lyondell directors breached their duty of care. But Lyondell's charter includes an exculpatory provision, pursuant to *8 Del. C. § 102 (b) (7)*, protecting the directors from personal liability for breaches of the duty of care. Thus, this case turns on whether any arguable shortcomings on the part of the Lyondell directors also implicate their duty of loyalty, a breach of which is not exculpated. Because the trial court determined that the board was independent and was not motivated by self-interest or ill will, the sole issue is whether the directors are entitled to summary judgment on the claim that they breached their duty of loyalty by failing to act in good faith.

This Court [recently] examined "good faith." * * * In *In re Walt Disney Co. Deriv Litig.*, the Court discussed the range of conduct that might be characterized as bad faith, and concluded that bad faith encompasses not only an intent to harm but also intentional dereliction of duty. * * *

The trial court reviewed the existing record under a mistaken view of the applicable law. Three factors contributed to that mistake. First, the trial court imposed *Revlon* duties on the Lyondell directors before they either had decided to sell, or before the sale had become inevitable. Second, the court read *Revlon* and its progeny as creating a set of requirements that must be satisfied during the sale process. Third, the trial court equated an arguably imperfect attempt to carry out *Revlon* duties with a knowing disregard of one's duties that constitutes bad faith. * * *

The Court of Chancery identified several undisputed facts that would support the entry of judgment in favor of the Lyondell directors: the directors were "active, sophisticated, and generally aware of the value of the Company and the conditions of the markets in which the Company operated." They had reason to believe that no other bidders would emerge, given the price Basell had offered and the limited universe of companies that might be interested in acquiring Lyondell's unique assets. Smith negotiated the price up from $40 to $48 per share—a price that Deutsche Bank opined was fair. Finally, no other acquiror expressed interest during the four months between the merger announcement and the stockholder vote.

Other facts, however, led the trial court to "question the adequacy of the Board's knowledge and efforts" After the Schedule 13D was filed in May, the directors apparently took no action to prepare for a possible acquisition proposal. The merger was negotiated and finalized in less than one week, during which time the directors met for a total of only seven hours to consider the matter. The directors did not seriously press Blavatnik for a better price, nor did they conduct even a limited market check. Moreover, although the deal protections were not unusual or preclusive, the trial court was troubled by "the Board's decision to grant considerable protection to a deal that may not have been adequately vetted under *Revlon*."

The trial court found the directors' failure to act during the two months after the filing of the Basell Schedule 13D critical to its analysis of their good faith. The court pointedly referred to the directors' "two months of slothful indifference despite *knowing* that the Company was in play," and the fact that they "languidly awaited overtures from potential suitors...." In the end, the trial court found that it was this "failing" that warranted denial of their motion for summary judgment:

> * * * [T]he Directors made *no apparent effort* to arm themselves with *specific knowledge* about the present value of the Company in the May through July 2007 time period, despite *admittedly knowing* that the 13D filing effectively put the Company "in play," and, therefore, presumably, also knowing that an offer for the sale of the Company could occur at any time. It is these facts that raise the specter of "bad faith" in the present summary judgment record ...

The problem with the trial court's analysis is that *Revlon* duties do not arise simply because a company is "in play." The duty to seek the best available price applies only when a company embarks on a transaction—on its own initiative or in response to an unsolicited offer—that will result in a change of control. Basell's Schedule 13D did put the Lyondell directors, and the market in general, on notice that Basell was interested in acquiring Lyondell. The directors responded by promptly holding a special meeting to consider whether Lyondell should take any action. The directors decided that they would neither put the company up for sale nor institute defensive measures to fend off a possible hostile offer. Instead, they decided to take a "wait and see" approach. That decision was an entirely appropriate exercise of the directors' business judgment. The time for action under *Revlon* did not begin until July 10, 2007, when the directors began negotiating the sale of Lyondell.

The Court of Chancery focused on the directors' two months of inaction, when it should have focused on the one week during which they considered Basell's offer. During that one week, the directors met several times; their CEO tried to negotiate better terms; they evaluated Lyondell's value, the price offered and the likelihood of obtaining a better price; and then the directors approved the merger. The trial court acknowledged that the directors' conduct during those seven days might not demonstrate anything more than lack of due care. But the court remained skeptical about the directors' good faith—at least on the present record. That lingering concern was based on the trial court's synthesis of the *Revlon* line of cases, which led it to the erroneous conclusion that directors must follow one of several courses of action to satisfy their *Revlon* duties.

There is only one *Revlon* duty—to "[get] the best price for the stockholders at a sale of the company." No court can tell directors exactly how to accomplish that goal, because they will be facing a unique combination of circumstances, many of which will be outside their control. As we noted in *Barkan v. Amsted Industries, Inc.*, "there is no single blueprint that a board must follow to fulfill its duties. That said, our courts have highlighted both the positive and negative aspects of various boards' conduct under *Revlon*. The trial court drew several principles from those cases: directors must "engage actively in the sale process," and they must confirm that they have obtained the best available price either by conducting an auction, by conducting a market check, or by demonstrating "an impeccable knowledge of the market."

The Lyondell directors did not conduct an auction or a market check, and they did not satisfy the trial court that they had the "impeccable" market knowledge that the court believed was necessary to excuse their failure to pursue one of the first two alternatives. As a result, the Court of Chancery was unable to conclude that the directors had met their burden under *Revlon*. In evaluating the totality of the circumstances, even on this limited record, we would be inclined to hold otherwise. But we would not question the trial court's decision to seek additional evidence if the issue were whether the directors had exercised due care. Where, as here, the issue is whether the directors failed to act in good faith, the analysis is very different, and the existing record mandates the entry of judgment in favor of the directors. * * *

[B]ad faith will be found if a "fiduciary intentionally fails to act in the face of a known duty to act, demonstrating a conscious disregard for his duties." The trial court decided that the *Revlon* sale process must follow one of three courses, and that the Lyondell directors did not discharge that "known set of *[Revlon]* 'duties'." But, as noted, there are no legally prescribed steps that directors must follow to satisfy their *Revlon* duties. Thus, the directors' failure to take any specific steps during the sale process could not have demonstrated a conscious disregard of their duties. More importantly, there is a vast difference between an inadequate or flawed effort to carry out fiduciary duties and a conscious disregard for those duties.

Directors' decisions must be reasonable, not perfect. "In the transactional context, [an] extreme set of facts [is] required to sustain a disloyalty claim premised on the notion that disinterested directors were intentionally disregarding their duties." The trial court denied summary judgment because the Lyondell directors' "unexplained inaction" prevented the court from determining that they had acted in good faith. But, if the directors failed to do all that they should have under the circumstances, they breached their duty of care. Only if they knowingly and completely failed to undertake their responsibilities would they breach their duty of loyalty. The trial court approached the record from the wrong perspective. Instead of questioning whether disinterested, independent directors did everything that they (arguably) should have done to obtain the best sale price, the inquiry should have been whether those directors utterly failed to attempt to obtain the best sale price.

Viewing the record in this manner leads to only one possible conclusion. The Lyondell directors met several times to consider Basell's premium offer. They were generally aware of the value of their company and they knew the chemical company market. The directors solicited and followed the advice of their financial and legal advisors. They attempted to negotiate a higher offer even though all the evidence indicates that Basell had offered a "blowout" price. Finally, they approved the merger agreement, because "it was simply too good not to pass along [to the stockholders] for their consideration." We assume, as we must on summary judgment, that the Lyondell directors did absolutely nothing to prepare for Basell's offer, and that they did not even consider conducting a market check before agreeing to the merger. Even so, this record clearly establishes that the Lyondell directors did not breach their duty of loyalty by failing to act in good faith. In concluding otherwise, the Court of Chancery reversibly erred.

QUESTIONS AND NOTE

1. Section 13(d) of the Securities Exchange Act of 1934 requires anyone who acquires more than 5% of a company's stock to file a Schedule 13D that reveals the ownership interest. Such a filing often causes the market price of the company's stock to increase, because the filing may indicate that someone may be considering an attempt to acquire the company.

2. Do the facts remind you of *Smith v. Van Gorkum*? Compared to the directors in *Van Gorkum*, did the directors in *Ryan* devote more or less effort to evaluating the offer for their company? Why the different result in *Ryan*?

3. Recall that after *Van Gorkum*, the Delaware legislature passed Delaware § 102(b)(7), which permitted Delaware corporations to eliminate their directors' liability for violations of the duty of care. However, § 102(b)(7) does not permit elimination of liability for violations of the duty of loyalty and good faith. Faced with such exculpatory language in Lyondell Co.'s articles, the plaintiff in *Ryan* attempted to recast conduct that had been characterized in *Van Gorkum* as a violation of the duty of care. Now the plaintiff asserted that it was a violation of the duty of loyalty and good faith. *Lyondell* blocked this attempt to avoid § 102(b)(7).

3. FEDERAL AND STATE REGULATION OF HOSTILE TAKEOVERS

Chesapeake, Unocal, Revlon, Time, QVC, and *Lyondell* involved "fiduciary duty" limits to takeover defenses imposed by a target company's board. However, there are no fiduciary duty limits to the takeover efforts of the bidder's board; the bidder does not owe a fiduciary duty to the target's shareholders.

Although no cases impose fiduciary duty limits on takeover efforts, there are federal and state statutory limits. In 1968, Congress regulated tender offers by enacting the Williams Act, which amended §§ 13 and 14 of the Securities Exchange Act of 1934. The Williams Act not only requires various disclosures by the bidder or perspective bidder, but also contains substantive rules that limit a bidder's high-pressure tactics and fraud. In addition, some states have enacted statutes that make hostile takeovers more difficult, regardless of whether there has been compliance with the Williams Act standards.

The next two cases involved such statutes.

CTS CORPORATION v. DYNAMICS CORPORATION OF AMERICA

United States Supreme Court, 1987
481 U.S. 69

POWELL, J. These cases present the questions whether the Control Share Acquisitions Chapter of the Indiana Business Corporation Law, is pre-empted by the Williams Act, or violates the Commerce Clause of the Federal Constitution, Art. I, § 8, cl. 3.

[T]he Control Share Acquisitions Chapter (Indiana Act or Act) * * * applies only to "issuing public corporations." The term "corporation" includes only businesses incorporated in Indiana. An "issuing public corporation" is defined as:

> a corporation that has:
>
> (1) one hundred (100) or more shareholders;
>
> (2) its principal place of business, its principal office, or substantial assets within Indiana; and
>
> (3) either:
>
> (A) more than ten percent (10%) of its shareholders resident in Indiana;
>
> (B) more than ten percent (10%) of its shares owned by Indiana residents; or
>
> (C) ten thousand (10,000) shareholders resident in Indiana.

The Act focuses on the acquisition of "control shares" in an issuing public corporation. Under the Act, an entity acquires "control shares" whenever it acquires shares that, but for the operation of the Act, would bring its voting power in the corporation to or above any of three thresholds: 20%, 33 1/3%, or 50%. § 23–1–42–1. An entity that acquires control shares does not necessarily acquire voting rights. Rather, it gains those rights only "to the extent granted by resolution approved by the shareholders of the issuing public corporation." § 23–1–42–9(a). Section 23–1–42–9(b) requires a majority vote of all disinterested shareholders holding each class of stock for passage of such a resolution. The practical effect of this requirement is to condition acquisition of control of a corporation on approval of a majority of the pre-existing disinterested shareholders.

The shareholders decide whether to confer rights on the control shares at the next regularly scheduled meeting of the shareholders, or at a specially scheduled meeting. The acquiror can require management of the corporation to hold such a special meeting within 50 days if it files an "acquiring person statement," requests the meeting, and agrees to pay the expenses of the meeting. If the shareholders do not vote to restore voting rights to the shares, the corporation may redeem the control shares from the acquiror at fair market value, but it is not required to do so. Similarly, if the acquiror does not file an acquiring person statement with the corporation, the corporation may, if its bylaws or articles of incorporation so provide, redeem the shares at any time after 60 days after the acquiror's last acquisition.

On March 10, 1986, appellee Dynamics Corporation of America (Dynamics) owned 9.6% of the common stock of appellant CTS Corporation, an Indiana corporation. On that day, six days after the Act went into effect, Dynamics announced a tender offer for another million shares in CTS; purchase of those shares would have brought Dynamics' ownership interest in CTS to 27.5%. * * * On March 27, the board of directors of CTS, an Indiana corporation, elected to be governed by the provisions of the Act, see § 23–1–17–3.

* * * Dynamics sought a temporary restraining order, a preliminary injunction, and declaratory relief against CTS' use of the Act. On April 9, the District Court ruled that the Williams Act pre-empts the Indiana Act and granted Dynamics' motion for declaratory relief. * * *

[T]he Court of Appeals issued an order affirming the judgment of the District Court.

* * *

The first question in these cases is whether the Williams Act pre-empts the Indiana Act. * * * [T]he state statute can be pre-empted only if it frustrates the purposes of the federal law.

Our discussion begins with a brief summary of the structure and purposes of the Williams Act. Congress passed the Williams Act in 1968 in response to the increasing number of hostile tender offers. Before its passage, these transactions were not covered by the disclosure requirements of the federal securities laws. The Williams Act, backed by regulations of the SEC, imposes requirements in two basic areas. First, it requires the offeror to file a statement disclosing information about the offer, including: the offeror's background and identity; the source and amount of the funds to be used in making the purchase; the purpose of the purchase, including any plans to liquidate the company or make major changes in its corporate structure; and the extent of the offeror's holdings in the target company.

Second, the Williams Act, and the regulations that accompany it, establish procedural rules to govern tender offers. For example, stockholders who tender their shares may withdraw them while the offer remains open, and, if the offeror has not purchased their shares, any time after 60 days from commencement of the offer. The offer must remain open for at least 20 business days. If more shares are tendered than the offeror sought to purchase, purchases must be made on a pro rata basis from each tendering shareholder. Finally, the offeror must pay the same price for all purchases; if the offering price is increased before the end of the offer, those who already have tendered must receive the benefit of the increased price.

The Indiana Act differs in major respects from the Illinois statute that the Court considered in *Edgar v. MITE Corp.*, 457 (1982). After reviewing the legislative history of the Williams Act, Justice White, joined by Chief Justice Burger and Justice Blackmun (the plurality), concluded that the Williams Act struck a careful balance between the interests of offerors and target companies, and that any state statute that "upset" this balance was pre-empted.

The plurality [in *MITE*] identified three offending features of the Illinois statute. Justice WHITE's opinion first noted that the Illinois statute provided for a 20–day precommencement period. During this time, management could disseminate its views on the upcoming offer to share-holders, but offerors could not publish their offers. The plurality found that this provision gave management "a powerful tool to combat tender offers." This contrasted dramatically with the Williams Act; Congress had deleted express precommencement notice provisions from the Williams Act. According to the plurality, Congress had determined that the potentially adverse consequences of such a provision on shareholders should be avoided. Thus, the plurality concluded that the Illinois provision "frustrate[d] the objectives of the Williams Act." The second criticized feature of the Illinois statute was a provision for a hearing on a tender offer that, because it set no deadline, allowed management " 'to stymie indefinitely a takeover.' " The plurality noted that " 'delay can seriously impede a tender offer.' " The third troublesome feature of the Illinois statute was its requirement that the fairness of tender offers would be reviewed by the Illinois Secretary of State. Noting that "Congress intended for investors to be free to make their own decisions," the plurality concluded that " '[t]he state thus offers investor protection at the expense of investor autono-my—an approach quite in conflict with that adopted by Congress.' "

As the plurality opinion in *MITE* did not represent the views of a majority of the Court, we are not bound by its reasoning. We need not question that reasoning, however, because we believe the Indiana Act passes muster even under the broad interpretation of the Williams Act articulated by Justice White in *MITE*. As is apparent from our summary of its reasoning, the overriding concern of the *MITE* plurality was that the Illinois statute considered in that case operated to favor management against offerors, to the detriment of shareholders. By contrast, the statute now before the Court protects the independent shareholder against the contending parties. Thus, the Act furthers a basic purpose of the Williams Act, "plac[ing] investors on an equal footing with the takeover bidder."

The Indiana Act operates on the assumption, implicit in the Williams Act, that independent shareholders faced with tender offers often are at a disadvantage. By allowing such shareholders to vote as a group, the Act protects them from the coercive aspects of some tender offers. * * * The desire of the Indiana Legislature to protect shareholders of Indiana corporations from this type of coercive offer does not conflict with the Williams Act. Rather, it furthers the federal policy of investor protection.

In implementing its goal, the Indiana Act avoids the problems the plurality discussed in *MITE*. Unlike the *MITE* statute, the Indiana Act does not give either management or the offeror an advantage in communicating with the shareholders about the impending offer. The Act also does not impose an indefinite delay on tender offers. Nothing in the Act prohibits an offeror from consummating an offer on the 20th business day, the earliest day permitted under applicable federal regulations, *see* 17 CFR § 240.14e–1(a) (1986). Nor does the Act allow the state government to interpose its views of fairness between willing buyers and sellers of shares of the target company. Rather, the Act allows shareholders to evaluate the fairness of the offer collectively.

The Court of Appeals based its finding of pre-emption on its view that the practical effect of the Indiana Act is to delay consummation of tender offers until 50 days after the commencement of the offer. * * *

Even assuming that the Indiana Act imposes some additional delay, nothing in *MITE* suggested that any delay imposed by state regulation, however short, would create a conflict with the Williams Act. The plurality argued only that the offeror should "be free to go forward without unreasonable delay." * * *

Finally, we note that the Williams Act would pre-empt a variety of state corporate laws of hitherto unquestioned validity if it were construed to pre-empt any state statute that may limit or delay the free exercise of power after a successful tender offer. State corporate laws commonly permit corporations to stagger the terms of their directors. By staggering the terms of directors, and thus having annual elections for only one class of directors each year, corporations may delay the time when a successful offeror gains control of the board of directors. * * *

In our view, the possibility that the Indiana Act will delay some tender offers is insufficient to require a conclusion that the Williams Act pre-empts the Act. The longstanding prevalence of state regulation in this area suggests that, if Congress had intended to pre-empt all state laws that delay the acquisition of voting control following a tender offer, it would have said so explicitly. The regulatory conditions that the Act places on tender offers are consistent with the text and the purposes of the Williams Act. Accordingly, we hold that the Williams Act does not pre-empt the Indiana Act.

As an alternative basis for its decision, the Court of Appeals held that the Act violates the Commerce Clause of the Federal Constitution. We now address this holding. On its face, the Commerce Clause is nothing more than a grant to Congress of the power "[t]o regulate Commerce . . . among the several States . . . ," Art. I, § 8, cl. 3. But it has been settled for more than a century that the Clause prohibits States from taking certain actions respecting interstate commerce even absent congressional action. * * *

The principal objects of dormant Commerce Clause scrutiny are statutes that discriminate against interstate commerce. The Indiana Act is not such a statute. It has the same effects on tender offers whether or not the offeror is a domiciliary or resident of Indiana. * * *

The Court of Appeals did not find the Act unconstitutional for either of these threshold reasons. Rather, its decision rested on its view of the Act's potential to hinder tender offers. We think the Court of Appeals failed to appreciate the significance for Commerce Clause analysis of the fact that state regulation of corporate governance is regulation of entities whose very existence and attributes are a product of state law. As Chief Justice Marshall explained:

> A corporation is an artificial being, invisible, intangible, and existing only in contemplation of law. Being the mere creature of law, it possesses only those properties which the charter of its creation confers upon it, either expressly, or as incidental to its very existence. These are such as are supposed best calculated to effect the object for which it was created.

Trustees of Dartmouth College v. Woodward, 4 Wheat. 518, 636 (1819).

Every State in this country has enacted laws regulating corporate governance. By prohibiting certain transactions, and regulating others, such laws necessarily affect certain aspects of interstate commerce. This necessarily is true with respect to corporations with shareholders in States other than the State of incorporation. Large corporations that are listed on national exchanges, or even regional exchanges, will have shareholders in many States and shares that are traded frequently. The markets that facilitate this national and international participation in ownership of corporations are essential for providing capital not only for new enterprises but also for established companies that need to expand their businesses. This beneficial free market system depends at its core upon the fact that a corporation—except in the rarest situations—is organized under, and governed by, the law of a single jurisdiction, traditionally the corporate law of the State of its incorporation.

These regulatory laws may affect directly a variety of corporate transactions. Mergers are a typical example. In view of the substantial effect that a merger may have on the shareholders' interests in a corporation, many States require supermajority votes to approve mergers. By requiring a greater vote for mergers than is required for other transactions, these laws make it more difficult for corporations to merge. State laws also may provide for "dissenters' rights" under which minority shareholders who disagree with corporate decisions to take particular actions are entitled to sell their shares to the corporation at fair market value. By requiring the corporation to purchase the shares of dissenting shareholders, these laws may inhibit a corporation from engaging in the specified transactions.

It thus is an accepted part of the business landscape in this country for States to create corporations, to prescribe their powers, and to define the rights that are acquired by purchasing their shares. A State has an interest in promoting stable relationships among parties involved in the corporations it charters, as well as in ensuring that investors in such corporations have an effective voice in corporate affairs.

There can be no doubt that the Act reflects these concerns. The primary purpose of the Act is to protect the shareholders of Indiana corporations. It does this by affording shareholders, when a takeover offer is made, an opportunity to decide collectively whether the resulting change in voting control of the corporation, as they perceive it, would be desirable. A change of management may have important effects on the shareholders' interests; it is well within the State's role as overseer of corporate governance to offer this opportunity. The autonomy provided by allowing shareholders collectively to determine whether the takeover is advantageous to their interests may be especially beneficial where a hostile tender offer may coerce shareholders into tendering their shares. * * *

Dynamics argues in any event that the State has " 'no legitimate interest in protecting the nonresident share-holders.' " * * * We agree that Indiana has no interest in protecting nonresident shareholders of nonresident corporations. But this Act applies only to corporations incorporated in Indiana. We reject the contention that Indiana has no interest in providing for the shareholders of its corporations the voting autonomy granted by the Act. Indiana has a substantial interest in preventing the corporate form from becoming a shield for unfair business dealing. Moreover, unlike the Illinois statute invalidated in *MITE*, the Indiana Act applies only to corporations that have a substantial number of shareholders in Indiana. Thus, every application of the Indiana Act will affect a substantial number of Indiana residents, whom Indiana indisputably has an interest in protecting.

Dynamics' argument that the Act is unconstitutional ultimately rests on its contention that the Act will limit the number of successful tender offers. There is little evidence that this will occur. But even if true, this result would not substantially affect our Commerce Clause analysis. We reiterate that this Act does not prohibit any entity—resident or nonresident—from offering to purchase, or from purchasing, shares in Indiana corporations, or from attempting thereby to gain control. It only provides regulatory procedures designed for the better protection of the corporations' shareholders. * * *

On its face, the Indiana Control Share Acquisitions Chapter even-handedly determines the voting rights of shares of Indiana corporations. The Act does not conflict with the provisions or purposes of the Williams

Act. To the limited extent that the Act affects interstate commerce, this is justified by the State's interests in defining the attributes of shares in its corporations and in protecting shareholders. * * * Accordingly, we reverse the judgment of the Court of Appeals.

AMANDA ACQUISITION CORPORATION v. UNIVERSAL FOODS CORPORATION

United States Court of Appeals, Seventh Circuit, 1989
877 F.2d 496

EASTERBROOK, CIRCUIT JUDGE. States have enacted three generations of takeover statutes in the last 20 years. Illinois enacted a first-generation statute, which forbade acquisitions of any firm with substantial assets in Illinois unless a public official approved. We concluded that such a statute injures investors, is preempted by the Williams Act, and is unconstitutional under the dormant Commerce Clause. The Supreme Court affirmed the judgment under the Commerce Clause, *Edgar v. MITE Corp.*, 457 U.S. 624 (1982).

Indiana enacted a second-generation statute, applicable only to firms incorporated there and eliminating governmental veto power. Indiana's law provides that the acquiring firm's shares lose their voting power unless the target's directors approve the acquisition or the shareholders not affiliated with either bidder or management authorize restoration of votes. We concluded that this statute, too, is inimical to investors' interests, preempted by the Williams Act, and unconstitutional under the Commerce Clause. This time the Supreme Court did not agree. It thought the Indiana statute consistent with both Williams Act and Commerce Clause. *CTS Corp. v. Dynamics Corp. of America*, 481 U.S. 69 (1987). Adopting Justice White's view of preemption for the sake of argument, id. at 81, the Court found no inconsistency between state and federal law because Indiana allowed the bidder to acquire the shares without hindrance. Such a law makes the shares less attractive, but it does not regulate the process of bidding. As for the Commerce Clause, the Court took Indiana's law to be regulation of internal corporate affairs, potentially beneficial because it would allow investors to avoid the "coercion" of two-tier bids and other tactics.

Wisconsin has a third-generation takeover statute. Enacted after *CTS*, it postpones the kinds of transactions that often follow tender offers (and often are the reason for making the offers in the first place). Unless the target's board agrees to the transaction in advance, the bidder must wait three years after buying the shares to merge with the target or acquire more than 5% of its assets. We must decide whether this is consistent with the Williams Act and Commerce Clause.

Amanda Acquisition Corporation is a shell with a single purpose: to acquire Universal Foods Corporation, a diversified firm incorporated in Wisconsin and traded on the New York Stock Exchange. Universal is covered by Wisconsin's anti-takeover law. Amanda is a subsidiary of High

Voltage Engineering Corp., a small electronics firm in Massachusetts. Most of High Voltage's equity capital comes from Berisford Capital PLC, a British venture capital firm, and Hyde Park Partners L.P., a partnership affiliated with the principals of Berisford. Chase Manhattan Bank has promised to lend Amanda 50% of the cost of the acquisition, secured by the stock of Universal.

In mid-November 1988 Universal's stock was trading for about $25 per share. On December 1 Amanda commenced a tender offer at $30.50, to be effective if at least 75% of the stock should be tendered. This all-cash, all-shares offer has been increased by stages to $38.00. Amanda's financing is contingent on a prompt merger with Universal if the offer succeeds, so the offer is conditional on a judicial declaration that the law is invalid. * * *

No firm incorporated in Wisconsin and having its headquarters, substantial operations, or 10% of its shares or shareholders there may "engage in a business combination with an interested stockholder ... for 3 years after the interested stockholder's stock acquisition date unless the board of directors of the [Wisconsin] corporation has approved, before the interested stockholder's stock acquisition date, that business combination or the purchase of stock", Wis.Stat. § 180.726(2). An "interested stockholder" is one owning 10% of the voting stock, directly or through associates (anyone acting in concert with it), § 180.726(1)(j). A "business combination" is a merger with the bidder or any of its affiliates, sale of more than 5% of the assets to bidder or affiliate, liquidation of the target, or a transaction by which the target guarantees the bidder's or affiliates debts or passes tax benefits to the bidder or affiliate, § 180.726(1)(e). The law, in other words, provides for almost hermetic separation of bidder and target for three years after the bidder obtains 10% of the stock—unless the target's board consented before then. No matter how popular the offer, the ban applies: obtaining 85% (even 100%) of the stock held by non-management shareholders won't allow the bidder to engage in a business combination, as it would under Delaware law. Wisconsin firms cannot opt out of the law, as may corporations subject to almost all other state takeover statutes. In Wisconsin it is management's approval in advance, or wait three years. Even when the time is up, the bidder needs the approval of a majority of the remaining investors, without any provision disqualifying shares still held by the managers who resisted the transaction. The district court found that this statute "effectively eliminates hostile leveraged buyouts". As a practical matter, Wisconsin prohibits any offer contingent on a merger between bidder and target, a condition attached to about 90% of contemporary tender offers.

Amanda filed this suit seeking a declaration that this law is preempted by the Williams Act and inconsistent with the Commerce Clause. * * *

If our views of the wisdom of state law mattered, Wisconsin's takeover statute would not survive. Like our colleagues who decided *MITE* and

CTS, we believe that antitakeover legislation injures shareholders.* [5] Managers frequently realize gains for investors via voluntary combinations (mergers). If gains are to be had, but managers balk, tender offers are investors' way to go over managers' heads. If managers are not maximizing the firm's value—perhaps because they have missed the possibility of a synergistic combination, perhaps because they are clinging to divisions that could be better run in other hands, perhaps because they are just not the best persons for the job—a bidder that believes it can realize more of the firm's value will make investors a higher offer. Investors tender; the bidder gets control and changes things. The prospect of monitoring by would-be bidders, and an occasional bid at a premium, induces managers to run corporations more efficiently and replaces them if they will not.

Premium bids reflect the benefits for investors. The price of a firm's stock represents investors' consensus estimate of the value of the shares under current and anticipated conditions. Stock is worth the present value of anticipated future returns—dividends and other distributions. Tender offers succeed when bidders offer more. Only when the bid exceeds the value of the stock (however investors compute value) will it succeed. A statute that precludes investors from receiving or accepting a premium offer makes them worse off. It makes the economy worse off too, because the higher bid reflects the better use to which the bidder can put the target's assets. (If the bidder can't improve the use of the assets, it injures itself by paying a premium.)

Universal, making an argument common among supporters of antitakeover laws, contends that its investors do not appreciate the worth of its business plans, that its stock is trading for too little, and that if investors tender reflexively they injure themselves. If only they would wait, Universal submits, they would do better under current management. A variant of the argument has it that although smart investors know that the stock is underpriced, many investors are passive and will tender; even the smart investors then must tender to avoid doing worse on the "back end" of the deal. State laws giving management the power to block an offer enable the managers to protect the investors from themselves.

Both versions of this price-is-wrong argument imply: (a) that the stock of firms defeating offers later appreciates in price, topping the bid, thus revealing the wisdom of waiting till the market wises up; and (b) that investors in firms for which no offer is outstanding gain when they adopt devices so that managers may fend off unwanted offers (or states adopt laws with the same consequence). Efforts to verify these implications have failed. The best available data show that if a firm fends off a bid, its

---

* [5] Because both the district court and the parties—like the Williams Act—examine tender offers from the perspective of equity investors, we employ the same approach. States could choose to protect "constituencies" other than stockholders. Creditors, managers, and workers invest human rather than financial capital. But the limitation of our inquiry to equity investors does not affect the analysis, because no evidence of which we are aware suggests that bidders confiscate workers' and other participants' investments to any greater degree than do incumbents—who may (and frequently do) close or move plants to follow the prospect of profit.

profits decline, and its stock price (adjusted for inflation and market-wide changes) never tops the initial bid, even if it is later acquired by another firm. Stock of firms adopting poison pills falls in price, as does the stock of firms that adopt most kinds of anti-takeover amendments to their articles of incorporation. Studies of laws similar to Wisconsin's produce the same conclusion: share prices of firms incorporated in the state drop when the legislation is enacted.

Although a takeover-proof firm leaves investors at the mercy of incumbent managers (who may be mistaken about the wisdom of their business plan even when they act in the best of faith), a takeover-resistant firm may be able to assist its investors. An auction may run up the price, and delay may be essential to an auction. Auctions transfer money from bidders to targets, and diversified investors would not gain from them (their left pocket loses what the right pocket gains); diversified investors would lose from auctions if the lower returns to bidders discourage future bids. But from targets' perspectives, once a bid is on the table an auction may be the best strategy. The full effects of auctions are hard to unravel, sparking scholarly debate. Devices giving managers some ability to orchestrate investors' responses, in order to avoid panic tenders in response to front-end-loaded offers, also could be beneficial, as the Supreme Court emphasized in *CTS*. ("Could be" is an important qualifier; even from a perspective limited to targets' shareholders given a bid on the table, it is important to know whether managers use this power to augment bids or to stifle them, and whether courts can tell the two apart.)

State anti-takeover laws do not serve these ends well, however. Investors who prefer to give managers the discretion to orchestrate responses to bids may do so through "fair-price" clauses in the articles of incorporation and other consensual devices. Other firms may choose different strategies. A law such as Wisconsin's does not add options to firms that would like to give more discretion to their managers; instead it destroys the possibility of divergent choices. Wisconsin's law applies even when the investors prefer to leave their managers under the gun, to allow the market full sway. [One study] found that state anti-takeover laws have little or no effect on the price of shares if the firm already has poison pills (or related devices) in place, but strongly negative effects on price when firms have no such contractual devices. To put this differently, state laws have bite only when investors, given the choice, would deny managers the power to interfere with tender offers (maybe already have denied managers that power).

Skepticism about the wisdom of a state's law does not lead to the conclusion that the law is beyond the state's power, however. We have not been elected custodians of investors' wealth. States need not treat investors' welfare as their summum bonum. Perhaps they choose to protect managers' welfare instead, or believe that the current economic literature reaches an incorrect conclusion and that despite appearances takeovers injure investors in the long run. Unless a federal statute or the Constitution bars the way, Wisconsin's choice must be respected.

* * *

The Williams Act regulates the process of tender offers: timing, disclosure, proration if tenders exceed what the bidder is willing to buy, best-price rules. It slows things down, allowing investors to evaluate the offer and management's response. Best-price, proration, and short-tender rules ensure that investors who decide at the end of the offer get the same treatment as those who decide immediately, reducing pressure to leap before looking. After complying with the disclosure and delay requirements, the bidder is free to take the shares. MITE held invalid a state law that increased the delay and, by authorizing a regulator to nix the offer, created a distinct possibility that the bidder would be unable to buy the stock (and the holders to sell it) despite compliance with federal law. Illinois tried to regulate the process of tender offers, contradicting in some respects the federal rules. Indiana, by contrast, allowed the tender offer to take its course as the Williams Act specified but "sterilized" the acquired shares until the remaining investors restored their voting rights. Congress said nothing about the voting power of shares acquired in tender offers. Indiana's law reduced the benefits the bidder anticipated from the acquisition but left the process alone. So the Court, although accepting Justice White's views for the purpose of argument, held that Indiana's rules do not conflict with the federal norms.

CTS observed that laws affecting the voting power of acquired shares do not differ in principle from many other rules governing the internal affairs of corporations. Laws requiring staggered or classified boards of directors delay the transfer of control to the bidder; laws requiring supermajority vote for a merger may make a transaction less attractive or impossible. Yet these are not preempted by the Williams Act * * *. Federal securities laws frequently regulate process while state corporate law regulates substance. * * *

Any bidder complying with federal law is free to acquire shares of Wisconsin firms on schedule. Delay in completing a second-stage merger may make the target less attractive, and thus depress the price offered or even lead to an absence of bids; it does not, however, alter any of the procedures governed by federal regulation. Indeed Wisconsin's law does not depend in any way on how the acquiring firm came by its stock: open-market purchases, private acquisitions of blocs, and acquisitions via tender offers are treated identically. Wisconsin's law is no different in effect from one saying that for the three years after a person acquires 10% of a firm's stock, a unanimous vote is required to merge. Corporate law once had a generally-applicable unanimity rule in major transactions, a rule discarded because giving every investor the power to block every reorganization stopped many desirable changes. (Many investors could use their "hold-up" power to try to engross a larger portion of the gains, creating a complex bargaining problem that often could not be solved.) Wisconsin's more restrained version of unanimity also may block beneficial transactions, but not by tinkering with any of the procedures established in federal law.

* * *

The Commerce Clause, Art. I, § 8 cl. 3 of the Constitution, grants Congress the power "[t]o regulate Commerce ... among the several States". * * *

When state law discriminates against interstate commerce expressly—for example, when Wisconsin closes its border to butter from Minnesota—the negative Commerce Clause steps in. The law before us is not of this type. * * *

* * * A putative bidder located in Wisconsin enjoys no privilege over a firm located in New York. So too with investors: all are treated identically, regardless of residence. Doubtless most bidders (and investors) are located outside Wisconsin, but unless the law discriminates according to residence this alone does not matter. * * *

To say that states have the power to enact laws whose costs exceed their benefits is not to say that investors should kiss their wallets goodbye. States compete to offer corporate codes attractive to firms. Managers who want to raise money incorporate their firms in the states that offer the combination of rules investors prefer. Laws that in the short run injure investors and protect managers will in the longer run make the state less attractive to firms that need to raise new capital. If the law is "protectionist", the protected class is the existing body of managers (and other workers), suppliers, and so on, which bears no necessary relation to state boundaries. States regulating the affairs of domestic corporations cannot in the long run injure anyone but themselves. * * *

The long run takes time to arrive, and it is tempting to suppose that courts could contribute to investors' welfare by eliminating laws that impose costs in the short run. The price of such warfare, however, is a reduction in the power of competition among states. Courts seeking to impose "good" rules on the states diminish the differences among corporate codes and dampen competitive forces. Too, courts may fail in their quest. How do judges know which rules are best? Often only the slow forces of competition reveal that information. Early economic studies may mislead, or judges (not trained as social scientists) may misinterpret the available data or act precipitously. Our Constitution allows the states to act as laboratories; slow migration (or national law on the authority of the Commerce Clause) grinds the failures under. No such process weeds out judicial errors, or decisions that, although astute when rendered, have become anachronistic in light of changes in the economy. Judges must hesitate for these practical reasons—and not only because of limits on their constitutional competence—before trying to "perfect" corporate codes.

* * *

Even in Wisconsin, though, options remain. * * * Because every potential bidder labors under the same drawback, the firm placing the highest value on the target still should win. Or a bidder might take down the stock and pledge it (or its dividends) as security for any loans. That is, the bidder could operate the target as a subsidiary for three years. The corporate world is full of partially owned subsidiaries. If there is gain to be had from changing the debt-equity ratio of the target, that can be done consistent with Wisconsin law. The prospect of being locked into place as holders of illiquid minority positions would cause many persons to sell out, and the threat of being locked in would cause many managers to give assent in advance, as Wisconsin allows. (Or bidders might demand that directors waive the protections of state law, just as Amanda believes that the directors' fiduciary duties compel them to redeem the poison pill rights.) Many bidders would find lock-in unattractive because of the potential for litigation by minority investors, and the need to operate the firm as a subsidiary might foreclose savings or synergies from merger. So none of these options is a perfect substitute for immediate merger, but each is a crack in the defensive wall allowing some value-increasing bids to proceed.

At the end of the day, however, it does not matter whether these countermeasures are "enough". The Commerce Clause does not demand that states leave bidders a "meaningful opportunity for success". * * * "[A] law can be both economic folly and constitutional." *CTS*, 481 U.S. at 96–97 (Scalia, J., concurring). Wisconsin's law may well be folly; we are confident that it is constitutional.

Affirmed.

* * * * *

Before considering other business structures, think about how corporations and partnerships have become more similar and how they remain different. A couple of new similarities:

First, legal entity status. A corporation has always been a separate legal entity. Now a partnership is also a separate legal entity.

Second, management systems. Originally, unlike a partnership, a corporation was managed by its board of directors who did not have to be shareholders. Today, a corporation can eliminate its board of directors and have a system of shareholder management of the corporation that operates very much like partner management of a partnership.

A couple of important remaining differences:

First, owner liability. Shareholders are not (generally) personally liable for the debts of a business structured as a corporation. Partners are personally liable for the debts of a business structured as a partnership.

Second, owner transferability. There are no general statutory constraints on a corporation's shareholder selling to a third party her ownership interest, i.e., selling her rights as a shareholder. There are however significant statutory constraints on a partner selling to a third party his partnership interest, i.e., selling his rights as a partner.

In addition, a partner is statutorily empowered to trigger the partnership's buyout of his rights as a partner through dissociation. There is no general corporate statute counterpart to dissociation. Except for the limited situations that trigger a dissenting shareholder's right of appraisal, a shareholder is not statutorily empowered to trigger the corporation's buyout of her ownership interest.

Chapter Nine

What Is a Limited Partnership and How Does It Work?

■ ■ ■

In considering what business structure to use for Bubba's Burritos, Propp, Agee, and Capel of course want "the best of both worlds."* They want the favorable tax treatment of a partnership and the protection from personal liability of a corporation.

If their lawyer took a business associations course in law school that used a casebook other than ours, she probably would recommend that they structure Bubba's Burritos as a limited partnership. Limited partnership is an old form of business structure. The original Uniform Limited Partnership Act (ULPA) was promulgated in 1916. In recent years, there have been important changes in limited partnership law. A Revised Uniform Limited Partnership Act (RULPA) was promulgated in 1976 and further significant amendments were made in 1985. Moreover, several states have in recent years made significant changes in their version of RULPA.† As if that were not enough, in 2001, a new version of ULPA was promulgated. By 2009, 14 states had adopted this Act, which we will call "ULPA 2001". *See generally* Allan W. Vestal & Thomas E. Rutledge, *The Uniform Limited Partnership Act (2001) comes to Kentucky: An Owner's Manual*, 34 N. Ky. L. Rev. 411 (2007).

This activity has been prompted in part by (i) changes in the Internal Revenue Code under which unincorporated business entities can qualify for the more favorable partnership tax treatment and (ii) the creation of new forms of business structures such as limited liability companies (LLCs), which we study in Chapter 10, and limited liability partnerships (LLPs), which we discussed in Chapter 3.

---

* Epstein thought the phrase "best of both worlds" was too trite to use in a serious book like this until it was pointed out that it is the title of the theme song for the Hannah Montana TV show. Moreover, a Yale law professor used the phrase in an article published in the Harvard Law Review. *See* Bruce Ackerman, *The New Separation of Powers*, 113 Harv. L. Rev. 633, 714 (2000).

† "Since 1983, the General Assembly has amended the LP Act eleven times, with a view to continuing Delaware's status as an innovative leader in the field of limited partnerships." Elf Atochem North America, Inc. v. Jaffari & Malek LLC, 727 A.2d 286, 289 (Del. 1999).

Some experts conclude that these new business structures will replace limited partnerships. Indeed, this seems likely. Nonetheless, we need to understand what limited partnerships are and how they work because:

- there are a lot of old businesses and old lawyers who use the limited partnership form;

- there is a lot of limited partnership law in the law of LLCs and LLPs; and

- there are still situations in which structuring a business as a limited partnership is the best way to meet your client's needs.

A. WHAT IS A LIMITED PARTNERSHIP AND WHAT IS LIMITED PARTNERSHIP LAW?

The most obvious difference between a limited partnership and a general partnership is that a limited partnership has limited partners! (Not all of this business stuff is difficult.) The limited partnership must also have at least one general partner. A general partnership, in contrast, has only general partners. Limited partners are not personally liable for the debts of the limited partnership. Article 3 of RULPA deals with limited partners. The general partner(s) in a limited partnership have the same rights and duties as partners in a general partnership. Article 4 of RULPA deals with general partners in a limited partnership.

Because of the hybrid nature of limited partnerships, they have been subject not only to limited partnership laws but also to general partnership laws. Thus, RULPA § 1105 provides "In any case not provided for in this act, the provisions of the Uniform Partnership Act govern." Stated another way, limited partnerships have been said to be "linked" to partnership law, whether that general partnership law was UPA or RUPA (which we saw in Chapter 3). Scholars debated whether such "linking" was required as a matter of law or desirable as a matter of policy. *See,* Larry E. Ribstein, *Limited Partnerships Revisited*, 67 U. CINN. L. REV. 953 (1999).

ULPA 2001 can be seen as a response to this debate. It "de-links" the limited partnership from UPA and RUPA and accounts for the recent development of LLCs and LLPs. The Prefatory Note to ULPA 2001 makes clear that the new Act "targets two types of enterprises that seem largely beyond the scope of LLPs and LLCs: (i) sophisticated manager-entrenched commercial deals whose participants commit for the long term, and (ii) estate planning arrangements (family limited partnerships)."*

No matter what statute applies and no matter what the nature of the business, it is clear universally that a limited partnership is an entity. It is

---

* A family limited partnership is basically a form of estate planning. It permits family members to transfer wealth from one generation to another while maintaining control over the assets and lowering the amount of gift or estate tax that would be incurred by direct transfer.

also clear that a limited partnership is subject to federal securities laws such as 10b–5 and state securities laws. While the phrase "limited partnership" is not expressly included in the definition of "security" in § 2(a)(1) of the Securities Act of 1933, limited partnership interests come within the Supreme Court's interpretation of § 2(a)(1). *SEC v. W.J. Howey Co.*, 328 U.S. 293, 299 (1946) (security exists "if a person invests his money in a common enterprise and is led to expect profits solely from the efforts of the promoter or a third party.")

B. WHAT ARE THE LEGAL PROBLEMS IN STARTING A BUSINESS AS A LIMITED PARTNERSHIP?

Unlike general partnerships (but like corporations), limited partnerships do not come into existence until there has been a public filing, usually with the secretary of state of the state of organization. That document is generally called a Certificate of Limited Partnership.

We have set out below the certificate of limited partnership available from the website of (you guessed it) the Delaware Division of Corporations, http://corp.delaware.gov/lpform09.pdf.

STATE of DELAWARE
CERTIFICATE of LIMITED PARTNERSHIP

The Undersigned, desiring to form a limited partnership pursuant to the Delaware Revised Uniform Limited Partnership Act, 6 Delaware Code, Chapter 17, does hereby certify as follows:

First: The name of the limited partnership is _____

Second: The address of its registered office in the State of Delaware is _____ in the city of _____. Zip code _____. The name of the Registered Agent at such address is _____.

Third: The name and mailing address of each general partner is as follows:
_____

In Witness Whereof, the undersigned has executed this Certificate of Limited Partnership as of _____ day of _____, A.D. _____.

BY: _____
(General Partner)

NAME: _____
(type or print name)

QUESTIONS

1.   Why do limited partnership statutes condition the existence of a limited partnership on a public filing of a certificate of limited partnership when general partnership statutes do not condition the existence of a partnership on a public filing? Is the reason related to the fact that limited partners (like shareholders in a corporation) are not personally liable for business debts?

2.   Agee, Capel and Propp want to make and sell Southern-style burritos near a college campus in a state other than Delaware. Can they structure their business as a limited partnership organized in Delaware?

3.   What are the possible advantages of organizing a limited partnership in Delaware? (Reconsider your answer after you consider *Kahn v. Icahn* later in this chapter.)

4.   If your clients decide to organize their limited partnership in a state that has adopted RULPA, can you still use the Delaware form of Certificate of Limited Partnership? Review RULPA § 201 (and the Official Comment to that section).

5.   There are several requirements for naming the limited partnership. RULPA § 102. Why?

Even if the Certificate of Limited Partnership meets the requirements of your state's limited partnership law, that document alone will not meet the requirements of your clients. The more important document to your clients is the limited partnership agreement.

Although RULPA does not require that there be a written limited partnership agreement, almost all limited partnerships have detailed written agreements. In particular, these partnership agreements define the relative roles of the limited partners and the general partner(s).

Recall that limited partnership statutes require that

● a limited partnership must have at least one general partner;

● this general partner, unlike the limited partners, is liable for the debts of the partnership; and

● the name and the address of the general partner must be set out in the Certificate of Limited Partnership, which is filed in public records. The limited partnership statutes do not, however, require that the general partner be a natural, flesh-and-blood person.

The general partner(s) in a limited partnership is liable for the business debts. There are two ways, however, in which business people avoid personal liability in the limited partnership. First, some states now recognize a special form of limited partnership called the "limited liability limited partnership" (LLLP). This is similar to the "limited liability partnership" (LLP) we saw in Chapter 3. There, as here, the general partner may file with the secretary of state a certificate telling the world that the general partner will not be personally liable for what the business does.

Second, the business people may simply put a corporation in place as the general partner. *See* RULPA § 101. Indeed, this is very common. If Agee, Propp, and Capel want to structure their burrito business as a limited partnership and want to avoid personal liability, they take two simple steps: (1) organize a corporation, Bubba's Burritos, Inc., and (2) organize a limited partnership, Bubba's Burritos Limited Partnership, with Bubba's Burritos, Inc. as the only general partner and each of them as limited partners. Then they use the limited partnership, Bubba's Burritos Limited Partnership, to own and operate the business. Although Bubba's Burritos, Inc. will now, as general partner, be personally liable for the limited partnership's liabilities, the *owners* of the corporation will not be; the corporate form protects them from personal liability.

C. WHAT ARE THE LEGAL PROBLEMS IN OPERATING A BUSINESS AS A LIMITED PARTNERSHIP?

1. WHO DECIDES WHAT?

The answer to this question is found in the limited partnership statute and the limited partnership agreement. As a rule of thumb, the answer will be that the general partner decides. RULPA establishes this as the default rule. Unless the limited partnership agreement specifies otherwise, the general partner has the same rights as a partner in a general partnership. RULPA § 403(a). And recall that each partner in a general partnership has equal management rights. RUPA § 401(f).

What should a limited partnership agreement say about the role of limited partners in business decisions? Review the following two examples of limited partnership agreement provisions relating to the role of limited partners in making decisions:

Example 1: Voting Rights.

The business of the Partnership will be managed by the General Partners, and the Limited Partners will have no right to vote or participate in the affairs of the Partnership except as specifically provided in this Agreement.

(a) *Actions Requiring Unanimous Approval.* The unanimous vote or written consent of all Partners will be required to:

(i) increase the required contribution of a Partner;

(ii) compromise a Partner's obligation to make a required contribution or return an improper distribution;

(iii) alter the Percentage Interest of a Partner or the priority of a Partner as to distributions, except as provided in this Agreement; and

(iv) amend this Agreement so as to alter, directly or indirectly, the actions requiring unanimous approval of Partners.

(b) *Actions Requiring More than Majority Vote.* The vote or written consent of Limited Partners holding at least _____ [percentage, such as sixty percent (60%)] of the Percentage Interests then held by Limited Partners is required to _____ [list actions requiring greater than majority approval, such as:

(i) remove a general partner; or

(ii) admit a new general partner; or

(iii) elect to continue the Partnership after a general partner ceases to be a general partner where there is no remaining or surviving general partner].

(c) *Actions Requiring Majority Vote.* The vote or written consent of Limited Partners holding at least a majority of the Percentage Interests then held by Limited Partners is required to approve:

(i) the dissolution and winding up of the Partnership as provided in Article Eight;

(ii) the merger of the Partnership or the sale, exchange, lease, transfer, mortgage, pledge, or encumbrance of all or a substantial portion of its assets other than in the ordinary course of business;

(iii) the incurrence of indebtedness other than in the ordinary course of its business;

(iv) a change in the nature of the business of the Partnership; and

(v) transactions in which any of the General Partners have an actual or potential conflict of interest with the Limited Partners or the Partnership. 4 CALIFORNIA TRANSACTIONS FORMS–BUS. ENTITIES § 18.33 (1996).

Example 2: The Limited Partners

The Limited Partners shall not take any part in the management of the business or the affairs of the Partnership in dealing with third parties and shall have no right or authority to act for or bind the partnership in any way. Lewis R. Kaster, *Limited Partnership Agreement for Ownership of Existing Commercial Real Estate,* 938 PLI/CORP 187 (May 1996).

QUESTIONS AND NOTE

1. RULPA § 303(b)(6)(v) is the key provision in that Act relating to removal of a general partner. As you can see, the provision does not establish

that limited partners always have authority to remove a general partner. Instead, the provision indicates that, if the limited partnership agreement permits limited partners to remove a general partner, the exercise of this authority will not by itself cause the limited partners to lose their limited liability.

If Example 1 from the draft provisions above were the only provision in the limited partnership agreement relating to powers and rights of the limited partners, would the limited partners have any power or right to replace the general partner who was making the decisions for the limited partnership?

2.   Limited partners, in theory, are not liable for the acts or debts of the limited partnership. They are more like shareholders of a corporation—they make an investment, which is at risk, but are not liable for what the business does. The theory assumes, however, that the limited partner is essentially passive with regard to running the business. As the law developed, it became clear that a limited partner who exerted "control" over the business of the limited partnership would become liable for the acts and debts of the business; by exercising "control," the limited partner had essentially become a general partner for liability purposes.

This concern about exposing limited partners to liability for the acts or debts of the business was the principal reason for restricting limited partners' participation in making decisions for the business. The next part of the book considers the practical significance of that concern under modern limited partnership laws. To summarize, RULPA § 303(a) indicates that, even if a limited partner exercises "control," the limited partner will nonetheless be liable only when the limited partner acted in a way that caused the third party reasonably to believe that the limited partner was instead a general partner. Moreover, RULPA § 303(b) provides a safe harbor by listing activities that will not constitute "control" by the limited partner.

2.   WHO IS LIABLE TO WHOM FOR WHAT?

a.   To Third Parties

Each general partner of a limited partnership is personally liable for the partnership's debts to third parties as if the partnership were a general partnership. The first sentence of RULPA § 403(b) says:

> Except as provided in this Act, a general partner of a limited partnership has the liabilities of a partner in a partnership without limited partners to persons other than the partnership and the other partners.

Accordingly, if Capel is a general partner of Bubba's Burritos Limited Partnership, creditors of the partnership can collect from Capel to the extent allowed under RUPA §§ 306 and 307. Could a provision in the limited partnership agreement limit the liability of the general partners to third parties? To answer this, note that the second sentence of RULPA § 403(b) mentions the partnership agreement, but the first sentence above does not. Why?

If Agee and Propp are the limited partners of Bubba's Burritos Limited Partnership, creditors of the partnership generally cannot collect from Agee or Propp. Traditionally, however, limited partners had to be very careful not to exercise "control" of the business. If they did, by dominating the general partner or calling the shots for the business for example, courts might find that they had become general partners. They would be liable to third-parties as general partners.

This aspect of limited partnership law has changed in recent times. Specifically, RULPA § 303, which you should read carefully, creates "safe harbors" for limited partners. It provides that certain acts by the limited partners—even in the aggregate—will not be deemed "control." Thus, the section brings great certainty and solace to limited partners. Even more recently, ULPA 2001 § 303(a) has gone even farther. It abandons the "control rule" altogether and provides the limited partners with complete freedom from liability for business debts.

QUESTIONS

1. Under RULPA, if the Bubba's Burritos Limited Partnership Agreement includes a provision similar to Example 1 of the draft limited partnership provisions set out above, will limited partners Agee and Propp be personally liable for the limited partnership's debts?

2. Bubba's Burritos Limited Partnership owes $20,000 to Third–Party Distributing Co. (TP) for grits and other foods delivered by TP to Bubba's Burritos Limited Partnership on credit. Can TP recover the $20,000 from limited partner Propp if it can establish that (i) Propp was working at the cash register at the times that TP made deliveries to Bubba's Burritos Limited Partnership, (ii) Propp signed receipts on behalf of Bubba's Burritos Limited Partnership, and (iii) TP's managers believed that Propp was a general partner?

3. Compare the liability exposure of a shareholder of a close corporation under the rules for piercing the corporate veil in Chapter 5 with the liability exposure of a limited partner under RULPA § 303. Again, we see a similarity between a limited partner and a shareholder. In theory, each tends to be a passive investor risking only her investment and leaving management responsibilities to others (although shareholders in close corporations can have management responsibilities). But if either exercises too much control, she might become personally liable for the acts or debts of the business. How do the standards for piercing the corporate veil and for liability of a limited partner under § 303 of RULPA compare?

4. Recall that the general partner of a partnership is quite often a corporation. Would your answers to Questions 1 or 2 above change if Propp were the president and a director of Bubba's Burritos, Inc., the corporation that was the sole general partner of Bubba's Burritos Limited Partnership? *See* RULPA § 303(b)(1).

The next case will also be helpful. In it, the "responsible corporate officer" of the corporate general partner of a limited partnership was held not liable for a contract obligation of the limited partnership. In reading the case, please consider the following:

1.   With whom did the plaintiff, Shelley Zeiger, contract?

2.   Why isn't the plaintiff suing Trenton, Inc.? Why isn't the plaintiff suing Trenton L.P.?

3.   What facts does the plaintiff rely on in suing Wilf?

4.   What facts are most helpful to Wilf?

5.   Did the plaintiff believe that Wilf was a general partner?

ZEIGER v. WILF

New Jersey Superior Court, 2000
755 A.2d 608

LESEMANN, J.A.D. This case offers a virtual primer in the Byzantine relationships among various forms of business organizations employed in a modern venture capital project. It includes a limited partnership, a corporation, a general partnership and several sophisticated individuals all involved in the proposed redevelopment of a hotel/office building in downtown Trenton. It also demonstrates the significance of limited individual liability which is a key reason for employing some of those entities, and the inevitable risk that anticipated rewards from such a venture may not be realized.

At issue here is an agreement by which plaintiff, a seller of the property to be renovated, was to receive a "consultant fee" of $27,000 per year for sixteen years. The payments, however, ceased after two years. A jury found the redevelopers (a limited partnership and a corporation) liable for those payments, and an appeal by those entities has now been abandoned. As a result, the matter now focuses on plaintiff's claim that Joseph Wilf, the individual who led the various defendant entities, should be held personally liable for the consultant payments and that such liability should also be imposed on a general partnership owned by Wilf and members of his family.

There is no claim that Wilf personally, or his general partnership, ever guaranteed the consultant payments or that plaintiff ever believed Wilf had made such guarantees. Nor is there a claim that plaintiff did not understand at all times that he was contracting only with a limited partnership and/or a corporation, and not with Wilf personally or with his general partnership. For those reasons, and also because we find no merit in various other theories of individual liability advanced by plaintiff, we affirm the summary judgment entered in favor of Wilf individually, and we reverse the judgment against Wilf's family-owned general partnership.

The property in question was a rundown hotel on West State Street in Trenton, located near several State government buildings. In or shortly before 1981, plaintiff Shelley Zeiger and his associate, Darius Kapadia, purchased the property with the intention of renovating and operating the hotel. They undertook some renovation and began operations but could not obtain sufficient financing to complete the project.

In or around March 1985, Steven Novick, an experienced developer, approached plaintiff concerning a possible purchase of the property. Novick believed the building could be successfully renovated and operated as an office building, (with perhaps some hotel facilities included), particularly if he could lease some or all of the office space to the State. Richard Goldberger, another experienced developer, soon joined Novick in the project, as did another associate, said to have considerable contacts within the State government. Plaintiff was also well known in Trenton governmental and political circles.

As the negotiations proceeded, Novick brought defendant Joseph Wilf into the picture. Wilf was described as a "deep pocket partner," whose financial means could help insure the success of the project. He was also a well known and successful real estate developer and soon became the leader and primary spokesman for the purchasing group. Novick and Goldberger generally deferred to Wilf during the negotiations and structuring of the transaction.

On February 17, 1986, the negotiations culminated in a contract with a purchase price of $3,840,000 for the real estate, a liquor license, and miscellaneous assets connected with the hotel's operation. The contract was signed by a corporation formed by the purchasers, known as Goldberger, Moore & Novick, Trenton, No. 2, Inc., (hereinafter, "Trenton, Inc." or "the corporation").

As the deal was finally struck, the parties also agreed that plaintiff would receive a "consulting fee" of $27,000 per year, payable monthly for sixteen years. While plaintiff was to provide assistance when requested, it is clear that he was not expected to devote much time or effort to the project. The agreement specified he would not be required to spend more than two days per month in consultations. Plaintiff claims the consultation payments were, in reality, an additional part of the payment price, structured as they were to provide tax benefits to the Novick/Goldberger/Wilf group. In addition, plaintiff was to receive from the project two and one half percent of "annual net cash flow after debt service."

Closing took place on March 4, 1986. Trenton, Inc., was the purchaser and also signed the consultant agreement with plaintiff. The contract documents authorized the corporation to assign its property interests, as well as the consulting contract, to another entity, and on the day following closing the corporation did that by assignment to a limited partnership named Goldberger, Moore & Novick, Trenton, L.P., (hereinafter "Trenton L.P." or "the limited partnership").

The limited partnership then began the anticipated renovation and operation of the hotel/office building. Trenton, L.P. consisted of one general partner—the corporation just referred to (Trenton, Inc.), which owned 4.9 percent of the limited partnership. In addition, it had four limited partners: an entity known as Midnov, owned by Novick and Goldberger, which held a 42.7 percent interest; another entity known as Capitol Plaza Associates (CPA), controlled by Wilf and his family and described further below, which also owned 42.7 percent; George Albanese, a former State official, who held a 5.1 percent interest; and plaintiff Shelley Zeiger who owned a 4.9 percent interest.

The stock of Trenton, Inc. was owned fifty percent by Midnov (Novick and Goldberger's entity) and fifty percent by CPA (the Wilf family entity). Goldberger became president of Trenton, Inc.; Wilf was vice president; Novick was secretary/treasurer, and Bernadette Lynch was assistant secretary.

Thus, all of Wilf's interests in both the limited partnership and the corporation were held through his family entity, CPA. CPA was a general partnership and defendant Joseph Wilf was one of the general partners. While other family members were also general partners in CPA, Joseph Wilf was clearly its guiding and dominating force.

Shortly after closing, Trenton, L.P. began its attempts to secure both state leases for the property and a 9.5 million dollar mortgage to finance the required renovation. Wilf was the leader in that operation as he was in all aspects of the project. He maintains that in doing so, he was functioning as vice president of the corporation, which was the only general partner of the limited partnership. In substance, he claims that the limited partnership was operating (as it was required to do) through its general partner. Since that general partner was a corporation, the corporation was, in turn, operating in the only way that a corporation can operate: by the actions of its officers and agents. He maintains further that Goldberger and Novick soon abdicated most responsibility and simply stopped functioning as corporate officers—a claim not disputed by plaintiff. Thus, Wilf says, it was left to him to function as the responsible corporate officer.

Both the limited partnership and the corporation operated informally. There were few, if any, corporate meetings, resolutions or minutes. Wilf was less than meticulous in affixing his corporate title to documents or other papers which he says he signed as an officer of the corporate general partner. Significantly, however, plaintiff makes no claim that at any time he thought Wilf was operating in some other capacity, or that he believed Wilf or CPA were undertaking any personal responsibility or liability for any part of the project.

The limited partnership began making the monthly consultation payments to plaintiff in early 1986, and it continued to do so for approximately two years. In March 1988, however, the payments were stopped at Wilf's direction. An additional $12,000 was paid in May 1989 (which represented almost all the amount then due to plaintiff), but thereafter no further payments were made. Wilf said at the time that the money was needed for the renovation project and that (alone among all the participants), plaintiff was contributing nothing to the project. Plaintiff complained to Novick, and Novick promised to discuss the matter with Wilf. Novick did so, but Wilf continued to maintain that plaintiff should receive no further payments and thus, no further payments were made. Wilf subsequently acknowledged that he was not familiar with the terms of the consultation agreement or plaintiff's rights thereunder.

Trenton, L.P., did obtain its desired 9.5 million dollar renovation loan. However, by January 1987, those funds were exhausted and more money was needed. Wilf maintains that he invested an additional $565,000 in the project through his own company, and he then obtained a 2.8 million dollar mortgage loan from First Chicago Bank, which he, his brother and Goldberger personally guaranteed. Wilf subsequently paid off that mortgage but—presumably to repay his $565,000 investment and his payoff of the First Chicago loan—he took a $3,063,000 mortgage from Trenton, L.P., covering the office building/hotel.

Eventually, the project failed. The limited partnership and the corporation filed bankruptcy, as did Novick individually. On July 19, 1993, plaintiff sued Wilf, claiming that Wilf had become the "surviving partner and owner of the partnership assets" pertaining to the "purchase and transfer of" the hotel, and that he was in default respecting payment of plaintiff's consulting fees.

Wilf moved for summary judgment dismissing the complaint as to him, which the motion judge granted on December 23, 1996.

This appeal was filed by plaintiff, seeking reversal of the judgment in favor of Joseph Wilf.

Plaintiff claims the limited partnership statute imposes general partner liability on Wilf because he functioned as the operating head of the parties' renovation project. We find the claim inconsistent with both the policy and the language of the statute.

A basic principle of the Uniform Limited Partnership Law (1976), N.J.S.A. 42:2A–1 to –72, is a differentiation between the broad liability of a general partner for the obligations of a limited partnership, and the non-liability of a limited partner for such obligations. Preservation of that distinction and protection against imposing unwarranted liability on a limited partner has been a consistent concern of the drafters of the Uniform Act on which our New Jersey statute is based, and has been described as "the single most difficult issue facing lawyers who use the limited partnership form of organization." Indeed, the history of the Uniform Limited Partnership Act, and thus the evolution of our New Jersey statute, shows a consistent movement to insure certainty and predictability respecting the obligations and potential liability of limited partners. The framers of the Act have accomplished that by consistently reducing and restricting the bases on which a general partner's unrestricted liability can be imposed on a limited partner. Under the present version of the Uniform Act, the imposition of such liability (absent fraud or misleading) is severely limited.

The original version of the ULPA was adopted in 1916. That enactment dealt with the question of a limited partner's liability in one short provision. In § 7 it said,

> A limited partner shall not become liable as a general partner unless, in addition to the exercise of his rights and powers as a limited partner, he takes part in the control of the business.

In 1976, the original ULPA was substantially replaced by a revised version (on which the New Jersey statute is based) which "was intended to modernize the prior uniform law." One of the ways that modernization was effected was by a new § 303, which replaced the old § 7. [Section] 303 reads as follows:

> [A] limited partner is not liable for the obligations of a limited partnership unless . . ., in addition to the exercise of his [or her] rights and powers as a limited partner, he [or she] takes part in the control of the business. However, if the limited partner's participation in the control of the business is not substantially the same as the exercise of the powers of a general partner, he [or she] is liable only to persons who transact business with the limited partnership with actual knowledge of his participation in control.

The Commissioners' Report in the comment to § 303 states:

> § 303 makes several important changes in § 7 of the 1916 Act. . . . The second sentence of § 303(a) reflects a wholly new concept. . . . It was adopted partly because . . . it was thought unfair to impose general partner's liability on a limited partner except to the extent that a third party had knowledge of his participation in control of the business . . ., but also (and more importantly) because of a determination that it is not sound public policy to hold a limited partner who is not also a general partner liable for the obligations of the partnership except to persons who have done business with the limited partnership reasonably believing, based on the limited partner's conduct, that he is a general partner.

Following that 1976 version, more limitations on a limited partner's liability came in 1988, with a series of "Safe Harbor" amendments. The Commissioners' Report explained the reason for those additions to § 303 of the Uniform Act:

> Paragraph (b) is intended to provide a "Safe Harbor" by enumerating certain activities which a limited partner may carry on for the partnership without being deemed to have taken part in control of the business. This "Safe Harbor" list has been expanded beyond that set out in the 1976 Act to reflect case law and statutory developments and more clearly to assure that limited partners are not subjected to general liability where such liability is inappropriate.

Plaintiff's argument rests on Wilf's key role in the renovation project. Wilf acknowledges that role, but argues that his actions were taken as a vice president of Trenton, Inc.—the corporation which was the sole general partner of Trenton, L.P. Wilf argues that since the corporation is an artificial entity, it can only function through its officers, and that is precisely what he was doing at all times when he acted concerning this enterprise.

We agree with that analysis. As noted, the 1988 "Safe Harbor" provisions set out a number of activities which, under the statute, do not constitute participating in "the control of" a business so as to impose a general partner's liability on a limited partner. The provision to which Wilf particularly refers is subsection (b)(6) of § 27, which provides that,

> b. A limited partner does not participate in the control of the business within the meaning of subsection a. solely by[,]
> * * *
> (6) Serving as an officer, director or shareholder of a corporate general partner;

That provision clearly applies here and essentially undercuts plaintiff's argument: while plaintiff claims that Wilf's activities constitute "control" of the activities of Trenton, L.P., the statute says, in just so many words, that those activities do not constitute the exercise of control.

In addition to the "Safe Harbor" protections, § 27a itself sharply limits the circumstances under which the exercise of "control" could lead to imposition of general partner liability on a limited partner. It first provides that if a limited partner's control activities are so extensive as to be "substantially the same as" those of a general partner, that control, by itself, is sufficient to impose liability: i.e., if a limited partner acts "the same as" a general partner, he will be treated as a general partner. However, but for that extreme case, mere participation in control does not impose liability on a limited partner. * * *

* * * To accept the [plaintiff's] claim would inject precisely the instability and uncertainty which the statute is designed to avoid.

Here, there was none of the "reliance" which is a necessary basis for a limited partner's liability. It bears repeating that plaintiff, an insider in the project, does not claim he was ever misled as to the entities with whom he was dealing. Plaintiff is described as a sophisticated, experienced developer and businessman. He does not deny that description. He does not claim that he ever sought or obtained any individual guarantee or promise of payment from Wilf, and certainly not from CPA. Nor does plaintiff deny that he understood completely that he was dealing with a limited partnership and a corporation. He does not deny his understanding that those entities, by their very nature, provide limited resources and limited recourse for parties with whom they contract.

In short, there is no claim that plaintiff was misled, or that he relied on some impression that Wilf was a general partner of Trenton, L.P., and thus there is no basis for any finding of personal liability against Wilf under N.J.S.A. 42:2A–27a.

* * *

Finally, we note two cases which particularly emphasize and relate to the need for certainty and predictability in defining a limited partner's liability for actions of a limited partnership entity.

Redwing Carriers, Inc. v. Saraland Apartments, 94 F.3d 1489 (11th Cir.1996), concerned a claim for contribution to environmental cleanup costs under the federal Comprehensive Environmental Response Compensation and Liability Act (CERCLA). The issue before the court was whether, in determining a limited partner's liability for such payments, the court should apply state law (there the law of Alabama) or develop a federal common law.

The court concluded there was no need to develop a federal common law since, "there is significant agreement among the 50 states and the District of Columbia on the broad outlines of a rule governing the liability of limited partners. This is because nearly every jurisdiction in this country has adopted a version of the Revised Uniform Limited Partnership Act of 1976 (RULPA)." *Id.* at 1501 n. 14. Noting the importance of stability and the avoidance of uncertainty respecting the critical question of limited partner liability, the court concluded that it should avoid developing a new federal common law, which would inevitably contribute to just such uncertainty and instability:

> What makes [limited] partnerships ... attractive to investors is the very concept of limited liability: as limited partners, investors can participate in the partnership's profits without exposing themselves to liability for the partnership's debts. When determining whether to enter a limited partnership, however, investors naturally evaluate their ability to control their risk by participating in the management of the partnership. Existing state limited-partnership statutes define how far a limited partner can go in managing the partnership's business without losing its limited liability status. Given the popularity of the limited-partnership structure as a means of organizing businesses and attracting investment in this country, we hesitate to upset the expectations investors have under current state law rules by adopting a federal common law rule.

Antonic Rigging & Erecting of Missouri, Inc. v. Foundry East Limited Partnership, 773 F.Supp. 420 (S.D.Ga.1991), expresses similar thoughts, although it involved a Georgia statute significantly different from the Uniform Act. There, the court noted that in adopting its current version of the limited partnership statute, Georgia had specifically renounced the proposition that, "a limited partner may be held liable as a general partner for participating in the control of a limited partnership's business." The court quoted the report of the Joint Legislative Committee which had produced the new statute and which had pointed out that,

Under most modern limited partnership statutes, the "control" rule has been diminished to the point where there is no liability for participation in control without creditor reliance, and an extensive "safe harbor" is usually provided. Even so, uncertainty as to the degree of control which can trigger liability creates significant disincentive to limited partnership investments, and accordingly the proposed new law eliminates the control test.

We are satisfied that, were we to find individual liability against Wilf because of his "control" here, we would be encouraging precisely the instability and uncertainty which are anathema to widespread use of the limited partnership as a business entity. The modern, sound view, epitomized by the ULPA, the New Jersey statute and the well-reasoned decisions discussed above is in the other direction: to curtail the threat of personal liability unless there is some "reliance on the part of the outsider dealing with the limited partnership." There was no such reliance here, and there is no basis for imposing personal liability on Wilf.

QUESTIONS

1. Why would Wilf choose to own substantial interests both in the limited partnership's corporate general partner and in one of the limited partners?

2. After this case, can a person with a contract claim against a New Jersey limited partnership ever collect that contract claim from an officer or director of the corporate general partner?

3. What should Zeiger have done in structuring his deal with the limited partnership to guaranty a personal target for a suit for his consulting fees?

4. Why didn't the attorney for the plaintiff

- bring an action against the corporate general partner, Trenton, Inc.?

- obtain a judgment against Trenton, Inc.?

- rely on piercing-corporate-veil case law for the proposition that Wilf should be liable for judgments against Trenton, Inc.?

5. Recall that some cases on piercing the corporate veil distinguish between contracts claims and torts claims. Is it significant that the plaintiff's claim in this case was a contract claim? If you represented Vic, a tort victim who was injured by Trenton L.P.'s negligence in the renovation of its West State Street building, would you be willing to represent Vic in litigation against Wilf on a contingency fee basis?

b. To the Partnership and Partners

A general partner in a limited partnership has liability exposure not only to third parties for the obligations of the limited partnership, but also to the limited partnership and to the limited partners for breach of fiduciary duties. RULPA does not directly describe the fiduciary duties of a general partner in a limited partnership. Instead the last sentence of RULPA § 403(b) refers to general partnership law:

> Except as provided in this Act or in the partnership agreement a
> general partner of a limited partnership has the liabilities of a partner
> in a partnership without limited partners to the partnership and to
> the other partners.

Note that the partnership agreement can alter a general partner's liabilities to the partnership and other partners. In contrast, the first sentence of RULPA § 403(b) indicates that the partnership agreement cannot alter rights to third parties. Why the difference?

Most of the case law on partnership agreement provisions that impose limitations on the fiduciary duties of general partners of a limited partnership involve the Delaware counterpart of RULPA § 403(b). The next case is an example.

KAHN v. ICAHN

Delaware Chancery Court, 1998
1998 WL 832629

CHANDLER, CHANCELLOR. This case concerns how and why a limited partnership agreement can narrow, or redefine, the traditional fiduciary duties among and between limited partners under Delaware Law. Here, plaintiffs, who are limited partners and minority stakeholders of a Delaware limited partnership, allege the usurpation of a partnership opportunity. For the reasons that follow, I conclude that plaintiffs fail to state a claim and grant dismissal in favor of all the defendants.

I. Background

Plaintiffs, Amanda Heather Kahn and Kimberly Robin Kahn ("Plaintiffs")* [1] bring this action derivatively on behalf of American Real Estate Partners, L.P. ("AREP" or the "Partnership") against AREP's general partner American Property Investors, Inc. ("API"), the general partner's sole shareholder and chief executive officer, Carl C. Icahn ("Icahn"), and Bayswater Realty and Capital Corp. ("Bayswater"), a corporation affiliated with Icahn (collectively "Icahn Defendants"), and API's other directors (collectively "Defendants").

Plaintiffs are holders of depository units representing limited partnership interests of AREP. AREP is a Delaware limited partnership, whose business is conducted through a subsidiary. AREP is in the business of acquiring and managing real estate and attendant activities. AREP has two classes of depository units—Depository Units and Preferred Units. AREP's general partner, API, is a Delaware corporation. Defendant Icahn is the chairman of the board and chief executive officer of API, and owns

---

* [1] Counsel for the API directors point out in their reply brief in support of their motion to dismiss the derivative complaint that, "[p]laintiffs and their family appear to have been singularly unlucky investors—they are named plaintiffs in at least thirteen lawsuits (including this one) challenging allegedly improper conduct." It is unclear what nefarious intent the defendant directors would have me infer from this statistic. While the Kahns' experience might qualify them as icons of Delaware corporate jurisprudence, in my view, their wisdom in forum selection should hardly subject them to a presumption of misconduct.

100% of that company's stock. According to Plaintiffs, at the start of this litigation, Icahn, through another Delaware partnership, High Coast Limited Partnership, owned 54.1% of the Depository Units of AREP and over 88% of the Preferred Units. In addition, Plaintiffs allege that defendant Bayswater is a real estate and investment company owned and controlled by Icahn.

Plaintiffs assert a claim for the usurpation of partnership opportunities, or opportunities that rightfully belonged to the Partnership.* [2] More specifically, Plaintiffs' complaint alleges that Icahn breached his fiduciary duties to AREP and usurped, for himself, a corporate opportunity of AREP by failing to make the opportunities completely available to AREP and, instead, keeping a percentage of the profits for Bayswater and other affiliates.† [3]

Defendants argue that the complaint fails to state a claim. Their principal contention is that § 6.11 of AREP's partnership agreement (the "Agreement") provides that API, the general partner, may "compete, directly or indirectly with the business of the Partnership."‡ [4] Arguing that a partnership is free to modify traditional default rules and duties of partners, Defendants insist that Plaintiffs cannot properly claim a breach of fiduciary duty under the facts alleged in the complaint.

Plaintiffs respond by saying that there is a legal distinction, cognizable in the present case, between competing with the partnership and usurping the partnership's opportunities. They add that the Icahn Defendants' actions fall into the latter category and as such their claim should withstand the motion to dismiss.

---

* [2] This case is analogous to "corporate opportunity" cases, and I rely on the reasoning developed in the line of cases dealing with the usurpation of corporate opportunities to inform my analysis in this context of limited partnerships.

† [3] Among others, Plaintiffs identify two specific transactions that they claim qualify as AREP's missed opportunities. The first is an investment in another real estate limited partnership, Arvida/JMB Partners, L.P. ("Arvida"). That investment was made through a number of entities but ultimately, AREP received roughly 70% of the potential AREP share of the investment and Bayswater received approximately 30% of the investment. The second allegedly usurped opportunity involves the Stratosphere Corporation ("Stratosphere"), which owns and operates the Stratosphere Tower, Casino & Hotel in Las Vegas, Nevada. AREP invested $42.8 million to purchase certain mortgage notes of Stratosphere, with a face value of $55 million. According to Plaintiffs, an affiliate of Icahn has purchased $39 million face value of those notes. Plaintiffs have represented that Stratosphere has filed a voluntary plan of reorganization and AREP and the Icahn affiliate have submitted a proposal for the restructuring of Stratosphere that would entail additional investments.

‡ [4] In full, § 6.11 states:

6.11 Other Business Activities of Partners. Any Partner, Record Holder or Affiliate thereof (including, without limitation, the General Partner and any of its Affiliates) *may have other business interests or may engage in other business ventures of any nature or description whatsoever, whether presently existing or hereafter created*, including, without limitation, the ownership, leasing, management, operation, franchising, syndication and/or development of real estate and *may compete, directly or indirectly, with the business of the Partnership*. No Partner, Record Holder or Affiliate thereof shall incur any liability to the Partnership as the result of such Partner's, Record Holder's or Affiliate's pursuit of such other business interests and ventures and competitive activity, and neither the Partnership nor any of the Partners or Record Holders shall have any right to participate in such other business interests or ventures or to receive or share in any income derived therefrom. (emphasis added).

II. Analysis

A. Partnership Agreements under Delaware Law

Delaware law permits partners to agree on their rights and obligations to each other and to the partnership. This is so even where Delaware law might impose different rights and obligations absent such agreement. § 17–1101(d) of the Delaware Revised Limited Partnership Act provides in relevant part that:

> To the extent that, at law or in equity, a partner or other person has duties (including fiduciary duties) and liabilities relating thereto to a limited partnership or to another partner . . . (2) the partner's or other person's duties and liabilities may be expanded or restricted by the provisions in a partnership agreement.

Thus, as a matter of statutory law, the traditional fiduciary duties among and between partners are defaults that may be modified by partnership agreements. This flexibility is precisely the reason why many choose the limited partnership form in Delaware. Our decisional law also has recognized and given illumination to this principle. The cases have gone so far as to suggest that partnership agreements act as safe harbors for actions that might otherwise qualify as breaches of fiduciary duties under the traditional default rules.

Given this legal backdrop, the question then arises whether or not the conduct complained of by Plaintiffs falls within the provisions of the Agreement. I hold that, as a matter of law, it does. [Section] 6.11 of the Agreement anticipates the type of conduct alleged. That sections' language (which includes specific references to the types of real estate investments at issue in this case)—in light of the statements that "[a]ny Partner, Record Holder or Affiliate thereof . . . may compete, directly or indirectly, with the business of the Partnership. . . . [a]nd neither the Partnership nor any of the Partners or Record Holders shall have any right to participate in such other business interests or ventures or to receive or share in any income derived therefrom"—is clear on its face.

In fact, Plaintiffs do not contend that Defendants have misinterpreted § 6.11. Plaintiffs make no claim that § 6.11 says anything other than what it seems to say. There is no claim that the contested investments were intended to fall out of the scope of that provision, the simple terms of § 6.11 notwithstanding. It seems that Plaintiffs would have me ignore that section in favor of finding a legal distinction between competition, as it is normally understood and as provided under § 6.11, and the usurpation of a partnership opportunity. Plaintiffs ask me to craft a new principle of law by recognizing that partners have separate and immutable duties of loyalty irrespective of clear and unambiguous modifications of fiduciary duties provided in a legally enforceable partnership agreement. Under the facts alleged I cannot so hold, for Defendants' actions are covered by the Agreement and as such are permissible as a matter of law.

The Defendants' duties to AREP (including their fiduciary duties) are defined by the AREP Partnership Agreement that clearly permitted the Icahn Defendants to make the investments without bringing them to the limited partners. Plaintiffs' arguments, that the partnership Agreement did not allow the Icahn Defendants to make investments for themselves, simply overlook the statute, make no reasonable attempt to distinguish cases most directly on point, and ignore the unambiguous terms of the Agreement.

The corporate and partnership opportunity doctrine "represents but one species of the broad ... duties assumed by a [fiduciary]."* **[15]** The Delaware Supreme Court has taken the time to make sure that trial courts understand that the inquiry in corporate opportunity doctrine cases is a general one that is fact intensive. The relevant question is "whether or not a [fiduciary] has appropriated for himself something that in fairness should belong to the [partnership]...." To answer that question the Delaware courts have concentrated on a number of considerations including, "(1) ... the opportunity is either essential to the corporation or is one in which it has an interest or expectancy, (2) ... the corporation is financially able to take advantage of the opportunity itself, and (3) ... the party charged with taking the opportunity did so in an official rather than individual capacity."

First, I think it a correct legal conclusion that where a partnership, by virtue of an unambiguous clause in its partnership agreement which authorizes competition with the partnership, is on notice that the partners intend to compete directly with the partnership, it hardly can be said to have a legitimate "expectancy" to be informed of—let alone participate 100% in—relevant investments. Put simply, since Plaintiffs knew that the Icahn Defendants were authorized to compete—in fact, in these investments AREP was a co-investor—they cannot now claim derivatively that AREP had a legally sufficient expectation of 100% involvement. The Partnership Agreement successfully did what it purports to do: modify the underlying fiduciary duties of the partners.† **[16]** Thus, even if absent the Agreement AREP might have had a legitimate claim to an "interest" or "expectancy" in the contested investments, § 6.11 modified the legal effect of such an interest.

Second, there are no factual allegations from which I might infer that any of the Defendants received the investment opportunities in an official capacity and then used that information for individual gain. Plaintiffs do not make factual allegations that the information which lead to the investments in the first place was received originally by AREP in the normal course of its business and then somehow misappropriated by the

---

* **[15]** *Cf. Broz v. Cellular Information Systems, Inc.*, Del.Supr., 673 A.2d 148, 154 (1996) * * *. [Note from your authors: Remember we read *Broz* in Chapter 5, Part C, § 2(b)(about the duty of loyalty of directors).]

† **[16]** By the fact that the partnership agreement contained specific language authorizing competition "[some] of the fundamental concerns undergirding the law of corporate opportunity are not present." *Broz*, 673 A.2d at 155. In the present case, it seems to me, the language of the Agreement alone would justify dismissal.

Icahn Defendants. Nevertheless, no such facts were alleged and they cannot be reasonably inferred from the complaint.

I pause to note, with emphasis, that the Partnership was not entirely precluded from participating in the transactions in dispute. In each transaction the Partnership was involved and did invest. Plaintiffs only complain that AREP was not able to make 100% of the investment in the contested transactions. Presumably, Plaintiffs knew about the details of the deals (e.g., who found the investment opportunities, to what extent were those opportunities limited by the sellers, etc.), and they were able to describe with some specificity the structure of the investments. Plaintiffs, nonetheless, decided not to plead specific facts by which I might reasonably infer that there was misappropriation of information, unlawful redirection or personal use of partnership resources or some sort of misappropriation of proprietary investment research. The absence of such allegations in this case is disturbing and may, alone, justify dismissal for insufficient pleading of this partnership usurpation claim. Without some breach of fiduciary trust, I would be hard pressed to come to the conclusion that any fiduciary in this case has appropriated for himself something that in fairness ought to belong to AREP.

III. Conclusion

If anything, Plaintiffs have identified situations where they would have wanted AREP to fully take advantage of investment opportunities. That is not a sufficient basis to make a claim, however. In light of the Partnership Agreement, Plaintiffs have not alleged facts that, even viewed in the light most favorable to Plaintiffs, show that any of the Defendants acted unlawfully or in any way improperly. For that reason I dismiss Plaintiffs' claims. Furthermore, the facts alleged are unable to support a usurpation of partnership opportunity claim. Thus, all of Plaintiffs' claims are dismissed.

QUESTIONS AND NOTES

1. Why did the plaintiffs buy a limited partnership interest in AREP? Why are the plaintiffs suing the general partner?

2. Are the facts of *Kahn* distinguishable from *Meinhard v. Salmon* and *Northeast Harbor Golf Club*?

3. How would the Delaware Chancery Court have decided this case if § 6.11 had not been included in the partnership agreement? How would the Delaware Chancery Court have decided this case if the partnership agreement had simply provided "No Partner owes a fiduciary duty to any other Partner or to the Partnership?" Cf. *The Continental Insurance Co. v. Rutledge & Co., Inc.*, 750 A.2d 1219, 1235 n. 37 (Del. Ch. 2000) ("Many opt for the limited partnership form in Delaware precisely * * * to embrace this flexibility. Commentators considering the subject agree that limited partnerships' contract-theory-based structure provide incentives for parties to opt for the limited partnership over other forms of business organizations. As such,

parties, otherwise unwilling to shoulder fiduciary burdens, maintain the opportunity to form limited partnerships precisely because the parties can contract around some or all of the fiduciary duties the general partner typically owes the limited partners.").

4. Notice that the plaintiffs, limited partners, brought this action derivatively for the limited partnership. RULPA provides for such derivative actions in Article 10. Derivative actions by limited partners have been recognized and required even in states without such provisions. For example, in *Energy Investors Fund, L.P. v. Metric Constructors, Inc.*, 525 S.E.2d 441, 443 (N.C. 2000), the North Carolina Supreme Court stated:

> Scholars have also analogized the role of a limited partner to that of a shareholder because [l]imited partnerships resemble corporations in various ways. Formalities of creation are much alike. Both forms of organization can attract investment capital by offering limited liability with roughly similar effects in limited partnerships and corporations. Limited liability necessitates some rules to protect corporate creditors. It facilitates passive ownership—a separation of ownership from control—that permits some efficiencies as well as poses some risks from delegated management. Thus, limited partners are somewhat analogous to shareholders.... Information rights and fiduciary duties owed to limited partners are similar to those owed to shareholders. Limited partners, like shareholders, may bring derivative suits on behalf of the business entity against errant management.

> While it is true that a partner and shareholder are treated differently for tax purposes, their duties are still analogous. As such, we conclude that the Court of Appeals properly equated the status of limited partners in a partnership to the relationship that exists between corporate shareholders and the corporation.

5. Notice also that one of the defendants was an individual, Carl Icahn, the corporate general partner's sole stockholder and chief executive officer. It seems clear that (1) the corporate general partner of a limited partnership owes a fiduciary duty to the limited partnership and (2) an officer or director of that corporation owes a fiduciary duty to the corporation. Is it also clear that a person who is an officer or director of a corporation that is the general partner of a limited partnership owes a fiduciary duty both to the corporation *and* to the limited partnership? If so, will those fiduciary duties ever conflict?

6. Under the traditional "control rule," a limited partner would be liable to third-parties for business debts if she has engaged in control of the business. In such a case, should the limited partner also owe the fiduciary duties of a general partner? *See* ULPA 2001 § 305. *See also* Kenneth M. Jacobson, *Fiduciary Duty Considerations in Choosing Between Limited Partnerships and Limited Liability Companies*, 36 REAL PROP. PROB. & TR. J. 1 (2001).

The next case provides the best-known discussion of the duties that the manager of a corporate general partner owes to the limited partners. In reading it, please consider the following.

1.   Is it important that the Wylys own 100% of the stock of USACafes General Partner, Inc., the corporate general partner of the limited partnership?

2.   What does the plaintiff allege that the Wylys did wrong?

3.   Are the plaintiffs alleging that the $15,000,000 to $17,000,000 paid to the Wylys by Metsa in connection with Metsa's acquisition of the assets of the limited partnership should have been paid to USACafes General Partner, Inc., or to the limited partnership?

IN RE USACAFES, L.P.

Delaware Chancery Court, 1991
600 A.2d 43

ALLEN, CHANCELLOR. These consolidated actions arise out of the October 1989 purchase by Metsa Acquisition Corp. of substantially all of the assets of USACafes, L.P., a Delaware limited partnership (the "Partnership") at a cash price of $72.6 million or $10.25 per unit. Plaintiffs are holders of limited partnership units. They bring these cases as class actions on behalf of all limited partnership unitholders except defendants. The relief sought includes, *inter alia*, the imposition of constructive trusts on certain funds received by defendants in connection with the Metsa sale and an award of damages to the class resulting from the sale.

The Partnership was formed in the 1986 reorganization of the business of USACafes, Inc., a Nevada corporation. Also formed as part of that reorganization was USACafes General Partner, Inc. (the "General Partner"), a Delaware corporation that acts as the general partner of the Partnership. Both the Partnership and the General Partner are named as defendants in this action. A second category of defendants is composed of Sam and Charles Wyly, brothers who together own all of the stock of the General Partner, sit on its board, and who also personally, directly or indirectly, own 47% of the limited partnership units of the Partnership. Sam Wyly chairs the Board of the General Partner.

The third category of defendants are four other individuals who sit on the board of directors of the General Partner. All of these persons are alleged to have received substantial cash payments, loan forgiveness, or other substantial personal benefits in connection with the 1989 Metsa purchase.

The Theories of the Amended Complaint

The first and most central theory involves an alleged breach of the duty of loyalty. In essence, it claims that the sale of the Partnership's assets was at a low price, favorable to Metsa, because the directors of the General Partner all received substantial side payments that induced them to authorize the sale of the Partnership assets for less than the price that a fair process would have yielded. Specifically, it is alleged that, in connection with the sale, (1) the Wylys received from Metsa more than

$11 million in payments (or promises to pay in the future) which were disguised as consideration for personal covenants not to compete; (2) the General Partner (which the Wylys wholly own) received a $1.5 million payment right in consideration of the release of a claim that plaintiffs assert was non-existent; (3) defendant Rogers, a director of the General Partner and President of the Partnership was forgiven the payment of a $956,169 loan from the Partnership and was given an employment agreement with the Partnership that contemplated a one million dollar cash payment in the event, then imminent, of a "change in control"; (4) defendant Tuley, also a director of the General Partner, was forgiven repayment of a $229,701 loan; and (5) the other directors were given employment agreements providing for a $60,000 payment in the event of a change in control. In sum, it is alleged that between $15 and $17 million was or will be paid to the directors and officers of the General Partner by or with the approval of Metsa; those payments are alleged to constitute financial inducements to the directors of the General Partner to refrain from searching for a higher offer to the Partnerships. Plaintiffs add that, even assuming that Metsa was the buyer willing to pay the best price, some part at least of these "side payments" should have gone to the Partnership.

The second theory of liability reflected in the amended complaint asserts that the General Partner was (or the directors of the General Partner were) not sufficiently informed to make a valid business judgment on the sale. This theory focuses upon the absence of shopping of the Partnership's assets, or of any post-agreement market check procedure, and on the alleged weakness of the investment banker's opinion. Thus, this claim is that the defendants were uninformed when they authorized the sale to Metsa.

The Pending Motions

The Wyly defendants and the other director defendants move under Rule 12(b)(6) to dismiss the breach of fiduciary duty claims in the amended complaint asserting that, while the General Partner admittedly did owe fiduciary duties to the limited partners, they as directors of the General Partner owe no such duties to those persons. The whole remedy of the limited partners for breach of the duties of loyalty and care, it is said, is against the General Partner only and not its directors.

The gist of this motion is the assertion that the directors of the General Partner owed the limited partners no duty of loyalty or care. In their view their only duty of loyalty was to the General Partner itself and to its shareholders (i.e., the Wyly brothers). Thus, in alleging that the director defendants breached duties of loyalty and care running to them, the directors say the limited partners have asserted a legal nullity.

In my opinion the assertion by the directors that the independent existence of the corporate General Partner is inconsistent with their owing fiduciary duties directly to limited partners is incorrect. Moreover, even were it correct, their position on this motion would have to be rejected in any event because the amended complaint expressly alleges that they personally participated in the alleged breach by the General Partner itself, which admittedly did owe loyalty to the limited partners.

The first basis of this holding is the more significant. While I find no corporation law precedents directly addressing the question whether directors of a corporate general partner owe fiduciary duties to the partnership and its limited partners, the answer to it seems to be clearly indicated by general principles and by analogy to trust law. I understand the principle of fiduciary duty, stated most generally, to be that one who controls property of another may not, without implied or express agreement, intentionally use that property in a way that benefits the holder of the control to the detriment of the property or its beneficial owner. There are, of course, other aspects—a fiduciary may not waste property even if no self interest is involved and must exercise care even when his heart is pure—but the central aspect of the relationship is, undoubtedly, fidelity in the control of property for the benefit of another.

The law of trusts represents the earliest and fullest expression of this principle in our law, but courts of equity have extended it appropriately to achieve substantial justice in a wide array of situations. Thus, corporate directors, even though not strictly trustees, were early on regarded as fiduciaries for corporate stockholders. When control over corporate property was recognized to be in the hands of shareholders who controlled the enterprise, the fiduciary obligation was found to extend to such persons as well.

While the parties cite no case treating the specific question whether directors of a corporate general partner are fiduciaries for the limited partnership, a large number of trust cases do stand for a principle that would extend a fiduciary duty to such persons in certain circumstances. The problem comes up in trust law because modern corporations may serve as trustees of express trusts. Thus, the question has arisen whether directors of a corporate trustee may personally owe duties of loyalty to *cestui que trusts* of the corporation. A leading authority states the accepted answer:

> The directors and officers of [a corporate trustee] are certainly under a duty to the beneficiaries not to convert to their own use property of the trust administered by the corporation.... Furthermore, the directors and officers are under a duty to the beneficiaries of trusts administered by the corporation not to cause the corporation to misappropriate the property.... The breach of trust need not, however, be a misappropriation.... Any officer [director cases are cited in support here] who knowingly causes the corporation to commit a breach of trust causing loss ... is personally liable to the beneficiary of the trust....
>
> Moreover, a director or officer of a trust institution who improperly acquires an interest in the property of a trust administered by the institution is subject to personal liability. He is accounta-

ble for any profit. . . . Even where the trustee [itself] is not liable, however, because it had no knowledge that the director was making the purchase . . . , the director . . . is liable to the beneficiaries. . . . The directors and officers are in a fiduciary relation not merely to the [corporation] . . . but to the beneficiaries of the trust administered by the [corporation]. 4 A. Scott & W. Fratcher, THE LAW OF TRUSTS § 326.3, at 304–306 (4th ed. 1989) (citing cases) * * *.

The theory underlying fiduciary duties is consistent with recognition that a director of a corporate general partner bears such a duty towards the limited partnership. That duty, of course, extends only to dealings with the partnership's property or affecting its business, but, so limited, its existence seems apparent in any number of circumstances. Consider, for example, a classic self-dealing transaction: assume that a majority of the board of the corporate general partner formed a new entity and then caused the general partner to sell partnership assets to the new entity at an unfairly small price, injuring the partnership and its limited partners. Can it be imagined that such persons have not breached a duty to the partnership itself? And does it not make perfect sense to say that the gist of the offense is a breach of the equitable duty of loyalty that is placed upon a fiduciary? * * *

While these authorities extend the fiduciary duty of the general partner to a controlling shareholder, they support as well, the recognition of such duty in directors of the General Partner who, more directly than a controlling shareholder, are in control of the partnership's property. It is not necessary here to attempt to delineate the full scope of that duty. It may well not be so broad as the duty of the director of a corporate trustee.* **[3]** But it surely entails the duty not to use control over the partnership's property to advantage the corporate director at the expense of the partnership. That is what is alleged here.

> The amended complaint contains the following allegations:
>
> 16.   The General Partner and its directors, the named individual defendants, are in a fiduciary relationship with the plaintiffs and the other Unitholders of USACafes. . . .
>
> 17.   . . . Through their unit ownership and executive positions [the director defendants] have dominated and controlled the affairs of USACafes. Among other things, they have . . . failed to adequately solicit or consider alternative proposals for USACafes, have failed to negotiate in good faith to enhance Unitholders' values and, instead, have agreed to sell all of its assets to Metsa, which will result in the minority limited partners receiving the grossly inadequate price of $10.25 per Unit. As inducement to the

---

* **[3]** For example, I imply nothing on such questions as whether a director of a corporate general partner might be held liable directly to the partnership on a "corporate" opportunity theory or for waste of partnership assets (two possible consequences of characterizing such persons as fiduciaries for the partnership).

individual defendants to agree to the Metsa proposal, Metsa offered to pay and the individual defendants agreed to accept, certain additional payments (approximately $17 million) that were not offered to the classes. . . .

19. The individual defendants and the General Partner participated in the wrongdoing complained of in order to divert the valuable assets of USACafes for their own benefit by entering into highly favorable compensation arrangements with Metsa as part of the liquidation of USACafes.

I therefore conclude that the amended complaint does allege facts which if true establish that the director defendants have breached fiduciary obligations imposed upon them as directors of a Delaware corporation or have participated in a breach of such duties by the General Partner. The amended complaint does, in my opinion, state a claim upon which relief can be granted.

QUESTIONS

1. Could the plaintiff have sued only USACafes General Partner, Inc. for the $15,000,000 to $17,000,000 paid to the Wylys? If the plaintiffs received a $15,000,000 judgment, do you think they would have been able to collect that judgment?

2. Is *USACafes* consistent with *Kahn*?

3. In this case, the plaintiffs' story was about putative "bad guys"— about directors of the corporate general partner taking money for themselves that (plaintiffs thought) should have gone to the limited partners. Does the *USACafes* case help you in a story in which there are no "bad guys"? For instance, consider a story in which the directors of the corporate general partner make a decision that benefits the corporate general partner, and not themselves.

Hotel, Inc. is the general partner of Hotel Limited Partnership. Shepherd is a director of Hotel, Inc. Shepherd learns of a new hotel opportunity that might be of interest to both the limited partnership and the corporate general partner. Does the *USACafes* case help Shepherd decide what to do? *Cf.* Robert B. Robbins, *Fiduciary Duties of Corporate General Partners to Limited Partnerships*, AMERICAN LAW INSTITUTE–AMERICAN BAR ASSOCIATION COURSE OF STUDY, SE68 ALI–ABA 489 (2000) ("*USACafes* can be criticized for relying on trust law principles while ignoring a fundamental distinction between the trustee's fiduciary duty of undivided loyalty and the contractual relationship between general and limited partners. A general partner and its affiliated limited partnership will have adverse or competing interests on many matters. When the two interests diverge, it is unclear under *USACafes* how the director is to balance his or her fiduciary duties to the corporate general partner and the partnership. If the higher duty is owed to the limited partners, by what standards is the 'lesser' fiduciary duty to the corporation to be judged?"). *See also* Robert W. Hamilton, *Corporate General Partners of Limited Partnerships*, 1 J. SMALL & EMERGING BUS. L. 73 (1997).

4. Considering the parallels between corporations and limited partnerships, should a general partner be able to claim advantage of the business judgment rule? *See* Elizabeth S. Miller & Thomas E. Rutledge, *The Duty of Finest Loyalty and Reasonable Decisions: The Business Judgment Rule in Unincorporated Business Associations?*, 30 DEL. J. CORP. L. 343 (2005).

D. HOW DO THE OWNERS OF A BUSINESS STRUCTURED AS A LIMITED PARTNERSHIP MAKE MONEY?

The owners of a business structured as a limited partnership, like the owners of businesses structured as partnerships and corporations, make money by (i) being employed by the limited partnership and receiving salaries, (ii) sharing in distributions of the earnings of the business, and (iii) selling the ownership interest for more than it cost.

The first two—salaries and distributions—depend on contracts and contract law. The third—sale of ownership interest—depends in part on whether the buyer is the limited partnership or a third party and whether the seller is a general partner or a limited partner. Recall that the default rule for general partnerships (Chapter 3) is that distributions, profits, and losses will be allocated equally to each partner. In limited partnerships, however, distributions, profits, and losses are allocated in proportion to the contributions of each partner. *See* RULPA §§ 503, 504. (Of course, the partners may agree to the contrary.)

1. TRANSFER OF OWNERSHIP INTEREST TO A THIRD PARTY

Sale of an ownership interest in a limited partnership to a third party by either a general partner or a limited partner is governed by RULPA. Please read RULPA §§ 504 and 702 and compare these provisions with RUPA § 502.

If you actually did all of that, you saw that RULPA, like RUPA, limits a limited partner's ability to sell her limited partnership interest to a third party by limiting what such a third buyer will get—distribution rights, but no management or information rights unless the limited partnership agreement otherwise provides. Professor Larry Ribstein is critical of these limitations:

> Restricting transferability makes sense as a default rule in a standard form general partnership because members who are actively managing the business and are personally liable for business debts could be expected to be picky about the identity of their co-members. Moreover, this active management makes exit less important as a way of protecting the members from mismanagement. But restricted trans-

ferability is more peculiar in a firm such as a standard form limited partnership whose members resemble public corporation shareholders.

Larry E. Ribstein, *Limited Partnership Revisited*, 67 U. CINN. L. REV. 953, 988 (1999).

QUESTIONS AND NOTES

1.   Bubba's Burritos is a limited partnership in which Propp is one of several general partners. If Propp sells his interest in the partnership to Roberts, will Propp retain his right to participate in management? What if Propp sells a fifty percent share of his partnership interest to Roberts?

2.   Suppose Propp is the sole general partner of the Bubba's Burritos Limited Partnership, and that he transfers his entire interest to Roberts. What happens to the limited partnership? Does it still exist? Who is the general partner?

2.   TRANSFERS OF OWNERSHIP INTEREST TO LIMITED PARTNERSHIP

Recall that, under RUPA, the owner of a business structured as a general partnership has the power created by statute to force the business to purchase her ownership interest—this was dissociation. RULPA, like RUPA, contains default rules regarding an owner's right to force the business to buy her ownership interest. RULPA §§ 602, 603, and 604.

The language in these RULPA sections differs from the language in the RUPA sections—here, we speak of "withdrawal" instead of "dissociation." In addition, the RULPA default rules differ in § 602 and § 603, depending on whether the person who is withdrawing is a general partner or a limited partner.

QUESTIONS AND NOTE

1.   The assigned RULPA sections make it clear that a general partner can withdraw at will, while a limited partner must give six months' written notice (unless the partnership agreement said otherwise). Given the respective roles of general and limited partners, why does this difference make sense?

2.   Propp is the sole general partner in Bubba's Burritos Limited Partnership. Agee and Capel are the two limited partners. Propp withdraws.

a.   What options do Agee and Capel have if they want the business to continue?

b.   What options do they have if they want the business to end?

3.   Same facts as Question 2, except that Propp was also a limited partner. He withdraws as general partner, but does not want the limited partnership to continue.

a.   Does Propp retain his status as a limited partner after withdrawing as general partner?

b.   If so, can Propp ensure that the limited partnership dissolves? (See if RULPA §§ 602 and 702 are helpful here.) BTW, the Arizona legislature added this sentence to its version of RULPA § 602: "The withdrawal of a general partner who is also a limited partner does not constitute withdrawal of the partner as a limited partner or affect the partner's rights as a limited partner." ULPA 2001, in its Comment to § 603, resolves any ambiguity as well.

4.   Agee, a limited partner in Bubba's Burritos Limited Partnership, wishes to withdraw. The partnership agreement is silent on term and on events permitting a limited partner to withdraw.

a.   Can Agee withdraw?

b.   If so, how does she do it?

c.   Would the answer be different if the partnership agreement were for a term of years?

PROBLEM: WITHDRAWING FROM A LIMITED PARTNERSHIP

You are the attorney for a new limited partnership. You are meeting with L, who represents a person considering a major investment in the limited partnership. L asks why the general partners have a right to withdraw at any time, but under the limited partnership agreement:

> A limited partner shall have the right to withdraw his or her capital account only upon the termination of the partnership as provided in paragraph 19, except that no part of the capital account of any limited partner shall be withdrawn unless all partnership liabilities have been paid, or unless the partnership has assets sufficient to pay them.

How do you satisfy L? By the way, take a look at RULPA § 801(4).

CHAPTER TEN*

WHAT IS A LIMITED LIABILITY COMPANY AND HOW DOES IT WORK?

■ ■ ■

A. WHAT IS AN LLC AND WHAT IS LLC LAW?

Another form of business structure that offers Propp, Agee, and Capel the best of both worlds is a limited liability company, which everyone calls an LLC. An LLC offers all of its owners, generally referred to as members, both (i) protection from liability for the business's debts similar to the liability protection of shareholders of a corporation and (ii) the same pass-through income tax characteristics of a partnership.

The LLC is a relatively new business structure in the United States. Its origins trace to a statute enacted in Wyoming in 1978. In the years since then, the LLC has become increasingly popular. Most new businesses today are LLCs.

Each state has a statute authorizing the creation of LLCs. These statutes differ greatly. There is far more variety in state LLC laws than we find in the corporation or partnership laws of the various states. However, there are several important influences on states' LLC laws. The Delaware Limited Liability Company Act has much influence because, as with corporations, more LLCs are organized under Delaware law than under the law of any other state. In addition, the National Conference of Commissioners on Uniform State Law (NCCUSL) issued a Uniform Limited Liability Company Act (ULLCA) in 1996.[†]

Even though each state has an LLC statute, the law of LLCs is primarily contract law—much more so than the law of corporations, partnerships, or limited partnerships. As the Delaware Chancery Court recently observed, "For Shakespeare, it may have been the play, but for a

---

* This book, *Business Structures*, ends with Chapter 10. A significant number of businesses, however, end with Chapter 11, which is a type of bankruptcy. It is covered in another law school course, and by other West books, the most helpful of which, have been written by the senior author of this book.

† In 2006, NCCUSL issued a Revised ULLCA. *See generally* Daniel S. Kleinberger, *The Next Generation: The Revised Uniform Limited Liability Company Act*, 62 BUS. LAW. 515 (2007). Because the "Re–ULLCA" is so new, our discussion will focus on the Delaware statute and the ULLCA.

Delaware limited liability company, *the contract's the thing.* Ultimately, it is the contract that compels the Court's decision in this case because it is the contract that 'defines the scope, structure, and personality of limited liability companies.' " *R & R Capital, LLC v. Buck & Doe Run Valley Farms, LLC,* 2008 WL 3846318 (Del.Ch. 2008).

Typically, the members of an LCC enter into an operating agreement, which sets out the rules that govern that firm. Most LLC statutes establish default rules that govern if and only if there is no contrary provision in the operating agreement.

For example, § 103 of ULLCA provides in part:

§ 103.   Effect of operating agreement; nonwaivable provisions.

(a) Except as otherwise provided in subsection (b), all members of a limited liability company may enter into an operating agreement, which need not be in writing, to regulate the affairs of the company and the conduct of its business, and to govern relations among the members, managers, and company. To the extent the operating agreement does not otherwise provide, this [Act] governs relations among the members, managers, and company. * * *

COMMENT

* * * This section makes clear that the only matters an operating agreement may not control are specified in subsection (b). Accordingly, an operating agreement may modify or eliminate any rule specified in any section of this Act except matters specified in subsection (b). To the extent not otherwise mentioned in subsection (b), every section of this Act is simply a default rule, regardless of whether the language of the section appears to be otherwise mandatory.

The Delaware statute also gives great deference to the operating agreement. Section 1101(b) provides in pertinent part: "It is the policy of this chapter to give the maximum effect to the principle of freedom of contract and to the enforceability of limited liability company agreements."

B.   WHAT ARE THE LEGAL PROBLEMS IN STARTING A BUSINESS AS AN LLC?

In Delaware, a "limited liability company is formed at the time of the filing of the initial certificate of formation in the office of the Secretary of State." Delaware § 18–201. Similarly, under the ULLCA, "the existence of a limited liability company begins when the articles of organization are filed." *See* § 202(b). We have set out below the Delaware Certificate of Formation available from http://corp.delaware.gov/llcform09.pdf. Compare the Delaware requirements to those in § 203 of ULLCA.

STATE *of* DELAWARE
LIMITED LIABILITY COMPANY
CERTIFICATE *of* FORMATION

- **First:** The name of the limited liability company is _____
  _____.

- **Second:** The address of its registered office in the State of Delaware is _____
  _____ in the City of _____.
  The name of its Registered agent at such address is _____
  _____

- **Third:** *(Use this paragraph only if the company is to have a specific effective date of dissolution.)* "The latest date on which the limited liability company is to dissolve is _____."

- **Fourth:** *(Insert any other matters the members determine to include herein.)*
  _____
  _____
  _____
  _____
  _____
  _____
  _____

In Witness Whereof, the undersigned have executed this Certificate of Formation of
_____this _____ day of _____, 20_____.

[handwritten: 203 Requirements / Name of co / Address of Initials]

BY: _____
                 Authorized Person(s)

NAME: _____
                 Type or Print

QUESTIONS

1. Can you use the Delaware Certificate of Formation as an "articles of organization" in a state that has adopted ULLCA? Again, *see* ULLCA § 203.

2. Does the name of the business have to include the words "limited liability company" or the letters "LLC"? *See* Delaware § 18–102; ULLCA

§ 105. What if the certificate of formation shows the name as "Alabama Associates, LC"?

Regardless of whether relevant state law uses the term "certificate of formation" or "articles of organization" to describe the document that must be filed to create an LLC, that document is not the most important paper in the business. The most important document is the "Operating Agreement." As we have seen before, although the relevant statutes do not require that there be an operating agreement, the needs of your LLC clients require that there be one.

3. What happens if the articles conflict with the operating agreement? Does it matter whether the subject of the conflict is internal or external to the business? *See* ULLCA § 203(c).

4. Suppose Propp, Agee, and Capel operate a general partnership. They want to change the business structure to an LLC. Do they have to dissolve and wind up the partnership and then form an LLC? *See* ULLCA § 902.

C. WHAT ARE THE LEGAL PROBLEMS IN OPERATING A BUSINESS AS AN LLC?

1. WHO DECIDES WHAT?

The owners of an LLC can elect the form of management. Every state's LLC statute affords the owners (members) the option of electing to manage the business themselves—"member-managed company"—or have managers—"manager-managed company"—or some combination of member managed and manager managed.*

The decision-making authority of the members of a member-managed company is much like that of the partners in a general partnership. And the decision-making authority of the managers of a manager-managed company is much like a corporation with a board of directors, professional managers, and separation of ownership and management.

In a member-managed company, the operating agreement will answer such questions as: (1) how to determine how many votes each member has and (2) how to determine what matters require more than majority vote. In a manager-managed company, the operating agreement will answer questions such as (1) how members elect and remove managers and (2) what issues require a member vote.

Interests in general partnerships are not subject to federal securities laws, while the interests in limited partnerships and corporations are. The debate over whether interests in LLCs should be considered "securities" for these purposes remains open. In your view, should the answer to this question depend upon whether the LLC is member-managed or manager-managed? (Hint: does one seem more like a corporation than the other?)

---

* Professor Goforth suggests that the election of management structure be influenced not only by the owners' goals but also by accounting, securities law, and tax considerations. *See* Carol R. Goforth, *Continuing Obstacles to Freedom of Choice for Management Structure in LLCs*, 1 J. SMALL & EMERGING BUS. L. REV. 165 (1997).

PROBLEMS: DECISION-MAKING IN AN LLC

1. Your client C is about to contract with a business structured as a limited liability company. How does C know whether the company is member managed or manager managed? Does C need to know? *Cf.* ULLCA § 301.

2. Facchina is the manager of Child Care of Irvine, LLC, (CCI), which is a Delaware limited liability company. Although CCI retains a law firm to prepare an operating agreement, the six members (A, B, C, D, E, and Facchina) cannot agree on the terms. After a few months, five of the six members agree that they do not want Facchina to continue as manager. What can they do? *Cf.* ULLCA § 404; Delaware § 18–402. *See also* Child Care of Irvine, LLC v. Facchina, 1998 WL 409363 (Del. Ch. 1998).

2. WHO IS LIABLE TO WHOM FOR WHAT?

a. Members' Liability to Third Parties

An LLC is an entity. Delaware § 18–201(b), ULLCA § 201. It can carry on "any lawful business purpose or activity." Delaware § 18–106. An LLC can incur debts from the actions and inactions of its managers or its members. ULLCA §§ 301, 302. Creditors of an LLC can collect their claims from the earnings and other assets of the company.

LLC statutes protect the owners from personal liability for these claims against the company. Compare Delaware § 18–303 and ULLCA § 303. Note that neither provision distinguishes the personal liability of members in member-managed LLCs from the personal liability of members in manager-managed LLCs. The members are simply not liable for the company's debts.

And that protection from liability for the company's debts extends to all members. One advantage of the LLC over the limited partnership is that there is no general partner who is liable for the company's debts.

A more important point is that the members are protected from liability only for the company's debts. As the next case points out, a member is personally liable for her own conduct, even when she is acting for the company.

WEBBER v. UNITED STATES STERLING SECURITIES, INC.

Connecticut Supreme Court, 2007
924 A.2d 816

VERTEFEUILLE, J. [Retail Relief, LLC is a limited liability company, organized under the laws of Delaware. Michelle Master Orr and her husband Shawn are members. The Orrs sent an unsolicited fax advertisement to Plaintiff on behalf of Retail Relief. Sending such a fax advertisement violated a federal law, and violations of that law are treated as torts. Plaintiff sued the Orrs individually. The Orrs, here referred to as the "defendants," moved for summary judgment, alleging that they could not be held personally liable because they were acting on behalf of Retail Relief, a Delaware limited liability company. The trial court granted the defendants' motion.]

[W]hen a limited liability company is incorporated [sic] in another state, our statutes mandate application of the laws of that foreign state. Because Retail Relief was incorporated in Delaware, we look to Delaware law to determine the extent of the defendants' liability.

We begin our analysis with the text of § 18–303(a) of title 6 of the Delaware Code Annotated. Section 18–303(a) provides in relevant part: "Except as otherwise provided by this chapter, the debts, obligations and liabilities of a limited liability company, whether arising in contract, tort or otherwise, shall be solely the debts, obligations and liabilities of the limited liability company, and *no member or manager of a limited liability company shall be obligated personally for any such debt, obligation or liability of the limited liability company solely by reason of being a member or acting as a manager of the limited liability company.*" (Emphasis added.) * * *

The plaintiff claims that § 18–303(a) does not shield limited liability company members from individual liability based on their personal conduct. In response, the defendants argue that their mere status as limited liability company members with Retail Relief exempts them from all personal liability and they rely in particular on the following language from the Delaware statute: "[N]o member or manager of a limited liability company shall be obligated personally for any such debt, obligation or liability of the limited liability company *solely* by reason of being a member or acting as a manager of the limited liability company." (Emphasis added.) Del.Code Ann. tit. 6, § 18–303(a) (2005).

To resolve the plaintiff's claim, we must ascertain the meaning of the word "solely." ... "[S]olely" is defined to mean "to the exclusion of alternate or competing things...." Webster's Third New International Dictionary. Thus, the statute plainly provides that a limited liability company member cannot be held liable for the malfeasance of a limited liability company by virtue of his membership in the limited liability company alone; in other words, he must do more than merely be a member in order to be liable personally for an obligation of the limited liability company. The statute thus does not preclude individual liability for members of a limited liability company if that liability is not based simply on the member's affiliation with the company. * * *

Under Delaware law, a limited liability company formed under the Delaware Limited Liability Company Act is treated for liability purposes like a corporation." * * * "The default common-law rule is that corporate officials may be held individually liable for their tortious conduct, even if undertaken while acting in their official capacity. ... [V]arious courts of [the state of Delaware] have recognized that executives, directors and officers of an entity can be held *individually* liable for the fraudulent or tortious acts which they, in their official capacities, commit, ratify or approve, despite the fact that they may have acted as an agent for or performed for the benefit of that entity at the time the fraudulent or tortious act was committed, ratified or approved." Accordingly, we conclude that although § 18–303(a) of the Delaware Code Annotated shields the defendants from personal liability based solely on their affiliation with Retail Relief, it does not shield them from personal liability for their own tortious conduct.

As previously noted herein, claims under the act generally are viewed as sounding in tort. We agree with the cases that have characterized claims under the act as tortious in nature.

Because those claims sound in tort, and § 18–303(a) does not bar the defendants' liability for tortious conduct, we conclude that the trial court improperly rendered summary judgment in favor of the defendants on the issue of the defendants' personal liability for the plaintiff's claim. * * *

QUESTIONS

1. Was it important that "those claims sounded in tort"?

2. Would Retail Relief also be liable for the Orrs' sending the fax? If so, why did the plaintiff sue the Orrs instead of Retail Relief?

3. If Epstein was a member of Retail Relief and Epstein had done no more work for Retail Relief than he has done on this new edition of the Business Structures book, would Epstein be personally liable?

4. Is this case consistent with principles of corporate law? Principles of agency law?

Recall that, under principles of corporation law, the limited liability of a shareholder of a close corporation is limited by the concept of piercing the corporate veil. The question of whether courts will similarly pierce the veil of an LLC is the most frequently litigated question of limited liability company law. In some states, limited liability company statutes do not expressly address this question. In other states, such as Washington, the statute is clear: "The members of a limited liability company shall be personally liable for any act, debt, obligation, or liability of the limited liability company to the extent that shareholders of a Washington business corporation would be liable in analogous circumstances. In this regard, the court may consider the factors and policies set forth in established case law with regard to piercing the corporate veil, except that the failure to hold meetings of members or managers or the failure to observe formalities pertaining to the calling or conduct of meetings shall not be considered a factor tending to establish that the members have personal liability for any act, debt, obligation, or liability of the limited liability company if the certificate of formation and limited liability company agreement do not expressly require the holding of meetings of members or managers." Revised Code of Washington, § 25.15.060 (2009).

As the next case illustrates, some states' limited liability statutes are apparently not as clear.

IN RE SUHADOLNIK

U.S. Bankruptcy Court, Central District of Illinois, 2009
2009 WL 2591338

GORMAN, BANKRUPTCY JUDGE. [Michael Suhadolnik filed for Chapter 7 bankruptcy relief. He is what both the Bankruptcy Code and this bankruptcy court call a "Debtor." Before filing for bankruptcy, Debtor allegedly "owned and controlled" a limited liability company, Chatham. Denmar Builders, Inc. ("Denmar") claims that Chatham is indebted to Denmar, and that the Debtor is personally liable for this debt owed by Chatham to Denmar because, *inter alia*, the Debtor treated Chatham as his alter ego and, thus, the court should pierce the veil of the LLC.]

* * * [B]oth parties have concentrated on the issue of whether the veil of an LLC may be pierced under Illinois law. This issue is determinative of whether Denmar is able to state a claim for relief against the Debtor individually to establish personal liability for the debt owed by Chatham to Denmar. Only if Denmar is able to establish Debtor's personal liability for the debt can it then move on to state a cause of action to determine the dischargeability of that debt. Thus, the viability of Denmar's dischargeabilty complaint rests on whether Illinois law allows veil piercing of LLCs.

Veil piercing is an equitable remedy which is generally associated with actions against corporate shareholders. Under certain circumstances, a corporate veil may be pierced and shareholders of a corporation may be held liable for the corporation's debts. * * *

Although the concept of veil piercing is a well-established principal of Illinois corporate law, the Debtor argues that Illinois law precludes piercing the veil of an LLC. The Debtor relies on a portion of the Illinois Limited Liability Act ("Act") which provides in pertinent part as follows:

180/10–10. Liability of members and managers

(a) Except as otherwise provided in subsection (d) of this Section, the debts, obligations, and liabilities of a limited liability company, whether arising in contract, tort, or otherwise, are solely the debts, obligations, and liabilities of the company. A member or manager is not personally liable for a debt, obligation, or liability of the company solely by reason of being or acting as a member or manager. * * *

(c) The failure of a limited liability company to observe the usual company formalities or requirements relating to the exercise of its company powers or management of its business is not a ground for imposing personal liability on the members or managers for liabilities of the company. * * *

Clearly, the Act specifically provides that an individual is not personally liable for the debts of an LLC solely because that individual is a member or manager of the LLC or because the LLC has not observed required formalities. The Debtor argues, however, that the Act goes even further and bars veil piercing of LLCs under all circumstances including fraud.

One Illinois case, *Puleo v. Topel*, 368 Ill.App.3d 63, 856 N.E. 2d 1152 (2006), appears to provide some support to the Debtor. * * * Although *Puleo* did not directly address the issue of piercing the veil of an LLC, the Debtor seizes upon dicta in *Puleo* which suggests that a member or manager of an LLC might be shielded from personal liability under all circumstances. The *Puleo* court noted that in 1998, the Illinois legislature deleted language from the Act which explicitly provided that a member or manager of an LLC could be held personally liable for the actions of the LLC to the same extent as a shareholder or director of an Illinois business corporation could be held personally liable. Noting a lack of legislative history clarifying the intent behind the amendment, the court presumed "that by removing the noted statutory language, the legislature meant to shield a member or manager of an LLC from personal liability." * * *

Although the *Puleo* court correctly noted a lack of legislative history surrounding the 1998 amendment of the Act, it failed to note that the amendatory language appears to have come directly from the Uniform Limited Liability Company Act ("Uniform Act"). The drafters of the Uniform Act included commentary explaining the import of the provision including the following:

> A member or manager, as agent of the company, is not liable for the debts, obligations, and liabilities of the company simply because of the agency. A member or manager is responsible for acts or omissions to the extent those acts or omissions would be actionable in contract or tort against the member or manager if that person were acting in an individual capacity.

Unif. Ltd. Liab. Co. Act § 303, comment.

The original provision of the Act provided for identical liability for members and managers of LLCs as shareholders and directors have for corporations. The 1998 amendment substituted a prohibition of actions based solely on member or manager status or based on a failure to comply with statutory formalities. The amendment is silent as to liability for actual wrongdoing or fraud by members or managers. The *Puleo* court interpreted that silence to mean that those causes of action are barred also. The plain meaning of the statute as amended does not lead to that conclusion. Further, the choice by the legislature to use the language of the Uniform Act, which was published with commentary suggesting that causes of action for individual wrongdoing are not shielded by the limited liability veil of an LLC, suggests that the legislature did not intend to bar those causes of action. Creating a super business entity which would shield all wrongdoing and bar all civil causes of action against controlling owners of LLCs even for the most egregious acts of fraud or other wrongdoing would serve no public purpose. Thus, absent a clearly expressed intent of the Illinois legislature to create such an entity, this Court will not presume that such an entity exists. Accordingly, * * * veil piercing is available with respect to members and managers of Illinois LLCs under traditional veil piercing theories such as alter ego, fraud, or undercapitalization

QUESTIONS

1. Do we know whether it is possible to have a single owner LLC under ULLCA? If so, do we know whether Debtor was the only owner of Denmar? Should that be relevant? Was it relevant when we considered piercing the LLC veil?

2. Did the bankruptcy court limit its holding that "veil piercing is available with respect to members and managers of Illinois LLCs under traditional veil piercing theories such as alter ego, fraud, or undercapitalization" to tort claims?

3. This opinion distinguishes the legal issue in *Puleo* from the legal issue in the case. Is *Puleo* factually distinguishable from this case? Is *Puleo* correctly decided? Do you agree with following statement from a law review article by a former dean named "Bud" that misspells *"Puleo"*:

> [T]here are two other sound bases to support a claim against a "member" of a dissolved LLC.
>
> First, the defendant breached his warranty of authority when he entered into a contract on behalf of the dissolved LLC. An agent warrants the existence of a principal and the agent's authority.
>
> In this case, there was no principal because the LLC had been dissolved. The Illinois Supreme Court, in *Joseph T. Ryerson & Son v. Shaw*, 277 Ill. 524, 531–32, 115 N.E. 650, 653 (1917), stated that "a person who assumes to act as agent for a legally incompetent principal renders himself personally liable to the person with whom he deals unless such person knows of the want of authority."
>
> Second, section 35–7 (b) of the Illinois act provides that a member who knows of the dissolution of the LLC but binds it by an act not appropriate to wind it up is liable to the company for the consequences of such an act. Since the defendant's contract with plaintiffs was not consistent with winding up the LLC, the defendant then was liable to the LLC for the consequences of the contract. Accordingly, if the LLC did not have funds, which it apparently did not, plaintiffs could be subrogated to the LLC's claim against the defendant.
>
> We hope that the next time the question of the liability of members and managers of a *dissolved* limited liability company is reviewed, the court will note the significance of the fact of dissolution and recognize that there are numerous bases upon which to hold the defendant liable.

Lin Hanson & Charles W. "Bud" Murdock, *Puelo v. Topel: Respectfully, the Court Got it Wrong, The Puelo Court Held That a Dissolved LLC Was on the*

Hook for Liabilities Incurred After the Dissolution. Wrong Answer, the Authors Argue, 98 Ill. B. J. 158 (March 2008).

4. Bubba's Burritos, a general partnership, enters a five-year lease with L & L Realty for its restaurant location. After one year, the business converts to an LLC.

a. Is the lease still enforceable? If so, against whom? *See* ULLCA §§ 902(g), 903.

b. Would your answers change if the general partnership had dissolved and the proprietors then formed an LLC?

b. Members' and Managers' Liability to the Company

Generally, a member acquires her ownership interest in a limited liability company by making or agreeing to make a payment or other contribution to the company. The operating agreement usually lists the amount of each member's initial contribution. And while the operating agreement can provide for additional contributions, it more commonly contains language similar to the following: "No Initial Member shall be obligated to make any Capital Contribution other than the Initial Capital Contribution on Schedule E."

In addition to the members' contractual obligation to make contributions to the limited liability company, members of LLCs that are member-managed and managers of limited liability companies that are manager-managed also owe the company fiduciary duties. In contrast, members of a manager-managed limited liability company generally owe no fiduciary duties to the company.

The exact nature of the duties varies depending on the language of the state's limited liability company act and the language of the company's operating agreement. *See* ULLCA §§ 103 and 409 for an example of statutory provisions regarding fiduciary duties. The following case provides examples of an operating agreement provision regarding fiduciary duties.

In reading the case, consider the following:

1. Who is the plaintiff? Is it the LLC or a member of the company?

2. Who is the defendant? Is it a member of the LLC or a manager of the LLC?

[handwritten: Lynch sued Carson (member)]

LYNCH MULTIMEDIA CORPORATION v. CARSON COMMUNICATIONS, L.L.C.

United States District Court, District of Kansas, 2000
102 F.Supp.2d 1261

MARETEN, DISTRICT JUDGE. Currently before the court in this action are competing summary judgment motions by plaintiff and defendants. The parties were involved in a joint venture limited liability company (CLR Video). One of the companies (Lynch Multimedia) has sued one of the other member companies, its owners, and its agent, alleging that they breached the operating agreement and various fiduciary duties when they independently acquired other cable franchises, rather than securing them for CLR Video. For the reasons stated herein, the court finds that the motion of the defendants must be granted, and the court finds, under the facts presented here, there was no violation of the operating agreement/fiduciary duties. * * *

Under the Operating Agreement of November, 1995, CLR has three owners: Lynch Multimedia, Rainbow Communications and Electronics, and the Robert C. Carson Trust. * * *. CLR has a Board of Managers which manages its business; under the Operating Agreement Lynch names three of the managers, and Rainbow and the Carson Trust each name one. Robert C. Carson was the president of CLR. The Operating Agreement gives the president "general and active management" of CLR's business, and carries out orders and resolutions of the Board of Managers. * * *

The two provisions of the Operating Agreement which are central to this case are set forth below:

[§ 11.4] Other Cable Systems. Any opportunity which comes to the attention of a Member to purchase cable television systems (i) in Kansas from Cablevison of Texas, Tristar Cable, Inc. or Falcon Cablevision; and (ii) in Atchison, Brown, Clay, Cloud, Doniphan, Jackson, Jefferson, Nemaha, Leavenworth, Marshall, Ottawa, Pottawatomie, Republic, Riley and Washington counties in Kansas shall be first offered to the Company.

[§ 11.2] Other Interests. Any Member or Manager may engage independently or with others in other business ventures of every nature and description. Neither the Company nor any Member shall have any right by virtue of this Agreement or the relationship created hereby in or to any other ventures or activities in which any Member or Manager is involved or to the income or proceeds derived therefrom. The pursuit of other ventures and activities by Members or Managers is hereby consented to by the Members and shall not be deemed wrongful or improper.

Carson learned in 1996 that Falcon [Cablevision] might be for sale. According to plaintiff, at a subsequent meeting of the members in the fall of 1996, the members approved the possible acquisition of Falcon, along with the potential purchase of two other cable systems (Galaxy and Tristar).

After this 1996 meeting, Carson learned that cable systems owned by Westcom (a successor of Tristar) and Galaxy might become available for purchase. * * *

In August or September of 1997, Carson informed Lynch representatives of the Westcom and Galaxy opportunities at a meeting at Lynch Corporation headquarters in Chicago. He also discussed those opportunities at another meeting in Chicago on October 26 and 27. According to Lynch, it encouraged Carson to acquire these companies. Carson objects that "encouragement" is too strong a term, that they merely suggested continued study of the target companies. * * *

Carson and the plaintiff's representatives met on April 4, 1998 in Greenwich, Connecticut. * * * Again, the members discussed the acquisition of Falcon, Westcom, and Galaxy. By the end of the meeting, no agreement had yet been reached with Falcon, Westcom, or Galaxy about buying their cable systems. * * *

On October 7, 1998, Carson wrote to Dolan, proposing two plans for acquiring Falcon and Westcom. On November 11, he sent a term sheet to [Mario] Gabelli [a representative of Lynch], proposing to acquire Falcon and Westcom. He submitted another term sheet to Dolan on December 30, which proposed the acquisition of Falcon and Westcom properties but which attached terms not contained in the CLR Operating Agreement, and which would require changes in the Operating Agreement. Among the proposed changes was an increase in his salary, continuation as president of CLR, and an increase in the value of his equity interest upon the sale of his interest to other members. * * *

[In March or April of 1999, Carson purchased the Falcon and Westcom cable systems for himself.]

Conclusions of Law

The core of the dispute between the parties lies in the construction of § 11.4 of the Operating Agreement, and the scope of the duty created by the section's requirement that an "opportunity . . . to purchase cable television systems . . . shall be first offered to the Company." Carson argues that any duty under § 11.4 was met when he notified or told other members of the CLR Video that certain opportunities existed.

Lynch adopts a more narrow definition of "offer," citing the Restatement (Second) of Contracts, § 24 (1981): an offer is a representation which must "justify another person in understanding that his assent to that bargain is invited and will conclude it." Thus, Lynch argues that Carson could not fulfill the duty created by § 11.4 unless he presented the other members with a no-strings-attached purchase offer at a properly called special meeting of the members. Carson violated this obligation, according to Lynch, because he sought to add terms to any acquisition of the target companies and because there was no formal meeting informing Carson that he could acquire the companies for his own.

The court finds that this interpretation must be rejected. First, looking just to the plain language of § 11.4, it would appear that the Operating Agreement does not intend the standard legal definition of "offer." Under this provision, the member does not offer an "offer" to the other members in the sense that it could be "accepted" or concluded. The member merely offers knowledge of an "opportunity." The member notifying the other members is not an agent of the target company, and thus could not bind the target company to any contract.

Secondly, § 11.4 must be read in the context of the entire Operating Agreement. * * *. In the context of an Operating Agreement creating a cable television company, formed from other cable television companies, this [§ 11.2] provision's explicit statement that the members may engage "in other business ventures of every nature and description" is plainly directed at permitting the members to enter into separate and additional business relations in the cable television industry. * * *

Finally, the court will also grant summary judgment as to the general claims of breach of fiduciary duty advanced by Lynch. Lynch never articulates how these claims are distinguishable from the underlying claim of breach of § 11.4 of the Operating Agreement. Under Kansas law, the members of a limited liability company may expand or restrict their duties and liabilities by the terms of their agreement. * * *

In short, Carson informed the other members of CLR Video of certain opportunities to purchase cable companies. Only after the passage of several months or years, and at one point after the rejection of the proposal, did Carson independently acquire the companies. Under the facts presented to the court, the plaintiff has demonstrated neither a breach of the Operating Agreement nor of the defendants' fiduciary duties.

QUESTIONS

1. Does Carson owe a fiduciary duty to CLR Videos? To Lynch?

2. Why is Lynch the plaintiff instead of CLR Videos?

3. Epstein is a member of Bubba's Burritos, LLC, a manager-managed limited liability company. Epstein is interested in buying a building from Bubba's Burritos because Epstein has learned that the University of Alabama is considering building a new football stadium two blocks from the Bubba's Burritos building. Epstein has not disclosed this to Bubba's Burritos' manager.

  a. Epstein wants to know whether (i) there are any limitations on or (ii) special legal obligations in his buying from Bubba's Burritos. Advise Epstein as to his liability exposure, if any. *See* ULLCA § 409.

  b. What if the operating agreement had delegated authority to Epstein to manage the real estate transactions for Bubba's Burritos?

4. Dean Murdock, speaking of the *Lynch* case, has said: "Under a typical entity opportunity situation, Lynch's position might prevail. The court rejected Lynch's position, however, based on the language of the agreement." Charles W. Murdock, *Limited Liability Companies in the Decade of the 1990's: Legislative and Case Law Developments and Their Implications for the Future,* 56 BUS. LAW. 499, 547 (2001). Do you agree? Do you remember that he goes by "Bud" when he writes for the Illinois Bar Journal?

D. HOW DO THE OWNERS OF A BUSINESS STRUCTURED AS A LIMITED LIABILITY COMPANY MAKE MONEY?

Recall that an owner of a business generally makes money by sharing in the business's earnings or by selling her interest for more than she paid for it or by being employed by the business.

Usually, the operating agreement provides how and when a limited liability company's earnings are to be distributed to its members. Statutory provisions on distributions are only default rules: "[T]his section [ULLCA § 405] creates a simple default rule regarding interim distributions. Any interim distributions must be in equal shares and approved by all members." Comment to ULLCA § 405. *See also* Delaware § 18–504.

The most important limitation on a member's making money by selling her interest for more than she paid for it is imposed by the market, not by the legislature, the courts or even the operating agreement. It is usually difficult to find a buyer for an interest in a small business or even a large business that has relatively few owners.

Even if a member of a limited liability company is able to find a buyer for her interest, her ability to sell may be limited by statute or by the operating agreement or by both. Again, the statutory provisions relating to a member's sale of her ownership interest are likely to be a default rule. For example, Delaware § 18–702 provides in part:

(a) A limited liability company interest is assignable in whole or in part except as provided in a limited liability company agreement. The assignee of a member's limited liability company interest shall have no right to participate in the management of the business and affairs of a limited liability company except as provided in a limited liability company agreement and upon:

   (1) The approval of all of the members of the limited liability company other than the member assigning the limited liability company interest; or

   (2) Compliance with any procedure provided for in the limited liability company agreement.

(b) Unless otherwise provided in a limited liability company agreement:

   (1) An assignment of a limited liability company interest does not entitle the assignee to become or to exercise any rights or powers of a member;

   (2) An assignment of a limited liability company interest entitles the assignee to share in such profits and losses, to receive such distribution or distributions, and to receive such allocation of income, gain, loss, deduction, or credit or similar item

to which the assignor was entitled, to the extent assigned * * *.

See also ULLCA §§ 502, 503.*

PROBLEM: TRANSFERS OF MEMBERS' INTERESTS

Propp, Agee and Capel have decided to organize Bubba's Burritos, LLC as a Delaware limited liability company. You are drafting the operating agreement. What if anything should the operating agreement provide with respect to sales of ownership interests by members to third parties?

———————

Because of the market and legal restrictions on a member's sale of her ownership interest in a limited liability company to an outsider, the questions both of whether a member can compel the company to purchase her ownership interest and whether an LLC can compel the member to sell her ownership are often important. The questions are answered by operating agreements, LLC statutes, and in part by the next case. In reading this case, consider the following questions about its facts:

1. Was Lieberman expelled or did he withdraw? Do we know? Does it matter?

2. Is Lieberman seeking dissolution or dissociation or both? Do we know? Does it matter?

3. Does the defendant argue that Lieberman sold, gave away, lost or otherwise transferred his ownership interest?

4. Is Lieberman related to Senator Lieberman? Do we know? Does it matter?

LIEBERMAN v. WYOMING.COM L.L.C.

Supreme Court of Wyoming, 2000
11 P.3d 353

LEHMAN, CHIEF JUSTICE. In this case, we review a summary judgment in favor of appellee Wyoming.com LLC, directing it to return only the capital contribution made by a withdrawing member of the LLC, appellant E. Michael Lieberman (Lieberman). Although the district court correctly resolved the return of Lieberman's capital contribution, its order does not

---

* "To appreciate the statutory provisions, it is necessary to have an historical perspective. A major reason for organizing an LLC is to avoid an entity level tax and obtain pass-through, or partnership, tax treatment as opposed to corporate tax treatment. At one point, the issue of whether the IRS would recognize that an LLC could be taxed as a partnership hinged upon the extent to which the entity exhibited certain characteristics that are common to corporations, but are usually absent from partnerships. * * * Consequently, the first generation of LLC statutes was designed to facilitate pass-through tax treatment by having default provisions that would negate transferability or continuity of existence." Charles W. Murdock, *Limited Liability Companies in the Decade of the 1990's: Legislative and Case Law Developments and Their Implications for the Future*, 56 BUS. LAW. 499, 548–49 (2001).

resolve the question of what became of the rest of Lieberman's interest in the company. We affirm in part and reverse and remand for full resolution of the parties' dispute.

In his brief, Lieberman raises three issues:

Issue No. 1: Unless otherwise provided in the Articles or Operating Agreement, is a member withdrawing from a Wyoming Limited Liability Company entitled to demand and receive the fair market value of his share of the business as a going concern, if the Company elects to continue?

Issue No. 2: Absent agreement, is there authority for the withdrawing Member's contribution to be valued at less than the fair value of his equity in the Company?

Issue No. 3: Did the District Court err in granting Summary Judgment on disputed material issues of fact?

Appellee, Wyoming.com LLC, presents this statement of the issues:

1. Whether a member who withdraws from a Wyoming limited liability company is entitled to demand and receive only the return of his contributions to capital when the limited liability company elects to continue * * *.

2. Whether the trial court's grant of summary judgment in favor of appellee was proper.

On September 30, 1994, Steven Mossbrook, Sandra Mossbrook, and Lieberman created Wyoming.com LLC by filing Articles of Organization with the Wyoming Secretary of State. The initial capital contributions to Wyoming.com were valued at $50,000.* **[1]** Lieberman was vested with an initial capital contribution of $20,000, to consist of services rendered and to be rendered. According to the Articles of Organization, Lieberman's contribution represented a 40% ownership interest in the LLC. The Mossbrooks were vested with the remaining $30,000 capital contribution and 60% ownership interest. In August of 1995, the Articles of Organization of Wyoming.com were amended to reflect an increase in capitalization to $100,000. The increase in capitalization was the result of the addition of two members, each of whom was vested with a capital contribution of $25,000, representing a 2.5% ownership interest for each new member. Despite the increase in capitalization, Lieberman's ownership interest, as well as his stated capital contribution, remained the same.

On February 27, 1998, Lieberman was terminated as vice president of Wyoming.com and required to leave the business premises. The other members of Wyoming.com met the same day and approved and ratified the termination.† **[4]** On March 13, 1998, Lieberman served Wyoming.com

---

* **[1]** Wyo. Stat. Ann. § 17–15–107(a)(v) requires the articles of organization of an LLC to set forth the total amount of cash and a description and agreed value of property other than cash contributed to the LLC.

† **[4]** Paragraph 7.4 of the Operating Agreement provides, "Any officer may be removed at any time by the Members with or without cause."

and its members with a document titled "Notice of Withdrawal of Member Upon Expulsion: Demand for Return of Contributions to Capit[a]l." In addition to giving notice of his withdrawal from the company, Lieberman's notice demanded the immediate return of "his share of the current value of the company," estimating the value of his share at $400,000, "based on a recent offer from the Majority Shareholder."

In response to Lieberman's notice of withdrawal, the members of Wyoming.com held a special meeting on March 17, 1998, and accepted Lieberman's withdrawal. The members also elected to continue, rather than dissolve, Wyoming.com. Additionally, they approved the return of Lieberman's $20,000 capital contribution. However, Lieberman refused to accept the $20,000 when it was offered.

Wyoming.com filed suit in June of 1998 asking for a declaration of its rights against Lieberman. Lieberman filed suit the same month requesting dissolution of Wyoming.com, and the actions were consolidated. After a hearing on cross motions for summary judgment, the district court granted Wyoming.com's motion for summary judgment and denied Lieberman's motion for partial summary judgment. The district court ruled that, because the remaining members of Wyoming.com LLC agreed to continue the business under a right to do so in the Articles of Organization, the company was not in a state of dissolution. The district court further ruled that Lieberman had the right to demand return of only his stated capital contribution, $20,000, which the district court ordered to be paid in cash. Lieberman appealed. * * *

Because this case presents our first opportunity to interpret the Wyoming LLC act, we make a few preliminary observations. Wyoming initiated a national movement in 1977 when it adopted the first limited liability company act in the United States. As a business entity, limited liability companies are a conceptual hybrid, sharing some of the characteristics of partnerships and some of corporations. "In general, the purpose of forming a limited liability company is to create an entity that offers investors the protections of limited liability and the flow-through tax status of partnerships."

Little case law exists regarding a member's interest in a LLC. Regardless, the precedential value of cases from other jurisdictions is questionable: "Widely divergent rules on the effects of member dissociation will ultimately create confusion and inhibit the development of uniform case law. As a result, case law will have little precedential value from state to state." Therefore, we must focus our review on the Wyoming LLC act as well as Wyoming.com's Articles of Organization and Operating Agreement.

Under the Wyoming LLC act, a member's interest in an LLC consists of economic and non-economic interests. One interest is a member's capital contribution, which a member may withdraw under certain conditions. A member also generally has the right to receive profits. A member's interest also usually grants him the ability to participate in management. Overall, a member's interest is transferable, although the management rights of a transferee may be limited. While these statutory provisions provide some guidance regarding a member's interest, we must also look at an LLC's operating agreement and articles of organization.

Turning to the issues presented, we first address whether Lieberman's withdrawal triggered dissolution of Wyoming.com. Wyo. Stat. Ann. § 17–15–123(a)(iii)* **[5]** requires that, upon withdrawal of a member, the LLC must dissolve unless all the remaining members of the company consent to continue under a right to do so stated in the articles of organization. Paragraph 9 of the Articles of Organization of Wyoming.com LLC permits continuation:

> 9.   Continuity. The remaining members of the LLC, providing they are two or more in number, will have the right to continue the business on the death, retirement, resignation, expulsion, bankruptcy or dissolution of a member or occurrence of any other event which terminates the continued membership of a member in this LLC, in accordance with the voting provisions of the Operating Agreement of the Company.

The minutes of a March 17, 1998, special meeting of Wyoming.com reflect that the remaining members of Wyoming.com elected to continue the LLC after Lieberman's departure.* **[6]** This set of undisputed facts establishes there was no dissolution, and Lieberman is not entitled to distribution of assets under Wyo. Stat. Ann. § 17–15–126,† **[8]** as he claimed.

We next address the propriety of the return of contributions to capital. In his notice of withdrawal, Lieberman invoked Wyo. Stat. Ann. § 17–15–120, which provides in pertinent part:

---

* **[5]** WYO. STAT. ANN. § 17–15–123(a)(iii) provides:

(a) A limited liability company organized under this chapter shall be dissolved upon the occurrence of any of the following events:

* * *

(iii) Upon the death, retirement, resignation, expulsion, bankruptcy, dissolution of a member or occurrence of any other event which terminates the continued membership of a member in the limited liability company, unless the business of the limited liability company is continued by the consent of all the remaining members under a right to do so stated in the articles of organization of the limited liability company.

* **[6]** Although Lieberman argues he was expelled from the LLC, neither the Operating Agreement nor WYO. STAT. ANN. § 17–15–123(a)(iii) draws a distinction between expulsion and withdrawal.

† **[8]** Wyo. Stat. Ann. § 17–15–126, Distribution of assets upon dissolution, provides:

(b) Subject to any statement in the operating agreement, members share in the limited liability company assets in respect to their claims for capital and in respect to their claims for profits or for compensation by way of income on their contributions, respectively, in proportion to the respective amounts of the claims.

Even if Wyoming.com were in a state of dissolution, § 17–15–126(b) is "subject to any statement in the operating agreement," and Article VI of the Operating Agreement would appear to control liquidation of Wyoming.com's assets.

§ 17–15–120. Withdrawal or reduction of members' contributions to capital.

(a) A member shall not receive out of limited liability company property any part of his or its contribution to capital until:

(i) All liabilities of the limited liability company, except liabilities to members on account of their contributions to capital, have been paid or there remains property of the limited liability company sufficient to pay them;

(ii) The consent of all members is had, unless the return of the contribution to capital may be rightfully demanded as provided in this act;

(iii) The articles of organization are cancelled or so amended as to set out the withdrawal or reduction.

(b) Subject to the provisions of subsection (a) of this section, a member may rightfully demand the return of his or its contribution: * * *

(ii) Unless otherwise prohibited or restricted in the operating agreement, after the member has given all other members of the limited liability company prior notice in writing in conformity with the operating agreement. If the operating agreement does not prohibit or restrict the right to demand the return of capital and no notice period is specified, a member making the demand must give six (6) months prior notice in writing.

In applying § 17–15–120(b)(ii), we note that Wyoming.com's Operating Agreement does not prohibit or restrict the right of a member to demand the return of capital contribution. It is undisputed that Lieberman's stated capital contribution was $20,000 when the LLC was formed and that no subsequent amendment to the Articles of Organization changed the stated amount of his contribution. Furthermore, the remaining members of Wyoming.com agreed to return $20,000 to Lieberman, and neither party contends he is not entitled to the return of $20,000. Under these circumstances, Lieberman is entitled to the return of his capital contribution pursuant to Wyo. Stat. Ann. § 17–15–120.* **[9]** However, the question is whether the return is limited to the sum of $20,000.

Lieberman claims the term "contribution to capital" found in Wyo. Stat. Ann. § 17–15–120 should be interpreted to encompass the fair market value of his interest in the LLC and that his return should not be limited to the amount of his initial capital contribution. At this juncture, a

---

* **[9]** Pursuant to Wyo. Stat. Ann. § 17–15–121, a contributor who withdraws capital contributions remains liable:

(d) When a contributor has rightfully received the return in whole or in part of the capital of his or its contribution, the contributor is nevertheless liable to the limited liability company, for a period of six (6) years after return of the capital contribution, for any sum, not in excess of the return without interest, necessary to discharge its liability to all creditors of the limited liability company who extended credit during the period the capital contribution was held by the limited liability company or whose claims arose before the return.

distinction must be drawn between withdrawal of a member's capital contribution and the withdrawal from membership in an LLC, often termed dissociation. After a thorough review of § 17–15–120, we conclude nothing in that provision contemplates a member's rights upon dissociation. Besides the fact that § 17–15–120 speaks only to withdrawal of capital contributions, other provisions in the LLC Act support our conclusion that § 17–15–120 does not govern dissociation. The following passage from § 17–15–119, which controls division of profits, envisions withdrawal of capital contribution without dissociation: "If the operating agreement does not so provide, distributions shall be made on the basis of the value of the contributions made by each member to the extent they have been received by the limited liability company and have not been returned." This quoted material clearly contemplates a situation where a member has withdrawn some (or even all) of his capital contribution but has not dissociated as a member. We conclude a withdrawal of capital contributions pursuant to § 17–15–120 does not also govern a member's rights upon dissociation.

In addition, we conclude § 17–15–120 permits the return of only the initial or stated capital contribution of a member. First and foremost, nothing in § 17–15–120 indicates that fair market value of a member's interest is to be included in the amount to be paid to a member upon withdrawal of that member's capital contribution. In addition, § 17–15–129(b)(i) requires amendment to an LLC's articles of organization when the amount or character of contributions changes. Thus, the amount of a member's capital contribution is a constant not subject to market fluctuations. Numerous LLC acts from other states do allow a member to receive the fair market value (or fair value) of the member's interest. However, those provisions generally contemplate dissociation, not simply withdrawal of capital contributions.

The foregoing discussion disposes of Lieberman's claim that he is entitled to demand dissolution under Wyo. Stat. Ann. § 17–15–120(d), which provides in pertinent part:

> 17–15–120. *Withdrawal or reduction of members' contributions to capital.* * * *
>
> (d) A member of a limited liability company may have the limited liability company dissolved and its affairs wound up when:
>
> (i) The member rightfully but unsuccessfully has demanded the return of his or its contribution[.]

To compel dissolution under this provision, Lieberman's demand for the return of his capital contribution must have been unsuccessful. The record establishes, and Lieberman does not deny, that Wyoming.com offered to return his $20,000 capital contribution. Because Lieberman has been offered all that to which he is entitled, his demand for the return of his capital contribution has not been unsuccessful for purposes of § 17–15–120(d)(i). He, therefore, cannot compel dissolution under § 17–15–120(d)(i). This, however, does not end our discussion.

Having determined that § 17–15–120 does not control a member's rights upon dissociation, we must determine what became of Lieberman's interest, other than his capital contribution, in Wyoming.com. Unfortunately, it is unclear from the district court's decision letter precisely what became of Lieberman's ownership interest. The Articles of Organization of Wyoming.com credited Lieberman with a 40% ownership interest in Wyoming.com, and he now argues he is entitled to payment for this interest at fair market value. In the alternative, he contends he retains that 40% interest because the district court has not resolved that portion of the parties' dispute. Wyoming.com disagrees.

We begin by examining Lieberman's notice of withdrawal. Lieberman strongly disputes any contention that he has simply forfeited his interest, other than his capital contribution, in the LLC. After examining the notice of withdrawal, we cannot say, as a matter of law, that Lieberman forfeited his interest upon his withdrawal because nothing in his withdrawal indicates his intent to do so. Indeed, Lieberman's demand for "his share of the current value of the company," whose value he estimated at $400,000, "based on a recent offer from the Majority Shareholder," indicates he would not easily part with, much less forfeit, his interest. Because we cannot say that, as a matter of law, Lieberman's withdrawal amounted to forfeiture of his interest, and because there is no statutory provision governing dissociation, we look to Wyoming.com's Operating Agreement to determine Lieberman's remedy.

Under the Wyoming.com's Operating Agreement, a member's equity interest was to be represented by a membership certificate. The Operating Agreement provides:

ARTICLE IV
Membership Certificates and their Transfer

4.1 Certificates. Membership Certificates representing equity interest in the Company will be in the form determined by the Members. Membership Certificates must be signed by the President and by all other Members. The name and address of the person to whom the Membership Certificate is issued, with the percentage of ownership represented by the certificate, must be entered in the Certificate Register of the Company. In case of a lost, destroyed or mutilated Membership Certificate, a new one may be issued on the terms and indemnity to the Company as the Members may prescribe.

4.2 Certificate Register. A Certificate Register will be maintained showing the names and addresses of all members, their total percentage of ownership represented by Membership Certificates, and their respective amount of capital contribution. Any and all changes in Members or their amount of capital contribution may be formalized by filing notice of the same with the Secretary of State by amendment of the Articles of Organization.

4.3 Transfers of Shares. Any Member proposing a transfer or assignment of his Certificate must first notify the Company, in writing, of all the details and consideration for the proposed transfer or assignment. The Company, for the benefit of the remaining Members, will have the first right to acquire the equity by cancellation of the Certificate under the same terms and conditions as provided in the formal Articles of Organization as filed with the Wyoming Secretary of State for Members who are deceased, retired, resigned, expelled, or dissolved. If the Company declines to elect this option, the remaining Members who desire to participate may proportionately (or in the proportions as the remaining Members may agree) purchase the interest under the same terms and conditions first proposed by the withdrawing Member.

If the transfer or assignment is made as originally proposed and the other Members fail to approve the transfer or assignment by unanimous written consent, the transferee or assignee will have no right to participate in the management of the business and affairs of the Company or to become a Member. The transferee or assignee will only be entitled to receive the share of the profit or other compensation by way of income and the return of contributions to which that Member would otherwise be entitled.

Provision 2.5 provides:

2.5 Quorum. At any meeting of the Members, a majority of the equity interests, as determined from the capital contribution of each Member as reflected by the books of the Company, represented in person or by proxy, will constitute a quorum at a meeting of Members.

Provision 2.7 provides:

2.7 Voting by Certain Members. Membership Certificates standing in the name of a corporation, partnership or Company may be voted by the officer, partner, agent or proxy as the Bylaws of the entity may prescribe or, in the absence of such provision, as the Board of Directors of the entity may determine. Certificates held by a trustee, personal representative, administrator, executor, guardian or conservator may be voted by him, either in person or by proxy, without a transfer of the certificates into his name.

Under these provisions, it is clear that a member's interest in Wyoming.com was to be represented by membership certificates. There is nothing in the record indicating what became of Lieberman's membership certificate; there is no indication it has been canceled or forfeited. * * *

The parties remain uncertain as to their legal relationship because it is unclear what became of Lieberman's ownership or equity interest (as represented by a membership certificate). Therefore, we conclude it appropriate to remand to the district court for a full declaration of the parties' rights.

We affirm the district court's determination that Wyoming.com is not in a state of dissolution and that Lieberman is entitled to the return of his capital contribution, $20,000. However, questions remain regarding Lieberman's equity interest, which was to be represented by his membership certificate. This case is thus remanded for a full resolution of the controversy between the parties.

QUESTIONS AND NOTES

1.   How would a court have decided this case if Wyoming.com LLC were a Delaware LLC? *Cf.* Delaware §§ 18–603 and 18–801.

2.   ULLCA provides for member dissociation and the limited liability company's purchase of the dissociating member's distributional interest at "fair value" unless the operating agreement otherwise provides. *See* ULLCA §§ 601, 602, 701, and 702. Why would the operating agreement provide otherwise?

3.   Estate and gift taxes provide a reason for eliminating dissociation rights. The inability to transfer or liquidate an ownership interest in an LLC results in a lower valuation for purposes of both the estate and gift tax, and thus less tax. *See generally* Laurel Wheeling & Susan Pace Hamill, *Dissociation From Alabama Limited Liability Companies in the Post Check the Box Era*, 49 ALA. L. REV. 909 (1998).

4.   "There are many reasons to retain the default buy-out right in the LLC, including the illiquidity of private investments, the relative imbalance of power between majority and minority owners, the difficulty a minority has in achieving suitable contractual protection, the wide variety of enterprises conducted in the LLC form (some of which may lack operating agreements altogether), the substantive and procedural uncertainties regarding claims for violations of fiduciary duties and standards of care, the potential lack of built-in statutory protections other than buyout rights, and, most of all, the likelihood of continued failures both in human relationships and in contractual documents. The current trend away from the broad judicial monitoring of private business enterprises creates an increased need for statutory direction and express statutory protections for minority LLC owners." Sandra K. Miller, *What Buy–Out Rights, Fiduciary Duties, and Dissolution Remedies Should Apply in the Case of the Minority Owner of a Limited Liability Company?*, 38 HARV. J. LEGIS. 413, 466 (2001).

Recall that the Wyoming Supreme Court did not address questions regarding Lieberman's equity interests. There were two more Wyoming Supreme Court decisions (cleverly referred to by the Wyoming Supreme Court as *"Lieberman II"* and *"Lieberman III"*) that dealt with Lieberman's equity interests. We are only asking you to deal with a part of the *Lieberman* III opinion in what we think (and the Wyoming Supreme Court obviously hopes) is the last of the Lieberman litigation.

LIEBERMAN v. MOSSBROOK

Supreme Court of Wyoming, 2009
208 P.3d 1296

KITE, J. It is undisputed that Mr. Lieberman withdrew his membership from Wyoming.com and demanded return of his capital contribution on March 13, 1998. Additionally, it is now undisputed that in accordance with his demand, Wyoming.com wrote him a check for $20,000 and cancelled his membership certificate on April 16, 1998. From that date, Mr. Lieberman's investment in the company as represented by his capital account was zero and he was no longer a member. He did, however, retain his equity interest in the sense that he remained entitled to his share of the company's earnings while he was an investor.

Mr. Lieberman's situation it turns out was different from that of a transferee. In *Lieberman II,* we said:

> The operating agreements clearly anticipate a situation where a person could be an equity owner in Wyoming.com but not a member. Provision 4.3 of the Operating Agreement provides that, if a transferee of an ownership interest is not unanimously approved by the remaining members, the transferee maintains the rights of equity ownership but will not be a member. Logically, given the absence of any contractual provision to the contrary, there is no reason to treat a withdrawing member any differently from someone who buys into Wyoming.com without becoming a member. Thus, Lieberman is not a member of Wyoming.com, but he maintains his equity interest and all rights and obligations attendant thereto.

However, Paragraph 4.3 of the operating agreement dealing with transfers of shares does not address the situation where a member's capital contribution has been returned. In a transfer, the capital contribution remains with the company and the transferee receives the ownership interest commensurate with the capital contribution. In the present case, there was no remaining capital contribution as of April 16, 1998; consequently, Mr. Lieberman was neither a member nor an investor. To be consistent with the way in which the parties' agreements treat other situations, his interest must be treated as if it was "liquidated" upon the cancellation of his membership certificate and return of his capital contribution.

Article VI, paragraph 6.2, of the Wyoming.com operating agreement provided that upon liquidation of any member's interest in the company, liquidating distributions were to be made in accordance with the members' positive capital balances. Paragraph 6.2 further provided that the members' capital accounts were to be credited with the amount of money the member had contributed, the fair market value of property the member contributed and the member's distributive share of company income and gain; the members' capital accounts were to be debited with the amount of money the company distributed to the member, the fair market value of property distributed to the member and the member's distributive share of company loss and deduction.

Pursuant to these provisions, upon cancellation of Mr. Lieberman's membership and return of his capital contribution, Wyoming.com was required to make liquidating distributions to him in accordance with the amounts credited and debited in his capital account at that time or risk a claim for conversion. Wyoming.com did not make those distributions and, by its failure to do so, converted Mr. Lieberman's equity interest. The district court correctly concluded that Mr. Lieberman established the elements of conversion as a matter of law. That is, he was legally entitled to payment of his equity interest at the time his membership was cancelled and his capital contribution returned; Wyoming.com failed to pay him the value of his equity interest; he demanded payment; Wyoming.com rejected his demand; and he sustained damages.

While this conclusion is clear from the record presently before us, it was not clear from the record before us in the prior *Lieberman* cases. Without the cancelled membership certificate, Mr. Mossbrook's testimony that the certificate was in fact cancelled April 16, 1998, and the evidence showing that Wyoming.com paid the $20,000 capital contribution to the district court in the garnishment proceeding, questions remained as to the status of Mr. Lieberman's equity interest. There now being no question that Wyoming.com cancelled Mr. Lieberman's membership certificate and returned his capital contribution on April 16, 1998, it is clear that he was entitled to liquidating distributions as of that same date. Mr. Lieberman has never received those distributions * * *

Ordinarily, a determination by this Court that a party is entitled to payment in accordance with the terms of a written agreement would require remand to the district court for determination of the payment amount. This, however, is not an ordinary case. What began in 1998 with a declaratory judgment petition and complaint for dissolution evolved into an unnecessarily complicated and protracted legal battle. We are disinclined to send this back yet again for the district court to resolve.

We have consistently stated that the goal in awarding damages is to make the injured party whole to the extent that it is possible to measure an injury in terms of money. An injured party is made whole when he is placed in the same financial position he would have been in had the wrong not been committed. * * *

Having reviewed the record in its entirety, we conclude the elements of conversion were met in April of 1998. * * * The value of Mr. Lieberman's interest must be measured by his share of the value of the company at the time he withdrew and received his capital contribution, together with interest on that amount. In that manner he is made whole and placed in the same financial position he would have been had the wrong not been committed.

The evidence presented at trial showed that in his March 1998 notice of withdrawal, Mr. Lieberman demanded $400,000 in payment for his interest in Wyoming.com. Although his written demand stated that the $400,000 was based on a recent offer from the majority shareholder, there is no evidence in the record supporting that valuation of his ownership interest. Other than his unsupported $400,000 demand, Mr. Lieberman presented no evidence of the value of his equity interest as of the date he withdrew.

The Mossbrooks contend that a January 25, 1998, offer to purchase Mr. Mossbrook's interest represents the best estimate of Wyoming.com's value at the time Mr. Lieberman withdrew. Based upon the purchase offer, an independent appraiser retained by the Mossbrooks valued Mr. Lieberman's equity interest on the date of his withdrawal at $100,000. Subtracting from that amount the $20,000 returned to Mr. Lieberman as his capital contribution and the $7,965 paid to him in September 1999, the appraiser concluded his equity interest amounted to $72,035. No evidence was presented refuting the appraisal. From the evidence presented, we conclude the value of Mr. Lieberman's interest at the time and place of the conversion was $72,035 together with interest at the rate of 7% per year from the date of his withdrawal.

QUESTIONS

1. How much do you think Lieberman and the other parties spent on attorneys' fees?

2. What could/should have been done to avoid this costly litigation?

E. FROM LIMITED LIABILITY COMPANIES TO . . .

In an appropriately titled continuing legal education presentation, "The Alphabet Soup of Unincorporated Business Law: What Is Happening With LLCS, LPS, LLPS, GPS, LLLPS & BTS and Dealing with RUPA, ULPA 2001, Re–RULPA, Re–ULLCA, UNETA, MITA, & META, Thomas E., Rutledge, a prominent Kentucky lawyer, observes: "On a national and state basis, the law of unincorporated business organizations is evolving at a frenzied pace." VML0202 ALI–ABA 1.

Whatever the next new thing in business structures will be, legislatures and courts will look to the old things that you have studied such as partnerships and corporations and limited partnerships and limited liability companies in developing the law for new business structures.

INDEX

References are to Pages

†